ARCHAEOLOGICAL SURVEY OF INDIA

ANNUAL REPORT

1902-03

ARCHAEOLOGICAL SURVEY OF INDIA

ANNUAL REPORT

1902-03

GYAN

Published by

Gyan Publishing House
5, Ansari Road
Daryaganj, New Delhi-110002
Phone: 011-47034999, 9811692060
E-mail: books@gyanbooks.com

Distribution Network
gyanbooks.com
India, USA, Canada, UK, Australia, France

ISBN : 978-81-212-2800-8 (HB)

2nd Impression 2021

Printed at: Gyan Press, Delhi.

Annual Report 1902-03

TABLE OF CONTENTS.

LIST OF PLATES.

TEXT AND OTHER ILLUSTRATIONS.

INTRODUCTION.

SOME opening words of explanation seem needed in this the inaugural issue of a new "Annual," to show not only the object and scope of the publication, but the circumstances which have brought it into existence.

More than two years ago, while the idea of an Archæological "Annual" was being discussed in the Government of India, a correspondent in the *Journal* of the Royal Asiatic Society in London happened simultaneously to give expression to the popular need of such a publication. He had just chanced upon a summarised account at second hand of Mr. Rea's interesting excavations in Southern India (described in Mr. Rea's annual report to the Madras Government), and was moved thereby to the following remarks:—

"This annual report, being embodied in a 'G. O.,' is circulated among a few favoured individuals and institutions, but it does not reach the public. What we want are annual volumes, such as those produced by the Egypt Exploration Fund. These volumes are published every year. They embody the outcome of the previous season's work. They possess no finality. They are not kept back, as our Indian volumes are kept back, until some great specialist shall have assimilated everything that can be known, and can write with certainty his full and deliberate convictions. And the result is that, while in every civilised country the work going on in Egypt is watched with intense interest by numbers of people who do not profess to possess any great scientific knowledge of the subject, and while therefore the societies engaged are supplied with funds which enable them to carry on the excavations and print their volumes, the labours of the Indian Archæological Department fall, invariably, dead and lifeless. Whatever is being done in India is done almost n secret, and everybody knows that nothing will be heard of it for fifteen or twenty years, so that no one cares to support it. If we could have for India annual volumes such as we have for Egypt, I am confident that the Royal Asiatic Society and the Indian Exploration Fund would receive numbers of new adherents, and the value of their work would be greatly increased."

It will be observed that the complaint was not of the absence of publications but of the absence of regular periodical publications which should promptly announce to the world all the latest results of the current work of the Archæological Survey, while the interest of the discoveries was still fresh. In point of fact quite a number of notable archæological volumes had from time to time been produced in India,—notable for their splendid originality and scholarship; and some account of these works will be in place here as explaining why, notwithstanding their merits, they necessarily left a great gap unfilled. By such a retrospect also the reader will be enabled to perceive at once the essential difference in motive between all past publications of the Archæological Department in India and this new "Annual."

Of the yearly Provincial reports it is not necessary to speak here. They were (and still are) reports prepared for official perusal, and, though not withheld from the public, rarely came in the way of attracting general attention, nor indeed would their admixture of purely administrative detail with archæological material have afforded very inviting fare for the multitude. The literary works of the Survey which have brought Indian archæological research before the public in a worthy and permanent form are the massive reports of the *Imperial Series* (associated for the most part with the name of Dr. Burgess) and the *District Reports* of General Cunningham.

Of the quality of Dr. Burgess's reports it would not be easy to speak in overstrained praise. But Dr. Burgess made no pretence of conducting a comprehensive and connected survey of the Indian continent by a system of simultaneous progress in its various parts; nor did it occur to him to publish periodical reports of his own important discoveries, at the time they were made. A specialist in his tastes, Dr. Burgess concentrated his rare abilities on special classes of antiquities or on special tracts whose peculiar interest fascinated him. Such books as *The Buddhist Caves of Western India* and *The Antiquities of the Bidar and Aurangābād Districts* exemplify this trait. More than that, the publication of each report was usually delayed until enough material had been accumulated and studied to enable a complete monograph to be produced, that should be fit to stand as the final word on the subject for the next generation. During the 29 years from 1874 to 1902 as many as 32 miscellaneous volumes of the *Imperial Series* saw the light without any semblance of periodicity; that is to say, sometimes one volume appeared in five years, sometimes five volumes came out in one year; and there are still large tracts of India and Further India which have been left quite untouched. It should be added that Dr. Burgess had nine coadjutors, who were separately responsible between them for 19 of the 32 volumes, all of which contribute in varying degrees to the monumental value of the *Imperial Series*.

General Cunningham's reports were personal descriptions of archæological tours in specially interesting districts or areas, and the 23 volumes, which were produced in as many years between 1862 and 1884, contained a great mass of information, systematised to some extent, according to the light then available. Each volume embodied the results of a single complete tour, lavishly illustrated, but was published in a leisurely way some two or three years after the tour had been made. Like Dr. Burgess's works, though running in a different groove and on another plane of scholarship, General Cunningham's reports aimed at exhaustiveness, and thus in their time carried a certain final authority. In their entirety these 23 volumes may be said to bring together the results of the survey of the Central and Northern parts of India, which General Cunningham and his assistants patiently worked at for nearly a quarter of a century; and the reports ceased when this particular survey ceased, on General Cunningham's retirement twenty years ago. Western and Southern India, and of course Burma, were left quite outside the programme, and even in Northern India, in spite of the industry of the explorers, many ancient monuments still remain to be surveyed, perhaps discovered, and many inscriptions to be deciphered.

Two conclusions clearly emerge from this brief literary retrospect. First, that earlier archæological publications, with their long periods of gestation, had a value as to scholarship and finality which the new "Annual" cannot and need not emulate. Secondly, that because of their very finality those publications often tended to stifle rather than to stimulate further research in the particular paths trodden by their authors. Now, the pre-eminent object of the present publication is to inaugurate a new policy in just this very respect. Instead of silently accumulating during a long course of years the materials for some future volumes, and keeping these materials hidden, as it were, behind a hoarding until the finished structure can be disclosed, it is the intention to show year by year exactly what materials have been and are being collected, so that other labourers may know how they can add to the heap and, if possible, themselves build from it the ultimate edifice. In other words, it is the intention, by means of these progress reports, to show that the Department, so far from looking to monopolise the field of research, desires and facilitates the co-operation of every earnest student and learned society. More than this, it is the intention to attempt to do for India something of what the volumes issued by the Egypt Exploration Fund during the last 20 years have done for the Land of the Pharaohs,—to attract wider and more abiding attention to India's grand treasure-house of historical relics. Even if active co-operation should not always be forthcoming, generous interest and sympathy at least, it is hoped, will periodically be excited, and the public led to view the work of the Department as something not outside the range of their concern.

The primary object of the new "Annual" being thus explained, the scope and character of the contents next require some exposition. But a short account of the Department itself and of the transformation it has lately undergone must, for the sake of clearness, come first.

The history of the Archæological Department may be said to open with the appointment in 1862 of Major-General Sir Alexander Cunningham to be "Director of Archæology." Upon this officer was imposed the charge "to make an accurate description of such remains as most deserve notice, with the history of them so far as it is traceable, and a record of the traditions that are retained regarding them." There was no element of recognised permanence in this creation of a new office; on the contrary, archæological work was looked upon as something to be accomplished in a few years, duly recorded and then dropped. By the year 1871 ideas on the subject had become somewhat more expanded; General Cunningham's appointment was declared by a Resolution to be that of "Director-General of the Archæological Survey of India," and his duty was defined to be—"to superintend a complete search over the whole country and a systematic record and description of all architectural and other remains that are remarkable alike for their antiquity, or their beauty, or their historical interest." But, although now nominally the head of the Archæological Survey in all India, General Cunningham, owing to the geographical limitations of his work, actually remained the head of the Survey in Northern India only: indeed, the Survey was not introduced into the Madras and Bombay Presidencies until 1874, and on that extension being made, the charge of the two Presidencies was separately given to Dr. Burgess. Moreover, the Director-General lacked the support of a proper staff of provincial surveyors, so that virtually he "directed" no activities but his own and those of the assistants working with him. With what ability and industry General Cunningham discharged his mission, however, his 23 volumes descriptive of 23 years' touring sufficiently attest.

It is specially to be observed here that repair and conservation formed no part of the Director-General's responsibilities; these duties were assumed to be sufficiently looked after by the Local Governments on whom they had been urged by many successive orders. It was not until 1878 that some qualms began to be felt by Lord Lytton concerning this arrangement, and the then Viceroy wrote in a Minute:—"The preservation of the national antiquities and works of art ought not to be exclusively left to the charge of Local Governments which may not always be alive to the importance of such a duty. Lieutenant-Governors who combine æsthetic culture with administrative energy are not likely to be very common, and I cannot conceive any claims upon the administrative initiative and financial resources of the Supreme Government more essentially imperial than this." As a fact, this Minute was penned with definite knowledge that many of the greatest buildings and monuments of ancient India were steadily sinking into a deplorable condition. The outcome of Lord Lytton's ideas was a proposal to appoint a Curator of Ancient Monuments who, combining engineering with archæological knowledge, should hold the position of an Under Secretary in the Public Works Department and be fortified in dealing with difficult questions of repair and restoration by a Committee of Taste. It was to be the duty of the Curator "to prepare classified lists of the monuments of each Province, grouping them according as they required to be kept in permanent good repair, or were decayed beyond that point but still not in complete ruin, or were unimportant or irretrievably ruined." He was also to state the amounts required in each case for special repair or maintenance, and to what extent they were forthcoming from local resources. The Government of India were then to arrange with each Local Government as to the Imperial grant to be made to the Province in aid of local resources for the preservation of ancient monuments.

At first the proposal failed to commend itself to the Secretary of State, who took the view that the Director-General and the Governors of British Provinces combined could very well look after the interests of conservation, and that a curator would be a kind of fifth wheel in the coach. But when the Government, in a later despatch in 1880, argued that the Director-General was sufficiently busy with research without being burdened with conservation also; that much destruction and decay were meanwhile going on, leading to lamentable and irremediable losses; and that many of the great Indian monuments were not situated in any British Province but in Native territory, the Secretary of State (Lord Hartington) admitted that a strong case had been made out for a temporary special appointment. Accordingly, early in 1881, Major Cole, R.E., was appointed Curator of Ancient Monuments for a period of three years.

Gifted with the qualities of knowledge, industry and enthusiasm, Major Cole at once set about examining the most important ancient buildings in British and Native India, and the result was an output of three annual reports, formulating a valuable though naturally incomplete programme of conservation work for the future. Besides these reports, Major Cole was responsible for the series of folio volumes which appeared under the title "Preservation of National Monuments in India," and which contained some exceptionally fine illustrations, with brief explanatory notes, of the most famous buildings and antiquities in charge of the Curator. At the end of three years, Major Cole's appointment terminated, and his reports are to this day the sole works of permanent value dealing with conservation as distinct from research among all the bibliography representing 32 years' archæological activity in India. On the Curatorship ceasing to exist, the work of conservation relapsed into the hands of the Local Governments as before; but the energies of the Curator had not been expended wholly in vain, since they may be said to have laid the foundation, in theory at least, of an organised scheme of permanent conservation. To what limited extent this foundation has since been built upon in the intervening twenty years will be briefly indicated later.

When General Cunningham retired in 1885, Dr. Burgess, who till then by his labours as Archæological Surveyor for Madras and Bombay had provided the complement of General Cunningham's work in Northern India, was promoted to be head of the entire Archæological Department. At the same time the functions of conservation were amalgamated with those of survey and research. Moreover, five Survey areas were mapped out—namely, Madras, Bombay, the Punjab (with Sind and Rajputana), the North-West Provinces (with Central India and the Central Provinces), and Bengal (with Assam); and a Surveyor was to be assigned to each. As a matter of fact only three Surveyors were appointed—for the Punjab, the North-West Provinces and Bengal; Dr. Burgess being still expected to superintend, with the help of two Assistant Surveyors, the detailed operations in the Madras and Bombay Presidencies in addition to his new imperial duties.

There was no intention even then, however, of making the re-organised Department a permanent institution An archæological survey was still regarded as something which once done was done for ever; and in view of the extent of ground covered by General Cunningham's 23 years of touring, it was hopefully thought that in about five years more the new Director-General would be able to complete the whole task, disband the Survey, and safely hand over the subsequent simple duties of conservation to the Local Governments. Indeed, when, shortly after Dr. Burgess's promotion, the progress of archæological work in the Bombay and Madras Presidencies came under review, it was decided, "in order to bring it to a termination within a reasonable time," to engage the services of an additional officer, Dr. Hultzsch, as Epigraphist, for the translation of inscriptions in the Sanskrit, Pali, and Dravidian languages.

It is, by the way, significant of the views which were still entertained regarding the powers of the Director-General, that Dr. Hultzsch and also Mr. Rea, the Madras Surveyor, were made directly subordinate to the Government of Madras, and the other provincial Surveyors were instructed similarly to conduct their duties in regard to the repair and restoration of buildings of antiquity in direct correspondence with the local authorities; while Dr. Führer, Epigraphist for Northern India, had to submit his reports to Dr. Hultzsch. In 1886, however, these anomalous arrangements were reversed, and Dr. Burgess became a real as well as a nominal Director both of research and conservation.

Another incidental point to be noted here is that much importance was attached to the enlistment of native talent in the discovery and translation of inscriptions and records in the ancient native languages, and one of the secondary objects of Dr. Hultzsch's appointment was to impart to those native Surveyors who might be selected to assist him the training which would qualify them for more or less independent research.

In 1889, when only four years had passed, Dr. Burgess decided to follow General Cunningham into retirement. He had then rendered brilliant archæological service in various capacities for fifteen years; and it may be remarked here that since his retirement he has added another fifteen years of editorial work to the record. His withdrawal proved the signal for something like disruption in the Department. An era of retrenchment had just begun in Government offices, and drastic ideas of economy were finding favour. The Finance Committee, which the Government of India had appointed to overhaul expenditure in all branches of the Public Service, commented on what they regarded as the unduly high cost of the Archæological Survey, and the Government thereupon determined upon wholesale reductions. The post of Director-General was allowed to remain vacant; virtually, it was abolished. Provincial Surveyors were retained in Madras and Bombay, and the North-West Provinces continued to employ Dr. Führer on a small pay as well as an Assistant; but Bengal, the Punjab, Burma, and the Native States were left without Surveyors. Even this attenuated Survey establishment was sanctioned for only five years (from 1890); the official opinion then being that by the end of that period the work of the Archæological Survey in India would, so far as Government was concerned, be generally completed.

With the year 1890, then, the low-water mark in the checkered history of the Archæological Department in India was reached, and for the next five years, down to 1895, the situation remained uneventfully at that depressed level. It will be seen that the outlook was sufficiently gloomy. The Director-General, who had devoted his talents for the most part to research and discovery (including the exploration of buried sites and the collection of inscriptions), was gone. The Curator, whose one duty had been to arrange for the up-keep of recognised ancient monuments, was gone too. Half of India was shorn of its archæological staff altogether, and in the other half conservation was abandoned to the Local Governments, with no central authority to ascertain how the responsibility was being interpreted or whether it was being discharged at all: and although it is now known that much was undoubtedly done by the Local Governments from 1880 onwards to preserve the most important ancient buildings, no connected statement existed of what had been or was being done, while it was certain that the lists of monuments supposed to require official conservation were everywhere incomplete. The annual reports of the Surveyors in Madras, Bombay, and the North-West Provinces were confined to brief narratives of archæological tours and descriptions of buildings and ruins visited and surveyed. They gave no information as to the present condition of the great historical monuments, or as to the measures taken during the year by the Provincial Public Works Departments to preserve them, nor did they contain any suggestions or recommendations as to conservation. Besides the ancient monuments in the possession of the Government, there are two other important classes of historical relics,—those held by Trusts or Societies, and those held by private individuals; but the annual provincial reports contained no reference to these. It is now known that in the North-West Provinces, and especially in Lucknow, much was done by the Local Government to secure the proper application of endowments for the up-keep of such monuments, and to supplement the endowments by grants-in-aid, but this knowledge is not obtainable from the records of the Archæological Department.

In 1895 it became time for the Government to consider what the future of the Archæological Department was to be. After consulting the Provincial Governments, and after weighing the strong pleas for the continuance of archæological work submitted by such authorities as the Royal Asiatic Society of London and the Indian Museum, Calcutta, the Government of India, going back upon former ideas, came to the conclusion (at the end of three years) that it was neither possible to disband the Survey altogether, nor advisable to maintain it on its then reduced and ineffective scale. But this decision was associated with an emphatic declaration that the operations must in future be directed almost exclusively towards conservation, as possessing claims incomparably more urgent than those of research. At the same time, they were careful to disclaim any wish to discourage original work, but they held that the limited sum which they felt justified in spending on archæological work should primarily be devoted to conserving the known rather than to searching for the unknown.

Accordingly a fresh re-organisation of the Department was decided upon. The new scheme provided for the constitution of five Survey Circles,—namely, Madras (with Coorg), Bombay (with Sind and Berar), the Punjab (with Baluchistan and Ajmer), the North-West Provinces (with the Central Provinces), and Bengal (with Assam). Each Circle was to be placed in charge of an Archæological Surveyor, to be paid imperially but controlled provincially, whose duty it would be to compile a classified list of archæological remains, to advise and assist his Local Government concerning the effective preservation of these remains, and to fill up any spare time he might have by prosecuting archæological research. Each Circle was to be equipped with two draftsmen and a small travelling establishment for the collection of coins and inscriptions. The expenditure to be incurred on the local establishments was accepted as an Imperial charge, save in the case of Madras where, being already a Provincial charge, it was to continue as such. Burma was provided for separately by the continuance of the existing Imperial grant to the Local Government of Rs. 10,000 a year.

To round off the whole scheme, it was determined to make the appointment of Epigraphist permanent so long as Dr. Hultzsch—an officer of exceptional attainments—might continue to hold it. There had been a proposal during the time when the scheme was still being formulated, to abolish the appointment of Government Epigraphist and to discontinue the publication of the *Epigraphia Indica*, on the ground that private individuals and learned societies might more appropriately undertake both the expenditure and the labour; but the arguments against this idea appeared so forcible, that it was eventually abandoned. In particular, it was realised that Dr. Hultzsch and his staff were the only people living who could decipher the old Tamil inscriptions, and, further, that Epigraphy was not only a subject of scientific importance in which the learned world was much interested, but also one which might throw useful light on many problems of modern administration. But as Dr. Hultzsch was essentially a Southern Indian specialist, the Government of India, while deciding on his permanent retention, proposed to encourage the entertainment of Honorary Epigraphists in other Provinces, and to relax Dr. Hultzsch's editorial monopoly by allowing them to prepare inscriptions for publication in the *Epigraphia Indica*.

The foregoing scheme came into force in May 1899. It will be observed that it still contemplated that all initiative and responsibility in the matter of conservation should rest with the Provincial Governments, and that it made no provision either for enabling the Government of India to inform themselves as to how this responsibility was being discharged or for the systematised central guidance of the provincialised archæological staff.

In 1900, the mild reaction which had previously set in against past lethargy became greatly intensified and led to another development, destined, it may be hoped, to impart a sustained impulse to the resuscitated Archæological Department. The first note in this fresh movement was struck in a speech which the Viceroy, Lord Curzon, delivered at a meeting of the Asiatic Society at Calcutta on the 1st February, 1899, a few weeks after he had landed in India. He there accepted the encouragement of research, the promotion of archæological study, and the preservation of the relics of the past as "a part of our imperial obligation to India," and announced his intention to pursue an active policy in this respect during his term of office. A year later, before an audience of the same Society, he elaborated the same theme, and thus graphically condensed the checkered story of the past :—

"There has been, during the last 40 years, some sort of sustained effort on the part of Government to recognise its responsibilities and to purge itself of a well-merited reproach. This attempt has been accompanied, and sometimes delayed, by disputes as to the rival claims of research and of conservation, and by discussion over the legitimate spheres of action of the Central and the Local Governments. There have been periods of supineness as well as of activity. There have been moments when it has been argued that the State had exhausted its duty or that it possessed no duty at all. There have been persons who thought that, when all the chief monuments were indexed and classified, one might sit with folded arms and allow them slowly and gracefully to crumble into ruin. There have been others who argued that railways and irrigation did not leave a modest half-lakh of rupees per annum for the requisite establishment to supervise the most glorious galaxy of monuments in the world. Nevertheless, with these interruptions and exceptions, which I hope may never again recur, the progress has been positive and on the whole continuous. It was Lord Canning who first invested archæological work in this country with permanent Government patronage by constituting in 1860 the Archæological Survey of Northern India and by appointing General Cunningham in 1862 to be Archæological Surveyor to Government. From that period date the publications of the Archæological Survey of India, which have at times assumed different forms and which represent varying degrees of scholarship and merit, but which constitute on the whole a noble mine of information in which the student has but to delve in order to discover an abundant spoil."

Before the close of the year the definite proposals of the Government of India had gone home to the Secretary of State. They embraced a definite policy of more active work, of closer supervision, and of larger outlay. The Government of India declared it to be indefensible that they should divest themselves of all responsibility for the preservation of monuments which, in the words of Lord Lytton, are "for variety, extent, completeness and beauty unsurpassed, perhaps unequalled, in the world." They felt that it would be the Supreme Government, and not the Provincial Governments, who would always be held in the judgment of the civilised world primarily responsible for maintaining intact this great inheritance, and they thought it unsafe to trust that the subordinate Governments would always be alive to the importance of the duty or would always be willing or able, under the pressing exigencies of provincial finance, to devote funds to it. They felt the necessity of someone at the head of the operations, who could not only assist local effort from an imperial standpoint with that advice and guidance which had been lacking since the days of Dr. Burgess, but could also maintain a continuous record of the archæological needs of the various Provinces, and of the work undertaken to meet those needs. They accordingly urged the re-appointment of a Director-General of Archæology, and the expenditure of a sum of not less than one lakh of rupees per annum for a term of years—to be expended in grants-in-aid for archæological work of special importance and magnitude. These proposals were sanctioned by the Secretary of State in the latter part of 1901, and the new Director-General, who was appointed for a term of five years, arrived in India to take up his duties early in 1902.

But meanwhile—in 1901—another important reform had been put through. Although most of the great archæological monuments of India are situate within the territories administered by the various Local Governments, the Native States are by no means devoid of interesting historical relics ; yet until then no effective machinery had been provided for the work of archæological conservation in territories administered by indigenous rulers or chiefs. By an order of the Government of India in the Foreign Department, dated the 4th June, 1901, this serious omission was at last remedied. Kashmir, Rajputana, and the Punjab Native States, as well as Dir, Swat, and Chitral, were added to the charge of the Surveyor of the Punjab-Baluchistan-Ajmer Circle ; Baroda, Central India, Hyderabad (Deccan), and the Bombay Native States were added to the charge of the Surveyor of the Bombay-Berar Circle ; and the Native States within the political jurisdiction of the Governments of Madras and Bengal were added to the charge of the Surveyors of the Madras-Coorg and Bengal-Assam Circles, respectively. It may be added that the Circle Surveyors have been instructed carefully to avoid any action which might cause misrepresentation of the aims of the Government of India or give offence to the Darbars whom it is desired to assist. No orders or instructions are to be given by the Surveyors to the officials of any Native State, and all suggestions or criticisms are to be conveyed to the Darbar through the medium of the Political authorities. Hereafter it may be found possible to induce the more important of the Native States to entertain an Archæologist of their own, as in Mysore, where the conservation of monuments and other questions of archæological interest have received the special attention of the Darbar. In the meantime every endeavour will be made to enlist the sympathies of the Native States in the task temporarily entrusted to the Circle Surveyors.

In concluding this outline of the history of the Archæological Survey in India, it will be appropriate to describe exactly and in detail the duties of the new Director-General, because, although nominally the successor of Sir Alexander Cunningham and Dr. Burgess, he is charged with responsibilities extending considerably beyond the sphere of archæological research wherein his predecessors confined their labours. The most important of his functions is to secure that the ancient monuments of the country are properly cared for, that they are not utilised for purposes which are inappropriate or unseemly, that repairs are executed when required, and that any restorations, which may be attempted, are conducted on artistic lines. In this respect his position will be generally similar to that occupied by the Curator of Ancient Monuments, who held office from 1880 to 1883. But his duties extend to the exercise of a general supervision over all the archæological work of the country, whether it be that of excavation, or preservation, or repair, or of the registration and description of monuments and ancient remains, or of antiquarian research ; he is to assist the provincial Surveyors in ascertaining and formulating the special requirements of each Province ; and to advise the Government of India as to the operations for which special subsidies may be allotted from Imperial funds. He is to co-ordinate and bring up to date the local Survey and reports ; and he is to submit annually to the Government of India a report on the progress effected during each official year.

The salient fact to be gathered from the foregoing brief historical sketch is that archæological activities in India were originally turned into too narrow a path. They aimed primarily at research, instead of at conservation, as if oblivious of the fact that research is a work that can be taken up equally well at any period by any qualified person or organisation, with or without official aid; whereas conservation in these quick-moving times is a duty of urgency devolving upon the Government of the day with the certain knowledge that no future solicitude will be able to repair the consequences of past neglect. Further, it appears that even the research work, brilliant though it was in scholarship, was begun without system and continued in a desultory manner, entirely omitting large and important parts of the country. Finally, the reader may see how, after many years, opinion has at last swung round, bringing conservation uppermost for the time being and until the task has been discharged, but still allowing to exploration, excavation, epigraphy, and general research their due places in the official programme.

With the past thus set forth, the present almost explains itself. As now re-organised, the Archæological Department stands for the first time on a firm administrative basis, with a consistent policy, definite responsibilities, and a systematised programme. There can be but two main functions of an Archæological Survey,—investigation and conservation; and of these conservation is, for the present at any rate, to be paramount, on the ground that if the material is carefully preserved, it can be examined at leisure and by any qualified agency, paid or unpaid. Especially is this priority of conservation emphasised in the case of those architectural or historical monuments whose preservation may be regarded as a duty owing not to India alone, but to the whole civilised world.

In view of the stress thus laid upon the importance of conservation—a stress which the whole contents of the present publication will be found indirectly to emphasise,— it may be appropriate to quote Lord Curzon's strong views on the subject as expressed in the speech already noticed, which His Excellency delivered to the Asiatic Society of Bengal:—

"In the course of my recent tour, during which I visited some of the most famous sites and beautiful or historic buildings in India, I more than once remarked in reply to Municipal addresses that I regarded the conservation of ancient monuments as one of the primary obligations of Government. We have a duty to our forerunners, as well as to our contemporaries and to our descendants,—nay, our duty to the two latter classes in itself demands the recognition of an obligation to the former, since we are the custodians for our own age of that which has been bequeathed to us by an earlier, and since posterity will rightly blame us if, owing to our neglect, they fail to reap the same advantages that we have been privileged to enjoy. Moreover, how can we expect at the hands of futurity any consideration for the productions of our own time—if indeed any are worthy of such—unless we have ourselves shown a like respect to the handiwork of our predecessors? This obligation, which I assert and accept on behalf of Government, is one of an even more binding character in India than in many European countries. There, abundant private wealth is available for the acquisition or the conservation of that which is frequently private property. Corporations, Societies, Endowments, Trusts provide a vast machinery that relieves the Government of a large portion of its obligation. The historic buildings, the magnificent temples, the inestimable works of art are invested with a publicity that to some extent saves them from the risk of desecration or the encroachments of decay. Here, all is different. India is covered with the visible records of vanished dynasties, of forgotten monarchs, or persecuted and sometimes dishonoured creeds. These monuments are for the most part, though there are notable exceptions, in British territory, and on soil belonging to Government. Many of them are in out-of-the-way places, and are liable to the combined ravages of a tropical climate, an exuberant flora, and very often a local and ignorant population who see only in an ancient building the means of inexpensively raising a modern one for their own convenience. All these circumstances explain the peculiar responsibility that rests upon Government in India."

It will now be plain to the reader that, as the scope of this "Annual" is to be co-extensive with current archæological operations, the contents will relate first and principally to Conservation, secondly, to Exploration and Research, and lastly, to Epigraphy. Under each head a plain tale will be told of the year's work, without any straining after literary effect. As now constituted, indeed, the Survey staff has no leisure for the refinements of archæological disquisition; it is essentially an active, not a contemplative corps, and its duty will therefore be to place before European scholars material for elucidation rather than to attempt elucidation on its own account.

If, under the new conditions of work, there was a danger that the Survey might degenerate into a mere monument-repairing department, such a possibility is now precluded by the generous ideal which His Excellency the Viceroy has upheld to all concerned:—"It is in the exploration and study of purely Indian remains, in the probing of archaic mounds, in the excavation of old Indian cities, and in the copying and reading of ancient inscriptions, that a good deal of the exploratory work of the archæologist in India will in future lie. The later pages of Indian history are known to us and can be read by all. But a curtain of dark and romantic mystery hangs over the earlier chapters, of which we are only slowly beginning to lift the corners. This also is not less an obligation of Government. Epigraphy should not be set behind research any more than research should be set behind conservation. All are ordered parts of any scientific scheme of antiquarian work. I am not one of those who think that Government can afford to patronise the one and ignore the other. It is in my judgment equally our duty to dig and discover, to classify, reproduce, and describe, to copy and decipher, and to cherish and conserve." And in point of fact—as the reader will discern in the following pages—a considerable impetus is at the present moment being communicated to exploration not less than to conservation.

It may be hoped that the "Annual" will serve to stimulate the interest not only of the public but of the Survey Officers themselves in what is being done. Instead of feeling, as in the past, that they are working in the dark on desultory schemes to no consistent end, Survey Officers will henceforth be sustained by the knowledge that good work during the year will obtain regular and prominent notice, and that it will meet with the appreciation in the Archæological World, which it deserves.

As various pens are to be employed in the production of this "Annual," nothing like uniformity of style or of matter will be attainable. Some of the writers are Natives; some others are Continentals. Some of the subjects of the articles are popular; others technical. Some of the work described is of universal importance; other work is of comparatively minor significance. Editorial supervision can therefore go no further than to secure that what is admitted into the "Annual" contains that which justifies its being published. Beyond that point responsibility will rest distributively with the several contributors, each individual being allowed to tell his story in his own fashion.

Similarly as to the pictorial illustrations, the reproductions, the plans, and the sketches. Some of these have been prepared in England; some in Madras; and some in other parts of India or Burma. They are to be appraised, therefore, independently according to their unequal individual qualities, and not viewed as a single artistic whole.

J. H. MARSHALL.

CONSERVATION.

IN the following general account of the past year's conservation work and in the special articles which supplement it, only those operations which are considered of some importance are noticed. The object of this "Annual" would hardly be served by detailing fully and exactly all the small miscellaneous repairs carried out by the Survey. Minor works, it is true, seem to constitute the bulk of the yearly task in more than one province, but a description of these undertakings, however necessary they may have been to the preservation of the buildings, would entail a wearisome repetition of measures like the clearing away of overgrowing jungle, the erasing of hideous, if well meant, whitewash, and the resetting of crumbling masonry. Should, however, any information about them be desired, it may be found in the regular provincial reports of the Archæological Surveyors. The single aim of the present narrative is to give an account of those features of current archæological activity which are most likely to interest the general student of Indian architecture, particularly in cases where monuments of world-wide celebrity are concerned.

In order to amplify and to illustrate the general summary in cases where expanded treatment seemed requisite, various Archæological Officers have prepared special articles, each dealing descriptively at first hand with the work carried out upon a single building or group of connected buildings. As the subjects of these special contributions are *ipso facto* of preponderating importance, it will be convenient to begin here by indicating the monuments with which they deal. These are as follows:—

Western India .	Sidi Sayyad's Mosque at Ahmadābād; Mosque of the Gol Gumbaz, Bījāpūr.
Bengal . .	The Aśoka pillar in the neighbourhood of Rampurwa; the Jain caves at Khandagiri; the temple on the hill at Muṇḍeśvarī; the temples at Bhubanesvar; the Black Pagoda at Konarak, and several Muhammadan buildings at Gaur, Panduah, and Rohtasgarh.
United Provinces.	Jahāngīrī Maḥall, Salīmgarh, Dīwān-i-'Āmm, Angūrī-Bāgh, Machhī Bhawan, Motī Masjid, Fatḥpurī Masjid, Sahelī Burj, and the Tāj Maḥall at Agra; and the Tomb of Akbar at Sikandarah.
Punjab . .	Qil'a-i-kuhna Masjid, Delhi.
Rajputana . .	Aṛhāī-din-kā-Jhoṁprā, and Pavilions of Shāh Jahān, Ajmīr.
Southern India .	Chennakēśavasvāmi temple at Sōṁpalle. Old fortified wall of Madras.
Burma . .	The Palace at Mandalay.

All the buildings in the foregoing list, save the old wall of Madras, may justly claim to rank among the finest examples of Indian architecture extant, and there are few readers, it may be opined, who will not be pleased to turn to the special articles which describe their conservation, and to learn in detail the measures which have recently been taken to rescue them from misuse or decay and to restore to them some measure of their ancient beauty. To ensure, however, that the following summary may convey a connected and fairly complete idea of the year's sum of labour, it will be necessary to give a brief outline of the ground embraced by these articles, and to supplement it by a more leisurely description of those other measures, which, either because they are of less general interest or because they are still far from complete, do not require to be separately discussed at the present juncture. The consequence of thus giving prominence to the less important subject matter, while only briefly noticing the more important, will be to distort in some measure the true perspective of what is described; but this is a difficulty which cannot well be avoided, and, after all, it matters little if it is borne in mind that a perusal of the special articles is necessary to bring the whole picture into focus.

A word of explanation seems called for as to the geographical arrangement adopted in the following pages. The monuments are grouped according to archæological "Circles," the chief Province or Presidency in each circle being first referred to, and afterwards the Native States or lesser administrations grouped around it. The arrangement is not a very satisfactory one, inasmuch as the areas of these "Circles" are quite arbitrary, and correspond to no political or natural divisions of the country, but it has at least the advantage of Departmental convenience: while the route over which the reader will be taken—starting on the Bombay side and finishing in Burma—is one which any tourist in India might quite naturally follow.

Bombay.—At Ahmadābād the mosque of the slave nobleman Sīdi Sayyad is no longer perverted to mean utilitarian uses. The many deformities which were perpetrated in order to convert it into a modern district treasury and which, incredible though it seems, were allowed to obscure the exquisite beauty of its demi-lune windows, have been removed, while the precincts have been restored to their original state. For many years debarred by the stringent rules observed in all treasury buildings from crossing the official threshold, the public once more enjoys free access to the interior, and Ahmadābād has regained an acquisition to its architectural attractions which alone would reward the visitor for his journey there.

From the finely proportioned mosque of the Gol Gumbaz at Bījāpūr the unsightly *dāk* bungalow has been summarily obliterated, and the building, with its fine façade and slender, graceful minars, has been rescued from rapid decline. It is a misfortune that a portion of the bold and highly ornamental cornice of this mosque was so far decayed that its removal became imperative, but it is hoped that a complete restoration of this striking feature may at some future date be effected.

Of less importance are the improvements carried out at the rock-hewn temples at Elephanta. Past visitors to these caves may have a somewhat disagreeable recollection of the difficulties of debarkation on the small island which forms the site of these wonderful subterranean shrines. Future visitors will find their convenience consulted by an improved landing-stage. At both the Elephanta and the Kārle Caves a considerable sum of money has also been spent in rebuilding proper quarters for the custodians. These are not works to be dwelt upon descriptively, but their utility will be appreciated by everyone familiar with the ground. It may be mentioned, too, that the Archæological staff needs to be almost as assiduous sometimes in preventing harm as in attempting good; witness a recent proposal to colour-wash the figures in the Kārle Caves and to whitewash an old carved black-stone temple.

Other works in the Bombay Presidency that similarly call for only passing mention are the special repairs to the Ibrāhīm Rauza at Bījāpūr, to the Adālaj step-well in Ahmadābād, and to some of the buildings at Champāner. In view indeed of the ground covered by the special articles, it will suffice to add here, so far as Western India generally is concerned, that the largest share of attention has been given to Bījāpūr and Ahmadābād, where seventeen different buildings have been repaired at a cost of more than Rs. 7,000; while in the remaining districts of the Presidency some forty monuments—temples, mosques, caves, forts, and tombs—have come under repair.

Central India.—In Central India, by the desire of the Viceroy Lord Curzon, a comprehensive scheme has been prepared for the repair and conservation of the splendid monuments of the Mālvā kings at Dhār and Māṇḍū. This scheme of course applies only to relics already discovered and examined. But Dhār and Māṇḍū would well repay a more complete and exhaustive survey than has ever yet been attempted. Mr. Cousens writes in his annual report: "We hardly know what is in Māṇḍū yet, the place is so thoroughly overgrown with thick jungle and undergrowth. It would be a delightful bit of work to explore the hill completely, and I hope it may fall to my lot some day to do it. Even in our short visit we found many things that were new to us, both in constructive and decorative detail. . . All the country to the south and west of Dhār within the Central India Agency, is practically unknown so far as antiquarian remains are concerned. The few scraps of information I gleaned at Dhār give promise of many interesting remains and places. The Bāgh Caves to the west, which thirty years ago were intact, are now, I hear, falling in and are so ruined that it is now almost hopeless to do anything to them. This is much to be regretted, since they had upon their walls fresco paintings similar to those which make the Ajantā Caves so famous."

The conservation of the sites of Dhār and Māṇḍū is thus a subject calling for more than casual notice. Dhār, the capital of the State of the same name, in Central India, lies thirty-three miles due east of Mhow, the well-known British Military cantonment on the Rajputana-Malwa Railway; and Māṇḍū is twenty-four miles south of Dhār. Dhār, and occasionally Māṇḍū, were the old capitals of the Hindu kings of Mālvā, one of whom, the great Rājā Bhojadeva, who reigned in the eleventh century of our era, stands out pre-eminently for his prowess and literary attainments. During his time some of the finest temples, that adorned Mālvā, seem to have been erected. Later, when Central India fell under the sway of Islām, Māṇḍū became the capital of the Muhammadan Sulṭāns of Mālvā, who set about building themselves palaces and mosques, first with material pilfered from the old Hindu temples (already for the most part desecrated and ruined by the inconoclastic fury of their earlier co-religionists), and afterwards with their own quarried material. Thus, nearly all traces of the splendid shrines of the Paramāras of Mālvā have disappeared, save what we find utilized in the ruined mosques and tombs; and the remains at Dhār and Māṇḍū may be said to consist now, almost wholly, of the ruins of the palaces, mosques, tombs, fortifications, and reservoirs of the Muhammadan period. These have been often described, the last writer being Captain E. Barnes, who contributed a paper to the *Journal* of the Bombay Branch of the Royal Asiatic Society.[1] The late Sir James Campbell also wrote a long and exhaustive account of Māṇḍū for the same *Journal*,[2] and a "Bombay Subaltern" many years ago penetrated the wild and tangled jungle of Māṇḍū, and left behind him a most interesting and faithful description of its ruins. We may go back still further, and add a royal author to the list in the person of the Emperor Jahāngīr, and a British Ambassador to Jahāngīr in the person of Sir Thomas Roe, whose brief remarks, read as a commentary on the pretentious diary of the Emperor, are full of fascinating interest. Jahāngīr made Māṇḍū his capital for a short time, during which many of its old buildings were repaired and its glories to some extent resuscitated; but this was the last expiring flicker of Māṇḍū's greatness. To-day the jungle has closed in on its fortress. Many of its monuments have been swept away. The famous Victory Tower of Maḥmūd Khaljī has fallen, and other buildings—both mosques and tombs—are crumbling to their end. But the grandeur of the site must always remain impressive, and for the monuments which are still left to attest the magnificence and taste of the Mālvā kings, it may truly be said that there is hardly a group of remains in India upon which the halo of age has shed such a splendour, or which is more worthy of being saved to posterity.

Both Dhār and Māṇḍū were visited by His Excellency Lord Curzon in November 1902, when he left careful instructions for a systematic scheme of conservation. The buildings which were to claim the first attention were the Jāmi' Masjid, Hūshang's Tomb, and the Mosque of Dilāwar Khān at Māṇḍū, and the Lāt Masjid and the Kamāl Maulā Masjid at Dhār. The measures decided upon provide for the repair of such portions of these buildings as were still left comparatively intact, and for the protection of the remainder. It was determined also to clear the *débris* and later additions from the Hindola Maḥal and from the ruins commonly known as the Tower of Victory. These works are now proceeding apace, with the happiest results, under the guidance of Captain E. Barnes, the Political Agent, who has promised a full account of them for a future report.

In the meantime, at the risk of anticipating the ultimate report, two discoveries of more than ordinary interest made by Captain Barnes may be noticed. The first occurred in the *miḥrāb* of the Kamāl Maulā Mosque at Dhār. The mosque itself appears from local tradition and from the numerous indications and inscriptions found within it to have been built on the site of, and to a large extent out of materials taken from, a Hindu Temple, known to the inhabitants as Rājā Bhoja's School. This inference was derived some time back from the existence of a Sanskrit alphabet and some Sanskrit grammatical forms inscribed in serpentine diagrams on two of the

[1] Volume XXI, No. LVIII, 1902, p. 339. | [2] Volume XIX, 1895-97, p. 154.

pillar bases in the prayer chamber and from certain Sanskrit inscriptions on the black stone slabs imbedded in the floor of the prayer chamber, and on the reverse face of the side walls of the *miḥrāb*.

It is the discovery of the hidden inscriptions on the back of these side walls that makes a story. At the angle of junction of the side and back wall of the *miḥrāb* are some holes large enough to admit a hand and arm, and it was entirely owing to the fortunate chance of some one passing his hand through one of these apertures and discovering letters on the back surface of the stones that the existence of these inscriptions was revealed. The method employed to obtain a record of these inaccessible inscriptions is also worth telling. Partial impressions were taken in the first instance by an ingenious system of paper rolled round jointed rods which were inserted through the apertures into the space behind the wall, and then unrolled; the impression was then made by rubbing lamp black upon a pad fixed to the extremity of a similar rod. This process was of course extremely laborious but was deemed well repaid by the results, so long, at least, as there appeared no chance of removing the stones. When, however, Lord Curzon visited Dhār in 1902, he requested that the repair of the mosque should be taken in hand, and that while this was being done any slabs likely to bear inscriptions and the removal of which involved no danger, should be taken out and examined. This work is still in progress, and the following *interim* information regarding it has been furnished by Mr. K. K. Lele, the Superintendent of Education, Dhār State, who has been instrumental in recovering many other inscriptions from that part of Central India.

The finest inscription is engraved on a slab of black stone (5′ 8″×5′) which was set up in the northern wall of the *miḥrāb*. The language is Sanskrit and Prakrit. There are 82 lines in all, containing the first two acts of a drama, written in praise of the last great Paramāra King, Arjunavarman (*c.* 1210—1218 A. D.), the 19th in descent from the founder Upendra, and the 10th from the famous Bhoja. The remaining portion of this stone-inscribed drama has not been found. The drama commemorates in particular the King's victory over Jayasiṁha, the ruler of Gujarāt (?), in the neighbourhood of the mountain Parva Parvata (which Mr. Lele conjectures may be Pavagaḍ in the Panch Mahals). The corresponding slab on the opposite side of the *miḥrāb* bears a Prakrit inscription of 83 lines, containing two odes in the Āryā metre to the tortoise incarnation of Viṣṇu—one composed by King Bhoja himself; and the other by a poet of his Court. Both slabs have now been fixed securely in strong frames and for the present are being preserved in the mosque. Besides the above, eight other fragments of Prakrit inscriptions were brought to light, one of which, consisting of 75 lines, is stated to have been composed by Rājā Bhoja.

None of the fragments or of the more complete inscriptions possess any date. All of them, it is hoped, will be published *in extenso* in due course.

The second discovery relates to the Tower of Victory and the excavation of what was once the most spacious and lavishly decorated tomb in Māṇḍū. For the following account of the affair the "Annual" is indebted to Mr. H. Cousens, the Archæological Superintendent of Western India, who has recently paid a visit to the spot:—

"Jahāngīr, in the account of the buildings of Dhār and Māṇḍū in his diary mentions a seven-storeyed tower or *mīnār*, standing out in front of the great Jāmi' Masjid, which, he says, was erected by Sulṭān Maḥmūd Khaljī. It is said to have been built as a Tower of Victory after the Sulṭān had vanquished the forces of Rānā Kumbha of Chitor. Its height was 54½ *gas*, its girth at the base was 50 *gas*, while from ground level to the top there were 171 steps. Sir James Campbell makes the *gas* three feet. Upon the middle of a great platform, about 270 feet square, and at the same height above ground level as the courtyard of the great Jāmi' Masjid, supported upon arched colonnades around its four sides, with round bastions at the corners, stood, until the beginning of this year, a great unshapely mass of fallen masonry, out of which rose portions of the four walls of a great building. This had been pointed out as the remains of the great Tower of Victory, and up to the time of my visit was accepted as such. At that time the workmen had removed about three-quarters of the material in the interior and had brought to view the marble-lined walls of a great chamber nearly 65 feet square, containing some graves over which were the remains of some beautifully designed grave-stones. Instead of the basement of a Tower of Victory we found the remains of a magnificent tomb of white marble, which, when complete, must have been the grandest building in Māṇḍū, and ranked amongst monuments of the first class in India. There is little doubt, from indirect evidence, all pointing in the same direction, that we have here the tomb of the greatest of Māṇḍū rulers, Sulṭān Maḥmūd. Probably the first notable to be buried in it was Khān Jahān, the father he loved so well.

"The interior measurement of the tomb is 64 feet 9 inches square, far larger than Hūshang's. It is of white marble, within and without, decorated with bands of ornamental carving, the interstices of which have been filled in with black and yellow stone so closely fitted that it is only the difference in colour of adjacent parts which shows where the joints are. In addition to this there has been an abundance of inlay work of red and green polished blood-stone, not in patterns of itself, but as filling the interstices of scroll work carved in the marble. There is also a great deal of coloured tile work, blue, white, green and yellow. There were three openings in each of the four sides of the tomb, which were all, except the central one on the west, facing the Jāmi' Masjid,—the entrance doorway—filled with lovely *jālī* work; and there are indications of a row, all round, of clear-story windows above these.

"The workmen had cleared one grave of the remains of an exceedingly ornate superstructure in inlaid black and yellow stone, but this grave was to the north of the centre of the tomb. I got the men to clear the centre, when another grave was found occupying the exact centre, with another, partly fallen in, touching it on the east. A day or two later a beautiful white marble grave-stone, in one great block, was found to the south-east of these, forced out of its position by the falling masses of masonry above. The clearance of this building is still being pushed forward, and interesting discoveries may still be looked for. All the beautifully carved inscriptions, which ran in bands around the frames of some of the windows, seem to be extracts from the Koran.

"But the Tower of Victory, or its site, had still to be located. Ascending the roof of the porch of the Jāmi' Masjid for a better view of the surroundings, it was at once seen that, of the four bastions around the great basement of this ruined tomb, the one at the north-west corner was far larger than the others, and it was, moreover, solidly built, while the others are hollow with entrance arches. On measuring these we found the large one 150 feet in circumference, and the smaller ones only 89 feet. The ruined, but undisturbed, masonry upon the big bastion rose to about twice the height of the top of the basement, whereas the other bastions do not rise higher than that level. Up through this solid bastion is a narrow staircase. Here, then, without a doubt, is the stump of the *mīnār*, or Tower of Victory, with the beginning of its staircase, which contained 171 steps *from the ground*, as Jahāngīr is careful to state, for he gives its height, as may be gathered from the context, from the level of the top of the basement or terrace on which the great tomb stood. In the basement below, running all around, are rooms and colonnades, the arches supported upon massive pillars, and these run up to and abut upon the base of the *mīnār*. This was the college said to have been built in connection with the *mīnār*. Sir James Campbell, as already stated, took the *gaz* at 3 feet, so that the circumference of this stump tallies with Jahāngīr's measurement of 50 *gaz*. We can now understand Sir Thomas Herbert's account when he says it was a tower 170 steps high, supported upon massive pillars and adorned with gates and windows very observable. It was built, he adds, by Khān Jahān, who there lies buried.[1] There are a few of the corbel brackets, which supported the balconied windows of the *mīnār*, still intact.

"Another discovery we made was that, beneath the inclined plane or ramp leading up to the ruined porch of the great tomb, were the original steps. It was then decided to clear away the ramp, which it was at first proposed to put into better order; but as Captain Barnes has kindly undertaken to write a full account of the work carried out at Māṇḍū, for a future issue of the "Annual," it is unnecessary here to describe the work further. There are certain points it would be interesting to go into more fully. Did Hūshang build the great Jāmi' Masjid, or did Mahmūd build it in commemoration of Hūshang? Hūshang did not have his own tomb sufficiently far advanced to be buried in it when he died. Is not the building, in Hindu style, on the west of Hūshang's tomb, the College in which he is said to have been first buried? The style is half way between the purely Hindu erections of Dilāwar Khān and the solid, square, massive masonry of Maḥmūd—built apparently in imitation of the former buildings before the heavier style was introduced. Was not the Hindola Maḥal one of Maḥmūd's palaces? The answers to these questions will satisfy something more than passing curiosity."

Bengal.—Passing eastward to Bengal, a whole series of important projects has there been taken up. Aśoka's broken pillar near Rampurwa, the separate pieces of which lay half buried in a lonely swamp, is now being raised from its grave and re-erected on the site where in all probability the great Buddhist Emperor himself originally set it up. The weird Jain caves at Khandagiri, crumbling away under their two thousand years' burden of age, have been protected against the further ravages of heat and rain; and the two stone elephants, which lay broken in confused fragments hard by, have been re-pieced and placed upon their feet again, flanking the front of the Gaṇeśa Gumphā, where they originally formed a guard-of-honour. On the summit of

[1] *J. B. B. R. A. S.*, XIX, 1895-97, p. 168. The great tomb may have been known as Khān Jahān's tomb in Maḥmud's lifetime and before he was buried in it, and this name may have stuck to the building.

the deserted hill of Muṇḍeśvarī the queer octagonal temple which lay half smothered in its own accumlated *débris*, the whole heap overgrown to the very roof with the rank vegetation of the jungle, has been brought back to the civilised light of day, and though the structure cannot now be restored to the form it bore twelve centuries ago, efforts are being made to preserve all the essential features. Similarly, the numerous temples at Bhubanesvar, some of which are in their own way quite unique, have been rescued, not, it is true, from the same advanced stage of disintegration, but still from a condition of more than incipient decay. Portions of the building which by the loosening of stones had become unsafe have been dismantled and rebuilt, as far as possible with the ancient material. The magnificent and costly temple of the Sun God, known as the Black Pagoda, strangely reared six hundred years ago on what is now at any rate a desert of sea sand at Konarak, has sunk into a state sadly different from that which still delighted the world in the time of Abū-l-Faẓl, who wrote: "Even those whose judgment is critical and who are difficult to please stand amazed at the sight." Much, however, has been and is being done to remedy the inroads of time and mischief. The plinth of the temple, which was buried in sand, has been laid open, and is now seen to be full of startling carvings including representations of harnessed horses and wheels, showing that the temple as a whole was designed to symbolise the chariot of the glorious Sun God.

Among the Muhammadan buildings of Bengal—relics of the independent Sulṭāns who had their capitals at Gaur and Panduah from the middle of the fourteenth to the middle of the sixteenth century—there was and still is room for much protective and restorative energy. It is the misfortune of these curious buildings, with their soft brick façades chiselled as elaborately as if of sandstone, that the glazed tiles, which form their crowning ornament, excited general covetousness. Much of the spoliation was wrought by Hindus in the early days of the East India Company, for Gaur has always been famous for its glazed tiles, but even to-day the hankering eye of the curio hunter is not at rest. Of course the destruction of Muhammadan masterpieces with the object of securing ornaments for vulgar Hindu buildings is not more reprehensible (nor more common) than the demolition of Hindu architectural trophies to provide decorations for common Muhammadan use. Many indeed of the old Muhammadan mosques were themselves built up with materials plundered from still more ancient Hindu temples. Happily the time has at last gone by when some influential zamindar of Malda could boldly deface a venerable Gaur relic that his new house might be adorned with enamelled tiles. Instead of destruction, we have now re-construction. It is, by the way, a point of some interest that the inscriptions preserved on some of the monuments, combined with numismatic evidence, have served to establish the exact chronology of the Muhammadan rulers of Bengal, in place of the muddled tabulation of dates which satisfied the compilers of the native records. At Panduah the striking five-storeyed *mīnār*, evidently an imitation of the Quṭb Mīnār at Delhi, has lost its topmost storey and its pinnacle, but these are now in the way of being carefully restored. Finally, the famous hill fort of Rohtasgarh and the many curious buildings on the Rohtasgarh plateau, which form the only specimen of Mughal civil architecture in Bengal, have been marked out for preservation, mainly because of the interesting example they afford of the conditions of military life in those unrestful days.

Assam.—In Assam, which belongs to the Bengal Circle, the Archæological Department has so far done little more than survey the ground, and even the survey is far from complete or exhaustive. Dr. Bloch made a tour of the province in the cold weather of 1902-03, and visited all the principal remains whose existence is known to the Department. These lie in the districts of Kamrup, Darrang, Nowgong, Sibsagar, Cachar and Sylhet. One important result of the tour is that a scheme can now be set going for the conservation of, at any rate, the more important monuments. The temple of Mādhava-Hayagrīva at Hajo, 14 miles north of Gauhati, was found to have been badly damaged by the memorable earthquake of 1897. Indeed, it seems a wonder that the building was not altogether razed to the ground as the earthquake was particularly violent and destructive in that region. The relic in question is one of the oldest of all the Assam temples, and is of pre-Ahom origin, dating back to Śaka 1505, which is equivalent to 1583-84 of our era. As for the ancient capital of the Ahom Kings at Ghurgaon, near Nazira, time and the elements have almost entirely obliterated it, and the single notable signpost of its existence is a fine three-storeyed building, which, however, is so overgrown with jungle as to recall to the imagination the nursery story of the Sleeping Beauty. And here it seems worth remarking that the exuberance of wild vegetation in India is such that the fabled magical envelopment of the Sleeping Beauty's palace in a tangled mass of impenetrable forest is a phenomenon that in real life confronts the Archæological Department again and again. One of the most persistent and insidious enemies the archæological conservator has to fight is the jungle.

A further proposal relating to Assam concerns the curious remains of the ancient capital of the Kachari Kings at Dimapur. It is estimated that the wall which belted this strange old city was 1½ miles in circumference, but the whole area thus enclosed has long been buried from human sight by a particularly rampant jungle, with the exception of a small corner near the eastern gate which, however, has only lately been cleared. The woodman's axe seems likely to be productive of interesting results here, if funds for exploration can be made available. In any case something, it is hoped, can be done for the curious monolithic *chessman* pillars and bifurcated columns, which now lie scattered about in broken pieces.

United Provinces.—Leaving Bengal and moving up country to the United Provinces we pass into a tract, which is, so far as monuments are concerned, the richest in all India. Here, in keeping with the magnitude of the task, the relatively large sum of Rs.1,58,541 was expended during the year 1902-03 on works of conservation, and of this large amount no less than Rs.1,27,330 was spent in the Agra Division alone. Thanks to the Public Works Department, the results happily are not less conspicuous than the outlay incurred to produce them. Agra indeed can boast of, perhaps, the greatest successes that restoration has ever yet achieved in any part of India—greatest not only by reason of the superlative importance of the monuments themselves, which have been rescued from impending ruin, but by reason also of the exceptional skill of the local masons, which has enabled them to copy the original carvings with scrupulous fidelity. In particular, a most striking improvement in the Fort has been produced by the complete restoration of the imposing frontage of the Jahāngīrī Mahall, and of the dilapidated brick-supported kiosk, which stands on the south bastion flanking its great façade. The quaint square pavilion known as Salīmgarh, which adorned the highest point of Agra Fort, was until quite recently used as a canteen, and the better to adapt it to that ignoble purpose the fine arches which open the pavilion on all four sides had been bricked up and fitted with mistri-made doors and windows, while a barrack-room verandah had been built up against the sun. To-day happily the canteen is wiped out of sight, and the pavilion has regained its former beauty—except that the modern whitewash has not yet been removed, because special precautions will be needed to preserve the delicate paintings under the plaster.

In the square surrounding the Dīwān-i-'Āmm, or Hall of Public Audience, which visitors in the past used to remember only as an arsenal yard and convenient stand for carriages, the military authorities have generously allowed the hideous modern casemates to be demolished and the ancient arcades, which they screened from view, to be restored in their entirety. Only half of the quadrangle has been taken in hand during the past year, but the transformation of this part has been complete. Along with the repair of the *dálāns*, much *débris* has been cleared away, and the old roads and pavement, where the assembled audience stood before the Emperor, brought to light and repaired. Other parts of the Agra Fort have also received their share of attention. The Angūrī-Bāgh and the Machhī Bhawan have both been restored more exactly to their original condition, and at the Pearl Mosque much has been done to obliterate from its pure marbles the traces of rough usage and decay.

At the Tāj Maḥall and its surrounding buildings, the work of renovation has been energetically pushed forward. The squalid bazars have been cleared away from its gates. The Fatḥpurī masjid on the right, and the Sahelī Burj, corresponding to it, on the left of the approaching road, have been rescued from a state of sad neglect and once again recall their former selves. The colonnades flanking the approach have been opened out and repaired and the untidy quadrangle, which precedes the main entrance, has been converted into a well grassed and peaceful court.

Within the precinct of the tomb itself the gardens, with their watercourses, fountains and flower beds, have been laid out more strictly in accordance with their ancient designs, and considerable improvements have been made in the water supply of the grounds, while the stately Mosque and its *jawāb* have been structurally repaired and beautified by the renovation of their encrusted ornaments and sculptured panels. Across the River Jumna, the tomb of I'timādu-d-Daulah has been crowned again with its graceful balustrade of perforated marble, and much of its inlay of precious stones has been repaired; and at Sikandarah, in the main gatehouse of the Mausoleum of Akbar, the bold designs of coloured stonework have been renewed and another of its gates, which must inevitably have collapsed in a few more years, has also passed into the repairer's hands.

Outside Agra, the most important operations of the year have centred at Lucknow, Allahabad, and in the Bānda district. In Lucknow the most interesting undertaking was connected with that almost modern memorial of heroic history, the Residency. The bruised and battered condition of the once massive walls and the crumbling state of the more decayed portions of the ruins are too well known to need any description here. To the violent damage inflicted by shot and shell during the great siege, much wanton injury was added by the chagrined mutineers when the Residency was evacuated in November 1857, after the final relief. Since then, for nearly half a century, rain, and wind, and weather have carried on a more peaceful but not less effective bombardment of the old building, until, now that at last the work of conservation has tardily been taken up, the difficulty of making up for past neglect is immense. To restore the building out and out would of course be a comparatively straightforward task; but obviously neither reason nor sentiment would permit any solution of that sort. What has to be done is not to repair damage, but carefully to preserve all evidences of damage for the glory of the tale it tells. The Residency after, not before, the Mutiny is the spectacle that alone will thrill the visitor, and it is this picture which the Archæological Department has striven to fix and to perpetuate without betraying its handiwork. Two clear objects were placed before the Public Works Department:—(1) to preserve, as far as possible, the existing appearance of the ruins and prevent the obtrusion of any sign of new work, whether woodwork, brick-work, or plaster; and (2) to preserve carefully all holes made by shot or shell, and yet somehow to prevent the broken walls from yielding to further decay. The methods adopted to give effect to these instructions are worth stating, as illustrating the difficulty of carrying out elaborate works of preservation and at the same time of avoiding obtrusive evidences of artificial bolstering:—

(i) The mud in the old joints in the brickwork was raked out to a depth of about 2 inches; one inch of which was replaced by good lime mortar, and the other inch left vacant. This treatment of the joints serves to prevent further damage from rain beating in and washing out the cementing material, and is entirely unobtrusive.

(ii) The ends of all plaster work have been finished off with a slope of good lime mortar to prevent water getting in between it and the wall.

(iii) The tops of all walls have been cement-plastered and given an outward slope from the centre, to ensure no water lodging on the top.

(iv) In many cases over doors and windows the wooden bressummers supporting the superstructure were in imminent danger of collapse. In these cases iron bressummers have been carefully inserted without disturbing the superstructure. There is still some of this work remaining to be done.

(v) In cases where brickwork repairs were absolutely necessary to avoid collapse of any portion of a structure, the greatest care has been taken always to use bricks similar to those of which the Residency was built; the joints being treated as described above.

Anyone revisiting the Residency now would probably say that he could see no difference in the condition of the building, and this would be the greatest compliment he could pay to the repairer, whose one idea has been to avoid all outward semblance of patching up a ruin.

In addition to the Residency, three other buildings of archæological interest in Lucknow have been brought into the programme of conservation—namely, the Dilkushā Palace, the Sikandar Bāgh gateway and enclosure, and the Jāmi' Masjid. As, however, the work in all these cases is still in progress, detailed reports are reserved. Of the Jāmi' Masjid it may be incidentally remarked that its repair has been undertaken rather in the interests of the Muhammadan community than of Archæology, since the building is of a late inferior style and decorated with plaster and paint in execrable taste. Mention should also be made here of the partial repair, which has been carried out during the past year, of the Nawābī Bridge at Lucknow The repair of the central span has not yet been undertaken, owing to the great difficulty and danger of the work, and it is an open question whether the undertaking can ever be completed.

At Allahabad the repair of the tomb of the Sulṭān Khusrau and of the other mausolea in the Khusrau Bāgh has been very successfully finished.

In the Bānda District, the stone steps on the hill ascent to Kalinjar Fort have been repaired, and the approaching footpaths cleared. The broken pieces of the statue of Viṣṇu lying on the Nāga have been put together. The battlements of the Fort have been restored in places, and some 1,000 trees cut out of the masonry of the walls. At Jaunpūr, in the same neighbourhood, the enclosure of the Sharqī Kings' Tombs has been repaired.

Punjab.—Coming to the Punjab, we find that, with one notable exception, practically nothing was done here towards conservation until the very end of the year under report, when the Local Government made an allotment of Rs. 40,000 with the promise of a like sum annually for the next four years. A further grant-in-aid of Rs. 25,000 was made by the Government of India, and these united resources enabled the Archæological Department to take in hand the conservation of some important monuments that had long suffered from neglect. The exception referred to is the grand old mosque erected by Sher Shāh within the wall of the old Fort at Delhi, famous for its profuse decoration and rich colour. The repair of this mosque was taken in hand at the instance of the Viceroy, Lord Curzon, and the transformation it has undergone has been thorough. The broken marble of the arches and the façade, the damaged sandstone of the walls, and the missing decorative inlay of white and black marble, have all been made good, and the visitor may once more contemplate it with joy instead of with pain. Besides the mosque in the Purānā Qil'a, some 15 other buildings, in all, came under special repair, but owing to the fact that the year was already well advanced when the allotments were made, and that careful plans and estimates had to be prepared and other preliminaries settled in the first instance, only a small proportion of the scheme could be brought to completion before the end of the year. Among the buildings brought under conservation were the mausoleum of Jahāngīr and several other tombs and buildings grouped around it at Shāhdara, the mosque of Wazīr Khān in Lahor, and the exquisite tomb of Shamsu-d-Dīn Taga Khān near Delhi. A full description of these works will be given in a future report. Among the works actually finished should be mentioned the complete repair, involving some small measures of restoration, of the Zīnatu-l-masājid at Delhi—a mosque once used as a bakery for the troops and for many years in a ruined condition. It has now been put in thorough repair: structural weaknesses have been made good; the whitewash has been cleaned from its marble and sandstone façade and from the aisles within; the falling plaster has been renewed; the roof and courtyard swept of jungle; the approaching stairway rebuilt; and the balustrades around the platform restored.

Of important works in the Punjab not yet finished, special mention must here be made, by exception, of the recovery from England and restoration to their original places of the famous mosaics which once adorned the throne of S͟hāh Jahān at Delhi. The throne, as is well known, occupies the centre of the north side of the Dīwān-i-ʿĀmm, or the Hall of Public Audience, of the Great Mug͟hal. It consists of a raised platform of white marble, inlaid with coloured stones, with a marble baldachino, or canopy, above it.

The throne was approached by the Emperor from the back by a doorway, pierced in a recess in the wall. The main feature of this recess was the mosaic work of marble and coloured stones with which its entire surface was adorned. The decoration is more particularly famous for the panels of black marble, inlaid with a variety of coloured stones in designs of birds and flowers. These panels are the sole examples in India of this particular form of technique. The most justly famous among them is one representing the figure of Orpheus sitting under a tree, and fiddling to a circle of listening animals.[1] At the time of the Mutiny in 1857 a good many of these panels, which are quite small, were picked out and mutilated. Twelve of them, including the representation of Orpheus, as well as four larger and seven smaller panels, were appropriated by Captain (afterwards Sir John) Jones, and sold by him for £500 to the British Government, who deposited them in the South Kensington Museum.

In 1882 all the inlay in the lower half of the back wall of the recess was restored under the supervision of Major H. H. Cole, the then Curator of Ancient Monuments in India. The work was executed with great care, but unhappily some of the stones employed in the new work matched badly with the originals. The difference between them is particularly noticeable in the background of the panels; a greyish black Indian marble having been used to replace the intensely black and finely grained marble, only procurable in Italy. In some other respects also the new work is inferior, the designs being harsher and the technique coarser. The upper portion of the wall was not repaired by Major Cole, because he hoped that the panels in England might be recovered at some future time, and it appeared inexcusable to resort to artificial renovation so long as the originals were known to exist elsewhere. During the past year a strong appeal for the recovery of these panels was made by the Government of India, and the trustees of the Victoria and Albert Museum were kind enough to agree to their return.

It had been hoped that the plaques would reach India in time to be restored for the ceremonies of the Investiture of the two Indian Orders held in connection with the Delhi Darbar, and the occasion would indeed have been an appropriate one on which to emblemise, by the restoration of these mosaics, the generous policy which the Government has now adopted towards the relics of antiquity, as opposed to the proverbial vandalism of earlier days. Unfortunately the plaques did not arrive till the last days of December, and their restitution had to be deferred until after the Darbar. They have now been replaced behind the throne; and many other panels, also in the upper portion of the walls, have been cleaned of the *lac* with which they were covered, and their mutilated surfaces repolished. There still, however, remain some

[1] A beautiful chromo-lithograph of this is published by Major H. H. Cole in his Report on Delhi, in the series entitled "Preservation of National Monuments in India." He also gives a general view of the back of the throne.

gaps where panels are partly or wholly missing, and these will gradually be filled up, as opportunity offers, in accordance with the ancient designs. But it will take some time before the precise stones used can be identified and procured from Europe, and it will very probably be found necessary to get the panels executed in Florence or to obtain artists from Italy to do the work in India.

Something remains to be said concerning the date and style of these plaques. Tradition has it that the decoration of the throne was the workmanship of Austin de Bordeaux, the celebrated French artificer, who is said to have been employed by the Emperor Shāh Jahān both on his palace at Delhi and on the Tāj at Agra. The figure of Orpheus, indeed, is pointed out by the native guides as a portrait of Austin de Bordeaux himself. The story seems apocryphal. Perhaps it was suggested by the obviously Italian character of the panel designs; but it should be observed that the black marble of their backgrounds and the majority of the inlaid stones are of Italian, and not Indian, provenance, and it is not unreasonable to suppose, therefore, that they were not only designed but actually executed in an Italian studio and afterwards imported into this country.

The arabesques, on the other hand, which decorate the interspaces between the panels, are of pure Indian style and Indian workmanship without a vestige of foreign influence. Mr. Havell, referring to the decoration of the Delhi Throne, in a recent article in the *Nineteenth Century and After*,[1] has suggested that it has been wrongly attributed to Shāh Jahān's reign and ought rather to be referred to the early part of the eighteenth century. He rightly insists on its inferiority in point of style to that of the Tāj at Agra, and further argues that the naturalistic representations of birds and animals, had they existed in the time of Aurangzeb, would scarcely have been left unmutilated by that iconoclast Emperor. The latter argument is not convincing, since parallel instances may be cited of other figures which must often have been seen by Aurangzeb, yet managed to escape violation at his hands. Nor ought mere inferiority of style to be pressed too far as evidence of date. The *pietra dura* of Shāh Jahān's reign in the Lahore Fort is equally inferior to that of the Tāj, and in the case of the Delhi Throne the task of the artists was a peculiarly difficult one. The basis of this decoration was a number of square and oblong panels of varying sizes and of wholly unfamiliar styles. There are few artists who could create an harmonious design out of such material, and least of all a Mughal artist, tied down by the strictest traditions of form and colour, both alike unsuitable to the task he had to perform. With such limitations it is not surprising that the result appears grotesque, or that the arabesques, which serve to combine the panels into a general scheme of decoration, compare unfavourably in style with those of the Tāj.

A special reference is also called for here to another work, involving the restoration of *pietra dura*, and carried out about the same time as the work on Shāh Jahān's throne—namely, the repair of the tomb of Jahānārā Begam, the faithful daughter of Shāh Jahān. The tomb is situated in the same enclosure as the Dargāh of Nizāmu-d-Dīn Auliyā, but is further enclosed within a marble screen. The grave consists of a simple marble block, slightly hollowed out on its upper surface to form

[1] *Nineteenth Century and After*, June 1903, pages 1039 sqq.—"The Tāj and Its Designers."

a small bed in which grass grows; and at the northern end stands a headstone on which is inscribed the famous couplet, written, it is said, by the Princess herself:—

> Let naught but green grass ever mantle my grave,
> For grass is the coverlet meet for the poor.

The decoration of this headstone had suffered much at the hands of visitors to the tomb. Originally the letters of the inscription were inlaid in black marble, with a foliated border of coloured stones around; but almost all the tessellated pieces had been sacrilegiously picked out, and the adjoining surface of the white marble ground had been much chipped in the process. Of the coloured stones—agate, jasper, and malachite—it was fortunate that some small fragments still adhered in their places; enough to make the restoration certain in every particular.

Regarding the Persian inscription, it seems worth remarking that the text has not infrequently been mistranslated as if the whole were in verse, whereas only the couplet already quoted is rythmic, and the rest is in prose. The whole inscription may be rendered in English thus:—

> He is the living, the everlasting—
> Let naught but green grass ever mantle my grave,
> For grass is the coverlet meet for the poor.
> The humble (and) mortal Jahānārā, disciple of the Chis͟ht lords, daughter of the Emperor S͟hāh Jahān G͟hāzi. (May God endow him with wisdom.)

Ajmir.—From the Punjab we go southward again into Rajputana and Ajmīr, which is, nominally at least, included within the Punjab Circle. Here, on the side of the Ajmīr Lake, the stately marble embankment built by S͟hāh Jahān has been carefully restored, and the ugly modern offices and bungalows, which offended every sympathetic eye, have been made to yield place to the exquisite marble pavilions of the Mug͟hal Emperor—white and spotless as when first erected. The embankment is now largely visited by both Hindus and Muhammadans, who appear to enjoy and appreciate the transformation that has been effected there. At Ajmīr also, the Aṛhāī-din-kā-jhoṁpṛā Mosque, which, according to Cunningham, is the finest specimen of the early Muhammadan mosque that now exists, has been rescued from a sad state of dilapidation. The domes have been replaced, the tenements of squatters have been bought up and cleared, the cloister walls have been strengthened, and various missing pillars have been restored.

Madras.—Passing still further south into the Madras Presidency, we come to a region almost barren of narrative so far as the present chapter is concerned—a fact which certainly can afford no ground for satisfaction. Much attention has, it is true, been given, at the desire of the Viceroy, to the interesting temple at Sōṁpalle, built in the floriated Vijayanagar style, with its exquisitely carved four pillared marriage hall, and graceful *dīpdān* or lamp column, in front; and some solicitude has also been exhibited by the local Archæological Surveyor for the preservation of the old wall at Madras (or what remains of it) which encircled the ancient town and marked the limits of civic responsibility imposed upon old Pedda Naiḍu, the watchman, in quaint pre-Company times. But when the story of these two monuments has been told—and the special articles on the subject tell it adequately—the sum total of the conservation work in Madras has practically been stated.

If Madras were a country generally devoid of archæological interest, there would of course be nothing either remarkable or regrettable in bygone archæological inactivity. But the very opposite is the case, and it is a matter for wonderment that the conservation of the fine galaxy of ancient monuments for which the Southern Presidency is famous should not have appealed more strongly to the genius of the Local Government. During the last twelve years, that is, since the Acting Governorship of Mr. Garstin in 1891, official responsibility in the matter in question has in theory been limited to the maintenance of one hundred typical examples of the various classes of architecture represented in the Presidency, and in practice the preservation even of these has been carried on in a desultory manner As far as the Archæological Department is concerned, its energies have been directed to the preparation of sundry drawings and to exploration, rather than to conservation. A complete change in this policy has now happily been inaugurated, and a more liberal programme adopted. During 1903-04 a sum of nearly Rs. 20,000 (about ten times the amount hitherto given to the purpose) has been allotted to Archæology, and effective measures are accordingly being prepared for a comprehensive scheme of conservation. Madras names of places look a little formidable to unfamiliar eyes, but Southern Indian Archæologists will appreciate the statement that a large plan of campaign seems to await execution at Mahādānapuram, Ratnagiri, Śivāyam, Śuṇdakkā-Pārai, Muśiri, Perambalūr, Samayāpuram, Tiruvallarai, Nārtāmalai, Arumbāvūr, Vālikaṇḍapuram, Āduturai, Uyyakoṇḍān, Śrī Rangam, Jambukēśvaram, Uṛaiyūr, Trichinopoly, Vijayanagar, Velluru, Kāñchīpuram, and Tānjāvūr.

Burma.—Lastly, in Burma, conservation works have been in progress at the two towns of Mandalay and Pagān, but it is the Palace and Fort at Mandalay that have been, and still are, the central figures in the Archæological programme. The Palace was originally built at Amarāpura by Shwe Bo Min in 1845, and was removed with almost American boldness, to Mandalay by King Mindon in 1859. During the last three or four years the Archæological Department has been very busy here, and the rebuilding of some of the missing *pyathats*, or pavilions, around the Fort walls, and the drastic sweeping away of the various offices, private quarters, and other evidences of British occupation from the Palace precincts, will be found duly described in the special article devoted to this subject. It may appropriately be mentioned here that local opinion does not unanimously endorse the conservation of the Mandalay Palace, and that the ground of disagreement usually urged is that the building, being of wood, is necessarily doomed to early decomposition. Compared with more solid and enduring memorials of stone, the Mandalay Palace, constructed entirely of wood, may indeed seem wanting in some of the elements of permanence. But permanence is relative, and, at any rate, the hope may be confidently entertained that the moderate scheme of conservation now in hand will preserve the palace intact for fully a hundred years. Is a century of extended existence too small an end to justify the effort? When we remember that the palace is the one and only example of the ceremonial and domestic architecture of the Burmese Kings; that it embodies some of the finest examples of Burmese wood carving anywhere extant; that since royal patronage passed away with Thibaw the glorious skill of the native decorator languishes for want of encouragement; that under the uninspiring influence of Western utilitarianism, the great Palace in Mandalay almost alone remains to keep alive the ideals of the depressed craftsmen; and that the abandonment of this majestic landmark would probably be the signal for a more rapid and hopeless decadence of the wood-carver's craft in Upper Burma—when we think of all this, and when we hear the workmen of to-day acknowledge the inferiority of their handiwork compared with the masterpieces of King Mindon's and King Thibaw's times, can we say that the preservation of the Palace, if only for a hundred years more, is a thing of small account?

The Pagān Monuments call for no very extensive notice here, as an effective scheme for their conservation still waits to be developed. In the meantime, however, some measures on a modest scale have been undertaken by the Local Government for the repair of the Ananda, Gawdapalin, Thabyinnyu, and Shwekugyi pagodas, and for the Manuha and Nanpaya temples.

* * * * * * *

Before dismissing the subject of conservation, it will be appropriate to refer to the steps that have been taken to secure the preservation of minor and moveable antiquities by instituting small museums in some of the main centres of archæological interest, and by stimulating local officers to assist in bringing together any objects of value upon which they may chance. This is one of the most important aspects of conservation, inasmuch as many of the smaller monuments scattered about the face of the country are incapable of preservation on the spot where they have been found and often too bulky to be removed to the larger museums which exist only in the capital cities of India; and, even if their removal were practicable, there are few local officers with sufficient general interest in the preservation of antiquities to take the trouble to despatch them to some far off Museum, where they themselves may never have the opportunity of viewing them again. The Museums which have recently been arranged for—all, it should be added, at the instigation of His Excellency the Viceroy—are at Malda in Bengal, at Pagān and Mandalay in Burma, at Bījāpūr in Bombay, at Sarnāth near Benares, at the Tāj in Agra, and at Peshawar in the Frontier Province. The districts in which these Museums are placed are sufficient guarantee that they will be rapidly stocked with interesting and valuable antiquities. Already in Pagān the efforts of one native assistant and the outlay of a few rupees have brought together a collection of inscriptions, idols, terra-cotta plaques, enamelled tiles and the like, of first rate importance. By the institution of such collections it may be hoped also that the attraction of visitors to these localities will be increased, that fresh light will be thrown on the groups of monuments with which they are connected, and that the minor antiquities themselves, which go to make up the collections, will be studied to a greater advantage on the actual spot where they have been discovered, than they could be, if dissociated from their surroundings in some distant Museum.

J. H. M.

SĪDI SAYYAD'S MOSQUE, AHMEDĀBĀD.

THIS mosque, which is situated in the north-east corner of the Bhadr, or royal enclosure, at Ahmedābād, is notable for the two remarkable perforated windows which adorn it, and which have become world-famed. For many years it has been used as a Government Office, and its interior has been inaccessible to the public. The windows, therefore, which are inserted in the back wall of the mosque, could be viewed only from the outside. They are flanked by others of the same shape and size, filled with geometric tracery, which, with three more in the south end of the building, would themselves suffice to make the mosque a distinguished building. In the north end are three empty spaces for similar windows, but a close inspection of the openings shews that they were never inserted. The unfinished *mīnārs*, which have not been carried above the roof of the mosque, also indicate an abrupt termination and abandonment of the work. Some think there was a third tracery window above the central *miḥrāb*, and between the two existing ones, where the space is closed with plain ashlar masonry. It is certainly possible that the builder intended to put in a third, and, perhaps, a still more superb window, in this space, and that when the work was abandoned, the space was walled up in order to make the mosque fit to worship in. The three open spaces which were left in the north end did not so much matter as they were not upon the sun or weather side.

The actual date of the erection of the mosque is not known. "Sīdi Sayyad, according to Sir Theodore C. Hope, was a slave of Aḥmad Shāh's, who, like many of his race, rose to wealth and power. This is the tradition, but there is no record to corroborate it, and the style of the building does not accord with that of the Royal tomb and Rānī's Ḥaẓīrah which belong to the latter part of Aḥmad Shāh's reign. The introduction of the archings between the piers to support the roof, alone seems decisive against a date in the fifteenth century; but whilst it is probably subsequent to the tomb of Shāh 'Ālam, it may belong, at earliest, to about the end of Maḥmūd Shāh Bigarah's reign, though possibly later." [1]

In Marāthā times the mosque was desecrated and allowed to fall out of repair, and later on it was converted, under British rule, into a treasury and record-room for the

[1] *Ahmedābād Architecture, A.D. 1412—1520* (Burgess), page 41.

local magistrate, the Māmlatdār of Daskrohi *tālukā*. To fit it for this purpose the whole front was walled up, modern windows and doors were inserted, cross walls and iron-barred partitions were added, the great perforated windows were walled up from behind, and two of the *mihrābs* were converted into presses. The space before the mosque was closed in with surrounding out-houses and shut off entirely from public view.

The windows which have become so famous, have been drawn, photographed, and copied in wood-work times without number. "One of these windows was injured slightly at the apex when taking down the platform which was put up by Mr. Purdon Clarke for the purpose of paper casts being taken about five years ago.[1] The damage has grown since then, owing probably to the stone having lost its cohesive properties from age and birds trying to make their nests there. The sooner the damage is repaired the better. Mr. De Forest, an American gentleman, had *facsimiles* made of these windows in wood. One of them is now in the Indian Section of the South Kensington Museum, and the other is in New York."

In October, 1900, His Excellency the Viceroy visited Ahmedābād, and shortly afterwards, at Poona, gave me instructions to proceed to Ahmedābād, and, among other things, to see that arrangements were made for the restoration of the mosque to its original state and all necessary repairs carried out. This necessitated a new office being built for the Māmlatdār, and thus the carrying out of the work was delayed until estimates had been prepared for the new building and sanctioned, funds allotted, and the new building erected.

The restoration was to include the demolition of all added walls and partitions, window and door frames, out-houses and walls and gate. The whitewash was to be removed and the building thoroughly cleaned, and the broken part of one of the great windows was to be very carefully mended. All this was eventually accomplished, and we have now added another object of interest to the city, a building of which it can rightly be proud. The whole front is open to the road with a spacious courtyard before it. The exquisite lace-like tracery of the great windows, as seen from within, with the light filtering through the delicate filigree work, and backed by the glory of the setting sun, is something worth going back to Ahmedabad to see.

But, alas! with the permission to the Muhammadan community to use it under certain conditions, the building is likely to suffer at the hands of the worshippers unless a close watch is maintained. When I was at Ahmedābād, the first time after the restoration, they had stowed away the ugly bamboo frame-work of one of their great *tābūts* in one corner, and although I had it removed, it was again put back with, I was told, the permission of the Collector.

The accompanying photographs show the building before and after restoration. The first was taken in a very confined area, not far from the south-east corner. I was unable, owing to the out-houses pressing so closely upon it, to get a photograph from the front. However, sufficient of the front is seen to show the manner in which it had been walled up.

---

[1] Extract from Mr. Crawley Boevey's *Scheme for the Protection and Conservation of Antient Buildings*. Published in 1886.

a 

b 

(a) BEFORE RESTORATION. (b) AFTER RESTORATION.

Attention was called to this mosque by Major H. H. Cole, R.E., in his report of the 5th July, 1881, when he held the appointment of Curator of Ancient Monuments in India. He wrote "*The clearing and cleaning of its disfigurements and impedimenta are urgent remedies which I strongly recommend to Government;* but, to place the building in a suitable condition, an office will have to be provided for the Mâmlatdâr." (The italics are his.)

The total cost of the restoration of the mosque amounted to Rs. 1,702.

HENRY COUSENS.

THE MOSQUE AT THE GOL GUMBAZ, BĪJĀPUR.

IT was the custom, when a great tomb was built. to add a mosque and a tank for the private use of members of the household of the deceased, and this custom was so thoroughly carried out at Bījāpur that in some cases—notably the Ibrāhīm Rauza—there is nothing to choose between the tomb and the mosque, whether in point of size, execution, or embellishment. The great Gol Gumbaz, the tomb of Maḥmūd 'Ādil Shāh, built in A.D. 1656, formed no exception to the rule, and beside it, on the west, stands one of the best proportioned and best built mosques in the city,—a mosque which, had it not been dwarfed by the overshadowing mass of the great tomb, with its enormous dome, one of the largest in the world, would have commanded far more attention and respect than has fallen to its share. Its beautiful cornice, its slender graceful *mīnārs*, still perfect, and its noble façade combine to make it a building of much higher artistic merit than the tomb to which it is an adjunct.

But the hand of the utilitarian had fallen upon it. Major H. H. Cole, R.E., writes in his report of the 26th May, 1881:—"The adjoining mosque to the west is a building of interest which should be preserved. During the famine of 1876-77 part of the interior was enclosed for an irrigation office, and I learned, during my visit in March, 1881, that it is proposed to convert it into a travellers' bungalow—*a proceeding which I consider vandalistic and disfiguring, and which I strongly advise may be counterordered. The mosque should be cleared of all the enclosing walls and left as originally built and designed.*" (The italics are his.)

Cross-walls were built between the piers, enclosing spaces sufficient to form four suites of rooms. These were even carried forward on one side to the front arches, but were subsequently removed. Bathrooms were added at each end of the façade, as will be seen in the accompanying photograph, and the back of the central *miḥrāb* was knocked out in order to insert a back door giving access to some cookhouses situated at the back. As if this were not enough, a proposal was made in 1898 to pierce the solid masonry of the back wall of the mosque in order to introduce two additional windows. This I unhesitatingly vetoed.

I had several times urged the necessity of restoring the mosque, but want of funds to build a new travellers' bungalow was always the reason for postponing it. In my Progress Report for 1899-1900 I brought it forward once again, when it was proposed to convert the Yāqūt Mahal into a travellers' bungalow, but nothing more was done until His Excellency the Viceroy visited Bījāpur on the 10th November, 1900, when he gave instructions for the restoration of the mosque to its original condition. This order was subsequently carried out, and the second photograph shows the mosque as it appears to-day.

The beautiful deep cornice which spanned the whole length of the façade between the *mīnārs* had for some years past given us trouble, owing to much of the stone rotting and giving way; and the difficult position of the work and the height from the ground combine to make it a risky as well as an awkward undertaking. Much more difficult and risky, however, will be the work of restoring the higher and heavier cornice of the great tomb opposite, which it is now proposed to take in hand. These deep overhanging cornices, so very wooden-looking in their design and mode of construction, have invariably been the weakest points in the buildings. It is evident that the architects and builders of those days were strangers to the Dakhan and unaccustomed to working in the local trap rock, else they would never have dared to use such material for these heavy overhanging and but slightly supported cornices. The stone is of a friable and brittle nature, and when exposed to the air and weather gradually disintegrates. It is very unequal in quality, for we often find in a great expanse of well-built and well-weathered walling a single stone here and there that has completely rotted away. The harder and better basaltic trap is a good building stone in block, but for unsupported, or poorly supported, brackets and slabs of large area it is hardly suitable. The builders, who probably came from Northern India, had no experience with it, and the only local buildings they could examine at all, if even they took this trouble, were a few old ruined temples of the Hindus.

So long as the damaged cornice remained in the state described, it was not only an eyesore but also a menace to the lives of travellers and servants in the building below, since several of the great brackets had already fallen, while others were more or less cracked or decomposed. It was therefore considered expedient to have something done, and in 1895 the Executive Engineer submitted an estimate amounting to Rs. 876 for renewing certain brackets, removing the very heavy layer of concrete upon the cornice slabs, and substituting a much lighter and thinner layer of cement concrete. For various reasons, the famine being one, the work progressed but slowly. Later, at the beginning of 1898, Mr. Ahmadi, the new Executive Engineer, examined the cornice and came to the conclusion that his predecessor's estimate was inadequate. He framed two alternative estimates, one for complete restoration, costing Rs. 3,027, and the other for propping up the cornice with teakwood struts as a temporary measure, costing Rs. 271. In December 1898, Government, in the Public Works Department, referred the matter back to the Superintending Engineer asking whether the building was of such architectural beauty as to justify the expenditure proposed; if not, whether it would not be better to remove the cornice altogether, in the meantime substituting corrugated iron for the slabs. Then followed two more alternative estimates in one of which it was proposed to preserve that part of the cornice above the south bay of the façade, as a sample of the whole, dismantle the rest and stack the stones upon one side; while the second provided for teak supports by means of longitudinal beams and struts bearing upon a projecting moulding on the wall below, and screwed back by bolts let into the wall masonry.

The Superintending Engineer stated that he considered both the building and the cornice of considerable beauty, but that the appearance of the building was marred by the partition walls within which formed rooms. The cornice, he said, was one of the finest in Bījāpur, overhanging to the extent of 8¼ feet, and having a greater projection than any other except that of the Gol Gumbaz. He approved of the retention of the south bay as a sample, but disapproved of the use of corrugated iron. He had no objection to the proposal of the Executive Engineer to retain that portion of the cornice over the central bay as well. He submitted three tracings with estimates for Rs. 248, Rs. 600, and Rs. 309, respectively, for three different methods of supporting the portion of the cornice to be retained over the south bay. He considered the rates in the previous estimate for restoring the whole cornice too low for the class of work desired, and forwarded a revised estimate for Rs. 4,594. Upon the correspondence being forwarded to me for opinion, I replied that, much as I should wish to see the whole cornice restored, I thought we must be content at present with preserving a part only, and that the dismantled stones, instead of being thrown down as proposed, should be laid upon the roof above, where they would be secure from pilferers, and save re-lifting, if, at a future time, the cornice should be wholly restored.

In the end the damaged cornice over three bays was removed, while that over the south and centre bays was retained and supported by teakwood struts and beams.

HENRY COUSENS.

ELEVATION AND SECTION OF CORNICE.

PLAN OF CORNICE, LOOKING UPWARDS.

CONSERVATION IN BENGAL.

ALTHOUGH the modern provinces of Bengal, Behar, and Orissa—and especially Behar—have under other geographical designations played a part of great interest in the ancient history of Hindustan, the archæological relics of the eventful past which the ravages of time and of vandalism have spared, are in number less considerable and in character less important than the striking monuments found in most other parts of historic India. That many architectural remains of a bygone glory lie beneath the soil is indeed probable enough, but the spade of the explorer has yet to prove whether anything of the buried past may still be reclaimed. Here, as elsewhere, the Muhammadan invaders were wont to signalise the subjugation of territories by demolishing Hindu and Buddhist shrines and temples, and employing the materials in the building up of mosques and tombs.

It was the more fortunate fate of the more remote province of Orissa to enjoy a relatively long spell of independence free from foreign inroads, and the result is visible to-day in the survival of a number of mediæval Hindu temples, which in their completeness afford striking illustrations of the artistic taste of their period. Bengal proper and Behar, on the other hand, formed the outposts of the Mughal empire, and the local viceroys were stern soldiers, not luxurious monarchs, having either no artistic bent or no inducement to indulge it. It was only the independent Muhammadan kings, who, feeling that the lustre they shed was their own, adorned their capitals at Gaur and Panduah with elaborate works of art; and these buildings, notwithstanding the vandalism of later days, still commemorate the pomp of their fallen majesty.

But when all this is said, it is still true that the Lower Provinces contain a number of ancient monuments which, if less widely known and less generally visited than the celebrated buildings of other provinces, deserve to be carefully maintained, both as worthy memorials of a bygone power, and as objects of scientific interest to students of archæology. The aim of this article is to convey some general idea of the time, the style, and the artistic features of the principal of these monuments, and of the conservation work which has been undertaken to arrest the creeping process of ruin. The four sections into which the present article has been divided are based upon a classification of the buildings according to period and style. Section I deals with the most ancient remains, belonging to a period ending with the rise of the great Gupta empire, or approximately 300 A.D. Next come the mediæval monuments, which carry the historical connection up to the first Muhammadan invasion, or about 1200 A.D. Section III embraces the period of independent Muhammadan rule in Bengal; and the buildings of the Mughal empire form the subject of the concluding section.

SECTION I.

EARLIEST MONUMENTS.

The Aśoka Column near Rampurwa.

The northernmost of the four pillars erected by Aśoka along the course of the Gandak is generally called the Rampurwa pillar, and is situated in the Shikarpur *thāna* of the district of Champaran, about 37 miles north of Bettiah, close to village Pipariyā. Rampurwa is a small *tolah* or hamlet a little west of the pillar, and locally the column is well known as *Pipariyā-kā-laur*.

The pillar was first discovered by Mr. Carlleyle in 1877-78, but his report was not published until 1885 in Volume XXII of General Cunningham's Reports; whereas the report by Mr. Garrick, who visited the pillar three years later than Mr. Carlleyle, appeared two years earlier, in 1883, in Volume XVI of the same series. Mr. Carlleyle tells us that he found the upper portion of the capital of a pillar, closely resembling that of the Lauriya one, protruding from the ground in an oblique position and pointing northwards. The lion, which originally crowned the capital, had disappeared, and no trace of it could be found. He dug a long trench on each side of the pillar, up to a depth of 8 feet 8 inches, when water was reached, which soon percolated into the trench. By these excavations about 40 feet of the length of the pillar was exposed, and from the lowest visible point upwards to about 11 or 12 feet an inscription appeared on opposite sides of the pillar, of which Mr. Carlleyle took an impression—since lost. He further noticed, at a distance of some 850 feet to the south, the shattered stump of a stone pillar, about 6 feet in height, standing midway between two low, brick-covered mounds, but it did not occur to him to offer any suggestion as to the possibility of a connection between the broken pillar and this stump.

Subsequently, in 1880-81, Mr. Garrick was deputed to take a photograph of the capital of the pillar, and in order to do this, he states that he had the capital disconnected from the shaft to which it was fastened by a solid barrel-shaped bolt of pure copper, 2′ $\frac{1}{8}$″ long, 4$\frac{5}{16}$″ in diameter at the centre, and tapering slightly towards the ends, where its diameter was 3$\frac{5}{8}$″. This copper bolt was afterwards deposited in the Indian Museum, Calcutta, where it still is. A lithograph prepared from Mr. Garrick's photograph of the capital may be seen on Plate XXVIII of Volume XVI, Archæological Survey Reports. At the time of my visit, in 1901, the capital was still standing in the open field close to the shaft of the pillar, apparently as left by Mr. Garrick. Mr. Garrick also made an excavation around the pillar, which disclosed a portion of the inscription. Of this he took an inked impression, which has been published in Volume II of the *Epigraphia Indica*, together with Professor Bühler's article on the Pillar Edicts. It gives about one-third of the first and larger portion of the inscription, consisting of 20 lines of writing, each of about 20 letters, and containing fragments of Edicts I to IV. The text agrees almost letter for letter with the two Lauriya versions, which in the article referred to are called the Mathia and Radhia Edicts. The shattered stump to the south between two low, brick-covered mounds was also examined by Mr. Garrick, but he distinctly speaks of this as the base of another pillar, the missing portion of which according to him was broken into small fragments and carted away for road-making purposes.

It is, however, beyond any possible doubt that the small stump standing between the two mounds is the base of the same pillar which now lies broken in the field some 800 or 1,000 feet to the north. The pillar, it appears, was overthrown, not by self decay, but by human hands, but the attempt to carry the enormous monolith away had soon to be abandoned on account of the difficulty and costliness of the operation. The lion of the capital may have been broken by the fall of the pillar, and this was evidently the only spoil actually carried away. It seems likely that the pillar was pulled down by the same men who tried to destroy the Aśoka pillar at Lauriya-Navandgarh (Nandangarh), 22 miles south of Rampurwa. This pillar bears the distinct mark of a cannon ball below the capital on its northern face, and as the name of Aurangzeb together with the *Kalima* and the date 1071 (A.D. 1660-61) is inscribed on the pillar, General Cunningham suggests that the injury was done by some jealous followers of Mīr Jumla's army, on their way back from Bengal, after the defeat of Aurangzeb's brother, Sulṭān Shujā'.

Be this as it may, there can be no doubt that the small base between the two mounds marks the original site of the pillar, and that the broken shaft, together with the capital, should be re-erected on this spot, and I submitted a suggestion accordingly after my visit to the pillar in November 1901. I then found the pillar lying in a trench, evidently the excavation made by Mr. Garrick, but the stone must have sunk much deeper into the swamp, as only 20 feet of its upper portion was above ground and the inscription was entirely hidden below water and swamp. My suggestion was readily taken up by the Local Government, and estimates were called for. A closer examination of the broken shaft showed that it could not be fixed upon the small base without building supports which would entirely conceal the base, owing to the great difference in width and thickness between the pillar and the base. I accordingly suggested the re-erection of the pillar close to the original site instead of on the old stump. The capital will be re-fixed to the pillar, and the original copper bolt, by means of which it was fastened, will be obtained from the Indian Museum and used again if practicable. An iron railing will be erected around the pillar, to prevent idle visitors from scribbling or scratching their names on it. The total cost of the work is estimated at Rs. 6,300.

It seems probable, I admit, that the inscription on the pillar will be found to contain nothing additional to the well-known Edicts of Aśoka, as the fragment already deciphered agrees closely with the other pillar Edicts: nevertheless, there can be no question that sufficient interest attaches to the pillar to justify the proposed expenditure.

The Caves at Khandagiri.

The numerous caves which cluster around Khandagiri, a low, double-peaked hill, four miles west of Bhubanesvar, in Orissa, are not to be compared with the magnificent rock temples on the western side of the Peninsula: they are for the most part plain cells of small size, and only a few have verandahs in front, supported by pillars, and with carved friezes. To the antiquarian the most interesting object on this hill is perhaps the *Hāthigumphā* inscription of King Khāravela, surnamed *Mahāmeghavāhana*, meaning apparently "one whose elephant is as big as a large cloud," a familiar simile to readers of Sanskrit poetry. It is a purely historical record, the first of its kind in India, resembling in style the Behistun inscription of King Darius. Unfortunately the text was incised into a very brittle rock, offering but little resistance to the disintegrating influences of the climate, and many of the letters have disappeared.

There is, however, one special point of interest about these caves. They all appear to have been made for the religious use of Jains, and for many centuries to have been inhabited by Jain monks. We owe the discovery of this fact to the correct reading and translation of the *Hāthigumphā* and other minor inscriptions by Bhagwanlal Indraji, which formed the subject of an article of the Transactions of the Congress of Orientalists at Leyden. The *Hāthigumphā* inscription opens with a portion of the usual benedictory formula of the Jains, while another inscription in the Svargapurī cave declares that the cave was made by the grace of the Arhats by the chief Queen of the same King—whose name is lost, but who is said to be the daughter of King Lalāka—for the monks of Kaliṅga. The continued residence in later times of Jains in Khandagiri is amply evidenced by a number of mediæval Jain figures inside several of the caves, as well as by an inscription of the time of Uddyotakeśarī (eleventh century A.D.), which records the *kula* and *gaṇa* of Śubhacandra, whose disciple, Kulacandra, occupied one of the caves, and who, like his master, must have been a Jain. There is also a small modern Jain temple on the Khandagiri hill, where once a year a number of Jain merchants from Cuttack foregather for worship. It is true that the older carvings in the caves exhibit no characteristics peculiarly Jainistic, but, on the other hand, not the slightest trace of Buddhism is to be found: tree-worship, elephants, Lakṣmī, the Sun-god, the *svastikā* mark and similar symbols were common artistic devices of all creeds in ancient India. The only Hindu figure that I recall, besides a crude modern wall-painting of Jagannātha, is a rock-cut Gaṇeśa on the back wall of the Gaṇeśagumphā, probably about 800 or 1,000 years old. At that time Hindu monks may have had a share in the occupancy of the caves, but we have no record to show the exact period when the Jains deserted the caves, except a vague tradition in the Puri temple annals, that Madana Mahādeva, the grandson of Coḍagaṅga, persecuted the Jains and Bauddha *Sādhus* who were staying in the hills round Bhubanesvar, which, if true, must have happened close on the end of the twelfth century A.D.[1]

In determining the date of the caves, one has to depend mainly on the evidence of

[1] *See* page 9 of *Notes on the remains in Dhauli and in the caves of Udayagiri and Khandagiri*, by Babu Mon Mohan Chakravarti, M.A. Bengal Secretariat Press.

the inscriptions already referred to. The learned Bhagwanlal Indraji was the first to recognize that Khāravela, in his long *Hāthigumphā* inscription, synchronises the thirteenth year of his reign with the year 165 of the *Maurya-kāla*. The inauguration of this era is now, I believe, universally referred to the coronation of Candragupta, the founder of the Maurya Empire, and not, as Bhagwanlal would have it, to the conquest of Kaliṅga by Aśoka. The European equivalent of the date would thus be about 155 B.C. One of the caves, as already stated, was made by the chief Queen of Khāravela, while others were the gift of a king, whose name has been made out to be Vakradeva and who also calls himself *Mahāmeghavāhana*, and of a prince Vaḍuka, both of whom probably were sons of Khāravela. We thus arrive at the middle of the second century B.C. as the period during which a number of these caves were made. The style of the carvings inside the principal caves, such as Rāṇī Naur, Gaṇeśagumphā and Anantagumphā, agrees so well with this chronological theory, that I see no reason why an earlier date should be favoured. Yet Babu Mon Mohan Chakravarti, in the report already quoted, which has been printed by Government for private circulation, argues that the simpler and plainer caves must be older than those with elaborate carvings. Numerous instances might be quoted against this presumption. The richness of the carvings and the size of the structures depended probably more upon the liberality of the donor than upon developments of style and taste, and I would prefer to attribute the small and simple caves to a later period, when the royal patronage which the settlement enjoyed during the reign of Khāravela and his successor was withdrawn.

The mediæval carvings may be assigned to a period ranging from the eighth to the eleventh century A.D., and we have moreover in one of the caves, which contains the largest number of such carvings, the inscription of the time of Uddyotakeśarī, which, though not accurately dateable, probably belongs to the eleventh century A.D. But we must at the same time admit that the caves containing mediæval Jain figures need not necessarily be as late as that, for we have in the Gaṇeśagumphā, one of the old caves, an instance of an image of Gaṇeśa having been carved out of the back wall of the cave at a much later date.

I have already referred to the great damage which unfortunately the *Hāthigumphā* inscription has suffered on account of the brittle nature of the rock on which it is cut. To restore the missing portions of the text is of course out of the question, but in order to preserve the remaining parts of this invaluable record, a shade or verandah has been erected in front of it, to keep off the glare of the sun and the torrents of the monsoon—evidently the most destructive factors. The verandah is so built that the inscription, which is just below its roof, can be easily read. But as the inscription is very high above ground and many of the letters have become very faint and indistinct, a visitor will need a scaffolding to enable him to examine the letters more closely. Since the time when Kittoe prepared his eye-copy, about 1835, many letters appear to have vanished, and this copy must therefore be always consulted. It is a marvel of accuracy, considering that Kittoe was unable to understand the inscription. There is also a plaster-cast of the inscription in the Indian Museum, which was made by Mr. A. E. Caddy in 1896.

The steps leading up to the verandah in front of the Gaṇeśagumphā were flanked by two elephants' statues, each represented as standing and picking up some flowers or fruits with its trunk, a common device in ancient Indian art. Both these statues were found broken and overthrown in front of the cave. They have now been raised up again, and the missing parts of one of them have been restored in correspondence with the other statue. It is evident that the cave derived its name from the two elephants, though, of course, they were not originally meant to be representations of Gaṇeśa, but merely ornamental figures. A very similar elephant statue of about the same date now stands inside a small shrine near the Viṣṇupad temple at Gaya, where it is worshipped as *Gayā-gaja*. Its origin is unknown.

The *Tantua Caves* are two small cells, one above the other, on the southern peak of the hill, which is called Khandagiri proper, as distinguished from Udayagiri, the northern peak, although the whole group locally bears the generic name of Khandagiri. *Tantua* means a diving bird, and the caves derive their name from some birds which are carved over the arches of the doors as if in the act of plunging into water. The *Tentuli Cave* is close to them. Its name comes from a tamarind tree, standing in front of it. These three caves, although of smaller size and minor importance, belong to the old order and were in urgent need of conservation. Accordingly the broken parts of their pillars and roofs have been repaired, and the rubbish and rank vegetation which had accumulated around them have been removed. The *Satghara Cave*, which is one of those containing mediæval Jain images, has also received the benefit of some repairs. A modern brick structure in front of it was demolished, and a new support to its verandah was built up in the style of the old work. An attempt to clean the interior of most of the caves and especially the carved friezes unfortunately met with less success, but some improvement in this respect has been made. As long as the caves continue to be occupied by modern Yogis and Sannyasis, who cook their meals in them, there is little chance of protecting their interiors against grime; yet an effort to oust the intruders meets with no popular support, as even educated Hindus labour under the idea that structures of this kind can be claimed as of right as residences for ascetics, since that was their primitive use and object.

SECTION II.

MEDIÆVAL HINDU TEMPLES.

The Temple of Muṇḍeśvarī.

In the Bhabua sub-division of the modern district of Shahabad, seven miles south-west of Bhabua, is an isolated hill close to the village of Ramgarh, rising above the plain to a height of 600 feet. Ascending the hill along its eastern slope one meets with steps laid out with stones, traces of small brick buildings, statues, rock-carved figures, and other scattered relics of antiquity. Pilgrims have chiselled their names in the rock, and the letters employed belong to a remote time. In some cases they are adorned by shell ornaments, which is, I think, the only true case of the often mentioned "shell-characters."

The temple of Muṇḍeśvarī stands on the summit of the hill, and a fair is held there in the month of Caitra. When I first saw the building, it was externally merely a heap of broken stones, the *débris* hiding the walls almost entirely, and leaving openings only around the northern and southern windows and the two doors in the eastern and western side. Jungle and trees grew freely over the roof, and in front of the eastern door stood a few pillars, which evidently once supported a portico. The interior was intact; it was of octagonal shape with a flat roof, and in the centre stood a *caturmukha mahādeva*, or a liṅga with four heads, and an image of Durgā. There were also a large stone chest, probably used for hoarding the temple treasure, and another large stone vessel shaped like a kettle. Though the two statues inside the temple did not appear to be of remarkably great age, the carvings around the windows and doors as well as some detached statues close to the temple bore evidence of belonging to a remoter period, and the writing along the steps furnished additional proof that the place was one of comparatively high antiquity.

Since then the *débris* around the temple has been cleared away, and the structure, or what remains of it, has been laid open. It appears to have formed an octagon outside as well as inside. The principal door was to the east, and another door afforded ingress from the west. There were two windows each in the northern and southern sides filled with latticed stonework, and the intervening mural spaces were provided with small niches for the reception of statues. It is difficult to say now how the roof was shaped, but it must have been crowned by the usual melon-dome, fragments of which have been found among the *débris*. On the left-hand side of the eastern door is an inscription in three lines, in characters of the eighth century. It reads: *Śrī-para-vala-gambhīra-Marucaṇḍa*. I think, however, that the temple is still older, as among the *débris* the second half of an inscribed stone has been found, the first half of which had been sent to the Indian Museum, Calcutta, in 1891. This stone is dated *Saṁvatsare triṁśatitame Kārttika-divase dvāviṁśatitame* (year 30, the 22nd of Kārttika) which must be referred to the Harṣa era, thus corresponding with 635 A.D. The name of the ruling chief, one letter of which is lost, can be easily deciphered as Udayasena, and the inscription records various donations made to Maṇḍaleśvara, probably an incarnation of Śiva, then worshipped there. There is nothing in the style of the temple opposed to the view that the building dates from about 635 A.D. The statues, which were found among the rubbish, with the exception of one Agni, are representations of Śiva, Durgā, Gaṇeśa, Kārttikeya, Nandī, Liṅgas, and Ardhanārīśvara and Hari-Hara, the last two on both sides of a pillaster.

Now that the *débris* around this interesting little temple has been cleared away, further repairs will be undertaken within the limit of available funds.

The Temples at Bhubanesvar.

We possess very few true and reliable data for determining the age of the vast number of temples and shrines which still exist at the sacred *Ekāmra tīrtha* or the *tīrtha* of the single mango-tree. The Temple of *Brahmeśvara*, we know, was built by Kolāvatī, the queen of the King Uddyotakeśarī, who appears to have been connected with the so-called Somavaṁśī Kings, a dynasty whose copperplates have been found in large numbers in Cuttack, the Orissa Tributary States, and the adjacent district of Sambhalpur in the Central Provinces. The inscription, which, together with others to be dealt with presently, was submitted to the Asiatic Society in 1811, but returned to Bhubanesvar in 1838, is now lost. The reign of Uddyotakeśarī, of whom we possess a second short inscription from Khandagiri (see above, page 40), probably belonged to the second-half of the eleventh century A.D.

Next in chronological order comes another inscription, which evidently refers to the Temple of *Ananta-Vāsudeva.* It announces that Bhavadeva, a learned Brahmin minister of an otherwise unknown King Harivarman, at the place where the inscription is found, set up a stone image of Nārāyaṇa, founded a temple of the god, in which he placed images of Nārāyaṇa. Ananta, and Nṛsiṁha, dug a tank in front of the temple and laid out a garden in its neighbourhood.[1] The temple here referred to is evidently the temple of Ananta-Vāsudeva, which is the only shrine in Bhubanesvar dedicated to Viṣṇu. The inscription seems to have belonged to this temple and is still preserved inside its court wall. The date appears to have been about 1200 A.D.

Contemporaneous with it probably was the third and last temple record of this kind. It is now also inside the Ananta-Vāsudeva temple, but must have belonged to some other building. It records that a Temple of ***Megheśvara*** was built by Svapneśvara, a connection and general of the Gaṅga King Aniyaṅkabhīma (Anaṅga-bhīma) I. That king ascended the throne in 1192 A.D., and reigned for 10 years.[2] Hence the temple was built about 1200 A.D. There is, however, some uncertainty as to which of the present shrines represents the temple built by Svapneśvara. The Public Works Department have given the name Megheśvara to a temple which Mitra and others used to call Bhāskareśvara, and have conferred the latter name upon another shrine, some 100 feet to the east of it. Probably, however, the last-mentioned temple represents the true Megheśvara shrine, built by Svapneśvara, as the tank mentioned in the inscription still exists close to it, while the other temple has no tank.[3]

Concerning all the other temples and shrines, reliable records of a similar nature are entirely wanting. It has, accordingly, been the custom to refer to the statements contained in the Mādlā Pāñji or the annals of the temple of Jagannātha at Puri. What may be gathered from those records with regard to the history of the Bhubanesvar temples will be found embodied into the elaborate descriptions given by Mitra in Volume II of his work on Orissa Antiquities. But none of the records can be relied upon. Mr. Fleet has, I think, conclusively proved that up to the conquest of Orissa by the Gaṅga King Coḍagaṅga the annals contain nothing but pure fiction, and that they cannot be used for historical purposes.[4] The long line of Keśarī kings, who are said to have ruled over Orissa for many centuries and to have built the principal shrines at Bhubanesvar, may be regarded as a later fabrication, containing nothing historical, except a dim reminiscence of two actual kings of Orissa, Yayāti and Janamejaya, but even these have been entirely misplaced as regards

[1] *Epigraphia Indica,* Vol. VI, p. 204.
[2] *Ibidem,* p. 200.
[3] See *Journal As. Soc. of Bengal,* Vol. LXVI, 1897, Part I, p. 16.
[4] *Epigraphia Indica,* Vol. III, p. 334, *et seq.*

a

b

(a) BEFORE REPAIRS. (b) REPAIRED.

chronology. I do not think that the name of Uddyotakeśarī (see above pages 40 and 44) can be used as an argument to show that kings of the Keśarī line actually existed. The word *Keśarī* simply means "lion," and I have met with the corresponding name Uddyotasiṁha in two mediæval Buddhist dedicatory inscriptions, which I discovered at Kispa, in the district of Gaya. There is, moreover, no other name in the list of this king's ancestors formed in the same way, while I am unable to verify the statement that Kolāvatī, the queen of Uddyotakeśarī, is mentioned in the Puri temple records.[1] The Mādlā Pāñji list also omits the name of Uddyotakeśarī.

The history of Orissa in mediæval times is broken by a long gap, which it is as yet impossible to fill. We know, however, that during the tenth and eleventh centuries A.D. Orissa was ruled over by kings of the lunar race, whose names alternate between Bhavagupta and Śivagupta, the first two of whom bear also the surnames of Janamejaya and Yayāti. To this line also belonged Uddyotakeśarī, whose queen, Kolāvatī, built the temple of Brahmeśvara (above, page 43). The names Bhavagupta and Śivagupta both signify "protected by Śiva," and we may conclude from them that the kings who were thus called were worshippers of Śiva. Now, as Bhubanesvar is the great stronghold of Śiva-worship in Orissa, in opposition to the Viṣṇu-worship in the Padmakṣetra or Puri, and to the Sūrya-worship in the Arkakṣetra or Konarak, one may venture to assume that Bhubanesvar owes its importance as such to those very kings of the lunar race who ruled over it in the tenth and eleventh centuries A.D., and who were, as we have inferred from their names, devoted to Śaivism. However, I broach this theory only suggestively, merely noting that inside the *maṇḍapa* of the temple of Paraśurāmeśvara, on the lintel over the door leading to the *garbhagṛha* or sanctum, there are written in characters of the tenth or eleventh century the names of eight planets, the images of which are carved on the lintel; thus, *āditya, soma, aṅgāraka, budha, vṛhaspati, śukra, śaṇaiścara, rāhu*. Ketu, the last, is wanting.

The principal temple at Bhubanesvar, the *Great Liṅgarāj*, as well as a minor shrine of *Bhagavatī* within its compound, has been repaired by Government. But as the priests do not allow non-Hindus to enter the temple precincts, and as even the European engineers in charge were prohibited from inspecting the progress of the work, it was decided to discontinue repairs until the temple custodians had adopted more liberal views. Fortunately, the same restrictions do not exist at the numerous other temples, and any student of Archæology has ample liberty to examine them as closely as he likes.

On Plates IV and V, I have given two views each of the temple of *Mukteśvara* and *Rāja-Rāṇī*—before and after repairs. A reference to these plates, especially to Plate V(*a*) (Rāja-Rāṇī temple before repairs) will show at once the nature of the work to be performed, which was the same in all the temples selected for preservation. The temples, generally, were fairly intact, and no great damage had been done to them; the carvings also were well-preserved. But a number of stones had become either loose or unsafe, and in particular the roof of the *maṇḍapa* and the upper parts of the *rekhā* or spire were in a critical condition. These portions had to be

[1] *Journal As. Soc. Bengal*, Vol. LXVII, 1898, Part I, p. 377.

dismantled and built up again, and in doing this great care was taken to use, as far as possible, the ancient materials, new stones being made use of very sparingly. Carvings, when broken and lost, were replaced by new ones with careful discretion, and the work of the modern stone-mason, a native of Bhubanesvar, does not fall much behind the old work, except that modern restorations of human or animal figures are less graceful than their older models. I need scarcely remark that only such carvings have been replaced by new ones of which the original pattern was available.

In style the temples are all much alike. They consist of a square *maṇḍapa* in front, with a pyramidal roof, and the spire or *rekhā*, which is crowned by the usual melon-dome and vase. Only in the Liṅgarāj and Ananta-Vāsudeva temples are additional buildings added in front of the *maṇḍapa*. There are, however, a few exceptions to this general rule. The *maṇḍapa* of the Temple of *Paraśurāmeśvara* is oblong, and has a flat roof with a skylight. This temple, which has some exquisite carvings, has been thoroughly repaired; the whole roof of the *maṇḍapa*, which was in a very bad state, had to be dismantled and rebuilt. An exact replica of this, but of smaller size, exists in the courtyard of *Vetal Deul*, but it has not received any attention as yet. The Vetal Deul itself is of the style of a South-Indian *gopuraṁ*. It was well preserved and needed only petty repairs. Finally, the temple, which I think Mitra correctly calls *Bhāskareśvara*, is unique in style, and for this reason has been thoroughly repaired. It consists of a square tower, rising from a square platform, with a pyramidal roof, and is built over a large, natural *liṅga*, which reaches through the ground-storey into the spire. A photograph of the temple is given in Mitra's Orissa, Volume II, Plate XLIV.

The Temple of *Brahmeśvara* had four small shrines, one in each corner of its court. Though simple and unpretending, they as well as two similar ones standing in front of the temple court were repaired, after the principal shrine had been put in order, for the sake of the general effect. This principle has also been followed, to great advantage, I think, in regard to the Temple of *Mukteśvara*. This beautiful little temple with the exquisite arch or *toraṇa* in front is surrounded by a great number of small shrines, and close to it also stands the Temple of *Siddheśvara*, a larger structure. All the shrines are inferior works of art compared with the Mukteśvara, but nevertheless they have all been restored, and a tank east of Mukteśvara has been cleaned out and laid out with new stone facings. Finally, the *Sahasraliṅga Tank* in front of the big Liṅgarāj temple has also been thoroughly repaired. It was in a very bad state.

The Black Pagoda at Konarak.

We find ourselves in a far better position in dealing with the history of the Black Pagoda at Konarak, than at Bhubanesvar. Here the statement of the Puri temple annals, as well as the *Āīn-i-Akbarī*, that the temple was built by King Narasiṁhadeva, is amply supported by historical records. All the published copper-plates of the Gaṅga Kings of Kaliṅga in their historical portion relate that Narasiṁhadeva I. built a temple of the Sun-god at Koṇākoṇa. Koṇākoṇa appears to have been the ancient name, and the modern name thus stands for *koṇārka*, meaning "the *arka* (Sun-god)

TEMPLE OF RĀJA-RĀNĪ, BHUBANESVAR. PLATE V.

(a) BEFORE REPAIRS.

(b) REPAIRED.

at Koṇa."[1] According to the latest account of the chronology of the Gaṅga Kings of Kaliṅga, by Babu Mon Mohan Chakravarti, the reign of Narasiṁha I. lies between Śaka 1160 and 1186 (A.D. 1238-1264),[2] and I have no doubt that these figures, based as they are on minute calculations of all the available data, are substantially correct. The actual date of the temple thus comes very close to that ascribed to it by the temple records, while the statement by Abū-l-Fazl that at his time the temple was 730 years old must be due either to a clerical error or to misinformation.

What may have induced King Narasiṁha to erect such a magnificent and costly structure at a place which is now simply a sandy desert, 1½ miles off the sea-shore, with no navigable river near it, becomes an interesting subject for speculation. The *Kapila-saṁhitā* locates at Konarak the story of Sāmba and his miraculous cure from leprosy by the help of Sūrya. But the original *locale* of this tale was the north-west of India, and thence it was transplanted to Orissa in order to enhance the sanctity of Konarak, or to gain for Konarak popular recognition as the true place where sun-worship should be performed. Accordingly a *melā* or fair is still held there in January, at a little distance from the temple, where a small river, called Candrabhāgā, formerly opened into the sea. Sun-worship was, of course, not rare in Eastern India in mediæval times; witness the great number of images of Sūrya met with in Behar and in parts of Bengal. In Orissa sun images are less common, but almost every temple in Bhubanesvar and elsewhere has images of the sun and the planets carved over the lintel of its door to protect it from evil influences. Similarly, the *grahaśānti* ceremony forms part of the propitiatory rites performed whenever a new building is opened for use.

It is quite possible that the temple originally stood as close to the sea-shore as the Puri temple does now. It is also likely that one of the small rivers near it was then navigable for rafts at least during the rains, affording facilities of transport for the huge blocks of stones which were used in building, and which were brought from the hills near Khurda some 30 miles away, and from even more distant places. Should the famous temple of Jagannātha ever fall into disregard, it would no doubt soon stand as lonely on the noisy sea-shore as that at Konarak, for the modern town of Puri owes its origin entirely to the hundreds of thousands of pilgrims who annually flock to the shrine.

The first notice of the temple which we encounter, apart from the Orissa records, is in the *Āīn-i-Akbarī*. As the passage has been quoted by Mitra according to Gladwin's translation, which is incorrect and misleading, I here give the correct translation by Colonel Jarrett[3]:—

"Near Jagannāth is a temple dedicated to the Sun. Its cost was defrayed by twelve years' revenue of the province. Even those whose judgment is critical and who are difficult to please stand astonished at its sight. The height of the wall is 150 cubits high and 19 thick. It has three portals. The eastern has

[1] The name is generally misspelt Kanarak, evidently because the first *o* was taken for the Uriya-Bengali pronunciation of *a*. But it represents a long *ō*, and the word should always be spelt Konarak, although the first vowel now often sounds like a short *o*.

[2] See *Journal As. Soc. Bengal*, Vol. LXXII, 1903, Part I, p. 120.

[3] *Āīn-i-Akbari*, English Translation by Colonel Jarrett, *Bibl. Ind.*, Vol. II, p. 128.

carved upon it the figures of two finely designed elephants, each of them carrying a man upon his trunk. The western bears sculptures of two horsemen with trappings and ornaments and an attendant. The northern has two tigers, each of which is rampant upon an elephant that it has overpowered. In front is an octagonal column of black stone, 50 yards high. When nine flights of steps are passed, a spacious court appears, with a large arch of stone, upon which are carved the sun and other planets. Around them are a variety of worshippers of every class, each after its manner, with bowed heads, standing, sitting, prostrated, laughing, weeping, lost in amaze, or wrapt in attention, and following these are strange animals which never existed but in imagination. It is said that somewhat over 730 years ago, Rāja Narsing Deo completed this stupendous fabric and left this mighty memorial to posterity. Twenty-eight temples stand in its vicinity, six before the entrance and twenty-two without the enclosure, each of which has its separate legend."

A comparison of this account with the actual remains of the temple shows that it was based on very inaccurate information. The height of the wall may refer to the height of the spire, which may be guessed from the following calculation :—The height of the *maṇḍapa* in front according to accurate measurements is 128 feet. If we add to this 10 feet for the broken *kalaśa* on top, we get 138 feet altogether. Assuming, as we may reasonably, that the height of the *maṇḍapa* was two-thirds of that of the *rekhā* or spire, we get 184 feet for the latter, which comes very close to 150 cubits. The text is however not quite clear. The three portals of the wall must surely refer to the three doors of the *maṇḍapa*. The elephants, horses, and tigers (or, more correctly, lions) still exist, but although they were lying broken at the time when the earliest authentic records of the temple were written, the words of Abū-l-Fazl afford no guidance as to their original position. I shall refer to this again later, and need merely mention that the lions stood in front of the eastern gate, the elephants in front of the northern gate, and the horses in front of the southern gate. The western gate was inside the *maṇḍapa*, and led to the *garbhagṛha* or sanctum. The octagonal column of blackstone, which is next mentioned, has been carted away to Puri and now stands in front of the temple of Jagannātha. We then meet the *maṇḍapa* again under the curious description of "a spacious court," for which it would be more appropriate to substitute "a spacious hall." The nine planets are the famous Navagraha stone, which originally was used as a lintel over the eastern door and which has now fallen down. Above it, inside a niche, was a sitting statue of Sūrya, probably the image which was sent to the Indian Museum in 1891. As regards the minor temples around the big one, the remains of many of them are probably still to be found beneath the numerous small sand-hills in the neighbourhood.

A stupendous stone fabric of this kind, as Abū-l-Fazl truly remarks, must always have excited the admiration even of critical minds, and it has been a matter of much speculation how, without the help of modern machinery, the huge blocks of stone used in the building could be brought from distances of 30 miles and more, and then raised to a height of 100 or 150 feet. What the actual dimensions of the broken spire were may be conjectured from a huge piece of sculpture, which still lies among

THE BLACK PAGODA, KONARAK: SOUTH.

PLATE VI.

the *débris*, and which originally was placed high up in the eastern side of the spire, probably some 150 feet above ground. It represents the usual lion rampant upon an elephant, which is to be seen projecting from the front of the spire in every temple in Orissa. The height up to the top of the lion's head measures 20 feet; the base is 15 feet long, and 4 feet 7 inches broad. This colossal figure was cut out of two solid blocks of stone, but in falling the head of the lion broke off. As already observed, both these stones had to be raised to a height of 150 feet above ground, where they were fastened into the wall. I have already suggested the probability of some of the neighbouring rivers having then been navigable for rafts, thus affording an easier means of transport than by land. As regards the raising of the building materials, there is a story that the structure was embedded in a sand hill, and that the huge stones were carried up the slopes of the hill by rollers. This sounds very probable. Whether the spire was ever finished we do not now know. At the time when the first drawings were made, it formed, as at present, a mere heap of *débris* with only a tottering fragment still standing.

To erect a structure of such enormous dimensions and to make it really durable required of course great engineering skill, and it is very likely that the greatest damage done is due to faulty construction. Thus, it appears that the spire gradually collapsed, and that about one-third of it will be found to be still extant, when the big heap of stones has been removed. It is, however, evident that human agency contributed to the downfall of this magnificent temple. Major Kittoe, in his journal of a tour through Orissa,[1] mentions that the Raja of Khurda was then demolishing the entrances to the temple, and I have already mentioned that the pillar, which originally stood in front of the Black Pagoda, is now put up in Puri. Likewise, many other materials from Konarak have been used in Puri, and stolen stones or carvings may be found set up as objects of worship in the village shrines for a long distance around.

Until recently very few preventive measures were taken to arrest further destruction. Twice it was determined to transport the big Navagraha stone, which originally formed the lintel over the eastern door, to the Indian Museum. The first attempt was soon given up for want of funds. The second, made about ten years ago, was suddenly abandoned on the discovery that the stone had come to be used as an object of local worship, a man from Puri having been cured by its miraculous virtues. The lions, elephants, and horses, which were then lying broken around the three doors, were re-erected again in 1881 by Mr. Davies, a Subordinate of the Public Works Department, but unfortunately they were placed in a wrong position, facing the temple, not, as they should stand, with their backs towards the temple.

The reader referring now to the photograph on Plate VI, will see the southern side of the temple (with one of the horses) as it stood in 1893. At that time, Babu P. C. Mukherji was deputed to Konarak to take detailed drawings of the temple, and he perceived that the entire plinth of the temple was buried beneath the sand. He laid open about half of the wheel, figured on Plate VII (*b*), and also a portion of the building shown on Plate VII (*a*), and made drawings of both.[2] His report

[1] *Journal As. Soc. of Bengal*, Vol. VII, 1838, page 681.

[2] The publication of selected drawings of Babu P. C. Mukherji has been sanctioned, and will be supplemented by new ones showing details of the excavated parts, and by photographs.

recommended the further excavation of all the hidden parts of the structure, but no action was taken, and the temple was still in the same state when I first saw it in 1901. However, a proposal made by me to excavate the courtyard around the temple was readily taken up by the Local Government, and operations were started in the next winter. The result may be stated briefly thus:—

The plinth of the temple is still fairly intact. It is full of elaborate carvings, the most striking of which are the representations of eight wheels, 9 feet 8 inches in diameter, four on each side, and of seven horses, three on the northern and four on the southern side. The only complete wheel is shown on Plate VII (*b*); it is on the northern side. Others, as also the horses, can be restored. The horses run in front along the steps leading up to the eastern door; then follow the wheels, which terminate at the junctions of the northern and southern sides of the plinth with the flanks of the northern and southern stairs. The temple thus represented the chariot of the Sun-god, drawn by his seven chargers.

In front of the eastern stairs stands a very fine hall, with elaborate carvings. It is shown on Plate VII (*a*). Before the excavation began it was completely hidden by sand. It is a square of 52 feet, standing upon a platform, which is about 75 feet square. A door was placed in the centre of each side, with two windows, closed or open. The roof evidently was pyramidal, consisting of several bands of cornices, as that of the *maṇḍapa* (see Plate VI), but unfortunately it cannot be restored. The lions have been re-erected there by mistake, and they will now be set up in their correct places in front of the eastern door, as also the elephants in front of the northern door, and the horses in front of the southern door. The building was evidently used as a dancing hall, as the many carved figures around it represent musicians and dancers, and for this reason it may be called *nāṭ-mandir*, which is the name generally given to such buildings in Orissa temples.

The excavation also laid open a multitude of terraces and outhouses, and a great number of carvings up to a line drawn across the courtyard and running along the eastern side of the northern and western stairs, that is, about one-third of the whole area. What it would mean to carry out the excavations to the end may be gathered from the dimensions of the court walls, which are 535 by 885 feet. A further difficulty was experienced by the strong drift of sand from the sea re-filling the excavations. Probably continuous digging will be found necessary, unless some preventive measure can be devised against the sand drift. As an experiment it has been proposed to plant trees and shrubs along the east, south, and west sides, and to defer further operations until these have grown sufficiently high to afford shelter.

As regards the *maṇḍapa* of the temple, it has been decided to fill up the interior with stones and later on with sand. This is considered the best means of supporting it against collapse. Of course the interior will thereby be blocked up, but this is not a matter of much concern. I understand that access will be left to a finely carved chlorite door, an exact counterpart of that to the east of the *maṇḍapa*, which is inside, leading into the sanctum, but of course it will then be visible only by the light of a lamp.

The total expenditure incurred at Konarak up to the end of the financial year 1902-03 was Rs. 27,033.

a

(a) DANCING HALL IN FRONT, EXCAVATED.

(b) CARVED WHEEL IN NORTHERN PLINTH.

SECTION III.

BENGALI-MUHAMMADAN BUILDINGS.

Gaur and Panduah.

In Bengal proper the principal objects of archæological interest are the monuments erected by the independent Sulṭāns, who ruled the country from about 1350 to 1550 A.D. The finest buildings of the kind are to be seen at the ancient capital of Gaur and Panduah in the district of Malda,[1] but there are many others at various places, and I shall have occasion to refer briefly to the remains at Panduah and Tribeni in the district of Hooghly, and to the tomb of Ghiyāthu-d-dīn A'ẓam Shāh at ancient Sonargaon, the repairs of which have lately been under consideration.

Generally speaking, the style of these buildings is peculiar, for two reasons :— Firstly, as stones were rare, bricks were used, and the mural ornaments which the mason would ordinarily have cut out of stone facings were imitated in the softer material of bricks and tiles, often with great skill. As a rule, these brick decorations were not moulded, but were actually cut out with a chisel, and workmen trained in this art are still to be had and have been employed in restoring the ruins at Gaur. Gaur also was famous for its glazed tiles, but unfortunately these formed a much coveted spoil for vandals, who in the early days of the Company's rule wantonly destroyed many a fine building solely for the sake of the tiles. Secondly, in imitation of the native style of the country, the roof slopes towards the ends and is curved like the roof of a Bengali native hut. The same peculiarity is observed in almost every Hindu temple in Bengal, and it is evident that the architects employed by the Muhammadan rulers followed the fashion of the country, although no remains of earlier times have been left to us.

The Muhammadan architecture in Bengal has thus developed a peculiar style of its own, and for this reason has an interest for the student of Archæology. The general outlines of these buildings, to my mind, look clumsy, and cannot compare with other Muhammadan monuments of the same period, but I readily admit that many details are extremely fine and instructive. I may also add that the inscriptions preserved in the buildings, combined with the evidence of coins, have been the means of fixing the chronology of the Muhammadan rulers of Bengal, which, in the native chronicles, was entangled in confusion.

I have alluded to the wanton destruction done to the remains at Gaur and Panduah. According to Grant, the *niẓāmat daftar* received an annual payment of Rs. 8,000 from two local Zamindars for allowing them the exclusive right to demolish the venerable ruins at Gaur, in order to carry away the highly prized enamelled tiles and the so-called Gaur marbles.[2] The tomb of Ḥusain Shāh, which about 120 years ago, when Creighton made his paintings, was still quite intact, has now entirely disappeared, and only the basalt sarcophagus remains lying broken in two pieces inside the modern village of Mahdiganj, west of Gaur. The walls of the tomb as depicted by Creighton were covered all over with glazed tiles alternating in colour between white and blue.

[1] This is the official spelling. It should of course be Pāndua and Māldah.
[2] *Journal As. Soc. of Bengal*, Vol. XLIII, 1874, Part I, p. 303, note.

Likewise, all the stone facings of the Gunmant mosque, up to the springing of the arches, have been stripped off. The same vandalism has caused irreparable damage to the *Bāradwārī*, also called the Great Golden Mosque, which once was one of the finest mosques in Gaur. The finely carved basalt or trap stones, which were quarried from the neighbouring Rajmahal Hills, and were known as Gaur marbles, may be seen built into modern houses in all the larger native towns as far as Patna, while the modern city of Malda is almost entirely built up with bricks from Gaur. History in this respect has repeated itself. In order to erect mosques and tombs the Muhammadans pulled down all the Hindu temples they could lay hands upon for the sake of the building materials. And again, when their time was over and their ancient capitals were deserted, the monuments which they had left were again demolished and the stones and bricks used for common purposes. It is a lamentable fact that, but for this wanton destruction, the ruins of Gaur and Panduah would have come down to us partly complete and intact, whereas in their present state it is almost impossible to restore any of them entirely.

The oldest and best known of the buildings at Gaur and Panduah is the *Ādīna Masjid* at *Panduah*, built by Sikandar Shāh, the son of Ilyās Shāh. The date of its inscription may be read either as 776 or 770, which corresponds with 1374 or 1369 A.D.[1] Fergusson states that the mosque was an imitation of the great mosque at Damascus. It differs from the other buildings at Gaur and Panduah in the absence of the usual curved battlement, which would have looked awkward on a wall some 500 feet long. The materials employed consisted largely of the spoils of Hindu temples, and many of the carvings from the temples have been used as facings of doors, arches, and pillars Cunningham rather scathingly calls the mosque "a big barn," and it must be admitted that there is nothing imposing in the long lines of cloisters that surrounded the open court of the mosque. However, some of the carvings, especially in the central transept and the *bādshāh-kā-takht*, are of exquisite beauty. As it was out of the question to restore all the broken cloisters and walls, only the most interesting and, happily, best preserved parts of the mosque have received attention. These were the transept, the front wall, and arches of the northern wing of the mosque, and the raised platform which was built for the use of the zenana, but which is now generally called *bādshāh-kā-takht*. The transept is shown on Plate VIII (*a*). As will be seen from this photograph, the side-walls have been restored up to the spring of the arched vault, which is as far as the work will now be carried. Unfortunately the missing stones of the richly carved pulpit could not be found. The walls and arches of the façade of the mosque have also been rebuilt. In the *bādshāh-kā-takht* one of the fluted columns supporting the domes has been renewed, and the stone paving of the platform, together with the stone beams and pillars that were broken, have been made good. All the domes over the *takht* and the surrounding cloisters have been restored: they were still fairly intact, but some of them, especially those to the north, had to be rebuilt. In order to afford a support to the new domes, it was decided to erect a new masonry curtain wall across

[1] It is doubtful whether ستة 'six' belongs to the year, or whether one should read ستة رجب '6th Rajab'; see *Epigraphia Indica*, Vol. II, page 283.

(a) TRANSEPT, REPAIRED.
(b) NEW CURTAIN WALL.

the aisle, and this rather questionable innovation may be seen on Plate VIII (*b*). The wall is in the style of the façade, but makes an unnatural division of the aisle into two separate parts, and some other more suitable contrivance ought to have been possible for the support of the new domes. It was of course out of the question to rebuild the whole roof. Outside, adjoining the *bādshāh-kā-takht* or ladies' gallery, is a square building, which leads into the gallery. This is generally said to be the tomb of Sikandar Shāh, but I feel certain that it was nothing of the kind, as it contains no trace of a grave or vault beneath. It doubtless merely served as an entrance for the ladies, who were thus able in visiting the mosque to maintain the prescribed seclusion. Similar platforms still exist in other mosques at Gaur.

The *Eklākhī* Monument contains three tombs, which according to the *Riyāẓu-s-salāṭīn* are those of Jalāl-ud-dīn Muḥammad Shāh, who died in 1430 A.D., his wife, and his brother. This tradition seems more acceptable than another, which asserts that Ghiyāthu-d-Dīn A'ẓam Shāh, the son of Sikandar Shāh, lies buried inside the Eklākhī Mausoleum, as there is reason to believe that Sikandar Shāh's son was buried at Sonargaon, where his supposed tomb is still pointed out. The facings of the brick walls of this monument, as well as the huge hemispherical dome, have been repaired.

The third ruin at Panduah, which has been recently restored, is the *Sonā Masjid*, also called Quṭbshāhī Masjid, after its builder. It is one of the latest buildings there, as the inscriptions over its central door, the pulpit, and the gateway of the quadrangle are dated 990, 992, and 993 A.H., *i.e.*, A.D. 1582, 1584, and 1585. Its erection thus falls well into the beginning of the Mughal period. It is remarkable for the happy fact that the stone facings of the walls have not fallen a prey to vandal destroyers. Its late date is evidenced by a decline in taste and workmanship compared with similar mosques at Gaur. The repairs done to it have consisted in rebuilding broken parts of the walls and arches, and in restoring the pulpit.

The visitor to the ruins of *Gaur*, starting from the Piyasbari Inspection Bungalow, which is the most convenient point, will first arrive at the *Bāradwārī of Rāmkel*, also called the Great Golden Mosque, because its walls are said to have been originally gilded. The former name is a misnomer, strictly speaking, as there are only eleven arched openings in front, and not, as the word "*bāra*" would imply, twelve. It stands outside the citadel of Gaur, a little to the north-east. Its inscription has been lost, but a copy has been preserved by Francklin in his account of Gaur, and from this we know that the mosque was built by Nuṣrat Shāh, the son of Ḥusain Shāh, in 1526 A.D. It must have been a conspicuous building, and evidently was intended to be the principal place of worship for the new city,[1] which Nuṣrat Shāh appears to have built at Gaur. In the inscription it is accordingly called *Masjid-i-jāmi'* or "cathedral mosque." The irreparable damage done to it is all the more deplorable. Only the corridor in front with eleven domes is still left; the roof of the mosque proper, the pillars supporting the domes and large portions of the walls have entirely disappeared. Although many of the facing stones had been carried

[1] I agree with Mr. Lane-Poole that the names Ḥusainābād and Nuṣratābād, which occur on the coins of Ḥusain Shāh and Nuṣrat Shāh, are temporary epithets applied by them to their capital, Gaur (*British Museum Catalogue of Muhammadan Coins*, Introduction, page xxiii). They imply, however, that both kings made additions to the old city.

away, a careful search all over the neighbouring villages yielded enough to restore completely the eastern façade and the southern wall of the mosque, and sufficient material is at hand to repair the eastern gate leading to the courtyard.

The inner façades of the walls also have been repaired, as the stones there were bulging out in places, and the brickwork over the arches in the northern and southern walls has been restored. The carving in the outside walls is very simple, but the niches inside were embellished with beautiful basalt carvings, of which, unfortunately, nothing but a few traces have remained.

A much better preserved stone mosque is the *Soṇā Masjid* of Firozpur, a southern suburb of Gaur, which is named also the Small Golden Mosque, or the Eunuch's Mosque. It was built by Walī Muḥammad, the son of ʻAlī, in the reign of Ḥusain S̲h̲āh (1494-1524 A.D.); the end of the inscription showing the exact year is broken. The neglect with which this fine building has been treated appears to be due to its great distance from the other ruins of Gaur, the road leading to it being also in very bad condition. Some of its domes and a portion of the back wall fell down during the last great earthquake, but it is otherwise fairly intact and can easily be restored almost completely. Probably on account of its distance from the river, it escaped the hands of pilferers, and the stones that have become broken are almost all lying around it. Its walls, moreover, have some fine ornaments, while the front wall of the *Bāradwārī* was almost plain, with but one small rosette on each side of the arches. The repairs of this Firozpur mosque have recently been sanctioned, and an estimate is under preparation.

The *Dāk̲h̲il Darwāza*, or northern gate of the citadel, is very close to the *Bāradwārī*; its builder is unknown. Here the arches over the door, as also portions of the walls of the colonnades, were in a very dangerous condition, and the brick facings accordingly had to be relaid. The arches have some very fine mouldings, which have been restored by new work. At present only the northern arch has been repaired, while the southern one was merely propped up by modern bricks, which, apart from their hideousness, did not even afford sufficient protection to some parts of the arch, which hung over very dangerously. It has now been sanctioned to repair this arch in the same way as the northern one.

A little to the east of the citadel stands the famous *Fīrōz Mīnār*. Its erection is generally ascribed to Saifu-d-dīn Fīrōz S̲h̲āh, 1486-1489 A.D. It cannot however, as Cunningham believes, have been used as a Muazzin's tower, as no remains of a mosque are found near to it and indeed it stands much too close to the old ditch of the fort, which is west of it, to permit the assumption that a mosque once stood between it and the ditch. I therefore feel inclined to look upon it as a tower of victory, a *jaya-stambha*, as a Hindu would say, and I think that its name should be taken as a literal translation of this word, and not as referring to Fīrōz S̲h̲āh. That the short reign of this king was distinguished by any great victory seems very unlikely, and I am inclined to reject the doubtful authority of Francklin and his account of the inscription, said to have belonged to the *mīnār*; preferring to ascribe the tower to the reign of Ḥusain S̲h̲āh, the most glorious of the independent Muhammadan rulers of Bengal. Local tradition, moreover, is in favour of such an assumption, and one might further hazard the conjecture that the conquest of Assam and Orissa by this king was the event in commemoration of which the tower was built. Both in inscriptions and on his coins Ḥusain S͟hāh often calls himself "the conqueror of Kāmrūp, Jājnagar, and Orissa,"[1] and this certainly was an achievement worthy of such a memorial. The stone facings around the base of this tower unfortunately have entirely disappeared and cannot be replaced, as we have no ancient drawings to guide us. The broken top portion likewise cannot be restored, but an iron ladder has been erected in front of the door, to afford an easy ascent to the interior with its interesting winding staircase. The door-lintel also has been replaced, and the walls have been repaired.

The *Tantipara Masjid* contains the finest specimens of moulded bricks that I have seen anywhere in Bengal. There are good reasons for placing its date in 1480-81 A.D., although the inscriptions have been lost. Unfortunately some of the arches in front have broken away, and great damage has been done to the ornamentations around the niches and the arches. No attempt has now been made to restore the mouldings, and the broken facings have merely been replaced by plain masonry. The domes also have collapsed altogether.

As the only fairly complete building laid out with glazed tiles, the *Lattan Masjid*[2] has received considerable attention. It was erected in 1475-76 A.D., according to Creighton, who probably saw the inscription, which thereafter was taken out and has disappeared. The colouring of the walls is somewhat monotonous, consisting of alternating horizontal bands of green, yellow, green, and white, blue, white. The small domes over the corridor, however, have graceful designs, mostly in blue and white, while, unfortunately, the interior and especially the big central dome have been stained by smoke and dampness. In the outer walls old glazed tiles, as many as could be found, have been replaced to great advantage, while, unfortunately, a trial to prepare new tiles in order to repair the broken domes over the corridor met with no success, and ordinary bricks had to be employed. There was also not a sufficient number of old glazed tiles to repair all the damaged portions of the walls, and accordingly plain masonry had to be substituted.

Of the ancient city of *Sonargaon* in the Narainganj sub-division of the district of Dacca, very few remains have been left. The most interesting is the tomb of G͟hiyāt͟hu-d-Dīn A'ẓam S͟hāh, famous in literature as having invited Ḥāfiẓ to his court, receiving in reply the well known *G͟hazal*, wherein the words occur:

> "And now shall India's parrots revel all
> "On that sweet sugar borne to far Bengal."

The tomb consists of a plain basalt sarcophagus, resting on a stone platform. As early as in 1874, Dr. J. Wise urged the necessity of having this interesting monument properly repaired,[3] but, unfortunately, without avail. It appears that since then many of the stones, that were lying about, have been stolen, and a careful examination of all the available materials shows that not more than one-fifth of the total is still

---

[1] الفاتح لکامرو و جاجنکر و آرجشه

[2] The name is said to be a corruption of *noṭin*, "a dancing girl," and should be spelt more properly *Loṭan*. Tradition says that the mosque was built by a courtesan.

[3] *Journal As. Soc. Bengal*, Vol. XLIII, Part I, p. 86.

at hand. This is quite insufficient for an accurate restoration of the tomb, and the Local Government have accordingly accepted my recommendation to leave the tomb as it is.

Repairs have, however, been sanctioned to another group of remains of the independent Muhammadan rulers of Bengal, at *Panduah* and *Tribeni*, in the district of Hooghly. The most striking of these is the five-storeyed *mīnār* at Panduah, to the east of a large old mosque. It is evidently an imitation of the Quṭb *mīnār* at Delhi, and though somewhat clumsy-looking, an interesting monument worth preserving. The fifth storey and the pinnacle broke down lately, but will be restored according to a drawing published by Blochmann.[1] The *mīnār* as well as the mosque, close to which it stands, are believed to date from the beginning of Muhammadan rule over this part of the country, about 1300 A.D. The mosque is in a very bad state of repair: it had originally 63 domes, out of which only 27 remain. In fact only a small fragment of this long structure is still standing, and this will be protected against further decay to serve as a mere specimen of the original building. Another old mosque with only one large dome stands inside the Dargāh of Ṣafī Shāh which is close to the large mosque and *mīnār*. Its inscription date corresponds to the 15th April, 1477 A.D. It is better preserved than the large mosque, but certain repairs are needed in order to strengthen the walls and to make the roof water-tight.

The principal object of interest at *Tribeni* is the Dargāh of Ẓafar Khān Ghāzī. The chronology of this ruler may be deduced from two inscriptions, of which one has been fitted into the plinth of his tomb, while the other is inside the small mosque to the west of the tomb. Both refer to him, and the first tells us that he built the mosque close to the Dargāh, which dates from A.D. 1298, while the second records the erection by him of a Madrasah or college in the time of Shamsuddīn Fīrōz Shāh and bears a date corresponding to the 28th April, 1313 A.D. It was he who conquered the Hindu Rāja of Panduah, and introduced Islam into this part of Lower Bengal. To begin with the mosque built by Ẓafar Khān Ghāzī, it is certainly the oldest in Bengal, far anterior to any building at Gaur and Panduah. For this reason, principally, it has been decided to make an allotment for its conservation, although no great architectural interest attaches to it. The tomb is built out of the spoils taken from Hindu temples. It is oblong, with two compartments, and appears never to have been roofed over. There are some elegant carvings around one of the doors and windows, and as a place of both archæological and historical interest it is to be put into proper order.

The repairs in the district of Hooghly have only recently been sanctioned, and as the estimated cost of Rs. 27,723 is very large, the work will be taken up by degrees and be spread over several years.

Section IV.

REMAINS OF THE MUGHAL PERIOD.

The first monument to be dealt with here belongs to the period of Sher Shāh and his successors, whose short rule interrupted the beginning of the reign of

[1] *Journal As. Soc. Bengal*, Vol. XXXIX, Part I, Plate XI.

the Mughal Emperors. It is the *Dargāh of Bakhtiyār Khān* near *Chainpur*, a small town seven miles west of Bhabua, in the Shahabad district. I have been unable to discover what part Bakhtiyār Khān played in the history of the Sūrī Kings, but he must have been a personage of rank, and Chainpur, where stands a fort built in the style of that age, and close to which his dargāh stands, probably was his *jāgīr*. There can, however, be no question as to the assignment of the tomb to the Sūrī time, as it is the exact counterpart of the tomb of Ḥasan Khān Sūr, the father of Sher Shāh, at Sasseram. It differs merely in its larger dimensions, and also in that it bears a cupola on its dome, and not a pinnacle, as in the case of the tomb of Sher Shāh's father.[1] It well bears comparison with the two fine tombs at Sasseram, and for this reason its conservation has been undertaken. The preliminary estimate amounts to Rs. 5,072, and the repairs will chiefly consist in relaying stone facings of walls, repairing the domes restoring the eaves of the verandah and the small kiosks, and destroying encroaching trees and vegetation. The tomb, as it now stands, would otherwise be doomed to decay.

The famous hill fort of *Rohtasgarh*, as is well known, was taken from the Hindus by Sher Shāh in A.H. 945. No information has come down to us about the last Hindu chief, and apparently the only records from Hindu times connected with Rohtasgarh are a few short rock-cut inscriptions at various places on the plateau. The first is at Phulwari, and says that Pratāpadhavala, the Nāyaka or Chief of Jāpila, constructed a road up the hill. Its date corresponds to the 27th March, 1169 A.D. Jāpila is evidently the modern Japla, on the opposite side of the Sone, in the modern district of Palamau, now a station on the newly opened Daltonganj branch line of the East Indian Railway, although no remains of any importance exist at present there. Two more inscriptions of the same Pratāpadhavala are to be found, one on the Tārācaṇḍī rock near Sasseram, and the other at Tutrahi, 5 miles west of Tilauthu. From another short inscription at Rohtasgarh we learn that the Chief in question belonged to the *Khayaravāla-vaṃśa*, and Professor Kielhorn has pointed out that this name appears to survive in that of the tribe of Kharawars, who still occupy the tableland on which Rohtasgarh is situated, and who claim a descent from the sun.[2] To a descendant and successor of Pratāpadhavala, called likewise Pratāpa, belongs the second Rohtasgarh inscription, the date of which is equivalent to the 5th March, 1223 A.D. It is near the Lāl Darwāza, and it records that a certain Mādhava made a well. Apart from these short inscriptions we have no record of Hindu rule over Rohtasgarh, for the long inscription of Mitrasena and Śyāmasāhi, which was near the Kathautiya gate, and is now in the Indian Museum, Calcutta, belongs to the time of Jahāngīr, as it is dated in the Vikrama year 1688.[3] The latter gives a long list of the ancestors of Mitrasena and Śyāmasāhi who belonged to the Tomara clan of Gwalior, but is of doubtful value to history. Certainly the statement that Śyāmasāhi took Rohtasgarh away from Sher Khān cannot refer to Sher Shāh. Probably some rebellious chief, who had taken temporary possession of the stronghold, is thus designated.

---

[1] The tomb of Sher Shāh likewise originally had a small cupola, but when it was repaired by the Public Works Department, this was converted into a pinnacle, in imitation of that over his father's tomb.

[2] *Epigraphia Indica*, Vol. IV, p. 311, Note 10.

[3] *Journal As. Soc. Bengal*, Vol. VIII, p. 695.

It may not be generally known that the Oraons assert that Rohtasgarh originally belonged to their race, and that it was wrested from them by the Hindus who surprised them at night during one of their great national festivals, when the men had fallen senseless from intoxication, and only women were left to fight. Tradition alleges that Sher Shāh also conquered the fortress by means of a stratagem, although of a somewhat different kind.

Very few remains on the Rohtasgarh plateau can be attributed to the time of Sher Shāh. I believe, however, that the mosque with three domes on the road from the Palace to the Lāl Darwāza belongs to this time, if I am right in reading the date of its inscription as A.H. 950. It is generally called the *Jum'a Masjid*, or '*Ālamgīrī Masjid*, although it certainly was not built under Aurangzeb. It is one of the buildings which have been repaired. The three domes had become unsafe and had to be restored. The large ***Mausoleum*** of Hawass Khān, as it is now called, which, however, should be *Ḥabsh Khān*, may be the tomb of the Dārogha of Sher Shāh mentioned by Buchanan. There is nothing to show that Ḥabsh Khān, a eunuch, who built a mosque in front of it, lies interred there.

The remainder of the buildings appear to date from *Mughal* times. The date of the inscription over the *Hāthiyā Pol*, or principal gate to the palace, which was built by Mān Singh, corresponds in the Sanskrit to the 14th March, 1597 A.D., and in the Persian to the 16th of the same month and year. The Kathautiya gate bears another inscription, with a date equivalent to the 28th February, 1607 A.D. Ḥabsh Khān built the mosque already referred to in 1580 or 1581 A.D.,[1] and close to it the tomb of Shāfī Sulṭān has an inscription with a date equivalent to 1578 or 1579 A.D.[1] Lastly, an inscription over the door of a tomb at the foot of the plateau, from the time of Shāhjahān, throws some light on the management of the hill fortress. It tells us that at that time Ikhlāṣ Khān was the Qil'adār with the rank of a commander of 3,000, and Faujdār of Makrai, the ***parganas*** of Siris and Benares, and that his *jāgīr* consisted of the following ***parganas***: Jiwand, Sakror, Tilauthu, Akbarpur, Bilaunja, and Japla. The ***parganas*** mentioned now lie in the modern districts of Shadabad, Gaya, Palamau, and Benares, and most of the names still exist. The Dārogha of the fort was Malik Wiṣāl. It was probably only he who was stationed there permanently, and for this reason built a tomb for himself and his family close to the hill, while the commander of the fort perhaps paid merely temporary visits to it. The tomb was finished in January-February, 1638 A.D.

The mural evidence with regard to the history of Rohtasgarh goes no further than this. Many inscriptions appear to have been lost, and their vacant spaces are still visible. The buildings themselves cannot in any way compare with the relics of the same period in other parts of India. However, as the only specimen of Mughal civil architecture in Bengal, and as striking examples of the conditions of military life in those days, they have been thought worthy of conservation, and a total expenditure of Rs. 36,303 has been incurred in repairing them.

The ***Palace*** itself is a very irregular medley of buildings. The repairs done to it generally consisted in removing the whitewash by which the ancient wall painting was hidden. This painting, by the way, is very simple, generally brown, with bands

[1] The numerical value of the letters forming the *tārīkh* in both inscriptions is one below the numerical figures added

of white, red and yellow, and does not rise to a high standard of art. The eaves of the roof and kiosks have been restored to a large extent, almost completely.

The *Mosque of Ḥabsh Khān* was the best preserved at Rohtasgarh, and has been thoroughly restored. All the broken stones have been relaid, and the domes have been made watertight. The repairs done to the so-called tomb of Ḥabsh Khān and the Jum'a or 'Ālamgīrī Masjid have already been referred to above, page 58.

Three Hindu temples also received attention. The temple shown in the illustration on this page is now called that of Gaṇeśa from regard to a modern statue which has been placed inside the sanctum. The building had originally in its front an open *maṇḍapa* with a pyramidal roof resting on pillars. This was quite broken, but with the help of an ancient painting by Daniells the pillars have now been restored out of materials still lying about. No attempt has yet been made to re-construct the roof.

The *Temple of Rohitāśva*, to whom the hill is sacred, and after whom it is named, was originally a structure resembling that of Gaṇeśa. But the tower as well as the *maṇḍapa* have long fallen away, and all the old stones are lost. For this reason it was impossible to restore any of the missing parts, and only the long flight of steps leading up to it has been repaired. A wretched looking brick mosque, which Aurangzeb is alleged to have built just behind it, immediately on the edge of the precipitous cliff over which the temple stands, has been pulled down.

Close to the temple of Rohitāśva stands another, sacred to his father, *Hariścandra*. It is an interesting little temple, with five cupolas, supported by pillars. The eaves and broken parts of the domes have been rebuilt, and the temple is now in good order again.

Although the remains at Rohtasgarh can claim no distinction as works of art or architecture, yet, set off by the fine scenery of the lofty plateau, they will always afford an interesting object of study to the visitor, who will find himself amply rewarded for the fatigue of ascending the hill by the sights which await him at the end of the journey.

T. Bloch.

CONSERVATION OF MONUMENTS AT AGRA.

IN the ordinary course the duty of describing the year's progress of conservation work in Agra would have devolved upon the Archæological Surveyor of the United Provinces and Punjab Circle, within whose important charge the group of monuments at Agra holds the first place. But the untimely death of Mr. E. B. Shepherd at the moment when he would have been taking up his pen to give an account of what have been accomplished there, has imposed upon me the responsibility of discharging the task.

Nowhere else in India has recent conservation work been more systematic or more steadily guided by a large and comprehensive purpose than in Agra. Here no hap-hazard operations—the promptings of a pious but passing impulse—have been hastily undertaken or hastily conceived. Thirty years ago Sir John Strachey, while Lieutenant-Governor of the then North-West Provinces, deliberately outlined a most liberal scheme of conservation, and himself set about inaugurating the work upon lines which are, in a general sense, being followed to the present day. Unfortunately, however, the qualifying statement has to be added that the work which Sir John Strachey began so well did not after his departure continue always to receive the same vigorous stimulus. His successors doubtless all shared to the full his intense admiration for what he rightly regarded as the finest collection of Archæological buildings in the East; but either exigencies of provincial finance or other untoward causes prevented some of these from carrying forward his plans with the same vigour. Down till the year 1884 there was perhaps but little to complain of in this respect, but from that time onwards a period of depression supervened, broken only by occasional spasmodic outbursts of activity. It was not until 1899 that a re-awakening came, and that the work was resolutely resumed. During the five years which have since elapsed, the new spirit infused into the scheme has already been productive of remarkable fruit, and before another five years have flown it is hoped that all the chief undertakings will be nearing completion. By that time all the buildings that are worthy of conservation in Agra itself, or at Fatḥpūr Sīkrī, or at Sikandarah, will have been put into a state of thorough repair, and it will remain only to maintain them in that state and to add to their list a few perhaps of the smaller tombs or mosques scattered here and there about the surrounding country.

Some idea of the mere scope of these operations may be gathered from the fact that, since the start in 1872, a sum of 16½ lakhs of rupees has been absorbed, and probably before the end is reached, the total expenditure will have been raised to twenty lakhs. But in return, the Government will be able to show results which would more than justify an outlay of treble that amount. In all their former magnificence the monuments of Agra could hardly have looked much more effective than the work of the last five and the next five years will render them. For, on the one hand, it is restoring to them the full symmetry of their ancient form without adding any obtrusive element of newness, and on the other it is preserving to them the softened tones which time has substituted for the brilliant, and not seldom tawdry, colouring of the past.

In the account of conservation works which is to follow, such buildings as are still in the repairer's hands are only briefly noticed—a fuller description being reserved for future issues of the "Annual," according as each of them emerges finally from the scaffolding of the Public Works Department. For the details of the engineering operations I am indebted to the very full and lucid reports of Mr. A. C. Polwhele, the Executive Engineer in charge, who, it may be further remarked, has displayed an uncommon care and earnestness in his supervision of the work.

The operations themselves are the outcome of specific instructions issued personally by the Viceroy, Lord Curzon, who on other occasions also, and at the very outset of the year under report, made a minute examination of each of the monuments described.

THE AGRA FORT.

Jahāngīrī Maḥall.

Undoubtedly the greatest achievement in archæological work at Agra has been the repair of the *Jahāngīrī Maḥall*, the vast red sandstone palace which lies towards the south-eastern part of the Fort, between the palace of S̲h̲āh Jahān and what is now the military prison. This palace has been fairly fully described by several writers, and particularly by General Cunningham's assistant, Mr. A. C. Carlleyle.[1] Fergusson has not much to say of it, but his brief description is well worth quoting: "One," he says, "of the most remarkable and characteristic of Akbar's buildings is the old or Red Palace n the Fort, so called from being constructed entirely of red sandstone, unfortunately not of a very good quality, and consequently much of its ornament has peeled off. It is a square building, measuring 249 feet by 260 feet. In the centre is a courtyard 71 feet by 72 feet, on either side of which are two walls facing one another. The largest, 62 feet by 37 feet, has a flat ceiling of stone, divided into panels, and supported by struts of purely Hindu design, very similar to those used in the palaces of Man Sing and Vicramaditya at Gwalior. Every feature around this court is indeed of pure Hindu architecture. No arches appear anywhere, but the horizontal style of construction everywhere. The ornamentation too, which is carved on all the flat surfaces, is of a class used by Akbar, but not found in the buildings of others. Indeed, throughout this

[1] *A. S. R.*, Volume IV, pages 124 sqq.

palace arches are used so sparingly, and Hindu forms and Hindu construction prevail to such an extent, that it would hardly be out of place at Chittore or Gwalior, though it still bears that impress of vigour and originality that he and he only knew how to impress on all his works." [1]

There has been much argument about the date of this palace. Mr. Carlleyle,[2] on the evidence, I think, of its name alone, assigned it to the reign of Jahāngīr. He is followed by W. Hunter[3] and Syad Muhammad Latif.[4] Their opinion is not shared by General Cunningham, who concluded from Jahāngīr's own account that his palace must have been quite close to the water gate, between it and the Muthamman Burj. His argument, it may be noted, finds additional support in the statement of the court chronicler of the Emperor Shāh Jahān to the effect that Jahāngīr had erected marble halls (*aiwān*) on three sides of the Shāh Burj (Regal Tower), now called the Muthamman Burj.[5] The Red Palace itself is attributed by the General to Ibrāhīm Lodī.[6] Fergusson, as we have already seen, believed it to have been built by Akbar,[7] and in this view he is followed by Mr. Keene.[8] Professor Blochmann utilised the authority of native historians to show that it was not at any rate a *pre-Mughal* building, since the fort and palace, which existed before the time of Akbar, were brick buildings and entirely demolished by that Emperor; but the authorities he cites are not conclusive on this point.[9]

On the whole the authority and evidence—both historical and architectural—favour its assignment to Akbar, and we may perhaps assume that it was used as the residence of the Heir-apparent—afterwards Jahāngīr—and his Hindu wives, though it may not have been intended for him in the first instance.

The name by which the building is now known does not appear to be found in any Muhammadan history. Maulavī Nūr Bakhsh suggests that it was originally called the Bengālī Maḥall, a palace referred to in the Akbar Nāmah, in connection with Akbar's return to Agra in the fourteenth year of his reign. The passage runs: "On the 31st of Urdī Bahisht (April) of the Ilāhī era, corresponding with Thursday, 24th Dhu-l-qa'dah (A.H. 977=A.D. 1570), the Emperor spread the shadow of his glory on the capital of Agra, and lodged in the centre of the Palace of the city in the Bengālī Maḥall, whose fabric had recently reared its head to the sky, etc." It may be added that the name Bengālī is still applied to the bastion tower at the south-east corner of the Jahāngīrī Maḥall.

The preservation of the Palace was first taken in hand between the years 1876-1885, when a special archæological division of the Public Works Department existed in the North-Western Provinces. The works then carried out were confined to the

[1] *Indian and Eastern Architecture*, page 578.

[2] *A. S. R., loc. cit.*

[3] *Imperial Gazetteer of India* (London, 1885), Volume I, page 73.

[4] *Agra, historical and descriptive* (Calcutta, 1896), page 31.

[5] Bādshāh Nāmah, *Bibl. Ind.*, Volume I, part II, page 239. I am indebted to Maulavi Nūr Bakhsh for pointing this out.

[6] *A. S. R.*, Volume IV, Preface, page 12.

[7] *Op. cit.*, page 578. In the footnote Mr. Fergusson speaks erroneously of Mr. Carlleyle's theory as being shared by General Cunningham.

[8] *Transactions of the Archæological Society of Agra* (January to June, 1874). "Note on General Cunningham's preface to Report for 1871-72, Volume IV," by H. G. Keene, President of the Society, pages 27—28.

[9] *Op. cit.*, pages xxx—xxxi.

PLATE IX

b

THE EAST, OR RIVER FRONT.

north and south sides of the inner quadrangle. In 1885 the archæological division was abolished, and little or nothing more was done to the Maḥall until the year 1899-1900. During that and the three subsequent years the work of protection and restoration was extended to all the chief parts of the building, and its execution has left nothing to be desired. Structurally, indeed, it may be said that it is now, thanks to the resourcefulness of modern engineering, more stable than it could ever have been before. And this is not all, nor the chief merit of its restoration. All the massiveness of its proportions and the sculptured beauty impressed upon its stone-work have been revived. To the spectator viewing the Palace from a distance or standing within its walls it apears now almost as it did in the day of the Mughals. The ugly break which its ruin caused in the long imposing line of the fortress wall has disappeared, and in its place the facade of the palace has risen again to its full height, with hardly a detail wanting and with each detail true to the original. The photographs in Plates IX and X convey a very fair impression of the sad state of disrepair into which the eastern side of the palace had fallen, and the transformation it has since undergone. They show what has been done, under the care of the Public Works officers, in the reconstruction of its upper storey and of the kiosk surmounting the bastion at its corner, in the restoration of its projecting balconies and eaves, and of the high *pardah* screen on the roof above. But they fail to give any idea of the refinement of carving in the panelled frieze of elephants or in the more delicate geometric designs with which both the curtain and the back of the façade are enriched; and it is in these minuter details that the Agra masons of to-day have shown themselves capable of a technique and finish as exquisite as any in the works of their forefathers.

For the following account of all that has been done since 1899 up to the end of the last season, I am indebted to Mr. A. C. Polwhele, the Executive Officer in charge of the works:—

"The first work undertaken was in the nature of general structural repairs to the brickwork and plaster of the interior walls and less prominent parts of the building, in order to prevent further disintegration. Simultaneously with this, the restoration of the following parts was carried out:—

(*a*) Of the pillared hall at the east end of the north side court, the roof of which had fallen in. The work consisted of restoring the red stone slabs (18 feet long and 12 inches thick) which formed the roof of the hall, and renewing the *chajja* or dripstone.

(*b*) Of the open pavilion at the south-east corner on the roof, which has been closed in with modern brickwork to form a dwelling house. The restoration comprised an entirely new *chajja*, or dripstone, with supporting brackets and bressummer, and the renewal of the plinth and bases of many of the decayed sandstone pillars. While this work was going on, the floor of the pavilion, which consisted of stone flags on wooden beams, gave way, owing to the rottenness of the latter.

(*c*) Of the hall on the north side of the central court. Here only six stone arch ribs and three heavy brackets had to be renewed.

"The above works were finished in 1899-1900, and at the end of the same year the restoration of the east side of the central court and of the north-west kiosk was taken in hand. This comprised :—

(*a*) The entire renewal of six of the twelve heavy carved sandstone brackets supporting the lower *chajja*, or dripstone, and portions of four others. (*b*) The restoration of the lower *chajja*. (*c*) The renewal of the frieze over the lower *chajja* and the greater part of the string course. (*d*) Thorough repairs to the colonnade of 22 arches on the upper storey, the facing stones of which were much decayed. (*e*) The renewal of 17 carved sandstone brackets supporting the horizontal eave stones above the colonnade. (*f*) Complete restoration of the projecting balcony in the centre of the colonnade and of the *chhatrī* on the roof above it.

"The kiosk at the north end of the west façade of the Jahāngīrī Maḥall was in a ruinous state, the domed roof having completely collapsed; the work of restoration comprised the reconstruction of the dome and the renewal of the two dripstones—one around the base of the dome and the other around the second storey of the tower; it also included the restoration of the two pieces of dripstones on the east side, one over the first storey and the other over the second storey facing the northern side-court, known as the *Tulsī Chibūtra* courtyard.

"The works mentioned in the preceding paragraph were completed in 1900-01, and the restoration of the west face of the inner courtyard, which was in a more ruinous state than the others, was then commenced. It entailed the following measures :—

(*a*) Restoration of the carved stone ceiling of the central room on the ground floor, which had fallen in. (*b*) Restoration of the jambs and five of the beautiful carved brackets which support the lintel of the main doorway. (*c*) Repairing and reroofing five small rooms on the first floor. (*d*) Entire restoration of the façade with its carved brackets, dripstones, colonnade, and central balcony. (*e*) Rebuilding of the small *chhatrī* over the centre of the façade. (*f*) Repairs to and renovation of the third storey and of the parapets and copings. This item involved the renewal of some very delicately carved pillars and brackets.

"All four faces of the inner courtyard having now been restored, it was decided to reconstruct the balustrade around the edge of the flat roof. The original balustrade had entirely disappeared, but the presence of mortice holes for the uprights afforded ample evidence that a balustrade once existed. The position of these mortice holes, which were, as usual, directly over the upper row of brackets, fixed the lengths of the several panels of the balustrade, but its height had still to be determined. This and all the designs of the panels were kindly worked out and drawn to scale by Mr. E. H. Hankin, who has made a special study of the *jālī* patterns of the Mughal period. The restored balustrade was completed in 1901-02.

"Simultaneously with the above the restoration of the missing parts of the *pardah* screen on the east edge of the roof, facing the river, was undertaken. A considerable portion of the original screen still existed, which made the restoration of its carved details a straightforward matter. At the north end, however, where a portion of the building has evidently disappeared, there was no evidence except the uncertain

a

b

EAST OR RIVER FRONT, RESTORED.

testimony of an ancient drawing to show the precise spot where it ended. In the absence of additional proof this question must always remain uncertain. The screen appears to have been added as an after-thought, and at neither end can its abrupt termination be worked in successfully with the lines of the original design.

"Among minor works executed in 1901 may be mentioned the following :—

(*a*) The perforated stone panels in the passage running around the south hall of the central courtyard were restored.

(*b*) The pieces of plain stone, with which the exquisitely carved pillars of this south hall had at some time or other been patched, were carved in relief *in situ*, according to the original designs.

(*c*) Some of the large brackets supporting the lower dripstone, which had been repaired with plain stone, were also sculptured.

(*d*) In one of the rooms on the south side of the narrow court to the south of the central courtyard, called the 'Tamolan kā Maḥall,' the walls and ceiling are decorated with delicate patterns moulded in plaster. The original work had suffered greatly from smoke and general abuse, and was in danger of perishing altogether. A small piece was therefore restored to give an idea of the beauty of the original.

"In 1901-02 was brought to completion the most important piece of work undertaken in connection with the Jahāngīrī Maḥall, or indeed of any other building in and around Agra; *viz.*, the restoration and repair of the wall on the east or river front, which forms part of the inner wall of the Fort.

"The face of this wall, which is 180 feet in length, consists of a series of panels slightly sunk in a beautifully carved ground; the lower panels are in the form of arched niches, in the centre of which are small windows giving light and air to the underground chambers behind the wall; on the upper panels are two elephants carved in relief; round every panel runs a plain border of white marble, but with this exception the whole of the face of the wall is of red sandstone. Above the panels is a balcony, which marks the level of the courtyard in front of the Maḥall, and above the balcony is a screen wall decorated on both sides with carved panels, and pierced with doorways, which give access to the balcony from the courtyard. The photograph in Plate IX(*a*), taken in 1901, will show how ruinous was the condition in which this wall then was. Its hearting had been disintegrated by the rains; the upper portion had disappeared completely, and in the lower part many of the panels had fallen, and the sculptured face of the majority of the remaining blocks had shaled off. It is much to be regretted that this photograph was not taken before the remains of the upper screen wall were touched, but it may be said that practically all that had then been removed consisted of modern repairs.

"Before the work of restoration was commenced, detail plans of both the outer and inner faces were prepared from the remaining traces of the original work on the wall itself and on the adjoining tower. No traces were found to indicate how the actual top of the screen wall was finished, but from the existence of a doorway in the tower at the south end and of a '*kangra*' pattern on the tower, it is reasonable to suppose that a walk extended along the top of the wall with a parapet on the outside.

"It is probable also that there was a balustrade along the balcony which would otherwise have been extremely dangerous, and also along the inner edge of the walk on the top of the wall. In fact, mortice holes are said to have existed in the jamb of the doorway leading out of the tower, but the original jamb could not be found. The existence of these balustrades, being uncertain, a small piece only has been erected as a suggestion of what the original may have been. This piece of balustrade can be seen in photographs X (*a*) and (*b*). It will be noticed that a piece of balustrade has been inserted in each of the doorways opening on to the balcony; this was done for safety, and, as no evidence could be found to show that the doorways were originally blocked in this way, the balustrades have been fixed behind, and not in the frame-work of the doorways, as they probably would have been, had they formed part of the original design.

Fig. 1.

"Of the restorations carried out up to the end of the year 1902-03 there remains only one more to be described, *i.e.*, that of the north-east bastion and the kiosk surmounting it. This bastion flanks the south end of the façade, the restoration of which is described in the preceding paragraph.

"The above photograph (Fig. 1) of the kiosk, taken before it was dismantled, shows that it was supported by modern brickwork and tied together by iron bands; besides which the upper part of the bastion itself was considerably out of the plumb, while the dripstone and balcony had entirely disappeared.

"A detail plan of the kiosk and bastion having been made, the kiosk was dismantled, and also the face work of the bastion down to the dripstone, every piece of stone, which was fit to be used again, being carefully preserved. The work of restoration consisted of renewing the red sandstone balcony and dripstone with the carved brackets supporting them, refacing the bastion, and re-erecting the kiosk. In the re-erection of the kiosk, one of the carved sandstone columns and some of the carved stone-work in the soffit of the dome had to be renewed. The photograph in Plate X (*b*) shows the restored bastion and kiosk."

Salimgaṛh.

The *bāradarī* known as the Salīmgaṛh (Fort of Salīm) stands near the modern military barracks, to the north-west of the Jahāngīrī Maḥall, and on the highest point within the fort. It consists of a single room, 34 feet 10 inches squarẹ, with arched openings on all sides. The name Salīmgaṛh is applied also, according to Mr. Carlleyle, to the irregular four-sided plateau on which the *bāradarī* stands, and which in his opinion marks the site of the Palace of Prince Salīm,[1] afterwards Jahāngīr. He doubtless believed that the *bāradarī* formed part of that Palace. But more usually the name Salīmgaṛh has been connected with Salīm Shāh, son of Sher Shāh, he who built a fort of the same name on an island in the Jumna at Delhi.[2] This was the opinion of Fergusson, who appears to have concluded on stylistic grounds also that the *bāradarī* should be referred to the reign of Sher Shāh. "In the citadel at Agra," this authority says, "there stands—or at least stood when I was there—a fragment of a palace built by Sher Shah, or his son Selim, which was as exquisite a piece of decorative art as anything of its class in India. Being one of the first to occupy the ground this palace was erected on the highest spot within the Fort, hence the present Government, fancying this a favourable site for the erection of a barrack, pulled it down and replaced it by a more than usually hideous brick erection of their own. * * * Judging from the fragment that remains, and the accounts received on the spot, this palace must have gone far to justify the eulogium more than once passed on the works of these Pathans—'that they built like giants, and finished like goldsmiths;' for the stones seem to have been of enormous size, and the details of most exquisite finish."[3]

If the fragment to which Fergusson refers is the same as the *bāradarī* now called the Salīmgaṛh—and there is no reason to suppose otherwise, nor can any trace be found of another building having existed here, which would answer to his description—then it must be said that the terms of admiration in which he speaks of it are somewhat overstrained and misleading. The eaves or *chajjas* are, it is true, unusually large and elaborately carved, but the general design and massiveness of its architecture, and the finish of its sculptured decoration, find close parallels among the monuments

---

[1] *A. S. R.*, Volume IV, page 124.
[2] *Tuzuk-i-Jahāngīrī* (Allygurh, 1864), page 65.
[3] *History of Indian and Eastern Architecture* (London, 1899), pages 572—73.

known to have been erected by Akbar, while the patterns employed are strikingly in the style that found favour during that Emperor's reign. The elaborate paintings, for instance, with which the interior is covered, are very like those in the Jāmi' Masjid at Fatḥpūr Sīkrī, and the clumsily drawn geometric figures, which ornament the quarter-dome-shaped recesses in the four corners of the hall, are found repeated in other buildings both at Agra and Fatḥpūr Sīkrī. These resemblances were noticed by Mr. Keene,[1] who remarks also that the Salīmgaṛh was considered by the natives "as having formed the *Noubat-khana*, or drumstand of Akbar's Palace." This last statement is probably inaccurate, since at the present day the natives know the Salīmgaṛh as distinct from Akbar's *Naubat-khāna*; nor does Mr. Keene seem to be correct in stating, as he does in the following sentence, that "Suleem's fort was called Badalgarh, and is generally stated to have been entirely demolished by Akbar in founding the existing Fort." At least there are good reasons for believing with General Cunningham[2] that the Bādalgaṛh was built by Hindus, while on the other hand there is no authority for assigning to it an Afghān origin.

Yet another suggestion made by Mr. Benson in the Provincial Gazetteer[3] is that the Salīmgaṛh may be the *bāradarī* of Bīrbal, Akbar's favourite Hindu Courtier, which "according to some native authorities exists in the Fort." What authorities these are that Mr. Benson refers to, has not yet been discovered, but the identification would accord well with the style of the pavilion.

Until quite recently the Salīmgaṛh was used as a soldiers' canteen, and for this purpose the archways had been bricked up, doors and windows fitted, and a verandah added on the west side. These modern accretions have now been removed, and the carved dripstone (*chajja*) has been restored around the building. The latter had completely disappeared, owing doubtless to the natural disintegration of the stone and the excessive strain due to the unusual length of the *chajjas*. Pieces of it were fortunately lying about on the ground, and from these the richly carved design on the under side could be faithfully copied. The modern whitewash, which covers the inside, has not yet been removed since special precautions have to be taken to prevent injury to the painted arabesques and medallions which it conceals.

Dīwān-i-'Āmm.

Those who have visited the Dīwān-i-'Āmm in the Agra Fort, will remember the quadrangle around it as nothing more than an arsenal yard, littered with *débris* and rubbish, and surrounded with hideous rows of modern casemates. This appears to have been the state of the quadrangle since shortly after the British occupation. Military exigencies demanded that none of the ancient buildings should be left visible, save the entrance gateways and the Hall of Public Audience alone, and even the latter was afterwards—at the time of the Prince of Wales' visit in 1875—disfigured by restuccoing its columns and clumsily renewing their decoration in red and gold. In one place, near the Motī Masjid, a breach was made in the ancient cloisters and a broad road carried through them. This was the road by which visitors used to drive

[1] *A handbook for visitors to Agra and its neighbourhood*, by H. G. Keene (Calcutta, 1874), page 26.
[2] *A. S. R.*, Volume IV, page 98, and note.

a

b

into the Fort, the open space in front of the Dīwān-i-'Āmm being used as a convenient stand for carriages. All this is now changed. During the past year the military authorities have generously consented to evacuate this quarter of the Fort, and a scheme has been taken in hand for reconverting the whole square, as far as possible, to its original form. So far, only the eastern half has been evacuated, but the remainder is to be given up during the ensuing year, and in the meantime the restoration of the eastern half has been practically completed.

The casemates that screened the red stone cloisters from view have been removed and the cloisters themselves repaired. In many places the dripstones and brackets were missing or badly damaged, and in many the stone facing had gone from the columns, and everywhere the shell plaster, with which the exterior of the cloisters appears to have once been stuccoed, had all but completely perished. The renewal of the stucco could not be attempted over the whole façade, nor would it have been in any way desirable. Only the repairs therefore which were limited to the red sandstone have been carried out. In removing the modern whitewash from the interior face of the columns and arches some ancient coloured decorations were disclosed. They are in an inferior style, and it has not yet been decided whether the rest of the painting is worth exposing to view. More interesting was the discovery of an ancient brick pavement a foot or two beneath the surface in front and on each side of the Dīwān-i-'Āmm. The bricks of which it is composed are laid edgeways in a checkered pattern of small alternating squares. Close by the Hall, the pavement was fairly intact. but further out, only broken patches survived. The line, however, where the pavement ended was quite clear, and the whole of it was restored up to this point. It is not unlikely that a rail, similar to the one around the Dīwān-i-'Āmm in the Lahor Fort, existed at its outer edge, but no trace of it could be found. The straight road, which formerly connected the two main entrances into the quadrangle, has also been relaid and remetalled, the modern curved road being abolished, and the breach in the cloisters, through which it was carried, repaired.

Pipes have been laid for irrigation from the large well in the western half of the quadrangle, and the grassing of all the parterres in the eastern half has been finished. When the pipes were being laid in connection with this work, some brick paving was struck in the north-east corner of the quadrangle about 2 feet below the general ground level, and on excavation a paved roadway, 16 feet wide and in a very fair state of preservation, was discovered leading straight out from the arched entrance into the Mīnā Bazar. Judging from the appearance of this pavement and from the buried plinth of the main gateways of the quadrangle, it seems more than probable that the roadway between the main gateways running north and south through the quadrangle was originally at a lower level than at present, and that it also was paved. The lower and earlier pavements may be contemporary with the surrounding buildings of Akbar, and may have been covered up when the Hall of Audience was built, and the pavement around it laid during the repairs carried out by the Emperor Shāh Jahān. The excavations at this point also brought to light an earthenware pipe embedded in masonry and evidently dating from the time of the Mughals, which, when opened, was found to be full of water under pressure. A fuller description of these works will be given in a future report, when the restoration of the whole quadrangle has been finished.

Angūri-Bāgh and Macchī Bhawan.

Other important work in the fort has been done in restoring the Angūrī-Bāgh more exactly to its original condition. The modern vine trellis over the marble pavements has been removed, the wilderness of common shrubs has been cleared away, the modern masonry watercourses have been demolished, and the whole garden has been grassed. In the Macchī Bhawan too, the quadrangle, which was formerly overgrown with rank jungle grass and covered deep in *débris*, has now been laid out in lawns intersected by paths, which delineate, so far as could be ascertained from trial excavations, the form of the ancient fish ponds.

Motī Masjid.

The Pearl mosque also has continued to receive its share of attention, and in another year this exquisite building should pass completely out of the repairer's hands. The red sandstone façade on the east has been renovated, and the interior of the prayer chamber and cloisters around has been beautified by the repair of breakages in the facing of white marble, and by the restoration of the black and yellow borders that surround the marble panels. The white marble flags in the north-east corner of the quadrangle, where a subsidence had occurred and caused water to pond, have been relaid and cleaned of their discoloration; and the flights of stairs on the north and south have been opened up again, and the descending corridors recoated with shell plaster.

The repairs to the white marble were principally in the form of patches in places where pieces had shaled off owing to the corrosion of the iron dowels with which the stones were held together; the work has a slightly mottled appearance which is not altogether satisfactory, but previous experience shows that this will tone down in a year or two. At the foot of the stairs on the southern side, the old solid wooden doors, which had rotted, have had to be replaced by smaller teak doors, with fanlights of pierced stone-work above. The insertion of fanlights was rendered necessary by the exceeding darkness of the passages, which for this very reason had long been unused and had become choked with an accumulation of rubbish. On the north side, where the doorways are only partially above ground, the doors have been omitted and pierced screens only inserted.

THE TĀJ AND ADJACENT BUILDINGS.

Fathpurī Masjid.

The red sandstone mosque, known as the Fathpurī Masjid, stands immediately outside the gateway by which the large quadrangle in front of the Tāj is entered on its western side. It is on the right of the approaching road, but raised well above it on a lofty basement. The mosque was built by Fathpurī Mahall, one of the *begams* of the Emperor Shāh Jahān, the same who erected another mosque similarly named at the western end of the Chandni Chowk in modern Delhi. An anonymous pamphlet on the Tāj, several manuscript copies of which are extant in India, mentions the Fathpurī

a

b

(*a*) BEFORE REPAIRS.

(*b*) AFTER REPAIRS.

Masjid among the Tāj buildings, and gives its cost as Rs. 29,000. There is nothing unique and nothing very grand about this building, but it is a characteristic example of the chaste and pure style of the period to which it belongs, and well worthy of its place among the buildings grouped around the Tāj. The prayer chamber, the interior of which is not visible in the accompanying photograph, consists of a central apartment, supported on two rows of arches, and surmounted by a dome of the same shape as that of the Tāj; it is flanked on either side by wings with double rows of columns, engrailed arches and flat roofs.[1] A charming feature of the interior is the delicate floral ornamentation in white upon a background of deep red, like that in the masjid of the Tāj itself. Of the ablution tank, forming the usual adjunct to the mosque, some remains have quite recently been excavated below the platform on the northern side, and this tank is now in course of restoration.

For many years this little mosque was in the care of the Muhammadan Community of Tāj Ganj, but they did nothing towards its preservation, doubtless because no funds could be found for the purpose; and long after the repair of the neighbouring monuments had been taken in hand by the Government, it still remained neglected, though every visitor on his way to the Tāj must have marked it as an eyesore and a blot upon the scene. A few odd repairs were, it is true, carried out in 1880-81, but not until 1900-01 did the Government decide to take in hand the complete conservation of the building. Several preliminaries had then to be arranged before the actual work could begin. The *dālāns*, or open colonnades, along the basement facing the main roadway had been hired out by the Muhammadan Community to shop-keepers or common curio-sellers, and an agreement had to be drawn up providing on an equitable basis for the ejection of these occupants, and for making over the care of the mosque to the Public Works Department; the Government, on their part, undertaking to furnish all the funds required for its preservation.

Both the structural repairs and the restorations have been of an extensive nature. The whole range of basement *dālāns* were shaky, and had to be restored, the disintegrated stone-work of their sills and columns being renewed and the chambers behind, which are of brickwork, being rebuilt in places and replastered. At the same time the remains of the shops with their hideous lean-to roofs of thatch and other dirty appurtenances were removed. The corner towers, surmounted by kiosks, had to be stripped to their masonry core, and then rebuilt on the model of the one at the north-east corner, which alone was still intact, but which also was in so dangerous a condition as to necessitate its subsequent re-erection. The projecting edge of the platform was broken and ragged, and many of its supporting brackets had fallen out. All these defects had to be repaired, and the whole length of the pierced balustrade surmounting it renewed. On the platform a considerable area of the pavement was relaid and a small tank for the use of the worshippers was sunk beneath it. In the Masjid proper the four corner towers, which were cracked and out of plumb, had to be dismantled down to the level of the roof, and the stone facing, which was loose and bulging, had to be stripped off as far down as the platform itself, before restoration could be effected. The shafts at the angles of the central archway were shaky and the masonry had to be

[1] *Cf. The Monumental Antiquities and Inscriptions in the N.-W. P. and Oudh* (Allahabad 1891), page 63.

relaid; the missing slabs of marble in the spandrels and panels being replaced. The finials and carved battlements were also restored, and many of the broken eaves, or *chajjas*, were replaced by new ones. In the interior of the prayer chamber the carved stone facing of three of the pendentives and a large part of the soffit of the central dome were renewed, as well as the stone-work of the niches in the back wall. It was not until 1902-03 that these various works were completed, and the finishing touch is now being put by repairing the dilapidated parts of the flooring within the prayer chamber, by lowering the ground around the plinth of the platform to its original level, and by restoring the tank together with its fountains, which lies between the mosque and the roadway.

Sahelī Burj.

Facing the Fatḥpurī Masjid, and corresponding to it on the opposite side of the road, is another high platform, on which stands the octagonal building known as the Sahelī Burj No. 4, there being several other Burjs of the same design round about the Tāj—all of them said to have been erected to the memory of maids-of-honour in the service of the Empress. The Burj itself and the miniature kiosks at the corners of the structure were repaired in 1901, and nothing remained but to relay the pavement of the platform on which jungle grass was fast encroaching, to restore the balustrade on the north and west sides, and to reconstruct the balcony of the north-west corner *chhatrī*. The first mentioned of these works was carried out during the past year. Unfortunately only a few broken fragments of the original red sandstone flagging could be found, but the marks of the ancient mortar joints were traceable in places on the concrete foundation, and the indications thus afforded were sufficient to show precisely what pattern should be followed in laying the new flags.

The Outer Quadrangle.

Within the quadrangle before the main or southern entrance of the Tāj several striking improvements have been effected. The roads have been metalled and the one leading to the Sīṛhī Darwāza widened to correspond—as it must have done in Mughal times—with the flanking column of the doorway. The cloisters around the quadrangle have been repaired to the extent of having their broken dripstones, brackets and all the dilapidated parts of the plinths, pillars, etc., renewed in red sandstone, and the modern brick wall on the north side of the road near the east gate has been demolished. It is not clear why this wall was ever built, for it merely served as a screen in front of an alley, which had once been the site of cloisters, but had since become a receptacle for *débris* and was overgrown with rank jungle. Following the removal of the wall the *débris* and jungle have all been cleared away.

The Tāj Gardens.

Within the actual precinct of the Tāj itself, operations were chiefly directed to the further restoration of the gardens to their ancient form, and to the repair of the Masjid attached to the tomb. The former work was much facilitated by the discovery sometime earlier of some ancient plans of the *Mughal* buildings in Agra, including a very detailed one of the Tāj and its gardens. The precise date of this plan is not known, but probably it is not much later than the building of the tomb. Besides this drawing, there exists the small anonymous pamphlet previously referred to, which among other things contains several items of information confirming the accuracy of the plan.

The most striking change effected—and one which has contributed greatly to the beauty of the gardens—has been the restoration of the central causeway running east and west, and the reconstruction of the water channels which had been filled up and converted into flower beds. At the same time, twenty-four fountains around the marble tank in the centre of the garden were replaced. This latter work involved the removal of a water main, and the laying down of nearly a thousand feet of iron piping for the irrigation of the garden, and of branch pipes for the fountains around the central tank.

Hitherto all the fountains in the Tāj gardens have been supplied from a high level tank outside the wall, filled by a manual pump, but with the substitution of cast-iron pipes for stone-ware, it has been possible to connect all the fountains with the irrigation main, thereby saving the cost of pumping without at the same time involving any appreciable diminution of " head " at the fountains.

The ancient copper pipes of the fountains around the central tank, and the copper vessels, which formed the connections between the main supply pipe and the fountain pipes, were discovered beneath the floor of the channel and have been preserved. At the west end of the causeway a trench was found in the floor of the central channel, and excavations brought to light an earthenware pipe embedded in masonry. It is fairly certain that this was the original main that fed the fountains, and the oldest inhabitants state that they remember many attempts to put it into working order, but always without success.

The Masjid.

The repairs to the Masjid attached to the tomb were in continuation of those commenced in 1901-02, and now brought to completion. In addition to general structural repairs, which were essential to the safety of the building, and among which may be noticed the renewal of many of the sandstone blocks in the honey-combed pendentives of the domes, the façade and interior of the mosque have been much beautified by the restoration of the black and white marble encrustation and sculptured panels of the dado, and of the rich frieze or band that surrounds the central archway. The recarving and repair of both frieze and panels constituted a work of great delicacy, and it is not a little to say that the result is a complete success. In the copying of the Mughal designs upon fresh slabs of stone, and in the careful fitting in of new patches, where bad fractures had occurred, in such a manner as to save every inch of the original that could be saved, the native sculptors displayed all the ingenuity and skilful mastery over material acquired by hereditary instinct.

In concluding this account of the repairs to the Tāj buildings it should be mentioned also that the pierced sandstone screens in the back of the pavilions in the east and west walls of the garden have been restored, and that suitable wooden doors have been inserted in the same pavilions in place of the unsightly iron barred ones, which existed before.

TOMB OF I'TIMĀDU-D-DAULAH.

Passing over the Jumna to its further bank—the only monument in that part of Agra that has been under repair is the tomb of I'timādu-d-daulah, a building which has long been famous for its profuse decorations in *pietra dura*—the earliest and perhaps the best preserved examples of that class of work in India. This tomb was one of the first to receive attention in the early days of conservation at Agra, and much appears to have been done at that time to preserve and renovate its inlaid ornaments; but for several years past it has been evident that further protective measures were imperative, and it was accordingly decided to examine, piece by piece, the whole of the *pietra dura*, resetting those which were loose, and replacing those which were shattered or missing. This work has now been done, and some ten thousand separate pieces of marble and other stones of various kinds and sizes have been replaced. In all cases where a piece had to be reset, which was itself inlaid with a stone of another variety, the smaller stone was first inserted from the back of the larger stone and wedged in with *lac*, so that there is no possibility of the smaller stone at any rate becoming loose and falling out.

A most striking feature of this mausoleum, which has now been restored to it, is the fretted balustrade of white marble, carried round the four sides of the roof and serving at once as a useful protection and a singularly graceful ornament. The work of replacing this missing balustrade was begun in 1901-02 and only completed towards the end of the past year. The length of each side is 63 feet, and the height of the balustrade 2' 0½". Each of the panels is divided off, as usual, by upright posts, technically known as *muttakās*, which correspond with the brackets beneath the projecting edge of the roof, or with other perpendicular features in the façade of the tomb, and thus determine exactly the length of each panel. As many varieties of geometric patterns have been introduced into the *jālī* work of this balustrade, it should be explained that the designs have in every case been sedulously copied from other parts of the tomb, and that in selecting one or other of the patterns for any particular panel the fixed principles, invariably observed by the Mughal builders when adapting their patterns to a given space, have been rigidly followed. We can thus feel morally certain that the majority at any rate of the restored patterns are the same as the originals. It may be remarked that only recently has the existence of such principles governing the construction and adaptation of geometric designs on Mughal buildings been observed, and that we are indebted to Mr. E. H. Hankin both for this useful discovery and for working out the particular designs for the new balustrade.

A word should be added about the position of this balustrade, which has been set back some feet from the edge of the roof. It would have been more in accordance with the usual practice of the Mughal architects if it had been erected within a few inches of the edge itself, and supported by the projecting brackets, and there are, indeed, some marks here and there in the pavement which seem to indicate that this was the position originally intended for it. But a more complete series of *muttakā* holes existed along the line where it has been restored, and from them it seemed

EAST GATEWAY: OUTER FACE.

reasonable to conclude that the original intention was given up, either because the carrying power of the brackets was mistrusted, or, more probably, on account of the extra cost which would have been incurred in carrying the balustrade around the outside of the corner towers.

SIKANDARAH.

Main Gateway.

In the Mausoleum of Akbar at Sikandarah operations have been concentrated entirely on the gateways. The main gateway on the south had already come under

Fig. 2.

extensive repair in previous years, and the crowning touch has now been put to the work by completing the restoration of its bold ornaments of carved and inlaid coloured stones. The most serious of its defects lay in the damaged spandrels of the six archways on its east and west faces, which had lost much of their beautiful inlay of white marble set upon a ground of black marble or red sandstone. Of the central archways the spandrels were comparatively sound with the exception of the upper archway on the west face, the inlaid work of which had entirely disappeared and been replaced by plain sandstone. Of the archways on the flanks a fragment of the inlaid pattern was left in one only, the remainder having been at some time filled in with plain stone; this piece of the original pattern served as a guide to the restoration of the spandrels of all the flank archways on the lower storey. Besides the spandrels, most of the inlaid panels in the plinth and large parts of the mosaic borders had been destroyed and afterwards repaired with patches of plain stone. All of these have now been faithfully restored to their original designs.

East Gate.

The false gate in the east wall of the enclosure had fallen into a much worse state of disrepair. On the inner face indeed the dilapidations were so serious that it was decided to confine the restoration in the first instance to the outer face and adjoining pieces of wall on the flanks of the gateway, which consisted at one time of seven bays with pierced sandstone screens similar to those existing at the south and west gateways; and merely to repair the inner face sufficiently to prevent further deterioration.

In the restoration of the outer face a variety of different kinds of work were involved, including the renovation of the red sandstone panels inlaid with geometrical patterns in white marble, and the repair of the carved borders and panels of yellow and red sandstone, and some other minor details which are shown in the photographs [Plate XIII (*a*) and (*b*)] taken before and after the repair of the façade. In the restoration of the screens on the flanks of the gateway (see Fig. 2) the existing screens at the south and west gates proved useful as guides. To protect the gateway from damage by cattle, a wire fence has been fixed around it and an iron gate has also been provided to make it accessible.

The cracks in this gateway are probably, in a great measure, due to the state of disrepair of the platform and tank in front of it, the paving of which has to a large extent disappeared, so that rain water can soak freely into the foundation. A portion of this paving has now been restored, and it is proposed to complete the remainder during the coming year.

North Gate.

The false gate on the north side of the garden was in altogether too ruinous a condition to be restored; such protective works only were therefore carried out, as would prevent the dilapidations spreading further, without in any way interfering with the character of the gateway as a picturesque ruin. To secure this end, the much-broken and overhanging parts of the gateway were built up with ordinary brickwork and any irregular ledges, where water was liable to lodge and percolate into the masonry, were roughly sloped off. The open joints of the exposed brickwork hearting were grouted with mortar; several dangerously cracked lintel stones were renewed, and some of the facing stones, which were on the verge of falling out, were reset and firmly supported.

J. H. MARSHALL.

THE QIL'A-I-KUHNA MASJID AT DELHI.

TWO miles south of the Delhi Gate of Shāh Jahānābād, or modern Delhi, lies the village of Indrapat, which retains the name and may conceivably occupy the site of Indraprastha, the city of the Pāṇḍavas. The present village is enclosed within the walls of the Old Fort (Qil'a-i-kuhna or Purānā Qil'a), which was the citadel of Delhi from its commencement by Humāyūn till the foundation of Modern Delhi by Shāh Jahān. Towering over the clustering huts which now fill the space between the lofty walls rises the magnificent mosque which Sher Shāh erected here in 1541.[1]

The Qil'a-i-kuhna Masjid belongs to that particular style of Indo-Muhammadan architecture which was designated by General Cunningham (and, following him, by Carr Stephen) as "Afghān," and forms the connecting link between the "Paṭhān" and "Mughal" styles. The name "Late Paṭhān," used by Fergusson, and recently adopted by Mr. H. C. Fanshawe, would seem to be more appropriate and, moreover, preferable from a practical point of view.[2] But it should be understood that the latter term by no means implies a degeneration from, or even a development of, the preceding "Middle Paṭhān" style. A greater contrast is hardly imaginable than exists between the mosques of Fīroz Shāh (1351-88) at Begampura, Khiṛkī and Delhi City (Kalān Masjid) on the one hand, and the Moṭh-kī-Masjid (1488) near Mubārakpūr, the Jamālī Masjid (1536) at Mahrauli, and the Qil'a-i-kuhna Masjid (1541) on the other. The former are characterised by sloping buttressed walls and very flat domes, and give the appearance of uncouth masses of stone without elegance of line or variety of colour, suggesting by their stern and gloomy aspect the idea of a mediæval stronghold. The mosques of the "Late Paṭhān" period, on the contrary, are generally distinguished by a profusion of decoration and richness of colour, vying in their splendour with some of the master-pieces of Mughal art. A difference so characteristic exhibited by buildings of the same class can hardly be explained by a mere divergence of taste on the part of their founders. Evidently there were other influences at work which at present can only be surmised but may

---

[1] Sayyid Ahmad, *Athāru-ṣ-ṣanādīd*, I, 49, ascribes it to Humāyūn, but does not quote any authority. *Cf.* Cunningham, *Archæological Survey Report*, I, page 222, and Carr Stephen, *Archæology of Delhi* (1876), page 190.

[2] Cunningham, *A. S. R.*, III, page 9. Carr Stephen, *loc. cit.*, VI. Fergusson, *History of Indian and Eastern Architecture* (London, 1899), page 518. H. C. Fanshawe, *Delhi Past and Present* (London, 1902), page 3?9.

not improbably have been carried into India on the wave of Mughal invasions. The Qil'a-i-kuhna Masjid belongs to the brief period (1540-54), when the Mughal power, already established in India by Bābar, was temporarily replaced by an Afghān dynasty. Historically the building might almost be said to belong to the Mughal period, and indeed shows a far greater affinity to the early Mughal style, as exhibited in the Khairu-l-manāzil (1561) of Akbar's reign, than to the stern and severe structures of the previous period.[1] It possesses, however, so many features of its own that we are fully justified in assigning it to a special style in common with the edifices of the fifteenth century.

A peculiarity which strikes us first is the absence of a cloister around the quadrangle in front of the prayer-chamber—an almost indispensable adjunct of the mosques both of the "Middle Pathān" and the "Mughal" periods. The cramped position of the mosque and the fact that it was finished in the early years of Sher Shāh's reign preclude the supposition that a cloister was ever intended in the original design. The absence of corner towers (*mīnārs*) is a feature which it has in common with the majority of earlier mosques as opposed to those of the Mughal period.[2] Their place at the back of the edifice is supplied by engaged octagonal turrets, richly ornamented and provided with balconies, but rising not higher than the roof of the mosque. In the centre of the courtyard is a sixteen-sided tank once used for the ablutions of the faithful.

The photographs [Plate XIV(*a*) and (*b*)] will give a sufficiently clear idea of the main features of the façade of the prayer-chamber itself, the only part of the building which has been recently repaired, but the following supplementary details may also be noticed. The lower parts of the ornamental bands, engaged columns and pilasters of the central portico, and of some of the narrower bands flanking the two adjacent archways, are faced with white marble rising to irregular heights and continued above in red sandstone. The bands surrounding the outer arches in the centre and both adjacent porticoes are decorated in relief with the inwoven Naskh and Kūfic characters, bordered with a geometrical design, that form such a conspicuous and lovely feature in the earlier mosques of Altamsh at the Quṭb and Ajmīr. The smaller band and the wall immediately above, within the central recess, are inlaid in geometric designs of white and black marble mingled with red sandstone. The outer half of the wings at either end of the mosque and their portal archways are of rougher construction and less elaborately ornamented than the rest of the building. These give the appearance generally of having been added at a later date, and in support of this view may be noticed, on the one hand, the material (grey stone) used in the construction (sandstone and marble being used to face the rest of the building); the meaningless ornamental bands with a *kangra* design cut in relief, carried horizontally across this part of the façade at half its height; the disproportionate heights of the inner and outer arches; and the total lack of ornament below the springers of the latter; and, on the other hand, the absence of the marble facing, of the borders of inscriptions, and of the fringe of lotus-buds beneath

[1] The style of the first half of the sixteenth century may "be considered as the last expiring effort of the Pathāns or the first dawn of that of the great Mughals, and is well worthy of either." Fergusson, *loc. cit.*, page 518.

[2] "The Pathāns seem to have regarded the *mīnār* as the Italians viewed the Campanile,—more as a symbol of power and of victory than as an adjunct to a house of worship." Fergusson, *loc. cit.*, page 518.

(*a*) BEFORE REPAIRS.

(*b*) AFTER REPAIRS.

the soffits of either inner or outer arch. Many other more minute details of difference might be added, but these perhaps will be sufficient to show that there is good reason for assuming that the wings do not belong to the original building. The roof is surmounted by a central dome, the contour of which shows a transition between the flat domes of the previous epoch, and the bulbous ones which came into vogue under Mughal rule. It is raised on a drum—unknown in "Paṭhān" mosques—of sixteen-sided form, the sides facing the cardinal points being pierced with arched windows, and the others recessed. Originally there appear to have been two flanking domes, of which traces [1] still exist, but these had already disappeared in Sayyid Ahmad's time. It should be noted that these domes surmounted those portions of the mosque which we believe to be later additions. It follows that, if our supposition be true, the original building was one-domed. And this is exactly a peculiarity of mosques of this period, such as the Khairu-l-manāzil and the Jamālī Masjid.

Sayyid Ahmad, writing about 1850, notices in his brief description of the Qil'a-i-kuhna Masjid that the building was in a state of disrepair, and it appears to have continued so until 1883, when it was repaired on the recommendation of Major H. H. Cole, Curator of Ancient Monuments in India. In his second report for the year 1882-83, p. cxii, Major Cole pointed out "that the floor should be repaired in concrete, the stone and marble mosaics repaired, the fallen *Chajjas* (*i.e.*, eaves) renewed, the bracketed window over the central arch repaired and leaks in the roof stopped. All the interior stone and marble work should be thoroughly cleaned." And again in his third report, p. 21, paragraph 45, we find that an estimate for special repairs to the Qil'a-i-kuhna Masjid amounting to Rs. 4,864 had been sanctioned in November 1883. "The whitewash of the interior has," he says, "been removed, but it should have been done without scraping the marble and stone. The mosaic work has been well repaired. The security of the structure requires attending to and insuring."

It is doubtful whether any action was ever taken on the strength of Major Cole's concluding remark. At any rate it is certain that, when His Excellency Lord Curzon visited the building, it was much in want of repair, and it was at His Excellency's instance that the following measures were carried out:—(1) Breakages in the marble of the arches and façade of the mosque, and decayed and damaged sandstone at the base of the face wall, have been repaired in new stone. (2) The decorative inlay of white and black marble and sandstone and also the vertical marble bands have been restored where broken or missing. (3) The face of the mosque has been cleaned. The effect of these repairs, the cost of which has been Rs. 1,301, and of the earlier ones of 1883, may be appreciated from a comparison of the photographs.

J. PH. VOGEL.

[1] These traces consist of two platforms measuring a little less than 20 feet square raised about 2 inches above the level of the roof. In the case of domes one would expect an octagonal plan, and it may be questioned whether perhaps, instead of domes, there were open cupolas or kiosks, such as are sometimes found on mosques of this period.

RESTORATION WORK IN AJMĪR.

THE archæological work carried out at Ajmīr between 1900 and 1902 includes restoration work on the embankment of the Āna-Sāgar Lake and protective work in the Arhāī-din-kā Jhoṁpṛā Mosque, "the finest and largest specimen of the early Muhammadan Mosque that now exists." [1]

The Mosque.

The first protective work on the Mosque of which we have any record, was carried out under the orders of the Maharaja Daulat Rao Sindhia, by whom the centre dome was restored and by whose order a stone tablet, still existing, was inserted in the gateway, prohibiting the removal of stones belonging to the Mosque by either Muhammadans or Hindus. After Ajmīr became a British possession in 1818, but little seems to have been done to the Mosque until Lord Mayo's Viceroyalty, although General Cunningham made a careful survey of it in 1864.[2] In 1870, when Lord Mayo held a Darbar at Ajmīr, and when the scheme for the establishment of the present Mayo College was publicly announced, a triumphal arch composed of pillars brought from the Mosque was erected, under which the Viceroy and the principal Chiefs of Rajputana passed in procession. The pillars were afterwards returned to the Mosque, and Lord Mayo gave directions for the repair of the well-known and beautiful Saracenic screen which was then falling to decay. These repairs were carried out in 1875-76 at a cost of Rs. 14,000.

From that time nothing was done until after His Excellency Lord Curzon's visit in November 1899, when it was found that, in spite of Lord Mayo's interest, the building had since been much neglected and stood in urgent need of repair. The five large and five small domes in the roof of the pillared hall were in the same condition in which Mr. Garrick found them in 1883. His report regarding the state of the roof at that time was as follows :—" The roof of the Arhai-din-ke-Jhopri has been covered with a most astonishing and heterogeneous collection of temple *sikris* or *kalas*, *i.e.*, the cog-wheel-shaped ornaments which surmount the *sikris*, or steeples, of Hindu temples. These appear to have been planted about wherever

[1] Cunningham, *A. S. R.*, II, 259.

[2] Cunningham, *A. S. R.*, II, page 258.

(a) GENERAL VIEW OF EMBANKMENT IN 1893.
(b) GENERAL VIEW OF EMBANKMENT IN 1903.

NEG. LENT BY RAJA DEEN DAYAL
RAJPUTANA PHOTOGRAPHIC CO

caprice dictated, and assuredly do not improve the appearance of this illused building."[1] One of the larger domes was missing altogether, and the hall beneath was thus exposed to the sun and rain. The surviving outer cloisters of the Mosque were in disrepair and in places were falling in. The same was the case with the exterior front wall. Squatters had encroached and built houses against the outer walls of the Mosque, while a protecting outer wall was needed at the rear.

The old domes have now been removed and replaced by plain segmental domes, the outlines of which are designed to be more in keeping with the arches of the screen, through which they are visible. The fifth missing dome has been newly built. The stone caps, or "*kalas*" of the older steeples have been retained. The tenements built by squatters have been purchased, and their sites cleared. The ruined cloister walls, where possible, have been strengthened with cement, which will arrest further decay, while, where the walls had fallen in altogether, they have been rebuilt in rough rubble masonry. The missing pillars in the lofty wall at the back of the Mosque have been replaced and the gaps in the outer front wall built up in cut stone. The whitewash coating over the marble *miḥrāb* also has, as far as possible, been removed, and, lastly, the numerous carved stones that belonged to the early Hindu temple, which the Muhammadans incorporated into their Mosque, have been collected and arranged in the low modern cloister on the right of the gateway.

The Mosque was visited for the second time by His Excellency Lord Curzon in November 1902, and the following additional measures were decided on: the removal of the common and modern stone supports found in the curious aperture (or *dīdwān*) above the *miḥrāb*; the cleansing and removal of whitewash from the interior of the domes in the roof; and the replacing of two marble stones that are missing in the *miḥrāb*. It is hoped that arrangements will also be made for the return of the six inscribed stones, dug up in the court-yard and sent to the Lucknow Museum in 1894. These carved stones, which were doubtless buried by the Muhammadans, contain Sanskrit plays in honour of the Chāhamāna King, Vigraharāja IV or Vīsaladeva, and in one of them mention is made of an expedition against the Turuṣkas, *i.e.*, Muhammadan invaders.[2] The operations of 1903 provide for a further excavation in the court-yard which may lead to interesting discoveries. In 1902 a large white marble *liṅga* was discovered in the course of excavation in the court-yard. This confirms the Brahmanical character of the early temple, which has often been incorrectly described as Jain.

The Pavilions.

In the works on the embankment of the Āna-Sāgar lake more extensive restoration has been necessary. The marble pavilions, or pleasure houses, erected here by Shāh Jahān in 1637 A.D., numbered originally five, and there was also erected a *ḥammām* or Turkish Bath. The embankment and the grounds below, known as the Daulat Bagh, formed a favourite garden-house of the Mughal Emperors when they visited Ajmīr.

[1] Garrick, *A. S. R.*, XXIII, 35.

[2] *Cf.* Professor F. Kielhorn, *Indian Antiq.*, XX, page 201, and "Bruchstücke Indischer Schauspiele in Inscriften zu Ajmere" in the "Festschrift zur Feier des 150 Jährigen Bestehens der Königl. Gesellschaft der Wissenschaften zu Gottingen. 1901."

The Āna-Sāgar lake is said to take its name from Arnorāja, one of the old kings of Ajmīr.[1] Formerly it was, perhaps, the greatest of the various natural beauties that combine to make Ajmīr one of the most remarkable of the old native cities of India. Now it is but seldom full, its catchment area having been diminished by one-half by the construction of a modern reservoir. The embankment, which dates from Hindu times, is broad and massive, and is faced with stone, rising from the waters of the lake. Between point and point its length is 11,122 feet. In Mughal times it was lined with a parapet of white marble and built over with pavilions of the same material. "*Bāradarīs*" (the twelve doors) is the name by which they are locally known.

On the British occupation in 1818 the embankment was selected as a site for the dwelling-houses of the Commissioner of Ajmīr and his subordinate officers, and public offices were also erected there. The house of the Commissioner included the two marble pavilions at the west end, which were imbedded in and concealed by the walls of the inner rooms. These are the pavilions now referred to as numbers 1 and 2. Between these and the third, the largest and most perfect of the pavilions, an office and a court room were erected, while another office was built on to the adjacent *ḥammām*. The third pavilion was permitted to remain intact and, save that it was repaired in 1884, has never, as far as is known, been added to or adapted. The fourth pavilion was converted into a station reading room and library, the spaces between the marble pillars being blocked in with masonry, while two masonry wings were added to the building. It was also used at one time as a Municipal Office. The fifth pavilion wes built into another dwelling-house. The embankment was divided into gardens and enclosures. The marble parapet was much neglected, such repairs as were necessary being carried out in common stone. A general view of the embankment in this condition is shown in Plate XV(*a*). Its restoration was first commenced in 1892, when the modern additions to the fourth pavilion [Plate XVI(*b*)] were demolished, and the pavilion itself renovated under the direction of Mr. Martindale, C.S.I., the then Commissioner, at a cost of Rs. 1,234.

In 1899 the rains failed and the lake became entirely dry. In consequence the foundations of the Commissioner's house subsided and the house became uninhabitable. The second house on the embankment suffered in the same way. An opening was thus presented for the restoration of the entire embankment and the beautiful buildings on it, and a scheme was accordingly prepared (under His Excellency the Viceroy's direction and supervision) for the demolition of the Commissioner's and the other houses, for the careful preservation of the original marble buildings contained in them and for their re-erection. At the same time all modern buildings were to be removed, the gardens were to be opened up, and the embankment, as far as was possible, restored to what it was when the Mughal Emperor first beautified it. The scheme has now been completed. The pavilions (numbers 1 and 2) in the Commissioner's house, were fortunately found to be nearly intact. Step by step, as the house was demolished, the marble work was carefully removed, and pillars, brackets and panels were numbered and re-erected *in situ* after the modern building material had been cleared away. [Plate XVI(*a*).] An idea of the completeness of the demolition may be gathered from Fig. 1, which shows every part of the pavilions lying prostrate on the ground, and a modern office, since removed. Comparatively little of

RESTORATIONS ON THE ÂNA SÂGAR EMBANKMENT, AJMER. PLATE XVI.

(*a*) PAVILIONS 1 AND 2 (RESTORED).

(*b*) PAVILIONS 3 AND 4 (RESTORED).

the original marble was missing, and the missing portions have been replaced by new marble work. The pavilions were re-erected by Mr. F. St. G. Manners Smith, the Executive Engineer of Ajmīr, to whom credit is due for a very delicate and successful piece of restoration work. In the case of the fifth pavilion the marble remains, which emerged after the demolition of the house, proved disappointing, as but little of the original marble building could be found. The three arches fronting the lake remained and corner wing-pieces of marble, indicating the shape of the original pavilion, were found standing, but that was all. Marble brackets were found imbedded in modern masonry without supports, and the shape of the original building can only be conjectured. No trace was found of any marble pillars, save those fronting the

Fig. 1. Showing pavilions dismantled before re-erection.

lake. It was proposed at first to retain the marble corner pieces, or wings, incorporating them in buttresses to support the front arches and pillars. The new buttresses, however, were not successful, and it was decided, after His Excellency's inspection in November 1902, that the wing-pieces should be removed altogether, and that the front arches and pillars should be supported by light buttresses of a simple character. This work is still in progress.

The completion of the parapet in marble, the removal of enclosures and buildings, the turfing of the two ends of the embankment, and the preservation of the marble floor of the former *ḥammām* are minor works that have been carried out under the advice and guidance of Mr. Marshall. There now remains but little to be done on the embankment, but some more levelling of the ground has to be judiciously carried out. Steps have been taken to protect the embankment by the appointment of a custodian, who lives on it in a small stone house of a design in keeping with the other buildings on the embankment. A marble inscription in Persian and English, recording the dates of the construction of the pavilions and of their restoration, has been inserted in the cliff in the south-west corner. The embankment is now largely visited by both Hindus and Muhammadans who appear to enjoy and to appreciate the transformation that has been effected.

A minor work unconnected with the mosque on the embankment has been carried out at the Ajmīr Fort in the cleansing and freeing from whitewash of the gateway facing the city. The gateway is that used by the Mughal Emperors for their State appearances at Ajmīr where they resided in the Fort, a massive rectangular structure built by the Emperor Akbar, and a good specimen of the architecture of that period. The immediate neighbourhood of the latter has been so much built over, and so many additions have been made to it during the British occupation, in which it was long used as an Arsenal, that its fine proportions are greatly obscured and marred. The centre building in the Fort has lately been examined with a view to restoration, if possible. Other measures are in contemplation for removing modern obstructions that have been erected near or built on to its wall.

A. L. P. TUCKER.

CHENNAKĒŚAVASVĀMI TEMPLE, SŌMPALLE.

THE village of Sōṁpalle stands at the base of a rocky hill, about 4 miles east of the South Indian Railway station at Mulkalacheruvu, in the Cuddapah District.

The tradition as to the origin of the village, which survives locally, is closely connected with the Polegar family, whose descendants still occupy the place. It relates that, during the reign of King Kṛṣṇa Dēva Rāya of Vijayanagar (A.D. 1509-1530), some cowherds who dwelt in the neighbouring jungles, erected a fort in order to enclose and protect the village; but, owing to oppression, the cowherds were compelled to flee from the place; leaving everything in charge of two brothers named Basi Nāyuḍu and Mullappa Nāyuḍu. Descendants of these named Śivi, Pedda, Vīramallappa, Muttumallappa, and Kumāramallappa continued the line of ruling zamindars, and in course of time cleared the surrounding forest, constructed temples and a fort on the Koṇḍamma hill, dug tanks, and laid out gardens. They in fact established their capital there, and the villages of Guṇḍlapalle, Chaṇḍasamudraṁ, Gaṇgareḍḍipalle, Diguvapālaiyaṁ, Koṭlapallē, Guḍupallē, Mulkalacheruvu, and Vēda-Śiri became outlying suburbs. This family continued to reign for a space of 422 years, and the rulers devoted themselves so far as the times would allow, to the well-being of their subjects.

It is stated that there are records to show that, during the times of the Mahraṭṭās and Mughals, the local rulers paid Rs. 5,000 *Kundani*, and an additional sum of Rs. 1,201 as *Pesh kist.* They celebrated the daily *utsavaṁs* at the temple, and built *maṇḍapaṁs.* Under the orders of the Mahraṭṭā Tahsīldārs Mādhava Rao, Mahāpati Rao, Kṛṣṇayya, and Bāji Raghunādha Nāmanāth, they strengthened the walls of the fort, and from it governed the surrounding country. When the Mughals conquered this part of the country, in the cyclic year *Hēvilaṁbi*, the inhabitants of Sōṁpalle were driven out by Mīr Sāhib, and the temple was partly destroyed. Evidences of this are at present seen in the headless and limbless images still in the temple. The country came under the rule of Mīr Rajā 'Ali Khān, who died in A.D. 1780, and whose tomb stands at Gurraṁkoṇḍa, in the Cuddapah District. In the cyclic year *Saḍhārana*, the Polegar Zamīndār Kumāramallappa Nāyuḍu again entered Sōṁpalle; and daily *pūjā* at the temple was resumed.

There are said to be accounts in the Vāyalpāḍ taluk, to the effect that the *utsavaṁs* of the temple were celebrated, partly by subscriptions raised by the ryots and partly by donations from Government.

In the year 1210 *Fasli*, Colonel Munro gave a *paṭṭa* to Mallappa Nāyuḍu, to the effect that *Izāra* had been granted for Rs. 2,120.

Condition of the temple.—The temple is built in the floriated Vijayanagar style. It is a comparatively small building, enclosed in a single court. The shrine and court walls are constructed of plain masonry with ornamental brick niches on the wall heads. Though the building, as a whole, is not very remarkable, there are some portions of it which are unique and well worthy of conservation. These are a beautifully carved four-pillared *Kalyāṇa maṇḍapaṁ*, a similarly carved *ratha* in front, and an unusually lofty *dīpdān* or lamp pillar, which stands outside the front. Several parts of the temple were a few years back in a partly ruined state; but they are all now thoroughly repaired at the instance of His Excellency the Viceroy.[1]

The building is briefly referred to in the "Lists of Antiquities, Madras" (Volume I, page 133). Local tradition states that the architect was a goldsmith, who also constructed the well-known temple in the fort at Vellore (*Lists*, page 164) in the North Arcot District; and the large temple at Lēpākṣā (*Lists*, page 122) in the Anantapur District.

The temple is entered through a *gopuraṁ* or gateway on the east side. The lower part is constructed of stone, and the superstructure of brick, with plaster ornaments. The brickwork was partly ruined, and masses of it often fell down after rain. All these defects have been repaired.

In the south-east corner of the court, are two small rooms, the *yāgaśālā* and the *maḍapaḻḻi* or cooking room. Both have flat stone roofs, which were partly ruined. They have now been repaired.

On the south of the court, are a grain store, and three *āḻvār* shrines, for containing images placed in a position as if worshipping the chief deity. Only one shrine at present contains an image.

In the south-west corner, are three shrines with finely figure-carved fronts. The centre of these shrines has a finely sculptured image of *Lakṣmīnārāyaṇasvāmi*, which is worshipped. The side shrines are for *āḻvārs*; but only one contains a headless worshipping image.

In front of these, is the *Kalyāṇa* or marriage *maṇḍapaṁ*. In the centre is an elaborately carved blackstone pedestal, supporting four finely sculptured piers, with images and shafts attached to them, and circular floral drop brackets on the capitals. On the top of the pedestal is a rectangular seat, for placing the god on festival occasions. It is most minutely carved in polished blackstone, and has almost the appearance of marble. At either end stands a small figure of a horse rampant, and at each side is sculptured a female attendant. The roof of this *maṇḍapaṁ* is a lofty circular dome, intricately carved with numerous projecting figures, as in some of the

[1] *Vide* my report embodied in G. O. No. 871 Public, dated 30th August, 1900.

fine Chalukyan temples in the Bellary District. It is somewhat similar in design to Plates VIII and XVII of Volume XXI, of the Imperial Series of Archæological Survey Reports. A more plainly carved colonnade stands in front of the *Kalyāṇa maṇḍapaṁ*, and connects it with the main shrine.

Between the entrance *gopuraṁ* and the *mukha maṇḍapaṁ* or colonnade in front of the main shrine, are two small pedestals. One of these is designed to support the *dhvajastambhaṁ*, a lofty wooden post generally placed in front of the temples; and the other is the *balipīṭaṁ*.

The *mukha* or front *maṇḍapaṁ*, forming the direct entrance to the main shrine, is an open colonnade of carved piers with small shafts attached to each. In front is a small stone shrine in the form of a *ratha* or car with four wheels. Its entrance door faces the main shrine, and it at one time contained an *āḷvār* or worshipping image. The lower part of the shrine is constructed of granite. The upper part or roof is of finely carved blackstone.[1] By its side is a flat circular stone slab, on four supports, for grinding sandalwood. The ceiling of the *mukha maṇḍapaṁ* is of flat stone slabs, covered with plaster, on which are painted some scenes from the *Rāmāyaṇaṁ*. The roof formerly leaked, and, in consequence, these paintings have been much injured, but the leakage has now been stopped. A deep curved cornice runs round the building externally and at its angles are drop rings, cut out of the stone. The front portion was ruined, by the collapse of a broken beam which hung down and partly rested on the top of the stone *ratha*. This beam has been replaced and some repairs done where necessary. Above the cornice are ornamental niches in brick and stucco.

The *mahāmaṇḍapaṁ* is the large enclosed hall in front of the main shrine. Its outer façade has plain stone walls, with a carved moulded base and a carved cornice. On each side of the door are two headless *dvārapālakas* or door-keepers. Inside are six massive stone piers, with bracket capitals. The roof is of plain flat stone slabs.

The *ardha maṇḍapaṁ* is the small antechamber to the shrine.

The *garbhagṛhaṁ*, or main shrine, contains the image of *Chennakēśavasvāmi*; it is finely carved in blackstone, and *pūjā* to it is performed daily. In the house of the *Dharmakartā*, or manager of the temple, are three copper images, one of the god *Chennakēsavasvāmi*, and the others of his spouses, *Srīdēvī* or *Lakṣmī* and *Bhūdēvī*. These are brought out and used on festival occasions. Over the shrine is a ruined brick tower. On the exterior of the back wall is a small niche.

By the side of the main shrine is another shrine for the *amman* or goddess, named *Peruṅdēvitāyār Sannidhi*. There is, however, no image there now, but the blackstone pedestal on which it stood still remains. The building is plain, and has a small brick tower with an open colonnade in front.

In the north-east corner of the court is the *utsava vigraha maṇḍapaṁ*. Inside is a platform, on which images were placed. A pillared porch in front was enclosed by mud walls to provide a room in which to cook rice for the god, as the original room on the opposite side of the court was partly ruined. These walls have been removed. On the wall is a Telugu inscription, somewhat illegible, bearing the date

[1] Other good examples of such *rathas* exist at the Viṭṭala temple in Vijayanagar and at Taḍpatri.

of the cyclic year *Vijayasamvatsaraṁ* and commemorating the name of Kṛṣṇama Nāyuḍu as one who had made a grant to the temple. On the exterior wall is a deep cornice with carved figures of climbing monkeys, and a drop ring carved out of the stone at the corner, similar to that at the angles of the *mukha maṇḍapaṁ.*

The courtyard walls are built of large thin stone slabs set on edge, on each face, with packing in between. Some of the stones are as much as nine feet long. The outer face of the wall by the south side of the *Kalyāṇa maṇḍapaṁ* had fallen out, and the inner facing stood in a somewhat dangerous position. This has been repaired. On various parts of the walls are carved representations of the *matsya* or fish.

Outside the courtyard, by the north side of the entrance *gopuraṁ*, is the *Golladāna* or *Peddanāyana maṇḍapaṁ*. It is named the cowherd's *maṇḍapaṁ* in commemoration of the part taken by these people in the foundation of the place. It contains a raised platform, on which the god is placed when brought out on festival occasions. Four channelled piers stand on the pedestal. In front is an open colonnade partly ruined. The side walls have mostly fallen away, and only a few of the piers remain standing. These piers have worshipping images attached. The ruins of another *maṇḍapaṁ* lie opposite, on the south front of the temple.

A short distance to the north of the cowherd's *maṇḍapaṁ*, is the *uyyāla* or *ūnjal maṇḍapaṁ*. It was used for fixing a swing, in which to place the god. It has a plain base, on which stand four lofty square piers each in a single stone. On the top is a plain stone cornice with a weather-worn superstructure of brick.

In front of the entrance *gopuraṁ*, in a line with, and south of the front row of piers of the cowherd's *maṇḍapaṁ*, a stone shaft or *Garuḍa stambhaṁ* stands on a basement.

Slightly further to the east, is an unusually lofty stone *dhvajastambhaṁ*. measures 51 feet 6 inches from the ground to the summit and is a monolith. The full length of the stone must be even greater, as the base is sunk into the ground, to ensure stability. It has a well-carved double square basement, on which is inscribed in Telugu the two words "*Vijaya samvatsaraṁ.*" These also appear in another inscription inside the courtyard, before referred to. From the centre of the base, rises the tapering square shaft, carved with figures and floral winding ornament on each face. Surmounting it, is a square capital, with iron rings suspended at each corner. To these rings, chains or ropes were attached for drawing up the lamps. Above the capital is some brickwork. On the east side of the *dhvajastambhaṁ*, is a mound, raised by a former official, who proposed to lower and remove the pillar; but fortunately, the intention was not carried out.

Glossary.

ĀLVĀRS :—(Tamil) meaning saints according to the belief of Srīvaiṣṇavas, the superior sect among Brahmins in the Hindu community.

BALIPIṬAṀ :—*Bali* (Sanskrit) means sacrifice; *Piṭam* (also Sanskrit) meaning a seat. This is the principal seat or spot for sacrifices. Such seats are also set at the eight cardinal points, where sacrificial food or rice is put to propitiate the deities presiding over them. But the *balipiṭaṁ* by the side of the *dhvajastambhaṁ*, and in front of all the temples, is the principal one, before which all caste visitors prostrate themselves before entering into the other parts of the temple.

BHŪDĒVI :—*Bhū* or *Bhūmi* (Sanskrit) means earth ; *Dēvi* (also Sanskrit) meaning goddess. The term therefore means goddess of earth. See *Śridēvi.*

DHARMAKARTĀ :—*Dharma* (Sanskrit) means charity or gift ; *Kartā* (also Sanskrit) meaning one who does or makes. The term consequently means one who conducts worship, *utsavaṁs*, etc., in a temple. In short it means a manager or agent of a temple.

DHVAJASTAMBHAṀ :—See *garuḍastambhaṁ.*

DVĀRAPĀLAKAS :—(Sanskrit) gate-keepers. *Dvāra* (Sanskrit) gate ; *pālaka* (also Sanskrit) one who protects. Their names are *Jaya* and *Vijaya*. There is an interesting account about them current among Hindus, and recorded in their sacred books, the *Rāmāyaṇaṁ*, etc., which led to the incarnations of the god *Viṣṇu* into *Rāma*, *Kṛṣṇa*, etc.

FASLI :—(Hindustani) name of an era. Used for revenue accounts.

GARUḌASTAMBHAṀ :—*Garuḍa* (Sanskrit) means a kite. *Stambhaṁ*, also Sanskrit, meaning a post or a pillar. A large post in front of the temples. The other post in front of the temples is the *dhvajastambhaṁ*. *Dhvaja* (Sanskrit) flag ; *stambhaṁ* (Sanskrit) pillar. A flag staff.

GOLLADĀNA :—(Telugu) meaning a milk-maid or milk-woman. The masculine form of it is *Gollavāḍu*. The term means a cowherd.

IZĀRA :—(Hindustani) a gift or present.

KALYĀṆA :—(Tamil) marriage.

KALYĀṆA MAṆḌAPAṀ :—Is the place where the marriage of the Hindu god and his spouse in a temple is celebrated annually.

KUNDANI :—To be ascertained.

MAṆḌAPAṀS also MANTAPAṀS :—(Sanskrit) large open halls.

MATSYA :—(Sanskrit) a fish.

MUKHA OR MUKHYA :—(Sanskrit) face ; or main or principal.

PESH KIST :—(Hindustani) a kind of tax.

SANNIDHI :—(Sanskrit) presence, *e.g.*, *Perumāḷ sannidhi* means in the presence of god. *Ācārya sannidhi* means in the presence of the priest. It also means a place close to the god, *i.e.*, generally a shrine. Hindus colloquially use "*Svāmi sanniḍhi*" when conversing with people of superior authority and rank.

STAMBHAṀ :—(Sanskrit) means a post or a pillar, *e.g.*, *Dhvaja stambhaṁ*. *Garuḍa stambhaṁ.*

ŚRI DĒVI :—(Sanskrit) goddess of wealth and prosperity. One of the spouses of *Viṣṇu*.

ŪNJAL :—(Tamil) a swing.

UTSAVAṀ :—(Sanskrit) festival occasion, or a procession.

UYYĀLA :—(Telugu) a swing.

VIGRAHAṀ :—(Sanskrit) an idol or image of god.

YĀGAŚĀLĀ :—(Sanskrit). The place where the sacred fire is kept and worshipped. It is also applied where sacrifices, such as those of the horse or a sheep, are made. It used to be made by Brahmins in the performance of the great *yajña* or *yajnaṁ*. This is the sacrifice referred to in Hindu religious books. *Yāga* (Sanskrit), a milder term for *yajñaṁ* (also Sanskrit); *Śālā* (Sanskrit) means a place.

A. REA.

THE OLD FORTIFIED WALL OF MADRAS.

THE remaining portion of the ancient fortified wall of Madras built to protect the northern part of the town (formerly occupied by merchants and native inhabitants), is situated outside the limits of the more modern walls and beyond the range of the protection of the guns of Fort St. George. It marked the northern limit of the old town, and the open country was to the north of it.

The wall runs from a point near the sea on the east, in a westerly direction, and is constructed of a north outer and a south inner facing of brickwork, with an earthwork rampart between. A large bastion, which stands about the centre of the length of wall yet remaining, is of great interest and in fair preservation. It still retains all its features including the embrasures for the guns. It is closed on the inner or south side by a wall with an arched gateway, through which a brick causeway ascends to the level of the ramparts. At some distance on the east length of the wall, and again on the west of the bastion, are square platforms approached by sloping brick pathways. These have each a brick-domed room underneath, probably used formerly as a magazine, or as a rest-house for the defenders; but the rooms are now rented out, one of them being occupied by the Mutiālapēt Hindu Union. At intervals, the curtain wall is pierced by brick-arched subways, which are probably the lesser gates or posterns hereafter referred to. The wall itself has been much altered in parts, and utilized for the support of adjoining modern buildings. This is especially the case at the east end, opposite the municipal water pumping station, where the earth of the ramparts has been removed, and the space between the exterior and interior brick walls used to form a large water cistern.

To the west of the wall, and near the Moṇēgār Choulṭry, is another detached portion of it, with a large bastion. On the latter, is a building until lately occupied by students, but now vacant. In the Wall Tax Road is an old magazine, and in the same road, some of the old walls have been utilized as a manure depôt.

The full extent of the wall is shown in a large plan preserved in the Secretariat of Fort St. George. The date of the erection of the wall, and other historical particulars regarding it, may possibly be contained in the military records of the Secretariat. But to these I have unfortunately had no access. Although the greater part of the wall above ground has now been demolished, it is probable that the foundations may yet in parts remain. Originally the wall apparently commenced at the southern extremity of the General Hospital, and passing along the Wall Tax Road as far as Basin Road, turned thence towards the east to Clive's battery on the sea coast. This last is the part now remaining.

Bastions, mounted with guns commanding all external approaches to the walls, were situated at sufficient intervals, and for six hundred yards (or gun range) outside the walls, the ground was kept clear for the fire from the bastion guns. The wall was provided with five chief entrances, *viz.*, one near the central railway station, one known as the Elephant gate, one as the Mint Street gate, another as the Moṇēgār Choultry gate, and the last in Tambu Cheṭṭi Street near Clive's battery. Between these there were other small gates or posterns; one opposite to Rasappa Cheṭṭi Street, one near the Salt Cotaurs, one at Muṇiyappa Mudali Street, and another between the Moṇēgār Choultry gate and the Tambu Cheṭṭi Street gate. The walls are said to have remained intact up to about 45 years ago, and during that time the doors of the gateways were regularly closed each evening at 8 P.M., after which no one could pass in or out.

The tradition assigned to the name of the Elephant gate is, that a certain priest had occasion to enter the old town of Madras, bringing with him a large retinue including some elephants, but the gateway was so low, that it had to be broken down to allow the elephants to enter. The rebuilding was however completed before the elephants reached their destination, and the gateway received and retained the name.

The old town of Madras, within these walls, is known as Pedda Nāiḍupet, after the watchman of that name. Pedda Naiḍu, a Poḻēgār, who was granted a *cowle*, was in possession of several villages, and was appointed watchman of the city of Madras, for which he was allowed certain villages free. He had also certain privileges, which were at a later date resumed by Government. A pension of Rs. 350 was granted to Pedda Naiḍu's son, Tyāgappa, in 1808. On his death, the same pension was continued to his brother, Cheṅgal Naiḍu, in 1825, and on his death, a reduced pension of Rs. 200 was given to his son, Aṅgārappā, in 1841. After him a moiety of Rs. 100 was granted to his widow, Ravaṇamma, and son, Cheṅgal Naiḍu, in 1856.

The deed of appointment of the watchman, by the Council of Fort St. George, states, that "having constituted and appointed you to be watchman of the city of Madras and the liberties thereof on the following terms, you must keep one hundred good peons for the preventing of robberies and other disorders in the said city and its liberties and for their maintenance we allow the following duties,"[1] which are therein duly detailed.

The *cowle* granted to Pedda Naick also states that "when any person paying custom to you has been robbed, such person shall acquaint you, and if satisfaction is not obtained in due time application shall be made to the Governor in due time who will take proper measures to cause you to do justice." In connection with this, stories are current as to how Pedda Naiḍu performed this part of his duties. One relates that an influential inhabitant lost a valuable ring, and reported the loss to

[1] Extract from a *cowle*, dated 13th May 1768, granted to Pedda Naiḍu.

Pedda Naiḍu, who endeavoured to trace it without immediate success. But, meanwhile, the ring had been swallowed by a fish, which was caught by a fisherman, who, on cutting it up, found the ring inside. The watchman happened to hear of this, and, recovering the ring, delivered it to its owner. Another version of the story is that he was "allowed ten fish out of every draft of a large net cast at sea," and that he found the ring in one of the fishes so rendered to him.

A part of the town, towards the east of the present Popham's Broadway, is still known as Mutiālapēt, after the name of Pedda Naiḍu's daughter Mutiālamma, on whom he conferred the income from this part of the town, while he reserved to himself the income of that portion towards the west, which is still known after his name Pedda Naiḍupet. Between these two portions of the town lies a Parachēri or street occupied by Pancamās. Regarding the origin of Pedda Naiḍu, the following tradition, narrated by one of his own descendants, is of interest.

Pedda Pedda Naiḍu and Pedda Naiḍu were two brothers, who owned some *pāḷayaṁs* (hamlets) in the northern countries. Being defeated in a fight, by invaders from the nörth, they fled from their village of Pīdapalli and settled at Rāyapuraṁ in Madras. Meanwhile Chennappa Naick, the chief of Kālahasti, was at war with the chiefs of the surrounding 77 *pāḷayaṁs*, and in one of his incursions he invaded Igavari *Pāḷayaṁ* and conquered it. Igavaru, the chief, had a fortress on a hill, where he had placed his wife. The hill is known after the name of his wife, as Iga Vabhusāṇi *durgaṁ*. When she heard that her husband and his followers were defeated, and slain in the battle, she donned man's attire, and sallied forth to contend with Chennappa Naick, whom she defeated in a single battle. The vanquished chief fled and took shelter in Rāyapuraṁ. The heroine, though successful in the fight, was so dejected at the loss of her husband and so many of his followers, that she put an end to her life.

The two brothers Pedda Pedda Naiḍu and Pedda Naiḍu afterwards met and defeated Chennappa Naick and slew him. The Navāb of the Carnatic, who had hitherto been much molested by the incursions of Chennappa Naick, was so pleased when he heard of the death of this chieftain, that he sent for the two brothers and appointed Pedda Naiḍu as *kotwāl* or watchman of the old town of Madras.[1] In "The Vicissitudes of Fort St. George," page 23, it is mentioned that "as early as 1659, the Black Town was guarded by a police force under a Pedda Naick. In 1686 the inhabitants complained that robberies were very frequent, and that the Police peons were in league with the thieves and shared their plunder. The Pedda Naick did not deny the fact, and he even made good the losses. But he hinted that it was a generally admitted principle that salary and income were not exactly the same thing, and that the town had increased so much that his force was unequal to the task required of it. He was accordingly granted 18 paddy fields, and the right to collect a variety of petty customs, and in return he engaged to employ not less than fifty peons for the

---

[1] Pedda Naiḍu is the name of the person. Here *Naiḍu* is an appellation showing that he belongs to the caste of *Nāiḍus:* while Pedda is his proper name. But Pedda in Telugu means 'great.'

Pedda Naick is the name given to the same person in books of reference. Here it is only his official designation meaning Great Master or Great Lord, *Pedda*, పెద్ద meaning in Telugu, "Great;" *Nāick* (నాయక) a corrupted form of Sanskrit *Nāyaka* meaning master, chief, or lord. Its feminine form is *Nāyiki*.

future. His memory is preserved to us in the Street that bears his name. Within the fort the Police duties were entrusted to a small company of soldiers, for many years under the command of a turbulent fellow named Seaton. The officers added to their pay by becoming proprietors of the Punch-houses which were frequented by their men."[1]

The ancient wall defined the extent of the town guarded by the peons of Pedda Naick or Naiḍu, and formed an enclosure to that part of the town now also known as Peddanaiḍupēttai and Mutiālapēt. The Kotwāl Chāvaḍi, now used as a vegetable market, was probably connected with the office of the watchman.

Glossary.

CHĀVAḌI :—Telugu చావడి (Chāvaḍi). A hall ; a choultry or caravansarai.

DURGAṀ :—Telugu దుర్గం (Durgam). A hill fort.

IGAVARI :—A proper name.

KOTWĀL :—Telugu కొత్వాల్ (Kotwāl). A watchman.

MONĒGĀR OR MONIGAR :—Tamil மநேகார் (Manēgār). Is a common term in Tamil for the correct appellation of *maṅiyagāḍu* in Telugu. This means the Headman of a village, or of a Hindu temple. It literally means one who collects money.

MUTIĀLAPĒT :—Telugu ముత్యాలపేట (Mutyālapēttā). The street named after Pedda Naiḍu's daughter Mutiālamma, from *mutyam*, Telugu for a pearl.

PĀLAYAṀS :—Tamil பாளயம் (Pālayaṁ). A country under a Poḻēgar.

PAÑCAMĀS :—Sanskrit पञ्चमाः (Pañcamāḥ). Pariahs. Literally means people of the fifth class or non-Hindus. Hindus are all classed as of one or the other of the four castes, Brahmins, Kṣatriyas, Vaiśyas and Śūdras.

PARACHĒRI :—A street of pariahs now known as Pañcamas.

PŌḺĒGĀR OR PŌḺIGĀR :—Tamil பாளெகார் (Pāḷēgār). Petty chieftains or landholders, who, in the troublous times of a century ago, occupied many parts of the Madras Presidency. Occasionally a revolted ryot set himself up as such. They fought amongst themselves, made raids, levied blackmail when possible, and sometimes combined to oppose the British. In many instances they were simply heads of fortified villages ; in others, they occupied regular hill forts of which numbers of examples remain. They were installed, and kept up, so far as their means permitted, the state and armed retinue of a petty rājah. They were with difficulty crushed by the British. Some of their descendants retain lands or pensions granted for services rendered to the British.

AṄGĀRAPPA :—A proper name అంగారప్ప.

RASAPPA CHEṬṬI :—A proper name రసప్పచెట్టి.

RAVANAMMA :— Do. రవనమ్మ.

---

[1] The Vicissitudes of Fort St. George," by David Leighton. (Madras and Bombay, A. J. Combridge & Co.)

MUṆIYAPPA MUDALI :—A proper name முனியப்பமுதலி.

TAMBU CHEṬṬI :— Do. தம்புசெட்டி.

PEDDA NAYUḌUPĒTTAI :—A proper name பெத்தநாயுடுபேட்டை.

TYAGAPPA :—A proper name త్యాగప్ప.

IGA VABHUSĀṆI DURGAṀ :—A proper name ఇగవభూసాణిదుర్గం.

ṘĀYAPURAṀ :—A proper name రాయపురం.

A. REA.

a

b

(*a*) BRIDGE OVER MOAT AND WALL OF FORT DUFFERIN.

(*b*) KING MINDON'S TOMB.

THE MANDALAY PALACE.

THE city of Mandalay, built in 1857 by King Mindon, is in the form of a square, each side of which is 10 furlongs in length. The battlemented wall of brick and mud mortar has a total height of 27 feet (the crenellations being 7 feet high), is 10 feet thick in the lower portion and 4 feet 4 inches in the crenellations, and is backed by an earthen rampart. There are twelve gates, three on each side at equal distances from each other, surmounted by *pyathats* or pavilions, and there is also a *pyathat* at each corner of the wall, making 48 in all. The central gate on each side is larger than the others, and, in Burmese times, was reserved for the passage of Royalty.

The *pyathats* over these four main gates have seven storeys each, the others only five. A moat averaging 225 feet wide and 11 feet deep surrounds the city, and was formerly kept full by a channel from the Aungbinle lake, but, since 1902, the supply has been drawn from the Mandalay Irrigation canal. The moat is now crossed by five road bridges, one to each main gate and one to the south-eastern gate which was formerly reserved for funeral processions, a corpse being an object of desecration and taboo. There are also two railway bridges entering by modern gates on the south and north faces, and a foot bridge on the north; in former times, there were, in all, twelve bridges corresponding to the gates. Each gateway is guarded by a masonry curtain, and is under the protection of a tutelary *nat* or spirit represented by a stone image. Tradition says that the city is also under the protection of the disembodied spirits of human beings, who were buried alive under jars of oil at each corner of the walls.[1] To the right of each curtain stands a massive teak post bearing the name of the gate. The *pyathat* over one of the northern gateways has been extended along the ramparts at each side and forms a residence for the Lieutenant Governor.

Plate XVII(*a*) gives a view of a portion of the wall and moat on the western face together with the pavilion over the gateway, the curtain in front, the "Alawi" or "Funeral bridge" crossing the moat, and the ancient post on which is inscribed the

[1] This burial of human victims as spirit watchers at each corner of the walls of Mandalay affords an interesting example of a sacrifice, that has been common at all ages and in many lands for the purpose of securing the foundations of cities and of rendering their walls impregnable. *Cf.* Tylor, *Primitive Culture*, 1, p. 106 sqq.; B. Schmidt, *Das Volksleben der Neugriechen*, p. 196 sqq.; Frazer, *Pausanias' Description of Greece*, Comm. Vol. III, p. 468. [Ed.]

name of the gate and the date of the foundation of the city. The Palace occupies the central space in the city. It was removed from Amarapura by King Mindon in 1857 A.D., and was re-erected at Mandalay. It was originally built by Shwebomin in 1845 A.D. Its architecture is unique, and recalls its prototypes of Nipal and Magadha. The Palace stood within two enclosures: the outer consisted of a stockade of teakwood posts, 20 feet high, and the inner was a brick wall about 15 feet in height. There was an esplanade, 60 feet wide, between the two enclosures. Each side of the outer enclosure measured about three furlongs. The inner enclosure was cut up into numerous courts surrounded by high walls, and in the very centre was a third brick enclosure containing the Palace. (The stockade and the brick walls were removed after the British occupation of Mandalay.)

The Palace faces east and the east gate is the main entrance. As one enters the grounds by this gate the clock-tower (A-1 on plan) is seen on the right and the tooth-relic tower (A-2 on plan) on the left. A water-clock was used and a big bell and drum were beaten every third hour. According to this reckoning, day and night each consists of four watches, and begins at 9 o'clock. The tooth-relic tower is probably a heritage from the Talaings of Pegu. There was much intercourse between the Peguans and the Sinhalese, and, in the seventeenth century A.D., the King of Ceylon palmed off on the King of Pegu an adopted daughter and a false tooth of Gautama Buddha.

A little to the north of the clock-tower is King Mindon's tomb [A-3 on plan, and Plate XVII(*b*)]. It is gilded and covered with glass mosaic, and is a simulation in brick and mortar of the usual seven-storeyed spire built of wood. It is a beautiful specimen of Burmese art, and, like the Tāj Maḥall, is seen at its best by moonlight, when the scintillations of the glass mosaic transform it into a fairy-like structure. This was renovated by the Public Works Department in 1898, and the work now seen is of quite recent date. Nothing of the old work remains.

To the south of the tooth-relic tower, and resting against the inner wall, was the *Hluttaw* or Supreme Council Hall [A-4 on plan and Plate XVIII(*a*)]. Here all State business was transacted. It was the highest tribunal in the realm, as all cases were decided by the King in Council. In the absence of the King, the powers of the presiding Judge were relegated to the Heir Apparent, or to some other member of the Royal Family, who was specially chosen for his tact, talent, integrity and sound judgment.

The building consisted of two three-roofed wooden structures recalling to mind the cognate architecture of Nipal. The outer structure was reserved for the officials and the litigants; and the four *Wungyis* or Chief Ministers sat each leaning against a heavily gilt column and facing a throne placed in the inner structure. The Throne was separated from the seats of the *Wungyis* by a gilt wooden railing [Plate XVIII(*b*)]. The railing consisted of an upper and lower band of rosettes enclosing cylinders with central bulbs.

The Throne is a gorgeous structure covered with gilding and glass mosaic (Plate XIX). It was treason for anybody but the King to sit on it. It is called the "Sihāsana" or the Lion Throne, and is an exact replica of that in the Great Audience Hall. A gilt wooden figure of the Lion is placed on each side of it.

(*a*) THE HLUTTAW, OR COUNCIL CHAMBER.
(*b*) GOLDEN RAILINGS AT THE HLUTTAW.

It is approached by steps from behind, as in the case of the Throne of the Great Mughal at Delhi, through a folding door of gilt iron screen work. In shape it is like the ordinary pedestal supporting an image of Buddha, narrowing at the centre and expanding above and below. The lintel of the doorway consists of two curved, dragon-like ornaments, which are surmounted by a row of the figures of 16 *nats* or *devas* with Śakra n the middle. Śakra or Indra is the lord of all *devas*, and is the "Recording Angel of Buddhism," and his presence as a tutelary deity is required in the transaction of public business as well as in the performance of religious ceremonies. Śakra's abode is called the "Tāvatiṁsa" or the "Heaven of the Thirty-three *devas*." What Sakra is to Tāvatiṁsa, *i.e.*, supreme and dominant, so is the sovereign to his kingdom.

On the outer edge of each jamb and attached to a line of rosettes is a row of the figures of seven *devas;* and, at the foot of the inner edge of each jamb, is also the figure of a *deva*. Below the lintel the number of *devas* represented, exclusive of the two figures on the top of the jambs and of the sun-god and moon-god, is 16; and above it, the number is the same; over all presides the Śakra. Thus the total number of *devas* shown is "Thirty-three," corresponding to that of the "Tāvatiṁsa."

The Burmese Kings claimed descent from the Solar and Lunar dynasties of India; hence it was essential that this genealogy should be symbolized on the centre of the jamb; to the left of the occupant is depicted the figure of a peacock, which represents the sun, and facing it on the right jamb is the figure of a hare, which represents the moon. According to the Aryan or Indian custom, the right is the side of honour, as with the right hand are associated dignity, courage, and strength; but, according to Mongolian or Chinese custom, the left is the side of honour, because the right is the working or servile hand, and because with the left hand are associated repose and peace, which are enjoyed by the master rather than by the slave. It is to harmonize with Mongolian custom that the sun, as the superior of the two, is represented on the left, and the moon on the right. This is, indeed, a striking instance of the commingling of Aryan and Mongolian ideas in Burma. Over the peacock and the hare are placed respectively the sun-god and the moon-god. On the top of each jamb is a *deva* holding a fan or *chowri* made of Yak hair, which is included in the regalia of a king. These two *devas* are bearers of the emblem of sovereignty of their King Śakra.

There remain only two more figures requiring explanation. They are attached to the centre of the folding door of gilt iron screen work. On the left is Brahmā, and on the right Śakra, the former being the superior of the two. At the coronation of a Burmese King, the assistance of these two deities, as well as that of Viṣṇu, was invoked, in their capacity as Hindu gods, rather than as *devas* of the Buddhist cosmogony.

The *Hluttaw* and its appurtenances, having become unsafe, have been demolished, and the Lion Throne has been deposited in the Indian Museum at Calcutta.

To the east of the Tooth-relic Tower is King Thibaw's monastery (A-5 on plan and Plate XX). It is an elaborately carved building of exquisite proportions, and serves as a perfect model of similar structures throughout the country. On the site of this *Kyaung* lived Thibaw when he was an obscure Prince, whom nobody ever expected to see on the throne of Upper Burma. He donned the yellow garb, and passed his time laboriously and strenuously in the midst of Pali palm-leaf manuscripts. It was from the cloister that he was suddenly and unexpectedly summoned to assume regal power. When he became king, he built this monastery in order to commemorate his past happy life in learned seclusion.

This building faces north on account of circumscribed space. It consists of four divisions, *viz.*:

(*i*) The *Pyathat saung* with the seven-roofed spire, or the chapel, where images of Buddha are kept;
(*ii*) the *Sanu zaung*, or the Master's quarters, where the *Sadaw*, or presiding Abbot, lives;
(*iii*) the *Saungmagyi* with triple roofs, or the hall, where lectures are given, ceremonies are held, and junior monks are provided with apartments;
(*iv*) the *Bawga zaung*, or the dormitory of junior monks.

When completed by Thibaw in 1879, it was heavily gilt. Its loss of gilding has made it somewhat tawdry; but the carving is still well preserved.

After the British annexation, it was used as a Military Protestant Chapel.

Entering the second enclosure by the main or Eastern Gate to the right of the *Hluttaw*, one is confronted by the seven-roofed *Shwepyathat*, the golden pyramidal spire over the Great Audience Hall, which is the pride and glory of the Burmese Palace as well as its most distinctive feature [A-6 on plan and Plate XXI(*a*)]. It is surmounted by a *ti* or umbrella of iron-work resting on a *sikra*. The umbrella is the symbol of sovereignty, and the *sikra* of divine right. Next comes a lotus-bud capital of duplicated and inverted form. Below these are the seven pyramidal roofs with carved gables. The original plank roofing of this and other Palace buildings was replaced with corrugated iron by King Mindon. Prince Siddhārtha, before he became Buddha, had, for his summer residence, a palace or mansion with seven storeys; and this model was probably adopted in Burma presumably because of its tropical climate. Under the spire is placed a Lion Throne facing the Great Audience Hall. The Chief Queen was invariably present sitting on the right of the King, whenever a *levée* was held. The Heir Apparent and the principal Ministers of State took their seats on the left of the king, while the seats on the right were reserved for officials of lesser dignity. Foreign embassies were received in this Hall, and three times a year, *viz.*, at the Burmese New Year in April, at the beginning of Buddhist Lent in June, and at the end of Lent in October, the King and his Chief Queen received the homage of their subjects. No ladies were admitted into this Hall, their homage on the above occasions being received in the Lily Throne Hall at the west end of the Palace.

The spire, as the emblem of sovereignty, must be *shikoed* or *kowtowed* to by all tributary Chiefs and their Ministers, whenever they visited the capital, or whenever they received Royal presents or decrees in their own States. He who refused to conform to this custom was declared to be a rebel and was accused of high treason. Even criminals, before execution, had to kneel down and prostrate three times towards the Palace spire as a farewell act of allegiance and fidelity to the

Throne and Person of the King. A similar custom obtains in China, and it finds a arallel among Moslems facing towards Mecca, and among Jews facing towards Jerusalem whenever they are engaged in prayer, and in the eastward position of Christians reciting the creed.

It would be interesting to trace the migration of this seven-roofed spire from the land of its birth, *viz.*, Kapilavastu (Nipal) and Magadha (Bihar) to Kashmir, Tibet, Assam, Manipur, Burma, China, Siam, Cambodia, and Java. In China, it may be remarked, the shape of the structure is not tapering or pyramidal, but cylindrical and uniform, while the inside is hollow and may be ascended to the uppermost storey by means of steps. But there, as elsewhere, the number of storeys is always odd, *viz.*, 3, 5, 7, or 9, reflecting the prototype in Kapilavastu.

The separation of the sexes in State ceremonies necessitated the provision of a different hall for ladies, and the Lily Throne Hall [VIII on plan, and Plate XXI(*b*)] was assigned for this purpose. This Hall is an exact counterpart of the Lion Throne Hall and was used for similar ceremonies. In November 1901, the Viceroy, Lord Curzon, held a Darbar in it, and its surroundings and associations lent an air of splendour and magnificence befitting the occasion. It is now occupied by the Upper Burma Club, but the quarters of the latter are to be removed as soon as possible.

In this connection, it may be interesting to note that in the Palace there were eight thrones provided for the King and Chief Queen.

These were (marked I to VIII on plan) :—

(1) The Lion Throne in the Great Audience Hall ;
(2) The Brahmani Goose Throne in the Ancestral Hall ;
(3) The Elephant Throne in the Privy Council Hall ;
(4) The Bee Throne in the Glass Palace ;
(5) The Conch Throne in the Morning Levée Hall ;
(6) The Deer Throne in the Southern Hall ;
(7) The Peacock Throne in the Northern Hall ;
(8) The Lily Throne in the Ladies' Hall.

The distinctive name of each Throne, with the exception of the Lily Throne, is due to the nature of the two figures placed before it as well as of those placed in the small square niches cut in the pedestal. The Lion Throne or Sīhāsana was evidently derived from Kapilavastu. The lion is the king among beasts and denotes courage, strength, endurance, and power. Gautama Buddha was called "Sākyasīha," the "Lion of the Sākya Clan," and "Narasīha," the "Lion amongst Men." When Suddhodana, the father of Buddha, died, his remains were placed in a coffin, which was set "upon the throne ornamented with lions."[1] Ruli, son of Pasenadi, King of Kosala, was sitting on a Lion throne "when he was sarcastically reviled by members of the Sākya clan for presuming to sit on the throne, he being of ignoble birth."[2] At the first Buddhist Council, held immediately after Buddha's death in 543 B.C., "Kashiapa appointed that Ananda should sit on the Lion Throne, with a thousand secretaries before him. They took down his words while he repeated the *Dharma* as he had heard it from Buddha."[3]

[1] Edkins' *Chinese Buddhism*, page 44. [2] *Ibid*, page 45. [3] *Ibid*, pages 64, 65.

The Bee Throne (Bhamarāsana) in the *Hman Nan* or Glass Palace; the Elephant Throne (Gajāsana) in the *Byedaik* or Privy Council Hall, and the Brahmani Goose Throne (Haṁsāsana) in the Ancestral Hall, were evidently derived from the Talaings, whose power was supplanted by the Burmese. A beehive was regarded as an omen of power and prosperity; and it is recorded in Talaing history that, during the reign of Wareru (1281-1306 A.D.), a hive of bees settled on one of the city gates of Martaban, and gladdened the heart of the King.

"*Byedaik*" is a Talaing word signifying a room for young Ministers in attendance, and, as a State Department, it corresponds to the Board of Civil appointments at Peking. Whenever the King attended in person the Council of the *Atwinwuns*, he would sit on the Elephant Throne. A *Cakravartin* or Universal Monarch must have a white elephant called the Uposatha; and the elephant serves as one of the symbols of sovereignty.

The Haṁsa bird or Brahmani Goose was sacred to the Talaings. It signifies purity, dignity, and gentleness. One of the three main divisions of their country was named after it and called "Haṁsavatī," (the modern Hanthawaddy). It was in the Goose Throne Hall that golden figures of the Kings and Chief Queens of the Alompra dynasty were kept and adored by the reigning sovereign. Prayers in the Pali language were specially composed for recitation whenever offerings were made to these figures.

The Conch Throne (Saṅkhāsana) and Lily Throne (Padumāsana) were apparently derived from Vaiṣṇavaism. One of the many hands of a figure of Viṣṇu holds a Conch Shell, and Viṣṇu and Lakṣmī are depicted as seated on a throne supported by a lotus. The Lily Throne also stands on a lotus in full bloom.

The Deer Throne (Migāsana) and Peacock Throne (Mayurāsana) recall the hunting habits of the Kings of the Maurya dynasty of Magadha. Hunting was of two kinds; hunting of quadrupeds with dogs,[1] and hunting of birds with falcons. The quarry of deer, etc., was exhibited in the Southern Hall, and that of birds in the Northern; and seated on the throne, the King would discuss the topics of the chase with his attendants. The introduction of Buddhism, which forbids the taking of life, changed the character of these two thrones. Seated on the Deer Throne the King would inspect the offerings to be made to monks, and seated on the Peacock Throne,[2] he would review troops, races, and tournaments.

At one time, it was seriously suggested that the Palace should be demolished lest hopes as to the revival of the Burmese Monarchy should be kept alive; but fortunately wiser counsels prevailed, and the main buildings were kept intact. In this connection, the words of the Viceroy, Lord Curzon, recorded in his Minute dated the 2nd December 1901, may be cited:—

"Moreover, its survival and maintenance are both a compliment to the sentiments of the Burmese race, showing them that we have no desire to obliterate the relics of the past sovereignty, and a reminder that it has now passed for ever into our hands. I attach no value to the plea that the Burmans will be led by the preservation of the

[1] The ancient Indian custom of hunting with dogs is referred to at page 363 of McCrindle's *Ancient India: its invasion by Alexander the Great.*

[2] The ancient Indian custom of rearing tame peacocks and tame pheasants is referred to at page 362, *ibid.*

KING THIBAW'S MONASTERY.

(a) PALACE PAVILION, CALLED THE CENTRE OF THE UNIVERSE

(b) WESTERN FACADE OF THE PALACE.

FACADE OF THE PALACE.

Palace to think that there is a chance that the Monarchy will one day be restored. Any such fanciful notion, even if it exists, cannot long survive. No one believes for a moment, because we preserve and are restoring the palaces of the Mughals at Agra, that we contemplate placing that dynasty again on the throne."

In November 1901, Lord Curzon made a minute inspection of the Palace, and arranged for its evacuation by the Upper Burma Club, Garrison Church, and certain Government Offices, as also for the dismantling of the *Hluttaw* and the repair and restoration of the wooden pavilions on the walls of Fort Dufferin. As stated above, the Lion Throne in the *Hluttaw* was removed to Calcutta and set up in the Indian Museum there. In accordance with the orders issued by His Excellency, estimates were framed and sanctioned as follows :—

Construction of new pavilions on the walls of Fort Dufferin .	Rs. 43,968
Repairs to existing pavilions	,, 23,000
Restoration of Palace buildings	,, 5,280
TOTAL .	Rs. 72,248

Originally, there were 48 *pyathats* or pavilions on the walls of Fort Dufferin, namely, 4 at the corners, 12 over the gateways, and 32 occupying intermediate positions between the gateways. The corner *pyathats* are larger than the intermediate ones, but have the same number of roofs, namely, 5. Seven out of the 48 pavilions had disappeared owing to destruction by fire or natural decay ; and, by March 1903, 5 new ones had been constructed. Out of the remaining 41, 37 were in need of minor repairs, as re-roofing, putting in new eaves and carving, and substituting new posts for those decayed. The execution of all the necessary repairs has been nearly completed, only three pavilions remaining to be taken in hand.

In the Burmese King's time, the gateways, the curtains masking them, and the bridges across the moat were all whitewashed, white no less than red being the colour of Burmese Royalty. After the British annexation of Upper Burma, the Public Works Department had these structures coloured light grey. Under His Excellency's orders, the original whitewash has been restored.

As stated above, in the early days of the British annexation, some of the Palace buildings were fitted up for use as offices, churches, or residences. These, namely, the Post Office, Telegraph Office, Forest Office, four private quarters, Carver's Workshop, Irrigation Superintending Engineer's Office, Conservator of Forests' Office, Western Division, Major General's quarters, and two elephant sheds were vacated and dismantled, as they were of no architectural or historical value, and the materials were sold by public auction. The Protestant Church, Roman Catholic Church, and Upper Burma Club still continue to occupy buildings on the Palace platform, because the question of the British troops remaining in Mandalay is still under consideration. But, as soon as the question is settled, the present quarters will be vacated. It has been decided to maintain the building now used as the Roman Catholic Church as long as it lasts. All traces of the recent occupation of the rooms, such as wall-papers, punkah brackets, doors, windows, and skylights not forming part of the original buildings, have been removed, together with the whitewash. The buildings from which whitewash has been removed, with the exception of three interior rooms mentioned below, have been painted red.

In King Thibaw's time whitewash was applied to three interior rooms, because of their darkness. They have now been re-whitewashed.

The crimson throne, upon which stood the small gold images, has been replaced behind the throne door where it stood in King Thibaw's time. The lions that stood on either side of the Lion Throne in the Audience Hall have been recovered, re-gilt and replaced. One was recovered from the Palace garden, and the other had to be made. Perforated zinc doors behind the throne entrances have been repaired ; and all thrones have been properly placed with reference to the relative position between them and the umbrella stands. The masonry pillars outside the Peacock Throne have been re-erected perpendicularly. The panels, with glass incrustations, have been replaced in their original position with the exception of the Club dining-room panels. The latter will be restored when the Club quits its present quarters. The water tanks, which were originally too near the platform, have been removed further away. All the vacated buildings have been cleaned, and great care has been taken to preserve, as far as possible, the original gilding or red lacquer paint. The gilt or painted portions were carefully washed, and the accumulated dirt of years, which gave the buildings a tawdry and dilapidated appearance, has been removed. A new Circuit house also has been built, and the Circuit rooms in the Palace have been vacated.

TAW SEIN KO.

Plan
of
MANDALAY PALACE.
SCALE: 300 FEET = 1 INCH.

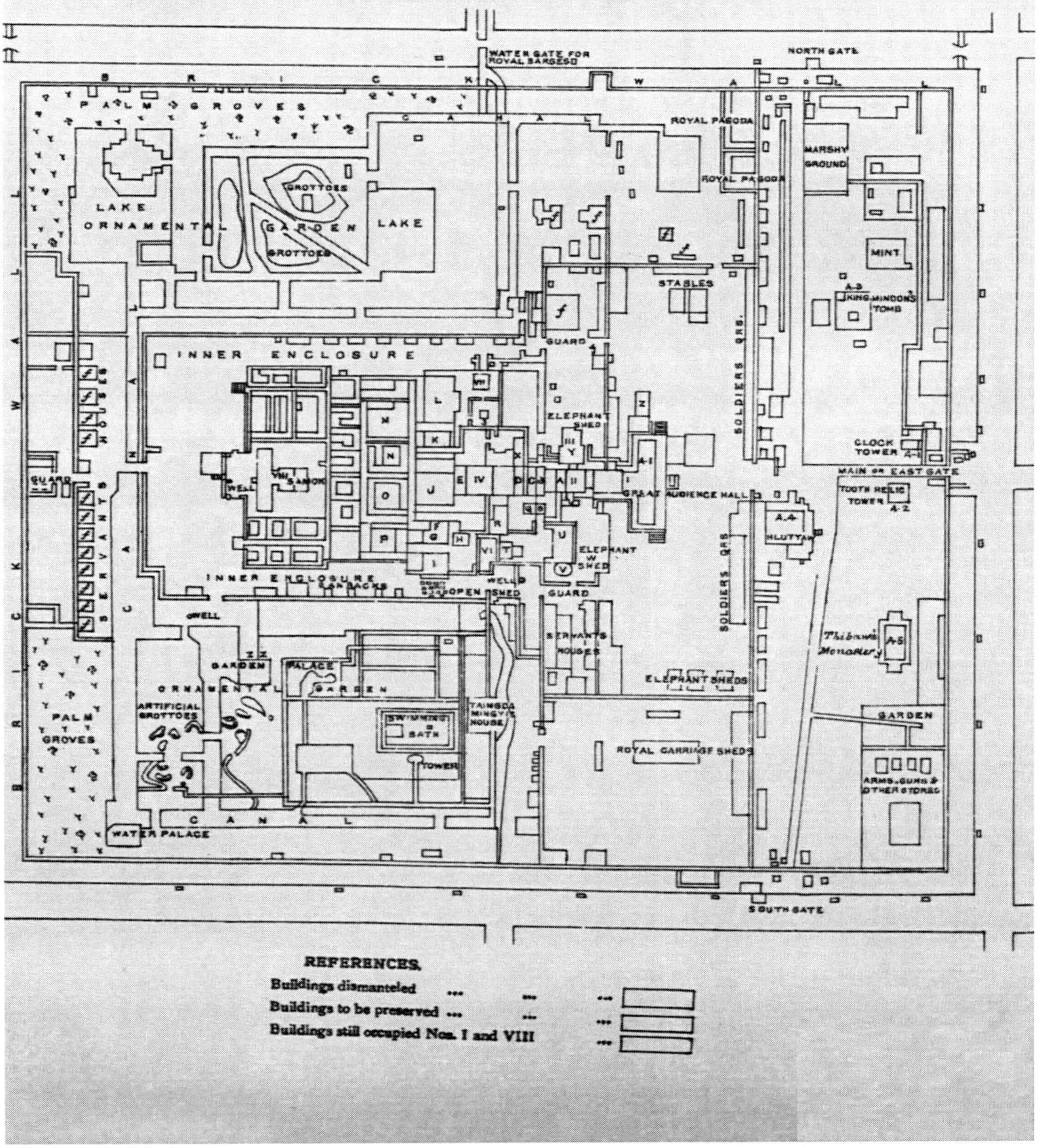

REFERENCES.

Buildings dismanteled	
Buildings to be preserved	
Buildings still occupied Nos. I and VIII ...	

References to Plan.

A.— } Zetawun Figures of the Royal ancestors
B.— } were kept here.

C.—The King here held his morning *levée*. It is an open passage between two rooms, in the western of which (D) the King was seated with his attendants.

E.—The Glass Palace. The western half is one large room of great height. Here the Royal nuptials were celebrated. It was also a Royal nursery, and offerings were here presented to Royal infants. The body of King Mindōn lay in state here. on the Water Feast throne, which stands at the western side of the room. The western half of the building is divided into smaller rooms used as robing rooms.

F.—Nursery.

G.—Daily attendance room for Queens.

H.—The King and Queen's special living room.

I.—A kind of drawing room, where the Court met to witness theatrical displays in the theatre on the south side. The stage is now cleared away.

J.—Originally the Queen's room. Thibaw's eldest child was born here, but Supayalat never regularly inhabited it.

K.—Tabindaing House. Made over by King Mindōn to the Salin Princess, the daughter of the Linban Queen, whom he intended to be the bride of the next King. On the death of the Salin Princess, it was made over to Supayalat's sister.

L.—Seindōn House. The residence of the Dowager Queen, Supayalat's mother.

M.—The Northern Palace. N.—The Western Palace. O.— P.—The Southern Palace, and the range of houses behind.	Houses made over to inferior Queens in King Mindōn's time; in King Thibaw's time, to Princesses, and used as waiting rooms for maids-of-honour.

The road running down the centre, east and west, was called the Samōk road and led to a courtyard, in the centre of which stood the Lily Throne. This courtyard was called the Samōk, and in the month of May, a maze was constructed and brilliantly illuminated, through which the Court passed in procession. The houses on the north and south of this courtyard were inhabited, in King Mindōn's time, by Queens, in Thibaw's time, by Princesses.

fff.—Servants' houses.

Q.—The King's private treasury.

R.— } Quarters of the personal body-guard.
S.— }

T.—An evening sitting room.

U.—Privy Council Chamber.

V.—Observatory tower and favourite resort of Supayalat. From it she watched the British troops enter Mandalay.

W.—The new house built for, but never used by, the white elephant.

X.—Cut up into various small rooms for tea-making, kitchen, and a photographic studio.

Y.—Byèdaik, or Treasury office, where the Atwin Wuns or Privy Councillors sat.

Z.—House for Pwès, native theatrical performances. The open space east of Z was used for races and various sports on horseback.

A-1.—The Clock Tower where the gong and drum sounded the watches.

A-2.—Also a high tower in which a tooth of Gautama Buddha was enshrined.

A-3.—King Mindōn's Tomb.

A-4.—Hluttaw or Supreme Council Hall.

A-5.—A richly decorated Monastery, on the site of which King Thibaw spent the period of his priesthood.

A-6.—Golden Spire over the Great Audience Hall.

ZZ.—The South Garden Palace. It was used as a kind of picnic house by King Thibaw, and it was in the front verandah of this house that he was taken prisoner by Colonel Sladen in November 1885.

I.—Lion Throne in the Great Audience Hall, used three times a year for the reception of Feudatory Chiefs, Ministers, and Members of the Royal Family.

II.—Goose Throne.

III.—Elephant Throne in the Byèdaik.

IV.—Bee Throne.

V.—Conch Throne.

VI.—Deer Throne.

VII.—Peacock Throne.

VIII.—Lily Throne, where the ladies were received.

EXPLORATION AND RESEARCH.

CONSIDERING the vast and promising field which India offers for exploration, the record of what has been done in it during the past year may appear to be a somewhat meagre one. But it must be remembered that it is the preservation of the known monuments rather than the exploration of the unknown which has the first claim upon the time of the Survey Officers, and in the majority of the Circles the duties connected with conservation have recently demanded almost uninterrupted attention. Only two excavations have been carried out—the one in the extreme south of the Peninsula, the other within a few miles of its northern frontier; and in neither case has the digging been on an extensive scale. In Madras, Mr. Rea has continued his exploration of the prehistoric site at Ādittanallūr, confining himself, as in the previous season, to excavating in the vast cemetery—said to cover more than a hundred acres—from which nearly thirty years ago Dr. Jagor obtained his collection of antiquities for the Berlin Museum. In details this cemetery is of a generally uniform character; waste or rocky ground, as usual, has been selected for the burials, and the graves are either sunk in rows in the solid rock, or excavated at irregular intervals in the gravelly soil. Each of the pits thus formed contains one or, occasionally, two urns, ranging from four to nine feet in diameter and from six to fifteen in height, in which the corpse, or some portion of it, was placed. A few of the urns are fitted with spouts, and a few with horns on the inside of the rim, from which Mr. Rea conjectures that vessels or other articles were suspended. Complete skeletons are rare; more usually a selection of bones only is found, or in some cases none at all. As none of the bones show signs of having been calcined, and no other traces of cremation occur, it must be inferred that in the majority of cases mutilation was resorted to, before the bodies were placed in the urns, or, possibly, that they were exposed to the vultures, and only such bones collected for burial as remained after the flesh had been devoured. It might conceivably be imagined that many of the bones had rotted away through age, the bodies themselves having been buried intact, but such an hypothesis is effectually disproved by the smallness of some of the urns and the narrowness of their mouths. A noteworthy feature of these burials are the swords, spears, and other weapons found point downwards around the urns, as if thrust there by the mourners at the grave. Weapons and implements of iron are the usual offerings in all the graves, along with a variety of earthenware vessels of fine fabric, sometimes containing the husks of grain, household utensils, or occasionally stone beads. In the richer class of graves are found gold frontlets[1] bound over the forehead of the dead, bronze ornaments, and other objects denoting a certain degree of *luxe*. A description of selected specimens from all these offerings, except the ceramic wares, which are reserved for a future Report, will be found in the special article devoted to the Tinnevelly excavations. The whole collection made during the past season, amounting to over 4,000 objects, has been conveyed to the Madras Museum, where, I understand, it will be kept together and exhibited along with the previous season's finds in a room to be built for the purpose.

As regards the period and people to which these inhumations belong, the excavator himself conjectures that they are to be ascribed to the Pāṇḍyas and the era when those people were supreme in this part of Southern India, and that the complete disappearance of any trace or tradition of the peculiar mode of sepulture revealed by these and other excavations is due to the overthrow of the Pāṇḍya power by the Chōlas. The same burial custom, he thinks, may have extended to the Pallavas also. The general considerations upon which Mr. Rea bases his conjectures are as follows:—A considerable number of cemeteries, of precisely the same class, are known to exist within the limits of the ancient Pāṇḍya territory, and are almost invariably found in close proximity to (and usually on the south side of) the sites of ancient towns. These towns are one and all by tradition of Pāṇḍya origin, and Pāṇḍya coins are commonly found among their remains; hence it is reasonable to conclude that the cemeteries are to be ascribed to the same people. That the neighbouring habitations of the living are related to, and probably contemporary with, the resting places of the dead seems likely enough, and the likelihood is strengthened by the discovery on two of the town sites of ceramic wares similar to those found among the tombs. But on other town sites Mr. Rea remarks that the bulk of the pottery is quite different from any found among the tombs. This difference, however, might be explained in several ways; for instance, there may be a considerable disparity in age between the pottery found in the uppermost strata of the towns and that from the adjoining cemeteries, for it is hardly probable that the bones exhumed represent the latest generations of those who inhabited the town sites. Or again, it may be that a particular class of ware was used for burial purposes, in much the same way as the Etruscans used their peculiar cinerary urns, or the Athenians their *lekythoi*.

In the case of the Ādittanallūr remains, Mr. Rea suggests that they mark the site of the well known capital seaport of the Pāṇḍyas, which was afterwards abandoned,

[1] The gold frontlets are of thin gold leaf, so flimsy that they could not possibly have been used as jewellery in real life. They are mere imitations of the genuine article, substituted by the relations of the dead, who no doubt kept the more substantial jewellery for themselves. For similar instances of this economical piety towards the dead, see Frazer, *Pausanias*, Vol. III, page 107; Schliemann, *Mycenae*, page 156, etc.; E. Gardner, *New Chapters in Greek History*, p. 343; E. B. Tylor, *Primitive Culture*, I, p. 439.

when the sea had receded from it, in favour of the more modern Kōrkai,[1] to which also its name was presumably transferred. If Mr. Rea is right (and the physical features of the country, and the importance of the Ādittanallūr site, as compared with that of Kōrkai, certainly warrant his supposition), then it is inspiring to reflect that in the site of *Koṅgarāyakurichi* we may rediscover the ancient Κόλχοι, as it was known to the Greek writers, and possibly, too, some definite traces of an early connection with the trade of the Western world. On the other hand, it must be admitted that this theory is as yet unsupported by evidence from any of the finds themselves, and it is useless perhaps to speculate as to where the truth lies, either in regard to this identification or in regard to the date and ethnic origin of the graves, until further excavations have been prosecuted among both the cemeteries and the town sites, and the material already accumulated subjected to a more critical study than has yet been possible.

At Chārsada, near the North-Western Frontier, some preliminary excavations were carried out during March and April by Dr. Vogel and myself. The site there had long been identified as that of Puṣkalāvatī, the ancient capital of Gandhāra, and the most important historical centre in the Province, and hopes were entertained that we might light upon some remains of the ancient Akropolis, or some antiquities of a different character to those which have been yielded with monotonous regularity by the exploration of Buddhist religious buildings. The most conspicuous among the vast number of mounds which cover the face of the country, either singly or in connected groups, is that known as the *Bālā Ḥiṣār*, or High Fort; and it has usually been supposed that this was a fortified citadel in pre-Muhammadan as well as in Muhammadan days, though a recent writer would have us believe that it marks the site of a gigantic *stūpa*. Digging on this mound was begun by sinking three lines of trial pits along its edges. Most of these pits yielded nothing but potsherds and minor antiquities, but on the western side some massive walls of the typical Buddhist masonry came to light, which could not well have been erected for any but defensive purposes, and which consequently dispose of the theory of the *Bālā Ḥiṣār* being nothing but the remains of a Buddhist *stūpa*. A further trial trench, descending some twenty feet in the centre of the mound, revealed only a Muhammadan building of comparatively little interest.

Another considerable mound, on the further bank of the Svāt River, is that known as *Mīr Ziyārat*, where an earlier excavator believed that he had struck the foundations of a Buddhist *stūpa*, and where topographical considerations suggested that the famous memorial of the Eye-Gift might be located. The supposed foundations proved, on excavation, to be the walls of some dwelling-houses

[1] Kōrkai, in Tamil properly *Kōlkai*, euphonised into *Kōrkai*, and still called *Kolka* in Malayalam, was identified by Bishop Caldwell with the Κόλχοι mentioned by the author of the *Periplus Maris Erythræi*, and other Greek writers. When the silting of the river Tāmraparṇi, and the consequent recession of the sea, caused Ādittanallūr to be forsaken, Kōrkai was no doubt on the sea coast. It is now some five miles inland. In like manner, and through the same geological causes, Kōrkai at a later date gave place to Kāyal, the *Cail* of Marco Polo, which has in turn been superseded by Tuticorin. As regards the transference of names, it may be noted that the name of Kāyal has now been given to the village Kāyalpaṭṭanam on the coast. (*Cf.* Yule's *Marco Polo*, Vol. II, p. 373; *Indian Ant.*, VI, p. 80, sqq.)

belonging, approximately, to the twelfth century A.D.; but not far from the base of the hillock were afterwards discovered some walls of the ordinary Buddhist masonry, and beneath them, in an earlier stratum, the remains of some brick structures, which, from the evidence of several coin finds, would seem to date back to the first century B.C. The discovery of these early brick remains was made only two or three days before the season's work was brought to close, but the few minor antiquities which they yielded augured hopefully for future excavation on the spot.

Prominent among the considerations which caused Chārsada to be placed first on the list of sites to be excavated in the Frontier Province, was the fact that two inscriptions in Kharoṣṭhī had been found there, and the hope that others might be recovered. One of these inscriptions, now in the British Museum, had been unearthed by the peasants in a small mound, known as *Pālāṭū Ḍherī*, about 3 miles to the north-west of Chārsada, and it seemed advisable to follow up the clue by excavating further on the same spot. Our hopes were not disappointed, for we obtained another votive inscription cut on the stone pedestal of a statue, and three more written in ink on earthenware vessels, recording their presentation to a community of monks. The inscriptions on these vessels are of special interest, as the practice of inscribing pottery in this way with dedicatory records was peculiarly common in ancient Greece, but almost unknown, I believe, in India,[1] and we should, perhaps, be justified in seeing in them another trace of Hellenic influence. Among the minor finds from the same place were a considerable number of well-executed, but unfortunately mutilated, sculptures. The building, among the remains of which these antiquities were found, was undoubtedly a *vihāra*, but practically all that was left of it was a paved courtyard surrounded by low walls, and a paved area towards the west; masses of charred remains showed that the superstructure had been of wood.

In another small mound, known as *G͟haz Ḍherī*, not far from the one above, the base of a ruined *stūpa* was brought to light, containing at its centre a relic casket with some fragments of bone, a copper coin, identified as one of Zeionises, and some other minor objects. Other sculptures were also found in the courtyard of this *stūpa*, but they betray for the most part a distinct decadence of style as compared with those from *Pālāṭū Ḍherī*. If any reliance could be placed on the evidence of a single coin,[2] we might use it to prove that this *stūpa* was erected either during, or not long subsequent to, the reign of Zeionises, and we might even go a step further and surmise that some at least of the sculptures found around the *stūpa* are contemporary with it, and then we might infer, from their generally superior finish, that the sculptures from *Pālāṭū Ḍherī* are of a still earlier date. But the evidence, in my opinion, seems too slender on which to build any such conclusions, though it cannot be altogether passed over in silence.

From the same country of Gandhāra comes the small collection of gold

---

[1] Masson mentions "an inscription written in ink" around an earthenware vessel found in a tope at Hiddā in Afghanistan. *Ariana Antiqua*, p. 60.

[2] Both General Cunningham and Mr. Fergusson assume that one of the topes, discovered by the former at Manikyāla, was erected in the reign of Zeionises, because one of that Satrap's coins was found in it. *Cf. A. S. R.*, Vol. II, p. 167, and *Indian and Eastern Architecture*, p. 79.

jewellery, shown in Plate XXVIII (*a*), the greater part of which was rescued by Colonel H. A. Deane from a large find made by the peasants at Torḍher, and deposited by him in the Lahor Museum. The extreme rarity of ancient Indian gold-work, whether Hindu or Buddhist, makes the recovery of these ornaments of exceptional value, and it is instructive, in view of what has been written about the origin of Gandhāra art, to observe the semi-Eastern. semi-Western character of their style and technique, and the close connection which exists between them and certain articles of jewellery belonging to the pre-Christian era from Western Asia.

A hasty visit which Mr. Cousens paid to the little village of Ter, near the western borders of H. H. the Nizam's Dominions, resulted in the discovery there of a very early site containing important Hindu, Buddhist, and Jaina remains, and among them several structural buildings, in a comparatively first-rate state of preservation. The village of Ter had already been identified by Dr. Fleet with the ancient Tagara, mentioned by Greek writers as the great trading centre of the Dakhin as early as the first century A.D., and referred to in native epigraphic records of the tenth and eleventh centuries as still being a town of some considerable importance. Dr. Fleet's identification was based upon the similarity of the two names and the indications as to the position of Tagara given in the ancient geographers; but no actual examination of the site had ever been made, and it was in the hope of finding some monumental remains either to prove or disprove Dr. Fleet's theory, that Mr. Cousens undertook his journey to the place. This hope was not, unfortunately, fulfilled, in so far, at least, as he failed to discover anything yielding conclusive evidence on the point, but the extensive remains upon which he lighted attest at any rate the existence of an important town on this spot as early as the fourth century A.D., and in this way they give very practical support to Dr. Fleet's identification. These remains consist of a series of extensive mounds, covered with brick and pottery *débris*, and containing at one point the foundations of brick walls of an early type of construction; a complete Buddhist *Chaitya* Hall of a date not later, in Mr. Cousens' opinion, than the fourth century A.D., and possibly much earlier; and two other temples with highly ornate brick and wood-work, of a slightly later age than the *Chaitya* Hall.

With such well preserved and important architectural remains, as these are, above ground, there is every reason to hope that excavations here will result in valuable discoveries, and possibly also in settling beyond doubt the ancient name of this town.

At Hinīdān on the Hab river, a series of structural tombs of a remarkable and, so far as India is concerned, unique type was brought to the notice of the Archæological Department by Major M. A. Tighe, late Political Agent in Southern Baluchistan; they were subsequently visited by Dr. Vogel, and a number of drawings and photographs were obtained. The characteristic features which distinguish these monuments, are their pyramidal form of construction, the over-ground mode of burial, and the decorative slabs carved in relief with figures of men and horses. That they are of Muhammadan origin there can be little doubt, and it is this fact which makes the presence of the ornamental slabs difficult to explain. Dr. Vogel suggests that the figures on these slabs are a Hindu survival, and he compares them with the figures on certain *Satī* stones in the Himalayan districts of the Punjab, but one cannot help feeling that there is a suspicion of something un-Indian in these carvings, especially in the more developed specimens; and the form of the tombs with their steps or tiers diminishing towards the summit, coupled with the name *Shāmī* (Syrian), given locally to the over-ground mode of burial, would certainly seem to connect them with the West rather than the East. Perhaps the immediate neighbourhood of Persia on the west might warrant the suggestion that these sarcophagi are the remote descendants of the early Persian structural tombs, like the famous one in the valley of the Murgh-āb, identified as the resting-place of Cyrus, the son of Cambyses; [1] or it may be that they were actually introduced by immigrants from Asia Minor, where many examples may be found of analogous structures.

Dr. Vogel's description of the Hinīdān tombs concludes the account of new archæological discoveries made by the Survey. The other special articles included in this section of the 'Annual" are concerned with inquiries into the origin or history of monuments that have long been known to us. These monuments are the Iron Pillar at Dhār, and the Mughal buildings in the Lahor Fort. As regards the former, Mr. Cousens advances good reasons for disbelieving the generally accepted opinion that the pillar was erected as a lamp-post or support for a beacon fire, and argues with a greater show of probability that it was a *jayastambha*, or column of victory, set up before one of the temples, and surmounted originally by some image or symbol, perhaps a *Garuḍa* or *triśūla*. The history which Mr. Cousens reconstructs for the pillar previous to its attempted removal by Sulṭān Bahādur Shāh, of Gujarāt, is somewhat more problematical. In speaking of this attempted removal, Jahāngīr mentions that the pillar was on that occasion accidentally broken into two pieces, measuring 22 and 13 feet, respectively. These two pieces still exist at Dhār, and Mr. Cousens is of opinion that a third and smaller piece, which until recently was lying at Māṇḍū, belonged originally to the same pillar. He ingeniously surmises that the pillar was set up in the first instance at Māṇḍū—perhaps by Arjunavarmadeva—in commemoration of a victory over Gujarāt; that it was overthrown and broken into two pieces by the Muhammadans, when they conquered Mālvā at the beginning of the fourteenth century; that the larger of the two pieces was removed to Dhār by Dilāvar Khān Ghūri about a hundred years later, and placed in front of the mosque just erected by him; and that this was the piece which Jahāngīr states was broken into two pieces by Bahādur Shāh.

In his notes on the Lahor Fort, Nūr Bakhsh has collected together a number of

[1] *Cf.* Perrot et Chipiez, *Histoire de l'art dans l'antiquité*, Tome V., Figs. 329, 375; and Curzon, *Persia* Vol. II. pp. 75 sqq.

passages from native authorities which throw much fresh light on the history of its buildings. The fact which these passages establish beyond a doubt, is that the Chhotī Khwābgāh and the Dīwān-i-'Āmm (both here and in Agra Fort) were built by Shāh Jahān. They make it practically certain, too, that the building known as the Shīsh Mahall, or Muthamman Burj, is no other than the Shāh Burj, erected by Shāh Jahān, and that the Naulakha also is to be ascribed to the same Emperor, and not, as formerly supposed, to his successor, Aurangzeb. Other conclusions of interest, which Nūr Bakhsh deduces from the authorities cited, are that the famous tile work on the exterior of the Palace wall, which hitherto has invariably been attributed to Jahāngīr, belongs in reality to Shāh Jahān's reign; that Akbar's Dīwān-i-'Āmm was the building in the rear of the present Dīwān-i-'Āmm, once surrounded by an arcade, which has now disappeared; and that the marble pavilion between the Khwābgāh and the Shāh Burj probably dates from Shāh Jahān's reign.

J. H. M.

PREHISTORIC ANTIQUITIES IN TINNEVELLY.

PREHISTORIC burial sites are especially numerous in the gravelly mounds or low hills of the Tinnevelly District, adjoining the valley of the Tāmraparṇi river.

These slopes, as Dr. Caldwell has pointed out,[1] occur along the course of the river, and formed its primeval banks. On them ancient remains may be looked for. The ground, between them and the river, being low and marshy, and at times subject to sudden floods, no ancient remains of habitations or sepulchres may be there expected to exist.

In a very extensive series of explorations of the many sites, situated along the course of the river, from Pālamcōṭṭah to the sea, I have generally found this to be the case, though there are a few exceptions. The mounds and hills stand at very frequent intervals ; and on almost all of them these remains are found. These sites are thirty-eight in number, and are situated at the following places. That at Ādittanallūr is the most important of all. There may still be others that I have not seen. Rājavalliporambu (1), Pālāmaḍai (2), Manappaḍai (3), Kiḷanattam (4), Pālamcōṭṭah (5), Kṛṣṇāpuram (6), Vaḍakku Vallanāḍu (7), Vallanāḍu (8), Agaram (9), Murappanāḍu (10), Vasavappāpuram and Anavaradanallūr (11), Viṭhalāpuram (12), Koṅgarāyakurichi (13), Karuṅgulam (14), Ādittanallūr (15), Srīvaikunṭham (16), Tiruppuliayamkuḍi (17), Pudukuḍi (18), Vellūr (19), Kālvai (20), Malavarāyanattam (21), Ālvār Tirūnagari (22), Alagiyamaṇavālapuram and Shembatu Parachēri (23), Tirukōlūr (24), Appankōil (25), Tentiruppērai (26), Poraiyūr (27), Aṅgamaṅgalaṁ and Kurumbūr (28), Nālumāvaḍi (29), Nallūr (30), Sugandalai (31), Kōrkai (32), Mārāmaṅgalam (33), Kāyalpaṭṭanam (34), and Vīrapāṇḍiyapaṭṭanam (35).[2]

In a few places, such as those near Kurumbūr, thė ground is not high and gravelly, but it is at a sufficient elevation to be beyond the reach of encroachment from the river. At Vellūr, near Ādittanallūr, a group of these remains stands in the bed of what is now a large irrigation tank ; the site is covered with water for the most of the

---

[1] *History of Tinnevelly*, Appendix IV.

[2] The numbers in brackets refer to the accompanying map ; (11), (23), and (28) include two places each.

year. This tank originally contained seven small tanks or wells, and it has been constructed in its present form, subsequent to the British occupation. In early times, before the river was enclosed by flood banks, the site must have been subject to frequent inundations.

The rule, however, not only in this, but in other districts where I have examined such remains, is, that, whenever possible, high land, waste or rocky, or such as is unsuitable for cultivation, is that which has been generally selected for burial sites. I have already remarked on this peculiarity.[1]

Another fact which these investigations proved is, that in the neighbourhood of these sepulchral sites, there is almost invariably found a site of an ancient habitation. So much was this impressed on me that, in the course of my investigations, whenever I saw an ancient town site,—known by the dark earth strewn with pottery, etc., and the presence of ancient coins—I generally found a sepulchral site with urns adjoining.

The latter is usually situated on the south side of a town, the south being the abode of Yama, the god of death, and thus having, from time immemorial, been selected—whenever possible—as the site for burials. It was on this side therefore, of a newly found site that I first looked, and I was seldom disappointed. When I was, I think it may be put down to the alteration of the ground, and removal of the soil, caused by extensive clearance of mounds so as to convert the land into flat rice fields. I observed some instances of this, one of which was at Ādittanallūr and another at Tirukōḷūr.

As to the precise age of these sepulchral remains, I think the proximity of the two classes of sites in this district may supply a clue. This may, of course, be simply a coincidence, and the town site may be much the more modern, being simply the re-occupation of a deserted site which may have been a town or village in prehistoric times contemporary with these burials. But it occurs so often that some connection is more than probable.

If it were only a coincidence that the neighbourhood of a prehistoric site had been ages after selected for habitation, there would be more than one deposit of strata of pottery and such like remains—the prehistoric and the more modern one. I have not, however, found such to be the case, and at Koṅgarāyakurichi, adjacent to Ādittanallūr—but now on the opposite or left bank of the river, through the latter having shifted its course during one of the floods—there is only one continuous stratum. This is clearly apparent, as the river has cut right through the site, and doubtless washed the most of it away. The pottery stratum is distinctly defined in the steep river bank some feet below the surface.

Admitting the theory of adjacent sites, I searched for one which would suit the conditions in the neighbourhood of the Ādittanallūr Cemetery, but at first without much success beyond hearing of a traditional account of a town having existed here.

It was only on my third visit that I found the town site of Koṅgarāyakurichi. The existing portion is less than a mile north of Ādittanallūr, on the other side of the river, being thus correctly placed in relation to the burial ground. Before the river

[1] Some prehistoric burial places in Southern India, *Journal As. Soc. Bengal*, 1888.

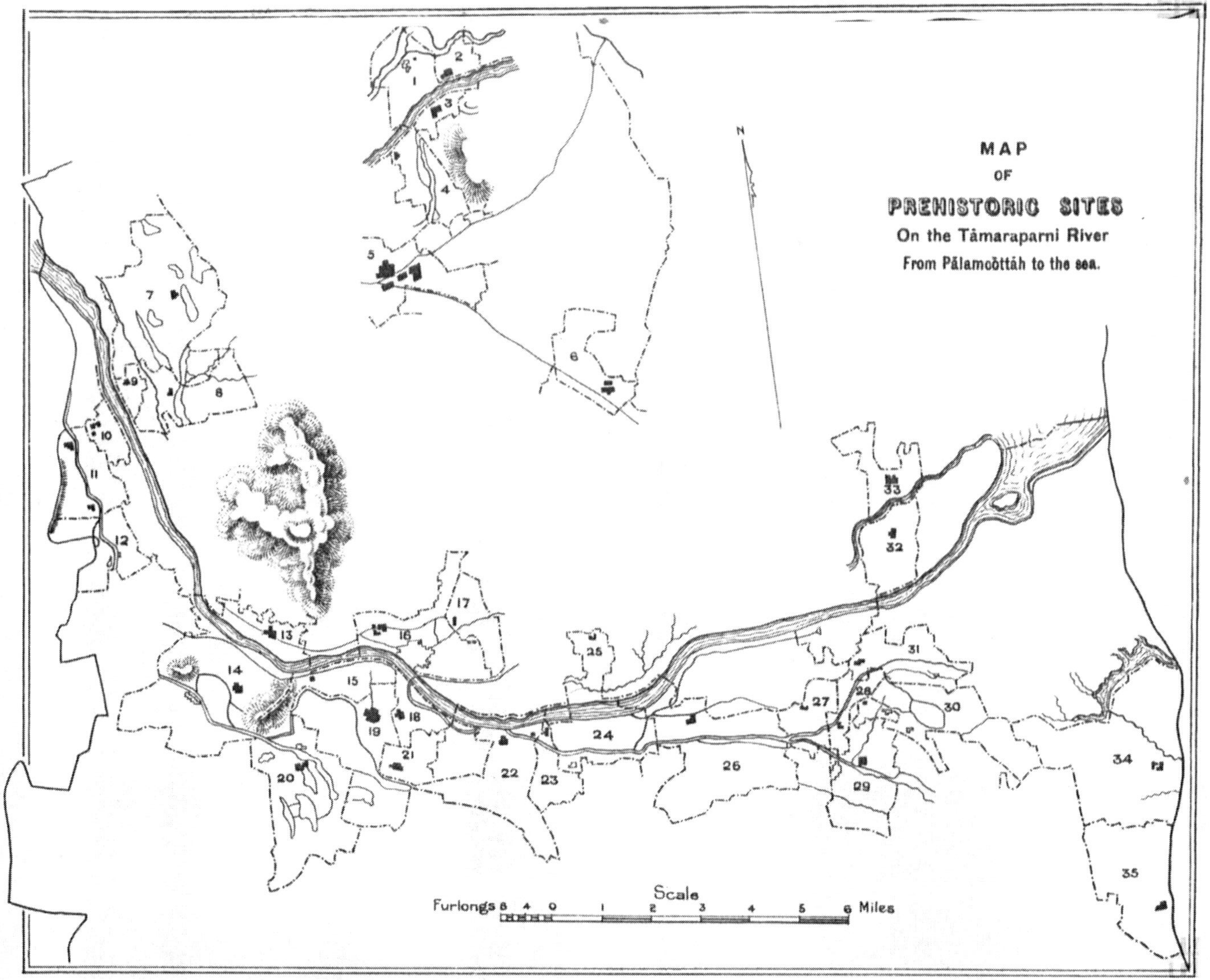
MAP
OF
PREHISTORIC SITES
On the Tâmaraparni River
From Pâlamcottâh to the sea.
N
Scale
Furlongs 8 4 0 1 2 3 4 5 6 Miles
1
2
3
4
5
6
7
8
9
10
11
12
13
14
15
16
17
18
19
20
21
22
23
24
25
26
27
28
29
30
31
32
33
34
35

Fig. 1.

changed its course, the two sites were doubtless connected, and the intervening ground, now swept over by the river, must almost certainly have been occupied by a part of the town.

The town site may supply some evidence as to the age of the neighbouring prehistoric remains. Kōrkai is a prominent example. They are all by tradition Pāṇḍiyan sites, they yield Pāṇḍiyan coins, some have Pāṇḍiyan temples, and at two of them, Vallanāḍu Agaram and Koṅgarāyakurichi, I found numerous fragments of prehistoric polished black and red pottery identical with that found in tombs in the adjoining sites. The bulk of the broken pottery, however, is quite different from any found in the tombs. This might perhaps be accounted for by some of the latter being specially made for the purpose, and not for general household use, for which it is too fragile. There are pots from the urns nevertheless which, for strength and shape, might have been so used. During a visit to Mārāmaṅgalam—near Kōrkai—I got a pot which had been dug out of one of the urns some time previously by a villager, who had since used it for household purposes.

In remains, such as these sepulchres, which have no unquestionable but only circumstantial evidences of date, which can be variously interpreted, speculations as to their age have of course been and will be many. It has been said they may be 400 or they may be 4,000 years old, and none can disprove either assertion.

It used to be the custom to assign an immemorial antiquity to everything Indian, of which the date was unknown, and now perhaps the scale has turned too far in the opposite direction; for some will, without sufficient or perhaps any data, at once confidently state that the tombs cannot be more than a few centuries old; while at the same time they will readily accept unquestioned a date of as many thousands of years before the Christian Era for a Greek or Egyptian tomb or monument as devoid of actual evidences of date as these are.

Possibly in these early times, civilized India was confined to the seaports, to the river-side towns, and to the north of the Peninsula, the interior of Southern India being then forests, inhabited by migratory tribes.

I have no evidence as to the occurrence of such remains in parts of India north of the Madras Presidency; but they exist at Kōrkai, a seaport well known in ancient times, and possibly intimately connected with some of these not far distant sites under note, which are scattered along the banks of the river Tāmraparṇi.

The river is thought to be the "Solen" of Ptolemy, by whom also Kōrkai is mentioned. Kōrkai is said to have been the Capital of the early Pāṇḍiyans, and one of the most important trading places in India, being mentioned in A.D. 80.[1] It is 9 miles east of Srīvaikunṭhaṁ and 11 miles from Ādittanallūr.

The prehistoric remains near Kōrkai are not to be compared in extent to those at Ādittanallūr, and if this is any criterion of early importance, the latter must, in prehistoric times, have been much the greater place. Ādittanallūr has undoubtedly been a place of some population or extent; and how near it originallv stood to the sea is now unknown; but as the sea there is receding, it must have been much nearer than at present.

[1] Sewell's *Lists*, Vol. I, page 312.

The site of Kōrkai was at one time covered by the sea, and though originally founded on the sea-shore, is now some 5 miles inland.

Ādittanallūr may have been the early seat of trade, and when the sea receded Kōrkai may have been founded as its seaport. The extensive remains existing at Kōrkai are mostly of mediæval times, some of them dating from the times of the European trading companies.

Against any theory of a comparatively modern date, for these burials, it may be urged that, in a country so conservative of its customs as India, some form of the non-cremation mode of urn burial—which is that invariably adopted in these sites—would undoubtedly have survived more or less to the present day; but such is not the case. What circumstances could have arisen to cause its adoption at a late period and its sudden rejection after a few years' use? All evidences are against it. Were it otherwise, the use of the word prehistoric would be a misnomer.

Even the traditions of the people, some of which are quoted by Dr. Caldwell,[1] have no hint to give which can help to throw light on the facts revealed by these excavations, nor can any trace of connection between the two be found. Either extreme antiquity or some other sufficient cause, there must be to account for this. The method of sepulture was peculiar to the indigenous people of the country, and was changed through some great cataclysm, such as an invasion, which resulted in the adoption of the conquerors' customs, or it ceased with a general exodus of the original inhabitants.

The Pāṇḍiyan Kingdom existed from a very early time, and is referred to, in an Asōka inscription B.C. 250 in Northern India.[2] Earlier and later writers mention it. In the Rāmāyana and Māhabhārata, Pāṇḍiyans, Dārviḍas, and Chōlas are mentioned.[3]

The Pāṇḍiyans were in possession of the Tinnevelly District from the earliest historical times.[4] The original line of kings seems to have continued down to their conquest by Rājēndra Chōla in A.D. 1064.

The reigning king at that time was Vīra Pāṇḍiya, son of Vikrama Pāṇḍiya. To this time may be ascribed the cessation of urn burial. I do not think any of the examples are of a later date, and some of them may be much earlier. Even on the Ādittanallūr site, in several parts of the ground, the contents of the urns differ from those found elsewhere. Thus the bronzes are only found at certain places, skulls and complete skeletons with few utensils at another, and so on. This may either indicate a difference in their age,[4] or in the castes which simultaneously made use of the several parts of the burial ground.

Burial urns are largely confined to the Tinnevelly District, and extreme south of the Peninsula,[4] or precisely in that portion of the country occupied and ruled over by the Pāṇḍiyans.

They similarly exist at different places in the Maḍura District, the chief centre of the Pāṇḍiyan kingdom.[5]

I have also found them at other places further north, in the Pallava country,

[1] *Ind. Antiq.*, Vol. VI, 280.
[2] Sewell's *Lists*, II, 221.
[3] Breek's *Prim. Tribes of the Nilgiris.*
[4] Sewell's *Lists*, I, 303.
[5] Rea. Some prehist. burial places in Southern India. *Jour. As. Soc. Bengal*, 1888.

such as Pallāvaram, near which is a Pallava cave temple; and it has been suggested that it was a contemporary Pallava custom also.

It is scarcely possible to suppose that the age of the urns is anterior to that of the Pāṇḍiyans,—though even this would give them a respectable antiquity—and, if that is so, this mode of sepulture must have been practised during their epoch, either by themselves, or by tribes residing within their limits. It could scarcely have been introduced at a later period, or subsequent to the height of the Pāṇḍiyan power. I have remarked on the proximity of these burial sites to Pāṇḍiyan settlements, and it seems more than probable, that the custom of urn burial was general in not only the Pāṇḍiyan, but the Pallava Kingdom also. It is found outside these boundaries, but a custom such as this would not have any arbitrary territorial limits. It seems most probable that it fell into desuetude on the overthrow of the Pāṇḍiyan and Pallava Kingdoms by the Chōlas; and scattered parties of the conquered peoples, fleeing from their conquerors, may have carried the custom with them to other parts of the country, as with the Kurumbas of the Nilgiris,[1] where they may have continued their customs for a time, but gradually changed them in favour of the Hindu practice of cremation

The Prehistoric Site at Ādittanallūr.

This is the most extensive prehistoric site as yet discovered in Southern if not in the whole of India. It covers an area of 114 acres, within which burial urns are found, at some places close together, and at others more widely apart. The site was first brought to notice in 1876, when it was visited by Dr. Jagor of Berlin, accompanied by the Collector of Tinnevelly and the District Engineer.

Some excavations were then carried out, and a considerable number of articles found. These consisted of "upwards of fifty kinds of baked earthenware utensils of all sizes and shapes, a considerable number of iron weapons and implements, chiefly knives or short sword blades and hatchets, and a great quantity of bones and skulls."[2] These articles were taken away by Dr. Jagor for the Berlin Museum.

At that time, the ground was used for the excavation of gravel, and as the workmen had a superstitious dread of disturbing the urns—which they have since got over—the exhumed urns, found in the course of the digging, were left standing exposed. Thus a good collection of objects was found ready for removal without much trouble or expense.

A proposal was afterwards made to continue the excavations, by removing the whole of the soil from certain areas, leaving the urns standing exposed,—which would have been rather a stupendous undertaking. But fortunately the proposal was dropped.

Orders were given by Government to leave the site undisturbed, but these appear to have been unattended to, for quarrying has been going on continuously ever since, with the result that vast quantities of these interesting relics must have been destroyed.

---

[1] Breek's *Prim. Tribes of the Nilgiris*, 55.

[2] Proceedings of the Madras Government, Public Dept. (No. 329 of the 27th March 1876).

Lately it has at my suggestion been conserved, and a watchman has been appointed to guard it.

Close to the west of the village, a low hill stands on the south bank of the river. From it a low wide gravelly ridge extends some distance to the south-west. On this is the prehistoric site. It is partly in the villages of Ādittanallūr, partly in Karuṅgulam and Kālvāi.

The road from Tinnevelly to Āḻvār Tirūnagari and Tiruchendūr, at this place runs close to, and parallel with, the river; and cuts through the mound at the base of the hill.

On the summit of the hill is the Pāṇḍiya Rāja Koil. It is said to be of ancient date, but was rebuilt with stones taken from the Pālamcoṭṭāh Fort, when the latter was demolished by some "Nawābs." There is no image or deity in the temple, but two bricks are set up in the form of a triangle, inside which a light is set, and worship is then made to the Pāṇḍiyan King. It is probably a survival of homage formerly paid to the reigning Pāṇḍiyan monarch. Every Friday the light is lit and water sprinkled at the threshold of the temple.

Festivals take place in the month of *Kartiki*[1] when *Poṅgal*,[1] flowers, and fruits are offered; and five days in the month of *Chittiri*[1] when sacrifices of sheep, etc., are made. The worshippers formerly were higher caste Hindus, but now they are Pallars who make offerings to Rāma, Lakṣmaṇa, Kṛṣṇa, Dharmarāja, Bhīma, Arjuna, Nakula, Sahadēva, Dhṛtarāṣṭra, Duryōdhana, and others.

Adjoining the temple and also a short distance south of it, are Sāśtan temples. These consist of a number of small stone images of deities, snakes, etc., grouped under a tree. Some of them are of archaic carving, resembling, in this respect, specimens of the bronze animals dug out of the adjoining tombs.

The spot to which the excavations have been chiefly confined, and where most of the discoveries have been made, is near the centre of the ground, and covers an area of about five acres. At this place, a loose quartz rock with its strata dipping about an angle of 45° to the north-west, appears close to the surface, and large wells or pits have been sunk in it in rows to contain the urns. Walls of rock are left between. The wells are of various sizes from 4 feet to 9 feet in diameter and from 6 feet to 12 feet or 15 feet in depth. The bottom is concave with a small hole in the centre in which the leg of the urn is placed. Sometimes two urns are found close together at the bottom. The wells were filled up to the surface with gravel, small or sometimes large stones that required several men to move. There was no surface indication of their presence. But when two adjoining wells were found, other pits sunk in line with them at similar distances apart, almost invariably struck the adjoining wells without the necessity of touching the intervening ground.

Outside the limits of the rocky ground, wells were found in the hard ground. They are not placed in regular lines like those cut in the rock, and they also had no surface indication; but in digging over the surface, the difference between the hard natural ground and the filled-in soil of the pits was easily apparent to the diggers, and there was thus not much difficulty in finding them.

---

[1] *See* Glossary.

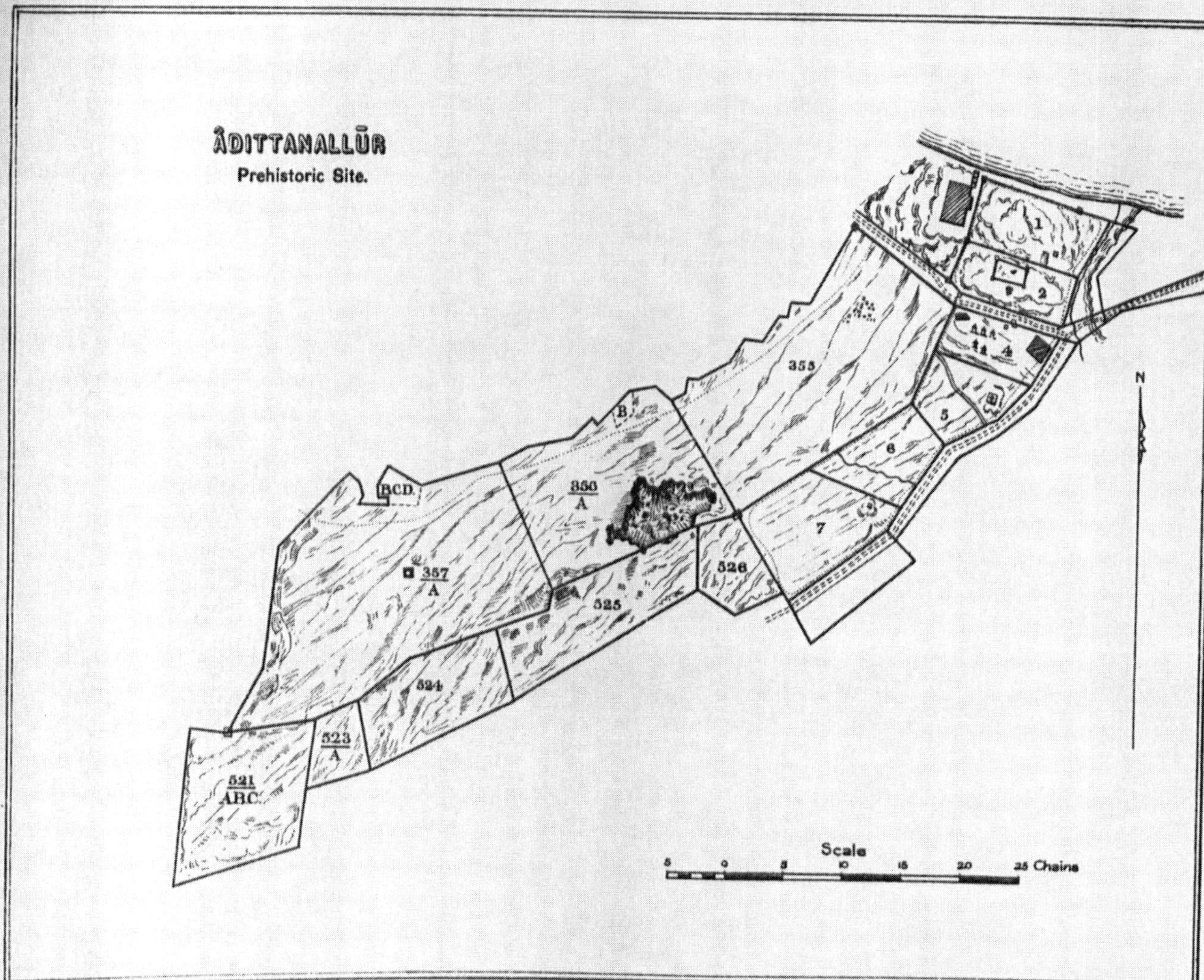
ÂDITTANALLŪR
Prehistoric Site.
1
2
4
5
6
7
353
356
A
357
A
B.
BCD.
526
525
524
523
A
521
ABC.
N
Scale
5
0
5
10
15
20
25 Chains

Fig. 2.

Bishop Caldwell speaks of a circle of stones in some cases being placed on the surface, over the urns, as an indication of where they may be found,[1] but I have not seen any traces of them at the sites I visited. Possibly they once existed, and have been removed for road metal.

Contents of the Urns.

In the first excavations, the objects discovered amounted to 1,872; and afterwards over 4,000 were unearthed.[2] Space only permits of the illustration and description of a very few typical examples of the first collection.

The objects yielded by these burial sites, are finely made pottery of various kinds in great number;[3] many iron implements and weapons; vessels and personal ornaments in bronze; a few gold ornaments; a few stone beads; bones; and some household stone implements used for grinding curry or sandalwood. Traces of cloth and wood preserved by rust or oxidation in contact with metals are found. In a number of urns there were quantities of mica in pieces about an inch in size. Husks of rice and millet were found in quite a large number of pots inside the urns. All the implements and weapons are in iron; there are none in bronze.

No palæolithic or neolithic stone implements of any kind occur.

The vessels are mostly in earthenware, with a much smaller proportion in bronze. Lamps are of iron; no other vessels are of this metal.

The comparative rarity of bronze objects and their use for personal ornament, show that this metal must then have been scarce, highly valued, and used only by the higher class of people. The only gold ornaments found in the tombs are diadems.

Thus the people who made these objects appear to have been skilful in moulding pottery, in casting or brating metals, in weaving, and in working stone and wood. That they were acquainted with agriculture is shown by the iron spades for digging, and the presence of husks of rice and millet. Some of the iron implements are for sacrificial purposes, others are for the chase or war. They have all been fitted with wooden handles. Their religion was probably devil worship, as evidenced by the various iron sacrificial implements discovered, which are similar to those used in this form of worship.

The attempts at art in casting animals in bronze and at ornamenting that metal, indicate a primitive workmanship. The ornamentation consists only of embossed dots, and incised lines for the most part in triangular or simple geometric designs.

The domestic animals represented in bronze are the buffalo, goat or sheep, and the cock, while the wild animals are the tiger, antelope, and elephant. Of these only the antelope is now known in a wild state in the locality, and that at the Vallanāḍ hill, where also this species would have disappeared, but that it is a Government reserved forest.

In the collection formerly made by Mr. Breeks on the Nilgiris, illustrated in his book,[4] and now in the Madras Museum, are a number of representations of animals in pottery; there are none of these in this material here. In other respects

[1] *Ind. Ant.*, Vol. VI, p. 280.
[2] Subsequently another 3,000 have been found.
[3] It has not been found possible to have these illustrated at present.
[4] *Prim. Tribes and Mon. of the Nilgiris.*

also, the pottery and metal implements from the Nilgiris and Tinnevelly differ widely from each other.

I have mentioned that bronze was the metal in which personal ornaments were made. But there was one instance of iron covered with gold plating being so used. It is a ring from Vallanāḍ (No. 30). The section of the metal is square $\frac{3}{16}''$ thick and $\frac{3}{4}''$ in diameter. The outer surface is corroded, and has but slight traces of the precious metal. It is fairly complete on the interior surface, and retains the gold plating almost intact. The ring may have been for the toes or the fingers.

An instance of the use of pottery for ear-rings, is seen in No. 63. These specimens are of similar shape to the modern Madras *Kummal*,[1] which is fixed in the widened ear lobe. They are $\frac{3}{4}''$ in diameter.

Some fish vertebræ, evidently used for the same purpose, were found in the sandy town site of Vīrapāṇḍiyapaṭṭaṇaṁ, on the sea-coast. In the same site were found a number of white, chalky, irregular-shaped, pierced beads somewhat larger than ordinary peas. These have been used for necklaces, and may possibly be ancient decayed pearls, which assume that appearance after extreme age or long exposure.

Urns—

The funeral urns are large, one-legged, elongated, globular pots of thick red earthenware, averaging less than a yard in diameter by a slightly greater height. They are similar to those found at Pallāvaram and elsewhere. Around the mouth is a rim, in most specimens plain, but in some impressed with the thumb nail or incised with triangular and dotted ornaments. All have had flat conical covers, and on the preservation of these depends, to a large extent, the condition of the contents.

The majority of the urns are now filled with stones or soil, but this is invariably due to breakage of the lid. They have never designedly been so filled. Some urns have horns on the inside of the rim, evidently for hanging or suspending pots or other articles. I have seen the same, but on the outside, on urns from the Bangalore District. Some of the large sized vessels have single or double spouts on one side, and one large urn had a hole near the lower end.

Very few urns appear on the surface, and such as are near it, do not yield many deposits; and these, moreover, are in a more or less broken condition through the lid having fallen in, together with quantities of stones and gravel. The urns, too, are usually cracked, owing no doubt to the expansion and contraction of the surrounding ground through damp, heat, and drought.

In only a few instances do the urns contain the complete bones of a skeleton, and then the urn is always of large size, being nearly 3 feet in diameter. Generally, the modern system of interring a selection of the bones only, seems to have been the method followed. Such urns may contain a skull or parts of it only, or some other bones of the skeleton, and these occur either by themselves or in company with other articles in pottery or metal. The latter are occasionally very numerous, both outside and inside the urn.

In those urns which contained complete skeletons, and which were thus preserved by the lid remaining intact, the position of the bones made it obvious that

[1] *See* Glossary.

the body had been set inside in a squatting or sitting position. On its decay, the leg and arm bones fell over and rested against one side of the urn, while the skull, ribs, and vertebræ dropped down to the bottom. This was the position in which every complete skeleton, without exception, was found; and the urns in which they were placed were all devoid of earth.

Many urns contained no traces of bones whatever. This may have been due to decay, or to the fact that none were buried. None of the bones were calcined.

Some urns had earth and stones only; some had only chatties; and a very few had bones without vessels of any kind. Some had earthenware outside and nothing inside, and others *vice versâ*. One had a bangle and nothing more.

Some complete skulls may offer a clue to the identity of the race to whom they belong. A few of the skulls have holes in the brow, which would indicate a violent death. Mr. Thurston of the Madras Museum has measured some of the skulls, and finds they belong to a dolichocephalic people. In a few urns were traces of ashes, but these did not appear to be the results of cremation. They were apparently due to the combustion of wood used during some ceremony of burial.

Objects in Metal—

The bronzes exhibit a very high degree of skill in workmanship, and manipulation of the metal; this is also the case with iron implements. All this confirms historical accounts as to the early skill of the Indians in the working of metal. When bronzes are found, they are usually inside the urns, but not invariably; some instances occur of only one being placed inside, and half a dozen or so on the outside.

Implements, arms, or lamps in iron, are generally found in conjunction with bronzes, and are, as a rule, placed outside; but they are found inside also. There are several swords from the inside, which have been bent by fallen *débris* before they had corroded, and have retained that shape.

All swords, spears, arrows, and other weapons from around the urns, were always found point downwards, as if they had been thrust into the surrounding earth by the attendant mourners.

Many of the iron weapons, through corrosion, are thickly encrusted with particles of gravel, but the metal is fairly firm and strong. Others again, either wholly or in part, are simply a mass of fibrous black rust which it is impossible to remove or even touch without breakage. The metal of these could be crushed to powder between the fingers. Many of the swords and implements show traces of wood, permeated with rust, at the handles and even along the blade.

Some of the objects, both metal and earthenware, but especially the former, are either so decayed or fractured, that it is, on their first exposure to the air, quite impossible to move them. Soaked with the moisture of the soil, they are—even if not much broken—extremely fragile. But if the surrounding earth is partly cleared away, and they are left to dry for a time, they become fairly hard, and can then generally be removed without harm. Some, however, are so thoroughly corroded, twisted, or cracked throughout, especially if composed, like some of the bronzes, of very thin metal, that, though the outline of their probable form can be traced, they cannot possibly be removed except in fragments. Sometimes removal can be effected by soaking the porous oxidized metal with size, which, on drying, gives it sufficient hardness to allow of its being handled. Tissue paper pasted on, is also sometimes useful in facilitating removal.

Gold Diadems—

When these ornaments were first discovered, it was thought probable that they were badges[1] for affixing to the upper part of the arm, and formerly used by persons of rank. It now, however, seêms certain that they are diadems. Diadems of the same shape were found at Mycenae, and are described[2] as long, thin, oval, gold plates, bound round the head by a small gold wire, the holes for which are at each extremity. This description applies equally to the present examples, except as to the gold wire, of which none was seen. The tying material was probably thread, of which I found traces in some bronze necklaces. Now-a-days no custom is known in the neighbourhood of tying diadems on the dead, but what may be a relic of it is described as *paṭṭayam Kaṭṭaradu*, (பட்டயம் கட்டரது) literally meaning in Tamil "the tying of a plate" to the forehead of a corpse, but which now simply consists in the sprinkling of some grains of gold and silver on the breast of the dead.

I also learn that among some castes in the east of the Madura District, there still exists a custom of tying a plain rectangular strip of gold, an inch or two in length, on the forehead of the dead. In this case, the custom is known by the same name, and its forms have been preserved in their entirety.

In Ādittanallūr, the custom could not have been a general one, for out of many urns excavated, only a few gold ornaments were found. It must have been limited to persons of rank or importance. The urns in which they occurred, were invariably placed at a considerable depth, usually from 10′ to 15′, and protected by deposits of large stones or boulders extending from the surface right down to the urn. In other cases, smaller urns were placed at some height over them, either as a protection, or representing a more recent burial. The urns containing them, were always large, and usually had considerable deposits, both inside and out, of pottery, bronze vessels, and iron implements. When all these indications occurred, a gold ornament was almost sure to be found. In only two adjacent parts of the ground, so far as it has been examined, were these discovered. In most of the present examples, the diadems were lying at the bottom of the urn crushed and crumpled—apparently intentionally—at the time of deposit. Their condition may possess some significance, as others were procured unfolded. A few were in bronze, both folded and unfolded.

Some of these diadems are simple ovals, and others have thin strips of the gold extending beyond each extremity. A few are plain, but most of them have repoussé linear designs of dots.

No. 292, Plate XXII, Figure 1.—Size $\frac{15}{16}$″ by $\frac{1}{4}$″, weight 2 grs. Diadem. Narrow fillet of laminated gold with pointed end. The other end has also doubtless been pointed but is worn off. Through the pointed end is a small hole.[3] The front side is burnished, the reverse side

---

[1] *Bhāju band.* [2] *Jour. Soc. Arts*, No. 2595, Vol. I, p. 777. [3] This is the case in all the examples.

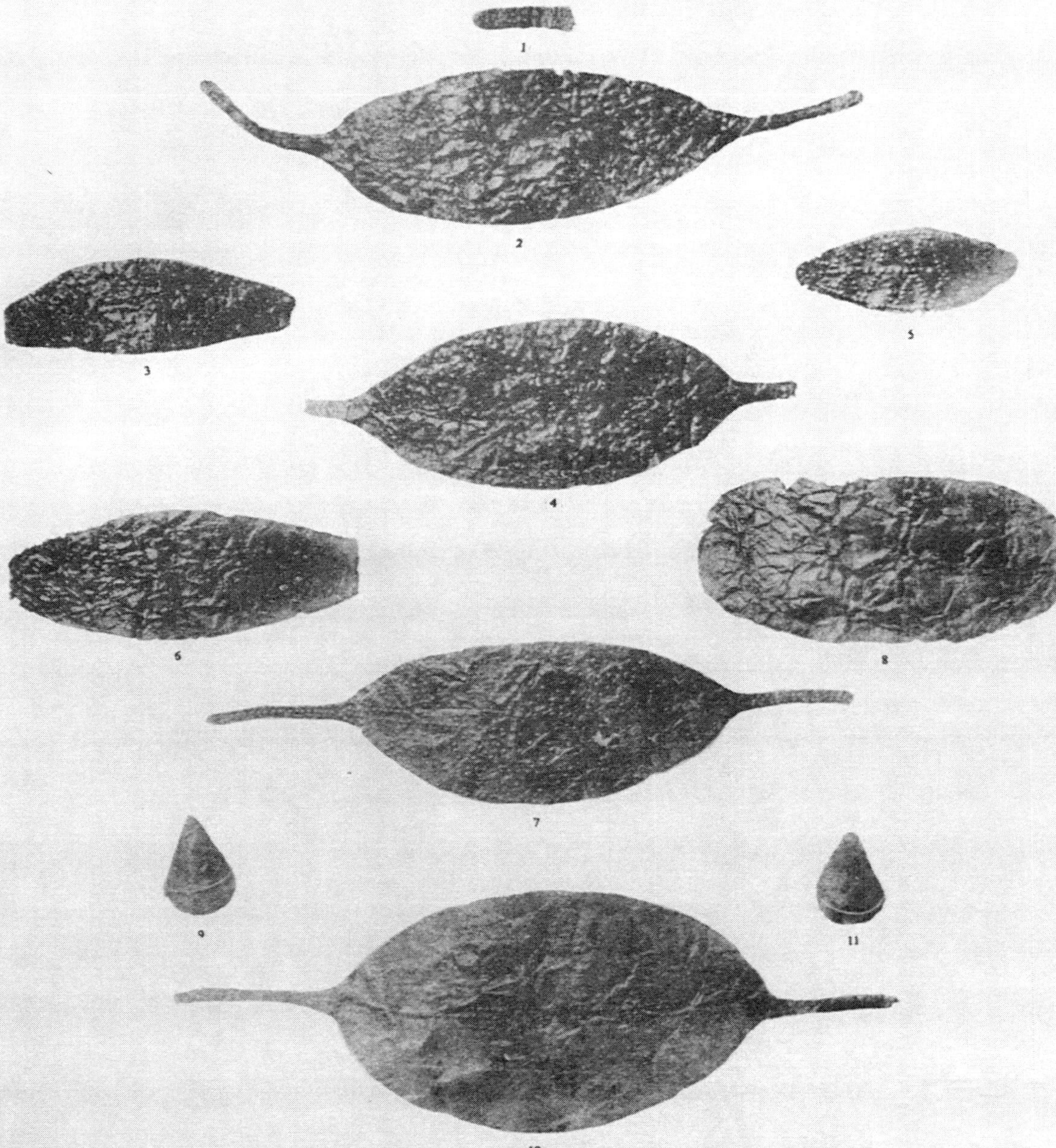

GOLD DIADEMS, ETC.

dull.[1] Three longitudinal lines of dots are impressed on the reverse side. Found inside a bronze jar.

No. 1088, Plate XXII, Figure 5.—Size $2\frac{8}{16}$" by $\frac{7}{8}$", weight 10 grs. Pointed oval diadem, with small hole at each extremity. Dotted line along the major axis and another around the edge. Dotted triangles between these lines. Front burnished, and reverse dull. Dots impressed on reverse.

No. 1231, Plate XXII, Figure 8.—Size $3\frac{1}{2}$" by $1\frac{11}{16}$", weight 35 grs. Oval diadem, with small hole at each end. Dotted lines along length and around edge. Crushed and folded.

No. 1467, Plate XXII, Figure 2.—Size $6\frac{3}{8}$" by $1\frac{1}{2}$", weight 32 grs. Oval diadem, with a strip extending beyond each end, at the extremity of each of which is a small hole. Dotted linear ornament. Folded.

No. 1468.—Six pieces of gold-leaf folded. Roughly rectangular about an inch in size.

No. 1481, Plate XXII, Figure 10.—Size $6\frac{5}{8}$" by $2\frac{5}{32}$", weight 47 grs. Oval diadem, with a strip at each end and perforated holes at the extremity. Three parallel lines of dots along centre of length and around edge. Double diagonal lines from central lines to edges. Folded.

No. 1508, Plate XXII, Figure 6.—Size $3\frac{15}{16}$" by $1\frac{5}{16}$", weight 20 grs. Oval diadem, with truncated ends. Finely dotted lines along centre of length and across centre of breadth, connected by diagonal lines. Folded.

No. 1509, Plate XXII, Figure 3.—Size $2\frac{13}{16}$" by $\frac{15}{16}$", weight 15 grs. Oval diadem, with ornament similar to 1508, but with deeper dots. Folded.

No. 1587, Plate XXII, Figure 7.—Size 6" by $1\frac{9}{16}$", weight 30 grs. Oval diadem, with strip at each end. Lines along centre and around edges, with triangular dotted lines between. Folded.

No. 1866, Plate XXII, Figure 4.—Size $4\frac{10}{16}$" by $1\frac{10}{16}$", weight 42 grs. Oval diadem, with strip at each end. Lines along centre of length and around edges, with diagonal lines between. Found folded.

Nos. 1867, 1868, Plate XXII, Figures 9 and 11.—Size 1" by $\frac{9}{16}$". Pear shaped drops of a glassy metallic substance covered with gold leaf. Without destroying a part of the gold covering, I have been unable to ascertain the material.

Bronze Ornamental Vase Stands—

In the earlier excavations, some of these curious objects were found, but as they were incomplete, their use was not at first apparent. In the recent excavations, however, a complete example was obtained and shows what the missing parts of the others were. It has a flat circular base, on which stand two tigers. On their backs rest two small shafts supporting a small ring and large flat bowl or vase.[2] Though the designs of all are varied, the general form of base, supporting animals or rods and surmounting bowl or vase, is the same in all.

There seems reason to believe that these vases were used as stands for the large bowls with ornamental lids, elsewhere described.

No. 528.—A circular stand of cast bronze, about 6" in diameter. The base and bowl are missing. The remaining portion in several pieces, which rested on the former and supported the latter, consists of six vertical rods $3\frac{1}{4}$" in length, with moulded circular bases and capitals. From the latter a bent rod curves upwards and inwards towards the centre on to a circular ring $2\frac{1}{4}$" in diameter. On this, stood the bowl. From each vertical rod another rod branches outwards and upwards, each supporting a flat circular disc, 3" in diameter, with another semi-circular disc projecting at right angles, from each. In the urn along with this, was the ornamental surmounting lid

[1] This is the case in all the examples.

[2] Illustrated in Madras G. O. No. 732 Public, dated 18th August 1903. Figure 12.

No. 539, which has similar bent rods and discs; an oval pot; a small chatti; a cylindrical lid, and fragments of a large chatti, two bowls, and a strainer, all in bronze. Outside the urn were an iron knife, iron ring, and a large eight-armed iron hanger.

No. 585.[1]—A cast bronze stand, 4" high, with base and bowl missing. Four buffaloes stand in a circle facing outwards. They are 3" in length, 2" in height, and have flat curved horns 2¾" across. Each animal stands on a cross, below which is a moulded knob. These would rest on the flat circular base or pedestal. On the backs of the animals, rest circular rods 2¼" in length, from the top of which flat rods slope inwards to a central ring 1¾" in diameter. The ring retains a fragment of the upper bowl. It is of very thin wrought metal separate from the cast buffalo stand.

In the same urn was found the ornamental lid No. 586, and various other bronze vessels.

No. 1225.—A vase of thin metal, much twisted and fractured. It has a moulded base, with a width of 5" narrowing above it, into a neck of 1" in diameter. Above this, it widens into a cup perforated with leaves. In the centre of the cup is a stem supporting circular discs. Height 8 inches.

No. 1455.—A cast vase stand similar to the preceding, but the four animals have wide, flat twisted horns, and are thus probably intended for rams. The length of the animals is 4½"; height 2¾"; width of horns 2¾"; and tail 1½". The diameter of the top ring, to which portions of the bowl are attached, is 1¾". The whole height is 5½". It was found lying outside the west of an urn; but one of the rams lay on the east side.

The ornamental lid No. 1456 was found outside the same urn.

Outside the same urn were 5 iron mamuties, an iron axe; a dagger, a long spear, a trident 3' 1½" long, a large iron hanging-lamp, and a saucer lamp with hooks and chain. On the west side a number of bronzes lay in a heap. They were—5 bowls with rice husks, a large flat bowl, fragments of a large bowl with embossed ornaments, fragments of 2 vessels, a sieve with fragments of its bowl, a bell-mouth of a large chatti with fragments, and a broken lid. In pottery there were—a chatti, 4 cups, a cover, and a bowl.

The inside of the urn was filled with earth, and had a cup and jar in bronze; a gold diadem No. 1467, and six pieces of gold leaf, folded as if at one time they had contained something.

No. 1840.—A moulded circular stand, with the top broken away. It has a sloping base 4" in diameter, narrowing to the neck above, to 1¾". The present height is 2".

Bronze Ornamental Bowl Lids—

Though these are evidently surmounting or terminal pieces to some kind of vessel, it was not till a complete example was found in the latest excavations that it could be definitely ascertained what the vessel was. This is seen in Figures 4 and 6 of the Report in Madras G. O. No. 732 Public, dated 18th August 1903.

There are two principal classes of these terminals. One has plain, moulded, pointed knobs, and the other has a vertical central column supporting an animal; while round it are numerous curved radiating rods surmounted by leaves, buds, or discs. A curious combination of the two is seen in No. 1862. They were fixed on to the cylindrical lids of certain kinds of bowls. Bowl No. 452 has the cylindrical lid in position on it with a ring top or handle for lifting it.

No. 484.—A cast moulded pointed circular knob of a cover. It is 3¼" high and 2" in diameter at the base. The lower half is concave moulded, with a ring around the centre: the top is conical. Below the base are pieces of the lid it surmounted, riveted on by a bronze nail.

No. 529, Figure 3.[2]—On a circular convex moulded base, an inch in height, stands a vertical rod, 2½" long, surmounted by triple winged discs. On the base is a circular plate from which

[1] See Plate III to Report in Madras G. O. No. 732 Public, dated 18th August 1903.

[2] Illustrated in Plate I of Report in Madras G. O. No. 732 Public, dated 18th August 1903.

twelve arms curve outwards and upwards. Each arm is surmounted by a flat circular disc, 1⅜" in diameter; each has a semi-disc on the outer face. The breadth across the arms is 6".

No. 586.[1]—A cast bronze lid terminal with a central column supporting a buffalo and twelve curved rods or arms—of which only five are complete radiating around. On each of the arms is a pointed pear-shaped bud. The length of the arms is 5", and the buds 2". The total height is 4½".

No. 1078.—Part of a cast bronze lid terminal, similar to No. 586. It has had eleven curved arms, radiating from a moulded centre piece, each of which has had a pointed bud on the end, all except one damaged by fallen *débris*. In the centre is a pillar supporting a buffalo 3¼" in length with wide, flat, curved horns. Under the circular plate is a circular moulded base. The full height is 6".

Fig. 3.

Fig. 4.

No. 1087, Figure 4.—Grotesque image of cock forming the op of bronze lid. It stands on and is riveted to a dome-shaped moulded circular base, which would be attached to the lid now almost entirely away. Base has a triangular ornament around. Body of the cock is of circular section, the comb flat, and the tail also, in two curved feathers, is of flat metal. It is of one piece of metal with a short column on which it stands. The total height is 6".

No. 103.—The remains of a cast bent armed lid. There have been eleven arms of 4½", each topped by a pointed bud. They radiate from a central circular plate in which is a hole for fixing the circular pillar seen in more complete examples.

No. 1234, Figure 5.—A cast knob top of a lid, probably for the bowl No. 1233. It is similar to the knob No. 484 but is more complete in that at the junction of the moulded convex lower half and the conical top, there is a portion of a wide moulding which has encircled it. At the base is a nail for fixing on to the broken-off lid.

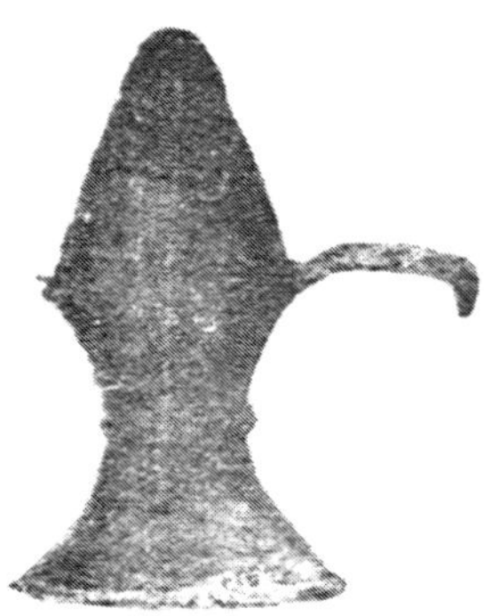

Fig. 5.

No. 1456.—The ornamental top of a lid found along with the stand No. 1455. It has twelve bent arms with branches, each bearing a round fruit radiating from a circular plate, and four birds perched on a central shaft Under the plate, as it lay in the earth, a fluted bulb was clearly visible, but as the metal was as thin as paper and completely oxidized, it was impossible to remove this part of it. The total height is 5". The arms curve outwards and upwards, then branch into two—one inwards and the other outwards. The round fruits on the outer branches are ⅞" in diameter, while those on the inner branches are slightly smaller, being ⅝" in

[1] Illustrated in Plate I of Report in Madras G. O. No. 732 Public, dated 18th August 1903.

diameter. The central pillar rises vertically for 2¾" and then branches into four, on the top which are the four birds. These are 1¾" long and 1¼" high with outstretched wings.

No. 1480.—An ornamental lid, much decayed and fragmentary, with curved branched rods supporting buds, a buffalo, etc.

Underneath is a circular moulded base with a circular plate over it, from which radiate nine curved arms, 5" long. At about the middle of the length a branch goes out, and each of them is surmounted by an elongated pointed bud. In the centre of the centre plate is a hole through which passed the pillar supporting a horned buffalo, as in other examples described. It is 3½" long and 2¾" high.

Along with this were found some disconnected objects which are probably fragments of the stand for the bowl of which the above was the lid. They are canoe-shaped with a short rod strutting out diagonally from near each convex end, and a short vertical pillar from the concave side. Two are fairly complete, and others are in fragments. They may have been placed between the pedestal and bowl of the vase, and would stand radiating from the centre as are the animals described in other examples.

No. 1507.—A surmounting top with under dome and bent arms with round fruits or buds and central buffalo above.

Over a dome of thin metal is a circular moulding, with a plate above, from which twelve bent arms radiate outwards and upwards. Five of these arms have each a bull on the top, the others are broken off. A central column supports a cross piece on which stands a horned buffalo. The total height is 6" by a width of 5½".

No. 1586.—A broken lid consisting of a small dome 1⅜" in diameter with a circular moulding above. Over this is a column with fragments of six radiating curved leaves, which seem to have been intended for those of mangoes. On the top of the column is an animal with a curved trunk, probably representing an elephant.

No. 1839.—Along with some bowls, a bell lid with a knob on the summit was found. It is similar to those so usual in pottery. It is 4" high with a diameter of 3". The knob is conical, with a rim at its base.

No. 1862.—This is an interesting example of a lid terminal consisting of a central pointed knob from which radiate a number of curiously twisted wires. It has probably been affixed to the cylindrical lid No. 1860. It was found among a heap of other bronzes in the bottom of an urn.

The knob is similar to the others before described, but it has, in addition, a small bell or dome below, of very thin metal vertically grooved in close lines.

Some of the twisted arms have been broken off. A reference to the plate will show their design.

Fragments of another object, with similar twisted wires, were found beside it. Their design is somewhat different from that of the other. These probably belonged to the supporting vase or stand. The central piece has a ring, which has had nine radiating arms, on which the twisted wires were fixed. A fragment of a thin flat plate adheres to the ring.

Bronze Bowls, Jars and Cups—

No. 244.—A semi-globular pot, 6" in diameter, with cylindrical rim, 4" in diameter. A plain bead moulding is at the junction of the rim. It is somewhat fractured.

No. 246.—A small bowl or cup, 3½" in diameter at the rim, body slightly wider, depth 3", and flat bottom 2½" in diameter. At the rim is a circular indented line.

It is smooth and somewhat polished in parts, and is complete except a slight fracture.

Nos. 286 and 287.—An elongated bronze jar with a cylindrical lid, lying in a platter. The metal is oxidized and the jar is unopened. The platter is in several pieces and is 9" in diameter.

The jar is 6½″ high by 4½″ broad. A fine jar in pottery (No. 266) of the same shape, with its cylindrical lid, were found in another urn.

No. 291.—A bowl 4¼″ in diameter and 2½″ deep. It has a flat base, 1¾″ in diameter.

No. 296.—A cylindrical cup with a taper inwards towards the flat base. A small bead moulding is around the rim. Diameter at rim 4¼″, at base 3½″, and height 2⅜″.

No. 299.—A plain jar with a slight crack on one side. At some places it retains a polish, but at others it is corroded. Its height is 5½″, the diameter at the rim is 3½″, and at the body, near the base, 4¼″.

No. 300.—A bowl 4″ in diameter by 2⅝″ deep. The rim is of slightly less diameter than the body. Around it is an ornamental incised band of diagonally crossed lines.

No. 344.—A semi-globular pot similar to No. 244, but of wider diameter. It is corroded and fractured in parts. At the mouth is a cylindrical rim and bead band, 5″ in diameter, separate from the pot. It is 6¼″ in diameter by 5″ deep. The bottom is concave on the exterior.

No. 397.—A small bowl, 4½″ in diameter by 3″ in height. It has been crushed into an oval shape. The surface is generally smooth and polished, and at one place, near the rim, is a dotted incised design of an upright line, with a small circle on its left, and two concentric circles on its right.

Fig. 6.

Fig. 7.

No. 452, Figure 6.—A pot similar to No. 344, but with a cylindrical lid and ring handle on the top. It has a cylindrical rim with an incised ornament under it, of parallel diagonal lines. The ring handle on the top is 3½″ high and is joined to the lid by a small moulded column. The metal in some parts bears a polish having the appearance of gilt. The vessel is 5¼″ in diameter and 4¼″ in depth.

No. 532.—A small flat saucer or plate, 7″ in diameter and 2″ deep.

No. 583, Figure 7.—A circular vessel fractured on one side. It is 5¾″ in diameter at the mouth by 5¼″ deep. The body is of greater breadth. Around it is a broad band of two bead mouldings with zig-zag incised lines between. These form a series of adjacent upright and reversed triangles, having the former filled with diagonal crossed lines and the latter plain.

No. 706.—A jar with cylindrical rim and lid. A bead moulding around the foot of the rim acts as a stop to the lid. The height is 5¼″, diameter of the body 5″, and lid 4″.

No. 707.—A bowl, broken on one side, with cylindrical rim, and a moulding of four narrow parallel beads around. It is 4″ in diameter and 2¼″ in depth. It has traces of cloth oxidized and adhering to the metal.

No. 1064.—A globular pot with one side crushed against the urn. The surface is smooth and retains a polish. It has a cylindrical rim with a fillet and bead moulding below. The diameter of the pot is 5½"; of the rim 4¼"; and the depth is 5".

No. 1077.—A bowl with two broad bead mouldings around it. It has a flat lid with a small conical projection in the centre. It is 5¼" in diameter and 3¼" deep.

No. 1086, Figure 8.—A bowl with a cylindrical rim. Around it are two spaced bead mouldings with a broad, flat, wavy bead between. It is similar to No. 1505, but in the latter, the ornament is flat, triangular, or zig-zag, instead of wavy. A small part of the lid yet remains, and on it are traces of cloth. It is 4½" in diameter; and 3¼" deep.

No. 1153.—A jar with the cylindrical lid tilted over on one side, and some bones adhering to the other. It has a cylindrical rim with bead moulding below. Its height is 5½", breadth at the rim 4¼," and diameter of the lid 4⅜."

No. 1161, Figure 9.—A small jar with a bead moulded mouth, ⅞" broad. It doubtless had the usual cylindrical rim above this. Its height is 4" and breadth at the rim 3½".

No. 1233.—A globular pot, cracked and twisted at one side of the rim. Inside, a portion not oxidized is as bright as gold. The flat base is convex outside. It is 4½" in diameter and 4⅞" deep.

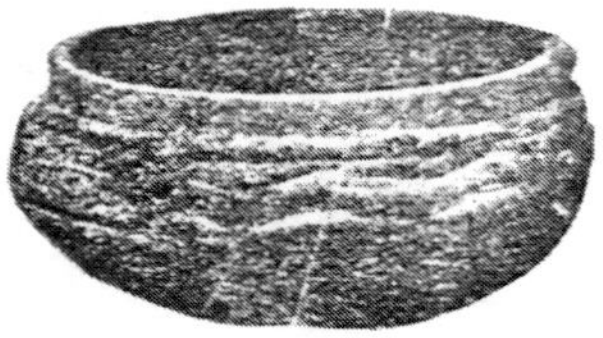

Fig. 8.

Fig. 9.

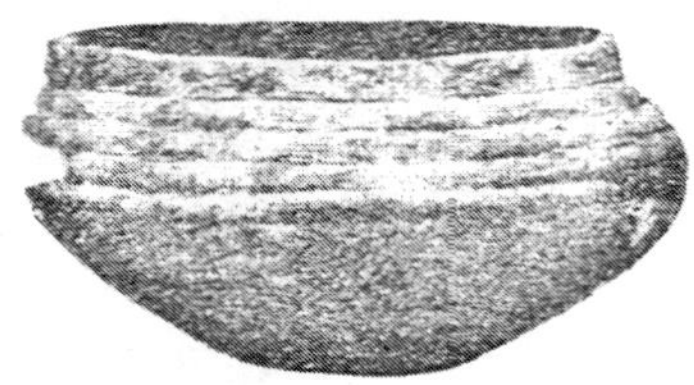

Fig. 10.

No. 1408.—A fragment of a bowl with a horizontal ornament, which would be repeated around it. Two slightly curved lines meet in an acute horizontal angle. The space inside the angle is plain except another small angle at its base. Outside the angle the space is filled with diagonal crossed incised lines. It is similar to that on bowl No. 1674.

No. 1445, Figure 10.—A bowl partly broken at one side, with narrow cylindrical rim and four broad bead mouldings around it. It is 4¾" in diameter and 4" deep.

No. 1448.—A cup with a small spout or handle ⅝" long projecting from one side. It is 3½" in diameter and 1⅜" deep.

No. 1449.—A large flat bowl or platter, much corroded, twisted and cracked. In its perfect condition it has been similar to the pottery platter No. 1429. The bottom is flat, and the side nearly vertical. It is 10" in diameter and 2" deep.

No. 1451.—Fragments of a large bowl with a series of embossed line and dot ornaments. The embossing is from the inside, so that all the ornamentation is raised. These bowls have been basin shaped; but being of large size and very thin metal largely oxidized, none was got unbroken. They were all found in a crushed condition, so that only the parts could be collected, and the size cannot be determined.

Some have horizontal parallel raised lines with an interspace of ⅜" of convex surface with small convex beads in rows, others have zig-zag lines in one space, with a row of beads below; then a series of horizontal set angles fitting into each other. Below this again are zig-zags and beads, all being separated by lines.

Another design has a row of small upright lines, 5" long, with a bead drop at the bottom of each. Below this are several rows of double beads.

No. 1505.—A bowl with one side broken; around it, is a zig-zag bead ornament. It is 5" in diameter; and 4" high.

No. 1575-1.—A cup with narrow cylindrical rim and wavy bead ornament below it. The bead meets in a point at each bend on the upper side. Diameter 3¾", depth 2¼". This was found inside No. 1575.

No. 1575-2.—A cup which lay inside No. 1575-1. Around it is an incised line ornament of a series of acute angles lying point to base horizontally. They are bounded by a horizontal line above, and another beneath. The space between them is filled with diagonally crossed lines. Size 3½" in diameter, 2" deep.

No. 1576.—A jar or cup with its cylindrical lid complete. A bead moulding surrounds the jar on which the lid rests. Height 4", diameter at top 2¾".

No. 1673.—A flat cylindrical vessel of thin metal with a beaded rim. It is evidently the lid of a jar. It is 4" in diameter and 1½" deep.

No. 1674.—A large vessel with incised triangular line ornament around. It is similar to but larger than that on No. 1572-2. Inside are some husks of rice and millet. Size 6¼" in diameter by 5" deep.

No. 1839.—A fragmentary crushed and twisted bowl with the ring mouth separate. The diameter of the ring is 4". A bell-shaped lid was also got inside it; and this is described under the same number along with the section on lids.

All the above bowls, etc., have been photographed. There are a number of others more or less fragmentary which have not been.

Bronze Sieve Cups and Strainers—

These sieves have been used for straining rice. They are in the form of small perforated cups fitted into small basins. The metal of the cup is extremely thin, and the basins only a little thicker. The perforations in the cups are by dots arranged in a variety of designs, chiefly concentric circles around the bottom, and concentric semi-circles sometimes interlacing around the rim. They are very finely made, and extremely fragile.

No. 295.—A sieve cup and attached basin found lying inverted on a bronze bowl. The bowl is 4½" in diameter and 2¾" deep. Attached to the sieve, and forming part of it, is a flat basin, 4" in diameter. Being of lesser diameter than the vessel on which it is lying and having been forced on to the latter, a part of it is broken off. The sieve has a bead moulding at its junction with the bowl, is pointed on the bottom, and is perforated with double dotted concentric lines. The sieve and basin are of separate pieces of metal.

No. 510.—A cup sieve, slightly pointed at the bottom, and wider at the body than the rim. It is perforated around the bottom with three concentric rows of triple dotted lines, and four double semi-circles around the rim. It is 2⅔" in diameter and 2½" deep.

No. 698.—A broken cup sieve which has been fitted on to a separate basin or strainer, a portion of which remains attached. The cup is round pointed at the bottom, around which are concentric lines of perforated dots. There are first three close lines, then two, and again three lines. At the rim are crescent shaped lines. The cup is 2¾" in diameter by 3" deep.

No. 803.—A perforated cup sieve, with its attached basin in fragments. Along with them is a bent thick wire handle to be fixed to the basin by small rivets which appear at each end of it. The cup is 3" in diameter by 2½" in height. The basin is 6¾" in diameter and 1¾" deep. The handle is semi-circular, 2" across, with the two ends bent outwards.

No. 1290, Figure 11.—A sieve cup and basin partly broken, similar to No. 1224. It has four concentric circles of perforations at the bottom; another row near the top of the cup and a row of triple semi-circular dotted lines between them. The cup is 2¾" in diameter and 2½" deep.

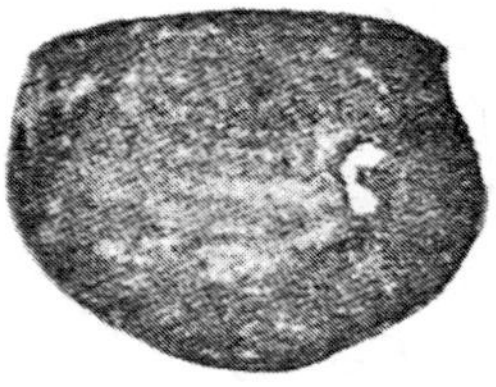

Fig. 11.

No. 1453.—A fractured sieve cup, with fragments of its bowl attached. It has the most elaborately perforated designs of any of these examples. Interlacing triple semi-circles are around the rim; while around the bottom are three concentric triple rows with rows of segments of circles between them. Diameter 3"; depth 3".

Bronze, Bell-mouthed Jars or Chatties—

All these vessels are made of very thin wrought metal, and are in consequence more or less fragmentary. The bell-mouth is in one piece, with a separate ring fitted on around the joint at the neck. The upper and the lower curved parts of the body are in separate pieces of metal jointed around the widest diameter. They are of broad flat form.

No. 249.—The fragmentary bell-mouth of a chatti. The rim is bent over; and at the neck is a band for covering the joint between it and the vessel. Diameter 4¾", height 2¼".

No. 252.—A broad, flat, globular vessel with bell-mouth. It has a bead moulding at its widest circumference, and another at the neck. The diameter of the chatti 8⅜", height 5¾". The bell-mouth is 3⅜" in diameter at the rim, and 2⅛ at the neck. It is 2¼" in height.

No. 1454.—A bell-mouthed chatti, 9" in diameter and 6" in height. The bell-mouth is 4⅛" in diameter at the rim and 2½" in height. It is similar to No. 252.

Nos. 1477 and 1477-1.—The upper and lower portions of a bell-mouthed chatti similar to No. 225, except that the bell-mouth has a wider curve. Diameter 9", height 4¾".

Bronze Plaques—

No. 241.—A round hollow platter, 5¾" in diameter and ¾" deep. The upper surface is hollow, the lower convex. There is a small chip off one part of the edge; and another break at the rim appears as if a handle had been fixed there, as the rim curves slightly outwards. No trace of a handle was however found. It probably may have been similar to that on No. 294.

No. 294, Figure 12.—A flat moulded plaque, 5¾" in diameter with flat triangular pointed handle, 1½" long, projecting from the rim. Around the circumference is a broad flat bead moulding, with a small concentric bead outside and another inside it. The under side is flat; the upper very slightly convex.

No. 577. Figure 13.—A flat moulded plaque, 7" in diameter. The metal is much oxidized. Around the rim is a flat fillet, ⅞" broad. In the centre is a knob, encircled by a bead moulding 2¼" in diameter.

The under side is flat.

No. 1856.—A broken irregular shaped piece of thin flat bronze, 9" broad, with a circular boss in the centre, 2¼" in diameter. Around the boss is a bead moulding, and in its centre, a small knob.

No. 1452 is a fragment of a similar boss.

Bangles—

Those below described are plain, but the later excavations discovered some with bells attached, such as are used by dancers. These are not here described.

No. 237.—Three bangles of thick wire, cut square off at the ends, which are some space apart. The circumference of each is about 6½".

No. 904.—A pair of wire bangles with pointed knob ends overlapping. Diameter 2″.

Fig. 12.

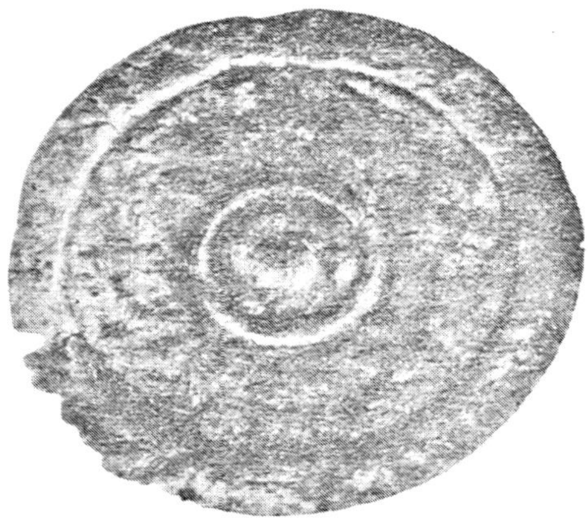

Fig. 13.

Necklace—

No. 1616, Figure 14.—A necklace composed of 373 minute finely made rings of square cut wire. They lay scattered about in the earth of an urn, and were collected in a sieve. They are now strung on a thread, and give a length of $8\frac{3}{4}$″.

Along with them were a small hollow cone, and two round hollow ball bells with a wire and ring attached. The bells are made in two pieces well fitted together. The cone has apparently been used as a fastening.

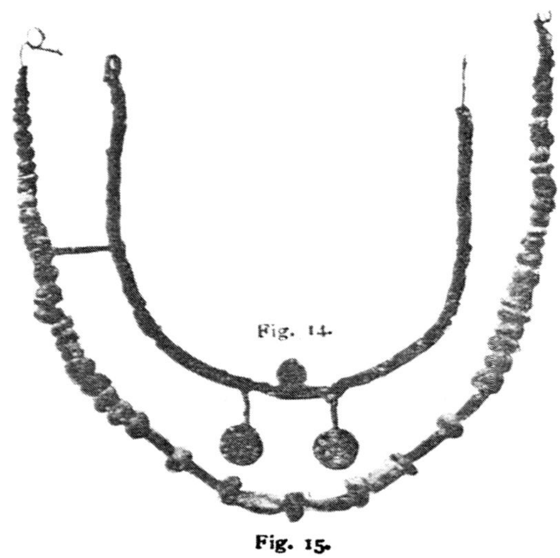

Fig. 14.

Fig. 15.

In some other examples of these necklaces afterwards found, there were traces of a thread, preserved by oxidation inside the rings, showing that this material, and not a wire, had been used in stringing them. They had also small bronze beads attached to alternate rings.

Ear Ornament—

No. 315.—A flat coil of thin wire, with one end projecting. It is seemingly an ornament for the ear. Diameter ⅜″.

No. 1552.—A small cylindrical coiled wire ring in pieces. It has probably been a finger ring. Diameter ½″.

Bronze Diadems—

No. 984.—A folded diadem of thin metal measuring 1¼″ in length and breadth. Several of the gold diadems were similarly folded, but owing to the greater flexibility of the latter metal, the folding was not confined to one direction as with this bronze example.

No. 1313.—An oval badge or diadem of thick metal retaining its bent form. It has a dotted ornament on the surface, as with the gold diadems, but owing to corrosion the design cannot be traced. It has traces of cloth attached. Length 5″, breadth 2¾″.

Though this is the same shape as the gold diadem, I am not prepared to affirm that it is one. It is of thick metal while the diadems of gold and bronze are thin. Arm badges are now used for various purposes, and the custom may have had an ancient origin. Its curved surface is greater than that which could fit a brow. This may thus be either an arm badge or a diadem. But I think it likely to be the former.

No. 1553.—An oval bronze diadem of thin metal with embossed dotted ornament and hole at each end, as with those in gold. Size 1¾″ by 1¾″.

Stylos—

Nos. 696 and 974.—Two rods pointed at each end, 7⅜″ and 5⅜″, respectively, in length, ⅛″ thick. The former has traces of having been wrapped in cloth. They are apparently stylos.

Moulded Tubes and Bulbs—

Nos. 975 and 1432. Figure 16.—Two circular tubes of similar shape resembling scent bottles. Narrow at the top, they gradually increase in width to a bulbous form at the foot. Underneath is a narrow neck which spreads out to a wide base. On the top is an umbrella-shaped stopper, broken, in the second example. The length is divided into three parts by horizontal bead mouldings. They are 4½″ and 4″ in length, the lesser length being due to the broken stopper. No. 1432 has a piece of cloth attached.

Fig. 16

No. 1275.—Two oval hollow bulbs with an opening at each end, 2½″ long by 1½″ in diameter.

Three other hollow bulbs are pear-shaped, with a circular opening at each end, and a slight moulding at the narrow end which is prolonged into a neck. These are 1⅝″ long by 1⅛″ broad.

It is doubtful what these are. They may either have been strung to form part of a belt, or put on the wooden handle of some implement.

Cornelian Beads—

Nos. 372 and 1058.—Crystal or other mineral beads are uncommon in these sites, and only a few were seen. None of the inlaid kind found in Madura and elsewhere were got.[1]

Two cornelian beads. The first is pointed pear-shaped, with a hole pierced at right angles through the broad end. The other is barrel-shaped, with a hole through it longitudinally.

[1] See *Prehist. Bur. places in S. India*, where some examples of inlaid and other beads are illustrated.

Iron Swords and Daggers—

All the swords and daggers have either a spike at the hilt or a curved pick-shaped piece of iron, on to which a wooden handle was attached. In this respect they are different from spears, javelins, and arrows which have hollow tube handles into which the wooden shaft was fixed. In several, wooden traces preserved by rust, remain. The spike is the most usual, and it has been preserved from splitting the wooden handle by the use of an iron ring which exists in some examples Those with the pick-shaped hilt have iron nails for fixing the wood. The sheaths have been of wood, as several specimens show. The blades are of various shape, and will be separately described. All are double-edged.

It is sometimes difficult to differentiate between javelins and arrows, especially with small specimens of the former. But it may be generally taken, as a rule, with possibly some exceptions, that those of spear-head shape are javelins, and the barbed weapons are arrows.

No. 201, Plate XXIII, Figure 9.—A sword of the concave edge and ribbed kind, like No. 300. It is 2′ 1½″ long by 2½″ broad. The rib on the flat surface runs from the hilt to the point. The concave edges are near the rim; above which they taper in convex shape to the point. There is a ring at the hilt for attaching the wooden handle, of which there are traces.

No. 230, Plate XXIII, Figure 14.—A parallel sided angular pointed sword with raised line up the centre from hilt to point. Handle worn and pointed, 2′ 4″ long by 2″ broad. Distinct signs of the sheath appear, some pieces of wood being attached to the blade.

No. 390, Plate XXIII, Figure 3.—A curious shaped short sword of which there are some more complete examples. It is in three pieces, and measures 1′ 9½″ by 1¾″ at its greatest breadth. From the hilt to near the middle of the length the two edges are concave, with a raised ridge in the centre of the breadth. Thence the edges gradually taper to the point, which is corroded and worn off. The iron handle tapers to a point and bears traces of the wooden handle. Signs of wood are also on the blade.

No. 445, Plate XXIII, Figure 8.—A sword in five pieces, 1′ 10½″ long by 2½″ broad. The handle is missing, and next it, as part of the blade, is a fillet. The blade has parallel edges, with a tapering point. It has been made of two plates of metal, as is clearly visible near the hilt where it is dented and split, probably caused by a blow of the weapon.

No. 478.—A sword with parallel sides, and angular point. Length 2′ 4½″ by 2½″. The spiked handle is 2¾″ in length. There are traces of wood on the blade.

No. 890, Plate XXIII, Figure 25.—A sword with spiked handle, and the point broken off. There is a slightly raised line along the centre. Length 1′ 1½″ by 2″.

No. 1004, Plate XXIII, Figure 15.—A triangular pointed sword with remains of wood on blade and handle, 2′ 1¼″ long by 1¾″ broad. A ring is attached to the hilt.

No. 1005, Plate XXIII, Figure 7.—A sword similar to No. 390, Plate XXIII, Fig. 3, with the point worn off. It has a rib up the centre, and concave edges near the hilt. Length 1′ 4½″ by 1¾″.

No. 1013, Plate XXIII, Figure 12.—A bent sword with parallel edges and curved angular point, 2′ 4″ long, by 2½″ broad. There is a fillet ring near the spiked handle. Signs of the wooden sheath appear on the blade.

No. 1101, Plate XXIII, Figure 13.—A long bent sword, 2′ 5½″ long by 2½″. The flat angle is rectangular, 4½″ long by 1½″ broad. A raised line runs up the centre of each side from hilt to point. The point is slightly concave angular. Wood appears both on the handle and blade.

No. 1232.—A bent sword with spiked handle, fillet band at the hilt, and angular point. It is 2¼″ broad throughout. On both sides are traces of wood. Length 2′ 3″.

No. 1262.—A curved edged sword with its greatest breadth at the centre of the length. From there it tapers convexly to the point, and with a flat concave curve to the hilt. The handle tapers from the hilt to a blunt point. From the hilt, a raised line proceeds up the centre of the blade for a length of 1′ 1″. Length 2′ 10½″ by 2″.

No. 1263.—A sword with the greatest breadth about the middle, from whence it sharply tapers by a flat convex curve to the point on the one side, and by a concave curve to the hilt on the other. A raised line appears along the centre for the length of a foot from the hilt. The flat handle has traces of wood and is 2¼″ long by an inch broad. Length 2′ 5½″ by 2½″.

No. 1311, Plate XXIII, Figure 5.—The point of a sword, 8″ by 2″.

No. 1336.—A spike-handled angular-pointed sword, with parallel edges. At the hilt is a broad fillet. Near the handle on one side are distinct traces of cloth and wood. Length 1′ 10″ by 2″

No. 1391.—A parallel edged sword with angular point. The handle is 4¾″ long, and is of curious shape, being 3″ broad at the convex curved extremity, and joining the hilt by concave curves. Through it project six nails, with traces of wood. Length 2′ 2¼″ by 1¾″.

No. 1420, Plate XXIII, Figure 11.—A parallel edged sword with angular point 2′ 4½″ long—including the handle, which is broken off—and 2½″ broad. It has a slightly raised line along the centre of each side of the blade, from hilt to point. There is a fillet at the hilt; and the handle is flat pick shaped, with traces of wood. When complete, the handle would resemble that on No. 1440.

No. 1440.—A parallel edged sword with angular point. The flat handle is a more pronounced form of that of No. 1391. The curved end is pickaxe-shape 5″ long curving in and upwards to the hilt. It has seven nails projecting through each side, and traces of wood. Length 2′ 8″ by 2¼″.

No. 1469, Plate XXIII, Figure 10.—A concave edged sword of the kind described under No. 390 and others. It is 2′ 4¾″ long by 2¼″ at its broadest. On each side is a ridge, highly raised for 10″ from the hilt, and thence to the point of slighter projection. The edges are concave near the hilt; and convex at the upper portion. There are traces of wood at the handle.

No. 1483.—A bent sword with parallel edges; spiked handle with fillet; and angular point. Has traces of wood on both sides. Length 2′ 3½″ by 2″.

No. 1642, Plate XXIII, Figure 42.—A sword with spiked handle and angular point, in three pieces. It is touched with wood throughout. Length 1′ 7¾″ by a uniform breadth of 1½″.

No. 1668.—A parallel edged sword, with spiked handle and fillet, and a curved angular point. A slightly raised line runs up the centre from the hilt to the point. There are wood traces on the handle and blade. Length 2′ 1¾″.

No. 1724, Plate XXIII, Figure 17.—A portion of a sword. The point and about half of the length are missing. The handle is spike-shaped, on the blade are traces of cloth. Length 1′ 4½″ by 2¼″ broad.

No. 1749, Plate XXIII, Figure 6.—A sword in two pieces 1′ 5¼″ by 2″. The pointed handle is 1½″ long. It has a tapering point. There is wood on the blade, indicating a wooden sheath.

No. 1820, Plate XXIII, Figure 16.—A much corroded sword with curved convex point, and handle broken off. A slightly raised longitudinal line appears on the centre. Length 1′ 6½″ by 1¾″ broad.

No. 1821, Plate XXIII, Figure 18.—A sword with curved convex point, and handle broken off. Slight line up the centre. It has traces of wood. Length 1′ 4¼″ by 2.″

Daggers—

No. 297, Plate XXIII, Figure 29.—A dagger with spiked handle and worn angular point. has indications of a coarsely woven cloth. Length 9¾″ by 1½″.

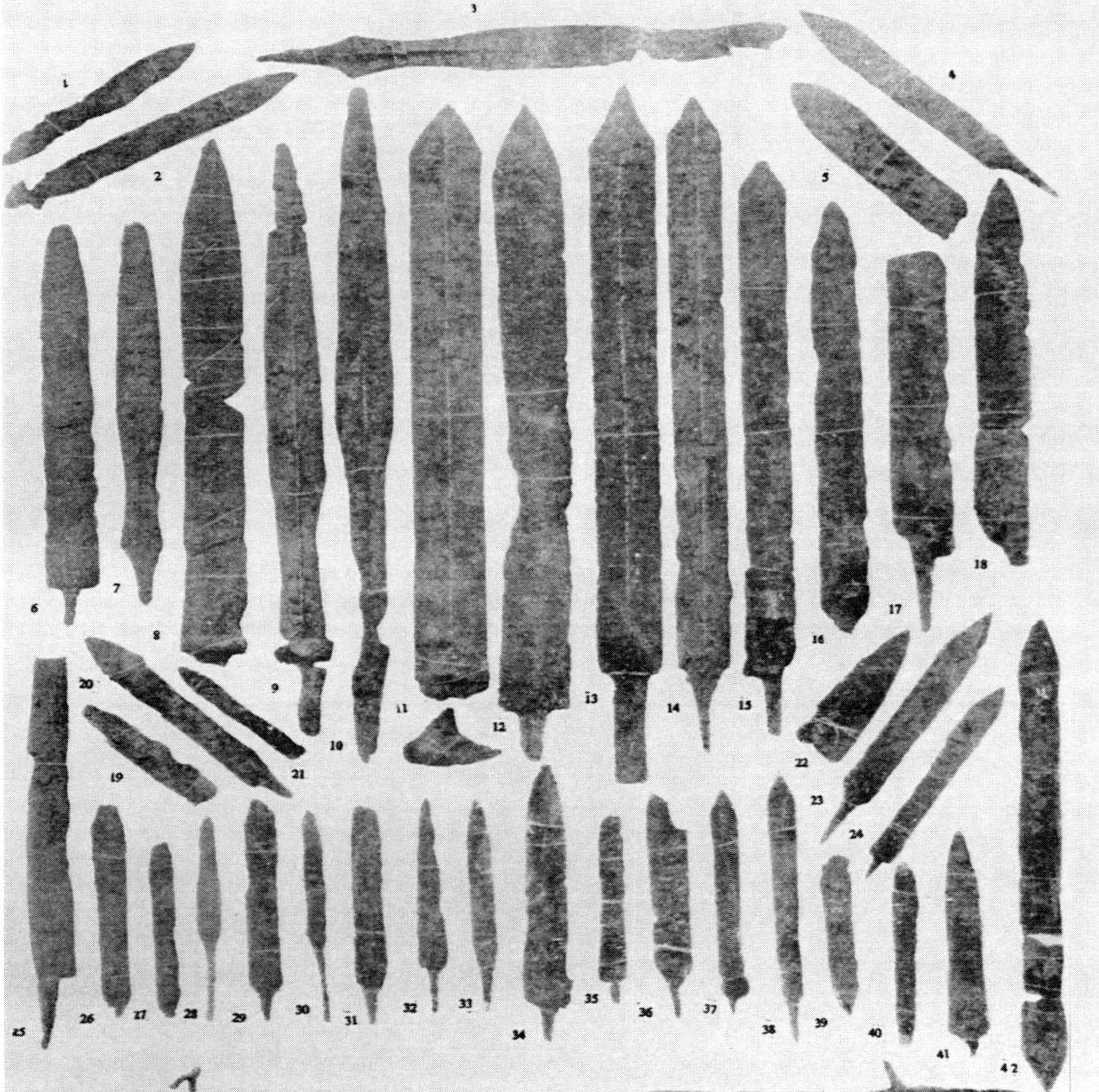

IRON WEAPONS AND IMPLEMENTS.

No. 305, Plate XXIII, Figure 28.—A dagger with a blade resembling a spear. The blade tapers to near the point where it is rounded. The spiked handle is of square nail section and is proportionately long, measuring 3½", while the blade is 5¼" by ¾".

No. 423, Plate XXIII, Figure 26.—A dagger with point and spiked handle slightly worn off. Length 11" by 1¼".

No. 451.—A dagger with spiked handle. Length 8½" by ¾".

No. 534, Plate XXIII, Figure 36.—A broad dagger with spiked handle and the point broken off. The centre is slightly raised throughout. Length 10" by 1½".

No. 534, Plate XXIII, Figure 41.—A spike handled dagger with the greatest breadth at the hilt, whence it gradually tapers to near the point, which is convex curved. Length 9¾" by 1¼".

No. 945, Plate XXIII, Figure 39.—A corroded dagger with point and handle worn off. Length 7" by 1".

No. 991, Plate XXIII, Figure 19.—A dagger, handle missing. Length 6½" by 1½".

No. 1012, Plate XXVIII, Figure 35.—A dagger, with a ring at the spiked handle. It bears signs of wood. Length 7¼" by 1".

No. 1110, Plate XXVIII, Figure 2.—A dagger, 12½" by 1¼". The pin for fixing into a wooden handle, and a ring for the latter remain. The tapering point is slightly broken.

No. 1149, Plate XXIII, Figure 1.—A dagger, 9" by 1¼". It is somewhat worn, and only a small part of the handle remains. The point is rounded angular.

No. 1216, Plate XXIII, Figure 33.—A dagger with spiked handle and rounded angular point. There is a slight trace of wood at the handle. Length 8¼" by 1".

No. 1265, Plate XXIII, Figure 20.—A dagger with spike handle and convex curved point. Traces of wood at the handle. Length 10" by 1¼" broad.

No. 1366, Plate XXIII, Figure 24.—A dagger with spiked handle and angular point. There is a ring at the hilt. Length 9¾" by 1".

No. 1367, Plate XXIII, Figure 27.—A dagger, much corroded, with handle and point worn off. Length 8" by 1".

No. 1416, Plate XXIII, Figure 21.—A dagger, handle missing. It has an angular point 6" by ¾".

No. 1417.—A dagger with spear-shaped blade. Length 6½" by 1¼". Handle 2¼" long.

No. 1438, Plate XXIII, Figure 4.—A dagger 12½" by 1½". The pointed handle is 2¼" long. It is similar to No. 1110, but without the handle ring. There are some wooden traces at the handle.

No. 1470, Plate XXIII, Figure 31.—A dagger with spiked handle having traces of wood. Length 9¾" by 1¼".

No. 1492, Plate XXIII, Figure 37.—A dagger with angular point, and a ring at the spike handle. There are traces of wood at the ring. Length 10" by 1" at the angular point, where the breadth is slightly more than at the hilt.

No. 1568, Plate XXIII, Figure 23.—A dagger with spiked handle and curved angular point. There is wood on the handle. Length 6¼" by 2¼".

No. 1667, Plate XXIII, Figure 38.—A dagger with angular point and spiked handle. The greatest breadth is at the angular point, where it is an inch broad. There are signs of wood at the handle. Length 1'.

No. 1723.—A dagger with a thin handle having a flat knob at its end. Length 1' 1" by 1¼".

No. 1748, Plate XXIII, Figure 34.—A large sized dagger with a spike handle and convex curved point. There is a ring at the hilt. Wood appears on the blade and handle. Length 10½" by 1¾".

No. 1787, Plate XXIII, Figure 30.—A spear-shaped dagger, resembling No. 305, Plate XXIII, Figure 28. The handle is thin and long in proportion to the blade. The total length is 6½" by ¾".

No. 1809.—A dagger with handle concavely curved and a flat knob at its end, pierced with a hole. Length 1' 2¼" by 1¼".

No. 1810, Plate XXIII, Figure 32.—A dagger with sharply tapering blade like a spear. It has a short spiked handle of 2" in length, with slight traces of wood. The total length is 9¼".

No. 1823, Plate XXIII, Figure 40.—A curved dagger with point and handle missing. The greatest breadth is near the point, where it is an inch across. Length 7¾".

Tridents and Śūlaṁ or Lances—

No. 1082.—A *śūlaṁ*, 2' 4" long. The round handle extends from half the length and is grooved. The remainder is flat.

No. 1261.—A lance or *śūlaṁ* 3' 4½" long. The shaft is corroded and bent, and is 1' 11½" long. It has a knob on the end, and traces of a spiral fluting can be seen. The lance is flat, with a blunt point. There is a cross-bar, but its arms are broken off.

No. 1368, Plate XXIII, Figure 44.—A *śūlaṁ* or lance with the handle worn away by corrosion. The flat blade also does not represent the original length. There is a cross-piece with remains of bent arms. Length 1' 3".

Fig. 17.

No. 1441, Figure 17.—A trident or *triśūlaṁ* 3' 1½" long. The handle is 2' long by half an inch square, with a round knob at the end. At the base of the three prongs is a cross-bar which extends out into a small knob on each side, and a curved rod underneath connects the bases of the central and side prongs. The prongs are flat and pointed at the extremities. The side ones spread out from a breadth of 6¼" at the base to 8¼" at the points.

No. 1569.—A lance or *śūlaṁ*, 2' 7" long. For a length of 4" the handle is spiral fluted, the remainder is plain. At the base is a knob. The lance is flat and pointed. At its junction with the shaft is a flat cross-piece, with four projecting bent arms, three of which are broken.

No. 1669.—A lance or *śūlaṁ*, 2' 10½" long, similar to No. 1569. The spiral portion of the shaft is 10" long, and the whole handle 1' 8". The arms of the cross-bar are slightly bent at each end, two of these are complete.

No. 1756, Plate XXIII, Figure 43.—A *śūlaṁ* or lance with worn corroded shaft and flat blade. At the top of the shaft is a cross-piece, which has had four bent arms like more complete examples elsewhere described. Length 1' 3¾".

No. 1757.—A lance or *śūlaṁ*, 3' 7½" long. The shaft is 2' 1½" long, is round, and has a knob at the end. The lance is flat with a flat point. A bent cross-bar is fixed at the top of the shaft.

No. 1825.—A lance or *śūlaṁ*, 1' 11½" long, with the point of the lance at the end of the shaft broken off. The handle is square in section, and 1' 2½" long The flat cross-bar has the remains of four bent arms.

Spears—

No. 1011.—A spear 1' 4½" long, with blade 2" broad at centre, tapering to handle and point. Extending up a portion of each centre of the blade is a raised line. The handle is 5" long, and has a nail or rivet through it, at ½" from the end. Inside are traces of wood.

No. 1267.—A spear or crowbar, 1′ 1¾″ long, 1¼″ broad at the base, and ½″ at the top, with blunt point. It has no flat blade; but is rectangular in cross section. The hollow in the end has traces of the wooden shaft which was fixed therein.

No. 1364.—A spear with long narrow blade similar to No. 1666. Length 17″ by 1″ at the handle where it is broadest. The handle is 3½″ long and has traces of the wooden shaft.

No. 1389.—A spear with the blade broadest near the handle. Length 1′ 4¾″ long by 1¾″. The handle is 4″ in length and contains traces of wood.

No. 1415.—A spear 1′ 11½″ long by 2½″. The blade is broadest close to the handle. The handle is 6¼″ long and has a nail through it, at ¾″ from the end. It has traces of wood.

No. 1439.—A spear 1′ 9¼″ long by 1¼″ breadth of blade. The blade is broadest in the middle, tapering to handle and point; and has a central ridge in the centre of each face ne. r the handle. The latter is 7½″ long and contains traces of wood.

No. 1482.—A spear of extra size, 2′ 4″ long by 2″. The blade is broadest near the handle. The latter is 4″ long, and has a nail through it, at ¼″ from the end. Inside are traces of wood.

No. 1635.—A spear 1′ 9″ long by 1¾″. The blade tapers from its greatest breadth near the handle. The latter is 5¼″ long, and contains traces of wood.

No. 1666.—A long spear with narrow blade, a diminutive of No. 1482. The greatest breadth of blade is near the handle. Length 1′ 6″ by 1″. The handle is 4½″ long, and has traces of wood.

No. 1725.—A broad bladed spear, 1′ 6½″ long by 2½″. The ends of the blade join the handle at right angles as with the swords. It is the only example of this. The edges are nearly parallel and end in a sharp point. The handle is 2¾″ long, and has remains of a nail and traces of wood.

No. 1726.—A spear with blade broadest in the middle, and tapering to point and handle. Length 1′ 4½″ by 1½″. Handle 4″ long, contains a piece of wood.

Arrows—

No. 512.—A barbed arrow, with part of hollow handle attached, 3″ by ¾″.

No. 1661.—A barbed arrow, with a barb and point broken, 6″ by 1″. Socket 2½″, has traces of wood.

No. 1662.—A barbed arrow, with a barb away, 6⅛″ by ¾″. Socket 2″, has wood inside.

No. 1663.—A barbed arrow, with a barb broken, 7″ by ⅞″. Socket 2½″.

Javelins—

No. 741.—A javelin, with the two sides of the blade differently curved, one side is almost barbed at the handle, and the other has a tapering convex curve. Length 6¾″ by ¾″. There is some wood in the tube.

No. 742.—A javelin with the point off. Length 6½″ by ¾″. The socket is 2½″ long, and has some mica attached.

No. 744.—A javelin with the ends of the blade at right angles to the handle, which is partly broken off Length 6″ by ¾″. The socket is 2¼″ long and contains a piece of wood.

No. 1374.—A javelin, with about half of the blade away. Length 3½″ by ¾″. The socket is 2″ long, is split and contains wood.

No. 1375.—A javelin, with part of the handle and point away. Length 4½″ by 1″. The socket contains wood.

No. 1376.—A javelin, 7¼″ long by ¾″ breadth of blade. Socket 2″ long, contains a piece of wood.

No. 1419.—A javelin, 5¾″ long by ¾″ breadth of blade. Socket ¾″ long.

Sacrificial Daggers—

No. 260.—A stiletto-shaped implement with spear point. The handle branches into four plates near the blade. The end of the handle is flattened, and has a nail through it. A similar implement is now-a-days used for impaling sacrificial fowls. Length 5¾″.

No. 307.—A sacrificial stiletto, resembling No. 260, but less complete, 3½″ long.

Iron Hatchets or Axes—

Iron axes are of a thick plate of flat metal with straight sides. The cutting edge is flat rounded, with a breadth greater than the butt. A number of them have flat oval detached rings, and probably all of them at one time had these rings placed diagonally near the butt end, through which the shaft would go. All these rings were found attached diagonally.

No. 311.—An axe 7½″ long by 2½″; with ring 3″ by 1¾″. Has traces of wood.

No. 480.—An axe 7½″ long by 2¼″; with diagonal ring 3″ by 1½″. Traces of wood on the axe and in the ring.

No. 481.—A corroded axe, an inch thick at the handle end, where it is of several thicknesses of metal. Length 7¼″ by 2½″.

No. 502.—An axe, 9″ long by 3⅛″ with diagonal ring 3⅜″ by 1½″. Has traces of wood on the blade and in the ring.

No. 503.—An axe, corroded and worn, 8″ long by 2½″; with half of a diagonal ring 3½″ long.

No. 863.—An axe, 5½″ long by 1⅞″; with diagonal ring, 2½″ by 1½″. Traces of wood on the axe.

No. 1779.—A corroded axe of great thickness, being an inch at the butt, where it is made of several plates. There are slight traces of wood. Length 7⅜″ by 2½″.

No. 1808.—An axe 8¾″ long × 3″; with broken diagonal ring, 4″ long. The edge is slightly broken; and there are traces of wood.

Mamuties or Spades—

These implements are numerous, and are of the same design throughout, though differing in form. They are made of thick metal, and all have a round projection or flange on each edge of the butt end, which is bent inwards on one side to form a hold for the handle, which would then be at right angles to the spade, as in the modern mamuty. Traces of the wooden handle in some cases remain.

They are all broadest at the digging point, which may be square, rounded, or convex pointed. There are two distinct forms, some with sides variously curved, and others with straight sides. These latter are of extra thick metal, and have the appearance of an edge, for which they may have been used.

No. 682.—A broad mamuty with round pointed edge. Length 8¼″ by 5″.

No. 683, Figure 18.—A mamuty with sharp oval pointed edge. Length 7″ by 4¼″.

No. 770, Figure 19.—A very large mamuty with pointed oval edge. Length 1′ 1½″ by 5¼″.

No. 816.—A mamuty with the flat rounded edge split into two, by a blow probably. There are wood traces in the flanges. Length 6″ by 3¼″.

No. 1001.—A round edged mamuty, with traces of wood in the flanges. Length 5¼″ by 4″.

No. 1002.—A straight sided mamuty. Length 7¼″ by 2¼″.

No. 1036.— A mamuty with flat round edge. Length 10½″ by 3¾″.

No. 2037.—A mamuty with the straight sides nearly parallel. Wooden traces remain. Length 5⅞″ by 2⅜″.

No. 1356, Figure 20.—A narrow mamuty with parallel sides and flat edge. It is of extra thick metal. Length 8″ by 2¼″.

No. 1360.—A large mamuty with sharp edge, and large traces of wood in the flanges. Length 9½″ by 4½″.

No. 1361.—A mamuty with straight parallel sides. Has traces of wood Length 5½" by 2".

No. 1436.—A narrow mamuty with the sides nearly straight and parallel and flat edge. Length 8½" by 2½."

No. 1754, Figure 21.—A very long mamuty, the largest found. It has a rounded edge, and straight sides. Length 1′ 2¾" by 4½".

Large Iron Hangers—

These implements have been used for suspending a number of objects, probably a series of the small iron saucer lamps, some of which are elsewhere described.

They have a strong broad suspending ring at the top of a vertical rod of thick square section, which again has four large hooks of various design at the bottom. Close to the top suspending ring, a series of from four to eight arms or ribs branch around, outwards and downwards, resembling in this respect the ribs of an ordinary umbrella. These also are terminated by hooks of thin flat metal at the extremities.

Fig. 18.

Fig. 19.

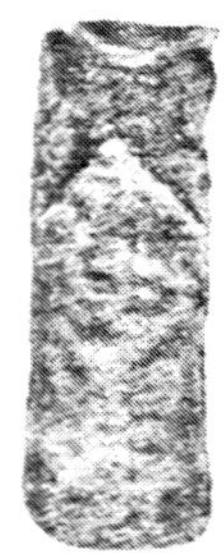

Fig. 20.

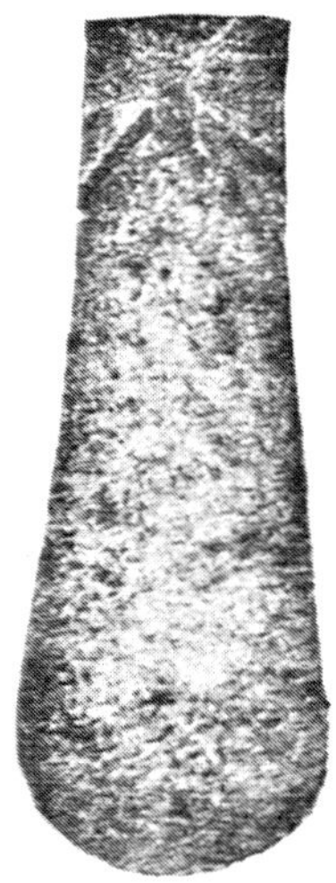

Fig. 21.

No. 335.—An extra large hanger with eight arms having a wide spread from side to side. Some of the arms are partly broken. The central rod has had four hooks, of which two remain complete. Height 1′ 10½"; arms 1′ 5".

No. 391.—A hanger which originally has had six arms, but of which only two or three remain complete. These have been crushed, so that they are nearly parallel to the central rod, like the ribs of a closed umbrella. One remaining part of an arm is at the angle at which all the arms originally were. The central rod has two and a half hooks remaining. Length 1′ 8"; length of arms 1′ 1".

No. 1080.—A hanger with two complete arms, out of six. They have pointed knobs at the ends of the hooks. The central rod has three out of four flat pointed hooks. Height 1′ 2".

No. 1213.—A hanger which has had six arms, but only parts of two remain. The central rod has had four hooks of which one remains. Height 1′ 7½".

No. 1402.—A hanger with four arms, having hooks at the extremities. The central rod has four curious hooks at the bottom. The diameter of the top ring is 3". Height 1′ 7½". Breadth across the arms 9½". Length of arms 1′ 2".

No. 1442.—A hanger with three out of eight arms complete and others partly so. The central rod has three hooks, with a fourth broken. Height 1′ 8"; arms 1′ 2".

No. 1670.—A hanger with three out of eight arms nearly complete. They have hooks with knobs at the ends. Four similar hooks are also at the extremity of the central rod. Length 1′ 8½″; arms 12½″.

No. 1755.—A hanger, much corroded and decayed, with most of the arms away. Originally it has had five, but only two without hooks remain attached. Only one hook at the base of the central rod remains. The height is 1′ 4¼″, and the longest arm is 12½″.

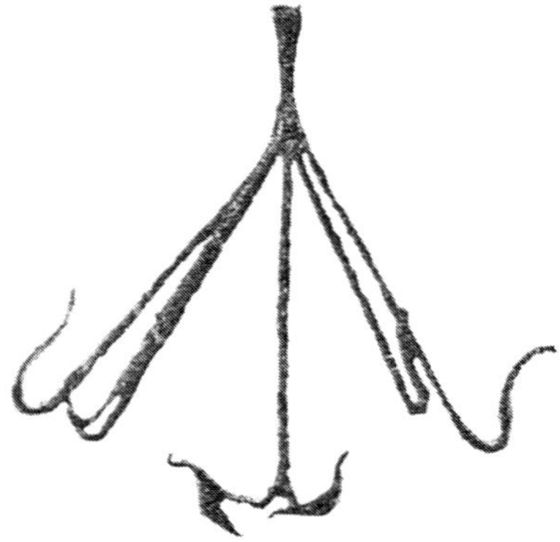

Fig. 22.

No. 1819, Figure 22.—A hanger with curious leaf-like hooks at the foot of the central rod. It has had seven hooked arms, but only five now remain. Length 1′ 9¼″, arms 14″, loop 1½″.

Saucer Lamps—

No. 371, Figure 23.—An iron saucer lamp 4″ in diameter, with circular arched bar complete. Height 6¾″. At the top of the arch is a hole for a suspender.

Fig. 23.

No. 564.—An iron saucer lamp, 4¼″ in diameter with bent suspending bar having a pin fixed in its centre.

No. 693.—An iron saucer lamp 3½″ in diameter with a suspending rod and chain in pieces.

No. 724.—An iron saucer lamp 3¾″ in diameter, with suspending rod fixed in the centre. The rod is 2¾″ long, and is flattened at the top, in which there is a hole.

No. 1056.—An iron saucer lamp 3½″ in diameter, with arched beam, springing from each side, hooked suspending rod and chain, all in pieces.

No. 1106.—An iron saucer lamp, 3¼″ in diameter.

No. 1112.—An iron saucer lamp, 3½″ in diameter. The arched beam is broken off. Parts of a chain, and rods—one of which is spiral fluted—remain.

No. 1212.—An iron saucer lamp, 4¾″ in diameter, with rods and chain separate. One rod has two links of the chain attached to it. Parts of two rods remain riveted to the sides of the lamp.

Fig. 24.

No. 1369.—An iron saucer lamp, 4½″ in diameter, with bent rod, hooks and chains separate.

No. 1403.—An iron saucer lamp, 3¾″ in diameter. Detached suspending hooked rods were found along with it.

No. 1443.—An iron saucer lamp, 3½″ in diameter, with overhead arched bar, fixed to each side. One side is broken. From the pan to the top of the arch the height is 5″. A portion of a suspending rod remains fixed in the top of the arch.

No. 1475, Figure 24.—An iron saucer lamp, 3¼″ in diameter. The hanging arched beam remains attached to the lamp complete. It is oblong with a hole and pin in the top bar. Hanging rods and a chain 8½" long remain detached.

No. 1564.—An iron saucer lamp, 4" in diameter, with arched bar broken off. Separate are five pieces of a rod, and a chain of 28 links.

Iron Beam Rods—

These objects are particularly all of one design or pattern. The only differences are in the size, or due to corrosion. They are long rods of round metal, with an elongated oval bulging in the middle, and a knob at each end. They resemble beams for weighing scales. The longest is 1′ 7″, by an inch diameter in the centre. There are eighteen of them, and pieces of six others.

No. 223.—Length, 1′ 4″ by 1″, knobs scarcely defined.

Chisels—

No. 33.—A chisel, 3" long.

No. 85.—A chisel, narrow in the centre and broad at the edge, and butt, 2¾" long by ½".

No. 133.—A chisel, tapering to a point at the handle end, and with a flat edge. Length 6⅓" by 1¼".

No. 936.—A flat chisel, with hollow tube handle. Length ·¾" × ¾". Some mica is attached.

Figs. 25 and 26.

Iron Tripods—

No. 1215.—An iron tripod, formed of a ring of flat metal ¾" broad resting on three legs. The legs partly curve outwards, and have a bent rest at the foot; they are 8" long. The diameter of the ring is 7". Two other tripods are of similar shape but of different size.

Miscellaneous—

No. 1111.—An iron cylindrical handle ring. Diameter 1½"; height 1¼".

No. 1260.—A reaping hook, 7¼" in length. From the handle to the point of the curved blade is 5⅜".

There are numbers of others of various kinds, in a more or less fragmentary condition.

Stone Implements—

No. 264.—Slab, 8" by 5½", 4½" high. The middle portion is hollowed out to a depth of ⅜", probably by use before it was buried.

No. 264 (*a*).—A stone curry grinding roller, 6" long. Circumference 8½" or 2⅔" diameter.

No. 422, Figure 25.—Sandal grinding slab on four legs, 12¾" long, 5" broad, 4½" high. Found outside an urn. The slab is marked with a cross inside a circle on under side.

No. 692, Figure 26.—Found afterwards near where the slab was found, is the grinder or curry grinding stone, 6½" long. Circumference in the middle 7". At the ends 7½".

No. 1782.—A four-legged (one leg missing) curry grinding stone, 8½" by 5", 4½" high The stone is curiously veined on the surface.

No. 1783.—Stone roller of No. 1782. Only the middle portion of 5" length is smooth surfaced, the two ends are rough and tapering unlike other rollers. Probably rings were attached to the ends. The whole length of the roller is 11½".

Pottery.

Time has not permitted of the numerous pottery being catalogued, and this must be reserved for a subsequent article.

Glossary.

CHAṬṬI :—A vernacular term for a pot.

CHITTIRI :— The first month of the Tamil year, March-April, when the full moon stands in Citra, the spring month, Spring.

KARTIKI :—The month Kārttika (October-November), when the moon is full and near the Kritti-kās; the eighth month in the Chāndramāna.

KUMMAL :—An earring of gold, etc., worn in the lobe of the ear of a female whose husband is alive.

MAMUṬI :—A broad hoe.

POṄGAL :—A preparation of boiled rice.

ŚŪLAṀ :— 1. A sharp or pointed weapon; a pike, a spear, a lance, a spike; the trident of Śiva. 2. A spit. 3. A stake for impaling criminals.

TRIŚŪLAṀ :—A three-pointed pike or spear; a trident.

A. REA.

EXCAVATIONS AT CHĀRSADA IN THE FRONTIER PROVINCE.

THE trial excavations in the neighbourhood of Chārsada, in the Frontier Province, undertaken by the Archæological Survey, lasted for only two months

Fig. 1. View of Svāt River and Bālā Ḥiṣār from Mīr Ziyārat.

between February 23rd and April 25th. A sum of Rs. 3,000 (£200) had been set apart by the Government of India from the special allotment of one lakh of rupees, annually devoted to Archæology, and this proved adequate for the undertaking, the actual expenditure incurred amounting to Rs. 2,999-15-11. Most of the plans and drawings reproduced have been executed by Bhairon Bakhsh and Ghulām Nabī, two draftsmen attached to the Survey, and practical assistance, especially in the matter of collecting antiquities and information from the surrounding villages, was also rendered by Sher Bāz, whose services were kindly lent to us by Colonel H. A. Deane, the Chief Commissioner of the Frontier Province.

Among modern travellers General Court, who seems to have visited the district previously to 1826, refers to the villages of Chārsada and Prāng under the name of Ashnagar or Hashtnagar. He speaks also of the Hissár[1] mound, and identifies the site generally with the Nysa of Alexander's Historians, in opposition to the then prevalent opinion that it represented Massaga, the capital of the Arsaceni. In 1863 General Cunningham[2] suggested its identification with Puṣkalāvatī, the ancient capital of Gandhāra, which would be rendered in Prākṛt by Pukkhalotī, and is referred to by the Greek writers under the forms Peukela, Peukelaōtis, and other variants.[3]

Nearly twenty years, however, elapsed before General Cunningham instructed his assistant, Mr. H. W. B. Garrick, to explore and excavate on this spot.[4] The reason for his postponing excavations at what he believed to be the most important historical site in the Province is no doubt to be sought in the fact that the presence of those Buddhist sculptures—which at that time were the almost exclusive aim of excavations—was more problematical here than in the well known hill sites of the Yūsufzaī. Mr. Garrick confined himself to preparing plans of the Bālā Ḥiṣār, and some irregular digging in and around the mound of Shahr-i-Nāpursān. About the same time a company of Sappers and Miners, under Lieutenant Martin, R.E., had been deputed to Chārsada by the Punjab Government, and some trials were made by them on the Bālā Ḥiṣār and Mīr Ziyārat mounds, but they withdrew again after twelve days, when excavations had been barely commenced.[5] One of the sculptures obtained by Lieutenant Martin in these trials was an inscribed pedestal now in the Lahor Museum.[6] From 1882 until the present year no excavations were made, but the accidental discovery of two other dated inscriptions has kept the attention of scholars fixed upon these banks of the Svāt. The first inscription was the well-known Hashtnagar pedestal, discovered in 1883 by Mr. L. White King, and referred to on a later page in connection with Pālāṭū Ḍherī; the second was found on an image of Hāritī,[7] some eight miles to the north of Chārsada. The topography of the district has been discussed by Colonel H. A. Deane,[8] and by M. Foucher,[9] who while differing between themselves in their location of the monuments referred to by the Chinese

[1] General Court describes the fortress of Hissár as situated on an island formed by two branches of the River Jind [*cf. J. A. S. B.*, Vol. V (1836), p. 479], but in a map compiled ten years earlier he places it to the east of these streams. [*J. A. S. B.*, Vol. VIII (1840), p. 312.]

[2] *Cf. A. S. R.*, II, 89; and *Ancient Geography of India*, p. 49.

[3] *Arrian. Ind.*, I, 8. Πευκέλα; *Ib.* IV, 11. Πευκελαιῆτις; *Anab.*, IV, 22-7, 28-6. Πευκελαῶτις; *Strabo.*, XV, 21, 27. Πευκελαῖτις; *Dionysius. Perigetes.* V, 1143. Πευκαλᾶις; *Periplus Mar. Eryth.*, 47, and *Ptolemaios*, VI, 1, 12. Π(ρ)οκλαῖς; *Pliny*, quoting *Baeton*, uses the form Peucolaitis. *N. H.*, VI, 21.

[4] For an account of Mr. Garrick's operations see *A. S. R.*, XIX., p. 96 sqq.

[5] A brief description of Lieutenant Martin's excavations is contained in his letter No. 84, dated February 19th, 1882, to the Secretary to the Punjab Government in the P. W. Department.

[6] Edit. by G. Bühler. *Indian Antiq.*, Vol. XXV, 1896, pp. 311-12.

[7] Now in the Lahor Museum. *Cf.* "Annual Progress Report" of the Archæological Superintendent, Punjab Circle, 1901-2, para. 16. Edited by Dr. Stratton in the *Journal of the American Oriental Society*, Vol. XXIV, p. 1.

[8] Note on Udyāna and Gandhāra. *J. R. A. S.*, Oct. 1896, p. 655.

[9] Notes sur la Géographie ancienne du Gandhāra, p. 14. (*Extrait du Bulletin de l'École française d'extrême Orient*, Vol. I, Hanoi, 1902.)

pilgrims agree in supporting General Cunningham's main identification. This identification has now found universal acceptance, and it is unnecessary for the purposes of this article to recapitulate the convincing arguments upon which it is based.

The legendary history of this city is referred to in the Rāmāyaṇa,[1] where Bharata, in obedience to Rāma, is related to have conquered Gandharva-deśa, a pleasant country on both sides of the Indus, and founded two cities in the conquered territory named after his two sons, whom he established as rulers in them. Takṣaśilā took its name from Takṣa, and Puṣkalāvatī from Puṣkala. A similar account occurs in Kālidāsa's Raghuvaṁśa.[2] Varāhamihira in his Bṛhatsaṁhitā[3] also mentions Puṣkalāvata[4] with Takṣaśila among the tribes who inhabit the north-west of India. But the city is best known, perhaps, from its connection with the campaign of Alexander the Great. Arrian states that Hephæstion took it by storm after a siege of thirty days, and that having slain Astes, the ruler of that district, he set up Sangæus as Governor.[5] Alexander himself afterwards visited the town, and having received its formal surrender established a Macedonian garrison there under Philippos.[6] When Buddhism was established in Gandhāra in the time of Aśoka, Puṣkalāvatī seems still to have been the first city in the Trans-Indus region, if we may judge from the number and antiquity of the Buddhist monuments described by Hiuen Tsiang, two of which he attributes to Aśoka himself.[7] To this evidence may be added also the statement of Fa-Hian that Dharma-vivardhana, the son of Aśoka, ruled in the place where Buddha had made a gift of his eyes, which must have been at Puṣkalāvatī, where the great *stūpa* of the Eye-gift existed.[8] At a later date the capital was transferred to Puruṣapura (the modern Peshawar), perhaps during the reign of Kaniska, who founded in the latter place his famous monastery and *stūpa*.[9] In the seventh century the size of Puṣkalāvatī was greatly exceeded by that of Puruṣapura. Hiuen Tsiang, who visited it between 629 and 645 A.D., speaks of its monuments as ruined, or cold and desolate. Possibly it may have suffered in the early part of the sixth century from the devastating wrath of Mihirakula, the ruler of the white Huns, who is said to have destroyed 1,600 *stūpas* and monasteries in Gandhāra.[10] After Hiuen Tsiang's time the city appears to have sunk into complete oblivion. Al-Bīrūnī at least, in describing the route from Kanauj to Ghaznī in the beginning of the eleventh century A.D., speaks of Waihind, the capital of Kandhār (Gandhāra), west of the River Sindh, and also of Purshāwar,[11] but makes no mention of Puṣkalāvatī, although it was situate on the main road between these two places.

---

[1] VII, 100,10. Unless this is an interpolation in the text, the reference proves the existence of Puṣkalāvatī as far back as the sixth or even eighth century B.C. It is noticeable that the commentator states that Puṣkalāvatī was in Gandhāra-deśa as distinct from Gandharva-deśa, in which Takṣaśila was situate.

[2] XV, 87-89.

[3] XIV, 26.

[4] In the Mārkaṇḍeya-purāṇa and the Adbhuta-sāgara we find the form Puṣkarāvata.

[5] *Arrian. Anab.*, IV, 22, 7 and 8.

[6] *Arrian. Anab.*, 28, 6.

[7] *Cf.* S. Beal's translation (1884), Vol. I, pp. 109 sq.

[8] *Cf.* J. Legge's *Si-yu-ki* (Oxford, 1886), pp. 31-2.

[9] *Cf.* Beal, *op. cit.*, Vol. I, p. 99.

[10] *Cf.* Beal, *op. cit.*, Vol. I, p. 171, and M. A. Stein, *Rājataraṅgiṇi*, I. 289, and note.

[11] *Cf.* Alberuni's *India*, Ed. E. Sachau, Vol. I, p. 206.

The modern Chārsada, the largest of the eight contiguous towns which constitute the well-known Hashtnagar, lies on the east bank of the Svāt River, some four miles to the north-west of its confluence with the Kābul, and roughly in the centre of the Peshawar Valley. At this point the river bends suddenly from a south-westerly to a south-easterly direction, thus forming a natural boundary on three, sides of the town. Westward, as far as the Frontier hills, the plain is watered by

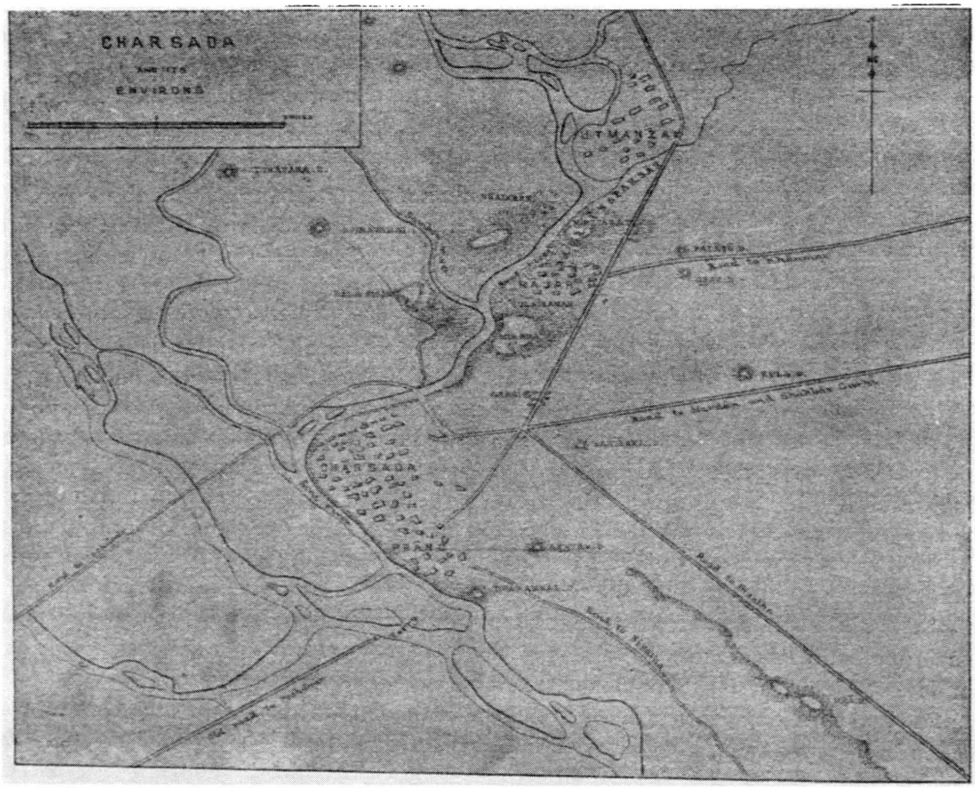

Fig. 2.

the many broken and meandering channels of the Svāt and Kābul Rivers, and to the north and east this natural irrigation is supplemented, as it may also have been in ancient times,[1] by a network of artificial canals. Independently, however, of the canals, this must always have been the richest corner of the whole Peshawar District. In addition to the fertility of the land, the convenient position of Chārsada in relation to the trade routes through the mountain passes to the west and north sufficiently

[1] Canal works can still be traced in Tangai above the line of the present Svāt Canal, and canals were undoubtedly taken out of the Svāt River opposite the modern canal head, and from the Kābul River two cr three miles above Warsak. *Cf. Peshawar District Gazetteer*, Ed. 1897-8, p. 15, and M. A. Court's remarks in *J. A. S. B.*, V, p. 480.

explains the growth and predominance of an ancient town on this spot, though it is not apparent why, if the Kābul and Svāt Rivers formerly met, as they now do, some four miles below Chārsada, a site was not chosen at their actual confluence, whence both waterways could be commanded. M. Vivien St. Martin has indeed located the old capital of the district at this spot, but on the other hand there are good reasons for believing that the ancient confluence was at Prāng, the village contiguous to Chārsada.[1]

At the back of the town, and in its immediate vicinity, stretches an interminable cemetery, dotted over with bare mounds that cover the ruins of bygone ages, and relieved only here and there by a copse of trees clustering round some Ziyārat, or by the avenues that indicate the main roads towards the east. The scene is singularly dreary, and one from which the eye turns instinctively to rest on the willows by the river's bank and the waving cornland beyond. The most conspicuous feature in this landscape is the artificial plateau or height, known as the Bālā Ḥiṣār, or the High Fort. It stands rather less than a mile to the north of Chārsada, across the main stream of the Svāt, and on the right bank of a branch rivulet known as the Ṣāmboṛ. Seen from the Chārsada side, its colour, rugged aspect, steep sides and flat top, sloping gently to the west, bring to mind the Akropolis rock at Athens, though the comparison may be prompted in part by the Western character of the surrounding country. North-east and south-east from the plateau extend two lines of lower mounds, the latter separated by only a saddle from the fortress itself, the former by a more extensive depression. To the south-east these mounds stretch towards the main channel of the Svāt, where they are lost in the low grounds over which the river sweeps in flood time, only to reappear on the opposite bank in the mounds on which the hamlet of Mīrābād is situate. That they originally formed a continuous ridge, and that the river has forced its way between them, cannot be doubted, especially when it is observed that a similar break occurs higher up the river in the line of mounds projecting to the north-east. Here the cutting through the artificial mounds of Shahr-i-Nāpursān is sheer and deep, and everywhere broken potsherds are visible imbedded in their sides. An examination of these sherds showed that the uppermost strata contained Muhammadan wares, and it may therefore be concluded that the change in the river's course took place at a date subsequent to the Muhammadan invasion. This is borne out by the survival to the present day of a tradition that the Svāt once flowed on the west side of the Bālā Ḥiṣār—a survival scarcely to be expected, if the change happened in pre-Muhammadan times. Hardly less certain is it that the lower reaches of the Ṣāmboṛ tributary also, which separate the Bālā Ḥiṣār and Shaikhān hill, are of comparatively modern origin; but that this rivulet has carried away much of the ancient site is unlikely.

[1] *Cf.* A. Foucher. Notes sur la Géographie ancienne du Gāndhara (*Extrait du Bulletin de l'École française d'extrême Orient*, Hanoi, 1902),—p. 15. M. Foucher adduces three arguments to prove that the confluence was at Prāng: (1) that the Chinese Pilgrim speaks of crossing one river only on the road from Pou-lou-cha-pou-lo (Peshawar) to Po-shi-kie-lo-fa-ti (identified with Chārsada), (2) that the name Prāng may be a derivative of Prayāg, signifying a confluence, (3) that the Kattiali stream, a branch of the Kābul, which joins the Svāt at Prāng, marks what was once the main channel of the Kābul, and is still known as such among the peasants.

[2] See Fig. 3. M. Foucher compares the Bālā Ḥiṣār with the famous mound of Babil at Babylon, and the wood-cut of the latter (*cf.* Perrot and Chipiez, Tome, II, Fig. 37) shows a close analogy.

In picturing then the appearance of the country in Buddhist times, we may eliminate these rivers and the ravages they have made, and imagine the Bālā Ḥiṣār as connected by an uninterrupted ridge with the elevation of Mīrābād, and separated by an intervening depression from the mound of Shaikhān. Southward from Mīrābād the *débris* of old habitations may be traced along the river bank beneath the modern villages of Chārsada and Prāng as far as the lofty mound of Dharmsāl, where they come to a sudden end, but nothing has yet been found to indicate that they possess a pre-Muhammadan origin. Our practical examination of the site has as yet extended only to trial excavations in the Bālā Ḥiṣār, and Mīr Ziyārat mounds, and in addition to these we have cleared the Pālāṭū and Ghaz Ḍherīs, two isolated hillocks towards the east, the former almost completely, the latter only partially.

The Bālā Ḥiṣār.

The Bālā Ḥiṣār is well known to have been occupied in turn by the Durānīs and

Fig. 3. View of the Bālā Ḥiṣār from the S.-E.

the Sikhs, whose walls and flanking towers of unburnt brick and rubble stone can still be traced around most of the fortress. The history of this occupation carries us as far back, perhaps, as the middle of the eighteenth century; before that date nothing definite is known, but a tradition is related by Mr. Garrick which points to the existence of a fortress here in the early days of Ghūrī rule in India.[1] Whether the tradition has any truth in it or not, it has generally been assumed that in early Muhammadan, and pre-Muhammadan days also, the mound served as a fortress. Recently, however, M. Foucher, in his brilliant discussion of the topography of the

[1] See Garrick, *A. S. R.*, XIX, p. 99 and footnote. The story seems entirely apocryphal.

district, has sought to identify the plateau with the great *stūpa* of the Eye-Gift,[1] stated by Hiuen Tsiang to have stood at a distance of four or five *li* to the north of Puṣkalāvatī.

The plan of the plateau is roughly pear-shaped, measuring some 250 yards north and south, and 220 yards east and west. A slight depression in the ground towards the north marks the position of an ancient well; for the rest, heaps of cobble-stones and broken bricks are all that are left of the buildings described by Garrick scarcely

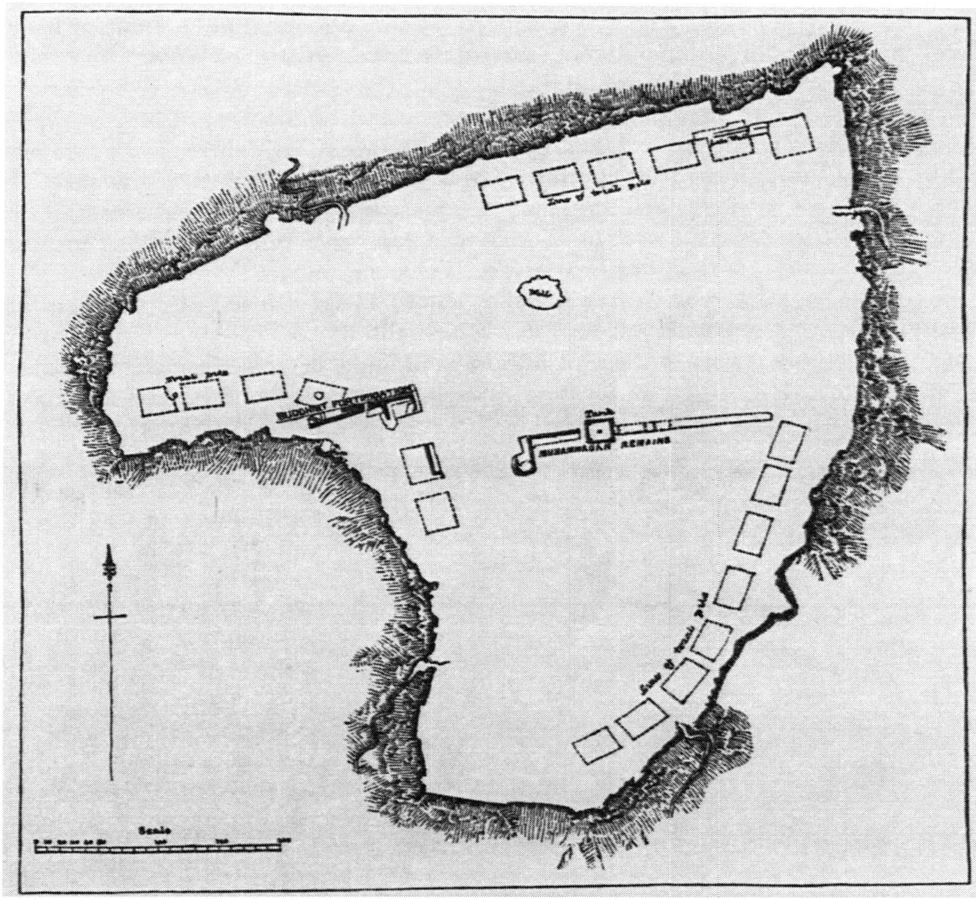

Fig. 4. Plan of the Bālā Ḥiṣār.

more than twenty years ago.[2] The eastern edge of the plateau rises about 75 feet above the level of the plain; the height of the western end is a few feet less. Almost the entire shell of the fortress has now crumbled away, and, in places, the accumulated

[1] A. Foucher, *op. cit.*, pp. 18 and 19.
[2] *A. S. R.*, XIX, 104 sq.

débris reaches to the full height of the mound. At other points the slopes are lower and more gradual, and above them the summit of the plateau rises in abrupt precipices, from the sides of which project here and there remnants of small buildings of typical Buddhist masonry, layers of pebble foundations, jars, pottery, bricks, and tiles—all evidences of the existence of an early settlement on the mound, and sure proof that most of the supposed fortifications, if they ever encircled the mound in pre-Muhammadan times, had long since fallen away and left its core exposed. At one point only, *viz.*, in the recessed angle at the south-west corner, were any traces of the walls left. Here the depredations of the peasants had lately brought to light, and almost demolished, a small turret (KK, Fig. 5) and parts of the adjoining walls, built of irregular but solid masonry of a comparatively early date, and leaving no room for doubt as to the purpose for which they were erected.

The main Muhammadan buildings which existed when Lieutenant Martin compiled his plan of the Bālā Ḥiṣār, are marked by him as situate in its centre, and as we wished to avoid cutting through their foundations, trial pits were sunk in three separate lines near the north, east, and western edges of the plateau. In those to the east no walls were revealed, and on the north side only the remnants of a late wall of loose construction appeared. In the western angle, however, close by the turret already referred to, the top of a wall (4 feet 4 inches thick) was disclosed at a depth of about 5 feet, and this, when opened out, proved to be built of the regular diaper patterned masonry [1] commonly found in the Buddhist buildings of this district. It was still standing to a height of 12 feet 6 inches. Towards the west it is broken away at the point A (Fig. 5). Its eastern end narrows slightly and is returned at a right angle towards the south by a smaller wall (BC, Fig. 5) 3 feet 4 inches thick. Parallel to the latter, and at a distance of 17 feet westward, is another cross wall of similar dimensions; both are broken away at their southern ends, their present length being about 16 feet. The space comprised between these two walls was packed with cobble-stones. Further south the line of the returning wall (BC) is continued by another wall (EF); which, however, from

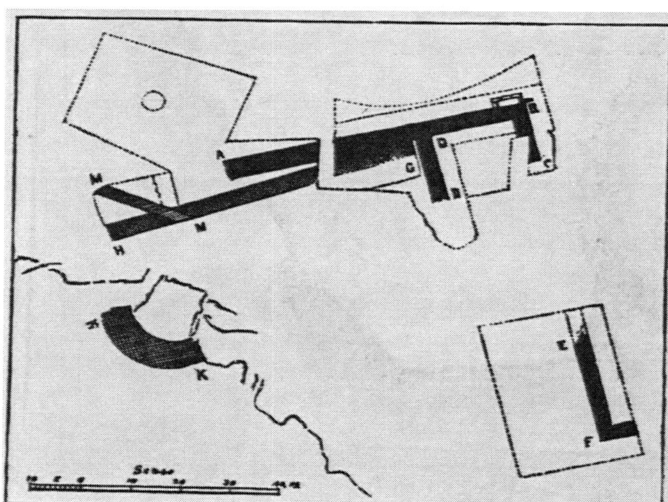

Fig. 5.

[1] *Cf.* W. Simpson, "Buddhist Architecture," *J. R. I. B. A.*, 1880, p. 39. "Stones more or less roughly squared are placed at intervals, with slates built in between each stone; a continuous layer of slates is then made forming a course in itself, and on this is placed the next course of stones with slates between them again—the whole presenting the appearance of a diaper pattern."

its different level and construction appears to have belonged to a separate building. The main wall (AB) is 63 feet long and batters toward the south. Its southern face is entirely rough, and must have been concealed from view. Its northern face is more carefully dressed, especially the upper portion within 4 feet of the top. We concluded that the lower courses to the height of 8 feet 6 inches served as foundations. At its eastern end and on the northern side is a perpendicular shaft of stone, some 7 feet high, which seems to have been set up at a later date at the head of a small grave, indicated by a quadrangle of boulders set against the side of the wall (*cf.* Fig. 5). That the grave was not Muhammadan seems likely in view of its orientation almost due east and west. From the main wall (AB) a second wall (GH), 5 feet thick, takes off at a slight angle towards the south-west. This was followed up for 66 feet but showed no sign of coming to an end. The style of its masonry is similar to that of the first, but the introduction of brickbats into the dividing courses proves it to be of later construction. This again is crossed above by a third and still later wall (MM) of a rougher type. It is 3 feet thick and about 4 feet high. No attempt has been made in it to preserve the regularity of the horizontal courses, and the interstices between the larger blocks are filled with mud and rubble.

The turret (KK, Fig. 5) at its nearest point is a little less than 16 feet from the western end of the second wall (GH), with which its similar style of construction seems to connect it. Its outer wall appears to have been about 7 feet thick and to have formed a little more than a quarter of a circle, abutting on to the angle of two walls, which once converged from the south and west, but have now fallen away. That all these walls are in the nature of fortifications there cannot be any reasonable doubt. Further excavations towards the west will make their history clearer, but in the meantime it may be conjectured that the earlier walls belonged to a gateway, the approach through which was constructed in such a manner as to compel an assailant to expose his flank to the defenders of the wall. Possibly the gateway was double and these walls formed part of an inner court. It may be surmised also that another wall of similar construction, battering to the north, existed parallel to the earliest wall AB, and about 16 feet from it on its southern side; between them would run the lighter cross walls, the chambers which they formed being filled with rubble. The thickness of the whole wall would thus be about 25 feet. At a later date the outer and part of the inner wall may have fallen, and the wall (HG) may have been built to take the place of the latter and relieve the batter of the remaining portion. The probability of these walls having belonged to an ancient gateway is strengthened by the existence of an entrance here in modern times,[1] and by the fact that at no other point in the whole circuit of the walls would an approach be so defensible as in this corner, where an attacking enemy would be exposed to a cross fire from the two walls projecting towards the south and west. These fortifications must not be confused, as they have been by Mr. Garrick, with the city walls and gates referred to by the Chinese pilgrims. The Bālā Ḥiṣār is, we believe, nothing more than the Akropolis of the ancient city, and its dimensions will be found to be in accord with this view.

[1] The entrance is marked in Lieutenant Martin's plan accompanying his letter referred to above.

Even in its present shrunken condition its superficial area is rather more than 31,000 square yards. The area of the Akropolis at Athens is approximately 33,000 square yards. If we include the small mound at the S.-E. corner, which undoubtedly belonged to the original fortress, and allow for the masses which have fallen on the eastern and northern sides, it will be seen that the areas of the two Akropoleis were much the same. How such a gigantic mass could be, as M. Foucher suggested, nothing more than the remains of a *stūpa*, it is difficult to understand.

The minor finds from the trenches alongside the fortification walls were comparatively few. Some mixed wares of Muhammadan date occurred near the surface, and at a lower level the following pre-Muhammadan objects :—

Pottery—

Broken saucers and bowls of the type shown in Fig. 24, Nos. 1, 3, 4, 5, 6 ; fragments of coarse *maṭans*, *gharās* and *cāṭis* (Fig. 24, Nos. 19, 20), and of others of uncertain shape ; a floral gargoyle forming the spout of a vase ; a fragment of a handle, with nail heads in imitation of a metal prototype ; and two earthenware lamps. *Cf.* Fig. 24, Nos. 12, 14.

Terra-cottas—

11 Figurines, mostly broken.

Coins—

1. Æ. ·95" Kaniṣka ? *Obv.* defaced. *Rev.* male deity. Crescent behind shoulders ; r. hand advanced ; l. on hip ; to l. symbol. *Cf.* Gardner, *Brit. Mus. Cat.*, p. 133, No. 39, and Pl. XXVII, No. 3 ; but the defacement makes the attribution uncertain. 2. Two Indo-Scythic. Æ. ·7", unidentifiable.

One Schist lamp. *Cf.* Fig. 24, No. 15.

Several fragments of blue (cobalt) glass, 3 cm. thick. Possibly it was used for tiles. Similar glass was found in Mīr Ziyārat mound.

Beads—

1 Amethyst, Amygdaloid, 1·4 cm. long.
12 Bone, disc and barrel-shaped.
4 pieces of shell bangles.
1 Lapis Lazuli, disc and barrel-shaped, 1·8 cm.
1 Onyx, 14-sided ; diam. ·8 cm.

Muhammadan Remains on the Bālā Ḥiṣār.

In the centre of the Fortress a trench was afterwards driven east and west for over 200 feet, and to a depth of over 20 feet at its western end, but it revealed nothing except Muhammadan remains. These consisted of a shallow tank, 20 feet square, of comparatively recent construction and near the surface. It may have been situate in the enclosure marked on Lieutenant Martin's plan as "Bathing houses." It is built of brick, faced with hard grey hydraulic cement, and coated with a thin layer of fine reddish stucco. Each corner is strengthened by a diagonal step. The supply pipe is in the centre and there is an outlet at one of the corners. East of this, and some 5 feet below it, was an earthenware pipe laid in sections averaging about 1 foot 7 inches in length, with flanged edges and socket joints. Some 14 feet below the tank, and 10 feet to its west, appeared an earlier building. A plain wall of brick faced with *chūnā* runs westward from this point for 40 feet, and is then returned for 20 feet towards the south.

Here it is pierced with three windows, 3 feet 2 inches broad and 4 feet above the floor level, the sills of which still retain portions of their wooden fittings (*cf.* Fig. 6.

Elevation and plan). A horizontal beam is carried right along beneath the brick piers that separate the window openings, and is secured with stout iron rails to wooden plugs, two of which are let into the brickwork beneath each pier. The wall here is 3 feet 6 inches thick; at its southern extremity is a chamber with arched entrance, and in each of the three other walls comprising the chamber is a shallow niche. The pilasters, from which springs the entrance arch, are raised on a step. Their base consists of a *cyma reversa* moulding with a fillet above. The springers of the arch are 6 feet above the base. In the construction of the walls the introduction of brickbats is noticeable; most of the material seems to have come from earlier—and probably Buddhist—buildings. The courses, however, are regularly laid and bedded in mortar joints of ½" thickness, composed of lime and powdered brick. The face of the walls was originally concealed with a coat of lime stucco. Digging here was particularly difficult, as the whole building was choked with heavy masses of fallen brickwork.

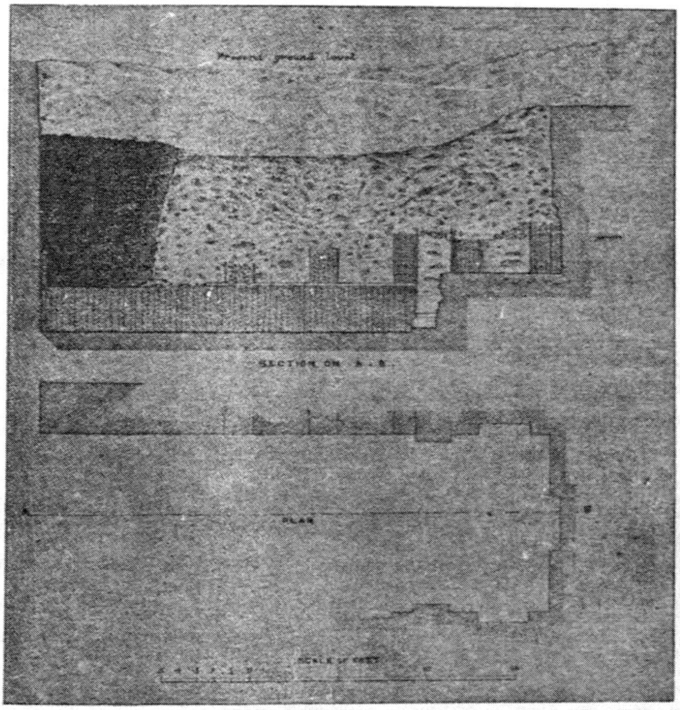

Fig. 6.

As regards the date of this building nothing can be affirmed, no coins or other evidence having been found to offer a clue.

Minor Finds in the Trial Pits on the Bālā Ḥiṣār.

In none of the trial pits on the Bālā Ḥiṣār could any certain evidence as to the date of the minor finds be obtained from stratification. Comparing them, however, with the finds from Mīr Ziyārat and from other sites of the Buddhist period, it was possible in the majority of instances to discriminate between the pre-Muhammadan and Muhammadan objects. Excepting the coins, the former only are included in the following list, an asterisk being placed against those about which there is any doubt.

Coins—

1. Æ. ·8″. Bas. Megas. *Cf.* Gardner, *Brit. Mus. Cat.*, p. 114, No. 2, and Plate XXIV, 2.

2. Æ. ·9″. Much defaced. *Cf.* Gardner, *op. cit.*, p. 122, No. 3.

3. Fourteen copper Indo-Scythic, of various sizes, unidentified.

4 Fourteen Muhammadan coins. Among these may be noted the Bull and Horseman type; and coins of Mu'izzu-d-Dīn Muḥammad ibn Sām (Muḥammad Ghūri); for types *cf. Ind. Mus. Cat.*, Part I, p. 4, No. 12613; *Ariana Antiqua*, Pl. XX, Fig. 14; and Rodgers, *Cat. of coins collected by C. J. R.*, Pt. II, p. 56, No. 11. Also of Alāu-d-Dīn ibn Takash of Khwārizm. Rodgers, *op. cit.*, Pt. II, p. 73, 29 ff. and p. 74, 41-44. A complete list of the Muhammadan and later coins from Chārsada will be given in a subsequent Report.

Sculptures—

Grey schist statuette in relief, ht. 14·8. cm. Male figure wearing necklace and loose upper garment, passing (like a Greek chlamys) over both shoulders and leaving the breast bare. The lower garment is rolled around the loins in Indian fashion. Face, feet, and hands missing.

2. Dark red (Agra ?) stone. Fragment of winged lion's head. Ht. 9 cm. Mane and wing feathers indicated by incised cross hatchings. Type common in Gandhāra sculptures. *Cf.* Grünwedel (Burgess), Fig. 56. The figure was intended to be seen from one side only.

3. Grey schist. Fragmentary. Ht. 12·8. cm. Upper half of body only. Holds lotus stalk in one hand.

4. Fragment, 7·6 cm. Miniature Indo-Corinthian pilaster and rosette.

5. Fragment, 5·1 cm., of capital of Indo-Corinthian pilaster.

6. Fragment, 12·8 cm., same as No. 5.

7. Fragment of decorative border of rosettes, 20·3 cm.

Pottery—

A great number of pre-Muhammadan and later wares were found in the trial pits. Examples of the former types are given in Figure 24, Nos. 1, 4, 7, 11, 12, 14, 19, 20, 23, 24, 25, 26, 31, and are discussed below on page 180 sqq. Among these may be noticed especially the fruit-shaped vessel of *bucchero nero* (Fig. 24, No. 24) which appears to have been used as an *alabastron*, and several fragments of a similar fabric with stamped designs, *e.g.*, Nos. 35 and 36. The uniform presence of so much pottery, and more particularly of vessels of every-day use (over 60 complete lamps, for instance, were recovered), affords additional evidence that the Bālā Ḥiṣār was covered with habitations at an early date.

Terra-cottas—

Several hundred terra-cotta figurines, nearly all mutilated. Many of these belong to the Muhammadan period, but the fabrics can generally be distinguished without difficulty. Some specimens of the earlier types will be described in a subsequent article dealing with the terra-cottas.

Shell Ornaments—

Thirteen fragments. Two have parallel lines incised on the outer surface, and one has a single row of circular bosses. The geometric pattern on another is shown in Fig. 7, No. 6. Similar shell ornaments have been found at several other early sites and notably in the lower strata at Brāhmanābād in Sindh.[1] The conch shell (*śankh*) is cut across in sections and joined together with wire, the minute holes, through which the latter passed, being observable in many specimens.

Nine fossilised *opercula* of Turbo, the Gasteropod. *Cf.* Fig. 7, No. 1. These *opercula* are found commonly in the Gāj (*Miocene*) beds of Sindh, and are at the present day an object of veneration among the Hindus. It may be taken for granted that a similar sanctity attached to them among the Buddhists, since a number of specimens were found at the base of the *stūpa* in Ghaz Ḍherī,

[1] See H. Cousens, *Progress Report of the Archæological Survey of Western India*, 1896-97, page 17, para. 44.

and in what we take to be the foundations of a monastery on Mīr Ziyārat. On the Bālā Ḥiṣār they were found in the pits close by some of the broken sculptures previously referred to, at the N.-E. corner of the mound, and it is probable, therefore, that some small *stūpa* may have existed at this point.

Iron Implements—

*1 knife
*4 rings } all badly corroded.
*8 nails

Miscellaneous—

*1 copper antimony rod (?) 11·2 cm. long, with incised cross hatchings.
*1 lead ditto, plain.
1 steatite lamp. *Cf.* Fig. 24, No. 16.
*8 schist lamps. *Cf.* Fig. 24, No. 15, for similar shape.
1 stone bowl. Fig. 24, No. 2.
Fragments of large steatite vessel.
1 lid of steatite vessel, turned on lathe.
*60 earthenware spindle whorls (?). *Cf.* Fig. 24B, Nos. 1 and 9.
*21 disc weights, pierced.
*12 pyramidal weights, pierced at their apices.

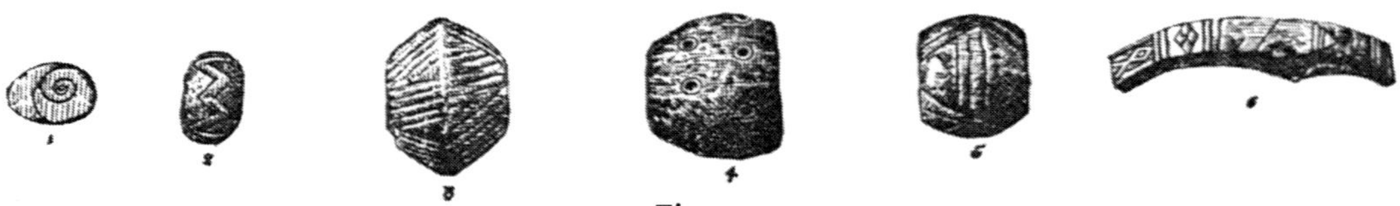

Fig. 7.

*10 stone rings, mostly of schist, the remainder of steatite. Some are slightly conical, with the lower base varying from 4 cm. to 1·8 cm. The centre hole, pierced perpendicularly, is roughly about one-third of the base diameter, narrowing to the top. The sides are curved and decorated with simple linear designs or concentric circles. *Cf.* Fig. 7, Nos. 2-5.
*10 rude stone implements.
*2 pieces of white marble.
Fragments of blue glass, coloured with cobalt. About 3 cm. thick. Similar glass was found in the lowest stratum at Mīr Ziyārat. It may have been used for tiles of some sort.
1 elliptical ring stone, unengraved.

Beads—

(*a*) Blue vitreous paste—3, round and fluted. *Cf.* Plate XXVIII (*b*), No. 2.
(*b*) Bone—Barrel-shaped, disc, round, and fluted, in large numbers.
1 fan-like pendant.
The miniature round bone beads are frequently cut in series of three or more from one piece.
(*c*) Crystal—1 pear-shaped pendant, ht. 1·9 cm.
2 round, diam. 1·3 and 1·1 cm.
1 ditto fluted, diam. 1·2 cm.
(*d*) Chalcedony—1 flat oval, bored through shorter axis, 1 cm. long.
(*e*) Amethyst—1 amygdaloid, 1·2 cm. long.
1 ditto, facetted.

(*f*) Agate—1 amygdaloid facetted, 1·2 cm. long.
1 fourteen-sided, diam. 1·4 cm.
(*g*) Lapis lazuli—1 amygdaloid, 2·2 cm. long.
1 ditto, unfinished.
1 semi-elliptical, the curved upper side with cross hatchings, 1·8 cm. long.
(*h*) Cornelian—1 irregular, inlaid with design in white paste, diam. 1·1.
1 fourteen-sided, diam. 1·4; burnt.
1 flat oblong with curved ends, length 1·1 cm.
1 irregular round.
(*i*) Steatite—1 three-sided prism, 1·3 cm. long.
(*j*) Limestone—1 fourteen-sided flat.
*(*k*) Turquoise—1 fanciful crescent, 1·6 cm. between horns.
*(*l*) Transparent glass—1 oblong, bored through longer axis; 2 cm. long.
(*m*) Clay—Several vase-shaped, *cf.* Fig. 24A, No. 7; length 1·4 to 2 cm. Also circular with compressed ends and fluted edges.

Various fragments of amethyst and mother-of-pearl.

Among the smaller finds from the Bālā Ḥiṣār must be mentioned a metal mould of earthenware picked up on the eastern slopes of the mound. The subject of the mould (*cf.* Fig. 8, from a cast) is a female, or effeminate male, figure riding on a swan. The bird carries a garland in its beak, and a band passes around its body behind the wings and legs. Below its neck is a heart-shaped depression, for the reception of a jewel. The figure on its back has the left arm uplifted and wears a necklace. Whether it is intended to portray the well known Greek type of Aphrodite, or the later type of Apollo, it is difficult to say. Probably, I think, the latter. Such representations of Apollo appear to have been in vogue in Asia Minor in Imperial times. On copper coins, for instance, of Julia Paula and Tranquillina, struck at Chalcedon in Bithynia, Apollo is depicted riding upon a swan.[1] The figure on the coins is nude and its proportions are effeminate, but the presence of the lyre above and behind the head makes the identification certain. The terra-cotta mould is unfortunately slightly broken, and it is impossible to say whether a lyre was originally depicted or not.

Fig. 8 (full size).

Mīr Ziyārat.

Mīr Ziyārat is the name given to the most considerable of the mounds in the Shahr-i-Nāpursān group, where some authorities have located the site of the famous Eye-gift *stūpa.* Its summit is marked by two boulders, lying side by side on its western edge. Notwithstanding the name Mīr Ziyārat, which might be expected to indicate a Muhammadan shrine, these stones are sacred to the Hindus, for they are said to mark the place where Gorakhnāth, one of their *Gurūs,* used to meditate with his disciples; in his honour a great *melā* is held at this spot twice a year. But the presence of so many Buddhist remains round about would seem to suggest that the

[1] *Cf. British Museum Cat.*, Pontus, Paphlagonia, etc.; p. 128, Nos. 34 and 35, and Plate XXVIII, 5.

sanctity of the place may date from a time when Buddhism was paramount here; and in this connection it must be remembered that the Hindus are peculiarly versatile in adopting foreign cults and observances.

In this excavation also Lieutenant Martin with his company of Sappers and Miners had been before us, and the site had long been the quarrying ground of the peasants of Rājaṛ. Lieutenant Martin had in true engineering fashion sunk two shafts, to a depth of 23 feet from the summit of the mound, and joined them by a subterranean

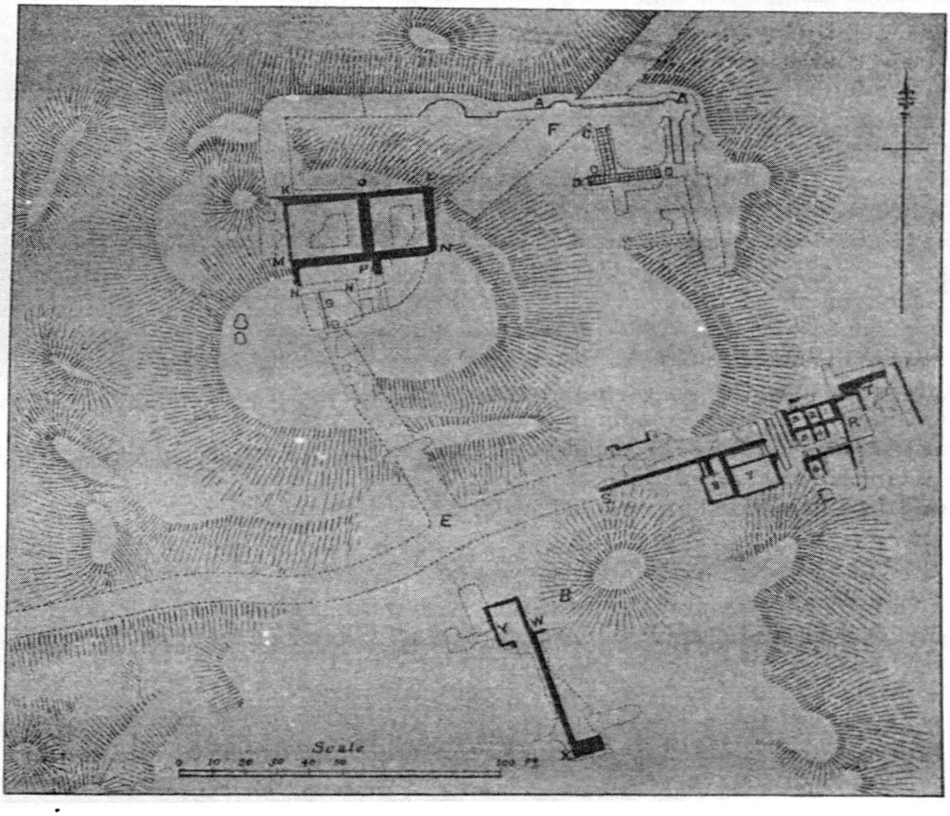

Fig. 9. Plan of Mir Ziyārat.

gallery some 20 feet in length. A description of his operations, with a section drawing, is given in a brief Report addressed to the Punjab Government.[1] The conclusion at which he arrived was that the boulders and a portion of a more regularly laid wall, which he seems to have struck at a depth of about 18 feet, were the foundations of a Tope, the plinth of which he believed to be marked by some rough walls, then existing on the top of the *ḍherī*, but since demolished. One immediate object of our excavations was to discover whether any further evidence existed to support this

[1] Letter No. 84 of 19th February 1882, from Lieutenant M Martin, R.E., to the Secretary to the Public Works Department.

hypothesis, or whether, as seemed more probable from the fragments of late pottery scattered about, and the loose nature of the soil—ill suited for the foundations of a solid superstructure—the walls on the summit of the mound belonged to some smaller Muhammadan building. The method adopted was first to skirt the mound with shallow trenches, in the hope, if a *stūpa* really existed, of striking the outer platforms and gradually feeling our way towards the centre. It soon appeared, however, that around the base of the hillock nothing more than foundations could be expected. On the north side these were exposed at a few inches below the surface, between the points A and B (Fig. 9).

They consist of two steps of cobble stones laid in mud, the upper step set some 18 inches further back than the lower one. The neat and regular courses of the latter as compared with the former seem to indicate an earlier date for its construction. The semi-circular projections, which belong to it, perhaps mark the foundations of buttresses. The line of these foundations was followed up some distance east and south, but no further trace of them could be found. On clearing the earth between here and the mound, two causeways (CC and DD, Fig. 9), crossing each other at right angles, came to light. The flat bricks, with which they were originally paved, measured $9\frac{1}{4}''$ square and $1\frac{1}{4}''$ thick, but at a later date the causeways have been repaired in parts with brickbats and cobble stones. A few inches below this pavement there were traces of another and older one, which the bricks measured 11 inches square, and $1\frac{3}{4}''$ thick. This earlier paving we associated with the lower course of the foundations to the north. On the south of the mound only a few fragments of paving similar the later kind on the north could be found, but a deeper trial lower down the slope disclosed some solid foundations of unbaked brick. These we deferred following up until we had penetrated the mound itself. New trenches were accordingly drawn from the points E and F towards the centre, and some portions of a wall of unbaked brick (KL, Fig. 9), covered here and there with patches of crimson stucco, were revealed at a low level on the north side. Higher up, on the summit of the mound, and within 2 feet of the surface were the remains of a later habitation, *viz.*, a row of fire-places backed by a low wall standing to the height of 2 feet 6 inches (GG, Fig. 9). The latter was built of pebbles, faced with bricks and clay mortar. At right angles to this and below it were the remains of a rubble wall faced with lime plaster (HH, Fig. 9). At this point our digging was interrupted by a deputation from the Hindu community of Rājaṛ, who begged us not to interfere with the two sacred boulders referred to above. For the time being therefore we contented ourselves with opening out the *kachcha* walls to the north-east. These—so far as they were eventually cleared—proved to consist of two parallel walls running east and west, intersected by three others towards the north and south. The two complete chambers on the north, which are formed by them, measure approximately 19 feet by 21 feet and 17 feet respectively. The south wall (MN) is standing to an average height of 6 feet, but the cross walls are broken away with the slope of the mound towards the north, and the north wall (KL) has a height of 1 or 2 feet only. The other chambers towards the south and centre of the mound were not cleared, as the removal of so much earth did not seem justified. All the walls are composed of sun-dried bricks of looser texture than those in he foundations to the south-east of Mīr Ziyārat. Over [illegible] icks of

(a) MĪR ZIĀRAT: VIEW FROM NORTH.
(b) MĪR ZIĀRAT: FOUNDATIONS TOWARDS S.E.
(c) GHAZ DHERĪ: N.E. CORNER OF STUPA.
(d) PĀLĀṬŪ ḌHERI: S.W. CORNER OF COURTYARD.

the bricks was laid a coating of clay plaster, and this was smeared with white lime (*chūnā*) and crimson paint ; only patches of this rough stucco remain on the upper surfaces of the walls. In the south-east room the north wall, towards its west end, was faced with half burnt bricks (11 inches square) laid flatwise. Around the base of the walls in the interior of the chambers runs a narrow projection or wainscot, the upper surface of which may have marked the level of the original floor. This seems the more likely as the stucco did not extend over the wainscot and there were no gaps in it to mark the existence of entrances to the two chambers on the north. In the room to the north-west was a confused mass of burnt wood and clay, and in this and the other rooms veins of charcoal in the soil made it evident that the building had been destroyed by fire. In the room to the north-west were also found (A) a broken sherd of coarse black clay, hand-polished, with some uncertain letters scratched upon it (Fig. 10), (B) several shapeless masses of iron, (C) three unidentified coins, (D) two pieces of coral. In the south-west room was a hoard of 87 copper coins. They were found in a heap with the fragments of an earthenware jar around. So far, an exact identification of these has not been possible, but they are almost certainly Ghaznavid coins, or coins of local rulers imitated from Ghaznavids.[1]

Fig. 10.

Besides the coins were found a clay disc weight, diam. 2·5 cm. ; a soapstone cylinder ; a fragment of white jade, and some bone, limestone, and cornelian beads. At a level about 3 feet higher than the above finds were two large *cāṭīs*, one of them plain, the other ornamented with spiraliform and simple geometric designs in black upon a ground of white limewash.

Enough had now been brought to light on Mīr Ziyārat to show that most of the mound consisted of Muhammadan remains belonging probably to a date not later than the end of the twelfth century A.D. This being so, it seemed unlikely that this could have been the site of the famous *stūpa* seen by Hiuen Tsiang in the middle of the seventh century, since it is difficult to believe that so vast a monument could have perished so effectually in the intervening period.

Abandoning, therefore, the centre of the mound, we returned to the south-eas corner and followed up the early walls of unbaked (*kachcha*) brick, referred to above. These resolved themselves into a network of foundations, with an average depth of 4 or 5 feet ; ordinarily the bricks are laid direct on the soil, but cobble stones are sometimes used to fill up depressions and afford a more compact and level bed. A plan of these foundations, so far as they were excavated, will be found in Fig. 9, and a photograph of the work in progress is given in Plate XXIV (*b*).

Originally they appear to have been surmounted by walls of well-burnt (*pakka*) bricks, a few remnants of which still survived in places, but the *pakka* bricks had at a later date been replaced by, or built over with, stone walls of the ordinary diaper

[1] We are indebted to Mr. E. Rapson for this general identification. He suggests that many of the coins, which bear the radiate circle, may have been derived from such an arc-type as that of Arsalān (*Brit. Mus. Cat. Or. Coins*, Additions I—IV, p. 248. No. 572 m), and he believes that he can read fragments of the name of Arsalān's successor, Bahrām Shāh, on some of them.

pattern. That *pakka* bricks were used here at an earlier date than stone for walls above ground, was made clear by another trial excavation a little to the south-west. At this point the foundations as well as the walls above (W, X, Y, Fig. 9) are in two distinct strata, and of two distinct styles of construction. The *kachcha* brick foundations are still surmounted by several courses of *pakka* bricks, while some feet above them are foundations of cobble stones mixed with brickbats, taken no doubt from the earlier walls, and a superposed wall of the usual stone masonry above.

We have spoken of the walls of unbaked brick as foundations, since they show no traces of entrances to the chambers within, but judging from the numerous small finds in the spaces enclosed by them, it seems not improbable that the house may have possessed chambers sunk below the ground and with entrances from above—a well-known device in the East for protection against the heat of summer.

Fig. 11.

In the lowest deposit, within the chambers marked 1, 2, 3, 4, 5, 7, and 8 (Fig. 9), were found the following objects :—

Coins—

Æ. ·55. Menander. *Cf.* Gardner, *Brit. Mus. Cat.*, p. 50, No. 68, and Plate XII, 6.

Two other coins of the same size and fabric, much defaced, probably belong to the same king.

Terra-cottas—

One broken figurine (Fig. 11). It is much worn, but the style is superior to that of the other terra-cottas. Probably it represents a Nāga, but the projections around the head may form part of a head-dress only.

Beads—

Vitreous paste with pale blue surface:—

(1) collection of 76 beads; round and slightly diminishing in size, with pendant; from room 2. Plate XXVIII (*b*), No. 5.

(2) ditto of 21 beads, round and fluted; the flutings vary from 7 to 20 in number, from room 5. Plate XXVIII (*b*), No. 2. Necklaces of a similar design in gold are still common in Northern and Western India.

(3) ditto, 62 beads, fourteen-sided, *i.e.*, cubes with the corners bevelled off. From room 1. *Cf.* Plate XXVIII (*b*), No. 4. Another collection of 107 beads of similar design, broken and calcined, was found in room 7.

(4) ditto of 73 beads, doubly flexured; each bead is pierced with two parallel holes. The upper side is bevelled at the edges, the lower flat; from room 2. *Cf.* Plate XXVIII (*b*). No. 3.

The chief materials and shapes of the other miscellaneous beads were:—

Bone and ivory—Cylindrical and barrel-shaped.
Lapis lazuli and soapstone—14-sided and round.
Cornelian—Lenticular.
Agate—Amygdaloid and tubular.
Blue transparent glass—10-sided.

Miscellaneous—

Shell ornaments—13 pieces, mostly broken; similar to those described on page 152 above.
3 fossilised *opercula* of the *gasteropod turbo*. *Cf.* page 152 *supra* and Fig. 7, No. 1.
37 cowrie shells, some pierced longitudinally for suspension.
1 lead disc, diameter 1·9 cm., bored through centre.
1 bone disc (Fig. 13) with incised designs.
2 pieces of mica.

14 fragments of rock crystal.

Numerous fragments of the blue and green glass, described above (page 153). It occurred especially in rooms 2 and 3.

From the soil about these foundations and the walls W, X, Y (Fig. 9), came the following:—

Coins—

1. Æ.·85 inch. Hermaios. Gardner, *Brit. Mus. Cat.*, p. 64, No. 28. *Cf.* also Plate XV, 6.
2. Æ.·95 inch. Hermaios. *Cf.* Gardner, *op. cit.*, p. 64, Nos. 27, 29, and Plate XV.
3. Æ.1·1 inch. Azes. Gardner, *op. cit.*, p. 86, No. 151.
4. Æ. Similar.
5. Æ.·5 inch. Basileus Megas. Gardner, *op. cit.*, p. 115, No. 17.
6. Æ. 1·1 inch. Ooemo-Kadphises. Gardner, *op. cit.*, p. 126, No. 12, and Plate XXV, 12.
7. Æ.·6 inch. Kaniṣka. Gardner, *op. cit.*, p. 135, No. 61, and Plate XXVII, 6.
8. Æ.·9 inch. Kaniṣka. *Cf.* Gardner, *op. cit.*, 133, No. 38, Plate XXVII, 3.
9. Æ. Kaniṣka. *Cf.* Gardner, *op. cit.*, p. 175, No. 2, and Plate XXVII, 14; Berl. Zeitschr. f. Num. 1879, Plate IX, 1. On the *Rev.* is Buddha, seated, facing, and cross legged; arms in position of one preaching. The legend is uncertain. Gardner reads] ΓΟΒΟΥΔΟ, with four or five uncertain letters preceding. The first two of these appear from this specimen to be MH.

16 other Indo-Scythic, unidentified.

Pottery—

Mostly small fragments. In room 2, were three standard goblets (Fig. 24, Nos. 8 and 9), and near the point S, 22 cups of coarse ware. Also some broken saucers (Fig. 24, Nos. 6 and 7) and a number of coarser fragments belonging to gharās, maṭans, etc.

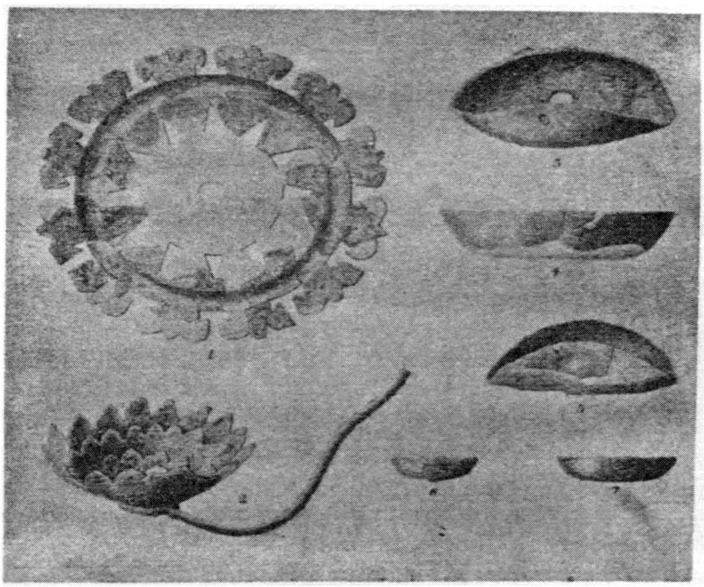

Fig. 12.

Bronzes—

Seven objects (Fig. 12) from above the foundations at Y. They are the type of objects which might be expected in a Buddhist shrine. All were originally gilded. No. 1, restored from small fragments, is a disc of conventionalised lotus form, used, perhaps, for offerings of flowers. The more natural lotus (No. 2) may have formed part of a candelabrum. The other 5 small bowls are of the same type, but different sizes. The larger hole in the centre was probably for a stem to pass through, the tiny holes around their edges for the attachment of ornamental *pipal* leaves or bells.

Sculptures—

From the same spot as bronzes.

1. Miniature head of Buddha, with halo around. In schist stone, greatest breadth 5·1 cm.
2. Corner of small pediment, with tail of hippocamp, in relief. Schist stone, 8·2 cm. long.

Gems—

1. Elliptical chalcedony intaglio, for ring; longer axis 1·3 cm. To r. cornucopia; to l. ship (?); across and behind cornucopia, a staff bound with fillet.

1 scaraboid sardoine, plain.

4 **Fossils—**

Opercula of *turbo*. (*Cf.* supra, page 152 and Fig. 7, No. 1.)

Also various fragmentary shell ornaments, terra-cotta figurines and beads.

So far as they have gone, then, these trial excavations on and around Mīr Ziyārat have revealed four distinct settlements—two of the Buddhist and two of the Muhammadan period. Of the former the earlier are represented by foundations of unbaked brick with remnants of *pakka* brick walls above. Their date, if the evidence of the coin finds may be adduced, seems to be earlier than that of Hermaios. The later are of the usual diaper-patterned stone masonry, and, to judge from the same evidence, belong to the reign of Kaniṣka or later. That both the earlier and later Buddhist buildings bore a religious character may perhaps be gathered from the nature of some of the small objects found in them—more particularly from the fragmentary sculptures and small fossils, the latter of which appear to have had a sacred value among the Buddhists, as they still have among the Hindus,—but further excavations towards the south and west are needed in order to determine this.

Fig. 13.

Pālāṭū and Ghaz Ḍherīs.

The two small *ḍherīs* known as Pālāṭū and Ghaz lie about three-quarters of a mile to the east of Mīr Ziyārat, the former on the north, the latter on the south of the road leading to Khānmai. A special interest attaches to Pālāṭū Ḍherī as the find place of the Buddha image to which the so-called Hashtnagar pedestal belongs. The details of this find are as follows. A *banyā* of Rājaṛ named Ratan selected this mound as a quarry, in order to obtain stones for a *dharmśālā*. Besides a considerable number of dressed stones he found also several specimens of sculptures.[1] Among these was a standing figure of *Śākyamuni*, in which the Hindus of Rājaṛ readily recognised their goddess Kālikā Devī. The image, clothed in some dozen dresses, was placed in the new *dharmśālā*, where it is still being worshipped. About 1883 Mr. L. White King, I.C.S., saw the Buddha thus metamorphosed, and noticed on the pedestal an inscription in Kharoṣṭhī. Finding the Hindus unwilling to part with their newly acquired *Devī*, he was constrained, with their permission, to have the pedestal sawn off, and presented it to the British Museum.[2]

Before excavation a slight depression divided the *ḍherī* into two mounds, which appeared, superficially, to contain separate groups of buildings. The mound (A) to the east was higher and roughly circular, that to the west (B) slightly smaller and rectangular. It was in the centre of the latter that the inscribed Buddha image had

[1] The most important of these sculptures we have been able to recover. They will be described along with those which were found in the course of our excavation.

[2] *Cf.* Vincent Smith, *Ind. Ant.*, XVIII (1889), p. 257, XXI (1892), p. 156 and *J. A. S. B.*, LVIII (1889), p. 144. G. Bühler, *Ind. Ant.*, XX (1891), p. 394, and XXV (1896), p. 312; E. Senart, *J. A.* 8 série, XV, p. 125, and 9 série, XIII, p. 530; Jas. Burgess, *J. I. A.*, VIII, No. 63, p. 31, and No. 69, p. 89.

been found at the point marked P, on the accompanying plan. This was ascertained from the finder himself, who asserted that, when discovered, it rested on a *takht* (base) of *chūnā*, and brought a copper coin found by him at the same spot. It proved to be one of Kadphises.

As soon as digging began we lighted upon the corner (C) of a brick wall running towards the north and east. Not more than three courses of bricks remained. On the south side it continued for a distance from the corner to the west for 17½′. At the further end only a few bricks were left buried under pebbles, which had apparently burst from the interior of the mound. From the point where the brick wall ceases, these pebbles were found to bar the main trench. The last bricks projected from the wall towards the west, indicating a continuation in that direction.

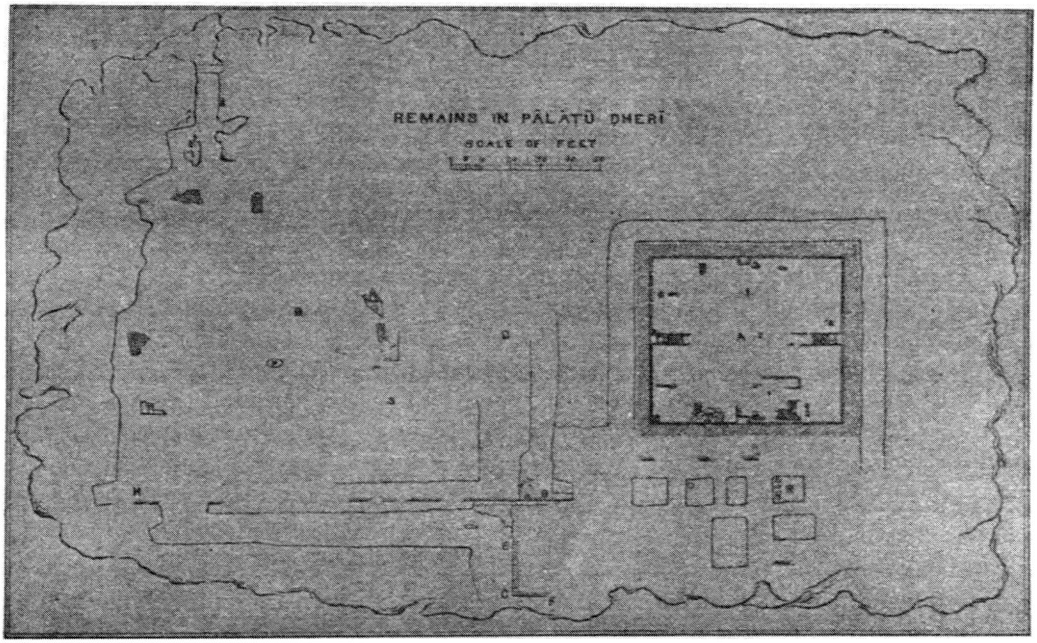

Fig. 14.

Behind the mass of pebbles was a stone wall of Buddhist masonry (G—H), facing north and continued westwards with considerable intervals for a distance of 103 feet. The width of this wall, the core of which consists of pebbles, is about 4 feet. But from the southern face all stones had been removed. The base has the same level as the brick wall first discovered. It is notable that to the north of this wall, at various places, pieces of pavement and a great number of sculptural remains were discovered, whereas south of it nothing whatever was found. It may be taken therefore that the stone wall marks the southern enclosure of building B.

About 14 feet from the eastern extremity of this wall on a level with its top the remnants of a pavement were found, consisting of square brick tiles. Further to the east (G), and at right angles with the stone wall, appeared the remnants of another brick wall, running north. Unfortunately neither this nor the lower brick wall could be traced farther north: nor were here any traces of walls on the south side of mound A.

The digging in the western half of this mound was more successful. Here a square courtyard was unearthed surrounded by low solid walls of Buddhist masonry and paved with square brick tiles. [*Cf.* Plate XXIV (*d*).] Four short flights of descending steps—one in the centre of each side—appear to have given access to the courtyard, but only those on the west side remain. These were joined by causeways which appear to have bisected each other in the centre of the court. The flat bricks with which they are paved are mostly bats, but some full-sized (11 inches square) still exist. It was obvious that they had either been taken from other buildings, or that the original paving had been relaid; probably the latter. The bed in which they are set is pounded earth. The causeways are bordered with bats set edgeways on the ground.

Similar paving extends over the rest of the court, the tiles being laid parallel with its sides and divided at intervals by bands of tiles set edgewise, which serve as bonding courses. On the southern side, and close by the entrance, was an open bowl-shaped vessel, 1′ 9¼″ across the mouth, sunk into the ground as far as its rim. Excavations proved that this was cased in a larger vessel, about 5 inches larger in diameter, the space between the two being intended for water—presumably for cooling the liquid in the inner bowl.[1] The larger vessel was imbedded in a layer of river sand, surrounded with a packing of brick dust and clay.

The backing of the surrounding wall exists complete on all four sides, but the facing is preserved only in the south-west corner as far as the middle of the southern and western sides; a small section also at the north-east corner and the lower portion at the south-east corner still exist. Its height averages a little over 2 feet. The backing consists of pebbles laid in earth to a width of 4½ or 5 feet. There is no defined outer face, and it is probable that the courtyard was in the nature of a depression, the top of the walls being level with the ground around. The facing is laid very regularly in the well-known diaper pattern; thin slab stones, laid horizontally and with their edges roughly cut, being used to indicate the mouldings. No doubt these and the face of the wall were originally finished off with plaster. A shallow projecting wainscot (8⅙″ high) runs around the base of the wall, and surmounting it is a torus and scotia moulding separated by a fillet. Above this the wall rises in a plain surface for 9 inches and then projects aga n about 3 inches. This projection marks another moulding of uncertain outline, which coincides with the original top of the wall. Around the quadrangle, close under the surrounding wall, especially on the southern side, were masses of burnt wood and fragments of iron. These apparently belonged to an early building; for, when the site was occupied at a later date, this fallen *débris*, instead of being cleared away, was covered over with a rough pavement, slanting downwards towards the centre of the courtyard.

Outside the quadrangle, at a distance of 30 feet from the inner facing of its southern wall (R, Fig. 14), four jars (*cāṭīs*) of the shape shown in Fig. 24, No. 19,

[1] The two vessels formed a sort of giant *Ψυκτήρ*, a vase well known in Greece for keeping wine cool.

were unearthed. They were standing in a row from north to south, each covered with a flat stone. The walls of these vessels are very brittle, the clay of which they are composed being mixed with a large percentage of sand, and worked up by hand to unusual thinness. They could scarcely have been intended for rough daily usage. Three of these jars bore Kharoṣṭhī inscriptions, but the characters, which were inscribed in a thin wash, were almost effaced, so that only by the application of moisture was it possible to trace their form. Considerable portions of the legends had completely disappeared. The inscriptions run in one line horizontally round the body of the vessel, the distance from the spring of the neck being 3 to 3½″ in A, 3 to 4⅓″ in B, and 1 inch in C. The largest circumference of the jars is 3 feet 4 inches. Of

A (1/4).

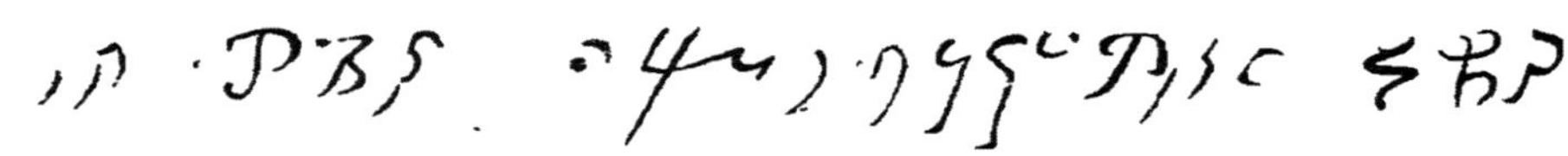

B (1/3).

C (1/1).

Fig. 15.

inscription A we possess two fragments which evidently represent its beginning and its end. Both fragments are 9 inches long and consist of 10 *akṣaras* each, the average size of the characters being 1⅓″. Inscription B, as far as it is traceable, is 18 inches long and seems to contain 22 *akṣaras*, the average size of which is 1 inch. The lettering of inscription C is fainter than that of the two others and could only be copied with the greatest difficulty. The reading is therefore even more uncertain here than in the two previous cases. The length of that portion of the inscription which can be traced is 6 inches, the number of letters 12 and their average size ½″.

We are not in a position to give even a tentative interpretation of these inscriptions, but would draw attention to the following points. The first 10 *akṣaras* of inscriptions A and B appear to be identical. The letters of A are more obliterated, especially their lower portions. So it may be supposed that some strokes which are plainly visible in B, are missing here. Compare, for instance, the 2nd, 3rd and 7th *akṣara*, which we read *gh*, *c* and *ṣ*, respectively. Assuming that the *anusvāra* over the first letter has been lost, the two initial *akṣaras* may be read *saṁgha* which can be the first member of a proper name. Secondly it should be noted that the last four syllables of A represent the word *dānamukha* meaning " an excellent gift " and regularly found at the end of votive inscriptions. If the interpretation of this part of the inscription is correct, it follows that these vessels were presented as a votive offering by some devotee whose name we may expect to be mentioned in the first part of the inscription. The character is that of the Kuṣaṇa period.[1]

What the original ground plan of these buildings was, it is difficult to determine. That there was a Buddhist sanctuary here is sufficiently proved by the discovery of numerous stone sculptures and stucco figures, among which may be noted several examples of the brackets belonging to a dentil cornice, such as is almost invariably found in Gandhāra *stūpas*. The fact that nearly all of these were found in the western half of the *ḍherī* suggested that a portion of the open space at B was once occupied by a small *stūpa*, and this was further borne out by the presence, at this point, of great quantities of water-worn pebbles, which, as we know, were regularly used for the cores of these structures. That nothing was left of the *stūpa* save fragments of its ornamental stone facing, need not be wondered at, seeing that the place has so long been the quarrying ground of the neighbouring villagers.

Mound A, in which hardly any sculptural remains were found, contained, on the contrary, numerous traces of habitation, such as pottery, ornaments, coins, etc., which were almost entirely wanting in mound B. We know from the Chinese pilgrims that *stūpas* and monasteries were invariably built side by side; and we know also that in the latter there was usually a central square, on the four sides of which the cells of the monks were erected. It is not unreasonable to suppose that the quadrangular courtyard described above was the centre of such a *vihāra*. The masses of charcoal and iron along the borders of the courtyard point to the existence of buildings on the platform round, and the presence of a perennial spring flowing along the north side of Pālāṭū Ḍherī, would mark it as a site especially suitable for a monastery; but the actual disposition of the buildings included in it can no longer be determined.

It is clear from the above that the Buddhist monument, which once stood on this spot, met with a violent end. About what time this happened may be surmised from the coins found in the courtyard which belong to the late Kuṣaṇa period. The date of its erection is more difficult to determine, but some hint may be obtained from the fact that the sculptures found here are of superior style, and presumably earlier, than

---

[1] Since the above was written, three of the best authorities on Indian Epigraphy—M. E. Senart M. l'Abbé Boyer, and Dr. H. Lüders—have kindly favoured us with the following readings of these inscriptions. To M. Senart is due the reading of the first half of inscription A, while that of the latter half is M. l'Abbé Boyer's. For the reading of B we are indebted to both M. Senart and Dr. Lüders, who arrived at precisely the same conclusions, and for the reading of C to M. l'Abbé Boyer.

A. *Saṁgh*[*e*] *catudiśe ṣama—da* — — — — — *ga amata eta danamukha.*
To the universal community of (?) monks (?) this jar (Skr. *amatra*) is a gift.

B. *Saṁgh*[*e*] *catudiśe ṣamaṇa* (*na*?) — — — To the universal community of monks — — — (For *ṣamaṇa*=Skr. *śramaṇa*, *cf.* inscr. on Chārsada pedestal, and also *ṣāvaka*=Skr. *śrāvaka*.)

C. *Yasavada samadaśadimitrasa.* [Gift] of Yasavat with his mother, relatives and friends.

SPECIMENS OF STONE SCULPTURES.

those from the adjacent *stūpa*, while such evidence as there is goes to show that the latter is to be referred to the reign of Zeionises.

Sculptures—

As might have been expected on a site situated in the open plain surrounded by villages, the stone sculptures and stucco figures were, for the most part, in a mutilated condition. This is the more regrettable as the fragments discovered in Pālāṭū Ḍherī were of particularly good style. Among them the most attractive perhaps is the Bodhisattva head figured in Plate XXV, A and B. There is a certain freshness about this head, which is seldom met with in the art of Gandhāra. The chiselling is rough, and the portrayal is sketchy, but it possesses, for this very reason perhaps, an originality which mere mechanical repetitions lack. There is no trace of drill-work on the stone. The figure was attached to a back-ground from which the head is broken, and the fracture produces a seeming irregularity in the profile of the skull. The facial angle is less obtuse than in the great majority of examples from Gandhāra. The features of the face, taken individually, hardly bear criticism. The ears and eyes are most at fault. The former are weighted down and distorted, in barbaric fashion, with heavy earrings; the latter are typically Mongolian and widely interspaced; the eyeball is full and round, but the pupils are turned upwards, and the lids are thick, heavy, and half closed, imparting an air of sleepiness which may not perhaps be unintentional. The modelling around the eyes, which might make them such telling vehicles of expression, is entirely wanting. The eyebrow is well arched and sharply cut; the bridge of the nose delicately indicated, but the nostrils over small, the cheek bones prominent, and the transition from nose to cheek pronounced. The charm of expression, such as it is, lies especially perhaps in the modelling of the lower half of the face. The curves of the mouth are simple, and the lips less fleshy than is usual. The hair is confined within a net—like the Greek *κεκρύφαλος*,—made of rows of beads, with small bosses to mark where they are tied. It is waved from the crown over the *uṣṇīṣa* (bump of intelligence), and falls upon the forehead in a schematic row of curls, which recall the conventional treatment of archaic Greek art. The two other heads (C and D, Plate XXV) come from Ghaz Ḍherī, and belong to a period when certain types of the Buddha had already become fixed in the art of Gandhāra. The features of both betray a conventional idealism, but of a widely different kind. That to the left (C) may be under a stronger Indian influence, but it must be admitted that the suggestion is based only on the conventional treatment of the hair, which is arranged, as the canon required,[1] in uniform rows of short spiral curls about the skull, and that a similar treatment of the hair is not uncommon in western Hellenic art. The *uṣṇīṣa* in this case is thrown forward and makes an ugly break in the otherwise regular curve of the skull, when seen in profile. The facial angle is obtuse, and there is a greater angularity about the features than in Figure D—a trait which is particularly noticeable in the prominent bone structure of the chin and jaw. The upper lip is short and fleshy and the lines of the mouth complex, the upward curve at the corner weakening its expression. The other head (Figure D) is of far superior style, and were it not for the unfortunate breakages in the chin and nose, might be

[1] *Cf.* Grünwedel-Burgess, *Buddhist Art*, p. 167, and Fig. 115.

classed, perhaps, as the finest from Gandhāra. Its pose is nobler and its proportions more perfect. The waves of the hair are soft and natural. The cheeks are full and the jaw massive, but with a well-rounded contour; the arching of the upper eyelid and the brow are more symmetrical; the nose is broad, the mouth more simply curved, and with a gentle curl in its under lip that suggests determination in its contemplative look.

Among the reliefs from Pālāṭū Ḍherī the one shown on Plate XXVII, No. 5, which we were able to piece together from ten fragments, is the most striking. The group is gracefully arranged, and the expression and posture of the individual figures natural and full of variety. Particularly noticeable is the contrast between the vigorous figure of the bearded Vajrapāṇi (Śakra ?), clasping the thunderbolt in his fist, and the lean monk behind him, his right arm wrapped up in his gown, and turning his shaven face away, as if in aversion from the things of this world.[1] The two figures to the left of the Buddha are unfortunately much mutilated, but not too much to prevent us admiring the vigour of their attitude, and the artistic arrangement of their drapery.

One of the sculptures obtained from the *dharmśālā* of Rājaṛ (No. 4) represents the familiar scene of Siddhārtha's riding out of the city gate of Kapilavastu. Two Yakṣas support the hoofs of the horse Kaṇṭhaka, which is shown in profile. At the side of the gate stands the city goddess (Śrī) wearing the mural crown and in an attitude of grief, which brings to mind the sorrowing figures on the funeral *stelai* of Greece—a good instance of the adoption of classical forms to Indian conceptions. No. 2 is a fragment of a panel representing Siddhārtha's conception, as can be ascertained from a comparison with a relief excavated by Colonel Deane at Sīkrī, now in the Lahor Museum. The latter shows Māyā lying on her left side on a couch, in front of which is placed a foot-stool. The upper part of her body is nude. Behind the couch, towards its foot, stands a female guard (Yavanānī ?) holding a spear in her right hand. In the upper corner of the relief we see the Bodhisattva, who in accordance with the scriptural legend is about to enter her womb from the right side in the form of an elephant. In the Chārsada relief, though the greater part of it is missing, the same scene can be recognised. The figure of Māyā agrees exactly in attitude with that on the Sīkrī relief, and the female guard can be traced behind the couch.

Figure 1 shows an empty throne, on either side of which stands an adoring figure, probably a *deva*, as indicated by the halo round the head. In the centre we natura y expect an image of the Buddha, but, strange to say, the surface of the throne does not retain any trace of it, nor show even a break.

In No. 3 the Buddha is confronted by a young ascetic, who, in his dress and attributes, closely agrees with the Sumedha of the Dīpaṅkara-Jātaka, as portrayed on Graeco-Buddhist reliefs. The two broken figures to the Buddha's right are also dressed like *tapasvins*.

The wealth of sculptures which once adorned the monument of Pālāṭū Ḍherī may be estimated from the fact that fragments of more than twenty Buddha and

[1] Elsewhere we find the monk with the right arm wrapped up, together with the Vajrapāṇi, in attendance on the Buddha (Cole, Pl. 30), which would lead to the supposition that he represents a definite character. *Cf.* also Cole, Pl. 13.

Bodhisattva statues were found. Among these fragments were eight pedestals, on which only the feet of the image, to which they belonged, still survive. On the face of these pedestals a relief is invariably carved, showing a seated Buddha or Bodhisattva in the centre, with worshipping figures (*bhikṣus* or *upāsakas*) on either side, enclosed between two Indo-Corinthian pilasters. It would be interesting to know if these reliefs have any reference to the persons dedicating the statue.

One of the pedestals found in Pālāṭū Ḍherī requires special notice, as it contains a Kharoṣṭhī inscription (Fig. 16) of seven *akṣaras* (*c.* ½" high), which is cut on the raised rim, beneath the front relief. The upper portion of the first *akṣara* is destroyed, so that only a vertical stroke remains for its lower part.

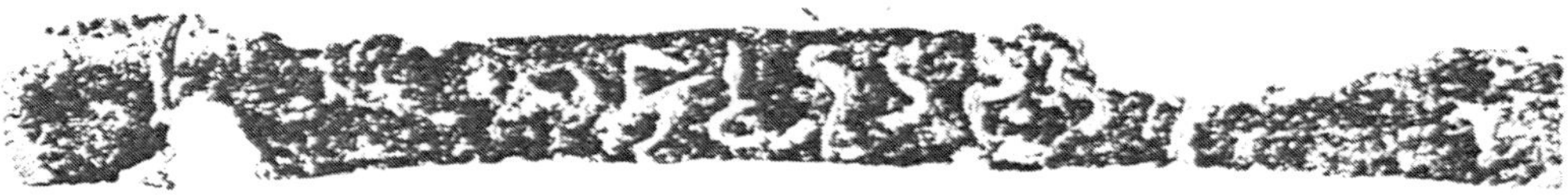

Fig. 16.

We read the inscription : ? *da-sa da-na-mu-khe* meaning "?-da's pious gift." The second word is well known from votive epigraphs. The only point to be noted is the nominative ending in *e* which also occurs on the Chārsada pedestal in the Lahor Museum. Unfortunately the name of the donor is uncertain. A proper name of two syllables, the second of which is *da*, looks neither Greek nor Indian, but it might be Parthian. The legend of Saint Thomas mentions a rother of Gudufara, called Gad. That this name is not purely legendary, appears from an intaglio recently acquired from the Frontier Province, which bears the Kharoṣṭhī legend *Gadasa*. The little that remains of the first letter on the pedestal does not preclude the possibility of its having been a *G*.

The following is a list of the stone sculptures found in Pālāṭū Ḍherī.

1. Pedestal (22 × 42 cm.) of a standing Buddha[1] statue, of which only the bare feet remain. On front, relief between Indo-Corinthian pilasters representing, in centre, Bodhisattva (Maitreya?) seated cross-legged on throne. Right hand *abhayamudrā* ; left hand holding ointment vessel. Vajrapāṇi behind his throne to his right. On both sides two worshippers (*bhikṣus* ?) . All the figures defaced. On either side of the pedestal a rosette ornament, partly missing. Beneath relief, a Kharoṣṭhī inscription of seven *akṣaras*. See above.

2. Pedestal (22 × 35 cm.) of a standing Bodhisattva statue, of which only the sandalled feet remain. On front, relief between Indo-Corinthian pilasters, representing, in centre, alms-bowl on throne under canopy. On both sides two worshipping *upāsakas*. On either side of pedestal a lotus rosette.

3. Pedestal (16 × 30 cm.) of a standing Buddha statue, of which only the bare feet remain. On front, relief between Indo-Corinthian pilasters representing Boddhisattva (Maitreya ?) in centre, seated cross-legged on throne ; right hand *abhayamudrā* ; left hand holding ointment vessel. On both sides two worshipping *upāsakas*. On each side of pedestal a palmette.

4. Pedestal (14 × 24 cm.) of a standing Buddha statue, of which only the bare feet remain. On front, relief between Indo-Corinthian pilasters (one missing) representing in centre Buddha

---

[1] In accordance with Grünwedel, *op. cit.*, p. 182, images in monk's dress are indicated as Buddha statues, those in princely attire as Bodhisattvas.

seated in *dhyānamudrā* with a worshipper standing on each side. On either side of the pedestal a rosette.

5. Pedestal (10 × 19 cm.) of a standing Buddha statue, of which only the bare feet remain. On front, relief between Indo-Corinthian pilasters, representing a Bodhisattva (Maitreya ?) seated; right hand *abhayamudrā*, left hand holds vessel. On his right two worshippers, on his left one. On either side of the pedestal a rosette.

6. Pedestal (7 × 21 cm.) of a standing Buddha statue, of which only the bare feet and a portion of the robe remain. On front, relief between Indo-Corinthian pilasters representing in centre Buddha seated cross-legged in *dhyānamudrā*, under *bodhi* tree, with two kneeling worshippers on each side, those to his left being *upāsikās*. On proper left side of pedestal a rosette; on right side an uncertain figure.

7. Pedestal (13 × 24 cm.) of a standing Buddha statue, of which only the bare feet remain. On front, relief between Indo-Corinthian pilasters representing Bodhisattva (Maitreya ?) seated cross-legged on throne; right hand *abhayamudrā;* left hand broken, holds ointment vessel (?). To his left, two *upāsakas*, standing with folded hands. On either side of the pedestal a palmette.

8. Pedestal (9 × 24 cm.) of a standing Bodhisattva statue, of which only the sandalled feet remain. The front relief defaced. On either side of pedestal a rosette.

9. Statue of a standing Bodhisattva with pedestal (height 1 m.) defaced. Arms missing. On front of the pedestal, relief enclosed between Indo-Corinthian pilasters representing in centre Bodhisattva, seated cross-legged on a lotus throne in *dhyānamudrā*. Two *upāsakas* are standing to his right, two *upāsikās* to his left. On either side of the pedestal a rosette.

10. Statue of a standing Buddha (height 86 cm.). Head, feet, and hands missing.

11. Statue[1] of a standing Buddha (height 56 cm.) in *abhayamudrā*. Head, hands, and feet with the pedestal missing.

12. Statue[1] of a sitting Bodhisattva, probably Maitreya (20·5 × 33 cm.). Upper part missing. Left hand holds ointment vessel.

13. Torso of a standing Buddha statue (40 × 28 cm.). Head, arms, and lower part of the body missing.

14. Statue of a standing Buddha (50 × 20 cm.). Head, arms, and feet missing.

15. Head of a Bodhisattva statue (height 14 cm.). Hair wavy, covered with beaded net; earrings.

16. Head of a Buddha statue (height 23 cm.). Considerably damaged. Hair wavy and arranged in *krobylos*. *Ūrnā*.

17. Head of a Buddha statue (height 11·5 cm.), well preserved.

18. Head of Buddha statue (height 7·5 cm.).

19. Head of Buddha statue (height 20 cm.), defaced. Hair arranged in *krobylos*.

20. Three Buddha heads (height 15 to 16 cm.), defaced.

21. Three fragments of Buddha masks.

22. Hand and part of the arm with bracelet (25 cm.) of Bodhisattva (?) statue.

23. A pair of hands in *dharmacakramudrā* (15 cm).

24. Twelve hands and fragments of hands.

25. Fragment of a relief (16·5 × 13 cm.) representing conception of Siddhārtha. Left and upper part of panel missing. The female guard (*Yavanānī* ?) standing behind Māyā's couch, is partly preserved. *Cf.* above, page 166.

26. Fragment.[1] of a relief (23 × 25·5 cm.) representing Siddhārtha leaving Kapilavastu. The proper right half of the panel is lost. To the left, an Indo-Corinthian pilaster encloses the scene. *Cf.* above, page 166.

---

[1] Obtained from the Dharmśālā at Rājar.

27. Fragments of a relief (23 × 25·5 cm.) representing Śākyamuni Buddha with three ascetics. The two standing to his right are broken. To the left of Buddha, a young ascetic, holding a vessel in his left hand. His right hand is broken. *Cf.* above, page 166.

28. Ten fragments of a relief (35·5 × 49·5 cm.). The upper proper left corner missing and the rest considerably damaged. In the centre the Buddha, larger than the surrounding figures, half turned to the left. Hishead, hands, and left foot are missing. To his right *Vajrapāṇi*, nude except for loin cloth and drapery over left arm. To his right a shaven monk turning away his face, the left arm wrapped up in his robe. Over Vajrapāṇi and the monk two figures are visible, one of which raises the right hand as in the act of showering flowers. The other is defaced. The proper left side of the relief is occupied by two figures in royal attire, which are much mutilated. One is standing in front of Buddha, with his knees slightly bent and his arms stretched forward in the direction of Buddha's left hand. The upper part of the body is nude, but decorated with collar and necklace. His head, left arm, and left leg are missing. The figure to the proper left wears a long gown, leaving part of his arms bare, and a royal head-dress. Over it another flying figure can be traced. The scene has not been identified. *Cf.* above, page 165 sq.

29. Two fragments of a relief (height 30·5 cm.), containing two adoring figures one over the other. The lower figure is standing with folded hands, the upper one is throwing flowers.

30. Fragment of a relief (height 22 cm.) representing a figure in monk's dress standing with folded hands. Head missing.

31. Fragment of a relief (height 20·3 cm.) containing two standing figures turned to the right. Feet broken. One is Vajrapāṇi, the other represents a woman. A third figure is partly visible over their heads.

32. Fragment of a relief (height 22·8 cm.) representing three figures turned to the right, probably *devas* showering flowers.

33. Fragment of a relief (20·3 × 19 cm.) representing a figure under a palm tree, turned to the left. Bust only preserved. Indo-Corinthian pilaster to proper right.

34. Fragment of a relief (25·3 × 10 cm.) representing a nude figure, of which the head and left leg are missing, turned to the right. Portion of the shaft and base of a pilaster to the proper left. Acanthus border beneath.

35. Fragment of a relief (height 28 cm.) representing a standing Buddha figure, defaced.

36. Fragment of a relief (height 17·8 cm.) representing a Buddha figure turned to the right, defaced.

37. Fragment of a relief (height 25 cm.) representing a nude figure to the proper right and two figures over each other to the proper left, defaced.

38. Fragment of a relief (height 19 cm.) containing three broken figures.

39. Fragment of a relief (height 15·2 cm.) containing part of a figure showering flowers, turned to the left. It probably belongs to a panel representing the *Dipaṅkara-jātaka.*

40. Fragment of a relief (height 20·3 cm.). The upper portion contains the legs of a standing figure and the base of a pilaster, the lower part a head with royal head-dress and the capital of a pilaster.

41. Fragment of a relief (height 23 cm.) containing a standing figure with folded hands. The head and legs missing.

42. Fragment of a relief (height 15·2 cm.) containing three women over a balcony.

43. Fragment of a relief (height 23 cm.) containing a standing figure of Vajrapāṇi, the head and left foot of which are broken. To the proper right a pilaster, the capital of which is missing.

44. Fragment of a relief (height 14 cm.) containing the lower part of a Buddha figure.

45. Fragment of a relief (height 17·8 cm.) containing part of a figure in royal dress with folded hands, turned to the right.

46. Fragment of a relief (height 15·2 cm.) containing two adoring figures (*devas?*) with folded hands, turned to the left.

47. Fragment of a relief (height 20·3 cm.) containing a head wearing a royal head-dress.

48. Fragment of a relief (height 12·7 cm.) containing a flying figure projecting from a disc. It probably belongs to a panel representing the *Dipaṅkara-jātaka*.

49. Fragment of a relief (height 14 cm.) representing a woman playing on a lute.

50. Fragment of a relief (height 12·7 cm.) containing part of a man on horseback. It probably belongs to a panel representing Siddhārtha leaving Kapilavastu.

51. Fragment of a relief (height 10 cm.) containing part of a soldier, his left hand resting on the hilt of his sword.

52. Fragment (height 11·3 cm.) containing the head and bust of a monk.

53. Fragments of a decorative border of reticulated stars, the largest one measuring 45 × 22 cm.

54. Fragments of an acanthus architrave (height 9 cm.).

55. Five fragments of a modillion cornice.

56. Four detached brackets of a dentil cornice. Indo-Corinthian capitals.

57. Fragments of a decorative border showing a rope ornament.

58. Fragment (11·3 × 15·2 cm.) containing the bust of a male figure.

59. Fragment of a border (28 × 20·3 cm.) showing female busts in sunk panels.

60. Two fragments of the solid dome of a miniature *stūpa*.

61. Fragment of a *stūpa* umbrella (12·6 cm.).

62. Fragment of a decorative border (15·2 × 16·5 cm.) showing a Cupid riding on a dragon. *Cf.* Grünwedel, *op. cit.*, No. 71.

63. Indo-Corinthian pilaster in sunk panel (28 × 12·6 cm.).

64. Three fragments (17·8, 12·6, and 9·5 cm.) containing portions of pilasters.

65. Fragment of a border (11·4 × 12·6 cm.) containing Buddha seated in *dhyānamudrā* flanked by trees, under acanthus architrave.

66. Fragment of a border (6·4 × 17·8 cm.) containing a Buddha figure seated in *dhyāna-mudrā* under an ogee arch to the proper left, and an alms-bowl on a throne under an ogee arch to the right, separated by miniature Indo-Corinthian pilaster.

67. Fragments of a decorative border (7·6 × 6·4 cm.) representing a pearl string and flowers. *Cf.* Grünwedel, No. 147.

68. Fragments of an *ūrdhvapaṭṭa* (the largest 25·4 × 14·6 cm.), containing panels with figure of Buddha in *abhayamudrā*, standing between two worshippers *upāsaka* and *upāsikā*, under arches of various shape supported by Indo-Corinthian pilasters. Only one panel is entire.

69. Fragment (height 23 cm.) of a Buddha figure seated cross-legged on a throne, the left hand holding his robe.

70. Fragment (15·2 × 21·6 cm.) containing an empty throne, on each side of which an adoring figure probably of a *deva* is standing. *Cf.* p. 166 above.

71. Fragment (10 cm.) representing a lion's claw.

72. Fragment (7·6 × 19 cm.) showing the head and arm of an Atlant.

73. Fragment (8·2 cm.) containing a miniature pilaster in a sunk panel.

74. Fragment (17·8 × 38·7 cm.) showing a panel with two women on a balcony and a rope border to the proper right. The rest is defaced.

75. Fragment (12·6 cm.) containing the foot of a throne.

76. Fragment of a border (10 × 14 cm.) containing Buddha figures seated cross-legged with intervening palm trees.

77. Fragment (11·4 × 12·6 cm.) representing a Buddha figure seated cross-legged on a throne in *dhyānamudrā* with a worshipper to his right; defaced.

78. Fragment (7·6 × 10 cm.) representing a Buddha figure of which the head is missing, seated cross-legged on a throne, with two worshippers standing to his right.

SPECIMENS OF PLASTER FIGURES.

79. Fragment of a vertical border (height 16·4 cm.) containing a series of standing Buddha figures (*abhayamudrā*).

80. Fragment (9 cm.) of a pilaster and an adoring figure.

Besides the stone sculptures a considerable number of stucco fragments were unearthed in Pālāṭū Ḍherī. The best specimen of these is the upper half of a Buddha figure, which we were able to reconstruct from three detached fragments (see Plate XXVI, 1). The position of the hands (*dharmacakra-mudrā*), which here as elsewhere is combined with a bare right shoulder, indicates that the image was a seated one.[1] But no fragments were recovered to prove this. On the same spot, where the Buddha was discovered, two stucco heads were found, one of them with part of the torso (Plate XXVI, 3). These must have belonged to figures of Bodhisattvas standing on either side of the seated Buddha, a combination commonly met with in Buddhist art. The stucco figures, including the above, consisted of the following :—

1. Head and torso of a sitting Buddha statue (Head, height 15·2 cm., circumference 40·6 cm.; torso, height 25·4 cm., width across shoulders 35·5 cm., but on each side about 2½ cm missing). Right shoulder bare. Hands joined in *dharmacakramudrā*. (Plate XXVI, 1.)

2. Head and torso of a Bodhisattva image, probably standing (head, height 11·4 cm. torso, height 20·3 cm.; width across shoulders 23 cm., but left shoulder broken). Ornamental head-dress; torso bare, but drapery over left shoulder; necklace and other ornaments similar to those commonly found on stone Bodhisattva statues. (Plate XXVI, 3.)

3. Head of a Bodhisattva statue, probably standing (height 12·6 cm., circumference 33 cm.). Ringlets round forehead and long locks at the back of the head; a *krobylos* on the top. (Plate XXVI, 2.)

4. Mask of a Buddha head (height 9·8 cm.) with *uṣṇiṣa* and schematic corkscrew curls. The surface is much decayed.

5. Small Buddha head (height 6 cm.) showing *uṣṇiṣa*, *ūrṇā* and prolonged ear-lobe. The top of the head is cut away at the back to a height of 2 cm. and depth of 2·4 cm., as if to make room for a projecting architectural member, passing behind it.

6. Fragment of an arm (9·5 cm.) partially concealed by drapery and a triangular raised ornament, countersunk with a smaller triangle and circle (?) within.

7. Right breast and shoulder as far as the elbow. (4·2 × 11 cm.) The biceps has the same triangular ornament as fragment 6. A strap passes across the right breast.

8. Mutilated mask (height 6·4 cm.); the breadth of the face is greater than its height. The nose is flat and short; the eyes are deep set, the cheeks full. The hair descends in straight strands from the crown of the head and ends in rows of bunched curls.

9. Head (height 7 cm), slightly turned to the left. Back destroyed; nose broken. Hair parted in the centre and drawn back over the ear, which wears a massive earring. Traces of red paint.

10. Buddha head (height 10·5 cm.) Back and left ear partly destroyed. Hair drawn back in waves from forehead and concealing *uṣṇiṣa* in form of Greek *krobylos*.

11. Head (height 7 cm.), broken off at the back. Hair parted from centre and retained in position by waved fillet.

12. Head (height 7·5 cm.), turned to the left and broken off at the back. Lower portion of the face destroyed; straight folded head-cover bunched together over the forehead.

13. Head (height 4 cm), broken off at the back. Round full face; hair arranged in corkscrew ringlets round the forehead. Traces of red paint.

[1] *Cf.* Cole, No. 1; Burgess, *J. I. A.*, VIII, 1 and 2; VII, 2. Grünwedel-Burgess, Nos. 121, 137, 140, 147, 152. In all these instances the Buddha is seated on a *padmāsana* and flanked by two Bodhisattvas.

14. Fragment of a head (height 5 cm.), broken off at the back. Lower portion of the face missing. Hair in double row of ringlets.

15. Head and torso (height 10 cm.). Arms missing; face turned to the left. Flat collar around neck and earring in left ear.

16. Fragment of Indo-Persian capital (5 × 8 cm.). Recumbent bullock to right; head facing front.

17. Fragment of Indo-Corinthian capital (5½ cm.), showing traces of blue and red paint.

The following *minor objects* were found in Pālāṭū Ḍherī :—

Coins—

1. Æ. 1·1 inch. Ooemo-Kadphises. Gardner, *Brit. Mus. Cat.*, p. 126, No. 12.

2. Æ. 1 inch. Defaced. Kaniṣka (?).

3. Twelve copper Indo-Scythic, unidentifiable.

4. A hoard of 57 copper coins of the late Kuṣaṇa period was found in the surface soil towards the north-east. The coins are too much corroded to make out more than a standing figure on the obverse of some of them, with Śiva facing, and a bull behind, on the reverse.

5. 1 Muhammadan, uncertain.

Gold—

1. Cylindrical gold ornament set with bluish garnet *en cabuchon*. *Cf.* Plate XXVIII, 16; the setting is strengthened by a projecting rim. The cylinder would seem to have fitted into a socket. At the back of the carbuncle is a small piece of silver foil, with a thin plate of gold behind, kept in place by a wire passed through the sides of the cylinder. The gold is pure but thin and flimsy.

2. Small fragment of gold, diameter ·8 cm.; with cylindrical sides pierced, as if for threading on a necklace.

Bronzes—

1. Small bronze bowl of good workmanship turned on the lathe (Fig. 17, 1).

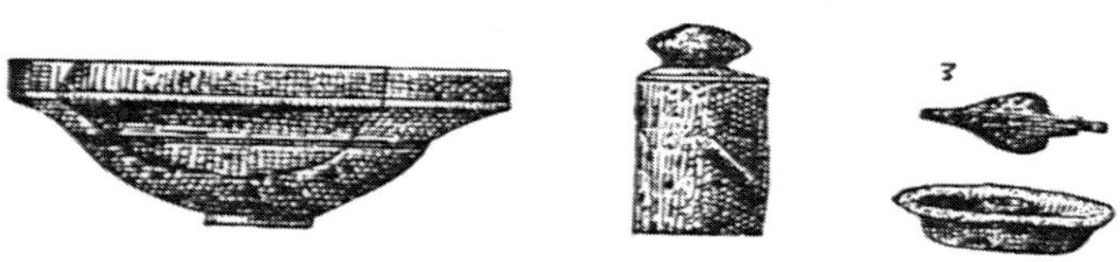

1. Fig. 17. 2. 3 4.

2. Two hollow cylindrical bronze objects (Fig. 17, 2) closed at one end, with projecting knob; twining leaves (Fig. 17, 3) were attached to the cylinders, and there were traces of gilding upon them. Probably they formed the ends of a reliquary worn about the neck. The centre of the cylinder may have been of crystal, or some perishable material, encircled, like the metal ends, with the leaves of the *pipal* tree. The cord, by which it would be suspended, would be fastened round the neck of the knobs at either end.

3. Miniature bronze dish (Fig. 17, 4) with rim turning outwards, and hole in centre.

4. Seventy bronze earrings. The simplest type is of plain copper wire with the ends twisted together (Fig. 18, 4). This type is elaborated by coating the wire with silver (Fig. 18, 1), and still further, by threading on it small beads of crystal, silver, or vitreous paste (Fig. 18, 2 and 3).

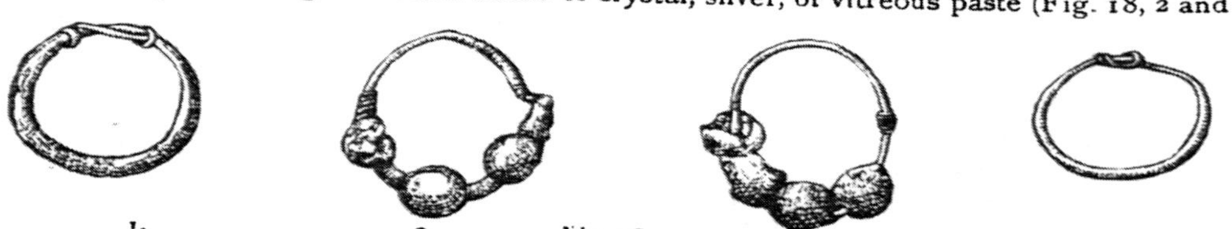

1. 2. Fig. 18. 3. 4.

5. Two finger rings, the one (diameter 1·4 cm.) a plain band, the other (diameter 1·7 cm.) encircled with a row of bead-like projections.

6. Round cup-shaped disc (diameter 2·4 cm.) gilt on convex side, with two holes at its edge for attachment.

7. Oblong bronze plate (3·5 cm. long) pierced with fragment of a nail at either end.

Beads—

Transparent glass. Plate XXIX (*b*), No. 1. The glass is manufactured in blue and white strata in imitation, apparently, of banded agate.

Amber—

Seventeen cylindrical beads, calcined. The amber is of the same deep hue as the Sicilian species, but somewhat similar amber has long been known in the Hukong valley to the north of the Myitkyinā district in Upper Burma. Other beads of vitreous paste, bone, ivory, agate, lapis lazuli, and cornelian—to the number of more than a thousand—were found in this *ḍherī*. They are of the same sizes and shapes as those of similar material, found on the Bālā Ḥiṣār and Mīr Ziyārat mounds. (*Cf. supra*, p. 153 sq.)

Pottery and Terra-cottas—

Besides the four *cāṭis* mentioned above, large numbers of pottery fragments and a few whole vessels and mutilated terra-cotta figurines were found in and around the courtyard. They are of the same fabric as the majority of the pre-Muhammadan wares from the Bālā Ḥiṣār and Mīr Ziyārat. A good specimen of a large store vessel, or *maṭan*, was found on the south side of the courtyard. It is ornamented with a rope pattern in relief, and would be difficult to distinguish from some of the pre-historic *pithoi* of the Levant. Of the other vessels the commonest forms were akin to the modern *piyālā*, *cāṭi* and *haṇḍi* (*cf.* Fig. 24, Nos. 3, 19, and 20), but flat dishes and lamps were also found in large numbers. Three terra-cottas came from the same spot; the first a female torso, the second a monkey playing on a stringed instrument, and the third a fragment of a miniature *stūpa*. Another fragment from here is figured on page 182 (Fig. 25, No. 7); on it is a stamped design of concentric rings, within which are rows of triskels, circles, and triangles.

Miscellaneous—

1. Two shell bangle ornaments. One with flanged edges and pierced with minute holes.
2. Fragment of iron ring (diameter 1·5 cm.) with plain bezel, much corroded.

Ghaz Ḍherī.

The first trench drawn through the middle of this mound from south-east to north-west for a distance of about 60 yards did not reveal any structural remains, but a parallel trench through its eastern part led to the discovery of the base of a *stūpa* measuring 32 feet square [Fig. 19, A, and Plate XXIV (*c*)]. Of the drum and dome of this monument no trace was left. The base, consisting of a solid mass of earth and rubble, must have been completely faced with a stone wall of Buddhist masonry of which some small portions still remain along its north side, partly covered with a layer of stucco (BB, Fig. 19). The outline of the base was traced by following up the flooring of square brick tiles (10 inches by 10 inches), with which the court around is paved on three sides. Along its western side no paving was found but at a distance of 7 feet from the base there was a parallel wall which belonged to a massive rectangular structure (C); on the far side of which the pavement was continued.

The southern side of this structure is in a line with the *stūpa* base, but its northern side projects two feet beyond that of the *stūpa*. There must be some connection between this circumstance and the fact that on this side, between the pavement and the *stūpa,* there is an open space corresponding in width exactly to the projection of the adjoining structure. The purpose of the latter cannot be determined with certainty. But the most plausible explanation would seem to be that it once served as the basement of a large recumbent figure of the dying Buddha. Its shape and position would well agree with this hypothesis, inasmuch as such images, which are known to have existed in India and are still commonly found in Burma, represented the Buddha lying on his right side with his head turned to the north, in close agreement with the scriptures.[1] There is a well-known example among the ruins of Māthā Kūar-kā-Koṭ near Kasiā. Here we find immediately to the west of the *stūpa* and in the

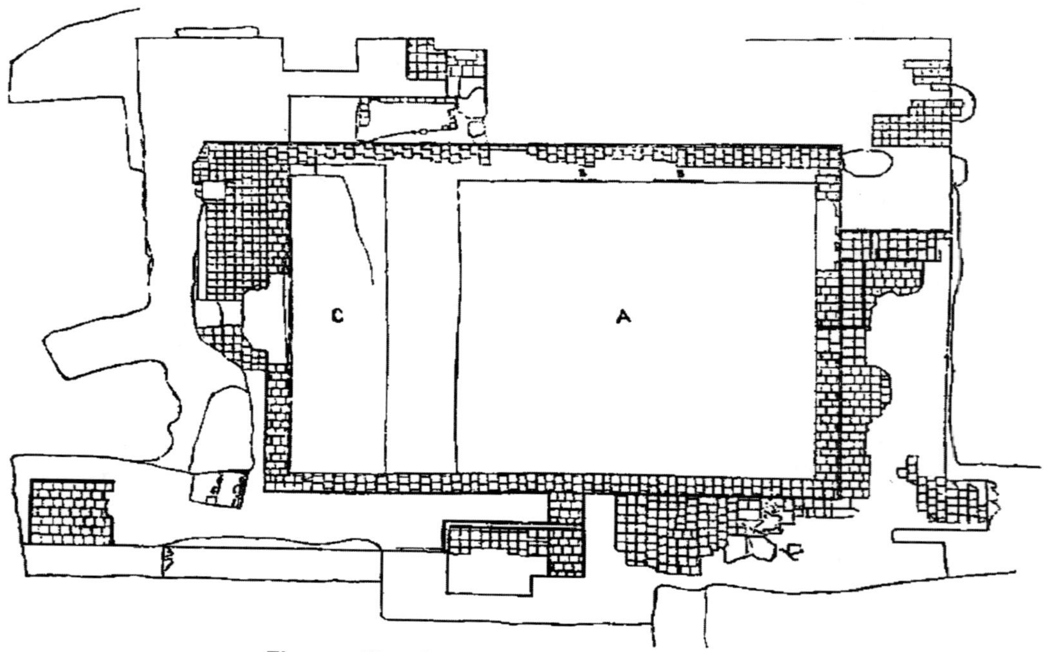

Fig. 19. Plan of *stūpa* base and courtyard in Ghaz Ḍherī.

same enclosure a shrine containing an image of the dying Buddha in the conventional position.[2] It is true that in Ghaz Ḍherī no fragments were found which can, with certainty, be attributed to it. Possibly it was moulded in perishable plaster, or possibly some of the colossal fragments of stone discovered here belonged to it, for it may be noted that a recumbent Buddha image is little else than a standing one placed horizontally.[3] It may be added also that on the Gandhāra reliefs representing

[1] *Cf.* Kern, *Manual of Indian Buddhism*, p. 43.
[2] *Cf.* V. A. Smith, *The remains near Kasiā*, Allahabad, 1896, p. 20 sq.
[3] *Cf.* Grünwedel, *op. cit.*, p. 122.

Sākyamuni's *parinirvāṇa* a small Buddha figure seated in meditation is invariably pictured, and three such images were found, one of them at the south side of the supposed basement, but unfortunately they are of too common a type to lead to any definite conclusion. That the main building really represents the base of a Buddhist *stūpa* cannot be doubted. For not only were several Buddhist sculptures and stucco figures (the latter including remnants of a railing; Fig. 20) found on its four sides, but in the exact centre only 9 inches below the surface were found the relics, for the sake of which the monument was reared. These consisted of some fragments of bone, placed, with a little gold, inside a small round casket of schist stone (Fig. 21, 2); this in its turn was placed in a larger box (Fig. 21, 1) of the same material, and the whole wedged tightly into a long narrow vessel of coarse earthenware, the space around being filled with hardened lime and earth. In order to remove the casket without breakage, the outer vessel had to be carefully sawn in halves.

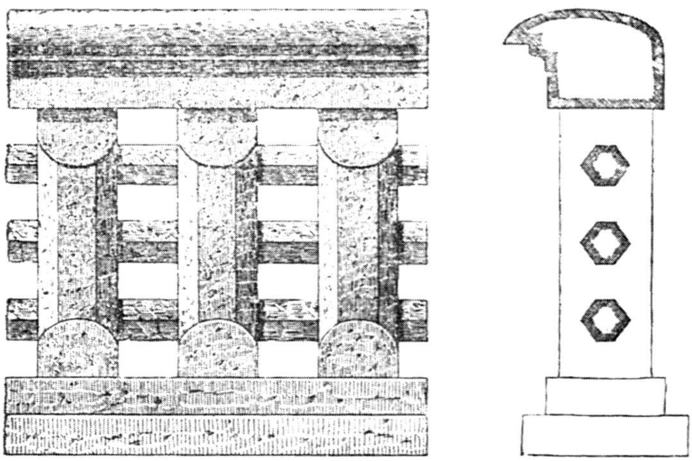

Fig. 20. Stucco railing (restored).

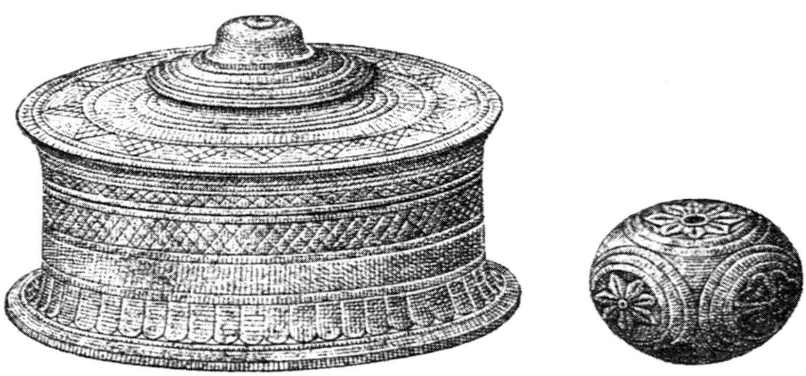

Fig. 21. Relic casket from Ghaz Ḍheri.

The smaller casket containing the relics is decorated with six flowers, in relief, each set within the innermost of four concentric circles. One of these flowers forms the lid of the casket, so carefully fitted, that the joint is indistinguishable. The centre of the lid is pierced with a small hole. The larger casket is something like a Greek *pyxis*, a shape commonly adopted for these relic boxes; the cover is incised with concentric rings, dividing it into bands of varying width, the broadest of which is decorated with hatched triangles; on the sides are four similar bands horizontally disposed, the two uppermost ornamented with cross hatchings, the third plain, the lowest with a row of conventional lotus leaves. Both caskets have been carefully turned on the lathe. Inside the larger one were found also :—

1 piece of pale amethyst, 3·4 cm. long.

1 coin, Æ. ·9 inch. *Obv.* Humped bull. *Rev.* Lion r. Both sides are defaced and no legend is visible. It has been assigned by three separate authorities to Zeionises, but the attribution cannot be absolutely certain.

In the earthenware vessel were—

7 laminated discs of silver (diameter 1·3 cm.) which crumbled to the touch.

1 scaraboid-shaped piece of crystal, pierced through its longer axis (2·2 cm.), and with it the corroded fragments of an iron hoop, to which it was affixed, and some traces of bronze or copper. The impression in the lime showed that the hoop was in the form of a three-quarters circle, with a diameter of 4 cm., and ornamented with three bulbs moulded in the copper or bronze. (*Cf.* Fig. 22.)

Fig. 22.

At the north-west corner of the *stūpa* base was unearthed the lower half of a standing Bodhisattva with a pedestal, on which there are traces of a Kharoṣṭhī inscription. The proper right part of the legend is completely destroyed. On the left side the lettering can be traced for a distance of 8 inches, but here also several characters are missing or injured. This part, containing the first half of the inscription, probably contained 16 *akṣaras*, the distance between the letters, as well as their average height, being about ½". We read it—*kha* (?) *la vi śa e cha* (?) *tra* (?) *pa* (?) *sya* (?)——*da* (?) *dha* (?) *sa*.—

Fig. 23.

It will be seen that the greater part of the reading is doubtful. The only *akṣaras* which may be said to be certain are *la vi śa e* in the beginning, and *sa* at the end. Before *la* there is room for not more than three letters, but as the initial letter probably stood at some distance from the edge we may assume that there were only two. Of these the second can still be traced and approaches most the sign for *kh*. If we insert *pu* for the missing initial, we shall read "*Pukhala viśae*" (Skr. *Puṣkala viṣaye*) "in the district of Puṣkala." The next word is perhaps the genitive of *chatrapa* (Skr. *Kṣatrapa*) "satrap," and for the third word we naturally expect a proper name. This interpretation is of course conjectural. It is noteworthy that this is the fourth inscribed pedestal found on the site of Puṣkalāvatī within an area of less than a mile.

The sculptures found in Ghaz Ḍherī are, on the whole, even more fragmentary than those of Pālāṭū Ḍherī. They include nineteen pieces of Buddha and Bodhisattva statues, among which are eight heads. Two of these are shown on Plate XXV, *c* and *d*, and referred to on page 165 above.

Among the remainder are a number of architectural pieces of a type common in the Buddhist monuments of Gandhāra, such as the frieze of sitting Atlantes[1] (Pl. XXVII, No. 11) alternating between pilasters and helping to support the architrave above them, or the frieze of Cupids carrying a garland[2] (No. 9). The latter is more elaborate than is the case in most similar specimens. The intervening spaces are filled with winged figures, one of which is beating on a cymbal, another playing on a flute. The corresponding place in the centre is occupied by a seated eagle with wide-spread wings. No. 10 is a fragment of an elephant similar to those which are commonly found arrayed along the base of *stūpas*, half projecting from the structure which they seem intended to support. In No. 12 we have the fragment of a pediment in the lower division of which the figure of the Buddha is visible with an attendant. In the central compartment a human figure descending into the form of a snake presumably meant to represent a Nāga. In the upper division the floral design, No. 6, is a fine specimen of a decorative border in exceptionally low relief.

Of the other sculptures, No. 18 is the most prominent. Evidently it formed the proper left portion of a panel, on which the preaching Buddha occupied the centre. This may be inferred from the attitude of the two figures turned to the right in the act of listening. Over them three women, much smaller in size, appear on a balcony. One of them joins her hands in adoration, the other seems to hold a bunch of flowers, whilst the third clasps a wreath in her left hand. These figures also point to the same conclusion. The scene probably represents an interview of Śākyamuni with some of his royal patrons. The introduction of such a balcony with adoring figures to fill the upper corners of the panel is a common device in Gandhāra art. It is regularly found on the scene representing the Dīpaṅkara-jātaka, *e.g.*, Burgess, *J. I. A.*, Vol. VIII, Plate XI.

No. 16 shows the Buddha standing, the right hand raised in the gesture of protection (*abhayamudrā*). In the other hand he holds the alms-bowl, under which a miniature figure, presumably of a child, with folded hands and quaintly crossed legs is stooping, another figure of like size standing behind it.

In fragment 15 we have two Buddha figures seated in meditation (*dhyānamudrā*) the one over the other under a leaf-covered hut (*parṇaśālā*). To their left an almost effaced figure in a long robe can be traced, the attitude of which reminds us of that of the Kuṣaṇa kings of the coins.

No. 13 is a fragment which contains the right leg of a Budhha, evidently seated in the European fashion. To his right a figure is standing which we may suppose to be a Bodhisattva.

The three other fragments, comprised in number 14, represent adoring figures.

---

[1] Supporting figures of this kind are also found in Cole's Plates 1, 13, 17, 29; Burgess, *J. I. A.*, Vol. VIII, Plate XXVI.

[2] For similar figures, *cf.* Cole, Plates 7, 14, 20, 28, 29; Burgess, *J. I. A.*, Vol. VIII, Plates VII, XXIII; Grünwedel-Burgess, Nos. 99, 100, 152.

No. 8 is a woman's head and bust, and No. 17 the much mutilated figure of an ascetic.[1] The full list of the stone sculptures from Ghaz Ḍherī is as follows :—

1. Pedestal of a standing Bodhisattva statue (height 95·4 cm.) of which only the lower half of the body and the feet remain. The body wears drapery, the feet sandals. The front relief (19 × 38 cm.) of which the proper right part is destroyed and the rest defaced, shows in the centre a Buddha or Bodhisattva figure seated cross-legged on a throne ; over its left shoulder the foliage of a tree is apparent. To his left two worshippers are standing. A pilaster encloses the relief on the proper left side. On the sides of the pedestal, a lotus rosette. Beneath the relief traces of a Kharoṣṭhī inscription ; see above, page 176.

2. Pedestal (25·4 × 29·3 cm.) of a standing Buddha statue, of which only the bare feet remain. On front, relief between Indo-Corinthian pilasters, representing Buddha seated cross-legged on a seat under *bodhi* (?) tree, in *dhyānamudrā*. To his right two *bhikṣus* and to his left one *bhikṣuni* (?) are standing in an attitude of adoration. On each side of the pedestal, a rosette.

3. Fragment of the pedestal of a standing Buddha statue (17·8 × 30·4 cm.), of which only the bare feet partly remain. On front, relief almost obliterated, representing a Buddha figure seated cross-legged on a seat under *bodhi* (?) tree. Two worshippers are standing to his right and left.

4. Fragment of the pedestal (12·6 × 26·6 cm.) of a standing Buddha statue of which only the bare feet partly remain. On front, relief almost effaced, apparently representing a seated Buddha with three worshippers.

5. Pedestal (9 × 17·8 cm.) of a standing Buddha statue of which only the bare feet remain. On front, relief enclosed between Indo-Corinthian pilasters, representing in centre a Bodhisattva seated cross-legged, with two worshippers standing on each side. On either side of the pedestal a rosette.

6. Statue (height 53 cm.) of a Buddha seated in *dhyānamudrā* on a throne, the front-relief of which shows two kneeling figures.

7. Statue (height 43 cm.) of a Buddha seated in *dhyānamudrā* on a throne, wholly defaced.

8. Fragment (height 19 cm.) of a Buddha seated in *dhyānamudrā* on a throne, the front of which has a Bodhisattva seated in *dhyānamudrā* between two kneeling worshippers.

9. Fragment (height 20·2 cm.) of a Buddha seated in *dhyānamudrā*, on the front of which is a kneeling figure.

10. Fragment (height 28 cm.) of the torso of a Buddha statue.

11. Fragment (height 17·8 cm.) of the torso of a Bodhisattva statue.

12. Buddha head (height 28 cm., circumference 70 cm.). Chin and nose injured. Hair drawn back in waves from forehead and concealing *uṣṇiṣa* in the form of a *krobylos*, retained in position by a fillet.

13. Buddha head (height 28·3 cm.). Considerably injured. *Ūrṇā* and *uṣṇiṣa*. Hair treated as in 12.

14. Buddha head (height 12·6 cm.).

15. Bodhisattva head (height 15·3 cm.) with *ūrṇā*, royal head-dress and ear ornaments.

16. Buddha head (height 19 cm.), defaced.

17. Buddha head (height 16·5 cm.), defaced.

18. Mask of a Buddha head (height 15·2 cm.).

19. Steatite Buddha head (height 10·1 cm.) ; hair in corkscrew ringlets.

20. Fragment (45·7 × 17·8 cm.) of a relief, representing two figures in royal dress seated in the European fashion, their feet placed on foot stools, and their faces turned to the right.

[1] *Cf.* Grünwedel-Burgess, No. 67.

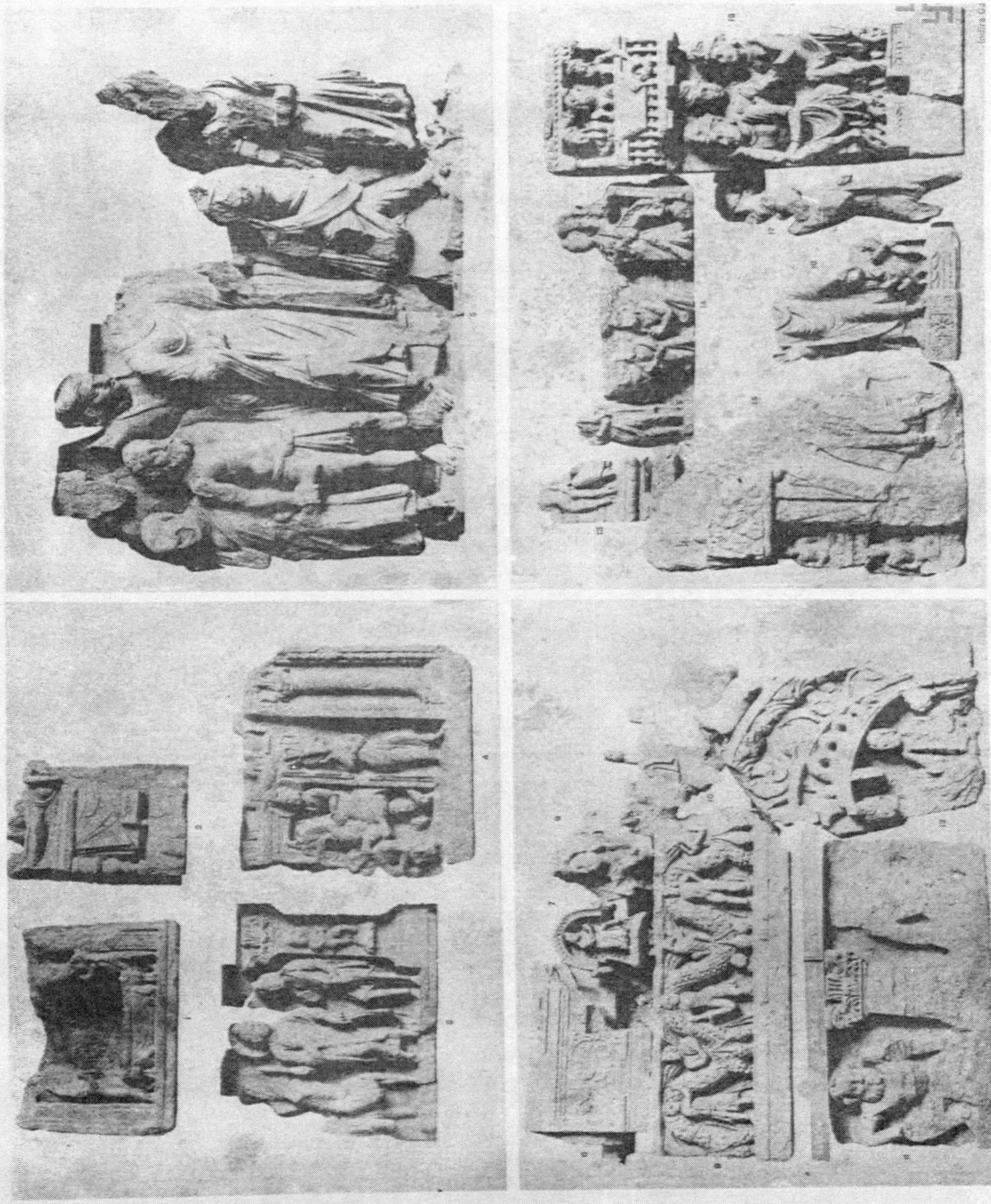

Between them a standing figure is partly visible. The upper portion of the relief shows a balcony with three women.

21. Fragment (height 20·2 cm.) of a relief, representing Buddha standing, the right hand raised in *abhayamudrā*, the left hand holding an alms-bowl. To his left two miniature figures, probably of children.

22. Fragment (height 12·6 cm.) of a Buddha seated in the European fashion with a worshipper or Bodhisattva standing to his right.

23. Fragment (height 14 cm.) representing the standing figure of a worshipper holding a vessel in his left hand. Head missing.

24. Fragment (height 15·3 cm.) representing the figure of a worshipper standing under a trefoiled arch.

25. Fragment (height 10·1 cm.) representing three figures of worshippers turned to the right, much defaced. The kneeling figure seems to be that of a woman, the two standing in front seem to represent children.

26. Fragment (height 11·4 cm.) representing head and bust of a female figure with necklace, ear-rings, and other ornaments.

27. Fragment (height 20·2 cm.) apparently of the figure of an ascetic.

28. Fragments (height 19 cm.) of an Indo-Corinthian capital, in the foliage of which a Buddha figure is introduced.

29. Fragment (height 50·8 cm.) of the dome of miniature *stūpa*.

30. Fragment (height 28 cm.) of a pediment, showing in the lower panel part of a Buddha figure with a smaller figure to his left.

31. Two detached brackets of a modillion cornice (height 11·4 and 7·6 cm. respectively).

32. Fragment (height 5 cm.) of a modillion cornice.

33. Fragments (the largest 35·6 cm.) of a *stūpa* railing.

34. Fragment (17·8 × 35·6 cm.) representing two seated Atlantes, of which the one to the proper left is defaced, separated by an Indo-Corinthian pilaster.

35. Fragment (14 × 42 cm.) of a decorative frieze representing Cupids carrying a garland.

36. Fragment of a border (15·2 × 55·8 cm.) showing figures standing under ogee arches, separated by pilasters. Defaced.

37. Fragment (40 × 30 cm.) perhaps of a pediment, showing two seated Buddha figures (*dhyānamudrā*), placed over each other, in a palm hut. A standing figure, defaced, to the proper left.

38. Fragment (20·3 × 14 cm.) of a decorative border showing vine leaf ornament.

39. Fragment (height 14 cm.) of an elephant figure carrying a bowl or relic casket on its back.

40. Fragment (height 10 cm.) showing the figure of a worshipper standing with folded hands to the proper left, under an ogee arch.

Stucco Figures—

1. A Buddha head (height 20 cm.). Plate XXVI, No. 6.
2. A Buddha head (height 23 cm.). Plate XXVI, No. 4.
3. A Buddha head (height 24 cm.). Plate XXVI, No. 5.
4. A small Buddha head (height 8·8 cm.).
5. A small Buddha head (height 10 cm.).
6. Fragments of a *stūpa* railing.

The minor finds made in G͟haz Ḍherī, which were comparatively few, consisted of—

Coins—

5 Indo-Scythian (uncertain).
6 Early Muhammadan.
2 Sikh.
12 Unidentified.

Pottery—

1 Miniature jug (Fig. 24, No. 27).
4 Clay lamps.
1 Fragment of miniature *stūpa* with frieze of rosettes.
4 Figurines; one, representing a buffalo, in *bucchero nero*; the others in red clay.
1 Stone lamp of form shown in Fig. 24, No. 15.
Several fragments of blue cobalt glass; *cf.* page 153 above.
2 Fossil *opercula* similar to those found in Mīr Ziyārat (Fig. 7, No. 1).
2 Plain bronze finger-rings, diameter 1·6 cm.
1 ditto ear-ring, diameter 1·9 cm. (Fig. 18, No. 4).
2 Shell bangles.
5 Clay beads, *cf.* Fig. 24 A., Nos. 3 and 7, for shape.
1 Cornelian ditto.
5 Bone ditto.
1 Fragment of amber.

Pottery from Chārsada.[1]

The specimens of Buddhist pottery recovered at Chārsada were comparatively few, and of little intrinsic merit, but, none of the wares from previous excavations in the Frontier Province having yet been described, and only a few fragments of them being preserved in the Museums, it may be worth while to record the following provisional notes, in the hope that they may eventually lead to a more complete classification of the pre-Muhammadan fabrics. Such a classification, if successfully accomplished, would be of particular value to explorers among the innumerable *ḍherīs* of Northern India, where the ever constant presence of pottery fragments on the surface of the mounds makes them the most serviceable index to the date of the remains buried beneath.

As regards the *technique* employed in the pre-Muhammadan fabrics, in the smaller and best specimens and notably in the bowls, cups, and terra-cotta figurines, the clay is finely levigated, and, when baked, of a pale pink colour; in the larger and coarser vases, it is red, reddish grey, or light buff. The former is light, and capable of being worked up to a very smooth surface, but brittle. The latter is more tenacious, and consequently more adapted to rough usage. Occasional specimens of intermediate degrees of colour and coarseness are found, apparently composed of a mixture of the light and stiff clays. In some of the larger vessels, used for storing grain or water, the clay is mixed with sand, which, to judge from the modern wares, amounts to about one-third of the weight of the clay. By this means the material is rendered more ductile and less liable to breakage in the firing. The tenacity of the clay is, however, diminished, and the thinness to which some of the vessels are worked, makes them extremely fragile. Another ware is of grey black colour, strikingly similar to the *bucchero nero* of archaic Etruria. It is of fine texture, and was used for smaller vessels only—especially if they were to be freely ornamented, *e.g.*, Fig. 24, Nos. 24, 30, 35, and 36. Whether the clay is a different variety or not, it is difficult to say. Possibly the colour was produced by the same process as

[1] Two of the pieces in Fig. 24, *viz.*, Nos. 22 and 32, are not from the excavations at Chārsada.

the modern one, *i.e.* by putting deodar wood or dung into the kiln, and stopping up the openings so that the smoke might penetrate the wares. With the exception of the larger storage jars, and of some of the *bucchero* vases, nearly all the pottery is wheel-made. The larger vessels, after being roughly formed on the wheel, were beaten out and worked up in much the same way as they are at the present day. Their inner surfaces retain the impressions of a circular convex instrument used in the beating process, which was probably of the same type as that now known as a *konera*.[1] Such an instrument (No. 34) was found in an early stratum on the Bālā Ḥiṣār. It is intended to be held with the left hand against the inside of the vessel to be operated on, while the concave side of a wooden mallet (*thatwa*) is used to tap the vessel over the spot where the *konera* is held. In working up some of the more ductile fabrics, in which sand is mixed with the clay, the thumb appears to have been used in place of the *konera*, and the clay to have been moulded rather than beaten. The bases of many of the vessels, especially the smaller, show the marks of a string used for severing the moulded vase from the lump of clay on the wheel. This method is still in vogue in the Frontier Province, and generally, we believe, in other parts of India. It may be noted also that it was the one adopted by the early potters of the Eastern Mediterranean. When the vases left the wheel, the more delicate ones and the figurines were coated with a smooth "slip," coloured a greenish buff, crimson, or reddish-brown—usually the last. In some instances a very thin wash of colour was added on this slip, and over this again in a few rare examples, traces of a design in white, if the ground is dark, are visible, or in crimson and black, if the ground is buff coloured. The white is observable only on fragments of small bowls, but as it was laid on in chalk, or some other powdery material after baking, and is very perishable, it is possible that other vessels may originally have been ornamented in the same way. In the absence of more abundant examples, the use of pigments in decoration must be looked upon as exceptional. More usually the ornament is incised or in relief, in which case it consists, in its simplest form, of plain ridges disposed horizontally, usually at the junction of the neck and body, or in several parallel bands above the shoulder. In some examples, there is a row of tooth-like projections along the edge of the lip, and rows of dots are punctured between the neck and the shoulder, or parallel wavy or angular lines are incised around the body of the vase. The last are especially common in the great storage jars. In one *bucchero* specimen, the incised design is in imitation of plaited wicker-work (Fig. 24, No. 30). More elaborate are the stamped impressions generally occurring around the shoulder of the *gharās*, but used also for other purposes, and, especially in some of the *bucchero* ware, to decorate the whole body of the vase in repeated bands arranged either horizontally (*cf.* Fig. 24, No. 35) or diagonally. The patterns employed on these stamps are circles, squares, triangles, stars (Fig. 25, Nos. 8 and 13), concentric circles, spoked wheels, to which a rotary motive is sometimes given (Nos. 9, 12, 15), triskels (No. 7), flowers (Nos. 16, 17), leaves (Nos. 10, 11), or ornamental lozenges. Other emblems are more fanciful. No. 14, showing the familiar tree growing from a pot and the *swastika* above, is

---

[1] *Cf.* "Monograph on the Pottery and Glass Industry of the Punjab" by C. H. Hallifax (Lahore, 1892), para. 16.

most worthy of notice. The same subject occurs on an amethyst gem recently secured in the district of Chārsada. On the *gharās* a single row of these stamps is usually found, two different designs usually alternating above a border of tooth ornament (*cf.* Fig. 25, 9). Appliqué work is used in the imitation of a rope passing round the body of the vase (*cf.* Fig. 24, No. 22, but more realistically in the case of the larger store jars); also to represent eyes on either side of the spout—a device well known on early Greek vases,—flowers and foliage (Fig. 25, Nos. 1, 3, 5), or birds and miniature lamps set on the rim of a bowl (Fig. 24. No. 28). This class of decoration is commonly found also on the early Khotanese pottery, discussed by Dr. Hoernle.[1] To it belong also some highly elaborated female figurines and elephants' heads from Chārsada, which form the spouts of vessels. These will be referred to in a subsequent publication. In some instances, rough ornaments of a similar nature to the above, are not made in separate pieces, but moulded in relief on the vase itself, *e.g.*, the bird's head (Fig. 25, No. 4).

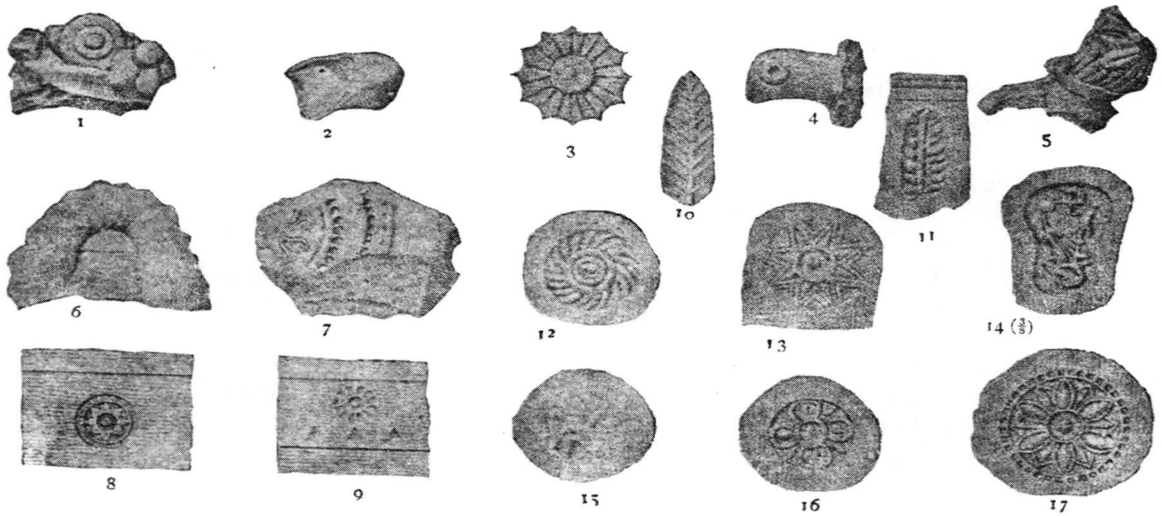

Fig. 25.

In connection with ***decoration*** we may note here certain examples which point to metallic prototypes. In Fig. 24, No. 33 (the handle of a vase), for instance, the metal flanges and the rivet of the original vase, from which it was copied, are observable; metal technique can be seen also in Fig. 24, No. 32 (the top of a lidless jug), and possibly in the spiral fluting of an unfigured vase of *bucchero*.

Turning to the ***shapes***, one is struck, first, by the almost entire absence of handles. Judging from the fragments turned up not one vase in five hundred could have been provided with them, and those which were, nearly always belonged to the finest class of fabrics. Nor can the absence of handles be merely accidental, since, owing to their strength, they are more likely to survive than the body of vessels. Spouts also are

[1] Antiquities from Central Asia. Extra No. to the *J. A. S. B.*, Vol. LXX, 1901, page 45.

Fig. 24. Forms of pottery from Charsada.

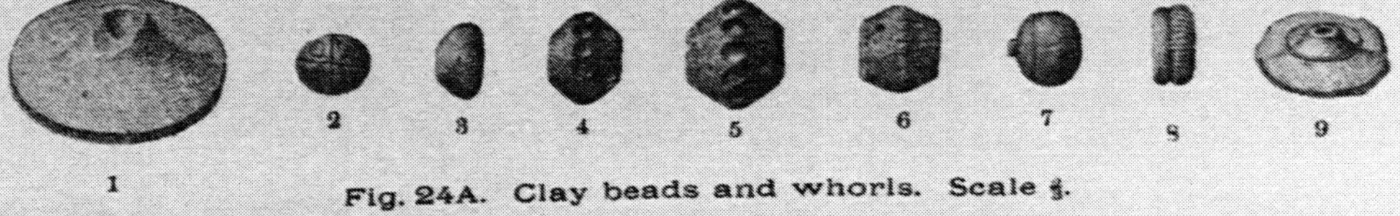

Fig. 24A. Clay beads and whorls. Scale ⅔.

restricted, for the most part, to the finer wares, and, as often as not, were made in grotesque shapes. Excluding mere fanciful types the shapes are very few and simple They may be roughly classified as follows :—

A. **Cups.**—(1) The simplest and commonest form is that of a shallow flower pot with straight sides. The examples, which numbered many hundreds, varied in diameter between 10 and 17 cm. across the mouth. All are of coarse ware, without slip or paint.

(2) Ditto, with rounded sides. For type, *cf.* Fig. 24, No. 2, but the base is generally flat. Of similar ware to the above ; diameter averaging 12·3 cm.

B. **Bowls.**—(1) Flat base, with curved walls narrowing at mouth. Clay finely levigated, often with red, brown, or crimson slip (Fig. 24, 1), like the modern *piyālā.*

(2) Similar, with rim turning outwards (Fig. 24, 3).

(3) Similar, with developed lip, narrowed neck, and bulging body. An example of this shape has a brown red slip with traces of cross hatching in white chalk.

(4) Larger than the last. Heavy lip and developed base. Diameter averages 22 cm. A fantastic form of bowl is that shown in Fig. 24, No. 28, with two miniature lamps and a bird perched on its rim.

C. **Saucers.**—(1) With deep, cup-like depression in centre, flat base, and rounded lip. *Cf.* Fig. 24, 4.

(2) Similar, with rim developed and sharply defined. *Cf.* Fig. 24, 5.

(3) Similar, with central boss or *omphalos* within, Fig. 24, 6. In the best specimens of this and No. (2) the inner outline of the rim takes the form of a *cyma reversa.*

(4) Similar, larger dimensions and decadent form ; the extra size is given by increasing the rim.

For the smaller saucers the best clays are used, and they are usually covered with a slip and painted. In some of the shallow specimens, the boss within makes them look like the lids of open-mouthed vessels, but in the majority of instances the bowl is too deep to serve this purpose, and the boss not sufficiently developed to do duty as a handle.

D. **Dishes.**—(1) Similar to the modern *ṭabāq* (*cf.* C. J. Hallifax, *op. cit.*, Plate 11, No. 7) with curved sloping sides, of coarse fabric. Diameter averages 48 cm.

(2) Similar, with taller sides, lips, and perforations in base, for cooking purposes.

E. **Goblets.**—The standard drinking cups (Fig. 24, Nos. 8, 9, 10) are exceptional, only a few specimens having been found. It is not improbable that their shape is under Western influence. The fabric is debased, but the natural divisions of the vases—the foot, base, body, and lip—are well indicated and combined in a manner unusual in indigenous wares. A somewhat analogous form occurs in the Ajantā Cave Paintings. *Cf. J. I. A.*, Vol. VIII (parts 61–69), page 22.

(2) A derivative of the above is Fig. 24, No. 11, a goblet standing inside a bowl. The purpose of this vessel is not apparent.

F. **Jars for keeping water, grain, etc.**—Including those akin to the modern *gharās*, *cāṭis*, and the like. All of these are thrown on the wheel in one piece, the mouth being broad enough to admit the potter's hand.

(1) With rounded bottom, short neck, and well defined rim. Fig. 24, No. 19.

(2) Similar, with flat bottom and developed neck and lip. The juncture of the neck and body is indicated by a ridge and the shoulder is almost invariably ornamented. Average height about 19 cm. A variant between this and the following, but without rim or lip, is Fig. 24, No. 22.

(3) Squat jars, with flat base and undeveloped neck. Fig. 24, No. 20.

(4) Similar, with high necks and rims like those of No. (2).

G. **Small Jugs.**—(1) With broad mouth and flat bottom. *Cf.* Fig. 24, Nos. 18 and 21.

(2) Similar with spout, and with or without handles, like the modern *loṭā*. Average height 13 cm.

(3) Narrow necked water pourers, of the type of the modern *ṣurāḥī*. The body of these is thrown in two pieces, joined horizontally in the middle, and the neck is made separately. *Cf.* Fig. 24, No. 17.

H. **Large Store Jars,**—like the modern *maṭan*, or the Greek *pithos*. The only complete specimen was ornamented with a rope design in relief, but numerous fragments of others with incised patterns were also found. The latter ornament generally takes the form of horizontal bands of several lines, between which run other bands in undulating waves, but several other varieties also occur.

I. **Lamps.**—Forming the most numerous class of objects found. They are usually round or slightly elongated with a depression at one side for a single wick. (*Cf.* Fig. 24, Nos. 12 and 14.) Another more developed form is No. 13, for four wicks. Fig. 24, Nos. 15, 16 are in stone, and their shape does not appear to have been copied in earthenware. The stones used for these lamps are steatite or schist.

J. **Vessels with handles.**—No complete specimens were found. The tall nondescript jar (Fig. 24, No. 26) has the remnants of three handles, which appear to have met above. They are loosely attached to the shoulder, the clay being merely kneaded on, when soft. In Fig. 27, which is a miniature vase of fine texture, the handle has been restored in accordance with the indications given by the fractures. The form of the vase, to which the fragment No. 33 belongs, appears to be that of a bowl similar to No. 1.

K. **Miniature vases.**—Several miniature specimens of superfine texture were found, imitating generally the shape of the larger vases. One particularly good example is fashioned after the human form. It will be referred to in a subsequent article dealing with the terra-cottas from Chārsada.

L. **Miscellaneous.**—Among miscellaneous vessels may be noted (1) the *mortars* (*cf.* Fig. 24, No. 25) with a pestle of stone or earthenware.

(2) *Oil or unguent flasks.*—Fig. 24, No. 24. The rim of lip in this specimen is broken away. Fig. 30 is another example of the same type from the Jhelum district, and several more, obtained from various sites in the Frontier Province, exist in the Lahor and Calcutta Museums. No. 24 would seem to be in imitation of some fruit; No. 30 of a flask covered with plaited wicker. Somewhat similar vessels are held in the hand of certain Bodhisattva figures, but of these latter some approximate more closely to the Greek *alabastron* type; *cf.*, for instance, Grünwedel-Burgess, *op. cit.*, p. 186, Fig. 132.

(3) No. 23 in Fig. 24 appears to have been used as a *sprinkler* of some sort, possibly for oil. The base is perforated with a number of small holes, and the mouth is narrow enough to be closed by the finger tip. From its find-spot it is uncertain if this vase is of Buddhist or later origin.

(4) Fig. 24, No. 31, is the fragment of what seems to be a large earthenware *horn*, of rough fabric, decorated with incised lines.

(5) *Spindle-whorls and beads* of pottery were turned up in great quantities. Typical specimens of the former are given in Fig. 24(*a*), Nos. 1 and 9, and of the latter, *ib.*, Nos. 2-8.

J. H. MARSHALL.
J. PH. VOGEL.

BUDDHIST GOLD JEWELLERY.

CONSIDERING the abundance of gold for which India has at all times been famous, and the inordinate fondness shown by the natives of the country for personal ornaments, it is surprising what a few objects of gold or silver jewellery have come down to us from ancient times. Amid all the rich collections of Indian antiquities to be found in India itself or in Europe, jewellery is represented by only a few and for the most part scarcely noticeable objects, the insignificance of which is most apparent when they are compared with the splendid displays of ancient gold and silver work which Western countries have produced. This comparative scarcity of jewellery is observable almost as much in the collections of Buddhist as in those of Hindu antiquities, and in both cases the cause is the same. For, whereas in Western countries—thanks to the prevailing custom of burying the personal ornaments of the dead along with their remains—the museums are stocked with the spoils of ancient cemeteries, in India, so far as the Buddhists or Hindus are concerned, there are no such happy hunting grounds for the excavator. In the case of the Buddhists, however, there is always the hope that their *stūpas* or *topes* may yield some interesting ornaments or precious vessels along with the sacred relics which many of these monuments were built to enshrine. Indeed, few as they are, practically all the pieces of jewellery which we possess have been found in monuments of this class—notably in the *stūpas* of Hiddā and Dih Bīmārān in Afghanistan, of Piprāvā in Nepal, and of Bhaṭṭiproḷu in Madras. I mention this fact because, although the personal ornaments figured in Plate XXVIII (*a*) and described in the following pages are different in character and superior, perhaps, in technique and design to anything of their kind hitherto discovered, the find-spot of the majority at any rate of the pieces appears to be no exception to the general rule.

Nos. 3 to 10 and 13, 14, and 15 belong to a find made some years ago at Toṛdher, a village not far from the Indus in the Yūsufzaī district of the Frontier Province. The amount of treasure recovered was said to be very considerable, but most of the objects were appropriated by the villagers on the spot, and many of them, no doubt, found their way, as generally happens, to the melting pot of the local goldsmiths. It is due to the energetic action of Colonel H. A. Deane that the 13 pieces referred to were recovered from the peasants and afterwards placed in the Lahor Museum. With them were found also some coins of Huviṣka and Kaniṣka; a cylindrical gold plated charm, ornamented with some fine designs; and a small casket, of what material is not known, containing a calcined bone, which was identified by Dr. Charles as the third phalanx of the second toe of a human foot. The cylinder, which was of copper covered with a thin lamina of gold, was of similar design to the small reliquaries represented on many of the Gandhāra sculptures as worn on a chain around the neck, and was filled with some organic matter, which looked, says Colonel Deane, like sealing wax, but was believed to be inspissated blood, although its precise nature could not be ascertained by chemical analysis. The actual spot where this jewellery was unearthed, was in the mound round which the village of Toṛdher has grown up, and the presence of the relic bone in the casket leaves no doubt, to my mind, that the whole find came from the relic chamber of some *stūpa*, which once existed there. Of the other objects in Plate XXVIII (*a*), the exact provenance of only one, Fig. 16, is known; it was found in the Pālāṭū mound in the neighbourhood of Chārsaḍa, and is described on page 172 above. The remaining pieces (Figs. 1, 2, 11 and 12) were recently acquired from a dealer at Rawal Pindi, who stated that they came from the neighbourhood of the ancient Taxila, but as dealers invariably have their reasons in these cases for concealing the truth, we should not be far wrong in concluding that Taxila is the one place from which they did not come. Judging from the similarity of their workmanship, it seems by no means improbable that they are from the same stock as the Toṛdher jewellery, and that fear of the law relating to treasure-trove prevented their being offered for sale at an earlier date. But whatever their exact provenance may have been, there can be no doubt that they are approximately of the same date and exhibit the same peculiarities in both style and technique as the objects from Toṛdher, and I feel justified, therefore, in representing them in the same plate and designating them, one and all, as of Buddhist origin. I shall revert later to the main points of similarity which exist between these various objects, and shall discuss individually some of the features which they have in common, but first it is necessary to explain such details of the several pieces as are not fully apparent from their photographs.

The two pendants (Figs. 1 and 2) are identical in all respects, save that the second is slightly better preserved, and a description of this one, therefore, will suffice for both. It consists of two separate pieces, the upper attached to the lower by means of a hook which passes through a hollow cylinder. It was stated that they were thus fastened together at the time of finding, and as the marks caused by the rubbing of the hook at the edges of the cylinder bear out this statement, we may believe that the two parts were originally combined to form one ornament, although it must be remarked that the combination is a clumsy one, and that the cylinder seems more suited for the reception of a jewel encircled with a setting of gold, such as that shown in Fig. 16. The upper portion of the ornament is built up on a frame-work of flat gold wire, which is twisted into the form of a square, sub-divided into four smaller squares. Beneath this is a somewhat broader band of gold ending in two hooks,

a

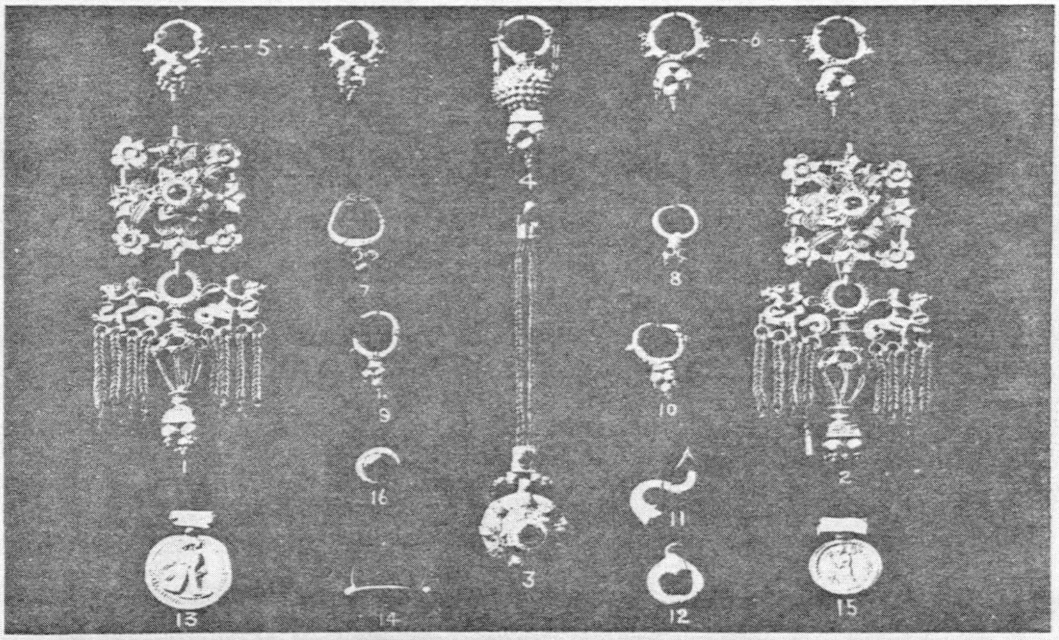

b

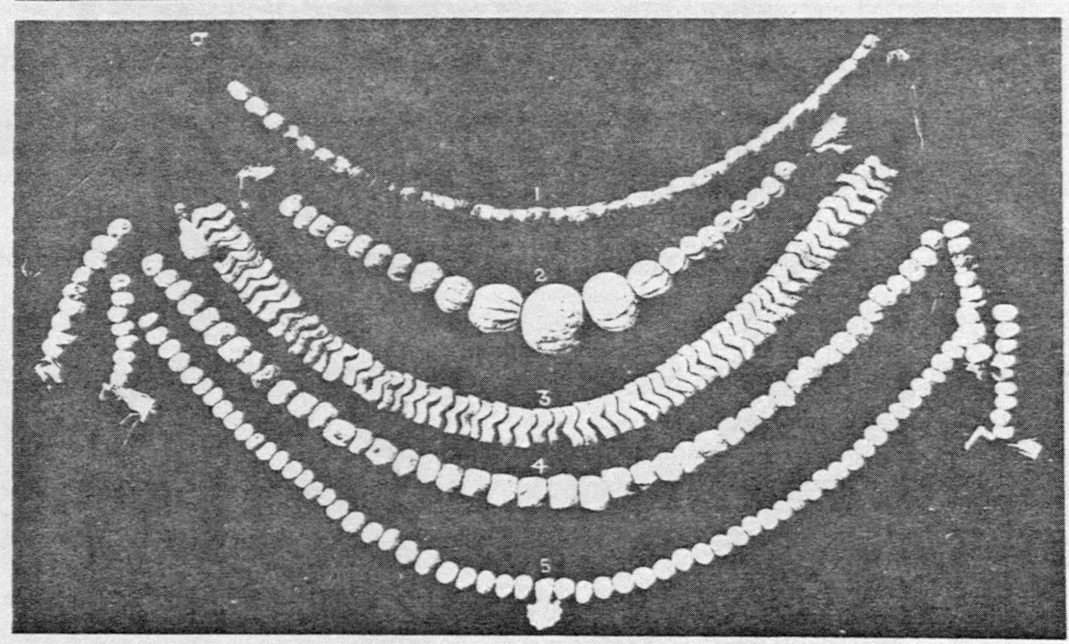

(*a*) BUDDHIST GOLD JEWELLERY.

(*b*) NECKLACES FROM CHĀRSADA.

which project beyond the frame-work on either side; at the point of projection the base of the hooks is enriched with a small circlet edged with granules. The ornament attached to this frame-work consists of a large central flower with trefoil leaves springing from the border of its obcordate petals, and with four smaller blossoms—one at each corner of the frame-work—united to it by means of tendril-like bands. The corolla of the central flower is formed of a sheet of gold roughly cut to the required shape, with a fine gold wire soldered round its edge, which serves to delineate more precisely the contour of its petals. The surface visible within this wire is covered with granules. The six smaller petals above the corolla, which seem to constitute a sort of corona, are composed of two laminæ united only at their edges by a narrow band soldered between them. Above these, again, are five smaller obcordate petals, each forming a *cloison*, from which unfortunately the coloured jewel paste has disappeared. In the centre of the flower is a raised cylinder with flanged edge, bordered with particles of gold of larger size than those which decorate the petals of the corolla; the flange of the cylinder is separately attached, and the cylinder itself was once, no doubt, closed with a gem cut *en cabuchon*. Gems also were originally inlaid in the small blossoms at the corners, and coloured paste or stones (probably lapis lazuli and garnet) in the trefoiled leaves which alternate between them.

The lower half of the ornament consists of a fanciful design, on either side of which is an infant Eros riding on a winged sea-lion, with four chains and bells suspended beneath him. The vase-shaped ornament in the middle is set upon a three-stepped base, from which hangs a cluster of five drops of gold, with a pyramid of five tiny granules clinging to each; the granules are of solid metal, but the larger drops are hollow, being formed of half globes beaten out and soldered together. The body of the vase-shaped design in the centre, for the *motif* of which we may compare the top of a silver casket from one of the Hiddā topes,[1] is a mere skeleton of filigrain work, with tiny rosettes of gold granules disposed about its shoulder, but the foot, neck and cylinder above consist of hollow tubes ornamented with granulated beadings. The cylinder, which rather suggests a Buddhist *cakra* or wheel, is, like the one in the centre of the flower above, flanged with a separate band of gold. The Erotes and sea-monsters appear to have been cast in a mould, and afterwards chased with a graver's tool; the hair of the boys is very carefully worked, and falls on their shoulders in a natural row of ringlets. Their wings, and the wings and ears of the monsters, both front and back, were inlaid with paste, a fragment of which, of blue green colour, still remains in one of the ears. A very similar figure of a boy riding on a sea-lion, but without wings, occurs on a golden plaque discovered with a great many other relics, on the northern bank of the Oxus in ancient Persia.[2] Between the rings from which the chains are suspended, are small bosses like nail heads, and to the lower extremity of the chains miniature bells were attached; only one of these bells is now left, and within it, at the time of finding, a small pearl is said to have been hanging.

The round medallion hanging from a chain (Fig. 3) is particularly interesting as

[1] Wilson, *Ariana Antiqua*, Plate II, Fig. 3

[2] See *J. A. S. B.*, Vol. LII, 1883, p. 259 sq., and Plate XXI (*f*).

being in the form of a *stūpa*. Its base consists of two concentric cylinders of gold, the smaller ·6 cm. less in diameter than the larger, the space between which is filled with a hard paste, while the back is closed with a plain gold plate soldered to the edges of the cylinders. The rest of the pendant is hollow, each member being separately formed. Above the base is a smaller domed drum, from which projects the *chatra*, crowned with a carbuncle. On the dome are six heart-shaped *cloisons* of garnets and lapis lazuli, alternately disposed, above and below which are trefoils and rosettes of gold granules. The edge of the projecting *chatra* is ornamented with drawn threads of finest filigrain, bordered by a granulated beading. To the side of the pendant is attached a ring, by which the chain is hinged, the gold pin of the hinge having a small pearl affixed at either end. The gem at the base of the chain, like the one in the pendant, is a garnet.

Fig. 4 is an elaborate ear-ring with a base and cluster of gold drops beneath, similar to those of Figs. 1 and 2. The body of the ornament is hollow and its outer surface completely covered with granules of a more developed type than are found in the preceding examples. Each granule is a half globe of beaten gold to which a single grain is affixed, like so many miniature breasts. Connecting the ring with the body of the ornament are two round bosses, fixed firmly at the point of contact; one of these bosses is set with a garnet, the stone from the other has disappeared. The ring is further strengthened in position by two *cloisons* of a fanciful heart-shape, soldered tangentially to the side. In one of these *cloisons* can be seen the silver foil which formed the backing for a transparent gem, but the gem itself is no longer there. Similar silver foil is found beneath the carbuncle in Fig. 16, and both these pieces are of interest in connection with the reference which Pliny the Elder makes to this particular method of mounting certain stones. He says—"*In India* (*sardae*) *trium generum: rubrae, et quas pionias vocant ab pinguitudine; tertium genus est quod argenteis bratteis sublinunt.*" [1] As stated above, the gem of Fig. 16 is a garnet *en cabuchon* (*carbunculus, ἄνθραξ*), and not a cornelian (*sarda, σάρδιον*), and it is probable that the missing gems in Fig. 4 were of the same kind, since there is no other instance of a cornelian or sard being used in this jewellery. The ring of Fig. 4, as of all the others except No. 10, is a hollow tube; in No. 10 the gold appears to be beaten out upon a core of silver or of an amalgam of other metals.

Among the other objects the workmanship of the ear-ring, Fig. 7, deserves notice. The ends of the gold wire have been drawn out thinner and thinner, and then looped and twisted back on themselves. The pair of ear-rings (Figs. 11 and 12) are also remarkable for the skilful ball hinges and carefully concealed clasps, with which they are fitted. Both are of solid gold and first-rate workmanship; their shape, it may be noticed, is similar to that of a pair of bracelets worn by one of the figures in the Ajantā cave paintings,[2] and brings to mind the barbaric torques of Northern Europe. Each of the remaining three pieces has a gold coin attached to it. The coin in Fig. 15 belongs to the Kuṣaṇa king Huviṣka, whose kingdom com-

[1] Pliny, *Nat. Hist.*, XXXVII, 7 (31). It is not clear from the context whether we should understand "Indians" as the subject of "*sublinunt*" or not. Of the Egyptian cornelians Pliny says—"*Brattea aurea sublinuntur.*"

[2] Griffiths, *The paintings in the Buddhist cave temples of Ajantā*, Vol. I, p. 18, Fig. 53.

prised the whole of N.-W. India and the Kābul valley,[1] and whose reign is generally placed in the second century A.D. Fig. 14 is a finger ring, the hoop of which is beaten out and flattened on one side, so as to afford a bed to which the reverse side of the coin is soldered; the coin is of Vāsudeva, who is usually regarded as a successor of Huviṣka. The third coin, Fig. 13, belongs to Ardas͟hīr-i-Bābagān,[2] the founder of the Sāsānian dynasty in Persia, whose empire is asserted to have extended as far as the Indus,[3] and whose reign is assigned to the years between 226 and 238 B.C.[4]

The presence of these three coins is important as furnishing evidence for the probable date of the jewellery, but their evidence is not conclusive, since we have no knowledge of the circumstances in which they were discovered, and it is conceivable that the coins may form part of a later deposit in the *stūpa* than the rest of the jewellery; or that many of the objects may long have been in use—perhaps as treasured heirlooms—when they were deposited in the *stūpa*; an hypothesis to which some colour is given by the marks of constant wear on the gold. Or, on the other hand, the rest of the jewellery may be later than the coins. But, in the absence of other evidence, we shall do well to assign it provisionally to a slightly later date than the most recent of the coins, *i.e.*, to about the middle of the third century A.D. Fig. 16 is probably later, and Figs. 1, 2, 11, and 12, from Rawal Pindi, may be of a different, and, if anything, earlier date than the objects obtained from Torḍher, but, on the whole, for the reason previously stated, I should prefer to regard them as belonging to one and the same stock.

We may consider now the main features of technique or design which the majority of these ornaments have in common, and the first point which we shall notice is the method of decorating the surface of the metal with fine granules—*pulvisculus aureus*, as they were known in Italy. This particular form of ornament appears to occur also (I rely upon the illustration in Wilson's *Ariana Antiqua*)[5] on the base of the famous gold casket discovered in a *stūpa* at Dih Bīmārān, where it is used to indicate the stamens of a conventional lotus and to enrich the field around the flower. The existence of the *pulvisculus aureus* on this jewellery is of peculiar significance, inasmuch as the art of granulating was a favourite one among the ancient gold workers of the countries bordering on the Eastern Mediterranean, and the process employed being at once ingenious and extremely laborious, it is unlikely that its discovery was made independently in these countries and in India. A description of this process is given by Benvenuto Cellini in the second chapter of his *Trattato dell' Oreficeria*,[6] from which it appears that each grain was separately soldered on, and we may suppose that the same was the technique practised by the ancient jewellers whether in Europe or in India; but in the case of the finer kind of granulated work, especially of some of the exquisitely minute work from Etruria, it is

[1] *Cf. Brit. Mus. Cat. of Greek and Scythic Kings*, p. 137, No. 12.
[2] *Cf. Zeitschrift der D. M. Gesellschaft*, Vol. VIII, 1854, p. 29, and No. 3, p. 31.
[3] *Cf.* Wilson, *Ariana Antiqua*, p. 383.
[4] The discovery of a coin of Ardas͟hīr side by side with one of Vāsudeva may possibly support Mr Vincent Smith's chronology for the Kus͟hān kings, *J. R. A. S.*, 1903, pp. 1-63.
[5] Plate IV, Fig. 3.
[6] Ed. Milanesi, p. 20.

not improbable that the grains were sprinkled, like dust, over the parts of the surface which had to be covered.[1] That the art of granulating gold was not originally borrowed by peoples of the West from India seems fairly well established by the number, as well as the extreme antiquity, of some of the granulated ornaments discovered in Egypt, Greece, and the neighbouring countries, of which it may be worth while to note here a few examples. The earliest known, perhaps, is from the treasure of Dahshur, referable to the sixth dynasty of Egypt,[2] in which the particles are of the finest description and the workmanship of exquisite quality. At a later date occasional specimens occur among the Trojan[3] and early Mycenæan[4] gold work, but they seem to have become commoner towards the end of the Mycenæan age,[5] and particularly when Phœnician influences became disseminated over the Mediterranean.[6] Some beautiful examples have also come from Geometric graves of about the eighth century B.C.[7] Whether the spread of this particular art was actually due to the so-called Phœnician influence, is a question with which we are not now concerned; it may be observed only that the art is found widely prevalent in those countries, like Cyprus,[8] Sardinia[9] and Etruria,[10] where there are other reasons to suppose that that particular influence was strongly felt. Belonging to the classical age there are numerous examples both from Greece proper and from the Greek colonies in Italy and Asia Minor.[11] In Asia Minor, the art must have continued to flourish on at least until the second century B.C., and probably very much later, for we have a good example of it in a cup mounted with gold from the Cossack village of Siverskaia at the western limit of the Caucasus, which is assigned to a date not earlier than the reign of Pairizades III(?), or the last part of the second century B.C.[12] In second-rate and imitative gold work, especially in barbaric plate or jewellery of the Christian era, we find the granules replaced by mere dots stamped on the metal; an instance of this technique is a gold *phaleræ* from Auvers (Seine-et-Oise),[13] but it is generally confined to gold-work of the flimsiest nature.

We have, then, from the Eastern Mediterranean a long list of examples of this granulated work belonging to the historic and pre-historic epochs, and we cannot be far wrong in considering it indigenous to that region. It, follows, therefore, that it must have been imported into India, unless we are prepared to maintain that the art was independently discovered in different countries. Such an hypothesis is of course always admissible, but in view of the difficulties involved in the technique, and the fact that it was long forgotten by the jewellers of Europe, and never re-discovered

[1] *Cf.* G. Karo, *Le oreficerie di Vetulonia* (*Estratto dagli studi e materiali di archeologia e numismatica pubblicati per cura di Luigi A. Milani*, Vol. I, *Puntata* II, 1901, p. 45).

[2] *Cf.* G. Karo, *op. cit.*, p. 45. No reproduction of this has yet been published.

[3] Schliemann, *Ilios*, p. 546.

[4] Perrot et Chipiez, *Histoire de l'art dans l'antiquité*, Vol. VI, 973. Fig. 549.

[5] *Cf.*, for instance, a pendant from Enkomi in Cyprus. (Murray, *Excavations in Cyprus*, p. 18, Fig. 35.)

[6] For an example from Phœnicia, *Cf.* G. Karo, *op. cit.*, p. 43, Fig. 46.

[7] *E.g.*, a pair of ear-rings from Eleusis; *Athene*, n 10960.

[8] *E.g.*, Perrot et Chipiez, *op. cit.*, Tome III, p. 817, Figs. 570 and 571.

[9] *E.g.*, *Ib.* p. 818, Fig. 575; p. 821, Fig. 577, etc.

[10] *Cf.* G. Karo, *op. cit.*, passim.

[11] *E.g.*, *Gazette Archéologique*, 1879, p. 75, Plate 11.

[12] *Les Fouilles de Siverskaia. Gaz. Arch.*, 1887, p. 149.

[13] *Gaz. Arch.*, 1883, p. 340, et Pl. 53.

until Castellani found it still being practised in an obscure Italian village; in view, too, of the obviously Western character of the winged Erotes riding on sea-lions, it seems more reasonable to suppose that the art was introduced into Northern India at a time when the influences of Western Asia were imprinting themselves so deeply on the coinage, gem-engraving, architecture and sculpture of the Gandhāra country. I may mention here a theory of Signor Castellani, which, if it could be proved, would materially serve to confirm the supposition that this art originated among the Mediterranean peoples. Signor Castellani, starting with the axiom that primitive people invariably borrow from the nature which surrounds them the typical elements of their ornamentation, was confident that he had discovered the natural prototypes, from which the conventional granulated devices were copied, in the sea molluscs (*diademiae* and *pseudodiademiae*), which abound along the shores of the Eastern Mediterranean.[1] The analogy between them is, no doubt, striking, but it would be dangerous to put forward an imaginative theory of this kind as evidence of the art having been first discovered by people living on the seaboard.

Another noticeable feature of this jewellery, and of the gold casket from the Dih Bīmārān tope, is the incrustation of gems. If the art of granulating is a Western one, it is certain that the art of incrusting is of Eastern origin, and that it was not generally known in the Mediterranean area until the Graeco-Macedonian period, when the conquests of Alexander had opened up the Orient.[2] In this connection the passage in Theophrastus,[3] where the braggart boasts of having taken part in Alexander's expedition and brought back ποτήρια λιθοκόλλητα, is particularly instructive, as indicating that vessels incrusted with jewels were regarded essentially as a product of the East. The same ποτήρια λιθοκόλλητα are also mentioned among Alexander's Persian booty.[4] Again, the Indian King Sopeithes is said to have worn golden sandals studded with jewels, and to have carried a golden staff in his hand set with beryls.[5] That this oriental luxury should gradually have spread to the courts of Alexander's successors was natural, and thus, in the first century B.C., we find Cicero telling of golden bowls inlaid with precious stones among the princely treasures which Antiochos set before the rapacious Verres,[6] from which it may be inferred that such bejewelled plate was, in Cicero's opinion, typical of what might be expected among the royal possessions of a Syrian Prince.

Numerous ornaments with incrustate jewels have been recovered from tombs in Western Asia, and some of these, in which the incrustation is combined with granulated devices, furnish close analogies to our Buddhist jewellery. Such, for instance, are a pair of ear-rings from Tortosa, the ancient Antaradus, in Phœnicia, and now in the Luynes collection at the Bibliothèque nationale in Paris, which are

[1] Degli ori e dei geioelli nella Esposizione di Parigi del 1878, Rapporto di Alessandro Castellani giurato della classe XXXIX, all Onor. Comm. S. Maiorano Calatabiano, Ministro di agircoltura, industria e commercio; Roma, 1879.

[2] *Cf.* Furtwaengler, *Antike Gemmen*, III, pp. 153 sq.

[3] Theoph. *Char.* 23.

[4] Athenaeus, XI, 17, quoting from Parmenion's letters—ποτηρίων λιθοκολλήτων σταθμὸς τάλαντα Βαβυλώνια νσ', μναὶ λδ'.

[5] Q. Curt. *Hist. Alex.*, 9, 1, 5.

[6] Cicero, *In Verrem*, 4, 62.

said by M. S. Trivier to belong undoubtedly to the Seleucid era.[1] In the same collection is another piece of jewellery, a medallion and necklace of strongly oriental character, which was found in the neighbourhood of Nola, and may well have been imported from Asia Minor during the third or second century B.C., by the Greek colonists settled in Southern Italy; the medallion is in the form of a shield set round with five garnets, while a sixth is placed at the point of attachment to the necklace.[2] Some few incrusted objects from the Levant are referable to a pre-Alexandrian date, as, for example, a gold pendant also in the Luynes collection, which is said to have come from the island of Melos;[3] its design is that of an open flower, highly conventionalised, with a beading of gold granules separating its petals, and in its centre an oriental sapphire, which points to a connection with Kashmir or Ceylon. But in this earlier jewellery the gems are used either singly or very sparingly, and not with the lavishness which characterises many of the post-Alexandrian specimens.

Of the objects from Western Asia, in which incrustation is an important *motif* in the design, the cup from Siverskaia, previously referred to, is perhaps the most instructive for the purpose of comparison. Around the upper part of this cup is a broad band of gold bordered above and below with four lines of filigree, and ornamented at equal intervals with carbuncles alternating with bosses of granulated gold.[4] The striking analogy, which this decoration offers to our Indian jewellery, is further borne out by a row of square chains ending in pendants of cornelian and gold drops, which hang from the lower part of the gold band. The chains are of precisely the same pattern as those on Figs. 1, 2, and 3 in Plate XXVIII (*a*), and they constitute what appears to be an essentially Indian element in the scheme of decoration. In the case of Figs. 1 and 2 their Indian character is demonstrated in part also by the little imitation bells of gold, with which the chains are terminated, but of which, unfortunately, only one still survives. In the Siverskaia cup these bells are replaced by hollow balls of gold, similar to those beneath the bases of Figs. 1 and 2, and present in the majority of the other pieces in Plate XXVIII (*a*). Chains with bells or other pendants attached figure extensively in Hindu, Buddhist, and Muhammadan[5] architecture, sometimes the whole length of the chain being most skilfully carved, link by link, in the round, and sometimes represented in relief. Some early examples of the latter are to be found in the lower decorative lines of some of the reliefs on the Buddhist *stūpa* at Barāhat,[6] which is usually ascribed to the first-half of the second century B.C. Grünwedel has rightly divined that the little bells and chains in these reliefs are borrowed from ornamented jewellery,[7] and there can be no doubt that the *motif* was a common one in the most ancient as it is in the most modern Indian decoration. Thus in the Mahābhārata, among the treasures which Yudhiṣṭhira loses at the gambling match at Hastināpura, we find the mention of a

---

[1] *Cf. Gazette Archéologique*, 1879, p. 75; Plate XVII.

[2] *Cf. Gazette Archéologique*, 1879, p. 75; Plate XI.

[3] Perrot et Chipiez, *op. cit.*, Tome III, p. 829, Fig. 591.

[4] *Gazette Archéologique*, 1887, p. 122.

[5] *Cf.*, for example, the ornaments on some of the Bījāpūr monuments. Captain Meadows Taylor, *Architecture at Beejapoor*, Plate LXXIV.

[6] Cunningham, *Stupa of Bharhut*, Plates XL—XLVIII.

[7] Grünwedel-Burgess, *Buddhist Art in India*, p. 31.

chariot adorned with a network of little bells. The closest modern parallels to these chains, bells and pendants are to be found among the modern Turkoman ornaments, which preserve, too, the same make of chain and the same proportionate length; it is significant, perhaps, that these ornaments are freely incrusted with gems and that the Turkomans assert that their designs are derived from immemorial antiquity.[1]

I would add here that the art of incrustation appears to have penetrated more generally to Western Europe during the first century B.C., after the Orient was opened up to Rome by the Asiatic conquests of Pompeius,[2] and the *motif* of chains and bells may have found its way westward about the same time. Caylus, in the *Recueil de mon. ant.*,[3] describes the figurine of a man riding on a marine beast, from which are suspended little chains ending in bells, which cannot but suggest a connection with the sea-lions and pendant chains in our Buddhist figures. Another figure—a bust of Mercury, from Vaucluse—with similar bells and chains, is published in the *Gazette Archéologique*,[4] and various unsatisfactory attempts have been made to explain the presence of its chains and bells as connected with religious ceremonial, or on other grounds.[5] For my own part, I feel that both in these and other examples we have a purely decorative and conventional device imitated from oriental prototypes.

I have reserved for the last the mention of a curious and striking parallel to some of our Buddhist ornaments furnished by a gold ring from Cyprus.[6] The date of this ring, if it has ever been ascertained, is not known to me, but from the connection in which it is mentioned by M. Perrot, I gather that it has been assigned to a date very considerably earlier than can be claimed for our Indian work. Its simple ornament consists of a cluster of round gold drops with little pyramids of granules clinging to each, which M. Perrot describes as "*des grappes de raisin mêlées à de gros fruits, qui ressemblent à des pommes.*" Whatever their *motif* may be, it is certainly identical with that which the little clusters on our Indian jewellery were designed to express, the only difference between them being that the Cypriote ornament is, if anything, slightly more naturalistic and original;[7] and this fact, taken in conjunction with what I have said about the origin of the granulation, would seem to point to this decorative device having been borrowed from the West.

To sum up the foregoing remarks as to the influences traceable in the designs and technique of these articles of jewellery, the seemingly Western features which they exhibit—apart from the Western character of the coin devices—are the Erotes riding on sea-lions, the granulated decoration, and the clusters of gold drops; while the Eastern and Indian elements are discernible in the incrustate gems, the pendant chains and bells, the *stūpa*-like design of the medallion, Fig. 3, and perhaps also in the floral *motif* of the upper portion of Figs. 1 and 2. The hybrid character

---

[1] *J. I. A.*, 1885, p. 53; with two plates.

[2] See M. R. de Lasteyrie, *Gazette Archéologique*, 1883, p. 346.

[3] Tom. VII, p. 477, and Plate XXXVII, Fig. 2.

[4] 1884, p. 7, and Plate III.

[5] M. R. Mowat sought to find in them an allusion to a story of Augustus and Jupiter Tonans told by Suetonius (*Aug.*, 91) and Dion Cassius (LIV, 4).

[6] Perrot et Chipiez, *op. cit.*, Tome III, p. 822, Fig. 584

[7] In stating this, I rely entirely upon the illustration cited in the previous note.

of these ornaments as well as of the gold casket from Bīmārān, and the comparisons instituted in the foregoing pages between them and analogous ornaments of the pre-Christian era from Asia Minor, point to their being the outcome of that widely diffused cosmopolitan art of Western Asia, which was chiefly developed from the fusion of Hellenic and Oriental influences in the fourth and third centuries B.C., and which gradually permeated eastward and was assimilated at a later date into the Buddhist art of Northern India.

J. H. MARSHALL.

TER.—TAGARA.

IN an article which appeared in the "Journal of the Royal Asiatic Society" for July 1901, Dr. Fleet identifies Ter, a town on the western confines of H. H. the Nizam's Dominions,[1] with the ancient Tagara, the great central emporium of trade in India about the beginning of the Christian era, the site of which scholars and antiquarians have hitherto sought in vain. There have been almost as many different identifications as there have been men who have taken the subject up. Even Dr. Fleet himself had previously identified Tagara with Kolhāpur, but not, as he says, with very great confidence. As the maps almost invariably spell Ter as Ther or Thair, he devoted a considerable portion of his article to prove that the spelling was wrong. But though he was not aware of it at the time, the proper official spelling as "Ter" is given in a published list, No. 167, Home Department Notification, of the 2nd February 1883.

Being anxious to ascertain whether there were any remains or indications of great age upon the spot to support his identification, I made a flying visit to the place in the beginning of November 1901. This visit, though eminently satisfactory in other respects, yielded no direct evidence of the identification. That it is, however, a very ancient site, containing early Hindu, Jaina, and Buddhist remains, the following account will show.

Ter is situated about 30 miles east of Bārsi, a great cotton centre in the Sholāpur district of the Bombay Presidency, upon the west bank of the Ternā river, which was, at the time of my visit, nearly dry but very broad. The town appears to have shrunk very considerably from its former proportions, being now but a half or a third of its original size. Extensive mounds to the south of the present town, as well as upon the opposite bank of the river, show the extent of previous occupation by their size and the amount of brick and pottery *débris*. Beyond the present south wall of the town, which is a more or less modern mud one in a ruinous state, we came across the foundations of brick walls, where the old bricks measure 16½″ × 8″ × 2¾″. From the mounds running parallel with the town walls, and which look like the ruins of the former town walls, the people still dig out old bricks for use in the village. The town

[1] Long. 76° 12′ 30″, Lat. 18° 19′ 20″.

seems to have shrunk away from the south side, and the only remains left of the extensive suburb upon the opposite bank of the river is the small hamlet with no special name of its own, but which is called the Peṭh. Mounds covered with potsherds, brickbats, and prickly pear extend for some distance along, opposite to the town. There is one lofty stone gateway on the town side of the river, of comparatively late construction, which now stands alone, the adjacent walls having fallen; the principal thoroughfare has been diverted and goes round it. Near this gateway is a platform on which is a red-daubed Māruti, while beside the platform stands a slab containing a long but much abraded Devanāgarī inscription with a date which is hardly legible. Above the writing, in a compartment, is carved a *liṅga*, with a standing four-armed figure beside it, while above are the sun and moon. A copperplate grant, which I obtained at Ter, written in Persian, states that the Qāzi of Ter, ratified certain privileges to the head of the Telī community in A.H. 1070 (A.D. 1659), thus showing that the town was called Ter at that date.

Dr. Fleet in his article says: "that as the Atlas sheet marks the town as having three 'pagodas,' it is not at all unlikely that the place possesses a *māhātmya* or local *purāṇa*, which would in all probability present the ancient name of Tagara under some pretext or another." I obtained a manuscript copy of the *māhātmya* of Ter on the spot and sent a photographic copy of it to Dr. Fleet. He writes of it thus: "It claims, in the colophon of each chapter, to be a part of the *Padmapurāṇa*; see, for instance, folio 8 *b*, lines 1, 2, and folio 65 *b*, lines 3, 4. This last colophon is followed by the statement that the book belongs to Kēśavavyāsa, son of Krishṇavyāsa. And this statement is followed by the date,—*Śakē* 1679 *Īśvara-nāma-saṁvatsarē āshāḍha vadya 2 dinē sampūrṇam astu*. This date falls in A.D. 1757. It may indicate either the date of composition, or the date of finishing this particular copy.

"The Māhātmya attaches itself to a town which, it says, was called Satyapura in the Kṛita age, and Śāntapura in the Trētā age, and Kaṅkavatī in the Dvāpara age, and Siddhāśrama in the Kali age; see folio 1 *b*, line 8, and folio 62 *b*, line 1. In other passages, Satyapurī occurs instead of Satyapura (for instance, in the colophons), and Śāntipura instead of Śāntapura (for instance, in folio 1 *b*, line 7). And it undoubtedly identifies that place with Tēr, and, in so doing, stamps itself as the *Māhātmya* of Tēr; for, it says, from a certain time when Yudhiṣṭhira bathed in the Kukulyākuṇḍa at the command of the god Vishṇu, that town was always known as Tērā; see folio 53 *b*. But the assertion that the town was originally called Satyapura, Śāntapura, Kaṅkavatī, and Siddhāśrama, is, of course, pure fancy, in simple accordance with the general style of *Māhātmyas*. There is not the slightest reason for supposing that the town ever really passed under any of those names.

"The *Māhātmya* mentions a river, which it calls Pippīlikā (folio 12 *b*); and some *tīrthas*, such as the Kālakuṇḍa (folio 45 *a*), and the Nāgavāpī (folio 48 *a*), and the Kukulyākuṇḍa (folio 52 *b*); and some gods, such as a *liṅga* called Uttarēśvara (folio 59 *b*), and another *liṅga* called Bilvēśvara (folio 62 *a*). But it does not present anything of a historical and practical nature; except, no doubt, in establishing Pippīlikā as the former name of the river which is now known as the Tērnā.

"It introduces the word *tagara* in folio 33 *a*, line 7; but only, with the *Karavīra* shrub, in the description of various flowers prescribed to be used in worship. It does not seem to make any attempt to connect the word *tagara* with the name of the town."

To return to the ancient remains at present found at Ter. By far the most important is a complete Buddhist *chaitya* temple, built in brick, which was subsequently converted into a Hindu temple and is still used as such; and it is to this conversion and use that we owe its perfect preservation. The temple of Trivikrama, for by that name it is now known, hoary with age, stands in a small crowded courtyard in the middle of the village, and is shut off from it by a high wall all round. It faces the east. The silt of years has buried its basement and the original floor of the court some three or four feet. The temple as it stands consists of a shrine—the original *chaitya*—and a low flat-roofed closed *maṇḍapa* or hall. The shrine is a long chamber, 26 feet long by 12 feet broad inside, with apsidal end and wagon-vaulted ridge roof. The walls of the shrine, which are about 3½ feet thick, and the roof are constructed of the very best brickwork, laid in mud cement, with exceedingly fine joints, the bricks measuring 17″×9″×3″. Those of the *maṇḍapa* are not so well laid, nor are the bricks so uniformly large, a smaller size being mixed with the larger. Several reasons lead me to think that the *maṇḍapa* is a later addition, probably added by the Hindus when they first took possession of the *chaitya*, but yet not so very far removed in point of time from the building of the latter. The present wooden door-frame of the shrine is so small that the great black Hindu stone images, which are in the shrine, could not possibly have been taken in through it. Through the plaster around it are indications of the outlines of a much larger aperture into which the smaller door-frame appears to have been inserted. The wooden pillars of the hall or *maṇḍapa* struck me, immediately on entering, as being not quite in keeping with the more archaic aspect of the shrine. They seem to be of a more advanced style—immediate precursors, in fact, of the stone pillars of the Chālukyan work. One would have expected to find massive square pillars with square and simple roll bracket capitals, not the turned capitals, narrow mouldings, and constricted necks of these.

Passing through the brickwork of the upper roll moulding of the eaves of the *maṇḍapa*, and leading off the flat roof, are four rough-hewn channelled black stones serving as gargoyles, whereas there is no stone whatever used in the shrine. These do not appear to have been inserted after the building of the *maṇḍapa*, but with it, since the original brickwork around each does not seem to have been disturbed for their after-insertion. The roll mouldings around the eave of the *maṇḍapa* are not carried round on the same level and in continuity with those of the shrine but slightly lower. Had the shrine and *maṇḍapa* been built at one and the same time, these would no doubt have been carried round on one level. There appears to be no bonding of the walls of the two chambers, those of the *maṇḍapa* being built against, not into, those of the shrine.

The façade of the shrine, as it rises above the roof of the *maṇḍapa*, follows the outline of the true Buddhist *chaitya* arch as found in the caves. The wooden arch frame is reproduced most literally, and the wooden construction of the earlier *chaityas* is, moreover, repeated most markedly where the ends of longitudinal beams project and rest upon the tops of the two pilasters. The whole façade, with its inner arching, cross-beams, pilasters, and toothed ornament, is practically the same design, in the rough, as that of the Viśvakarma cave at Elurā.[1]

The niche, now filled with a coarse image of Hanumān in plaster, and arched over, was, without doubt, originally a plain square opening, as in the Viśvakarma façade, to let light in upon the *dāgoba*. The whole shrine, then, is just such a structural *chaitya* hall in brick, with its arched roof and apsidal end, as was more elaborated in stone in the caves. The vaulted roof is but a reminiscence of the bamboo and thatched dwellings of earlier times, such as we see reproduced in the Sāñchi bas-reliefs, and find even at the present day amongst the aboriginal tribes. The ribs of the *chaitya* caves are but the bent bamboos of the grass huts. In *Glimpses of India*, page 441, is the photograph of the façade of a grass Toda hut, which is almost a rough copy of the front of this temple, even to the little square opening.

The arched roof of the *chaitya* is, like the walls, constructed wholly of brick masonry, each horizontal course having a slight offset inwards as it rises to the ridge. There is no true arching with radiating bricks. The interior thus follows the curve of the exterior, and there is no intermediate or false ceiling within.

The only decoration upon the exterior of both shrine and *maṇḍapa* are the heavy roll mouldings, which General Sir A. Cunningham calls "Gupta mouldings,"[2] running horizontally round the building, and a series of thin shallow pilasters[3] at intervals along the wall representing the original wooden pillars supporting the frame-work of the thatched roof. The heavy overhanging lower edge of the roof reminds one much of the lower, thick, trimmed edge of a thatch. The whole of the exterior has been plastered, and that, I believe, originally.

Upon entering the shrine we find a common-looking Kāla Bhairava image upon a seat, against what at first sight seems to be the backwall. This is but a dummy set up in troublous times when Muhammadan fanaticism spared nought that was fashioned in the image of god, man, or devil. This cross-wall, at the back of the image, is but a partition screen, which is sufficiently high to be lost in the gloom of the ceiling, and which has a small entrance through it, in the dark corner, to one side, which leads to the proper images behind. A very small hole or window in the middle of this wall, opposite the shrine door, allows those, who do not go beyond the door, to get a glimpse of part of the features of a shiny, black, oily image behind it. Both these apertures, in times of need, could quickly and easily be closed up. Behind the cross-wall, then, in almost absolute darkness, are two colossal images, one in front of the other, of Viṣṇu and Trivikrama. They are, as far as I was able to judge from a glimpse through the port hole, and the help of a magnesium light, executed in the very best style and workmanship. The image-breaker had evidently been here before the cross-wall was built, or perhaps in spite of the cross-wall, for the former image has lost its legs, and these have been replaced by wooden ones which, in their turn, are

[1] See Fergusson's *Indian and Eastern Architecture*, p. 128.

[2] *Reports*, Vol. IX, p. 32.

[3] Precisely the same as are found decorating the exterior of the *stūpa* near Moro in Sind, but which are there rather more ornamental in the capitals.

PLATE XXIX.

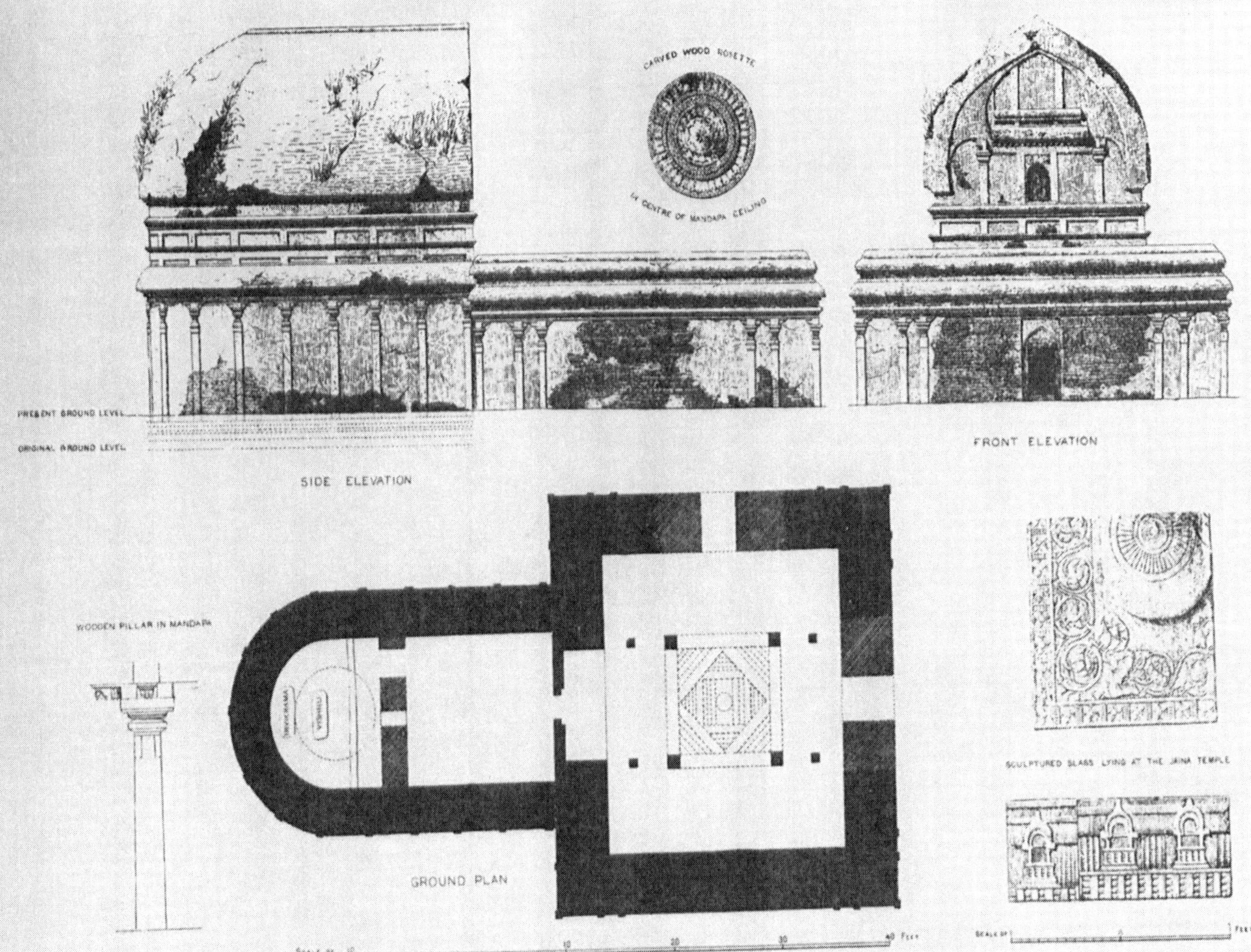

TEMPLE OF TRIVIKRAMA—AN APPROPRIATED BUDDHIST CHAITYA—AT TER.

rotting and crumbling away. Behind this image is that of Trivikrama, or the Bali or three-strides *avatāra* of Viṣṇu. The figure sits upon a bench against the backwall with its right leg hanging down, while the left is stretched straight out along the edge of the seat, as if in the act of kicking something away. The body sits upright, and the two arms are akimbo. Beneath this outstretched leg are Bali, Sukrāchārya, Bali's wife, and at the point of the toe, touching it, Viṣṇu's wife. Across the shrine, in front of Viṣṇu's image, is fixed a stout wooden beam, let into the side walls, a short distance above the floor, as if intended for an altar rail. The position of Viṣṇu, facing the door of the shrine—Trivikrama being hidden behind him—would seem to indicate that the temple, when converted to their use by the Hindus, was consecrated to Viṣṇu. The subsequent damage and desecration of this image may have led them to transfer their worship to Trivikrama who, however, is but another form of Viṣṇu. That there was a great temple to Viṣṇu at Ter in olden times is clearly shown by these images, together with an old corroded image of his *avatāra* Narasiṁha placed in a comparatively modern temple to the south of the town, and by the remains of the original temple itself scattered about the place.

But the original object of worship in the shrine or *chaitya*, when occupied by the Buddhists, was, without doubt, the *dāgoba*. In the Jaina temple of Mahāvīra and Pārśvanātha, to the west of the town, and marked on the Atlas Sheet as a "pagoda," I found four carved Buddhist stones which had been carried there, with ordinary stone, for building purposes. Two of these have been built into the end wall of a *dharma-śālā*, on the outside, as ordinary block-in-course stones; another has been thrown down carelessly to form a temporary step before the door of Pārśvanātha's shrine, while the fourth was serving a similar ignoble purpose before the entrance to Mahāvīra's temple. Those in the wall were contiguous blocks in the work for which they were originally cut, and are carved to represent three small *chaitya* arched windows with little Buddhist railings before them. A railing on a larger scale runs along below these, while between them are panels of basket-work in convex rolls as we find it on the face of the Koṇḍāne *chaitya*.[1] The slab lying before the entrance of Pārśvanātha's temple is a quarter of a huge *pādukā* slab. It has the back part or heel of one of the footprints, raised, and having the sacred wheel upon it, while the rest of the slab is decorated with beautifully designed lotuses, birds, and a *makara* in low relief, outside of which runs a narrow lozenge-shaped flower border. The slab before Mahāvīra's shrine is flat and plain, with one edge worked to a segmental curve, with a raised ring around, much like a piece of a very large flat saucer.[2] This stone might well be part of the basement of a *dāgoba*, and the first described stones, built into the wall, part of a decorative band passing round the cylinder, tee, or neck of the same;[3] and they would suit just such a size of *dāgoba* as we might imagine occupying this shrine in Buddhist days. They are in a light drab or creamy coloured limestone very much like the Shāhābād limestone.

The *maṇḍapa* has a flat roof. It has doorways on the east and north side only,

---

[1] *Reports of the Archæological Survey of India, Imperial Series*, Vol. IV, Frontispiece.

[2] See saucer tray under *dāgoba* in illustration, p. 29, *Buddhist Art in India*, translated by J. Burgess, C.I.E., LL.D.

[3] See illustration, p. 227, *Cave Temples of India*.

the present frames having been roughly inserted at some late period to take the place of other earlier ones removed. The south wall is intact and has never had a doorway. Four wooden pillars, with corresponding pilasters, support the wooden beams and joists of the roof. The central space of the ceiling is of flat boards, set diagonally in the square contained within the four beams over the pillars, so as to form two other squares, one within the other, like the ordinary later temple ceilings. In the centre is a very prettily carved wooden boss or rosette about 2 feet in diameter. Over the beams is brick and plaster. The present shrine door-frame is entirely of wood, with very little ornament, what there is being made up of dog-tooth and chequer designs in narrow bands. There are two rather well carved brackets over the entrance to the shallow antechamber before the shrine door. The whole of the woodwork is perfectly black with age and perhaps the smoke of lamps. To prevent the splitting of the pillars, iron bands have been fixed round the necks of the capitals and the edge of the abaci or square tiles surmounting them.

The only other Buddhist structural *chaitya*, hitherto discovered in any tolerable state of preservation, is one, almost identical with this in size and design, found by Mr. Alexander Rea at Chezarlā in the Madras Presidency some fourteen years ago.[1] Like this one, it, too, has been appropriated to Hindu worship. There, also, a *maṇḍapa* or hall seems to have been added at an early period by the Hindus, who have not been sparing in the use of whitewash, from which the Ter *chaitya* has hitherto escaped. While the latter was converted to Vaiṣṇava worship the former appears to have been dedicated to Śaiva. Mr. Rea's *chaitya*, without the *maṇḍapa*, measures 30 feet 3 inches outside, which includes a wall 2 feet 9 inches built across the east or open end, while the Ter building without such a wall measures 30 feet 2 inches. Without seeing Mr. Rea's plan I am unable to say whether the wall mentioned by him is built across and within the ends of the *chaitya* walls, or outside and against them. If the former, the two *chaityas* are exactly of the same size. The bricks used in the Chezarlā example measure 17″×9″×3″, just the same as at Ter.

With these *chaityas* might be compared the rock-cut *ratha* at Mahāvalipuram with wagon-vaulted roof and apsidal end, but the simplicity of the Ter example, its archaic and primitive appearance, and absence of all decoration, point to a very early period. The absence of ornament was not due to the material in which it was built, for we have some very fine ornamental work in brick and terra-cotta upon the *stūpa* near Moro in Sind. Moulded and carved brickwork was used at Ter later on in the building of the old Hindu temples of Uttareśvara and Kāleśvara, where *makaras* with florid tails were executed in that material, of the same type as we find in stone on the decorated temples of the seventh and eighth centuries at Kukkanūr and Paṭṭadakal. Taking all these points into consideration, I do not think we can place the Ter *chaitya* later than the fourth century; it is possible it may be very much older. My visit was too short to study the question of age as fully as I could wish.

And now to the old temples of Uttareśvara and Kāleśvara, which themselves would have rewarded me amply for the trouble of my visit. These two are very old shrines, built in moulded or carved brick, the decoration being carried out in the

[1] *Progress Report of the Madras Archæological Survey* for December 1888 and January 1889, p. 12.

same style as we find it in stone in the old temple of the Navaliṅga at Kukkanūr, Kailāsa at Elurā, and the oldest temples at Paṭṭadakal.[1] But whether due to the more easily disintegrated material of which they are built, or to other causes, they certainly wear a more venerable appearance than those. Another sign of great age is the absence of stone in their construction. Just before the brick age merged into the stone-building age, brick temples were fitted with stone door-frames, sometimes with beams, and occasionally with the pillars of the porch in the same material; but here we have wooden beams and wooden door-frames, now crumbling to dust, the latter being very ornate. The bricks measure 16″×9″×2¼″, showing a somewhat later period than that of the Buddhist *chaitya*. As time wore on, the size of bricks gradually lessened and never returned to the great size they were in early years of the Christian era. The *śikharas*, or towers, rise in the Dravidian style in horizontal storeys, with heavy overhanging roll mouldings, decorated with boldly fashioned *chaitya*-arch ornaments. The whole of the brickwork has had a thin coat of plaster.

The shrine of Uttareśvara is situated in a small courtyard in the midst of the town, its basement and the lower portions of its walls being buried in the accumulated *débris* of ages. It is but a small building, now terribly dilapidated. The upper portion of the *śikhara* has been clumsily rebuilt at a late period, but the whole of the south-east corner and its walls have collapsed, showing the hollow core, with the old beams of the shrine ceiling still in position. The temple faces the east and has now a small *liṅga* in the shrine tended by a solitary *pūjāri*. The brickwork has been beautifully moulded, *makaras* with flowing arabesque tails being sharply and crisply worked. The walls have been decorated with upright pilasters at intervals, between which were ornamental niches, the tops of which are formed of *makaras* supporting foliated arches. This is now very much ruined, and not much of it remains. The carved wood door-frame of the shrine, like the rest of the building, old and crumbling, is a gem of the wood-carver's art. It is of much the same pattern as the old decorated stone Chālukyan doorways, but the details are bolder and freer in treatment. There is a grand band of small figures which are carved out in full relief across the top, above the deep overhanging cornice. Seated in the centre is a figure which might almost be the same quadruple deity that we found on a temple at Dilmāl in Gujarāt,[2] a combination of Śiva, Viṣṇu, Brahmā, and Sūrya, only that it has six hands instead of eight, and three faces. In the upper left hand is a hooded snake, such as Śiva usually holds; in the middle left hand, on a level with the breast, is a full-blown lotus such as we generally find in the hands of Sūrya; and in the lower, a citron or *śaṅkha*. In the upper right is the *gadā* or mace, with a *liṅga* upon its top. The other two hands are gone, but the middle right appears, from the position of the broken surface, to have been in the same position, and to have held a lotus, as the corresponding hand upon the other side. The central face has the central eye of Śiva. It is possible this is a trimurti, and I am inclined to look upon it, with its three sets of arms, as composed of Śiva, Sūrya, and Viṣṇu or Brahmā. We do not usually meet the Trimurti as a full figure, but as a bust simply.

[1] *Reports of the Archæological Survey of India, Imperial Series*, Vol. I, Plate XXXVIII.

[2] See my *Progress Report* for months March and April 1890. p. 9.

Upon the right of this image is another three-faced figure with four arms, seated, but leaning and looking towards the central figure. It is probably Brahmā. In the upper right hand is the staff or *gadā* with the *yoni* on the top. The upper left does not appear, the lower right rests, palm downwards, on the extreme outside of his right knee, while the lower left presents the palm of the hand to the front, finger tips upwards. Upon the left of the central figure, and also leaning and looking towards it, is what I take to be Śiva, as he seems to have matted or rolled hair. He has had four arms, but they are broken away. These three images occupy the position over the doorway where, in later temples, we so often find Brahmā, Viṣṇu and Śiva. The present arrangement, in which Brahmā and Śiva are relegated to the flanks, leads me to think the temple was originally dedicated to Viṣṇu or Sūrya. Upon the dedicatory block, below the cornice, is an image, somewhat corroded, but remarkably like the usual Jina upon Jaina temples, with pendant ears, and but two arms, the hands apparently laid upon one another in the lap. It has four attendant figures, two on each side, with their hands joined in adoration towards the seated figure. Seeing this alone, without the upper band, I should unhesitatingly have said the temple was originally Jaina. Or can it possibly have been a late Buddhist temple? The present name of Uttareśvara belongs, of course, to the subsequently placed *liṅga*.

But we have not finished with the figures over the cornice. On the right of the image of Brahmā is a seated figure with a five-hooded snake canopy over him which at first sight looks like Pārśvanātha, but it has four arms and a high jewelled head-dress. The body is apparently nude to the waist at least, and there is neither neck-lace nor sacred cord, which the other images have. The two lower hands repose, Jina-like, in the lap, palms upwards; in the upper right seems to be a mace, now broken, while the upper left holds a hooded snake. On either side of him stands a *chaurī*-bearer, that on his left wearing what seems like a snake round his neck. Balancing this figure, on the other side of Śiva, is a seated figure with but two arms. A sword (?) in the right, and a bowl in the left. It has two female attendants, one on either side, who hold over him, by the rim, a flat, tray-like disc, or umbrella without a handle. Going to the other side again, we have, on the right of the snake-hooded figure, a well carved group of figures, apparently musicians, while at the other end, on the left of the man with the umbrella, is a well-carved *jogī*, seated and turned inwards, whose arms are broken, but his hands, with the palms together, seem to have been in the attitude of devotion or respect towards the umbrella figure.

Beneath this very remarkable band of figures is a deeply projecting quarter round roll cornice, decorated along its front, at intervals, with boldly cut little *chaitya*-arch ornaments, four in all. These are cut with great vigour and depth; later on they became shallower, and were repeated more frequently. Under this cornice is a band of geese with a central lotus. The side mouldings of the door-posts are very similar to the later stone Chālukyan work. The outer moulding is a running scroll, next a succession of griffins rampant, then pairs of human figures; after this comes the main pilaster, and finally an inner band of the usual lozenge-shaped ornament. The figures which were upon the other side, at the bottom of the door-frame, are destroyed.

Through the gap in the *śikhara* the method of its construction can be seen. There

PLATE XX

is the flat wooden ceiling of the shrine, from which level the walls slope inwards to form the spire by corbelling forward the horizontal layers of bricks until they meet, as was done in the *chaitya*. Standing before the shrine there was, perhaps, a porch, but this has been ruined, and at a later date was probably added a stone *maṇḍapa*, signs of which still exist. Within the shrine is placed a small *liṅga*, but it has practically no worshippers. In the enclosure near the temple are some loose stone images, amongst them being those of Viṣṇu and Bhairava, and some memorial stones indifferently carved but with no inscriptions.

The other old brick temple, of the same age and style, is upon the high bank, on the other side of the River Ternā from the town, and to the north of the latter. The original shrine with its Dravidian *śikhara* is complete, but the *maṇḍapa* attached to the front of it, constructed of heavy Muhammadan arching, is quite modern. Unfortunately the original walls of the shrine have been buttressed up with heavy brickwork, set in mortar, to strengthen them and prevent their bulging or falling outwards by the weight of the tower upon them. This brickwork is as high as the cornice all around, and from it spreads out, pyramid fashion, to the floor of the courtyard. A very similar buttressing up of the walls of a temple is to be seen at the temple of Galgeśvara at Galaganātha in the Dharwar district, only that the latter is all in stone. The crowning member of the spire is similar to that of Kailāsa at Elurā. The temple has been very coarsely replastered, probably when the buttressing was added, as it was carried down over that. Into the modern *maṇḍapa* walls are built several memorial slabs where, in each case, as in so many more through the village, the hero plunges a short sword or dagger into the bowels of his opponent.

Within the shrine is a *liṅga*, but upon the dedicatory block over the shrine doorway is Garuḍa, as well as over the outer doorway of the courtyard, but these may be of a much later date. I was not allowed to enter the temple to examine the shrine door. Lying loose against the front of the *maṇḍapa* are some four slabs which formed the balustrades or flanking slabs to some Chālukyan temple steps. They are carved upon one side to represent a tiger attacking an elephant. A number of *satī* stones, with a bent arm with open palm upon them, lie about or are used in the masonry of some of the modern walls. Out in front of the temple are a number of *yonis* for *liṅgas*, there being no less than nine of them. Mutilated figures of Śiva, Śiva-Pārvatī, Bhairava, and Gaṇapati, and the capitals of pillars of some Chālukyan temple lie about. These fragments seem to have been brought here for building purposes. Beside the old temple is another very modern one, with a great hall attached, enshrining *Viṭhobā's* footprints, while in a niche, in the back of this same temple, is an old image of Viṣṇu.

The next temple perhaps, in point of age, is the small ruined shrine of Tripurantakeśvara, built upon a rock in the middle of the river. The outer casing of the walls, which are entirely of stone, has disappeared, but it seems to have been an ordinary mediæval Chālukyan shrine. Within the shrine is a *liṅga*, while Nandi sits outside before it.

Another temple, that of Narasiṁha, is situated about half a mile to the south-east of the town, and is a more or less modern brick-and-mortar temple built in the hybrid style so common at the present time, in which Musalman domes, arches, and minarets, in modified forms, play so great a part in the designs. There is nothing of interest about the building, save that it contains, as the principal object of worship, the old corroded image of Narasiṁha already alluded to. This is, no doubt, the one referred to in the *Māhātmya*, and probably with that of Trivikrama belonged to a set of the *avatāras* of Viṣṇu originally set up in some old stone temple now no more.

The Jaina shrines on the west of the town, and the temple of Rāmeśvara within the town are all very modern and are of no particular interest. The country around is flat, and composed of rich arable land all under cultivation.

My visit was very short, as I was only able to spare a few days. I certainly went unprepared to find so much within twelve miles of Dhārāsiṁha, a place at which our camp was pitched under Dr. Burgess for some days in December 1875. It shows how very difficult it is to get information concerning these old remains from the villagers, for no one was more persistent than he in his endeavours to glean every scrap of information as he went along. Even in the forms distributed to the officials all over the country for filling in, when I was compiling my lists of remains for the Hyderābād State, nothing at Ter was entered.

HENRY COUSENS.

THE IRON PILLAR AT DHĀR.

LYING at Dhār, in Central India, are three portions of a great iron column with a total length of 43 feet 4 inches, and an average width of 10¼" each way. The longest portion measures 24 feet 3 inches, and is square in section throughout; the second 11 feet 7 inches, of which 8 feet 6 inches is square and 3 feet 1 inch of octagonal section; and the third piece, 7 feet 6 inches in length, and, with the exception of a circular collar at the end, about 8 inches deep, is of octagonal section throughout. In February last (1903) the longest piece was lying outside, and at a short distance from the north entrance to the great courtyard of Dilāvar Khān's mosque, known on this account as the Lāt Masjid. The second portion was lying at the Ānand High School, where a museum has lately been established, while the shortest length was set up and fixed in a masonry basement in the public gardens known as the *Lāl Bāgh*, not far from the High School.

The length at Dilāvar Khān's mosque, which has attracted most attention, lies with its lower end tilted upwards and resting against the high masonry basement upon which it was set up by Dilāvar Khān. The proper lower end, now the highest, though square like the rest of its length, is, as in the case of the Delhi iron column, slightly bulbous, being 11 to 11¼" wide at 2 feet from the end, while the rest measures 10½ to 10¼". At 6 feet from the proper upper end is a short inscription of Akbar's, dated in the 44th year of his reign, recording his halt here on his way to the Dakhan, but which, if the column were re-erected, would be upside down. This is due to the inscription having been engraved while the column was lying in its present position, it being upon the upper side as it lies, and in the easiest position for an engraver to work at it, standing at the side of the pillar with the slant, like a desk, before him. Were the column standing in its last position, the inscription would be over 16 feet above the point where the pillar emerged from the basement, and, as already said, upside down!

Upon other parts of the pillar are names and letters in the Devanāgarī character, all apparently later than the fourteenth century, but which, unlike Akbar's inscription, are engraved with the proper side up. Among these is a group of several names of visitors of the goldsmith caste, each name having "*soni*" for *sonār* attached to it, the last of which seems to read "Jasu soni" for Yesvant Sonār. There appears also to be a date immediately after the names, but it is very indistinct. These names are between 6 feet 11 inches and 7 feet 6 inches from the proper lower end of the pillar. Twenty inches of the end was let into the socket in the great boulders when it stood upright on its present site, which would leave the inscription between 5 feet 3 inches and 5 feet 10 inches from the level upon which the engraver might have stood, a fairly easy height for him to work at. When the pillar was entire and unbroken, set up in its original postion, probably another foot or more of it was embedded in the basement, and this would make the position of these names, if they then existed, the very best possible for the greatest ease in engraving. There are also several small symbols and a Persian word or two, but they are all rather scratched in than engraved. It will be noticed from the drawing which accompanies this that all these Devanāgarī letters and names are about the same level, and none occur upon the upper parts of the pillar, nor upon the other two fragments, showing clearly that these characters were not engraved after the final fall of the pillar.

Upon the masonry basement stand the three great rock boulders, which were bound together by iron bands and had a socket in the top, 20 inches deep, in which the foot of the pillar was gripped. The iron bands securing these passed round them horizontally, and their pressure was spread over the boulders by vertical flat iron bars inserted at intervals under the bands in slots cut for the purpose. In fact the whole was faggotted around the end of the pillar.

The piece lying at the Ānand High School is, for 8 feet of its length, of the same section as the last, and was, no doubt, a continuation of the Lāt Masjid length. In this piece the square changes to an octagon, but a very irregular one.

The piece in the Lāl Bāgh, which has lately been taken out of its masonry basement in order to get its measurements correctly, was, without doubt, a further continuation of this second piece. Mr. Lele, the State Superintendent of Education, who made the measurements, doubts this on account of its smaller perimeter measurement, but, I think, he overlooks the fact that, in two figures, a square and an octagon formed off the same square, with the same diameter from side to side, the perimeter measurement of the octagon will be very much less than that of the square. His own perimeter measurement of 34½", taken about the middle of the length, works out to a diameter from side to side of fully 10⅜". The upper end of this piece has a round neck, about 8 inches deep, a little smaller in diameter than the rest of the pillar, as if it were intended to hold a collar or fit into a socket of a capital.

One curious thing about all three sections of this great column is the presence of a number of small holes at intervals in its sides, varying in depth from 1¾" to 3 inches, and in diameter about 1¼". They run up each of the four sides of the square shaft and the corresponding faces of the octagon. In the drawing I have shown the four faces of each of the three lengths of the pillar; but whether, in my arrangement, I have hit off the proper continuation of the faces, one above the other, I cannot say, since I have nothing to guide me. To find out properly which end fits which end, and which faces are the proper continuations of those on the other pieces, it would be necessary to take casts of the joining ends of the different lengths and to fit them together by trial, since the columns themselves are too unwieldy to experiment with and are not even near each other.

PLATE XXXI.

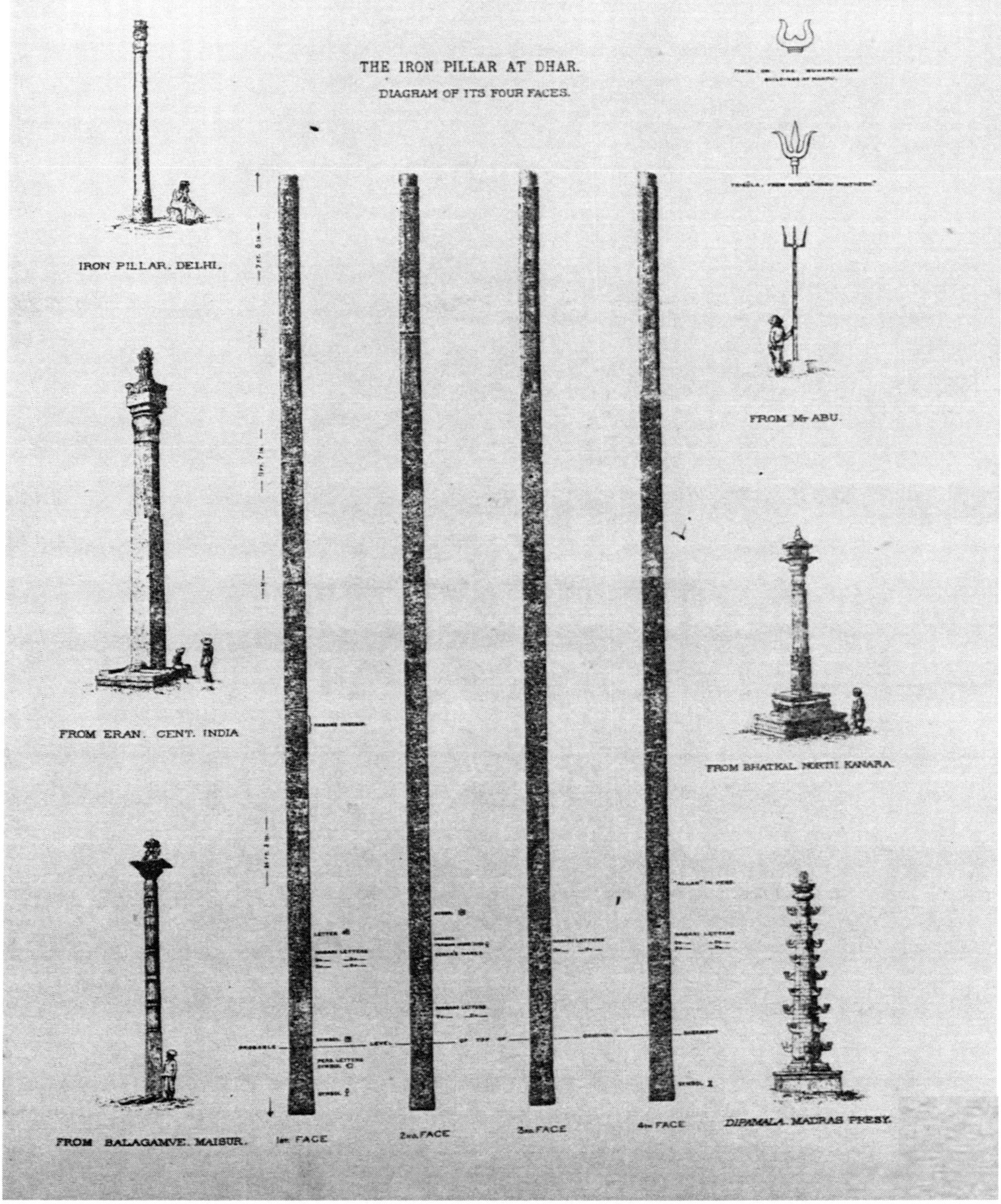
THE IRON PILLAR AT DHAR.
DIAGRAM OF ITS FOUR FACES.
IRON PILLAR. DELHI.
FROM ERAN. CENT. INDIA
FROM BALAGAMVE. MAISUR.
FROM Mt ABU.
FROM BHATKAL NORTH KANARA.
DIPAMALA. MADRAS PRESY.
1st FACE
2nd FACE
3rd FACE
4th FACE

It has been thought that these holes were intended for pegs to carry lights, presuming the column to have been a *dīpadāna* or lamp-post, or to form a ladder for a person to climb to the top to light a fire there. My own opinion is, for reasons I will endeavour to show, that the column was not used as either a *dīpadāna* or beacon, and that no pegs ever occupied the holes for that purpose. Had the holes been intended for any such permanent use, the pegs would have been welded in hot with the rest of the metal, and would not have come out so easily as they seem to have done. One only refused to move, and it has been broken off; there are none in any of the other holes, which, I think, shows they were worked in cold, in order that they should not be permanently welded to the rest of the metal, and were only used for temporary purposes. The holes, in all probability, were made as the mass of the pillar was built up, in order to hold the ends of crowbars or levers with which the workmen could the better handle and roll over the great heavy column as bit by bit of semi-molten metal was added and welded on to the white hot stump of the shaft. The crowbars were removed and shifted from place to place as required; one stuck and was chipped off, leaving the end in the hole.

At the bottom of the length at the Lāt Masjid is a hole about 3 inches deep. This was evidently intended for an iron peg in the basement to fit into, to prevent the column from slipping sideways from its bed when it was set up.

The very meagre details of its history give us no clue as to who caused it to be made, or for what purpose it was forged. I think there was but one purpose to which it could have been put—to carry an image or symbol, set up before a temple, either as a special gift to the temple or as a *jayastambha*, or column of victory. *Jayastambhas* were common enough all over the country, two, at least, of which were of iron, *viz.*, that at Delhi and another of more modest proportions on Mount Ābu. This latter, which stands 12 feet 9 inches high, is set up in the courtyard of the temple of Achaleśvara and is surmounted by a Śaiva *triśūla*. I have given a sketch of it upon the accompanying drawing. This pillar is said to have been made out of the arms cast away by the flying Muhammadans when chased down the hill by the bees.[1]

The only thing recorded in an inscription[2] of a certain southern King Tiluṅgavidya is that he erected a pillar of victory, with a figure of Garuḍa on the top, at Ujayapurī. That the Paramāra kings of Mālvā were no strangers to such erections we learn from the Udaypur *praśasti* of those kings,[3] where it is stated that Vairisiṁha, one of the early kings of that line, composed his own eulogy by erecting pillars of victory; and, curiously enough, this is practically the only thing recorded of him.

The earliest columns or *lāts* that we have are the round Aśoka *lāts*, bearing his edicts, and generally surmounted by one or more lions. Following them are the Gupta columns, generally square below, rising into octagonal, sixteen-sided, and circular section as they ascend, such as the Eraṇ[4] and Paṭhāri examples. A very interesting pillar, erected for quite a different purpose, is that at Bijayagaḍh, set up as a sacrificial pillar (*yūpa*) by Vishṇuvardhana in A.D. 371.[1] This pillar, of a single

[1] It is dated Sam. 1468 (A.D. 1412), about the time that general revolts were raised against 'Alā-al-dīn, just before his death.

[2] *Epig. Ind.*, Vol. VII, p. 121. [3] *Epig. Ind.*, Vol. I, p. 237.

[4] See drawing, also General Sir A. Cunningham's *Reports*, Vol. VI.

block of red sandstone, rises to a height of 26 feet 3 inches, 3 feet 8 inches of which is square, while the rest is a tapering octagonal shaft broken off at the top. Later on we have frequent references to the setting up of *jayastambhas* or pillars of victory. The Narwār pillar of the Tomara Kings is such a one, supposed to have been erected in the reign of Shāh Jahān.[2] In two copperplate grants, Bīchaṇa,[3] the governor of the southern provinces under the Yādava king Siṅghaṇa, is recorded to have set up a pillar of victory upon the banks of the Kāverī about A.D. 1238. Again the Chola King Rājendradeva is said, in a copperplate grant, to have erected a *jayastambha* at Kollāpuram.[4]

That the pillar was probably surmounted by an image of Garuḍa I should think not unlikely from the fact that most of the copperplate grants of this dynasty have a representation of Garuḍa engraved upon them by way of a seal.[5] It was evidently a royal device used by many of those rulers. In this case it would have stood before a Vaiṣṇava temple, and that Vaiṣṇava worship was prevalent in this State is shown by the numbers of images of Viṣṇu already gathered together at the lately established museum at Dhār. Or, as at Ābu, it might have been surmounted by a *triśūla*. The two great columns in the courtyard of the monolithic temple of Kailāsa at Elurā were also surmounted by *triśūlas*.[6] At the village of Balagāṃve in Maisūr, not far from the southern borders of the Bombay Presidency, stands a tall graceful column surmounted by an image of Gaṇḍabheruṇḍa,[7] which was, as an inscription upon it tells us, set up before a temple of the god Jagadekamalleśvara.

In connection with the possibility of the iron column having been surmounted by a *triśūla* a curious idea presents itself. The finial adopted by the Muhammadans for the domes of their earliest buildings at Māṇḍu is practically a *triśūla* with the central prong removed, or rather dwarfed. On the accompanying drawing I have given sketches of both. Did the Hindu *triśūla*, which for so long had presided over the city of Māṇḍu, give them the idea for their finial? Or did they, as they adapted so many Hindu things to their own use, press this idolatrous symbol, in its new guise, into the service of Allah?

Stone columns, generally very ornamental in design, were set up in front of Jaina temples, especially in the Kanarese country, where we still find many examples, such as the one at Bhatkal sketched in the drawing. They carried little images within a small canopy upon the top. I have found these with their images in North Kanara. Fergusson gives illustrations of two, Nos. 149 and 155, and another, No. 188, where the image and canopy have been removed and a five-branched iron brazier placed in their stead. I do not believe this was originally so. Curiously enough we find just such a pillar as the first two, surmounted by a little canopy for an image,

[1] General Sir A. Cunningham's *Reports*, Vol. VI, p. 59, and *Corpus Inscriptionum*, Vol. III, p. 252.
[2] General Sir A. Cunningham's *Reports*, Vol. II, p. 324.
[3] *Journ. Bom. Br. R. A. Soc.*, Vol. XV, p. 383, and Vol. XII, p. 43.
[4] *Epig. Ind.*, Vol. VII, p. 145.
[5] See Mandhata plates, *Epig. Ind.*, Vol. III, p. 46. Ujjain plates, *Ind. Ant.*, Vol. XIX, p. 345; and see also note 87, *Epig. Ind.*, Vol. I, p. 237; and *Ind. Ant.*, Vol. VI, p. 49.
[6] *Cave Temples of India*, pp. 452-3.
[7] A fabulous bird which preyed upon elephants, represented sometimes as a man with two birds' heads looking different ways; see drawing.

in the middle of a tank at Nalcha, on the roadside between Dhār and Māṇḍu. It is illustrated in Captain Barnes' account in the *Journal of the Bombay Branch of the Royal Asiatic Society*, No. LVIII, Vol. XXI. This was not a *dīpamālā* or *dīpadāna* as supposed. In the middle of a tank, on a dark night, it would have been a veritable *ignis fatuus*.

All these Jaina columns are of stone, and are comparatively unimportant and non-essential adjuncts to the temples they adorn, and it is hardly likely anyone would have lavished so much money and labour upon so colossal an undertaking in iron, a material they were not in the habit of working up in those days into anything more massive or important than military and agricultural implements. It was, no doubt, made long before the people had learnt to manipulate large masses of metal in making cannon.

Even far less important and essential to a temple is a *dīpadāna*, and the very design of the Dhār column excludes the supposition that it was made for that purpose. Where were the lights to be placed? *Dīpadānas*, as we know them, are generally clumsy conical, or pyramidal towers of masonry covered from top to bottom with innumerable little projections or pigeon-holes, at perfectly regular intervals, to hold lights. In the accompanying drawing I have given a sketch of one from Harihar,[1] which is much more attenuated and graceful than they are generally found. The *dīpadāna* is for a display of lights after dark. In the case of the iron column there would have been but a poor display with one solitary oil light placed some 50 feet above one's head, and there were certainly no arrangements for lights upon the pillar elsewhere. As a beacon, with a brazier on the top, it will be seen that the holes, if they ever held pegs to climb by, are in some instances too far apart to enable a man, even unencumbered with fuel for the fire, to scale the column. In some places they would, for the same purpose, be unnecessarily close together, while they also start nearer the ground than there would be any occasion for; in fact, some of them would have been actually embedded in the basement with the foot of the column.

We must therefore dismiss at once the idea of a *dīpamālā* as its purpose. It would have been far cheaper and more effective to have had a masonry *dīpamālā* with its scores of ledges for lights. The *dīpamālā* is so very subordinate and non-essential an adjunct to a temple that it seems too much to suppose that such a costly *chef-d'œuvre* of the blacksmith's skill should be degraded to so unworthy a purpose. This was to have been its lot, had Jahāngīr succeeded in carting it to Agra as he wished.

It might be mentioned, in passing, that the Jains have no *dīpamālās* attached to their temples, since the bright lights would lure myriads of tiny lives to sudden death, and even the setting up of columns crowned with images, as already referred to, does not seem to have been practised by the Jains so far north.

What we know of the column, from history, is very little. My idea is that it was originally set up before the principal temple of Māṇḍu,[2] probably a Vaiṣṇava one, which occupied the site of the present Jāmi' Masjid. We know, and they have

[1] *Chālukyan Arch.*, by A. Rea, Plate CIX.

[2] Possibly the Muhammadan tower of victory of Maḥmūd I. was raised upon the spot occupied by the iron column.

exultingly recorded the fact, in many of their inscriptions, that the Muhammadans, when they first overran the country, made a practice of destroying the chief temple at most places they visited and building their first Jāmi' Masjid upon its site. The pillar was probably entire when 'Ainu-l-Mulk Multānī was sent to effect the conquest of Mālvā in A.D. 1304. After being thrown down by the Muhammadans, and its shaft broken into *two* pieces, which lay about for a hundred years, the greater length was brought down by Dilāvar Khān Ghorī, about A.D. 1405, to be erected before the mosque he had just built at Dhār. Here it remained until Sulṭān Bahādur of Gujarāt, in A.D. 1531, reduced Māṇḍu and wiped out its dynasty. He is said, by Jahāngīr, to have wished to carry the pillar to Gujarāt, and, in attempting to do so, allowed it to fall, when it broke into two pieces of 22 and 13 feet. The longer of these *two* pieces, which is really 24 feet 3 inches in length, is lying where it fell, while the shorter piece seems to have been carried away, and was set up in the garden of the Agency or Guest House at Dhār, where Dr. Führer says he saw it surmounted with a bell-capital[1] in 1893. It was subsequently taken to the newly started museum at the Ānand High School, where it now lies.

This piece must not be confused with the smaller piece, 7 feet 6 inches in length, set up, as already stated, in the Lāl Bāgh. This third piece, that which was broken off when the pillar was first thrown down at Māṇḍu, remained up there until recently, when it was brought down to Dhār. This same piece, Dr. Führer tells us in his Progress Report, was then standing opposite the Jāmi' Masjid at that place. The late Sir James Campbell, in his account of Māṇḍu,[2] says: "In front of the gateway of the great mosque, in the centre of a masonry plinth about 3 feet high, stands an iron pillar about a foot in diameter at the base and 20 feet high." Upon this same basement, at our visit in February last, we found a tall iron flagstaff, known as Allauddal's *sāng* (spear), wrapped round with an old flag. It is but a few inches in diameter. Perhaps Sir James has, in his notes, substituted the perimeter measure of this for the diameter. Mr. Lele's information on this point is that this piece of the column was brought from the front courtyard of the Hindolā Mahal at Māṇḍu. In an account of Māṇḍu by a "Bombay Subaltern," published in 1844, it is said, in describing the buildings in front of the Jāmi' Masjid entrance porch, "On the left, in front of the present quarters of some sepoys of the Dhār Raja, is an iron pole now used as a flagstaff."[3] And again, speaking of the Taweli Maḥal it is said that, outside that building, "is a large piece of iron several tons in weight—a remnant of the blacksmith's stock-in-trade, which he forgot to convert into gold."[4] The first undoubtedly refers to the present iron flagstaff, while the second refers to the small piece of the *lāt* subsequently brought down to Dhār. It is curious how both Sir James Campbell

[1] See his *Progress Report* for the year ending 30th June, 1893, p. 21. In reply to enquiries made through Captain Barnes regarding this bell-capital, Mr. Lele writes: "As soon as your letter came, I drove to the Agency House and made a search for the bell-capital near the Havaldar's house. Nothing like it was found there or anywhere else. But on further enquiries I found, near the *bāghbān's* house, a flat octagonal slab of ordinary black-stone, which old people say rested upon the *lāt* while it was standing in the Agency garden. It formed the seat of a stone figure of Napoleon Bonaparte on horseback by which the *lāt* was surmounted. When Dr. Führer visited Dhār this slab with its support might have looked to him bell-shaped."

[2] *Jour. Bom. Br. R. A. S.*, Vol. XIX, p. 157 (1895).

[3] *Hist. of Mandu, the ancient capital of Malwa*, by A Subaltern (a reprint: Bom. Ednl. Secy.'s Press), p. 13.

[4] *Id.* p. 16.

and Dr. Führer make the same mistake, unless the one simply copied his account from the other.

Who made the column and where was the iron got from? I take it for granted it is of iron, and from a superficial examination it certainly appears to be so: I am not aware of any analysis of the metal having been made. It is remarkable that the column contains no original record, but it may be that the shaft, as it is, is in an unfinished state, or that the inscription, if any, was upon the basement upon which it was set up. The discovery of the capital, which is quite possible, would, perhaps, give us a clue. I should not be surprised to know that the image which crowned the column, together with the mutilated image of the principal deity of the temple, lies buried ignominiously beneath the floor, or is embedded in the walls of the great mosque, at Māṇḍu. Stone images, so stowed away, are seen peeping out of breaches in the wall of most of the buildings there.

Although we know absolutely nothing of its origin, still there is a certain fascination in hazarding guesses and building up pretty theories which may or may not be true. Presuming it to have been a *jayastambha,* or column of victory, such as the only two other iron pillars we know of were, we might discard the reference to those set up by Vairisiṁha I., as being too remote and mythical. We can only recall the occasions upon which, as matters of history, these kings claimed to have scored decisive and crushing victories over their enemies, and to imagine any one of these to have been the occasion for its erection. One of the most important of the early victories was that gained by Rājā Bhoja's General Kulachandra over Bhīma Deva I. of Gujarāt. These two kings and their successors were lifelong and natural enemies.

This General took and entered Anhilvāda, sowed cowries at the gate of the palace, and brought away with him a *Jaya pattra* or official acknowledgment of victory from the enemy.[1] Not long afterwards the Gujarāt king, Siddharāja invaded Mālvā and carried off King Yaśovarmadeva as prisoner. This disgrace was to be wiped out, and Arjunavarmadeva, a later king, did it. We are told that he laid Gujarāt waste. What more natural than that having completely conquered the country, he should disarm it; and what better calculated to commemorate this great victory than this unique iron column, made from the very arms and booty taken from the enemy? No wonder then Bahādur Shāh wished to carry back to Gujarāt that which was its own.

The people believe the column to be made of *pañcarasa* or *aṣṭa dhātu*, an alloy of five or eight metals. Some light silvery looking spots have given rise to this

[1] *Ep. Ind.*, Vol. I, p. 231.

"*Note*:—The measurements of the three sections of the iron pillar, given in the article above, were made by Mr. Lele, the Superintendent of State Education of Dhār, but since the article was written I have personally taken fresh measurements of the two smaller sections, as a doubt was expressed as to their both having been parts of the same pillar. The smallest piece, with the collar or neck at one end, measures 2' 9¼" round its octagonal shaft, while the other measures 3 feet 2 inches round the octagonal end. The first gives 10½" diameter from one face to an opposite face, through the pillar, and the breadth of the square shaft of the largest section at the Lāt Masjid is 10⅜" at its upper end, while the breadth of the square part of the middle section is 10⅛". The width then of the smaller section is practically the same as the square part in the other two sections. But the perimeter of the octagonal end of the middle piece gives a diameter of 11⅜", which shows how unequal the diameter is in different parts. It seems quite clear, however, that the shortest piece does not immediately join on to the middle piece as there would be a sudden lessening from 11⅜" diameter to 10½", and I think we must conclude that there is a missing piece which fitted between these. The proportion of the octagonal part of the whole pillar to the square portion, as shown in the drawing, seems also to require greater length in the former. The total length of the orignal pillar was probably little short of 50 feet."

idea, and Mr. Lele, in his measurements, marks the positions of these. May not these really be silver imperfectly mixed with the iron, from silver mounted weapons. Tradition ascribes the column to Vikramāditya or Bhoja, but I would rather place it in the time of Arjunavarmadeva, say about A.D. 1210. It would have been a better finished piece of work from the hands of Rājā Bhoja.

HENRY COUSENS.

TOMBS AT HINĪDĀN IN LAS BELA.

HINĪDĀN is a place on the right bank of the Hab River, the boundary between Las Bela and Sindh, at a distance of some fifty miles from Karachi. Major M. A. Tighe, late Political Agent of Southern Baluchistan, was the first to draw my attention to the existence of tombs of a very remarkable type at that spot. Not only is the mode of burial which they exhibit exceptional, but on one of them Major Tighe believed that he recognised the rude representation of a crucifix. The following account is the result of a personal inspection of those monuments.

The place is situated near the confluence of a rivulet of the same name and the Hab River in the territory of the Chattas. To-day the only habitation is a police station, close to which is an extensive cemetery. Popular tradition ascribes its origin to the tribe of the Jākharas, which at present is settled in Sindh. It contains a considerable number of ordinary Muhammadan graves — oblong mounds of boulders with a large slab erected at the north end and a smaller one at the south end. Scattered among these are seventy-one sepulchres of the type shown in Fig. 1. Once the number must have been greater, as slabs of old tombs are found used for the ordinary graves. Their direction is universally from south to north. The material is yellowish sandstone. They may be divided into two sub-divisions: twenty-seven small ones consisting of one sarcophagus, and forty-four large ones having

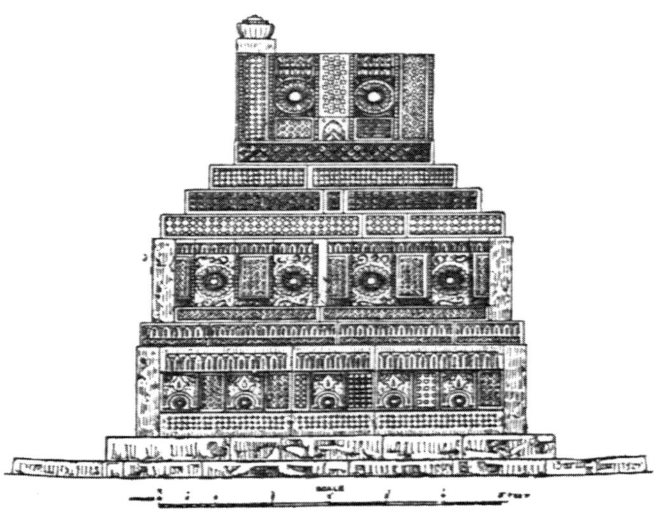

Fig. 1.

two, and in one instance even three, sarcophagi placed one upon the other. The tombs are either single or built in rows numbering from two to eight, sometimes raised on a common plinth. The lower sarcophagus is generally constructed of eight vertical slabs, three on each long, and one on each short side. These are covered by three slabs on which the second sarcophagus is raised, similar to the lower one, but slightly smaller in its dimensions. On the upper sarcophagus four or five layers of slabs are laid horizontally, gradually diminishing in size so as to give the whole structure the general appearance of a slender pyramid. The topmost slab is set vertically, its northern end carved in the form of a cylinder, which projects above it and is terminated in a knob.

The slabs are all carved. The vertically placed stones show a succession of deep-cut squares with a horse-shoe or lotus rosette, in high relief, in their centre, enclosed by high borders of a plain geometrical, often chequered, design. The latter is also found on the horizontal slabs, except those of the plinth, which are plain. A peculiar feature of the ornamentation is a pair of square or cylindrical knobs ending in a lotus, projecting on the north and south side of the slab which covers the uppermost sarcophagus.

The most curious part of the ornamentation is the figure, referred to by Major Tighe as the rude representation of a crucifix. It does not occur on all the tombs, nor is it the same in every instance where it is found. Out of the seventy-one tombs there are only fourteen, *i.e.*, about 20 per cent., which have a panel showing this particular design on the vertical side of the top slab. It is generally found on the side turned to the west, in three cases both on the west and east sides, and twice at the east side alone. As regards the design, in a few cases it certainly bears some resemblance to a crucifix showing a human figure with widely outstretched arms and deep lines cut all around (see Plate XXXII, Figs. A, B, and E). But the circumstance of this figure being placed on the back of an animal, either horse or camel, precludes the possibility of any relation to the Christian symbol.

A close examination of the other tombs afforded a clue to the meaning. On the top-slab of a tomb, comprising two sarcophagi and situated in the north-west corner of the grave-yard, I found the well executed figure of a horseman with lance on shoulder and sword and shield hanging at the side of his horse (Fig. C). It is one of the two cases in which the panel is found on the east side of the top-slab. Local tradition claims that it represents a Rājpūt, and it must be admitted that the shape of its head-dress seems to confirm this assertion. In the northern part of the cemetery there is a partly ruined group of three detached sarcophagi placed on a common plinth. On two of them the top-panel shows a horseman holding the reins in his right and a lance in his left hand and having a curved sword and shield hanging at the side of his horse (Figs. F and G). The figure suggests the idea of a knight in armour. He is preceded by a footman with matchlock on shoulder and a sword and shield, similar to that of the horseman, hanging at his side. On one of these two panels (Fig. F) a Latin cross is cut out above the head of the horse; on the other we find a small cross on the face of the horseman.

On five tombs the top-panel represents a shield crossed by a sword, invariably

SEPULCHRAL RELIEFS FROM HINĪDĀN, BALUCHISTĀN.

A

B

C

D

E

F

G

turned to the west; whereas in three out of the five cases the horseman-figure is found on the opposite side. On two tombs we find female ornaments carved on the top-panel. To return to the crucifix-like figure, there can be little doubt, after comparing them with the other reliefs, that they are merely clumsily executed effigies of a man on horseback. Even the footman is indicated on Figs. A and B beneath the head of the horse. Above it, we discern a bow and at the other side of the horseman there seems to be a quiver.

The occurrence of a human figure on what evidently are Muhammadan tombs is hardly less puzzling than the supposed presence of a crucifix. The only explanation which occurs to me is to consider it as a Hindū survival. The custom of erecting sepulchral slabs on which the effigy of the deceased is rudely carved is practised in different parts of India. In Kāngṛā and other Himālayan tracts such slabs are commonly found in the courtyards of temples, near tanks and under *banyan* and *pīpal* trees. That in many instances the stone exhibits more than one figure, is explained by the fact that women, who became *Satī*, were represented on the same slab with their husband. Curious examples of this kind are found in the so-called *Satī* slabs of the Rājās of Maṇḍī.[1] Here they are called *barselās*, because they are worshipped for one year (*baras*), but the general name by which they are known in the Kāngṛā valley is *mūhrā*. Near Nagar, the ancient capital of Kuḷḷū, there is a collection of *mūhrās*,[2] several of which have a figure said to represent either a *Rānī* who died before her husband, or a Rājā who became an ascetic. On some of them the effigy of a horse will be seen at the bottom of the slab, as is always the case with the Maṇḍī stones.

Opposite Kalesar on the Biyās, six miles below Nadaun, I found some specimens of *mūhrās*, which reminded me of these figures in Baluchistan. They exhibit a horseman armed with lance, sword, and shield, and are said to be the *mūhrās* of Rājpūts. At a place called Kharūhī between Bāmla (Maṇḍī State) and Hamīrpūr I saw one which bore a remarkable resemblance to the more primitive-looking figures at Hinīdān, showing a man with wide-stretched arms, standing on a horse. It is of interest to note that the Jākharas, to which the Hinīdān tombs are ascribed, are a sub-division of the Burfat tribe, which is believed to be of Rājpūt origin.

Another un-Muhammadan feature of the Hinīdān tombs is the peculiar form of overground burial which most of them exhibit, locally known as *Shāmī*, *i.e.*, Syrian, whereas the underground burial is said to be *Rūmī*, *i.e.*, Turkish. Whether its origin is really Syrian, I must leave undecided. In any case it is foreign, as no instances of overground burial are known in India. Probably their origin is Western. Captain Showers, Political Agent at Kalāt, has since informed me that he had noticed similar tombs, but not quite so large, between the Hab River and Samniani on the Makrān coast, and mentioned also that the overground burial occurs in Sīstān.

That for the rest the Hinīdān tombs are Muhammadan, *viz.*, are built by people who professed Islām, I infer from the following facts :—

1st—The tombs, without any exception, are placed with the head to the north.

---

[1] *Cf.* G. T. Vigne, *Travels in Kashmir* (1842), I, 85; and Cunningham, *A. S. R.*, XIV, 123 (Plate XXIX).
[2] *Cf.* A. F. P. Harcourt, *The Himalayan District of Kooloo, Lahoul and Spiti* (1871), p. 357.

2nd—On the plinth of the westernmost group I found a word in the Arabic character, which might be read *Jalāl*, an abbreviation of Jalālu-d-dīn. Evidently it is not meant to render the name of the person buried, but is more probably the name of the workman who executed the tomb.

3rd—The Hinīdān tombs are, with regard to their construction and ornamentation, similar to those at Magar Pīr in Sindh.[1] That those are Muhammadan appears from their inscriptions.

4th—The popular tradition retains some names in connection with the tombs at Hinīdān. One grave, distinguished from the others by some small cow-bells, talismans, and primitive ornaments hanging about, is said to belong to Ḥājī Mor Mubārak. On the same row are the graves of his father, mother, elder brother, and sister's son. The latter's name is given as Gunga. At some distance in a detached tomb of a somewhat different type, surrounded by a railing, is buried his sister's daughter, Māī Asūdī, with her infant child. It is the grave on which the female ornaments are carved. One other tomb deserves special notice. It is treated with peculiar attention, being surrounded by a wall of boulders covered with the same objects as Mor Mubārak's grave; it is said to contain the ashes of his mother's brother, Pīr Sumbak. It was the holiness of these two saints, presumably, which led so many people to have their own tombs built in the vicinity.

As regards the date of the Hinīdān tombs, the uniformity of their architecture and decoration points to their belonging to one period. Among the tombs at Magar Pīr referred to above, one is dated about the middle of the eighteenth century.[2] There, however, the mode of burial is *Rūmī*; for this reason I believe it to be later than the bulk of the Hinīdān graves. It is a plausible suggestion that the overground burial was replaced by the general method of interment; the reverse is highly improbable. For the same reason I believe those of the Hinīdān tombs, in which we find the *Rūmī* mode of burial practised, to be later than the others. If those are to be placed in the eighteenth century, the *S͟hāmī* tombs can scarcely have been constructed after 1700.

As to the *terminus a quo*, I may remark that on two of the panels the horseman is accompanied by a footman carrying a matchlock. Firearms do not appear to have come into use in India before the sixteenth century. In a remote tract like the south of Baluchistan it was probably at least half a century later. Unfortunately the matchlockman occurs only on the two graves, where the *Rūmī* mode of burial is followed, and therefore cannot help to fix the date of the *S͟hāmī* tombs, which I believe to be older. The general state of their preservation, which, I confess, is an unreliable criterion, does not seem to point to a very remote age. That several of them are more or less ruined, can easily be explained from the loose method of their construction. I should be inclined to think that the Hinīdān tombs were constructed in the seventeenth century. Popular tradition, it is true, calls Ḥājī Mor Mubārak a disciple

[1] Magar Pir is situated 10 miles north of Karachi. *Cf.* L. von Orlich, *Travels in India*, I, 84 and D. Ross, *The Land of the Five Rivers* pp. 17-19.

[2] The exact dates are A. H. 1157 and 1171. For a sketch of this tomb, which bears the names of four *maliks* of the Burfat tribe, see T. N. Allan, *Diary of a march through Sindh and Afghanistan*, p. 25.

of Shāh Bilāwal, the great Pīr of Las Bela, and places him in the seventh century of the Hijra, but, especially where the age of a saint is concerned, people are inclined to exaggerate.

Finally, it should be noted that a group of five tombs built in the same style as those at Hinīdān is found at a place called Gundar, at a distance of 5 to 6 miles north of Dinga, the last stage before Hinīdān. But here we meet with the underground burial, as appears from the presence of a projecting stone on the north side of the lower plinth, indicating the spot where the corpses were interred, only a few inches below the surface of the ground. The same peculiarity may be noticed with the dated tomb at Magar Pīr. Again, on a plateau called Kārpāsān, immediately south of Hinīdān, there are two large and two small sepulchres, each consisting of one sarcophagus, in which remains of human bones are contained.

J. PH. VOGEL.

HISTORICAL NOTES ON THE LAHORE FORT AND ITS BUILDINGS.

THE origin of the Lahore Fort is uncertain, but we find it mentioned in connection with Muḥammad Sām's successive invasions of Lahore in A.H. 576 (A.D. 1180), 580 (A.D. 1184), and 582 (A.D. 1186).[1] It was ruined by the Mongols in A.H. 639 (A.D. 1241),[2] but was rebuilt by Balban in A.H. 666 (A.D. 1267).[3] It was again destroyed by Amīr Tīmūr's army in A.H. 801 (A.D. 1398),[4] and again built with mud by Sulṭān Mubārak Shāh in the beginning of A.H. 825 (A.D. 1421). Nearly five months later the mud fort was attacked and damaged by Shaikhā Gakkhar.[5] In A.H. 836 (A.D. 1432) it was taken and repaired by Shaikh 'Alī.[6] Mention is made of its gates in connection with the arrival of Mirzā Kāmrān from Kābul in the first year of Humāyūn's reign.[7] Humāyūn's successor, the Emperor Akbar, demolished the old mud fort and rebuilt it in brick and solid masonry. The work is thus referred to in the Āīn-i-Akbarī :—

> "Lahore is a large city in the Bārī Dōāb. In size and population it has few rivals. In old books it is called Lohāwar. It lies in longitude 109° 22′, and latitude 31° 50′. In this everlasting reign the fort and palace have been built of burnt bricks. As it was for some time the seat of Government, lofty edifices were erected, and delightful gardens added to its beauty."[8]

The above passage does not give the date of the masonry fort. But a fort is mentioned in connection with Mirzā Muḥammad Ḥakīm's rebellion in A.H. 974 (A.D. 1566).[9] Assuming it to be the same as that built by Akbar, we conclude that the present fort was built before the twelfth year of the reign of that Emperor.

No particulars regarding Akbar's buildings in the Lahore Fort are available except that it contained a Dīwān-i-'Āmm, as appears from Al Badāonī's account. It is of interest to note that the number of bays enclosing the courtyard of the Dīwān-i-'Āmm, as shown on the old map, is nearly the same as that given by this historian, a fact which indicates that the Throne Room at the back of the present Dīwān-i-'Āmm with its arcade was the Daulat Khāna-i-'Āmm of the Emperor Akbar. The

---

1 *Tārīkh-i-Farishtah* (Cawnpur, 1884), Vol. I, p. 56.
2 *Siyāsatu-l-amṣār fī tajribati-l-a'ṣār* by Minhāj-i-Sirāj, p. 50.
3 *Farishtah*, Vol. I, p. 77.
4 *Farishtah*, Vol. I, p. 159.
5 *Ṭabaqāt-i-Akbarī* (Lucknow, 1875), p. 137.
6 *Farishtah*, Vol. I, p. 168.
7 *Akbar Nāmah* (Calcutta, 1879—82), Vol. I, p. 125.
8 *Āīn-i-Akbarī*, ed. by H. Blochmann (Calcutta, 1877), Vol. I., p. 538.
9 *Ṭabaqāt-i-Akbarī*, p. 276.

bays were extant in Sikh times, but have disappeared since. The following is the passage referred to above :—

"The 22nd.Rabī'u-th-thānī, A.H. 996 (29th December, A.D. 1587) was the New Year's day and the commencement of the 33rd or 34th year of the accession. The Daulat Khāna-i-'Āmm (hall of public audience) which consists of 114 bays (*aiwān*) was wrapped in fine stuffs and painted curtains, and decorated with all kinds of ornaments attractive to the vulgar. Various practices contrary to the Muḥammadan Law were introduced, and *Shuyu'-i-ma'ṣiyat* (Propagation of Heresy) expressed the date in a chronogram."[1]

The Emperor Jahāngīr continued the work commenced by Akbar. The following Persian inscription over an archway to the west of the Dīwān-i-'Āmm records the date of the completion of Jahāngīr's palace :—

بسال دراز دهم از جلوس مقدس بندگان عالیحضرت شاهنشاه ظل الهه سلیمان جاه کیو مرث بارگاه
سکندر سپاه خلافت پناه نورالدین پادشاه ابن جلال‌الدین پادشاه غازی مطابق سال هزار و بیست و هفت
هجری عمارت این دولتخانه همایون باهتمام کمترین مریدان و غلامان فدوی معمور خان صورت اتمام پذیرفت

"In the twelfth year of the blessed accession of His Imperial Majesty, the shadow of God, a Solomon in dignity, Kayomarth in state, an Alexander in arms, the asylum of the caliphate, the Emperor Nūru-d-dīn Jahāngīr, the son of the Emperor Jalālu-d-dīn Ghāzī, corresponding with A.H. 1027 (A.D. 1617-18), the building of this auspicious palace was completed under the superintendence of his most humble disciple and slave, the devoted servant, Ma'mūr Khān."[2]

It was in order to see this palace that Shāh Jahān made a hasty visit to Lahore from the royal camp of his father on the banks of the Beās. The Emperor Jahāngīr refers to this journey in his Memoirs :—

"On Monday the 30th (Muḥarram, A.H. 1029, 12th October, A.D. 1619) my son, Shāh Jahān, took leave for ten days to see the buildings of the royal palace which had been newly erected, and hastened to Lahore."[3]

The Emperor paid a visit to it himself in the beginning of A.H. 1030, an account of which is given below from his Memoirs. From the passage cited it may perhaps be concluded that the so-called Jahāngīr's quadrangle is correctly ascribed to him.

"On Monday the ninth of the month of Ādhar of the Ilāhī era, corresponding with the 5th of Muḥarram, A.H. 1030 (6th September, A.D. 1620), I rode from the garden of Momin (on the Rāwī) on an elephant called Indra, and, scattering money (as alms), went in the direction of the city. After the lapse of three *pahars* and two *gharis* (*i.e.*, towards evening) of that day I entered the palace in an auspicious and approved hour, and found a joyful and blessed lodging in the buildings recently completed under the superintendence of Ma'mūr Khān. Without ceremony I may say that these are delightful buildings and charming abodes, extremely fine and faultless, all *painted* and *sculptured*, and embellished by the labour of rare masters. The smiling, green gardens with various kinds of flowers and sweet scents are eye-captivating.

From head to foot how sweet, turn where I please!
Soft glances at my heart cry, 'Take thy ease.'

---

[1] The *Muntakhabu-t-tawārikh* of 'Abdu-l-Qādir Bin Malūk Shāh Al Badāoni, ed. by Captain W. N. Lees, LL.D., and Munshī Aḥmad 'Alī (Calcutta, 1865), Vol. II, p. 365. *Cf. Voyages de François Bernier* (Amsterdam, 1699), Vol. II, p. 54.

[2] *Cf. Public Inscriptions at Lahore*, by Henry Cope, *J. A. S. B.*, Vol. XXVII, pp. 309, 312; *Lahore: its history, architectural remains and antiquities*, by Syad Muḥammad Laṭif (Lahore, 1892), p. 125.

[3] *Tuzuk-i-Jahāngīrī*, ed. by Syud Ahmad (Allygarh, 1864), p. 284.

"In short, this building cost seven lacs of rupees which is equal to twenty-three thousand tumans as current in Persia." [1]

Thomas Herbert who visited Lahore one year before Jahāngīr's death speaks of the Palace in the following words :—

"In Lahore are many things observable; Palaces, Mosques, Hummums or Sudatories, Tancks, Gardens, etc. The castle is large, strong, uniforme, pleasant, and bravely seated ; of stone, white, hard, and polished ; arm'd with twelve Posterns three of which respect the Towne, the rest the country : within, a Palace sweet and lovely, entered by two gates and Courts ; the last pointing out two wayes : one, to the King's Durbar and Jarneo (where hee daily shewes himselfe unto his people) the other to the Devon-Kawn or great Hall (where every eve from eight to eleven he discourses with his Umbraves :) On the wall are pictur'd sundry stories and pastimes, *vis.*, Jagheer (otherwise called Shah Selym) crosleg'd upon a rich carpet under a stately Throne of State, his sonnes Perwees on the right hand with Curron and Tymoret, his brothers, D'han Shaw, and Sha Morad ; about him Emirza Sheriff, Can Asom's elder brother, of such wealth and pride, that having above a hundred concubines, he clad them daily, and each night tearing them off, buried them in the ground where they rotted, Mirza Rustam (once King of Candahor) Can Channa, Rajea Manisengh, Can Asam, Asaph Chan, and Radgee Jugonath (at whose death, his wives, sister, Nephew, and seven other friends burnt themselves with him for complement sake in the fire :) And on the left hand, Rajea Bousing fly-skarer, Rajea Randas sword-bearer, Mocrib-Chan Parasite, Rajea Rodorow rebelle, Radgees Ransingh, Mansingh, Bersingh, and Bossou, etc. In another Goozelchan (and neere the former) is painted the Mogull, under a state crosleg'd : upon the dores the Images of the Crucifix, and of the blessed virgin Mother. In another, the King's Progenitors, of whom, Babur, and thirty Nobles in the habit of Pilgrim Kalenders, etc." [2]

Although we find very few particulars regarding the buildings of Akbar and Jahāngīr in the Lahore Fort, we possess full details of Shāh Jahān's work in it. It was in the first year of his reign that he ordered a hall of forty pillars, now known as the Dīwān-i-'Āmm, to be built in the Forts of Agra and Lahore, as appears from the following passage [3] of the Bādshāh Nāmah of Mulla 'Abdu-l-Ḥamīd Lahorī, the court chronicler of the Emperor :—

"In the reigns of their departed Majesties (Akbar and Jahāngīr) and after the accession of the lord of the world (Shāh Jahān) till this date (4th Dhu-l-ḥijjah, A.H. 1037, 10th May, A.D. 1628), in front of the *jharoka* of the Daulat Khāna-i-Khāṣṣ-o-'Āmm (hall of public and private audience) where all servants gain the fortune of admittance (to the royal presence) and of interview, there was no building (in the Agra Fort) to protect the courtiers (*lit.*, adherents of the royal carpet) from rain and heat, and a portico of cloth used to be erected as has been mentioned above. As in this august age all means of comfort that a ruler can give have passed from the region of potentiality into that of actuality, and every ornament of the world has hastened from the nadir of non-existence to the zenith of existence, in accordance with the royal order, masons like magicians and carpenters like Āzar [4] finished a lofty palace, that has raised its head to Saturn, and a high building that has reached the entrance [5] of the seventh heaven, in front of the *jharoka* of the Daulat Khāna-i-Khāṣṣ-o-'Āmm, 70 imperial yards long and 22 imperial yards broad, in forty days, as had been conceived in the enlightened mind of the world-conquering Emperor. Those who stand before the royal throne (thus) acquired a fresh

[1] *Tusuk-i-Jahāngiri*, p. 318.

[2] Th. Herbert. *Some years' travels into divers parts of Asia and Afrique* (London, 1638), p. 68.

[3] The first part of this quotation refers to the erection of the Dīwān-i-'Āmm in the Agra Fort which, as the passage shows, has been rightly ascribed to Shāh Jahān by Mr. A. C. L. Carlleyle. *A. S. R.*, IV, p. 144.

[4] Name or title of Abraham's father who was an idol-maker.

[5] *Lit.*, the lote-tree in the seventh heaven beyond which the angel Gabriel cannot go.

shelter from the rain and the sun, and the face of the heavenly court also gained an immeasurable ornament. On the three sides of this high palace, each of which has an entrance for the *Amirs*, servants, and other officials of note, has been pitched a silver balustrade. In this palace, the servants stand in order of rank, and in an appointed place, and in a manner worthy of the assembly of mighty Emperors. Most of them stand with their backs towards the balustrade, several who are distinguished by a closer connection (stand) by the two pillars which are near the *jharoka*, and armour-bearers with golden banners and flags, in royal armour, towards the left hand with their backs turned to the wall. In front of this heaven-like building is a spacious court-yard with a coloured wooden balustrade around, on which are stretched canopies of brocaded velvet. In this place those whose rank is less than two hundred (horsemen), and bow-bearing *aḥadīs*,[1] and skilled musketeers, and some of the attendant *Amirs*, receive admittance. At the doors of the Daulat khāna-i-khāṣṣ-o-'Āmm, and of both the balustrades, stand trustworthy mace-bearers, staff-bearers, and door-keepers, all in fine clothes, to refuse entrance to strangers and those who are unworthy of such an honour. The gleaner of good meanings and ornamenter of poetry, Ṭālib Kalīm, wrote this quatrain in praise of this lofty building, laid before his most holy Majesty, and the skirts of his hope became heavy with the royal reward.

This new edifice of which the Divine throne is a neighbour,
Of whose rank Height is but a letter,
Is a garden, each pillar of which is a cypress,
In whose shade repose both nobles and common folk.

And the holy order was issued that in the capital of Lahore also should be constructed a high palace in front of the *jharoka* of the Daulat khāna-i-khāṣṣ-o-'Āmm, in the same style (as at Agra), and that the building of the Shāh Burj should be completed."[2]

The above passage corroborates what we have already said regarding the position and existence of Akbar's Daulat Khāna-i-'Āmm. It also speaks of the Shāh Burj. The name occurs again in the following Persian inscription over the *Hatyā Paul*:—

شاه جم جاه سلیمان قدر کیوان بارگاه - کز سپهر و مهر برتر برده رایات جلال
ثانی صاحبقران شاه جهان کز عدل و جود - نیستش نوشیروان مانند را فریدون همال
شاه برجے حکم کرد احداث کز فرط علو - هست بیرون همچو عرش اعظم از وهم و خیال
در صفا و رفعت و لطف و هوا برجے چنین - از حصار چرخ ننمودست و ننماید جمال
بنده یکدل مرید معتقد عبدالکریم - بعد اتمام عمارت یافت این تاریخ سال
دائما چون دولت این بادشاه جم سپاه - این همایون برج عالی باد از آفت بے زوال
سنه ۱۰۴۱ هجری ۴ جلوس

"The king, a Jamshed in dignity, a Solomon in grandeur, a Saturn in state,
Who has carried the banners of his glory beyond the sky and the sun,
The rival of the Ṣāḥibqirān,[3] Shāh Jahān, to whom in justice and generosity
Naushervwān is no equal nor Afredūn a peer,
Ordered a Shāh Burj to be erected which for its immense height
Is like the Divine Throne beyond imagination and conception.
In purity, height, elegance and airiness, such a tower

---

[1] Aḥadīs, a class of Indian *manṣabdārs* of the time of Akbar, with a nominal rank, having with them no foot or horse soldiers from the Emperor.

[2] *Bādshāh Nāmah* (Calcutta, 1867), Vol. I, pp. 221-23.

[3] *Lit.* lord of the happy conjunction; one born under an auspicious conjunction of Jupiter and Venus; a fortunate and invincible king. It is the title of Amir Timūr. The Emperor Shāh Jahān is entitled Ṣāḥibqirān-i-Thānī or Thānī-i-Ṣāḥibqirān, *i.e.*, the rival of Amir Timūr.

Has never appeared from the castle of the sky nor will.
The sincere servant and faithful disciple, 'Abdu-l-Karīm.
After the completion of the building devised this date;
For ever like the fortune of this king, a Jamshed in arms,
'May this auspicious lofty tower remain safe from destruction'
A.H. 1041, 4th year of the accession." [1]

The tower thus eulogised is believed by some to have been a detached tower that has since disappeared. The name is not now applied to any part of the Fort. But it is evidently meant to indicate the N.-W. portion, now known as the Muthamman Burj. This is exactly that part of the Fort to which originally the *Hatyā Paul* gave access, though the arrangement is now entirely changed. Fortunately the same contemporaneous work removes all doubt regarding this point, for its description of the building goes on as follows:—

"On the first of the month of Ādhar, the 19th year of the accession of his late Majesty (Jahāngīr), they began to dig the foundations, and after the active spademen had carried them down to the water level with the strength of their arms, the wise, laborious mathematicians and the architects like Sinmār [2] filled them up with stones and mortar so as to be thoroughly strong and durable, and levelled them with the ground. On the foundations was raised the plinth of the heavenly mansions and everlasting buildings with bricks and lime like a platform, and was made seven yards high. From the accession of the world-conquering king (Shāh Jahān) up to the fourth year of his reign three more yards were added in the same fashion. So in each *radah* (layer), that is a row of bricks used by the builders, 1,80,000 bricks were used. When the overseers of the buildings of the capital laid before the king the plan that had been approved of in the reign of his late Majesty (Jāhāngīr), and this plan did not satisfy the fastidious disposition (of Shāh Jahān), by the royal orders Yamīnu-d-daulah who is well versed in the subtleties of this art laid before the royal eye several plans which the masters like Sinmār had made in consultation with him. One of these received the honour of approval and improvement of the king. The plinth of the heavenly edifice was raised eleven yards higher. The sky-reaching structures were built up to correspond to it. On this flat platform which is 21 yards high from the level of the ground, was erected a hall [3] (*aiwān*), 26 yards in length and 12 yards in breadth. Its dado and twelve pillars are of marble. The middle and the borders of the dado have been inlaid with stones of different colours. Verily it is from the sparkling of the particoloured objects of this heaven-exalted palace that the turquoise-coloured firmament every morning and evening comes to shine like pearls and rubies. From the intermingling of colours in this sky-reaching structure and lofty mansion the spring adorns the cheeks of the tulip and the face of the jasmine. Behind it is a *tambi khāna* (an open-fronted summer-room), 12 yards in length and 7 in breadth, with a dado like that of the (above) hall, over-looking the river, Rāwī. [4] On the edge, in the east and west, it has an octagonal chamber with a diameter of six yards, each with a domed ceiling. On the two sides of the large hall (*aiwān*) are two paradise-like halls, each in length 10¼ yards and in breadth 3¼. On each of the east and west sides of the Shāh Burj is erected a fine hall, in length 9 yards and in breadth 6. Round these paradise-shaped buildings there are six sitting-rooms besides, extremely fine and beautiful, the dado of all which is of marble, and the ceilings and walls are ornamented with Aleppo glass. Towards the west of the Shāh Burj they have made a pavilion [5]

[1] Public Inscriptions at Lahore, *J. A. S. B.*, Vol. XXVII, pp. 310, 312; Laṭīf, *Lahore*, p. 121.

[2] Sinmār (Ar. Sinimmār) is the name of the architect who built in Babylonia, by order of the king Nu'mān Bin Mundhir, a wonderful palace, called Khawarnaq, for the prince Bahrām Gor of Persia. But on the completion of the edifice the king killed him by rolling him down from its top, lest he make a like palace somewhere else.

[3] Now known as the Shīsh Maḥall.

[4] MS. Jamna, which is certainly one of the numerous misprints found in this book.

[5] Now called the Naulakha.

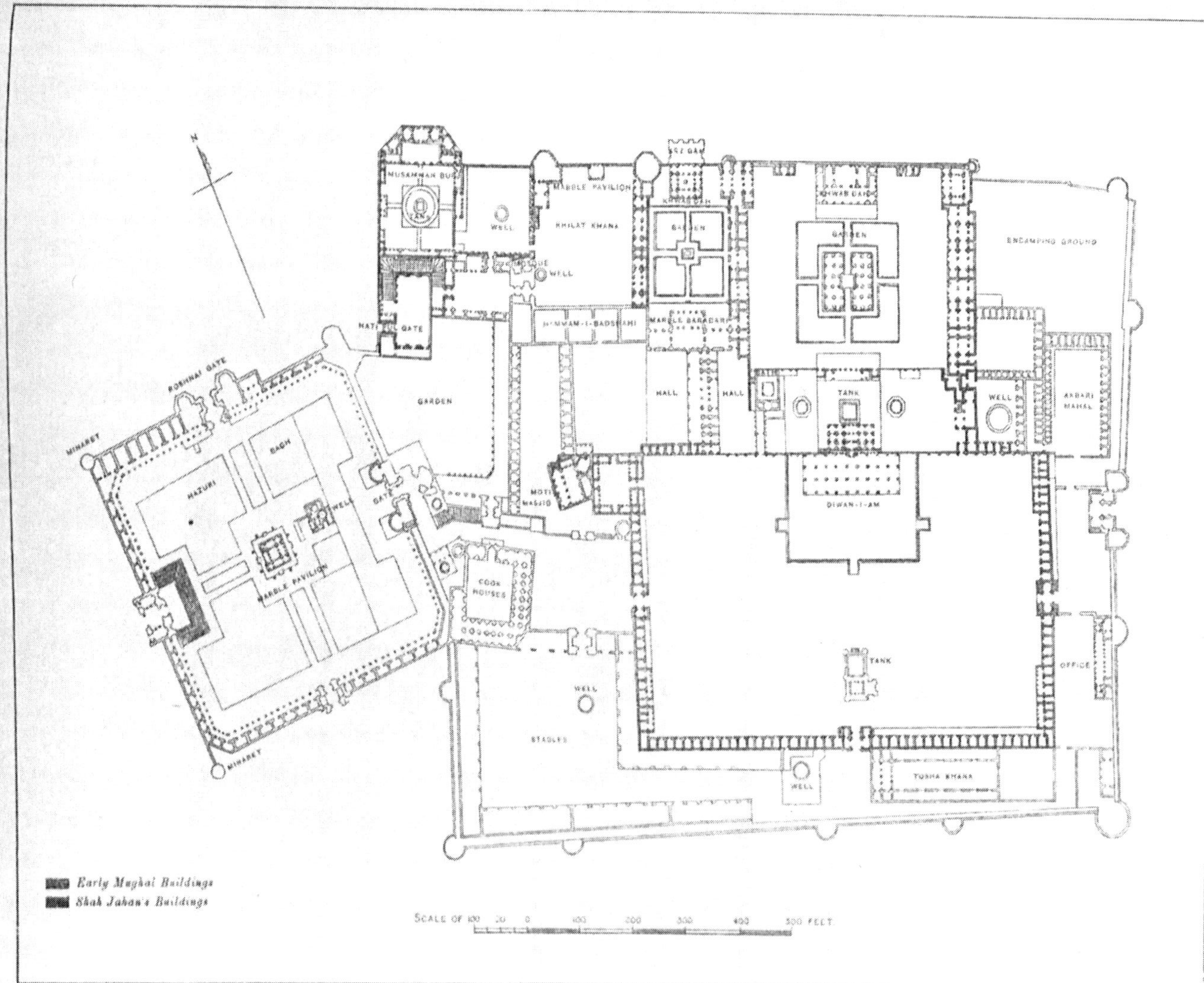

Ghulam Nabi del. Archæol. Survey Panjab & U. Provinces.

PLAN OF LAHORE FORT.

(*banglah*) of marble, whose mosaics of cornelian, coral, and other precious stones excite the emulation of the workshop of Mānī.[1] To the north and south of this pavilion are two halls facing east The floor of the court-yard of these fine buildings, which is 50 yards by 50 yards, is inlaid with black marble and *sang-i-maryam.*[2] In the middle of the court-yard is a reservoir, 20 by 20 (yards), with a height of three *tassūs* (⅛ yard), from the level of the court-yard. Towards the south of the said court-yard there is a square sitting-room, in length and breadth 3½ yards, with two royal seats (arched recesses?), and in the east and west two beautiful chambers each 9½ yards long and 3 broad. Adjacent to each chamber is situated a long narrow room. Adjoining each narrow room there is a hall facing north, in length 10 yards and breadth 4, behind one of which is a *tambi-khāna* which is the blessed khwābgāh (sleeping-room) in length 9 yards and breadth 5, with a dado of marble. Wonder-working painters and magical artists have made it (khwābgāh) a model of the world-exhibiting cup[3] with a variety of colouring and gilding, and figures and pictures, especially the pictures of cities and gardens. To the east of the said court-yard below the plinth of this building is situated another court-yard, in length 55 yards and breadth 51½."[4]

The above description so closely agrees in all details with the Muthamman Burj that there is little room left for doubting the identity of the two. It is of special interest to note that the Naulakha, which has been wrongly ascribed to Aurangzeb by previous authors,[5] formed part of the Shāh Burj buildings erected by Shāh Jahān. Another point of still greater interest is the date of the tile-work on the Palace front hitherto ascribed to Jahāngīr. From the passage in question I am inclined to ascribe it to Shāh Jahān. The height of the floor of the Shāh Burj from the bottom of the wall is stated to be 21 yards. Jahāngīr had made only a platform 7 yards high, and Shāh Jahān added 14 to make up the number. It is evident then that in Jahāngīr's time there was no such wall as we find now extending from the *Hatyā Paul,* bearing an inscription of Shāh Jahān, to the farthest end of the lower courtyard of the Shāh Burj; hence the tile-work on this portion of the Palace front, amounting to 3,655 square yards, is the work of him who built the wall. We shall presently learn from the quotations given further on that the Khwābgāh and the marble pavilion of the old map were also erected by the same Emperor in A.H. 1043 (A.D. 1633) and 1055 (A.D. 1644), respectively; hence the tile-work on this part of the wall is also of Shāh Jahān's time. As for the rest, it is possibly of the same period and might have been executed during Shāh Jahān's repairs to Jahāngīr's buildings in the seventh year of his reign. The uniformity of style seems to speak in favour of such a possibility. The following account of Shāh Jahān's repairs is taken from the contemporaneous work of Muḥammad Ṣāliḥ :—

"Having performed these things (kind treatment of the pious, and enquiries into the behaviour of authorities towards their subjects), the Emperor turned his whole attention to repair the buildings of the Palace of the capital of Lahore, which had long remained uncared for. As

[1] The Persians credited Mānī with a miraculous power of painting pictures.

[2] The same as the Indian architects call *sang-i-abri*, a variegated highly fossiliferous kind of marble.

[3] The reference is to a cup made by Kai Khusrau, the King of Persia, with geometrical figures in it by means of which he foretold the future events of the whole world.

[4] *Bādshāh Nāmah*, Vol. I, pp. 223-25.

[5] T. H. Thornton, *Lahore* (Lahore, 1876), p. 56; Latif, *Lahore*, p. 126. The *pietra dura* work above the dado is possibly of a later date; the ceiling evidently dates only from Sikh times.

the buildings of the Ghusl Khāna[1] (bath-room) and Khwābgāh were not in reality pleasing to the Imperial mind in their plan and style, architects versed in geometry according to the exalted orders sketched new, wonderful and charming plans and laid them before the fastidious eye of their master. The Emperor put it under the superintendence of Wazīr Khān and other overseers of Lahore to lay the foundation and execute the plan which was selected from these, (ordering) that they should finish it before his return from his successful journey to Kashmīr."[2]

In A.H. 1055 Shāh Jahān built another building, most probably the marble pavilion on the old map, which has already been mentioned. His court chronicler speaks of it in the following passage :—

"On the 2nd of the said month (Ṣafar, A.H. 1055, 1st November, A.D. 1644) the Faiḍ Bakhsh and Farḥ Bakhsh gardens[3] received a new freshness and beauty from the royal visit. The next day the Emperor went to see the buildings of the exalted palace and inspect the building, which is entirely of marble and overlooks the river, and had been recently founded, but had not yet come under the royal eye. Owing to his fastidious and critical disposition, he suggested some changes and returned to the said gardens."[4]

Muḥammad Ṣāliḥ, who has already been quoted, in another book[5] eulogises, in very flowery language, the Palace in the Lahore Fort with its various buildings : the Ghusl Khāna, the Khwābgāh with its inlaid floor and courtyard, the *jharoka* and the forty-pillared hall of the Dīwān-i-'Āmm with its silver railing, and the Shāh Burj including the marble pavilion now known as the Naulakha and the courtyard with its reservoir and fountain.

To sum up the result of the above investigation, the buildings marked red on the accompanying map, *viz.*, the *jharoka* with the arcade surrounding the square in front, and edifices round the square behind it, existed prior to Shāh Jahān's reign. But with the material at hand it is impossible to distinguish between the buildings of Akbar and Jahāngīr. The date of the Motī Masjid is unknown. But from its connection with Jahāngīr's palace and the silence of Shāh Jahān's historians about it we may perhaps ascribe it to the former. Those marked yellow—the hall of forty pillars, now called the Dīwān-i-'Āmm ; the Shāh Burj, now known as the Muthamman Burj, including the Shīsh Maḥall, the Naulakha, and other adjoining buildings ; the Khwābgāh ; and very probably the marble pavilion between the last two—were added by Shāh Jahān. Of the buildings left uncoloured on the map we cannot say now with certainty by which of the Emperors they were built. So much seems certain that no more additions were made after Shāh Jahān except some unimportant structures raised by the Sikhs, which can easily be distinguished by their style.

NŪR BAKHSH.

[1] Mulla 'Abdu-l-Ḥamid of Lahore remarks on this term as follows :—" In the reign of his Majesty (Akbar), whose abode is heaven, between the Dīwān Khāna (hall of audience) and the royal *harem* there was a room, in which the Emperor used to bathe. In this place some courtiers (*lit.* adherents of the royal carpet) received admittance, and the Dīwān (Prime Minister) and the Bakhshi (Paymaster) also, being honoured by the royal presence, presented to the Emperor their urgent requests. In the course of time this *khalwat kadah* (private apartment), for the reason of having a *hammām* (bath-room) built near it, became known by the name of the Ghusl Khāna, and so it was on the lips of the high and the low, but now it is called by the Public the Daulat Khāna-i-khass (royal palace) as the most holy Majesty (Shāh Jahān) has named it." *Bādshāh Nāmah*, Vol. I, p. 148.

[2] *'Amal-i-ṣāliḥ* (MS. in the Public library at Lahore), fol. 262-3.

[3] Now called the Shālamār gardens.

[4] *Bādshāh Nāmah*, Vol. II, p. 414.

[5] *Bahār-i-Sakhun* (MS. in the Public library at Lahore), fol. 115-17.

EPIGRAPHY.

UNDER the head of Epigraphy there is much that is of interest to tell. The efforts of the Survey have not, it is true, been very evenly distributed over the country ; excepting, indeed, the inscriptions in the mosque at Dhār, which have already been referred to, and the copperplates from Ratlām published below by Dr. Hultzsch, no fresh epigraphic material worthy of notice has been discovered either in Western or Central India, or in the United Provinces. But any backwardness in this particular field of work, which may be noticeable in these districts, is amply made up for by the conspicuous results attained in other parts of India,—particularly by Dr. Hultzsch in Madras, and by Dr. Vogel in the Punjab.

It may be remembered from the short sketch of the history of the Archæological Department, which was given in the Introduction, that, under the reorganisation scheme of 1898, the appointment of Epigraphist to Government was to be continued only so long as Dr. Hultzsch should continue to hold it. The regrettable announcement has now been made that Dr. Hultzsch has decided to retire from India, after seventeen years of epigraphical work of unique value to India, and to the archæological world generally ; and the present opportunity cannot be allowed to pass without reviewing, however briefly and inadequately, the important results achieved by Dr. Hultzsch during his long tenure of office in Southern India.

Dr. Hultzsch joined his appointment in November 1886, and during his seventeen years' service has published three volumes of *South-Indian Inscriptions* and edited five volumes of the *Epigraphia Indica*. In the former he confined himself to the epigraphical records of the Madras Presidency, while the latter contains some inscriptions from other parts of India as well.

Prior to the appointment of Dr. Hultzsch, South Indian Epigraphy had been studied at odd intervals by Dr. Burnell, Sir Walter Elliot and the Rev. T. Foulkes, who made many contributions to the subject during the time at their disposal. But the history of their labours shows clearly that South Indian Epigraphy, if it is to be studied systematically at all, requires a specialist who can devote all his time and attention to it.

Among the chief dynasties that held sway over Southern India, the Pallavas were, at the time of Dr. Hultzsch's appointment, represented by a few copperplate grants published in the *Indian Antiquary*. Of the Chōlas several lists derived from local chronicles were known, but not even the names of kings could be definitely ascertained. The Eastern Chalukya kings of Veṅgi were mistaken for Chōlas and a wrong chronology was started. No regular genealogy of the Vijayanagar kings existed. Of the Pāṇḍyas a number of inscriptions were known, but no satisfactory transcripts or translations of them were published.

Dr. Hultzsch's researches have thrown considerable light on the history of the Pallavas and their monuments. The approximate period of some of the kings has been fixed with the help of the dated inscriptions of their Chalukya antagonists published mostly by Dr. Fleet. The monolithic caves at Trichinopoly, Vallam, Mahendravāḍi and Śivamaṅgalam, can now be definitely assigned to the first half of the seventh century A.D., as they were all excavated during the reign of the Pallava king, Mahendravarman I. of Conjeeveram. An important event of the period of Pallava supremacy, which Dr. Hultzsch has made known, was the Śaiva religious revival in the seventh century. The last known king of this dynasty was Nandivarman, who reigned about the middle of the eighth century A.D. Then came the later Pallavas, whom Dr. Hultzsch has called Gaṅga-Pallavas. Of this period a number of inscriptions have been published. Next came the Chōlas about the end of the ninth century A.D. Practically all that is now known of them is derived from the inscriptions edited by Dr. Hultzsch. The chronology of this dynasty presented serious difficulties, which were overcome by a patient and careful examination of synchronous records belonging to the Kanarese and Telugu countries published by Dr. Fleet and Mr. Rice. As a result of these researches, we have recovered a considerable number of Chōla kings and a regular succession of them for more than two centuries. Of these, Parāntaka I., who ascended the throne about A.D. 907, deserves particular mention, as he appears to have established the power of the Chōlas by conquering the Gaṅga-Pallavas. The two Uttaramallūr inscriptions, which give a detailed account of how village assemblies were managed in ancient times, belong to his reign. The Rāṣṭrakūṭa conquest of the Tamil country and the temporary eclipse of Chōla power during the third quarter of the tenth century are facts known mainly through the researches of Dr. Hultzsch and his staff. For the subsequent history of the Chōlas from A.D. 985 to 1135 we are indebted entirely to his publications. This was the period when the Chōla power was practically supreme in Southern India. It was occupied by the reigns of seven powerful kings, whose conquests are described at length in their inscriptions, and during whose time a number of South Indian temples came into existence. The great temple at Tanjore was built by the powerful Chōla king, Rājarāja I., who ascended the throne in A.D. 985. It signified apparently another period of religious revival in Southern India. A number of important copperplates of the Eastern Chalukyas of Veṅgi in the Telugu country have also been published and throw fresh light on the history of that family. A few of them have also been useful in correcting certain mistakes in the chronology of the Chōlas. The last powerful Chōla king was Kulōttuṅga III., who ascended the throne in A.D. 1178 and reigned at least thirty-seven years. The subsequent decline of the

Chōlas, the temporary ascendancy of the Pāṇḍyas and the invasion of the Hoysalas of Halebīḍ, to help the former against the latter, are facts which are now as good as established in the history of Southern India. The initial dates of a number of Pāṇḍya kings have been recently ascertained and will be very useful in working out the later history of that kingdom. Of the dynasties of Vijayanagara, a number of stone inscriptions and copperplates have been published, which are of material help in the history of Sanskrit literature. Regular genealogies have been made out of the three families and approximate dates assigned to a number of kings.

During the year more particularly under review, also, the most systematic and comprehensive work in the domain of Epigraphy has naturally been done by Dr. Hultzsch and the special staff employed solely for epigraphical work in Southern India. A detailed list of 347 new inscriptions copied by him during the year, with some remarks on the more important among them, is given in his Report to the Madras Government, which also contains an interesting account, based on the latest researches, of a certain Chōla king, who reigned from A.D. 1118 to at least 1135.

Of these the inscription on the bank of the Pakhal Lake, which attracted the attention of His Excellency the Viceroy in April, 1902, deserves particular mention. It is a record of the thirteenth century, belonging to the Kākatīya dynasty, whose capital, Warangal, is 30 miles to the south. The inscription records the construction of the lake by a Kākatīya feudatory, and the grant of "a lofty place" and some land to the poet who composed the inscription.

Two fresh inscriptions of the second Vijayanagara dynasty furnish some valuable details of the conquests of Kṛṣṇarāya, who reigned in the beginning of the sixteenth century, and add considerably to our knowledge of the history of his reign. The record of his donations to the god of Tiruvaṇṇāmalai and to other temples, and of the building of a *maṇḍapa* and *gōpura* at Kālahasti, are also of some interest. In connection with these inscriptions Dr. Hultzsch has drawn attention to the fact that the temple on the Tirupati hill near Chandragiri contains three statues representing, as certified by their inscriptions, Kṛṣṇarāya and his two queens. As no European is permitted to enter the temple, arrangements are being made for these statues to be photographed by a caste Hindu.

Eight more ancient temples in Madras have been marked out for so-called repairs by private individuals, and as a result the inscriptions which they contain will disappear with the demolition of the existing masonry, the stones being disposed of according to the whims of the masons. The Government have expressly divested themselves of all control over religious institutions, and cannot interfere to prevent the destruction of these ancient monuments. They have, however, ordered to be translated into the vernacular a letter of protest from the Royal Asiatic Society, in the hope that it may help to convince the temple trustees of the desirability of preserving their lithic records. So far, however, the letter has not had the desired effect, and the Archæological Department has been forced to make hasty arrangements for copying the inscriptions at these eight temples before they are destroyed. At the same time the Madras Government have succeeded in persuading the trustees to postpone further action until complete estampages have been prepared.

In Burma, nearly seventy inscriptions, found in the Mandalay, Myingyan, and Pakokku districts have been deciphered and published by Mr. Taw Sein Kho. Besides which, he has translated several other miscellaneous records from other parts of the country. One, from the Mergui district, is particularly interesting as showing the extent of the Burmese dominion before the break-up of the Empire, which followed on the invasion of the Chinese under Kūblai Khān. In those days Tenasserim, now an insignificant village in the Mergui district, was a frontier outpost and a flourishing centre of trade with Cambodi and Malaysia.

Another interesting find is a Grantha and Tamil inscription from Pagān in Burma. It was noticed by the Hon'ble Sir A. T. Arundel during a tour in Burma, and impressions of it were sent at his instance to the Government Epigraphist in Southern India. Dr. Hultzsch assigns the record to the thirteenth century on palæographical grounds. It proves the existence of a colony of Vaiṣṇavas in the Buddhist country of Burma, for whose spiritual welfare a temple had been built at Pagān. For the benefit of this temple a donation was made by a native of Cranganore in Malabar, who was apparently not the first immigrant from Southern India, as there is sufficient evidence in Chōḷa inscriptions to show that intercommunication between Burma and the Indian Peninsula existed as early as the eleventh century A.D.

In the plains of Northern India epigraphical material of the pre-Muhammadan period is rarely met with, owing partly to the early and permanent establishment of Muhammadan rule and partly to the absence of stone. In the hills, inscriptions may be expected to be more abundant. The Kangra Valley in particular has yielded a number of interesting inscriptions on stone—the rock inscriptions, for instance, of Paṭhyār and Kanhiyārā, and the *praśastis* of Baijnāth and Bhavan. Inscriptions on metal, however, have hardly ever come to light in this district, nor have they been found in Kashmīr, where they once must have existed in considerable numbers. Here, too, Muhammadan influence is probably responsible for their loss.

One of the very few districts where copperplate inscriptions still appear to exist is the Native State of Chambā. The oldest belong to the tenth and eleventh centuries and they are continued almost uninterruptedly up to modern times. The number of plates which Dr. Vogel examined during his tour in Chambā, and of which he obtained *fac-similes*, amounted to nearly fifty; but from official returns it was evident that the total figure is much higher, and may be estimated at two hundred or perhaps even more. The existence of a series of documents of this kind from pre-Muhammadan times up to the present day is remarkable, if not unique. The older plates throw much light on the ancient geography of the State; the later ones are linguistically interesting, as they are partly composed in vernacular and contain agricultural terms of the sixteenth and seventeenth centuries, which are now either modified or lost. For the history of Chambā they are practically the only reliable documents, and have already made it possible to correct the traditional list of Chambā Rājās, published by Cunningham (*A. S. R.*, XIV, p. 114), and to fix, approximately, the periods of their reigns. It is of special interest that some of the earlier rulers, whose names occur on copperplates, are also mentioned in the Rājataraṅgiṇī.

Dr. Vogel's finds are of palæographical value also in that they show the development of the ancient Śāradā to the modern Ṭākarī of the hills.

The oldest known inscription in Assam is incised on a big boulder of granite, lying on the northern bank of the Brahmaputra, about one mile below Tezpur. The rock, which from a distance resembles the head of an elephant, is locally known as Dhenkanal. In the dry season the inscription is eight or ten feet above the water level, but during the floods it is said to be partly submerged. From this cause some of the letters have become very faint or have vanished entirely, but the greater part of them are still readable. The date of this record, as recognised by Prof. Kielhorn from photographs and tracings, appears to be in the Gupta year 510, corresponding to 829-30 A.D. Prof. Kielhorn also found that the purpose of the inscription was to record a grant of land made to certain Brahmans. He was, however, unable, from the imperfect materials at his disposal, to read more than fragments of the inscription, or to recover the name of the ruling king and of the periodical governor. He accordingly asked for mechanical copies. When Dr. Bloch visited Tezpur in December 1902, he prepared a duplicate set of paper impressions of the inscription, which he made over to Major Gurdon for transmission to Prof. Kielhorn. A transcript and translation of this valuable document for the ancient history of the Assam Valley may thus be soon looked for from Prof. Kielhorn. In the meantime, Dr. Bloch states that from a preliminary examination the name of the king appears to be Harjjara, who is known to us already from the genealogical lists in the Tezpur and Nowgong copperplates, and that the provincial governor was the *Mahāsāmanta* Sucittra. The most interesting point is the date, which is recorded in the Gupta era, and proves that Assam once formed a portion of the dominions of the Imperial Gupta family, or of some minor dynasty, who used their era. Dr. Bloch suggests that this may have been the famous Śaśāṅka of Karṇa-Suvarṇa, who from a copperplate recently found in Ganjam is known to have followed the dating of the Gupta era. As far as is known yet, dates in the Gupta era of so late a period have been found only in Nepal and in Kathiawar; but at the last named place it went under the name of the Valabhī era. Śaśāṅka's plates are dated in Gupta 300.

A still older inscription has been found at the temple of Muṇḍeśvarī in the Bhabua sub-division of the Shahabad district. The stone is broken into two parts and the first half of it had been sent to the Indian Museum, Calcutta, in 1891, where it is marked as coming from Bhabua, without any specified locality. The second half was found recently in clearing away *débris* around the temple. The inscription is dated in the year 30, the 22nd day of Kārttika. From the style of the letters there can be no doubt that this must be referred to the Harṣa era, and we thus get A.D. 635 as the European equivalent. The inscription belongs to the reign of (Uda)yasenadeva, and records some grants made to the temple of Maṇḍaleśvara. This, says Dr. Bloch, may have been the original name of the goddess worshipped on the Muṇḍeśvarī Hill. The name of the ruling chief is new to history, and there is no evidence as to his possible connection with any of the known dynasties of that time. The first two letters of his name, as given above, are bracketed, as they are lost, but little doubt exists as to their correctness. Another inscription, of about the ninth or tenth century, was also found on the Muṇḍeśvarī Hill, but the stone, on which it is incised, seems to have suffered much damage, and the impression taken was not sufficiently clear to make its decipherment possible.

The curious inscription of Ādityasena, over the door of the temple of Vaidyanātha at Deoghar (Baidyanath), has again come under consideration. A reading of it, together with an English translation, may be found in the footnote to Dr. Fleet's publication of the Mandar Hill inscription of Ādityasena, in his Gupta Inscriptions. The inscription is written in Bengali characters, perhaps 300 years old, and it states that Ādityasena with his queen, Koṣadevī, who had come from the Chōla country near Madura, in Southern India, built a temple of Viṣṇu, and that a certain Balabhadra put up an image of the boar incarnation of Viṣṇu. The inscription concludes with the words :—" This is the chapter on Mandara." Dr. Bloch remarks that there are certain historical facts found among these statements. " As we know from an inscription close to it, the Pāpahāriṇī Tank on the Mandar Hill was dug out by Ādityasena's queen, whose real name however was Koṇadevī, and the many ancient shrines around it evidently belong to the same time. The last śloka, referring to Balabhadra, is actually found in characters of about the same time as Ādityasena on the top of the Mandar Hill, close to the modern Jain temple, which now stands there. But the statement that Ādityasena was a native of the Chōla country deserves no credit whatever. It gives us, however, a clue to the otherwise unexplained fact that the inscription is placed over the door of the temple of Vaidyanātha, with which seemingly it has no connection. We must remember that local tradition, as related by Buchanan, has it that a Chōla Rājā was once cured from leprosy by bathing in the holy tank to the south of Mandar Hill, and that he selected this place as his residence, and built a large city there, the traces of which are still visible. The author of the inscription evidently combined this tradition with the name of Ādityasena, which he had seen in the Mandar rock inscription. From the fact that he copied verbally another rock inscription on the same hill, it is evident that he had read those inscriptions, although he mistook the queen's name for Koṣadevī instead of Koṇadevī. Ādityasena thus became vested with the robe of the leper king from the Chōla country, whose cure was effected by the miraculous powers of Mount Mandar and its holy waters. At present the famous liṅga of Vaidyanātha at Deoghar, about 30 miles south of the Mandar Hill, enjoys the same fame for curing leprosy as the Mandar Hill formerly did. A connection thus appears to exist between the two neighbouring *tīrthas*, and to this it may be due that an inscription purporting to give a history of the Mandar Hill was placed over the entrance to the temple of Vaidyanātha."

Several new Muhammadan inscriptions also turned up in Bengal which had not been noticed before. While digging near the Khazanchi, a small ruined building inside the old citadel of Gaur, an inscription of Nuṣrat Shāh was found, recording the building of a mosque in the Hijrī year 926. It is the oldest inscription of this king and belongs to the first or second year of his reign. Another inscription of the same king, Nuṣrat Shāh, of a somewhat later date, 930 A.H., belongs to an old mosque at Bagha, in the district of Rajshahi. The stone is now lying in the court of the mosque, but will be replaced again when the restoration of the mosque has been taken in hand. Two new inscriptions of G͟hiyāt͟hu-d-Dīn Bahādur S͟hāh, of the Sūrī family, were discovered last year. One belongs to the mosque at Kusumbha in the district of Rajshahi, and the other to a ruined mosque at Kalna, in the district of Burdwan. The date of both inscriptions is equivalent to 1560 A.D.

When Dr. Bloch was at Bhagalpur, in February 1903, he found two old guns lying in the open field, close to the mausoleum of Ibrāhīm Ḥusain K͟hān, near the Khanjarpur road. One of them bears a Sanskrit inscription, written in that form of Bengali letters which is found in Assamese inscriptions. It states, says Dr. Bloch, that the cannon was taken away from the Muhammadans at Gauhati by the Assamese king, Jayadhvajasiṁha, in the Śaka year 1580 (A.D. 1658). The victory which gave this weapon into the hands of the Assamese happened during the troubled time when Sulṭān S͟hujā', the Governor of Bengal, had mobilised all his forces in order to resist his brother Aurangzeb. It is expressly stated that in this year, 1658 A.D., the Ahom king, Jayadhvajasiṁha, attacked the Muhammadan Governor of Kāmrūp, Mīr Luṭfullāh S͟hīrāzī, in order not to allow the Koch king to regain any of his former territories. Luṭfullāh seeing himself thus surrounded on two sides, and having no troops to check the invaders, took to his ships and retreated to Dacca. After the fall of Sulṭān S͟hujā', Mīr Jumlā invaded Assam, to resume the lost dominions of the Mug͟hals. He pursued the Ahom king up to Ghargaon, then his capital, which he conquered on the 17th March 1662. Prof. Blochmann in his article on the conquest of Assam by the Muhammadans, tells us that "the next day many guns were recovered from the tanks into which the Rājā had thrown them before his flight." Altogether 675 guns are said to have been captured, and evidently the gun now at Bhagalpur was one of them.

J. H. M.

RATLÂM PLATES OF DHRUVASÊNA II.

[GUPTA-]SAṀVAT 321.

THESE plates belong to the Ratlâm Darbâr and were lent to Messrs. Marshall and Cousens in December 1902 by the Dîwân of the Ratlâm State in Central India. I edit them from two sets of ink-impressions and one set of estampages, prepared by Mr. Cousens. The estampages are very excellent and show many letters which, owing to the corroded condition of the original, appear only imperfectly on the ink-impressions.

The copperplates are two in number and bear writing only on their inner side. There are two ring-holes at the bottom of the inscribed side of the first plate, and two corresponding ones at the top of that of the second plate. To judge from the impressions, each of the two plates measures about 9 inches in height and 11⅛" in breadth.

The alphabet resembles that of other Valabhî inscriptions of the same period. The *jihvâmûlîya* occurs twice (ll. 34 and 40), and the *upadhmânîya* once (l. 53). The date portion contains the numerical symbols for 300, 20, 1 and 3 (l. 54). The *anusvâra* is represented by guttural *ṅ* before *ś* and *h* (ll. 3, 5, 12, 23, 48, 50) and by dental *n* before *s* (ll. 15, 29, 34).[1]

The language is Sanskṛt. Almost the whole of the inscription is in prose; but three of the customary verses are quoted in ll. 51 to 53. The language of ll. 41 to 43 is incorrect. The dative *vinirggatâya* (l. 41) refers to *Dattasvâmi* (l. 42), which is, however, left without case-ending. Further, *Dattasvâmi* is joined by the particle *tathâ* to the following *Kumârasvâmi* (l. 43), to which the dual case-ending *bhyâm* is affixed.

The inscription records the grant of a field to two Brâhmaṇas by the Valabhî king Dhruvasêna II., who issued this edict 'from the victorious camp pitched at Va[n]ditapallî' (l. 1). His genealogy is described in the same words as in his previously published grant of Saṁvat 310[2] and has been translated by me elsewhere.[3]. The grant portion runs as follows:—

(L. 39.) "The devout worshipper of Mahêśvara (Śiva), the glorious

[1] But in *saṁsakta* (ll. 2, 5) and *saṁskâra* (l. 36 f.) the *anusvâra* is not changed into *n*.
[2] *Ind. Ant.*, Vol. VI, p. 3 ff.
[3] *Ep. Ind.*, Vol. I, p. 89 ff.

Dhruvasêna (II.) whose second name was Bâlâditya, being in good health, issues (the following) command to all according as they are concerned :—

(L. 40.) "Be it known to you that, for the increase of the spiritual merit of (my) mother and father, I have given to the Brâhmaṇa Dattasvâmin, who has come from Udumbaragahvara, resides at Nakâgrahâra, belongs to the Trivêdins of Daśapura, to the *gôtra* of the Pârâśaras and to the school of the Mâdhyandina-Vâjasanêyas, (and is) the son of the Brâhmaṇa Budhasvâmin, and to the Brâhmaṇa Kumârasvâmin, who resides at Agastikâgrahâra, belongs to the Caturvêdins of the above-said (town), to the *gôtra* of the Pârâśaras and to the school of the Vâjasanêyas, (and is) the son of the Brâhmaṇa Budhasvâmin, a field measuring one hundred *bhaktîs* at the southern boundary of the village Candraputraka in the above-said district (*viṣaya*) in Mâlavaka.

(L. 44.) "The boundaries of this (field are) :— to the east, the boundary of the village Dhammaṇahaḍḍikâ; to the south, the boundary of the village Dêvakulapâṭaka; to the west, the boundary of the field of the *Mahattara* of Vîrataramaṇḍalî; at the north-western corner, the small tank (called) *Nirgaṇḍî;* (and) to the north, Vîrataramaṇḍalî.

(L. 46.) "(I have given), as a meritorious gift, with libations of water, this field measuring one hundred *bhaktîs*, thus defined by (its) four boundaries, with the *udraṅga*, *uparikara* (and) *bhûtavâtapratyâya*, with the income in grain and gold, with the *daśâparâdha*, with (the right to) eventual forced labour, not to be meddled with by any royal officers, excluding gifts previously made to temples and Brâhmaṇas and the twentieth (share due) to Brâhmaṇas,[1] according to the maxim of *bhûmicchidra*, to last as long as the moon, the sun, the ocean, the earth, the rivers, and the mountains, (and) to be enjoyed by the sons, grandsons, and (further) descendants (of the two donees)."

Ll. 49 to 53 contain the usual admonitions and imprecations.

(L. 53.) "The messenger (*Dûtaka*) for this (grant is) the *Râjaputra* Śrî-Kharagraha. This (edict) has been written by the chief secretary (*Divirapati*) Skandabhaṭa, the son of the chief secretary Vatrabhaṭṭi, who was charged with peace and war. The year 300 (and) 20 (and) 1; (the month) Caitra; the dark (fortnight); the 3rd (*tithi*). (This is) my own signature."

The date of this inscription. [Gupta-] Saṁvat 321 (*i.e.*, A.D. 640-41), falls between that of the previously published grant of Dhruvasêna II.,—Saṁvat 310, and the earliest date of his son and successor Dharasêna IV.,—Saṁvat 326,[2] and thus extends the known period of the reign of Dhruvasêna II. by 11 years.

The first donee resided at Nakâgrahâra (l. 41), and the second at Agastikâgrahâra (l. 42). Each of them is styled a son of Budhasvâmin, a student of the Vâjasanêya-śâkhâ, and a member of the Pârâśara-gôtra (ll. 41 to 43). This suggests that they were the sons of the same father, and that the epithet 'who has come from Udumbaragahvara,'[3] which is applied to the first donee (l. 41), holds good for the second one as well. Further, as the first

[1] Compare Professor Bühler's remarks in *Ind. Ant.*, Vol. XV, p. 337.

[2] See Professor Kielhorn's *Inscriptions of Northern India*, p. 67, Nos. 479 and 481.

[3] Udumbaragahvara occurs also in a grant of Dharasêna IV.; *Ind. Ant.*, Vol. XV, p. 336.

donee is called a Trivêdin of Daśapura (l. 41), it appears that the expression 'a Caturvêdin of the above-said (town),' which is applied to the second donee (l. 43), is meant for 'a Caturvêdin of Daśapura.' This result is of some importance, as it enables us to explain the expression 'the above-said district (*viṣaya*) in Mâlavaka' (l. 44) by 'the Daśapura-viṣaya in Mâlavaka.' Mâlavaka is the present Mâlwâ, and Daśapura is the modern Dasôr or Mandasôr, the chief town of a district of the Scindia's dominions,[1] and situated to the north of Ratlâm, where these plates are now preserved. Nakâgrahâra and Agastikâgrahâra, where the two donees resided, were probably quarters or hamlets of the town of Daśapura (Mandasôr). The village Candraputraka (l. 44), to which the granted field belonged, will have to be looked for in the environs of Mandasôr. I have no detailed maps of that part of India and am therefore unable to identify Candraputraka and the other localities mentioned in connection with it. At any rate, this new grant proves that the territory of Dhruvasêna II. extended in the east as far as Mandasôr in Western Mâlwâ.

The *Dûtaka* of this grant, prince (*Râjaputra*) Kharagraha (l. 53 f.,) is perhaps the same person who later on ascended the throne as Kharagraha II. The writer of the inscription, the *Divirapati* Skandabhaṭa, occurs again in the grants of Dharasêna IV.;[2] his father Vatrabhaṭṭi in the grants of Śîlâditya I. and Dhruvasêna II.;[3] and his son Anahila in the grants of Dhruvasêna III., Kharagraha II. and Śîlâditya II.[4]

Besides the two plates now edited, the Ratlâm Darbâr possesses another Valabhî grant of two plates. To both sets of plates is affixed a single seal, whose ring was found broken or cut, and of which it cannot be said to which set it belonged originally. The seal is elliptical, measures about 2¼" by 2" in diameter, and bears, on a countersunk surface, in relief, a bull couchant which faces the proper right, and below the bull, the legend *Śrî-Bhaṭakkaḥ*. The second of the two additional plates is so much corroded that it cannot be published from the two ink-impressions which Mr. Cousens has sent me. These two plates were issued from Valabhî and record that Dhruvasêna II. granted one hundred *bhaktîs* in some village in Mâlavaka to two Brâhmaṇas, who had come from Udumbaragahvara[5] and Jambûsara[6] respectively, had studied the Vâjasanêya-śâkhâ, and were members of the Pârâśara and Kauśika *gôtras*. The name of the class of Caturvêdins to which they belonged is illegible; but, as the second donee is stated to have resided at Nakâgrahâra,[7] the lost word can be supplied as Daśapura. The *Dûtaka* and the writer are the same as in the subjoined grant, and the date seems to be Saṁ[vat] 300 (and) 20.

E. HULTZSCH.

[1] See Dr. Fleet's *Gupta Inscriptions*, p. 79 f. and *Ep. Ind.*, Vol. V, p. 38 f.
[2] *Ind. Ant.*, Vol. VII, p. 75, and Vol. XV, p. 340.
[3] *Ibid.*, Vol. VI, p. 16, Vol. IX, p. 239, and Vol. XIV, p. 328.
[4] *Ibid.*, Vol. VII, p. 79, and Vol. XI, p. 309; *Ep. Ind.*, Vol. I, p. 85, and Vol. IV, p. 81.
[5] See above, p. 2, note 3.
[6] This is the modern Jambûsar between Kaira and Bronch; compare *Ind. Ant.*, Vol. VII, p. 241.
[7] See the preceding page.

ii.

Ratlam Plates of Dhruvasena II.—[Gupta-]Samvat 321.

I.

E. HULTZSCH. SCALE 7/8 W. GRIGGS, PHOTO-LITH.

TEXT.

First Plate.

1 ओं[1] स्वस्ति [॥*] विजयस्कन्धावाराद्[न्दि]तपल्लीवासकात्प्रसभप्रणतामित्राणां मैत्रका-
णामतुलबलसम्पन्नमण्डलाभोग-

2 [2]संसक्तप्रहारशतलब्धप्रतापात्प्रतापोपनतदानमानार्ज्जवोपार्ज्जितानुरागादनुरक्तमौलभृतश्रेणी-

3 बलावाप्तराज्यश्रियः परममाहेश्वरश्रीभटार्काद्व्यवच्छिन्नराजवङ्क्षान्मातापितृचरणारविन्द-
प्रणति-[3]

4 प्रविधौताशेषकल्मषः शैशवात्प्रभृति खड्गद्वितीयबाहुरेव समदपरगजघट[ा]स्फोटनप्र-
[का]शि[त]-

5 [4]सत्वनिकषः तत्प्रभावप्रणतारातिचूडारत्नप्रभासंसक्तपादनखरश्मिसङ्गतिः[5] सक[ल]स्मृति-
प्रणी-

6 तमार्ग्गसम्यक्परिपालनप्रजाहृदयरञ्जनान्वर्त्थराजशब्दो रूपकान्तिस्थैर्य्यगाम्भीर्य्यबुद्धिसम्प-
द्भि[:*] स्मरश-

7 शाङ्काद्रिराजोदधित्रिदशगुरुधनेशानतिशयानः शरणागताभयप्रदानपरतया तृणवदपास्ता-
शेषस्वकार्य्य-

8 फलप्रार्त्थनाधिकार्त्थप्रदानानन्दितविद्वत्सुहृत्प्रणयिहृदयः पादचारीव सकलभुवनमण्ड-
ला[भो]गप्रमोदः

9 परममाहेश्वरः श्रीगुहसेनस्तस्य सुतस्तत्पादनखमयूखसन्तानविसृतजाह्नवीजलौघप्रक्षा-
लि[ता]शेष-[6]

10 कल्मषः प्रणयिशतसहस्रोपजीव्यमानसम्पद्रूपलोभादिवाश्रितः सरभसमाभिगामिकैर्गु-
णै[:*] [स]हज-

11 शक्तिशिक्षाविशेषविस्मापिताखिलधनुर्द्धरः प्रथमनरपतिसमतिसृष्टानामनुपालयिता धर्म्म-
दा[याना]-

12 मपाकर्त्ता प्रजोपघातकारिणामुपप्लवाना[7] दर्शयिता श्रीसरस्वत्योरेकाधिवासस्य [8]संह-
तारातिपक्षल[क्ष्मी]-

13 परिभोगदक्षविक्रमो विक्रमोपसप्राप्तवि[म]लपार्त्थिवश्रीः[9] परममाहेश्वरः श्रीधरसेनस्तस्य
सुतस्तत्पादानु-

---

[1] Expressed by a symbol.

[2] An indistinct symbol is engraved above the line between पा and त्प्र of °प्रतापात्प्र°.

[3] Read °वंशा°.

[4] Read °सत्त्व°.

[5] Read °संहतिः.

[6] Read °कल्मष°.

[7] Read °प्लवानां.

[8] Read संहता°.

[9] Read °संप्राप्त°.

14 ध्यात: [1] सकलजगदानन्दनात्यभुतगुणसमुदयस्थगितसमग्रदिङ्मण्डल: सम[र]शतविजय-शोभास-

15 नाथमण्डलाग्रद्युतिभासुरतरांसपीठोदू[ढ]गु[रु]मनोरथमहाभा[र]:[2] सर्व्व[विद्या]परा-पर[वि]भागाधिग-

16 मविमलमतिरपि सर्व्वतस्सुभाषितलवेनापि सुखोपपा[द]नीयपरि[तो]ष: समग्रलोका-गाधगाम्भी-

17 र्य्यहृदयोपि सुचरितातिशयसुव्यक्तपरमकल्याणस्व[भा]व: खिलीभूतकृतयुगनृपतिपथ-[वि]शोध-

18 नाधिगतोदग्रकीर्त्तिर्द्धर्म्मानुपरोधोज्ज्वल[त]रीकृतार्त्थसुखसम्पदुपसेवानिरूढधर्म्मा[दि]त्यद्वितो-[य]नामा पर-

19 ममाहेश्वर: श्रीशीलादित्यस्तस्यानुजस्तत्पादानुध्यात: [स्व]यमुपेन्द्रगुरुणेव गुरुणात्यादर-वत[ा] समभिल-

20 षणीयामपि राजलक्ष्मी[3] स्कन्धासक्तां परमभद्र इव धुर्य्यस्तदाज्ञासम्पादनैकरसत[ये]-वोद्वहन्खेदसुखरतिभ्या-[4]

21 मनायासितसत्वसपत्ति:[5] प्रभावसम्पद्वशीकृतनृपतिशतशिरोरत्नच्छायोपगूढपादपीठोपि परावज्ञाभि-

22 मानरसाना[लिङ्गित]मनोवृत्ति:[6] प्रणतिमेका[7] परित्यज्य प्रख्यातपौरुषाभिमानैरप्यरा-तिभिरनासादितप्र[ति]क्रि[यो]-

23 पाय: [8] कृतनिखिलभुवनामोदविमलगुणसङ्कृतिप्रसभविघटितसकलकलिविलसितगतिर्नो-[च]जनाधि-

24 रो[हि]भिरशेषैर्द्दोषैरनामृष्टात्युन्नतहृदय: प्रख्यातपौरुषास्त्रकौशलातिशयगणतिथविदक्ष-[क्षि]तिपाति-[9]

25 लक्ष्मीस्वयंग्रहप्रकाशितप्रविरपुरुषप्रथमसंख्याधिगम:[10] परममाहेश्वर: श्रीखरग्रहस्तस्य तनयस्तत्पादा-

26 नुध्यात: स[क]लविद्याधिगमविहितनिखिलविद्वज्जनमन:परितोषातिशय: [11] सत्वसम्पदा-त्यागौदार्य्येण च

27 विगतानुसन्धान[ा*]शमाहितारातिपक्षमनोरथाक्षभङ्ग: सम्यगुपलक्षिताषकशा[स्त्र]-[12]

28 [13] [क]लाथोकचरितगह्वरविभागोपि परमभद्रप्रकृति[र]कृत्रिमप्रश्र[यविनय]-

---

[1] Read °समुद°.
[2] Read °रांस°.
[3] Read °लक्ष्मीं.
[4] Read °म्भिद°.
[5] Read °सत्वसंपत्ति:.
[6] Read °नालिङ्गित°.
[7] Read °मेकां.
[8] Read °संहति°.
[9] Read °विपक्षक्षितिपति°.
[10] Read °प्रवीरपुरुषप्रथमसंख्याधिगम:.
[11] Read सत्त्व°.
[12] Read °तानेक°.
[13] Read °कलालोक°.

Second Plate.

29 शोभाविभूषणः समरशतजयपताकाहरणप्रत्यलोदग्रबाहुदण्डविध्वन्सित-[1]

30 निखिलप्रतिपक्षदर्प्पोदयः स्वधनुःप्रभावपरिभूतास्त्रकौशलाभिमानसकलनृपतिम-

31 ण्डलाभिनन्दितशासनः परममाहेश्वरः श्रीधरसेन[:*] तस्यानुजस्तत्पादानुध्य[ा*]त[:*] सच्चरितातिशयितस-

32 कलपूर्व्वनरपतिरतिदुस्साधानामपि प्रसाधयिता विषयाणां मूर्त्तिमानिव पुरुषकारः परिवृद्धगु-

33 णानुरागनिर्ब्भरचित्तवृत्तिभिर्म्मनुरिव स्वयमभ्युपपन्नः प्रकृतिभिरधिगतकलाकलापः कान्तिमा-

34 न्निर्वृतिहेतुरकलङ्कः कुमुदनाथः प्राज्यप्रतापस्थ[गि]तदिगन्तरालप्रध्वन्सितध्वान्तराशिः[2] सतती-

35 दितस्सविता प्रकृतिभ्यः परं प्रत्ययमर्त्थवन्तमतिबहुतिथप्रयोजनानुबन्धमागमपरिपूर्ण्णं

36 विदधानः सन्धिविग्रहसमासनिश्चयनिपुणः स्थानेनुरूप[मादे]शं ददद्गुणवृद्धिविधानजनितसं-

37 स्कारस्साधूनां [3]राज्यसालातुरियतन्त्रयोरुभयोरपि निष्णातः प्रकृष्टविक्रमोपि करुणा-मृदुहृद-

38 यः श्रुतवानप्यगर्व्वितः कान्तोपि प्रशमी स्थिरसौहृदय्योपि निरसिता दोषवता-मुदयसमयसमुप-[4]

39 जनितजनतानुरागपरिपिहितभुवनसमर्त्थतप्रथितबा[ला]दित्यद्वितीयनामा[5] परममाहेश्वरः श्री-

40 ध्रुवसेनः कुशली सर्व्वानेव यथासम्बध्यमानकान्समाज्ञापयत्यस्तु वस्संविदितं यथा मया मातापित्रोः

41 पुण्याप्यायनाय उदुम्बरगह्वरविनिर्ग्गताय [6]नकायाग्रहारनिवासिदशपुरत्रैविद्यसामान्य-पाराशरस-

42 गोत्रमाध्यन्दिनवाजसनेयसब्रह्मचारिब्राह्मणबुधस्वामिपुत्रब्राह्मणदत्तस्वामि तथागस्तिका-ग्रहारनिवासि-

43 [ड]म्बमानचातुर्व्विद्यसामान्यपाराशरसगोत्रवाजसनेयसब्रह्मचारिब्राह्मणबुधस्वामपुत्रब्राह्मण-कुमारस्वामिभ्या[7]

44 मालवके भुज्यमानविष[ये] चन्द्रपुत्रकग्रामे दक्षिणसीम्नि भक्तीशतप्रमाणक्षेत्रं यस्या-घ[ा*]टनानि पूर्व्वतः धम्मणह-

45 ड्डिकाग्रामकङ्कटः दक्षिणतो देवकुलपाट[क]ग्रामकङ्कटः अपरतः वीरतरमकलिमक्षेत्र-क्षेत्रमर्य्यादा उत्तरपश्चि-

---

[1] Read °विध्वंसित°.

[2] Read °प्रध्वंसित°.

[3] Read °शालातुरीय°.

[4] Read °मुदय°.

[5] Read °समर्त्थित°.

[6] Read नकाग्रहार°.

[7] Read °बुधस्वामिपुत्र°. The syllable स्वा is entered on the margin of the plate ; read °भ्यां.

46 मकोणे निर्म्मण्डीतडाकिका उत्तरतः वीरतरमण्डली एवमेतच्चतुराघाटनविशुद्ध भक्तीमतप्रमाणक्षेत्रं ग्रो-[1]

47 द्रङ्गं सोपरिकार[2] सभूतवातप्रत्यायं सधान्यहिरण्यादेयं सपद्मपराध[3] सोत्पद्यमान-विष्टिकं सर्व्वराजकीयानामह-

48 स्तप्रक्षेपणीय[4] पूर्व्वप्रत्तदेवब्रह्मदेयब्राह्मणविकृतिरहितं[5] भूमिच्छिद्रन्यायेनाचन्द्रार्क्कार्ण्णव-क्षितिसरित्पर्व्वं-

49 तसमकालानं[6] पुत्रपौत्रान्वयभोग्यं उदकातिसर्ग्गेण धर्म्मदायो निसृष्ट[:*] यतोनयो-र्चितया ब्रह्मदेयस्थित्या भुञ्जत[7]

50 कृषत:[7] कर्षयत:[7] प्रदिशतोर्व्वा न कैश्चिद्व्यासेधे वर्त्तितव्यमागामिभद्रनृपतिभिरप्य-स्मद्वंशजैरन्यैर्व्वा[8] अनित्यान्यै[श्व]र्य्याण्य-

51 स्थिरं मानुष्यं सामान्यञ्च भूमिदानफलमवगच्छद्भिरयमस्मद्दायोनुमन्तव्यः परिपाल-यितव्यश्चेत्युक्तञ्च ॥ बहुभिर्व्वसुधा भु-

52 क्ता राजभिस्सगरादिभिः [।*] यस्य यस्य यदा भूमिस्तस्य तस्य तदा फलं [॥*] यानीह दारिद्र्यभयान्नरेन्द्रैर्द्धनानि धर्म्मायतनीकृतानि [।*] [9]निभुक्तमाल्यप्रति-

53 मानि तानि को नाम साधुः पुनराददीत ॥ षष्टिवर्षसहस्र[ा*]णि स्वर्ग्गे तिष्ठति भूमिद[: ।*] आच्छेता[10] चानुमन्ता च तान्येव नरके वसेदिति । दूतकोत्र राज-

54 पुत्रश्रीखरग्रह[:*] लिखितमिदं सन्धिविग्रहाधिकृतदिविरपतिवत्सभट्टिपुत्रदिविरपति-स्कन्दभटेन ॥ सं ३०० २० १ चैत्र ब २ स्वहस्तो मम ॥

---

[1] Read सो°.
[2] Read °करं.
[3] Read सदशापराधं.
[4] Read °णीयं.
[5] Read °विंशति°.
[6] Read °कालीनं.
[7] Read °तः.
[8] Read °वंश°.
[9] Read निर्भुक्त°.
[10] Read आच्छेत्ता.

Fig. 1. Brahmaur, the ancient Brahmapura.

INSCRIPTIONS OF CHAMBA STATE.

CHAMBĀ, the hill-state on the upper Rāvī, owing to its secluded position, has had the rare fortune of escaping the wave of Muhammadan invasions and the almost equally destructive influence of Sikh ascendancy. This fact is borne out by a greater abundance here of archæological, especially epigraphical material than is met with in other parts of the Pañjāb.

Chambā was visited by General Cunningham in 1839, who here as in so many other places in India was the first to draw attention to the remnants of the past.[1] He gave an account of the ancient temples and of the inscriptions on copper and on stone found in the State. But his visit was too short to do full justice to the subject, especially as regards epigraphy, the acquisition of epigraphical material requiring no less time and labour than its decipherment. A prolonged stay in Chambā during the hot season of 1902 and a renewed visit in the following summer have enabled me to continue his work.

[1] *Report of the Archæological Survey of India*, XIV, p. 109, sqq. and XXI, p. 134, sqq. *Cf.* also *Ancient Geography*, p. 141.

INSCRIPTIONS OF MERUVARMAN.

The most ancient records as yet discovered in Chambā are the inscriptions of Meruvarman, one of the early rulers of the State. They are engraved on the pedestals of the brass images of Lakṣaṇā Devī, Gaṇeśa, Nandi and Śakti Devī, of which the three first mentioned are found at Brahmaur (map Barmaor), the ancient capital of the State, situated on the Budhil, a tributary of the Rāvī, whilst the temple of Śakti Devī stands at Chatrāṛī (map Chitrahi) half-way between Brahmaur and Chambā town.

The shrines in which the two *devī* images are placed, are of a type peculiar to the Western Himālayas. They consist of a square cella enclosed by a double wall, leaving a passage all around. At Chatrāṛī this passage must once have been an open verandah, as the outer wall is found to consist of twelve heavy wooden pillars with beautifully carved capitals, the intervening spaces of which have been filled with masonry walls. The wooden verandah running round the outer wall is evidently a later addition as appears from the different style of wood carving. The tasteless frescoes on the inner wall belong to a recent restoration, and by their glaring colours contrast strangely with the subdued antiquity of the building. Both the temples are surmounted by a sloping slate roof not different from that found on an ordinary village house in the Pañjāb Hills.

The special interest attaching to the *devī* shrines is their graceful wood-carving, which is far superior to the crude work found in Kuḷḷū and other Hill Districts. At Brahmaur the carving of the façade has been much defaced by a long exposure to the weather. A remarkable feature is the trefoil arch enclosed in a triangular pediment, analogous to those of the ancient Kaśmīr temples. But here the tympanum is decorated with reliefs, the central figure of which represents the twelve-armed Sun-god,[1] which is placed at the top of the numerous rows of miniature figures covering the façade. The finest carvings are those on the inner door and the ceiling and pillar-capitals of the Śakti temple, which being protected against the weather are still in an excellent state of preservation. Those of the outer entrance are inferior and evidently of a later date.

The shrine in which the Gaṇeśa image is placed is little more than a shed. The bull Nandi stands in front of a *Śikhara* temple of the ordinary type, containing a *liṅga* and known by the name of Maṇimaheśa. Opposite this temple is another, built in the same style, but smaller in size, which is dedicated to Narasiṁha (see Fig. 4). Tradition ascribes it along with the others to Meruvarman. Not only does the absence of any inscription plead against this assumption; but there is positive proof, as will appear in the course of my paper, that the Narasiṁha temple was founded considerably later than the others.

The four inscribed images which were made by order of Meruvarman exhibit a high degree of technique, rather than of artistic merit. In the *devī* statues the workman, whose name Gugga is perpetuated in the inscriptions, has realized that

[1] Cunningham asserts that it represents Kālı, but the figure evidently is a male deity. The position of the legs, the *vāhana* (Garuḍa), the number of arms (the twelve months?) indicate it as Viṣṇu-Sūrya. The seven crouching figures beneath I take to be the Sun, the Moon and five Planets, after which the days of the week are named.

(a) FAÇADE OF LAKṢAṆĀ TEMPLE.

(b) PILLAR IN ŚAKTI TEMPLE.

conception of female beauty so frequently portrayed in old Indian poetry, but so alien to Western taste. The Gaṇeśa figure is more fortunate and we cannot but admire the skill with which he has succeeded in imparting majesty to the grotesque features of the elephant-faced god.

Lakṣaṇā, apparently one of the numerous names of Durgā-Pārvatī,—she is also known as Bhagavatī—is represented in the act of slaying the Mahiṣāsura. Her right foot is placed on the head of the buffalo-shaped demon, and with the *triśūla* held in her right hand she pierces his neck.[1] Her left hand raises his body partly from the ground. Another right hand clasps a sword, another left hand a bell. The image proper is 3 feet 4 inches, the pedestal 9 inches high. Śakti Devī of Chatrāṛī, the personification of the divine power, is also four-armed. In her right hands she holds a lance and a lotus flower, in her left hands a bell and a snake. The first-mentioned attribute possibly implies an allusion to the name of the goddess, Sanskṛt *śakti* meaning both "power" and "lance." The images of Gaṇeśa and Nandi do not require any detailed description. The former is 3 feet high, its copper pedestal 14½". The bull is of considerable size, being 5 feet high, to which the pedestal adds 13 inches. It should be noted that of the Gaṇeśa statue the legs are broken and that of the tail of the bull a portion is missing. It is believed that this damage was done on the occasion of a foreign invasion, but tradition fails to supply any reliable information as to the nationality of these invaders. People agree in asserting that they were not Muhammadans. These certainly would have done the work of destruction more thoroughly. The *Vaṁśāvalī* of the Chambā Rājās relates that in the reign of Lakṣmīvarman, the grandson of Meruvarman, the Kīras invaded Chambā and killed the Rājā in battle.[2] It seems not unlikely that the damage done to the statues may be connected with this invasion.

Fig. 6.

The language of Meruvarman's inscription is Sanskṛt, but of a kind which, especially in the metrical portions, would certainly have startled Pāṇini. The

[1] *Cf. Durgāsaptaśati* (Bombay, 1871) III, 37 *evam uktvā samutpatya sārūḍhā taṁ mahāsuram pādenākramya kaṇṭhe ca śūlenainam atāḍayat.*

[2] *Suvarṇavarmā tat* (i.e., Meruvarma)-*sūnur Lakṣmivarmā tadātmajaḥ ‖ tasya rājye nipatitā mārī lokā rujā hatāḥ tadaiva Kīrair āgatya rājā raṇamukhe hatah ‖ Vaṁś.* 48.

substitution of *v* for *b* and the doubling of *t* before *r* (*gottra*, *puttra*) and of *g*, *c*, *t*, *m* and *v* after that letter (*durgga*, *arccā*, *kīrtti*, *varmman*, *pūrvvam*) are too common in Sanskṛt epigraphs to call for special notice. A more serious error is the substitution of *o* for *au* in *potra* and the use of forms like *kārāpita* for *kārita* and *karmīṇa* for *karmiṇā*. The Gaṇeśa and Lakṣaṇā inscription are in prose, the other two in verse, the Nandi inscription in the Vasantatilaka, the Śakti inscription in what is evidently meant for the Indravajrā metre. The numerous grammatical as well as metrical mistakes occurring in the two latter do not suggest great ability on the part of Meruvarman's *paṇḍits*. They obscure the meaning to such an extent that it is only possible to guess the purport of the inscriptions.

According to General Cunningham [1] the character used would be that of the ninth and tenth centuries. It should, however, be noted, that the script of Meruvarman is decidedly earlier than the Śāradā of the Hills, as found first at Baijnāth c. 800 A.D. Hence it is difficult to assign to it a later date than the eighth century, and on account of its striking resemblance to the script of *c.* 700 A.D., as found in the Multai copper-plates,[2] I am inclined to place it rather in the beginning than at the end of that period. *Oṁ* is regularly expressed by a symbol which is derived from the sign for *O*, as found in inscriptions of the seventh century, but which in some cases is placed vertically. In the Lakṣaṇā legend we find twice at the end of the sentence a symbol consisting of two concentric circles, the inner one approaching a dot.[3] In the same inscription the use of the *jihvāmūlīya* should be noticed.

The engraving of the Brahmaur inscriptions is well executed. The letters are clear and perfectly legible, especially those of the Nandi legend. In the Chatrāṛī inscription on the other hand the cutting is indistinct and hesitating; the value of several of the characters is therefore far from certain. The inscriptions are being edited from tracings, as a purely mechanical reproduction was found impossible owing to their position. The inscription on the image of Lakṣaṇā consists of two lines, 18½ and 17½" long. The average size of the letters is from ⅜ to ½".

Text A.[4]

1. Oṁ Moṣūṇasva-gottr-Āditya-vaṁśa-saṁbhūta-Śrī-Ādityavarmma-deva-pra-pauttro(tra)-Śrī-Va(Ba)lavarmma-deva-pauttra-Śrī-Divākaravarmma-deva-puttreṇa ‖

2. Śrī-Meruvarmmaṇā ‖ ātma-puṇya-vṛddhaye Lakṣaṇā[5]-devyā(a)rcca(ā)ḥ-kārāpitāḥ (kāritāḥ)‖Karmmīṇa (karmiṇā) Guggeṇa(na)‖.

Translation.

1. Born from the house (*gotra*) or Moṣūṇasva and from the Solar race, the great-grandson of Śrī Ādityavarma-deva, the grandson of Śrī Balavarma-deva, the son of Śrī Divākaravarma-deva

---

[1] *Ancient Geography*, p. 141.

[2] Bühler, *Indische Palaeographie*, Table IV, col. XX.

[3] *Ibidem*, p. 85; for the *o* see Table IV; 6, XVIII.

[4] This and the following inscription were edited by Cunningham, *A. S. R.*, XIV, p. 111, sq.

[5] Evidently a word meaning or indicating "an image" is wanted; the reading *Lakṣaṇā-devyārccaḥ* cannot be correct. I propose to read *devyarcāḥ* and to assign to *arcāḥ* (Plural of *arcā*-worship) the meaning of an object of worship, *i.e.*, an image.

2. Śrī Meruvarman, for the increase of his spiritual merit, has caused the image of the goddess Lakṣaṇā to be made. By the workman Gugga.

The Gaṇeśa image bears the following inscription in four lines of unequal length (13 to 5¾"). The fourth line is divided in two by the head of a grotesque figure crouching in front of the *siṁhāsana*. The size of the letters is from ¼ to ⅜".

TEXT B.

1. Oṁ namaḥ (mo) Gaṇapataye[1] ‖ Mūṣūṇasva-gottr-Āditya-vaṁśa-saṁbhūta-Śrī-Ādityavarmma-deva-papottra (prapautra)-

2. Srī-Va(Ba)lavarmma-dev-ānupottra(pautra)-Śrī-Divākaravarmma-deva-sūnunā‖

3. mahārājādhirāja-Śrī-Meruvarmmaṇa(ā)kārāpita(ḥ) (kārito) devadharmmo-yam‖

4. Karmmīṇa (karmiṇā) Guggeṇa (na) ‖

Translation.

1. Oṁ. Adoration to Gaṇapati. Born from the house (*gotra*) of Mūṣūnasva and from the Solar race, the great-grandson of Śrī-Ādityavarma-deva,

2. the grandson[2] of Śrī Balavarma-deva, the son of Śrī Divākaravarma-deva,

3. the *mahārājādhirāja* Śrī Meruvarman has caused this image[3] of the god to be made.

4. By the workman Gugga.

On the image of the bull Nandi we find two lines 38 inches long, the name of the maker being added in a third line of 4¾". Average size of letters ½".

TEXT C.[4]

1. Oṁ Prāsāda Meru-sadṛśaṁ Himavanta-mūrdhniḥ kṛtvā svayaṁ pravara-karmma-śubhair-anekaiḥ tac-candraśālā-racitam navanābha nāma prāg-grīvakair-cciviva (vividha ?)-maṇḍapa naiḥka-cittraiḥ‖

2. tasy-āgrato vṛṣabha pīna-kapola-kāyaḥ saṁśliṣṭa-vakṣa-kakud-onnata-devayānaḥ Śrī-Meruvarmma-catur-odadhi-kīrttir[5]-eṣāḥ mātā-pitṛḥ satatam-ātma-phal-ānuvṛddhaiḥ‖

3. Oṁ. Kṛtaṁ karmmīṇa Guggenaḥ‖

Translation.

1. After that he had himself built a temple like unto Mount Meru on the top of the Himavant through the manifold bliss of [his] excellent actions (*karman*), an upper chamber (*candraśālā*) was added to it with various (?) porches (*maṇḍapa*) and numerous ornaments (*citra*) turned towards the east ;[6]

---

[1] The dot over *g* apparently does not make part of the inscription.

[2] The anomalous form *anupautra* probably owes its origin to a wish of emphasizing the distinction between *pautra* and *prapautra*, the meaning being evidently the same as that of *pautra*.

[3] Here the word *dharma* is used in the sense of an image, as is *arcā* in the previous inscription ; one feels inclined to read *deyadharma* but for the verb *kārāpitaḥ*, i.e., *kāritaḥ*, with which it is combined.

[4] In this and the following inscription I have not attempted to correct the numerous grammatical mistakes which will be obvious to any one possessing the most elementary knowledge of Sanskṛt.

[5] An expression like *catur-udadhi-samatikrāntakīrti* is evidently meant; *cf.* Fleet, *Corpus Inscr. Ind.*, III, p. 288.

[6] The translation of the second part of the first line is problematic. For the term *navanābha nāma* (if this be the correct reading) I cannot offer any plausible explanation. Nor is it clear what is meant by *Candraśālā* and *prāggrīvaka*. The present temple has neither upper storey nor porches. But it can hardly be the original building erected by Meruvarman.

2. in front of it [was set this] bull, fat of cheeks and body, solid of breast and hump, the exalted vehicle of the god (*Śiva*). This is the glorious work [1] of Śrī-Meruvarman [famous] over the four oceans, [tending] to increase continually the [spiritual] fruit of his parents and himself.

3. Made by the workman Gugga.

The inscription on the image of Śakti Devī at Chatrāṛī consists of two lines 15 inches long. The maker's name is mentioned in a separate line of 3 inches, placed behind the former. Size of letters ¼ to ⅜".

TEXT D.

1. Oṁ Āsī viśuddha-kula-dhurya-vāho Śrī-Devavarmm-eti prasiddha-kīrttir-tasyas-sutaḥ sarvvaguṇātirāmaḥ Śrī-Meruvarmmā prathita prithivyāḥ‖

2. mātā-pitṛḥ-puṇya-nimitta-pūrvvaṁ kārāpitā bhaktita (to ?) dharma (?) Śaktyā jitvā ripūṁ durjaya-durgga-saṁsthā[ṁ] kīrttir-yaśor (?)-dharmma-vivṛdhyat-āyuḥ (vivardhit-āyuḥ ?)‖

3. Kṛtaṁ karmmīṇa Guggeṇa ‖

Translation.[2]

1. Oṁ. There was an eminent chief of a pure race Śrī Devavarman of accomplished fame. His son, charming by every virtue [is] Śrī Meruvarman renowned on the earth.

2. First for the sake of the spiritual merit of his parents and out of devotion, he caused the image of Śakti to be made, after having conquered the enemies in their invincible castles,[3] he who has prolonged his life by glory, fame and religious merit.

3. Made by the workman Gugga.

COPPER-PLATE INSCRIPTIONS.

In the course of his stay at Chambā, General Cunningham [4] noticed the existence of four inscriptions, one on stone and three on copper-plates. Of the latter the earliest one was fully discussed by Professor F. Kielhorn,[5] but owing to defects in the rubbings then available, no facsimile of the inscription was published. The number of copper-plates, however, existing in Chambā is considerably larger, as will appear from the fact that, by the valuable assistance of Miyān Bhūri Singh, C.I.E., the enlightened Prime Minister of the State, I was enabled to collect no less than forty-nine copper-plates, dating from the reign of Yagākaravarman, the son of Sāhilla, the reputed founder of Chambā, down to that of Rājā Śyām Singh, the present ruler of the State. In the absence of any other authentic records the later plates also are of great value for local history. They are of interest also to the linguist on

---

[1] For *kirti* in the meaning of any word which renders the constructor famous, *cf.* Fleet, *Corpus Inscr. Ind.*, III, p. 212. An analogy is found in the words *arca* and *dharma* as used in inscriptions A and B.

[2] The translation for reasons stated above should be considered merely as an attempt to render the probable meaning. The general purport in any case is sufficiently clear.

[3] This can as well be applied to the Rājā as to the demon-slaying goddess.

[4] *A. S. R.*, XXI, p. 135.

[5] *Ind. Ant.*, XVII (1888), p. 7.

Inscriptions on brass images in the Chamba State.

A.—Lakshaṇá image.

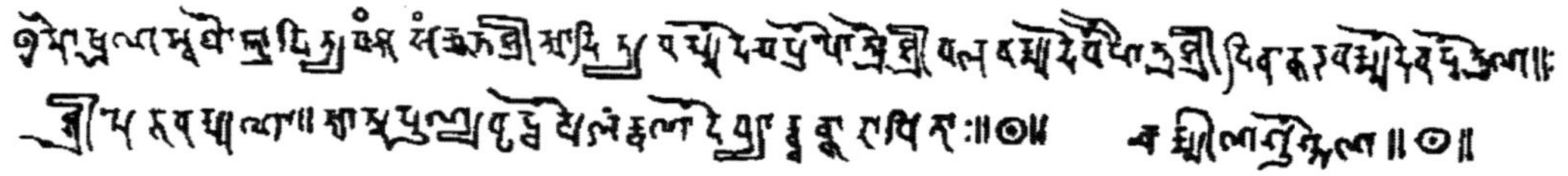

B.—Gaṇeśa image.

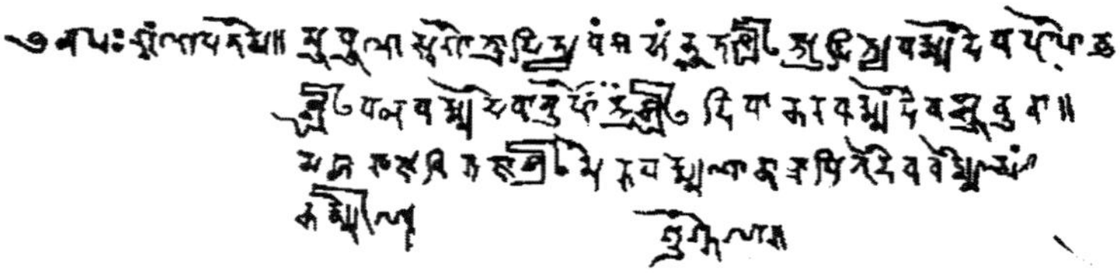

C.—Nandi image.

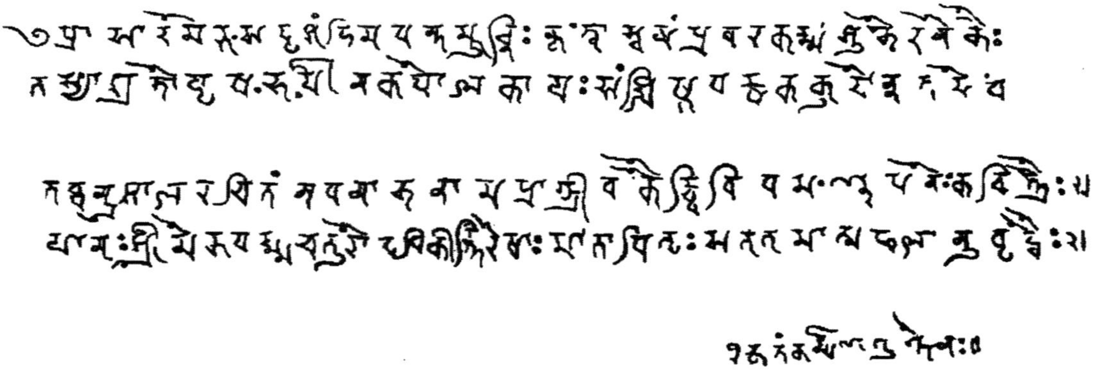

D.—Śakti image.

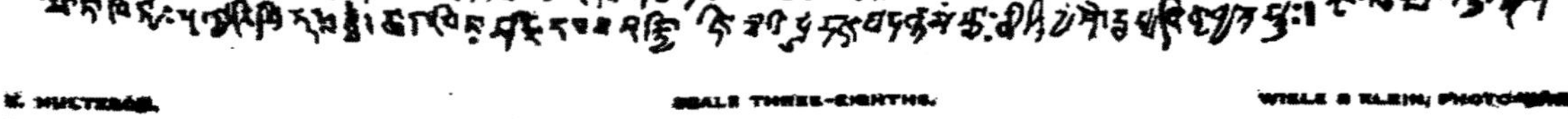

[illegible] SCALE THREE-EIGHTHS. WIELE & KLEIN, PHOTO.

[illegible] supplied by Dr. Vogel.

account of their being partly written in the vernacular, and contain a number of agricultural terms current in this part of the Western Himālayas.

The following is a chronological list of the plates recovered :—

I.	Yagākaravarman, son of Sāhilla.	Saṁ. 10, Vaiśākha, ba. ti. 10
II.	Vidagdha, son of Yugākaravarman.	Saṁ. 4, Māgha, śu. ti. 1.
III.	Somavarman, son of Sālavāhana	Saṁ. 7, Bhādrapada, kṛ. ti. 3 [o]. (Sūryagrahaṇa.)
IV.	Somavarman and Āsaṭa.	Saṁ. 1, Vaiśākha, sita 3, Śukravāra and Saṁ. 11, Bhādrapada, śu. ti. 12.
V.	Āsaṭa, son of Sālavāhana.	Saṁ. 5, Śrāvaṇa, śu. ti. 15.
VI.	Vairāsivarman.	Śāstra 6, Vikr. 1387, Kārtika, śu. ti. 12.
VII.	Bhoṭavarman.	Śāstra 80, Vikr. 1461, Āṣāḍha, śu. ti. 2.
VIII.	„	Saṁvat 12, Māgha, prav. 10.
IX.	Saṁgrāmavarman, son of Bhoṭavarman.	Śāstra 22, Jyeṣṭha, śu. ti. 11.
X.	Ānandavarman, son of Saṁgrāmavarman.	No date.
XI.	Gaṇeśavarman, son of Ānandavarman.	Śāstra 88, Śaka 1434, Māgha, Amāvāsyā.
XII.	„ „ „	Śāstra 97, Caitra 8, Navarātra.
XIII.	„ „ „	„ 34, Vaiśākha, ba. 27 (?).
XIV.	„ „ „	„ 34 (?).
XV.	„ „ „	„ 35, Kārtika, śu. ti. 11.
XVI.	„ „ „	No date.
XVII, XVIII, XIX.	Pratāpasiṁha, son of Gaṇeśavarman.	Śāstra 51.
XX.	„ „	„ 55, Vikr. 1636, Bhādrapada, su. 14.
XXI.	Balabhadra, son of Vīrabhāna (Vīravāhana ?) and grandson of Pratāpasiṁha.	Sāstra 65, „ 1646, Vaiśākha, śu. 3.
XXII.	„ „ „	Śāstra 67, Vikr. 1648, Bhādrapada, ba. 12.
XXIII.	„ „ „	„ 68, „ 1649, Caitra, śu. 3.
XXIV.	„ „ „	„ 75, „ 1656, Āṣāḍha, ba. 2.
XXV.	„ „ „	„ 75, „ 1656, „ „ 10.
XXVI.	„ „ „	„ 83, „ 1664, Bhādrapada śu. 7.
XXVII.	„ „ „	„ 84, (?) Phālguna 20.
XXVIII.	„ „ „	„ 84, „ 1600 (r. 1665).
XXIX.	„ „ „	„ 86, „ 1667, Kārtika, ba. 11.
XXX.	„ „ „	„ 5, „ 1686, Māgha, śu. 12.
XXXI.	„ „ „	„ 10, „ 1691, Bhādrapada, ba. 8.
XXXII.	„ „ „	„ 11, „ 1699, (1692?).
XXXIII.	„ „ „	„ 11, „ 1692, Vaiśākha, śu. I (?)
XXXIV.	„ „ „	„ 12, „ 1693, „ ba. 3.
XXXV.	„ „ „	„ 12, „ 1693, Kārtika, śu. 15.
XXXVI.	„ „ „	„ 12, „ 1693, Caitra, ba. 11.
XXXVII.	„ „ „	„ 12, „ 1693.
XXXVIII.	„ „ „	„ 13, „ 1694, Māgha, śu. 12.
XXXIX.	„ „ „	„ 15, „ 1695, Vaiśākha, śu. 5.
XL.	„ „ „	„ 16, „ 1697, Māgha.
XLI.	Pṛthvīsiṁha	„ 17, „ 1698, Vaiśākha, śu. 8.
XLII.	„	„ 21, „ 1702, Phālguna.
XLIII.	„	„ 21, „ 1702, Māgha śu. 7.
XLIV.	„	„ 36, „ 1717, Kārtika, śu. 12.
XLV.	„	„ 37, „ 1718, Śrāvaṇa, śu. 5.

XLVI. Śatrusiṁha	Śāstra 54, Vikr. 1734, Vaiśākha, śu. 12.
XLVII. Umedasiṁha	„ 24, „ 1805, Śaka, 1670, Māgha, Pūrṇamāsa.
XLVIII. Rājasiṁha	„ 52, „ 1833, „ 1698. Śrāvaṇa, śu. 8, Bhauma.
XLIX. Śyāmasiṁha	„ 60, „ 1941, Kārtika.

It should be understood that this list by no means represents the full number of copper-plates existing in Chambā which indeed must amount to some two or three hundred. But as far as I have been able to ascertain no more plates of the pre-Muhammadan period are found except the five, numbered I—V, which I intend to edit in the present paper. These five are far superior to the later plates both as regards scholarship and workmanship. They are neatly engraved on good-sized plates in well-arranged and clear-cut Śāradā letters, which up to the present are perfectly legible, except where the plate has become damaged by accident. The character is the same as that used in the Baijnāth inscriptions, and differs so little from the script once used in Kaśmīr, that a Kaśmīrī Paṇḍit would have little difficulty in recognising most of the *akṣaras*. It is noteworthy that the script of the oldest plate, that of Yagākara, differs considerably from that of the later plates in the mode in which the letters are finished at the top. Whereas in these later ones the letters are throughout finished at the top by means of a horizontal stroke, in the earliest one we find twc small strokes forming a fork of an angle of about 45°. This point is especially remarkable as between the plate of Yagākara and that of his son Vidagdha there can be but little difference in time.

The language of the five earlier grants is Sanskṛt, but intermixed with *bhāṣā* words in Plates I and II, where the boundaries of the granted land are defined. In the plates of the Muhammadan period such passages are invariably in the vernacular introduced by the words "*atha bhāṣā.*" As it was essential that this part of the deed should be intelligible to local officials, it was no doubt found more convenient to resort to the spoken language in a time when Sanskṛt learning was on the decline. That in the days of Somavarman and Āsaṭa Chambā still possessed men well-acquainted with the classical language, appears from the plates issued by those rulers. The lengthy compounds extolling the virtues of Sāhilla are good specimens of that literary skill which is most esteemed by indigenous scholars. Less favourable must our opinion be of the author of Yagākara's grant, as regards his knowledge of the *Dharmaśāstra*. His quotations from the *Smṛti* are extremely corrupt and contain some strange blunders. Vidagdha's plate is composed in a very tolerable Sanskṛt. In general, however, it must be confessed that our inscriptions are by no means free from grammatical errors. Offences against *Sandhi* rules especially are not uncommonly met with *svarga* I, 15; *bhūmi* II, 27; *mānasaḥ* III, 12; *vyāvasthaḥ* III, 13: *agrahāratveti* III, 23; *t* and *d* are often omitted at the end of the word *madhyā* I, 7; *prāmāṇyā* I, 13; *bhave* I, 14; *vyatikrame* I, 15.

To a certain extent mistakes are evidently due to vernacular influence, *e.g.*, in the substitution of *j* for *y praṇiji* III, 15; *vīrajātrika* V, 9; in the interchange of the sibilants *śāśanam* I, 15; *aśeśa* III, 17; *maśī* III, 7; IV, 7; *aseṣa-sāstra* IV,

11; *kuṣalī* V, 7; *sāsyamāna* V, 11; *vyāśa* V, 19; also in *siṁgha* IV, 10; *potra* IV, 31. The same influence is perhaps at work, when we find *ri* instead of ṛ, as in *trina* III, 21; *tritīya* IV, 27 (on the other hand *āśṛta* II, 24 for *āśrita*) and *ṇ* for *n*, as in *Triṇayana* I, 2; *māliṇī* I, 17; *lavaṇa* II, 23; *ṇāma* II, 28; *yāṇi* II, 28; *pratimāṇitāni* II, 28; *pravardhamāṇa* II, 29. The letters *b* and *v* are often interchanged. Instead of *ddh* we have *dh* in *caurodharaṇika* V, 9; *ddh* instead of *dh* in *śuddhyate* I, 16; *ṭ* for *ṭṭ* in *bhaṭāraka* I, 4; *kuṭita* III, 3. *Anusvāra* and *visarga* are often omitted *eka* I, 9; *savāsā* I, 11; *janapadānā* I, 11; *asmi* I, 14; *taḍāgānā* I, 17; *eka* II, 27; *va* I, 11; *sarvai* I, 13; *taru* II, 4; *yaśa* III, 15; *carita* III, 17. In *tilakaḥ parama*-V, 4 we find *visarga* instead of *upadhmānīya*; in *vaṅśa* II 4; *vaṅśe* IV, 24 and *saṅsāra* II, 19 the guttural nasal stands for *anusvāra* and in *Caṇpakā*[1] (I, 3; II, 1; III, 2; IV, 3; V, 2) the lingual for the labial nasal. A certain number of mistakes, especially in Plate V, are evidently blunders of the engraver, such as *vyāpna* V, 1; *śuru* V, 3; *śaulmika* V, 9; *bhitvaraśāna* V, 9; *tabhau* V, 12; *śocara* V, 13; *u* V, 19; *maramo* V, 19; *ato* V, 21; *tava* I, 2; *pariṣālanīyaś* II, 26; *paripāpālita* III, 13; *dāturṇām* IV, 29; *māprakāś* IV, 29.

This however is clearly not the case where we find ungrammatical forms like *bhuṁjāpayatu*, II, 21; *bhucyamāna* I, 8; IV, 16; V, II; and *vasāpayatu* I, 13 and un-Sanskritic words like *paripanthanā*="way-laying, opposition," which perhaps originates from a misreading of *paripaṅthinā* Instr. of *paripanthin*. Sometimes we find words used in a sense different from that which they possess in classical Sanskṛt, *e.g.*, *upadrava* II, 24; V, 17 meaning "misfortune, calamity," but here evidently to be taken in the sense of "vexation," and used neuter instead of masculine. Compare also *anupadrava* IV, 23. Another curious instance is the word *cāṭa* which is found combined with *bhaṭa* in the list of State officials II, 97 and in the expression *a-cāṭa-bhaṭa-praveśa* (II, 17; *cf.* also II, 22-23). The meaning of *cāṭa* in the classical literature is "cheat, deceiver, fortune-teller," which does not fit here. Dr. Bühler took *cāṭa-bhaṭa* to mean "regular and irregular troops," an interpretation which has been generally adopted since by editors of copper-plate inscriptions. That this however is not the true meaning of the words seems to me certain, as up to the present in Chambā State the word *cāṛ*, evidently a derivative of *cāṭa*, is used to indicate the head of a *pargaṇa* who is an executive officer responsible for the apprehension of criminals, and to whose duties it belongs to collect labourers and supplies on behalf of the head of the State and, now-a-days, of European travellers also. This explains why it was granted as a special privilege to holders of land that the *cāṭa* and his servants should not be allowed to enter it.

As to the contents of the Chambā title-deeds, it will be seen, that in their fullest form as represented by Plate IV they contain the following seven elements:

(1) One or two imprecatory or benedictory verses in honour of Śiva and other deities (not found in Plate II).

(2) Eulogy of the donor, his parents and sometimes more remote ancestors. This part, very brief in Plates I, II, and V, is much extended in the two remaining plates, where a considerable portion, in No. III almost half

[1] *Cf.* Dr. Stein's note at Rājat. VII, 218.

of the inscription, is devoted to the praise of Sāhilla, the great ancestor of the Chambā Rājās.

(3) Appeal of the Rājā to his officials to observe the grant. This interesting passage is best represented in Vidagdha's plate. It occurs also in Nos. IV and V, and in a very brief form on Plate I also. It is not found in III.

(4) Description of the position of the granted land and sometimes of its boundaries. This, the most essential part of the grant, is of importance for the ancient geography of Chambā.

(5) Definition of the rights and privileges which the grantee will enjoy in connection with the grant.

(6) Name and, if a Brāhman, pedigree of the grantee, found like 4 naturally on all the plates.

(7) Quotations from the *smṛti* regarding the *dānadharma*, most explicit in Plate I, where no less than six *ślokas* are quoted. In Plate III such verses are altogether omitted.

(8) Name of the "messenger(s)" (*dūta*) and writer(s) (*kāyastha*) of the plate, and subscription of the donor(s).

The grants are composed in prose except the parts 1 and 7, which are composed in couplets of various metre. Only in one case, namely in Plate IV, at the end of part 6 (l. 23-24) we find a verse introduced in the grant proper.

The inscriptions are being edited from the original plates. In the transcripts I have followed the system adopted by Dr. Fleet in the third volume of the *Corpus Inscriptionum Indicarum* (for particulars see there Introduction, page 193). So round brackets are used for corrections, and square ones for restorations, an asterisk being added in the latter case, if the sign supplied is omitted in the original.

I. Grant of Yagākaravarman.

The plate containing this grant is $13\frac{3}{8}$" broad by $8\frac{1}{4}$" high. The average size of the letters is $\frac{3}{16}$". It has 19 lines besides the subscription which is written vertically on the proper right margin. The plate is far from entire. The four corners are broken away, which has led to the loss of the symbol *oṁ* and the first two *akṣaras* of the signature in the upper proper right corner, and to the loss of the last five *akṣaras* of the first line and of the upper portion of the last four *akṣaras* of the second line in the upper proper left corner. In the lower corners the first four *akṣaras* of the last two lines are missing to the proper right, whereas the end of the last six lines is missing to the proper left in such a manner that of line 14 only the last *akṣara* is damaged and of line 20 some nine *akṣaras* are lost. In the upper part of the plate a broken piece of $2\frac{1}{2}$" by $1\frac{3}{4}$" has been fastened with clamps, by which several *akṣaras* of the first four lines have been injured or destroyed.

TEXT I.

1. [Oṁ] svastiḥ ‖ Oṁ Gaṇapataye nama [h*] ı (‖) A[vani][1] -salila-vahni-vyoma-vāyvā(a)ntarātma - - - - -

[1] Metre, Mālinī.

I.—Chamba Plate of Yagakaravarmadeva.

SCALE THREE-FOURTHS.

From an ink-impression supplied by Dr. Vogel.

E. HULTZSCH.

WIELE & KLEIN, PHOTO-ZINCO.

2. purāṇa svāṅga- saṁbhūta-yone । Hara Ta(Bha)va Śiva Śarva Tryambak Eśāna Rudra Triṇa(na)yana Vṛ[ṣabhā]ṅkā

3. nantamūrte namas=te ॥ Śrī-Caṇpakā-vāsāt=paramabrahmaṇya-deva-dvija guru-bhakta-parama-bhaṭ[*ṭ]āraka-ma-

4. hārājādhirāja-parameśvara-śrīmat-Sāhila-deva-pādānudhyāta-paramabhaṭ[*ṭ]ā rikā-mahārājñī--Śrī-Nennā-dev-yo(u)dara-samutpa-

5. nno nek[1] -ārāti-cakra-nirmūlana-mahādā(mā ?)na-salila-setu-samabhi[va*]-rdhita-yaśaḥ-pādapa[ḥ] ॥ (।) paramabhaṭ[ṭ*] ṭāraka-mahārajā-

6. dhirāja-parameśvara-śrīmad-Yagākaravarma devaḥ=kuśalī svaśāsyamāna-Brahmapura-maṇḍala-pratibaddha-Viḍavikā-

7. grāma-prativa(ba)ddha-pūrve Khaṇī-maṭhasya kolhika-satka-bhū. 2 eṣaṁ madhyā[d] Harihalla-Rāṁkila-sva(su)tasya praviṣṭaṁ Śabdabagga-

8. nāma kṣetraṁ tasya parivarte dattaṁ Grima-grāme candi (cāpi ?) Ākuṭanāga-vika-satka Rahaṅka-suta-gaṇa-bhucya(jya)mānā kuṭika vāpye-

9. ya dhānā-piṭakam=eka [ṁ*] dattaṁ । tathā Khaṇī-maṭhasya-sannikṛṣṭa-Yamalikā Śākavāṭikā tatra vāpye piṭaka-dvaya-

10. m=aṅkata 2? ubhau kuṭika-sahita pi-3 tathā dhā(dā)ruvāṭikārdham । Sarvān=eva niyoga-sthāṁ rāja-rājānaka-rājasthānī-

11. ya-sarva-savāsā [ṁ] bodhayaty=astu va[ḥ*] saṁviditaṁ prativāsi-janapadānā [ṁ] bhogikādīnāṁ sāṣṭādasa-prakṛtyādīnāṁ mahā-

12. rājñī-Śrī-Tribhuvaṇa(na)rekhā-devyā pratiṣṭhita-Narasiṁhasya[2] yomala-kaṁtasya[3] pratigraheṇ āgrahāratveti pratipāditaṁ

13. viditvā kīrtitānukīrtitai (kīrtitākīrtitaiḥ)[4] sarvai [ḥ*] rājapuruṣair=anumanta-vyaṁ yato smat-pradatta-śāśa(sa)na-prāmānyā (ṇyād) vasatu vasāpa-

14. yatu (vāsayatu) bhāge na prayachana kena cit=paripanthanā kāryā । Asmi [ṁ*]va[ṁ*]śe samutpanne(o) yaḥ-kaści[n] nṛpatir=bhave[t*] tasy=āham has[ta]-

15. lagno smi śāśa(sa)naṁ mā vyatikrame[t*] । Pālanāt=paramo dharma[ḥ*] pālapālanānāṁ (pālanāt paramaṁ) tapaḥ pālanā[t*] paramo(maḥ) svarga(o) garī-[yas=te-].

16. na pālanā (nam) । Yat=kiṁ [ś*] ci[t] kurute pāpaṁ janmaprabhṛti mānavaḥ tad= gocarma-ma(ā)treṇa bhūmihartā na[5] śuddhyate (śudhyate) । Phā[la]-kṛṣ[ṭāṁ mahīṁ da-].

17. [t]tvā sabījā[ṁ] sasā(sya)-māliṇi(nīṁ) yāvat-sūrya-kṛtaṁ(tā)loke(kās) tāvat=svarge mahīyate । Taḍāgānā [ṁ*][6] sahasreṇa [cāśvamedha-śate-

18. na ca gavāṁ] koṭī-pradānena bhūmihartā na śuddhyate (śudhyate) । Anai (u) dakeś(ṣ)u[7] ra(va)ne[ṣu*][śu]pka(ṣka)-koṭara-vāsiś(ṣ)u kṛṣṇa-sa [rpeṣu jāyante bhūmi-

---

[1] The *akṣara* which I read *ne* is not clear and has almost the shape of *e*. But on account of the preceding ending I take it to be *ne*, in which the vowel-stroke has become amalgamated with the letter proper.

[2] It deserves notice that this word except the last *akṣara* is written in a type much later than that used throughout in this grant, from which it would seem as if the name had been substituted.

[3] This word I cannot explain. A term like *udakapūrvakasya*, *hastodakasya*,' or *toyaculukasya* is evidently wanted.

[4] *Cf.* Plate II, 9-10.

[5] Instead of *bhūmihartā na* read *bhūmidānena*.

[6] The verse is restored from Plate IV, 26-27.

[7] This verse in a modified form is found in Fleet's *Corpus Inscr. Ind.*, III, 180, 108, 137. *Ind. Ant.*, XIV (1885), p. 319.

19. dāyaṁ hara]nti ye ॥ Saṁvat 10 Vaiśākha-ba-ti-10[॥*] Dūto-tra(ā)kṣapaṭi(ṭali) ka-Śrī-Vivakhala [ḥ॥ Li] khitaṁ kāyastha-Jāsa [ṭeṇa[1]]...

[Śrīma]d-Yagākaravarma-deva-svahastaḥ ॥

Translation.

[Oṁ], Hail ! Oṁ. Reverence to Gaṇapati. O Thou that art the soul of the earth, the water, the fire, the aether, and the air. . . . . . . ancient and self-created. Hara, Bhava, Śiva, Śarva, Tryambaka (three-eyed), Īśāna (Lord), Rudra, Trinayana (Three-eyed), Vṛ[ṣabhā]ṅka (Bull-marked), O Thou whose shape is endless, reverence to Thee.

(Line 3.) From (his) residence at the glorious Caṇpakā, he who reverentially remembers (*lit.* is meditating on the feet of[2]) the very devout worshipper of the deities, the twice-born and the spiritual preceptors : the *Paramabhaṭṭāraka*, *Mahārājādhirāja*, *Parameśvara*,[3] the illustrious Sāhiladeva, and was born from the womb of the *Paramabhaṭṭārikā*, *Mahārājñī*, the illustrious Nennādevī, he, the tree of whose glory is increased by damming back the great wave of pride[4] [arising from] outrooting the host of manifold enemies,—he, the *Paramabhaṭṭāraka*, *Mahārājādhirāja*, *Parameśvara*, the illustrious *Yagākaravarmadeva*, the prosperous one—[grants].

(L. 6.)—2 *bhū*[5] of the irrigated land[6] of the Khaṇī hospice[7] formerly belonging to the village Viḍavikā belonging to the Brahmapura district of his domain. A field Śabdavagga[8] by name which was enjoyed (*lit.* entered) by the son of the Harihalla[9] Rāṅkila is given in exchange. Also in the village Grima one *piṭaka*[10] of rice is given from the *kuṭika*[11] arable land(?) which was enjoyed by the sons of Rahaṅka collectively and belongs to the Ākuṭanāgavikā. Further, in the vicinity of the Khaṇī hospice [is] the Yamalikā kitchengarden ; out of the arable land there : two, in figures 2 *piṭaka* [are given]. [These] two together with that of Kuṭika [make] 3 *pi.* And, further, half the orchard.[12]

---

[1] The name Jāsaṭa, which occurs as that of a Chambā Rājā in the Rājataraṅgiṇī may be surmised here. The *akṣara sa* is partly preserved on the plate. Other names on *ṭa* peculiar to the Pañjāb Hills are Āsaṭa, Bhogaṭa, Dhammaṭa.

[2] *Cf.* Fleet, *Corpus Inscr. Ind.*, III, p. 17, n. 2.

[3] *Cf.* Fleet, *loc. cit.*, page 10, n.

[4] I translate according to the proposed correction *māna* for *dāna*, as the latter word does not produce any reasonable sense.

[5] A *bhū* or *bhūmi* sub-divided into four (*bhū*) *māṣaka* is equivalent to about 17 acres.

[6] The word *kolhika* is evidently sanskritised *kohli*, which in Chambā and neighbouring hill-tracts indicates an irrigated field used for rice-cultivation and is regularly found in the vernacular portions of the later Chambā title-deeds. (*Cf.* also A. H. Diack's Kuḷḷūī grammar, *i.v. khol.*) The word is derived from *kuhl(a)* meaning "a channel" Skr. *kulyā* Kaśm. *kul.*.

[7] For the use of the word *maṭha* in Kaśmīr place-names *cf. Rājat.* (transl. Stein), Vol. II, 369 n.

[8] The second member of the compound is the vernacular word *bag* meaning "a field."

[9] Perhaps a caste-name.

[10] It is the custom in Chambā as in Kaśmir to designate a certain area of land by the weight of rice seed required for its cultivation. *Cf.* Stein, *Rājat.*, V, 71. In Chambā *piṛa* (the modern form of Skr. *piṭaka* is the twentieth part of a *khāri* and contains 20 *mānī*, a *mānī* being equivalent to 4½ *ser*. A *piṭaka* consequently would amount to 90 *ser*.

[11] It is possible that by this word a special kind of land is indicated. In the Kullū dialect the word *kuṭ* means "cultivated land lying at a high elevation, yielding in the course of two years only two crops, buckwheat followed by wheat" (Diack's *Kūllūī grammar*, p. 75). But the term does not seem to be known in Chambā now-a-days.

[12] The passage in which the grant is stipulated is far from clear, owing partly to the number of proper names and what apparently are sanskritised vernacular words, and partly to the loose syntactical construction and absence of interpunctual signs. My translation should, therefore, be considered as entirely hypothetical. The names of localities mentioned will be discussed in the sequel in connection with the results derived from the inscriptions collectively for the ancient geography of Chambā.

(L. 10.) He (the King) informs all officials, every rājā, rānā,[1] Chief Justice,[2] and all house-owners. Be it known unto you, neighbouring country people,[3] landholders and others, who are the eighteen elements of the State. On [the temple of] Narasiṁha founded by the Queen Tribhuvanarekhā-devī is [by a formal libation of water?] this grant bestowed. Having understood [this], all servants of the King should observe it, so that on the authority of the charter[4] issued by us he (the grantee) should live and cause [others] to live.

[L. 14.] Whosoever born of this race may be king, I enjoin on him not to transgress [this] order. By [its] observance the highest religious merit, by [its] observance the highest ascetic merit, by [its] observance the highest heaven [will be attained]; [its] observance, therefore, is very important. Whatsoever sin, from his birth onwards, a man commits, it will be cleansed by a gift of land, be it only the size of a cow-hide.[5] He who gives land, tilled with the plough, provided with seed-corn and fertile (*lit.*, wreathed with grain) he will be blessed in Heaven, as long as light is produced by the sun. He who takes away [the land] is not cleansed by [the digging of] a thousand tanks, by a hundred horse-oblations, and by a gift of ten million cows. Those who confiscate a grant of land are born in black serpents, dwelling in the hollows of dried-up trees in waterless forests.

(L. 19.) In the year 10, [the month] Vaiśākha, the dark fortnight, the lunar day 10. The messenger on this occasion [was] the Great-Recordkeeper, the illustrious Vivakhala. Written by the writer of legal documents Jā[saṭa ?]

Signature of the illustrious Yagākara.

II. Grant of Vidagdha-deva.

The plate of Vidagdha measures 17 inches in width by 13 inches in height and contains 30 lines, of which two are written vertically in the proper right margin. On the cuneiform handle to the right side of the plate there are moreover three short vertical lines containing the donor's subscription. The average size of the letters is ¼". The plate is well preserved except for a small piece missing in the lower proper right corner, by which one *akṣara* has been partly lost. Through the central portion of lines 13-15 there runs a rent, which however has caused no damage to the inscription. The plate is now in possession of a Brāhman, Jyotiya by name, who lives at Suṅgal, and is one of the numerous descendants of the original grantee.

TEXT II.

1. Oṁ svastiḥ ‖ Śrī-Caṇpakā-vāsakāt=paramabhaṭṭāraka-mahārājādhirāja-parameśvara-śrīmad-Yugākaravarma-deva-pādānudhyāta [ḥ*] parama-bra-

2. hmaṇyo nikhila-sacchāsan-ābhipravṛtta-guru-vṛtta-devat-ānuvṛtta-samadhigata-śāstra-kuśalatayā samārādhita-vidvaj-jana-

[1] *Cf.* Bühler-Stein. *Epigr. Ind.*, II, p. 483.

[2] *Cf.* Fleet, *loc. cit.*, page 157 n. I and *Rājat.* (transl. Stein), Vol. II, p. 316 n. at VIII, 601.

[3] The word *prativāsin* means "neighbour," but possibly indicates the people living on the granted land. *Cf. sa-prativāsi-jana-sameta.* Fleet, *loc. cit.*, p. 289, l. 10. and beneath II, 21, *bhuñjamānasya prativāsi-janapadaiḥ.*

[4] *Cf.* Fleet, *loc. cit.*, page 99, n. 2.—In Chambā rent-free land is now-a-days called *śāsan*.

[5] I translate according to the proposed emendation.

3. hṛdayo nay-ānugata-pauruṣa-prayog-āvāpta-trivarga-siddhiḥ saṁ(m)yag-arjit-ābhikāmika-guṇa-sahitatayā phalita iva

4. mārga-taru[ḥ*] / sarva-satv-āśrayanī(ṇī)yo Moṣanāmnāya (Moṣaṇ-ānvaya)-Āditya-vaṅś-odbhava-parama-māheśvaro (raḥ)Śrī-Bhogamatī-devyā samutpanna[ḥ]pa-

5. rama-bhaṭṭāraka-mahārājādhirāja-parameśvara-śrīmad-Vidagdhadevaḥ-kuśalī / sva-śāsyamāna-gavdikaharaṇa-saṁbaddha-Tāva-

6. saka-maṇḍala-pratibaddha-Sumaṅgala-grāme samupāgatā[ṁ*] sarvān=eva rāja-rājānaka-rājaputra-rājāmātya-rājasthānīya-

7. pramātṛ-sarobhaṁga-kumārāmāty-oparika-viṣayapati-nihelapati-kṣatrapa-prāntapāla-hastyaśvoṣṭra balavyāvṛ(pṛ)taka-dūta-ga-

8. māgamik-ābhitvaramāṇa-Khaṣa(śa)-Kulika-śaulkika-gaulmika-khaṇḍarakṣa-tarapatika-chatracchāyika-veṭakila-vīrayātrika-

9. cauroddharaṇika-daṇḍika-daṇḍavāsika-bhogapati-viniyuktaka-bhāgika-bhogika-cāṭa-bhaṭa-sevakādīṁ sarvān=eva kīrtitā-

10. kīrtitā[ṁ*] rājapāda-prasād-opajīvino (naḥ) kuṭumbi-janapadā[ṁ*]ś=ca brāhmaṇottarā[ṁ] sāṣṭādaśa-prakṛtyādhiṣv(ṣṭh)ānīyo(yāṁ) Med-Āndraka-

11. dhīvara-Caṇḍāla-paryantā[ṁ*] sarva=savāsāṁ samājñāpayaty=astu vas=saṁviditaṁ yath-opari-likhita-Sumaṅgala-grāme Serī nā-

12. ma bhūr=ekā yasyām-āghāṭāny-amī bhavanti / Pūrva-digbhāge Pāṭalīyāgrahārika-bhū-sīmā dakṣiṇa-digbhāge bṛhavīḍā-nāma-

13. sīmā paścima-digbhāge Khanibagga-vīḍā-sīmā uttara-digbhāge Prāhabagga-nāma-sīmā evaṁ catur-āghāṭ-opetā upari-sthita-gṛ-

14. ha-śākavāṭikā-sametā bhūr=ekā [॥*] tathā nyā sminn-eva grāme Lavāla nām ārdha-bhūmī / yasyām=āghāṭāni bhavanti । Pūrva-digbhāge khaḍḍā । da-

15. kṣiṇa-digbhāge bṛhat-pāṣāṇaṁ paścima-digbhāge Majvalikā (?) nāma kuppaṭo(ṭa) uttara-digbhāge gocara-Puṣkarī-patha-sīmā [॥*] evaṁ catur-āghāṭa(ṭo)-

16. petam bhūmy-ardhaṁ uparilikhita-bhūmyā saha sārdhā bhū sva-sīmā-tṛṇa-goyuthī (gavyūti)-gocara-paryantā savā(va)naspaty-udaka-sīhāra-kullaka-pāṇī(nī)ya-

17. sametā sāgama-nirgama-praveśā sa-khilapolācya (?) sadaśāparādhā putra-pautrādy-anvay-opabhogyā anācchedyā aparipanthyā a-cāṭa-bha-

18. ṭa-praveśā akiṁcitkarā anāhārā ā-candr-ārk-ārṇava-kṣiti-sthiti-samakālīnā mayā mātā-pitror=ātmanaś=ca puṇya-hetave yaśo-bhivṛ-

19. ddhaye / paraloka-saṁśreyorthaṁ saṅ(ṁ)sār-ārṇava-tāraṇārthaṁ ca / Kurukṣetra-tīrth-āśrama-vinirgata-Brāhmaṇa-Devanna-pautrāya Dedduka-putrāya Śrī-Nandukā-

20. ya Kāśyapa-gotrāya Brahmacāriṇe tri-pravarāya Vāji(ja)se(sa)neyāya puṇye hany=uttarāyaṇa-saṅkrāntyām=udaka-pūrvaka-pratigraheṇā grahāratve-

21. na pratipāditaṁ / Viditvā smadīyāgrahāra-śāsanaprāmāṇyā[d*] yatheṣṭaṁ bhuṁjatu (bhuṅktām) bhuṁjāpayatu (bhojayatu) bhuṁjamānasya prativāsi-janapadaiḥ ā-

22. ñā-śravaṇa-vidheyair=bhūtvā yathā-samucita-bhāga-bhoga-kara-hiraṇy-ādi sarva-rāja-bhāvya-pratyāyam=asy opadeyaṁ / asya cāsmadīya-cā-

23. ṭa-bhaṭ-ānyatar-ādinā gṛh-āvataraṇa-harita-pakva-sasy-ekṣu-cāraṅa-lavaṇ(n)-apamardana-rocika (?)-ciṭolā (?)-grahaṇa-gokṣīra-grahaṇa-pīṭhaka-pīṭhi-

II.—Chamba Plate of Vidagdhadeva.

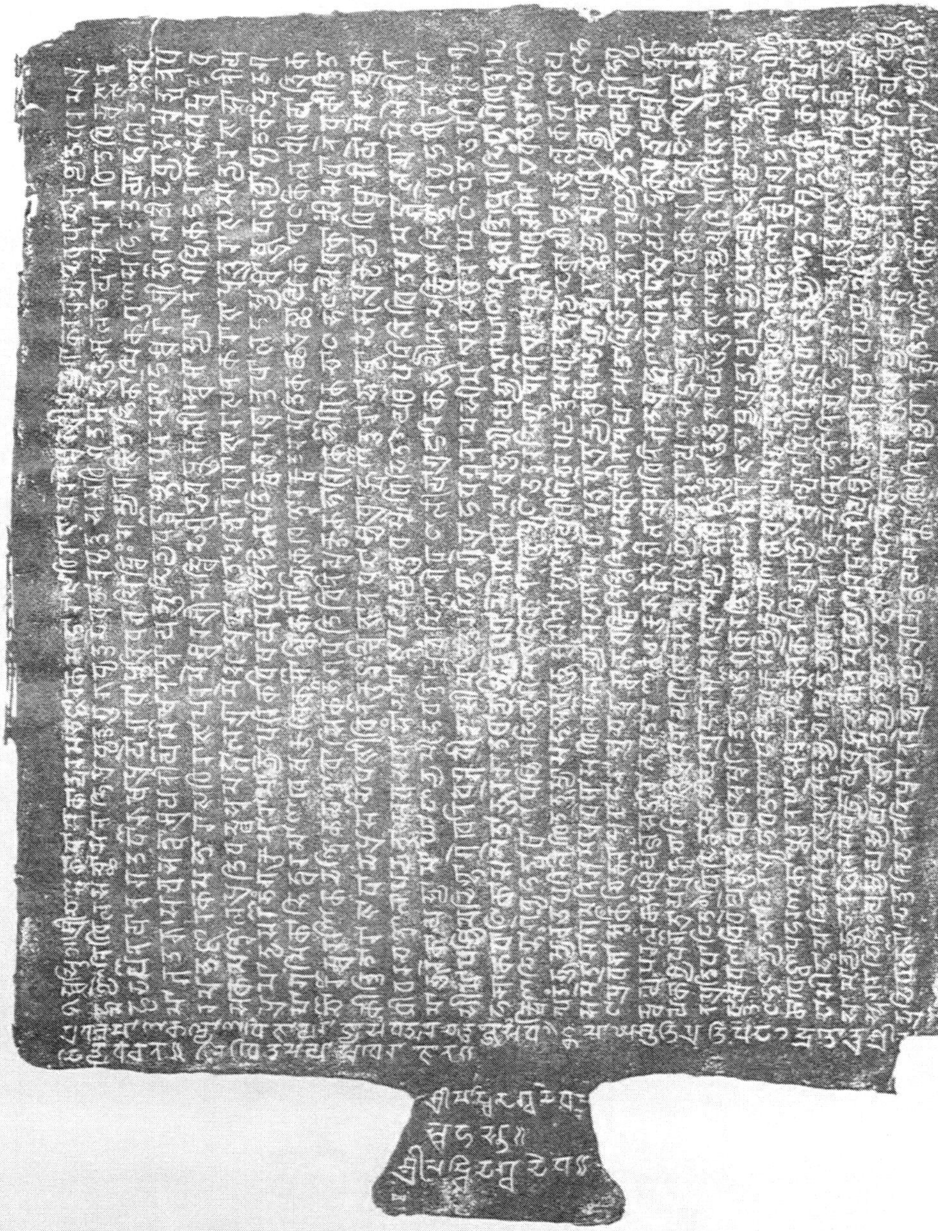

SCALE ONE-HALF.

From an Ink-impression supplied by Dr. Vogel.

E. HULTZSCH.

WIELE & KLEIN, PHOTO-ZINCO

24. kā-khaṭv-āpaharaṇa-kāṣṭh-endhana-ghāsa-bus-ādikaṁ na kena cit pragrāhyaṁ I svalpam=api piḍ-opadravaṁ na kartavyaṁ / etad=āśṛ(śri)ta-hālika-gopāla-

25. dāsī-dās-ādi-samasta-jana-sametasya ca / Ato nyathā śāsan-ātikrame dharma-hāni-nigraho(haḥ) syāt / Āgantu-rājabhir=asmad-vaṅśe-jaiś=ca

26. sāmānyaṁ bhū-dāna-phalam=avekṣyā yaṁ brahma-dāyo numantavyaḥ pariṣā(pā)lanīyaś=ca / Uktaṁ bhagavatā Veda-vyāsena / Bahubhir[1] vasudhā bhuktā rājabhi-

27. s-Sagar-ādibhiḥ yasya yasya yadā bhūmi[s*] tasya tasya tadā phalaṁ I Suvarṇam[1] - eka[ṁ*] gaur (gām)-ekāṁ bhūmi(me)r=apy=ekam=aṅgulaṁ haren (ran)-narakam-āpnoti yāvaś-ca-

28. ndra-divākarau I Dattāni[2] dānāni purā narendrair-yāṇ(n)y-atra dharm-ārtha-yaśas-karāṇi I nirmālya-van(t)-tat-pratimāṇi(ni)tāni ko ṇ(n)āma sādhuḥ-punar-ādadhītaḥ (ādadīta) (II*)

29. Pravardhamāṇa(na)-kalyāṇa-vijaya-rājya-saṁvatsare caturthe saṁvat 4 Māgha-śu. ti. pratipad I [II*] Dūto tra Śrī Ā-

30 dityavardhana[ḥ*]II Likhita[ṁ] mayā SukharājenaII

Śrīmad-Vidagdha-deva-svahasta [ḥ*]II Śrīmad-Vidagdha-deva [ḥ*] II

Translation.

Oṁ. Hail! From [his] residence at the glorious Caṇpakā, he, who reverentially remembers the *paramabhaṭṭāraka*, *mahārājādhirāja*, *parameśvara*, the illustrious Yugākaravarma-deva; he, who having attained expertness in the Law, by his obedience to the deities and by his deportment towards the spiritual preceptors, engaged in all good teaching, has propitiated the hearts of the learned; who by the practice of bravery combined with policy has acquired success in the three aims of life (*dharma*, *artha*, *kāma*), who by his complete attainment of desirable qualities resembles a fruit-bearing tree on the road-side; he the refuge of all beings, sprung from the house of Moṣaṇa and from the Solar race, born from the *paramamaheśvarī*, the illustrious Bhogamatī-devī, the *paramabhaṭṭāraka*, *mahārājādhirāja*, *parameśvara*, the illustrious Vidagdhadeva, the prosperous one,

(L. 5.) orders all who are concerned with[3] the village of Sumaṅgala belonging to the Tāvasaka district of his domain,[4] every rājā, rāṇā, rājpūt, royal minister, Chief-Justice, *pramātar*,[5] *sarobhaṅga*, counsellor of the prince,[6] *uparika*,[7] *viṣayapati*,[8] *nihelapati*,[9] *kṣatrapa*,[10] frontier-guard, those occupied with elephants, horses, camels, and the forces, every *dūta*, *gamāgamika*,

---

[1] Metre, Śloka (Anuṣṭubh).

[2] Metre, Indravajrā. The same verse modified. Fleet, *Corpus Inscr. Ind.*, Vol. III, p. 180.

[3] Literal meaning "arrived at."

[4] The strange term *gavdikaharaṇa* seems to be a synonym of *ch(kṣ)atrābhoga*, found in corresponding places (*cf.* beneath IV. 15 and V. 11).

[5] *Pramātar* (a measurer, taxator?) perhaps a synonym of *sīmakarmakara* "a maker of boundaries." *Cf.* Fleet, *Corpus Inscr. Ind.*, III, 217. The word is also found Bühler, *Epig. Ind.*, I, 118.

[6] *Cf.* Fleet, *Corpus Inscr. Ind.*, III, 16 n.

[7] *Ibidem passim.*

[8] *Ibidem*, 32, 69 n, 71.

[9] *Ibidem*, 291.

[10] *Kṣatrapa* probably stands for *kṣetrapa*.

abhitvaramāna,[1] Khaśa, Kulika, collector, inspector of police,[2] *khaṇḍa-rakṣa*, bridge-guard (?), umbrella-bearer,[3] betel-carrier,[4] those belonging to the expeditionary force (?), thief-catcher, jailor, executioner, *bhogapati*, *viniyuktaka*, land-owners, land-holders, district-officers[5] and their subordinates and servants,—all, whether named or unnamed, who subsist on the favour of His Highness, the Rājā, householders and country-people from the highest Brāhmans, who hold a prominent position among the eighteen elements of the State, down to the Medas, Andrakas, fishers, and Caṇḍālas, all inhabitants.

(L. 11). Be it known unto you, that in the above-said village of Sumaṅgala [there is] one *bhū* of land, Serī by name, of which the boundaries are these:—on the east-side the limit of the rent-free land (*agrahāra*) of [the village of] Pāṭala, on the south-side the limit known as the great slope,[6] on the west side the limit of the slope of the Khanibagga [field[7]], on the north-side the limit known as Prāhabagga. One *bhū* of land, thus bounded, together with the houses and kitchen-gardens[8] standing on it. Further, in that same village [there is] another half *bhū* of land, Lavāla by name, on the east-side the precipice,[9] on the south-side the large rock, on the west-side the rivulet (?) Majvalikā (?) by name, on the north-side the limit of the path to the pasture-ground Puṣkarī. Half a *bhū* of land, thus bounded, together with the above-described *bhū* makes one and a half *bhū* as far as its limits, grass, grazing and pasture-ground, together with fruit-trees and with the water of water-courses and channels,[10] with ingress and egress, with fallow lands large and small,[11] with [the fines for] the ten offences,[12] to be enjoyed by the succession of sons, sons' sons, and so on, uncurtailable, unopposed, [with the privilege that it is] not to be entered by district officers or their servants, free from tax, inalienable, for as long a time as the moon, the sun, the ocean and the earth shall endure, for the sake of the spiritual merit and for the increase of the glory of my parents and myself, for the sake of the bliss of the next world, and in order to cross the ocean of existence, have I granted by a formal libation of water,

(L. 19.) as an *agrahāra*, after his return[13] from the hermitage of holy *Kurukṣetra*, to the grandson of the brāhmaṇa Devanna, the son of Dedduka, the illustrious Nanduka the Brahman student of the house of Kāśyapa, the descendant of three pro-

---

[1] *Cf. Rājat.* (transl. Stein), Index. i. v. *Khaśa.*

[2] *Gaulmika* is a *vṛddhi* derivation of *gulmā*, to be taken in the sense of "patroll." *Cf.*, however, Fleet, *loc. cit.*, 5 n.

[3] *Chattracchāyika*, lit. "umbrella-shadower," must be synonymous with *chattradhāra.*

[4] *Ve(ai ?)ṭakila* from *viṭikā* "a preparation of the Areca nut enveloped in a leaf of the betel plant."

[5] *Cf.* above p. 247.

[6] *Viḍā* is sanskritised *biṛ*=a slope between terraced fields.

[7] *Bagga* sanskritised *bag*=field.

[8] The word *śākavāṭā* is preserved in the Chambyālī dialect in the form *śagvāṛ*, *śugāṛ*.

[9] *Khaḍḍā* another sanskritised *bhāṣā* word *nl. khaḍ.*

[10] *Sīhāra* seems to stand for Skr. *sīrā*=a stream; *kullaka* I take to be the vernacular *kuhl(a)*, *kulla*=a canal, from Skr. *kulyā.*

[11] In corresponding places we find *sakhilopakhila.* *Cf.* III, 21; IV, 20, and V, 13.

[12] *Cf.* Fleet, *Corpus Inscr. Ind.*, III, 189, n. 4.

[13] The meaning of *vinirgata* is really "departed from." It is probable that the purport of the grantee's visit to Kurukṣetra was the performance of the *śrāddha* in behalf of his employer. In later plates we often find stated that the grant was given by the Rājā to his *purohita* on a similar occasion.

minent sages (*ṛṣi*) and adherent of the school of the Vājasaneyas, on the auspicious day of the hibernal solstice.

(L. 21.) Having understood this, he should freely enjoy and make [others] to enjoy [this grant] on the authority of our charter. The subjects, resident in the enjoyed land, in obedience to our command, will have to deliver to him the regular share and use,[1] tax in kind and gold and every other tribute due to the king. And of our district officers and their subordinates and others, no one will be allowed to enter (?) his house, to cut,[2] or crush his corn, sugar-cane or pasture (?), whether green or ripe, nor to take *rocika* or *ciṭolā*[3] or cows'-milk, nor to carry off stools, benches or couches, nor to seize his wood, fuel, grass, chaff and so on. Not even the slightest oppression or vexation should be inflicted [on him], nor on his ploughmen, cowherds, servants, maid-servants, and all other people that are dependent on him. Otherwise in case of infringement of [this] order [the culprits] will be punished for breaking the law. Also the future kings, born from our race, considering the common merit of bestowing land, should recognise and preserve this brahmanical property.

(L. 26). It has been said by the venerable arranger of the Vedas: "Many kings from Sagara onwards have enjoyed the land. Whose is the ground, his is the fruit. Whosoever will take away one gold-piece, one cow or one inch of land, he will remain in hell for as long as moon and sun shall endure. Those gifts, which have been given by previous princes, causing here [in this world] spiritual and material gain and glory, and respected like the remnants of a sacrifice, what pious man, indeed, would take them back."

(L. 29.) In the fourth year of the increasing, fortunate reign of victory, anno 4, [the month] Māgha, the bright fortnight, the lunar day 1 (*pratipad*). The messenger on this occasion was the illustrious Ādityavardhana. Written by me, Sukharāja.

Signature of the illustrious Vidagdhadeva. The illustrious Vidagdhadeva.

III. Grant of Somavarma-deva.

This copper-plate is $14\frac{3}{4}''$ wide and $10\frac{3}{4}''$ high, and consists of 24 horizontal lines. In the proper right margin the subscription of the donor and two short lines containing the names of the officials concerned are written vertically. Over these the signature of the previous Rājā Sālavāhana, the father of Somavarman, can still be traced, partly running through the initial *akṣaras* of lines 5-17. The plate is in a fair state of preservation, except along the proper right margin. Both right corners are broken. In the upper corner the symbol *oṁ*, the initial *akṣaras* of the first two lines and the initial *akṣara* of the subscription are missing. In the lower corner four *akṣaras* of line 22, probably two of line 23 and one of line 24 have been lost, besides the lower portion of the two short vertical lines in the margin. Along the lower edge of the plate some rents are visible, one of which has been clamped. The average size of the letters is $\frac{3}{16}$ to $\frac{1}{4}''$.

---

[1] For *bhāga cf.* Fleet, *Corpus Inscr. Ind.*, III, p. 248; for *bhoga*, *ibidem*, p. 112. n.

[2] I translate according to the proposed emendation *lavana* instead of *lavaṇa*.

[3] These two terms are not found in any *kośa* and are presumably *bhāṣā* words; *ciṭolā* may perhaps be connected with Pañjābī *civoli*=Buchanania Latrifolia. *Cf.* Saligram, *Nighaṇṭubhūṣaṇam* (Bombay, Saṁvat 1953), Vol. VII, p. 589.

TEXT III.

1. [Oṁ sva]stiḥ ‖ Oṁ namaś=Śivāya‖Jayati[1] bhuvana-kāraṇaṁ Svayaṁbhūr=jayati Purandara-nandano Murāriḥ [।*] jayati Girisutā-niruddha-deho
2. [du]rita-bhay-āpaharo Haraś=ca devaḥ ‖ Śrī-Caṇpakā-vāsakāt=parama-brahmaṇyo lalāṭa-taṭa-ghaṭita-vikaṭa-bhrūkuṭī-praka-
3. ṭa-kuṭ[ṭ*]ita-kaṭaka-Saumaṭika-kṛta-sānāthya-Durgar-eśvara-samīra-sandhukṣita-Kīra-bala-balavad-dav-āśuśukṣaṇi-kṣaṇa-kṣapaṇa-
4. nava-jaladharasya । daṇḍ-opanata-Trigart-ādhip-ānunaya-prārthita-sandhānasya । sevā-vidhi-vyagra-svakulya-Kulūt-eśvara-karma-vyatihā-
5. ra-prārthyamāna-rājy-ārpaṇa-prasādasya । Kurukṣa(e)tre Rāhūparāga-samaya-samarthi(rpi)ta-mada-gandha-lubdha-madhukara-kul-ākula-kapola-pha-
6. laka-kari-ghaṭā-dāna-prīti-prasanna-mānasa-bhagavad-Bhāskar-ābhinandita-nij-ānvaya-prasūti-paramparā-sāra-Kari-varṣ-ābhidhān-ābhyu-
7. dayasya । tat-kāla-milita-nikhila-mahīpāla-mukha-maś(ṣ)ī-kūrcikā-[*kīrti[2]] surabhita-sapta-bhuvan-ābhogasya । niratiśaya-śaury-audārya-dhai-
8. ry-āgādha-gāmbhīrya-maryādā-dayā-dākṣiṇya-vailakṣaṇya-jarjarita-Jāmadagnya-Śivi-Karṇa-Yudhiṣṭhir-ādi-pravara-prasiddheḥ darśana-saphali-
9. ta-loka-locana-manorama-mūrti(e)r=bhagavac-Chrī-Śūdraka-svāmi-deva-prakhyāpyamān-ānanya-sāmānya-sphāra-sphurad-ura(u)-mahimnaḥ samara-sa-
10. hasra-saṁvidhāna-kāryita-(*read* saṁnidhāna-kop-ārjita [3])-Sāhasāṅka-Niśśaṅkamalla-Maṭamaṭatsiṅgh(siṁh)-ādy-apara-paryāyasya । Pauṣaṇa(ṣṇa)-vai(vaṁ)śa-bhūṣaṇa-mahāmaṇeḥ
11. Śrīmat-Sāhilladevasya ‖ nirmale kule tilaka-bhūtaḥ niravadya-vidyā-vinoda-rasa-rasikaḥ aśeṣa-śāstra-parimal-ādhi [*vāsita*]-
12. mānasaḥ(sa) agaṇita-vimala-guṇa-gaṇ-ālaṁkṛta-mūrtiḥ(tir) vivek-aika-vasatiḥ deva-dvija-guru-pūjā-nirata-matir=atiśaya(yi)-
13. ta-śauṭīrya-śāli-spṛhaṇīya-vikramaḥ krama-paripāpālita(paripālita)-cātu[r*]-varṇ[y*]a-vyavasthaḥ(stho) durvāra-vairi-bala-vipula-darpa-dalana-vya-
14. gr-ogra-karavāla-valga-dakṣiṇa-dor-daṇḍaḥ pracaṇḍa-pratāp-otkhāta-pratinā-(sthā)pit-āneka-naranātha-prathita-prauḍha-prabhu-śaktiḥ(ktir)
15. vāṁchita-vastu-vistara-paripūrita-sakala-praṇiji(praṇayi)-jana-manorathaḥ śaśadhara-kara-nikar-āvadāta-yaśa[ḥ*]-prasara-prakāśita-
16. sarv-āśaḥ sakala-kalā-keli-peśala-vilāsaḥ(sa) । udayaśe(ai)lo mitra-maṇḍalasya un(t)pāta-ketu-rahita-janasya । asādhā-
17. raṇa-śaury-ājita-yaśo-rāśi-prakāśit-āśeś(ṣ)a-viśva-pradeśaḥ Pauṣaṇ(ṣṇ)-ānm(ānv)ay-o[d*]bhavat-pitṛ-mātṛ-bhakti-vinirjita-Rāma-carita[ḥ*]
18. parama-māheśvaraḥ parama-vaiṣṇavaḥ paramabhaṭṭāraka-mahārājādhirāja-parameśvara-śrīmat-Sālavāhana-deva-pād-ānudhyāta-pa-
19. ramabhaṭṭārikā-mahārājñī-Śrī-Rarḍhādevī-kukṣi-kṣīranīranidhi-sudhādīdhiti-paramabhaṭṭāraka-mahārājādhirāja-parameśvara-śrī-
20. mat-Somavarma-devaḥ-kuśalī sva-s(ś)āsyamāna-Trighaṭṭaka-maṇḍala-pratibaddha । Kulikagoṣṭhe Raṅguka-suta-Raṇāditya-satka etat-putra-Udma-

---

[1] Metre, Puṣpitāgrā.

[2] *Cf.* beneath IV, 7.

[3] *Cf.* beneath IV, 9.

[4] *Cf.* beneath IV, 11.

21. [sth]it-āsī[d*] bhūr=ek=āṅkataḥ Raṅguka-suta-saṅ(t)ka bhū । evaṁ sva-sīmā-tri(tṛ)ṇa-goyūthī (gavyūti)-gocara-paryantaṁ sa-khil-opakhilaṁ sa-vanaspa-

22. [ty-udakaṁ sa] nirgama-praveśaṁ । ārāma-viśrāma-sahitam=ā-candr-ārkaṁ । brā । Kāś[y*]apa-gotrāgā(?)ya । tri-pravarāya । Vājisneya (*i.e.*, Vājasaneya)-śākhāya ।

23. [- - - -pau]trāya । Brahmaputrāya । Bhaṭṭarahaśāya । sūrya-grahaṇa-nimitte agrahāratveti (tvena) pratipāditaṁ ita ūrdh[v*]am=ā-candr-ārkaṁ putra-pau-

24 [tra]yo[r*] bhoktavyaṁ । Pravardhamāna-kalyāṇa-vijaya-rājye saṁvat 7 Bhā [kṛ] ti-3 [o*] Dūto tra mahāmātya-rājānaka-Śrī-Rīhilaḥ mahākṣapaṭalika-

25. rājānaka-Śrī-Kāhilaḥ ā - - - -

26. Lhuthukaḥ [॥*] Likhitaṁ kā. De[vapena? [1]]
[Śrī]mat-Somavarma-deva-svahastaḥ ॥ (*Original subscription:*) [Śrī]mat-Sālavāhana-deva-svahastaḥ.

Translation.

Oṁ. Hail! Oṁ. Reverence to Śiva. Victorious is the cause of the world, the Self-existent (Brahmā). Victorious is the son of the Destroyer of Castles (Śiva), the Enemy of Mura (Kṛṣṇa). Victorious is He, whose body is held by the Mountain-daughter (Durgā), He who removes distress and danger: Hara, the god.

(L. 2) From his residence at the glorious Caṇpakā, the highly devout [king Somavarman], who is an ornament of the spotless house of Sāhilladeva; who (Sāhilla) was a fresh rain-cloud to extinguish in a moment the mighty blazing fire of the Kīra forces, fanned, as by the wind, by the Lord of Durgara, assisted by the Saumaṭikas, whose camp was manifestly crushed by the fearful frown produced on the slope of his (Sāhilla's) forehead; whose (Sāhilla's) alliance was humbly sought by the ruler of Trigarta, subdued by force; who (Sāhilla) was asked the favour of bestowing royalty in return for services by his kinsman, the Lord of Kulūta anxious to render him homage; who (Sāhilla) had the fortunate name of Karivarṣa (elephant-rain) on account of the continuous and stable generation of his posterity joyfully granted by the Lord Bhāskara (the Sun-god), whose mind was contented with gladness by the gift of a multitude of elephants, whose flat cheeks were covered by a swarm of bees attracted by the scent of the rut-secretion and which were bestowed[2] in Kurukṣetra at the time of an eclipse; who (Sāhilla) has made the circuit of the seven worlds fragrant by his fame, [painted] with[2] the ink-brushes which were the mouths of all the princes assembled on that occasion; who (Sāhilla) by his unequalled kindness and compassion combined with unsurpassed bravery, generosity, firmness and unfathomable profoundness has impaired the fame of heroes like the son of Jamadagni (Paraśurāma), Śivi, Karṇa and Yudhiṣṭhira; by looking upon whose (Sāhilla's) lovely presence the eyes of the world have been made fruitful; whose (Sāhilla's) wide-spread greatness brilliant with matchless effulgence was renowned like that of Śūdrakasvāmi-deva; who (Sāhilla) by his fury in setting in array a thousand battles had acquired such names as Sāhasāṅka (marked by rashness) Niśśaṅkamalla (the dauntless wrestler) and Maṭaṁaṭatsiṁha (the roaring? lion).

[1] *Cf.* beneath V, 21.
[2] I translate according to the above proposed emendation.

(L. 11) [king Somavarman] who delights in passing his time in attaining faultless knowledge, whose mind is perfumed by the fragrance of every science, whose form is adorned with numbers of innumerable spotless qualities, he the only abode of discrimination, whose heart takes delight in the worship of deities, the twice-born and spiritual preceptors, who possesses enviable courage full of excessive manliness, who in their proper order maintains the status of the four castes, whose strong arm is dexterous in brandishing the fierce sword intent on crushing the great pride of the host of the irresistible foe, who (Somavarman) by his excessive majesty has uprooted and re-established[1] the mighty and wide-spread royal power of several princes, who has completely fulfilled the wishes of all his favoured ones by profusely granting to them their desired objects, who by the effulgence of his glory, bright like the multitudinous beams of the Hare-holder (the Moon), has illumined all regions, who takes an exquisite delight in every art and sport, he the eastern mountain from which the orb of the sun (*alias*, the circle of his friends) rises, by which the people are freed from the comet of calamity, he who has illumined all the quarters of the universe by his fame acquired by extraordinary heroism, who by his devotion to his parents, born from the Solar race, has outvied the piety of Rāma, he, the supreme worshipper of Maheśvara (Śiva) and Viṣṇu, he who reverentially remembers the *paramabhaṭṭāraka, mahārājādhirāja, parameśvara*, the illustrious Sālavāhana, and was born from the womb of the *paramabhaṭṭārikā mahārājñī*, the illustrious Rarḍhādevī, as the Moon was born from the Milk-ocean, he the *paramabhāṭṭāraka, mahārājādhirāja, parameśvara*, the illustrious Somavarmadeva, the prosperous one,

(L. 20) has granted one *bhū* in Kulikagoṣṭha, which belongs to the Trighaṭṭaka district of his domains and was occupied[2] by Raṅguka's son Raṇāditya and belonged to the latter's son Udma, in figures 1 *bhū* occupied by Raṅguka's son, as far as its limits, grass, grazing, and pasture-ground, with fallow-land, large and small, with fruit-trees and water, with ingress and egress, together with gardens and resting-places, for as long as the moon, and the sun [shall endure], to the Brā[hmaṇa] of the house of Kāśyapa, the descendant of three prominent sages (*ṛṣi*) and adherent of the school of the Vājasaneyas. the grandson of - - -, the son of Brahma, Bhaṭṭarahaśa, on occasion of a solar eclipse, as an *agrahāra*. To be enjoyed henceforward for as long as the moon and the sun [shall endure] by son and son's son.

(L. 24) In the increasing, fortunate reign of victory, anno 7 ; Bhā[drapada], the dark fortnight, the lunar day 3[o]. The messenger on this occasion was the Great-Councillor the illustrious Rānā Rihila, the Great-Recordkeeper the illustrious Rānā Kāhila . . . . . . Lhuthuka. Written by the Kā[yastha] De[vapa ?]

Signature of the illustrious Somavarma-deva. (*Original subscription* :) Signature of the illustrious Sālavāhanavarma-deva.

IV. Grant of Somavarma-deva and Āsaṭa-deva.

This inscription, as stated above, has been discussed by Prof. Kielhorn. In re-

[1] I translate according to the above proposed emendation.

[2] The word *satka* (also above I, 7 and 8) I presume to be an equivalent of Prākṛt *santaka* (Fleet, *Corpus Inscr. Ind.* III, 118, n. 2); *santaka* is evidently derived from Skr. *sant-* the pres. part. of *asmi*, whereas *satka* is derived from *sat* the weak form of the same participle. In l. 21 and also beneath IV, 17 and 18 *sthita* is used in exactly the same meaning.

editing it with a facsimile and a translation, I wish to acknowledge the great benefit derived from the previous work by so great an authority on Indian Epigraphy. My transcript—it will be seen—differs but slightly from that of Prof. Kielhorn, which was prepared from a rubbing. In my translation I have adopted the rendering of certain passages, as given by my predecessor in the course of his paper. The only point, in which my conclusions venture to differ from those of the distinguished scholar, is the topography, in elucidating which I had the enormous advantage of an investigation *in loco.*

Plate IV measures 18 inches in width and 12 inches in height. It contains 32 lines, of which 1-28 are written horizontally over the whole breadth of the plate, recording the original grant by Somavarman, whose signature is engraved vertically in the centre of the proper right margin. The addition by his successor Āsaṭa commences from the end of l. 28 and is continued along the lower, proper left and top margins, ending in the proper right margin near the first *akṣara* of Somavarman's subscription. After his name the signature of Āsaṭa is engraved.

The plate is well preserved, except for a rent running from the proper left edge over and partly through the last eight *akṣaras* of l. 12. A piece of the upper proper left corner is broken, by which about five *akṣaras* of the end of l. 30 and about three *akṣaras* of the beginning of l. 31 have been lost. In the upper, proper right margin two *akṣaras* are slightly injured, but still legible. The size of the letters is from $\frac{3}{16}$ to $\frac{1}{4}$". It would seem that originally there was a handle to the proper right, to which perhaps a seal was attached.

The plate is in possession of the temples of Hari Rāī and Campāvatī, but the lands, for which it is supposed to be the title-deed, are not those described in the grant. Moreover it appears, that the original grantees were the temples of Hari and Śiva. Of Campāvatī no mention is made in the inscription.

TEXT IV.

1. Oṁ namaś=Śivāya ı (ıı) Jayati[1] bhuvana-kāraṇa[ṁ] Svayambhūr=jayati Purandara-nandano Murāriḥ [ı*] jayati Girisutā-niruddha-deho durita-bhay-āpaharo Hara-

2. ś=ca devaḥ ıı Jayati[2] janam=aniṣṭād=uddharantī Bhavānī jayati nija-vibhūti-vyāpta-viśvaḥ=Purāriḥ [ı*] jayati ca Gajavaktras=so=tra yasya prasādād=uparamati

3. samasto vighna-varg-opasargaḥ ıı Śrī–Caṇpakā-vāsakāt=parama-brahmaṇyo lalāṭa-taṭa-ghaṭita-vikaṭa-bhrūkuṭī-prakaṭa-kuṭṭita-kaṭaka - Saumaṭika-kṛta - sānāthya-Durga-

4. reśvara-samīra-sandhukṣita-Kīra-bala-balavad-dav-āśuśukṣani-kṣaṇa-kṣapaṇa-nna(na)va-jaladharasya ı daṇḍ-opanata-Trigart-ādhip-ānunaya-prārthita-sandhānasya ı sevā-vidhi-vyagra-

5. svakulya - Kulūt - esva(śva)ra - karma - vyatihāra - prārthyamāna - rājy-ātp(rp)aṇa-prasādasya ı samara-bhara-bhagn-ārugṅāruṣka-Turuṣka-vipula-bala-viśāla-s(ś)ākhinaḥ Kurukṣetre Rāh-ūparā–

[1] Metre, Puṣpitāgrā.

[2] Metre, Mālinī.

6. ga-samaya-samarthi(rpi?)ta-mada-gandha-lubdha-madhukara-kul-ākula-kapola-phalaka-kari-ghaṭā-dāna[1]-prīti-prasanna-mānasa-bhagavad-Bhāskar-ābhinandita-nij-ānvaya-prasūti-

7. paramparā-sāra-Karivarṣ-ābhidhān-ābhyudayasya tatkāla-milita-nikhila-mahī-pāla-mukha-maś(ṣ)ī-kūrcikā-kīrti-surabhita-sapta-bhuvan-ābhogasya niratiśa-

8. ya-śaury-audāry-āgādha-gāmbhīrya-maryādā-dayā-dākṣiṇya-vailakṣaṇya-jar-jarita-Jāmadagnya-Śivi-Karṇa-Yudhiṣṭhir-ādi-pravara-prasiddheḥ darśana-saphalita-lo-

9. ka-locana-manorama-mūrti-bhagavac-Chrī-Śūdrakasvāmi-deva-prakhyāpya-mān-ānanya-sāmānya-sphāra-sphurad-uru-mahimnaḥ samara-sahasra-saṁvidhāna-kop-ārjita-

10. Sāhasāṅka-Niśśaṅkamalla-Maṭamaṭa[t]siṁgh(siṁh)-ādy-āpara-paryāyasya। Pauṣaṇa(ṣṇa)-veṁ(vaṁ)śa-bhūṣaṇa-mahāmaṇeḥ śrīmat-Sāhilladevasya। nirmale kule tila-

11. ka-bhūtaḥ niravadya-vidyā-vinoda-rasa-rasikaḥ as(ś)eṣa-s(ś)āstr-ārtha-pari-mal-ādhivāsita-mānasaḥ vivek-aika-saro-rājahaṁsaḥ agaṇita-vimala-guṇa-gaṇ-alaṅ-kṛ-

12. ta-mūrtiḥ tribhuvana-bhavana-vi[c*]churita-kīrtiḥ parama-bhaṭṭāraka-mahā-rājādhirāja-parameśvara-śrīmat-Sālavāhana-deva-pād-ānudhyātaḥ paramabhaṭṭārikā-mahārājñī Śrī-Rarḍhā-

13. devī-kukṣi-kṣīranīranidhi-sudhādīdhitiḥ paramabhaṭṭāraka-mahārājādhirāja-parameśvara-śrīmat-Somavarma-devaḥ=kuśalī। sarvān=eva niyogasthān rāja-rājā-naka-rājā-

14. mātya-rājā(ja)putra-parikara-sanniyuktaka-viniyuktaka-dūta-gamāgamika-bhitvaramānya[2]-Khaśa-Kulika-śaulkika-gaulmika-khaḍgarakṣa-tarapati-vīrayātrika-cauro-

15. ddharaṇika-daṇḍika-daṇḍavāsika-brāhmaṇa-kṣatriya-viṭ-chūdr-ādi-sāṣṭādaśa-prakṛtīḥ=prativāsi-janapadāṁś=ca samājñāpayaty=astu vas=saṁviditaṁ yathā sva-śāsyamāna-ṣa(kṣa?)trā-

16. bhoge Pānthila-maṇḍala-pratibaddha-mahārājñī-Śrī-Rarḍhā-devyā bhucya-(jya)māna-Kuloṭī-satka-bhūmayaś=catasraḥ tathā Muṅgale sūpakāra-Surambhaṭa-sthitā sīt bhūmi-dvayam। tathā

17. Vāṭāyāṁ chonneraka-goṣṭhika-sthitā sīt bhūmi-dvayam tathā Tāvasaka-maṇḍala-pratibaddha Bhadravarme Bhadrāvakāśīya-Vijjaula-sthitā sīt bhūr=ekā tathā Sarāhule

18. Bhaṭṭavasanta-sthitā sīd=bhūmir=ekā tathā Ḍhālyake=ṣṭaprahārika Denna-suta-satka Lartuke bhūmi-dvayaṁ tath=ātr=aiva dvitīy-āṣṭaprahārika-Rāmajjeya-suta-satka Jauḍhake bhū-dvayaṁ tathā Pāra-

19. kamaṭa-maṇḍala-pratibaddha-Maṅgale Ḍhaullikāyāṁ। Lutthuka-suta-satka-bhūmāṣaka-dvayaṁ tathā Huṁrtāka-suta-satka-bhūmāṣaka-dvayam=ubhau saṁśu-ddhaṁ bhūr=ek=āṅkataḥ Kuloṭī bhū 4 Muṅgale bhū 2 Vāṭāyāṁ

20. bhū 2 Bhadravarme bhū 1 Sarāhule bhū 1 Ḍhālyake bhū 4 Maṅgale bhū 1

---

[1] Prof. Kielhorn reads *dāra*; *cf.* above III, 6.

[2] Read *abhitvaramāṇa*; *cf.* above II, 8 and beneath V, 9.

IV.—Chamba Plate of Somavarmadeva and Asatadeva.

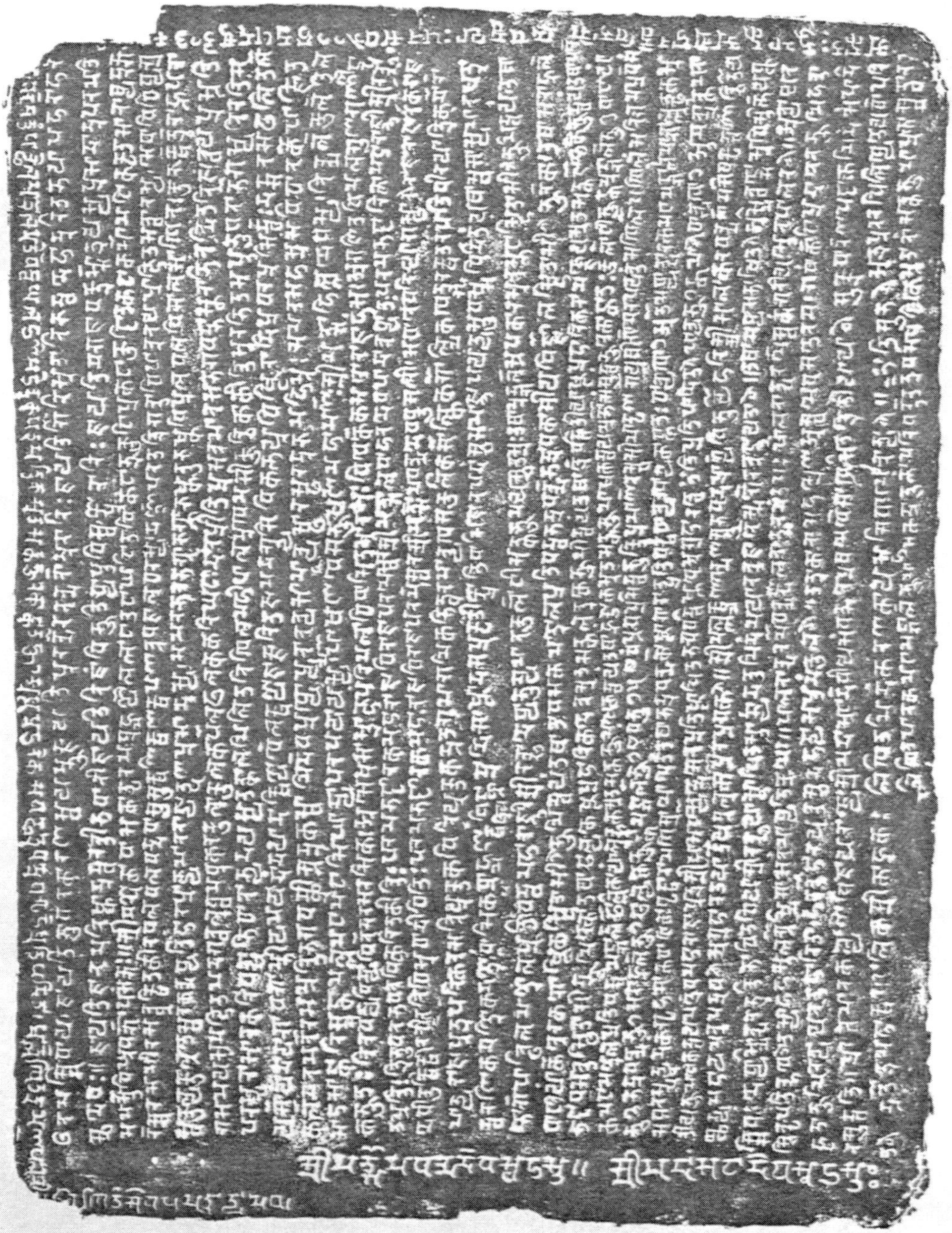

E. HULTZSCH.

SCALE FOUR-SEVENTHS.

WIELE & KLEIN, PHOTO-ZINCO.

evaṁ bhū 15 evaṁ pūrva-prasiddha-bhukti-pramāṇena sva-sīmā-tṛṇa-goyūthī (gavyū-ti)-gocara-paryantaṁ sa-khil-opakhilaṁ sanirgama-praveśaṁ

21. sa-vanaspaty-udakaṁ gṛha-śākavāṭikā-vṛkṣārāma-viśrām-opetaṁ tathā Bhadravarma-koṣṭhāgārāt=prativarṣaṁ dhānya-khāry=ek=āṅkataḥ dhānya-khā 1 ato madhyāt=Pārakamaṭa–Maṅgala-mārgāl=Lutthukasu-

22. tīya-bhūmāṣaka-dvayam=atr=aiva mahārājaputra-Śrī-Pāsaṭasy [1]=oddeśena pratiṣṭhāpita-bhagavad-Viṣṇave agrahāratve iti pratipāditaṁ pāṇya (?) bhū 14 mā 2 dhānya-khā 1 ā-candr-ārkam=anā-

23. cchedyam=ahāryam=anupadravam agrahāratayā toya-culuk-āpūra-pūrva-kaṁ ‖ Śrīmal[2]-Lakṣmaṇavarmaṇaś-śubhavada-prakhyo[3]=vibhur=yo Hariś=Śrī-Sālā-karavarmaṇe ca śiva-kṛd=vāṇ-ārcito ya-

24. ś-Śivaḥ [1*] devyā smin=parabhakti-bhāvita-dhiyā Śrī-Rarḍhayā sthāpitas=tābhyāṁ dattam=idaṁ mayā nanu janais=sarvair=anujñāyatāṁ ‖ Tathā ca Vyāsa-bhāṣitam[‖*] Asmin=van(ṁ)śe suvistīrṇe yaḥ=ka-

25. ś-cin=nṛpatir=bhavet[1*] tasy=āhaṁ hasta-lagno=smi śāsanaṁ mā vyati-krameḥ ‖ Pālanāt=paramo dharmaḥ=pālanāt=paramaṁ tapaḥ[1*] pālanāt=param-aiśvaryaṁ garīyas=tena pālanam ‖ Anyāyena

26. hṛtā bhūmir=anyāyena tu hāritā 1 haranto hārayantaś[4]=ca dahaty=ā-sa-ptamaṁ kulam ‖ Taḍāk(g)ānā[ṁ] sahasreṇa aśvamedha-śatena ca 1 gavāṁ koṭi-pradānena bhumi-hartā

27. na śuddha(dhya)ti ‖ Pravardhamāna–kalyāṇa-vijaya-rājye Śrīmad-Āsaṭa-devīye saṁvatsare prathame Vaiśākha-sita-tri(tṛ)tīyāyāṁ[5] Śukravāreṇa paṭṭakam=idaṁ sampādi-

28. taṁ [‖*] Dūto 1 tra mahākṣapaṭalika-Śrī-Kāhukaḥ ‖ Likhitam=idaṁ karaṇakāyastha-Śivapa-Mannābhyām[6] ‖ Iti śubham [‖*] Atra punar=api likhyate [‖*] Yathopari-

29. likhita-Pārakamaṭa-Maṅgale bhūmāṣaka dā(cā)turṇām parivarte tatr=aiva Savaryika-sutānāṁ satka-bhū-māpra(ṣa)kāś=catvāraḥ

30. aṅkataḥ bhūmā 4 agrahāratve vibhāge deva-dvayoḥ pana (punaḥ ?) Saṁvat 11 Bhādrapada-śu-ti. 12. sa - - -

31. vāre dattaṁ Pānthila-maṇḍala-pratibaddha-Ghalahaṇe Mahendraka-po(pau)-tra-Mantika-suta-satka-bhūr=ek=ānkato bhū 1 aṣṭapraha(hā)rika-savarphe treva (*read* sevārthe=traiva) devagṛhe pratipa(pā)ditā 1 prāṅ(g)-le(li)khita-krama(me)ṇa pālanī-[yam‖]

32. [Li*] khitaṁ Śivapa-Mannābhyām[6]=eva 1 (‖)
Śrīmat-Somavarma-deva-svahastaḥ ‖ Śrīmad-Āsaṭa-deva-svahastaḥ [‖*]

Translation.

Oṁ. Reverence to Śiva. Victorious is the cause of the world the Self-existent (Brahmā). Victorious is the son of the Destroyer of castles (Śiva), (Kṛṣṇa) the

[1] Prof. Kielhorn reads *Āsaṭa*, which probably is correct. The grant evidently was drawn up at a time when Somavarman was still Rājā and Āsaṭa consequently *mahārājaputra*.

[2] Metre, Śārdūlavikriḍita.

[3] Prof. Kielhorn has *prā[khye]*; the *a*-stroke however must belong to the second *akṣara*.

[4] Read *harato hārayatas*.

[5] Prof. Kielhorn reads *dvitīyāyām*.

[6] Prof. Kielhorn reads *Siva-Pamannābhyām*; *cf.*, however, *Manna-Devap-atmaja-Sivapābhyam* (V. 21).

Enemy of Mura. Victorious is he, whose body is held by the Mountain-daughter (Durgā), he who removes distress and danger, Hara, the god. Victorious is she, who saves mankind from misfortune, Bhavānī (Durgā). Victorious is he, who with his splendour has pervaded the universe, the Foe of the castles (Śiva). Victorious also is the Elephant-faced one, he, by whose favour the calamity of a host of obstacles ceases (Gaṇeśa).

(L. 3) From his residence at the glorious Caṇpakā, the highly devout [king Somavarman] who is an ornament of the spotless house of Sāhilladeva, who (Sāhilla) was a fresh rain-cloud, to extinguish in a moment the mighty blazing fire of the Kīra forces, fanned, as by the wind, by the Lord of Durgara, assisted by the Saumaṭikas, whose army (camp) was manifestly crushed by the fearful frown produced on the slope of his (Sāhilla's) forehead, whose (Sāhilla's) alliance was humbly sought by the ruler of Trigarta, subdued by force; who (Sāhilla) was asked the favour of bestowing royalty in return for services by his kinsman, the Lord of Kulūta, anxious to render him homage; who by the weight of battle had broken, like a wide spreading tree, the large force of the Turuṣkas, on whom wounds had been inflicted; who (Sāhilla) had the fortunate name of Karivarṣa (Elephant-rain) on account of the continuous and stable generation of his posterity joyfully granted by the Lord Bhāskara (the Sun-god), whose mind was contented with gladness by the gift of a multitude of elephants, whose flat cheeks were covered by a swarm of bees attracted by the scent of the rut-secretion and which were bestowed in Kurukṣetra at the time of an eclipse; who (Sāhilla) has made the circuit of the seven worlds fragrant by his fame [painted] with the ink-brushes which were the mouths of all the princes assembled on that occasion; who (Sāhilla) by his unequalled kindness and compassion combined with unsurpassed bravery, generosity, firmness, and unfathomable profoundness, has impaired the fame of heroes like the son of Jamadagni (Paraśurāma), Śivi, Karṇa, and Yudhiṣṭhira; whose (Sāhilla's) wide-spread greatness brilliant with matchless effulgence was renowned like that of Śūdraka-swāmi-deva; by looking upon whose (Sāhilla's) lovely presence the eyes of the world have been made fruitful; who (Sāhilla) by his fury in setting in array a thousand battles had acquired such names as Sāhasāṅka (marked by rashness) Niśśaṅkamalla, (the dauntless wrestler) and Maṭamaṭatsiṁha (the roaring ? lion).

(L. 11) [King Somavarman] who delights in passing his time in attaining faultless knowledge, whose mind is perfumed by the fragrance of every science, the royal swan of the only lake of discrimination, whose form is adorned with numbers of innumerable spotless qualities, whose fame is strewn over the dwellings of the three worlds, he who reverentially remembers the *paramabhaṭṭāraka, mahārājādhirāja, parameśvara*, the illustrious Sālavāhana-deva and was born from the womb of the *paramabhaṭṭārikā, mahārājñī*, the illustrious Raṛdhādevī as the Moon was born from the Milk-Ocean, he, the *paramabhaṭṭāraka, mahārājādhirāja, parameśvara*, the illustrious Somavarma-deva, the prosperous one,

(L. 13) enjoins on all the officials, every rājā, rānā, royal councillor, rājpūt, those appointed and commissioned of (the Rājā's) attendants (?), every *dūta, gamāgamika, abhitvaramāṇa*, Khaśa, Kulika, bridge-guard (?), those belonging to the expeditionary force (?), every thief-catcher, jailor, executioner, brāhmaṇa, kṣatriya, vaiśya, śūdra and all others, that constitute the eighteen elements of the state and the neighbouring country-people.

(L. 15) Be it known unto you, that in the domain under our sway in the Pānthila district there are four *bhūmis* of land belonging to Kuloṭi, enjoyed by the *mahārājñī* the illustrious Rarḍhā-devī, and at Muṅgala two *bhūmi* belonging to the cook Surambhaṭa, and at Vāṭā there were two *bhūmi* belonging to the *Chonneraka-goṣṭhika*, and in the Tāvasaka district at Bhadravarma there was one *bhū* held by the Bhadrāvakāśīya Vijjaula, and at Sarāhula there was one *bhū* held by Bhaṭṭavasanta, and at Ḍhālyakā two *bhūmi* in Lartuka which belong to the *aṣṭaprahārika*, the son of Denna, and in the same village two *bhū* in Jauḍhaka, belonging to the second *aṣṭaprahārika*, the son of Ramajjeya, and in the Pārakamaṭa district at Maṅgala in Ḍhaulikā two *bhūmāṣaka* belonging to the son of Lutthuka and two *bhūmāṣaka* belonging to the son of Huṁrtāka, both together making one full *bhū*. In figures: of Kuloṭī 4 *bhū*, at Muṅgala 2 *bhū*, at Vāṭā 2 *bhū*, at Bhadravarma 1 *bhū*, at Sarāhula 1 *bhū*, at Ḍhālyakạ 4 *bhū*, at Maṅgala 1 *bhū*, thus 15 *bhū*, thus on the previously established terms of occupancy as far as their limits, grass, grazing and pasture-ground, with fallow-land, large and small, with ingress and egress, with fruit-trees and water, together with houses, kitchen-gardens, orchards and resting places; also from the store-house of Bhadravarma annually one *khāri* of grain, in figures 1 *khā* of grain. Out of these (lands) the two *bhūmāṣaka* of the son of Lutthuka on the road of Maṅgala in Pārakamaṭa are bestowed as an *agrahāra* on [the temple of] the Lord Viṣṇu founded here by order of the illustrious Āsaṭa, the son of the [late] *mahārājā*.[1] The remaining 14 *bhū* 2 *mā*. and 1 *khā*. of grain are granted by me as an *agrahāra* for as long as moon and sun shall endure, uncurtailable,

(L. 23) to [the temple of] the Lord Hari (Viṣṇu) which is renowned by the auspicious word of the illustrious Lakṣmaṇavarman, and to Śiva who, praised with music, has blessed the illustrious Sālākaravarman, and [whose temple] has been established by the illustrious queen Rarḍhā, having fixed her mind on the highest devotion. Let then all people approve it.

(L 24) And this has been spoken by Vyāsa: "Whosoever of this wide-spread race may be king, I enjoin on him not to transgress [this] order. By [its] observance the highest religious merit, by [its] observance the highest ascetic merit, by [its] observance the highest sovereignty [will be attained]; [its] observance is therefore very important. The land which is unlawfully confiscated or unlawfully caused to be confiscated consumes (*lit.*, burns) up to the seventh generation of him who confiscates it and of him who causes it to be confiscated. He who takes away the land is not cleansed by [the digging of] a thousand tanks, by a hundred horse-oblations and by a gift of ten million cows."

(L. 27) In the increasing, fortunate reign of victory, in the first year of the illustrious Āsaṭa-deva, on the third day of the bright fortnight of Vaiśākha, on Friday, has this plate been presented. The messenger on this occasion was the Great-Record-

---

[1] I translate according to the proposed emendation. I have inserted "late" as Āsaṭa was the brother and not the son of Somavarman, the donor of the grant, as appears from Plate V, where Sālavāhana is mentioned as his father.

keeper, the illustrious Kāhuka.[1] This was written by the writers of legal documents Śivapa and Manna.

(L. 28) Here again is written that, in exchange for the four *bhūmāṣakas* of Maṅgala in Pārakamaṭa, four, in figures 4, *bhūmāṣakas*, belonging to the sons of Savaryika, are given as an *agrahāra* in apportionment to the two gods. Anno 11, [the month] Bhādrapada, the bright fortnight, the lunar day 12. One, in figures 1, *bhū* belonging to the son of Mantika, the grandson of Mahendraka, in Ghalahaṇa, situated in the Pānthila district, are granted for the service of the *aṣṭaprahārikas*[2] in the same temple. To be observed in the previously described manner.

(L. 32) Written by Śivapa and Manna. Signature of the illustrious Somavarmadeva. Signature of the illustrious Āsaṭa.

V. Grant of Āsaṭa-deva.

This plate is $13\frac{1}{4}$ to $13\frac{3}{4}''$ broad and $9\frac{1}{2}''$ high. It consists of 21 lines whereas the subscription of the donor is written vertically in the proper right margin. The size of the letters is from $\frac{3}{16}$ to $\frac{1}{4}''$. The plate is in an excellent state of preservation. It is now in the hands of a Brāhman at Tundu-Mundu, a village in the Hul-Gudiāl pargaṇa. To the proper right there is a pierced handle, to which possibly a seal was attached originally.

Text V.

1. Oṁ. Jayati janam=aniṣṭād=uddharantī Bhavānī jayati nija-vibhūti-vyāpna (pta)-viśvaḥ=Purāriḥ [1*] jayati ca Gajava-

2. ktras=sotra yasya prasādād=upaśamati samasto vighna-varg-opasargaḥ ‖ Śrī-Caṇpakā-vāsakāt=parama-brahmaṇyo deva-dvija-

3. śu(gu)ru-pūjan-ābhirato dīn-āndha-kṛpaṇ-ānātha-vatsalaḥ agaṇita-guṇa-gaṇ-ālaṅkṛta-mūrteḥ vivek-aika-vasatiḥ śa-

4. śadhara-kara-nikar-āvadāta-yaśaḥ-prasara-prakāśita-sarv-āśaḥ Pauṣaṇa(ṣṇa)-kul-aika-tilakaḥ paramabhaṭṭāraka-mahārājā-

5. dhirāja-parameśvara-śrīmat-Sālavāhana-deva-pād-ānudhyāta-paramabhaṭṭārikā-mahārājñī-Śrī-Ran(r)ḍhā-de-

6. vy-o(u)dar-odadhi-vivardhita akalaṅkaḥ paramabhaṭṭāraka-mahārājādhirāja-parameśvara-śrīmad-Ā-

7. saṭa-devaḥ=kuṣ(ś)alī samupāgatān sarvān=eva niyogasthān। rāja-rājānaka-rājaputra-rā-

8. jāmātya-brāhmaṇa-kṣatriya-viṭ-śūdra-rājasthānīya-parikara-sa[ṁ*]niyuktaka-viniyuktaka-dūta-gamāgami-

9. ka-bhitvaraśā(mā)na-khaśa-kulika-śaulmi(lki)ka-gaulmika-khaṇḍarakṣa-tara-pati-vīrajā(yā)trika-cauro[d]dharaṇika-da-

10. ṇḍika-daṇḍavāsik-ādim-āṣṭādaśa-prakṛty-ādīn। sarvān=sap(m)ājñāpayaty=astu va[ḥ] sa[ṁ*]viditaṁ yadhā(thā) sva-

---

[1] We may suppose this Kāhuka to be the same individual as Kāhila, the messenger of the previous grant (III, 25). In the same way we find the names Paituka and Paitala indicating the same person in an inscription in the Delhi Museum (*Epig. Ind.*, I, p. 95).

[2] *aṣṭaprahārika* possibly means "a temple watchman" called *pāhari* in Chambā and Kāngrā. This word, however, presupposes a Skr. "* *prāharika*, from *prahara*," a watch of three hours.

V.—Chamba Plate of Asatadeva.

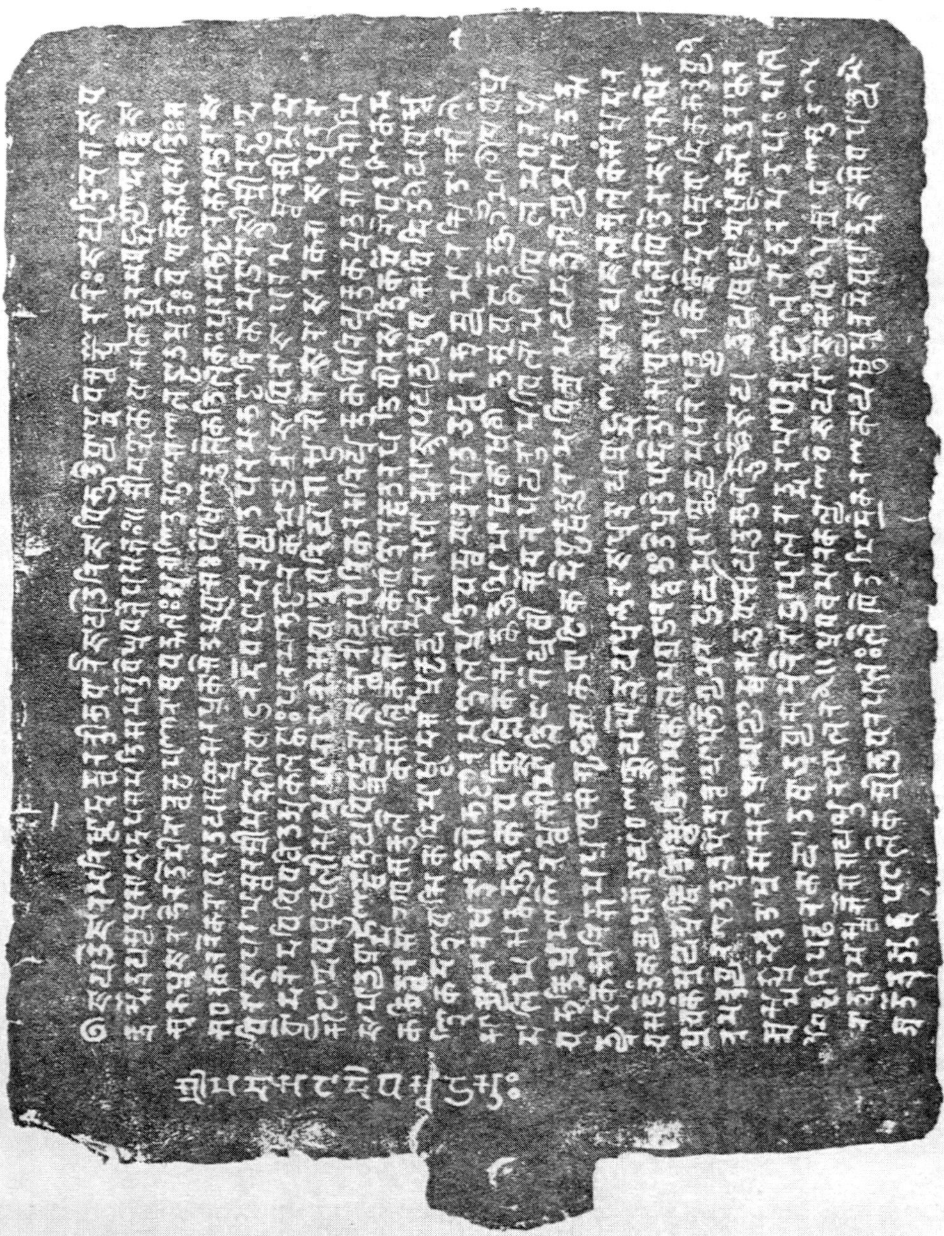

SCALE TWO-THIRDS.

From an Ink-impression supplied by Dr. Vogel.

E. HULTZSCH.

WIELE & KLEIN, PHOTO-ZINCO.

11. s(ś)āsyamāna- ṣ(kṣ)atrābhoge Bhaṭṭāra-maṇḍala-pratibaddha-Cānnasuta-Uddhara-bhucya(jya)māna-sthitā sīt

12. Dālima-satka-bhūr=ekā । Vañjāllika ?-satka-bhūmimāṣaka ṣaṭ ta(u)bhāv=aṅkato bhū 1 mā 6 evaṁ pū-

13. rva-bhukti-pramāṇena sva-sīmā-tri(tṛ)ṇa-goyūthī (gavyūti)-śo(go)cara-paryantā(taṁ) sa-khil-opakhilaṁ sa-vanapsa(spa)-

14. ty-udaka[ṁ*] sa-nirgama-praveśaṁ gṛha-śākavāṭik-ādi-vṛkṣa-ārāma-viśrāma yad=atra lagyamānaṁ tat-sa-

15. rva-sahitaṁ Kāśyapa-gotrāya Dhaṇa(na)ñjaya-pautrāya Pūrṇarāja-putrāya brāhmaṇa-Mācāya jala-śu(cu)luka-saṁpradāna-

16. pūrvakaṁ sūry-endu-kṣiti-sthiti-samakālam=agrahāratve iti pratipāditā (taṁ) । Sarvair=upari-likhitai[ḥ] rājapuruṣair=a-

17. numantavyaṁ । etat-putra-pautr-ānvay-opabhogyam=anāhāryam=anācchedyam=aparipanthyaṁ na kiñcid=upadravādika[ṁ*] kartavyaṁ[॥*]

18. Asmat-pradatta-tāmra-śāsana-prāmāṇyād=vasatu vāsayatu bhunaktu bhojayatu yath-eṣṭa-ceṣṭaṁ karotu na kena

19. cit=paripanthanā kāryā । Tathā u(ca) Vyāśa(sa)-munir=āha । Pālanāt=ma (pa)ramo dharmaḥ=pālanāt=paramaṁ tapaḥ pāla-

20. nāt=paramas=svargo-gaga(rī)yas=tena pālanaṁ ॥ Pravardhamāna-kalyāṇa-vijaya-rājye saṃvat 5 Śrāvaṇa-śu-ti-15[॥*]

21. A(Dū)to tra ākṣapaṭalika-Śrī-Bhuvanapālaḥ[॥*] Likhitam=idaṁ karaṇa-kāyastha-Manna-Devap-ātmaja-Śivapābhyam (bhyām)[॥*]

Śrīmad-Āsaṭa-deva-svahastaḥ[॥*]

Translation.

Oṁ. Victorious is she, who saves mankind from misfortune, Bhavānī (Durgā). Victorious is he, who with his splendour has pervaded the universe, the Foe of the castles (Śiva). Victorious also is the Elephant-faced one, he, by whose favour the calamity of a host of obstacles ceases (Gaṇeśa).

(L. 2.) From his residence at the glorious Caṇpakā, the highly devout [king Āsaṭa-deva] who takes delight in the worship of deities, the twice-born and spiritual preceptors, the friend of the distressed, the blind, the needy and the unprotected, whose form is adorned with numbers of innumerable virtues, the only abode of discrimination, who by the effulgence of his glory bright like the multitudinous beams of the Hare-holder (the Moon) has illumined all regions, the only ornament of the Solar race, who reverentially remembers the *paramabhaṭṭāraka*, *mahārājādhirāja*, *parameśvara*, the illustrious Sālavāhana-deva, and was reared by that other ocean, which was the womb of the *paramabhaṭṭārikā mahārājñī* the illustrious Rarḍhā-devī, but was without spot;

(L. 6) he, the *paramabhaṭṭāraka*, *mahārājādhirāja*, *parameśvara*, the illustrious Āsaṭa-deva, the prosperous one, enjoins on all the officials concerned, every rājā, rānā, rājpūt, royal councillor, brāhmaṇa, kṣatriya, vaiśya, śūdra, chief justice, those appointed and commissioned of (the rājā's) attendants (?), every *dūta*, *gamāgamika*, *abhitvaramāṇa*, Khaśa, Kulika, collector, inspector of police, *khaṇḍarakṣa*, bridge-guard (?), those belonging to the expeditionary force (?), every thief-catcher, jailor, executioner and all others, that constitute the eighteen elements of the state.

(L. 10) Be it known unto you, that within the circuit of the domain under my rule, in the Bhaṭṭāraka district there is one *bhū* of land belonging to Dālima, which has been enjoyed by Uddhara, the son of Cānna, and six *bhūmi-māṣaka* of Vañjāllika, together in figures, 1 *bhū* 6 *mā*. [This land], on the terms of its previous occupancy, as far as its limits, grass, grazing and pasture ground, with fallow-land large and small, with fruit-trees and water, with ingress and egress, with houses, kitchen-gardens etc., trees, gardens and resting-places, with all that is attached to it joined, has been granted as an *agrahāra* to the brāhmaṇa Māca, the son of Pūrṇarāja, the grandson of Dhanañjaya of the house of Kāśyapa, after a formal libation of a handful of water, for as long a time as the sun, the moon and the earth shall endure. This grant is to be observed by all above-named royal officers, to be enjoyed by the succession of [his] sons and sons' sons, inalienable, uncurtailable, unopposed. Let no hindrance whatever be caused [to him]. Let him on the authority of the copper-charter, issued by us, live and make [others] to live, enjoy and make [others] to enjoy. Let no one offer opposition.

(L. 19.) For thus has Vyāsa, the sage, spoken: "By the observance [of this grant] the highest religious merit, by [its] observance the highest ascetic merit, by (its) observance the highest heaven [will be attained]; [its] observance, therefore, is very important."

(L. 20.) In the increasing, fortunate reign of victory; in the year 5 [the month] Śrāvaṇa, the bright fortnight, the lunar day 15. The messenger on this occasion was the Recordkeeper, the illustrious Bhuvanapāla. This was written by the writers of legal documents Manna and Śivapa, the son of Devapa.

Signature of the illustrious Āsaṭa-deva.

CONCLUSIONS.

GEOGRAPHICAL.—Our first object will be to consider what conclusions regarding the ancient topography of Chambā can be drawn from the copper-plates. We find the State divided into districts (*maṇḍala*) of which the following are mentioned:—

1. Brahmapura (I, 6), the modern Brahmaur (map Barmaor) which name is applied to a *wazārat*, a *pargaṇa*, and a village. The Brahmapura *maṇḍala* must have corresponded to the Brahmaur *pargaṇa* comprising the valley of the Budhil, a tributary of the Rāvī. The village Khaṇī, which belonged to this *maṇḍala* and still retains its name (map: Kani), is situated east of the confluence of the Rāvī and the Budhil, on the ridge which forms the watershed between the two rivers. Mention is made of the hospice (*maṭha*) of Khaṇī. It is curious that up to the present day we find several rest-houses for travellers shaded by mulberry trees at the spot where the road from Ulānsa to the village of Brahmaur crosses the ridge near Khaṇī. It is evident from the name that Brahmapura, in the first instance, indicated a town or large village. The meaning would be "town of Brahmā" or "town of the Brāhmaṇas." It is interesting that the goddess Brahmāṇī, the female energy of Brahmā, is still worshipped at a spring above the present village of Brahmaur. Other villages mentioned in the *maṇḍala* are Viḍavikā, which perhaps is the modern Baṛei (map Barai), and Grima which is still known by the same name.

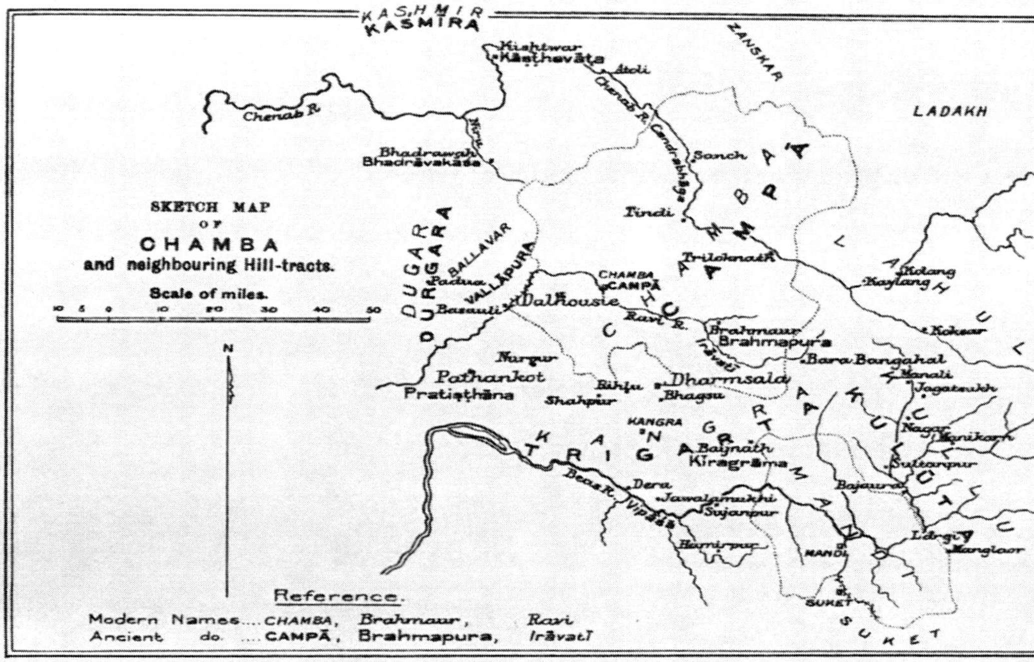
SKETCH MAP
OF
CHAMBA
and neighbouring Hill-tracts.
Scale of miles.
10 5 0 10 20 30 40 50
N
KASHMIR
KASMIRA
ZANSKAR
LADAKH
Kishtwar
Kāsthavāta
Atoli
Chenab R.
Candrabhāga
Bhadrawah
Bhadrāvakāśa
Sanch
Tindi
Triloknath
CHAMPĀ
DUGAR
DURGARA
BALLAVAR
VALLĀPURA
Padua
Basauli
CHAMBA
CAMPĀ
Dalhousie
Ravi R.
Irāvatī
Brahmaur
Brahmapura
Kolang
Kaylang
Koksar
Bara Bangahal
Manali
Jagatsukh
Nurpur
Pathankot
Pratisthāna
Rihlu
Shahpur
Dharmsala
Bhagsu
KANGRA
TRIGARTA
Baijnath
Kiragrāma
Nagar
Manikarn
Sultanpur
KULUTA
Bajaura
Dera
Jawalamukhi
Sujanpur
Beas R.
Vipāśā
Hamirpur
MANDI
Larji
Manglaor
SUKET
Reference.
Modern Names....CHAMBA, Brahmaur, Ravi
Ancient do. ....CAMPĀ, Brahmapura, Irāvatī

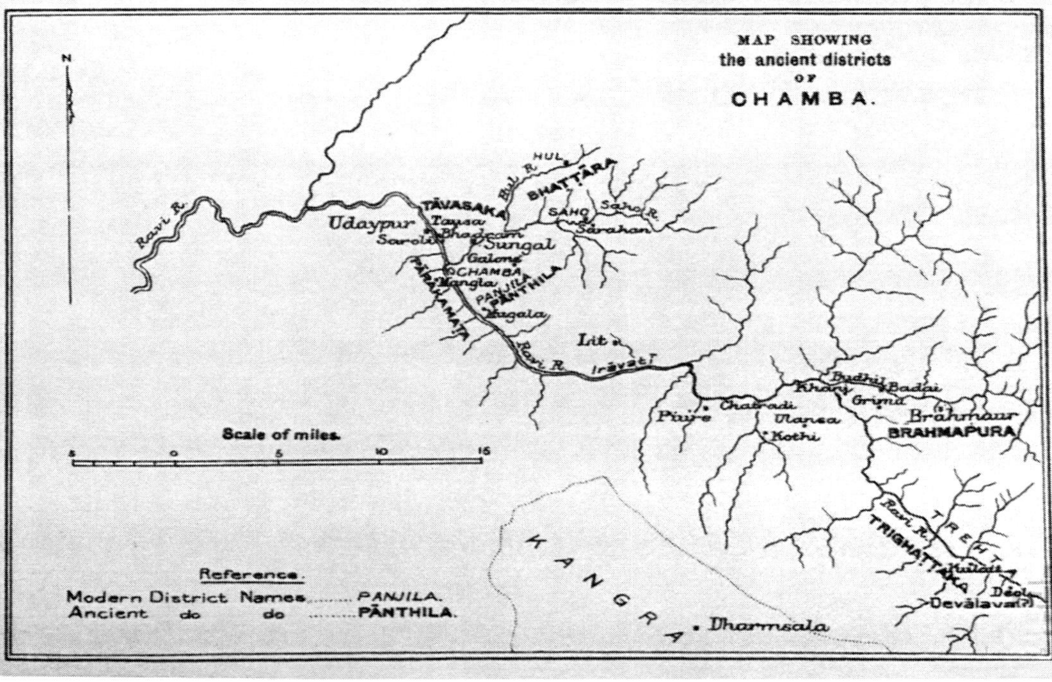
MAP SHOWING
the ancient districts
OF
CHAMBA.
N
Ravi R.
Udaypur
TĀVASAKA
Tausa
Bhadgam
Saroli
Sungal
Galong
CHAMBA
Mangla
PANJILA
PĀNTHILA
Yugala
Bul R.
HUL
BHATTĀRA
SAHO
Saho R.
Sārahan
Lit
Ravi R.
Irāvatī
Piure
Chatradi
Ulansa
Kothi
Khani
Budhil
Badai
Grima
Brahmaur
BRAHMAPURA
Scale of miles.
5 0 5 10 15
KANGRA
Dharmsala
TREHTA
TRIGHATTAKA
Deol
Devālava(?)
Reference.
Modern District Names......... PANJILA.
Ancient do do ....PĀNTHILA.

2. Trighaṭṭaka (III, 20), the present *pargaṇa* of Trehṭā (map Traita), a tract along the upper Rāvī above its junction with the Budhil. The name points to the existence of three passes (Skr. *ghaṭṭa*, H. *ghāṭ*) leading into this part of the Rāvī valley, presumably from the Cīnāb valley (Lāhul), from the Biyās valley (Kāngṛā), and from the Budhil valley (Brahmaur). The village Kulika-goṣṭha mentioned in this *maṇḍala* is represented by the modern Kulait (map Kolait) on the left bank of the Rāvī, 11½ miles above its junction with the Budhil. The name indicates that it was a settlement or station (Skr. *goṣṭha*) of Kulikas, a tribe mentioned elsewhere in our plates (II, 8; IV, 14) together with the Khaśas.

3. Pānthila (IV, 16, 31), the *pargaṇa* of Pañjilā, situated immediately above Chambā city between the right bank of the Rāvī and the left bank of the Śāho. It contains the villages Kuloṭi (not identified), Muṅgala, the modern Mugalā, 3 miles above Chambā on the right bank of the Rāvī, Vāṭā now Bāṭ, 3 miles north-east of Chambā, and Ghalahaṇa now Galone in a valley opening on the left bank of the Śāho, 3 miles east of Chambā.

4. Tāvasaka (II, 5; IV, 17), below Chambā town, between the right bank of the Rāvī and the right bank of the Śāho. The name is not preserved in the designation of a *pargaṇa*, but presumably is that of the village Tausa. The localities belonging to this *maṇḍala* are: Sumaṅgala (II, 6), the present village of Suṅgal (map Sungul), 1¾ mile above Chambā town on the right bank of the Śāho; Bhadravarma, now Bhadram, 2 miles below Chambā; and Sarāhula, now Sarol (map Saroli), 1½ mile below Chambā. The two latter villages situated on the right bank of the Rāvī belong now to the Rājnagar *pargaṇa*. The other localities of the Tāvasaka *maṇḍala*, Ḍhālyaka, Lartuka, and Yauḍhaka, I am unable to identify. They would seem to indicate cultivated fields rather than villages.

5. Pārakamaṭa (IV, 18, 21, 29), as the name indicates, is the district situated on the other side (Skr. *pāra*) of the Rāvī opposite Chambā town, now known as the Sāc *pargaṇa*. The ancient designation seems to be entirely lost. The village Maṅgala (map Mungla), still known by its original name, is situated on the road to Nūrpūr by the Cauhārī pass. Ḍhaullika, another locality in this *maṇḍala*, is evidently the name of a piece of land now known as Ḍholi near Maṅgala, between the village and the steep bank of the Rāvī.

6. Bhaṭṭāra (V, 11) is no longer the name of a district, but is now used to indicate fifteen villages in the Hul-Gudiāl *pargaṇa*. The local deity is still known as Bhaṭṭār Devī Śītalā, and the pilgrimage to her shrine is called Bhaṭṭār jātrā. It is said that the inhabitants of these villages combine against other villagers in the game of *chakṛī* (the same as *caunpaṭ*), thus preserving the tradition of their former unity as residents of one district.

From the foregoing it is clear that at the time to which our plates belong, the State of Chambā comprised the valleys of the upper Rāvī and its tributary the Budhil, and the tracts round Chambā town along both banks of the Rāvī and the Śāho. But as the plates are all dated from Chambā city as the seat of Government, which probably was in the centre of the State, there is reason to assume that its territory extended considerably lower down the river, perhaps as far as the Sivāliks, comprising the whole of the valley of the Rāvī and its tributaries during its course through the hills. Whether in those days any tracts on the upper Cīnāb now belonging to the State, or other territories outside the country drained by the Rāvī, were included in Chambā, it is impossible to say. But it deserves notice that mention is made of an inhabitant of Bhadrāvakāśa (IV, 17) *i.e.*, Bhadravāh, as a land-holder in Chambā. Bhadravāh occupies the valley of the Nīrū, a southern tributary of the Cīnāb, and belonged to Chambā before it became absorbed in the Jammū State of which it now is a district. That it did not belong to Kaśmīr in the beginning of the twelfth century is evident from the Rājataraṅgiṇī (VIII, 500-501), where we read that the pretender Sahasramaṅgala, being expelled from Kaśmīr by Sussala (1112-20), took refuge in Bhadrāvakāśa. That the name is only once mentioned in Kalhaṇa's chronicle makes its occurrence in a Chambā grant the more interesting.

In the passage relating to Rājā Sāhillavarman (III, 2-11 and IV, 3-10) several States and Tribes of the Pañjāb Hills are mentioned, which were either at war or in alliance with the Chambā ruler. His opponents were the Saumaṭikas, the Kīras, and the lord of Durgara.

Durgara appears to be the ancient name for the modern Dugar (Dogrā), the mountainous tract between the Jehlam and the Rāvī, or more definitely the ancient Jammū State on the Cīnāb.[1] The Kīras were a tribe located in the immediate neighbourhood of Kaśmīr.[2] The famous Baijnāth in Kāngṛā would seem to have been a settlement of this tribe, as the ancient name is stated to have been Kīragrām, a village of the Kīras. The Saumaṭikas I have not found mentioned anywhere else. But from the wording of the inscription it is clear that we shall have to look for them somewhere in the vicinity of Jammū. Now in the Basaulī *tahsīl* of the Jasroṭā district of the present Jammū State there is a tract (*'alāqa*) known as Sumarta (map Sambarta). This name in Prākritised form would be Sumaṭa, of which Saumaṭika would be a regular *vṛddhi*-derivative. It is certainly strange to find the older form used now-a-days. From a topographical point of view the identification seems very plausible.

The allies of Sāhilla were the ruler of Trigarta, *i.e.*, the Kāngṛā or Lower Biyās valley, and the lord of Kulūta, the modern Kullū on the Upper Biyās, which is now a sub-division of the Kāngṛā district.[3]

HISTORICAL.—The inscriptions of Meruvarman acquaint us with the names of his father Divākara-(or Deva-)varman, his grandfather Balavarman and his great-grandfather Ādityavarman. Assuming for palæographical reasons that Meruvarman ruled in the commencement of the eighth century, his immediate predecessors are to be placed in the second half of the seventh century. Unfortunately the inscriptions do not contain any information regarding these rulers. Of Meruvarman himself we can only surmise that, considering the number of temples founded by him, he must have been a

[1] Cunningham, *Ancient Geography*, p. 130. Stein, *Rājat.* (tranl.), II, p. 432.

[2] *Bṛhatsaṁhitā*, XIV, 29, mentions them as a people inhabiting the North-East together with the Kaśmiras. They are once mentioned in the *Rājat.* VIII, 2767, as auxiliaries of the pretender Bhoja. *Cf.* Stein, *Rājat.* (tranl.), II, p. 365. As noted above, p. 241, the *vaṁśāvali* of the Chambā Rājās refers to an invasion of Kiras in Chambā territory under the reign of Meruvarman's grandson.

[3] Cunningham, *Ancient Geography*, pp. 136 and 142. *Cf.* also *Mudrārākṣasa* (Telang), p. 32.

prince of some importance. From the title *Mahārājādhirāja* it would seem that he occupied a higher position than those *rāṇās* (Skr. *rājānaka*) who, according to tradition, held small portions of Chambā State before its consolidation by Sāhillavarman. That Brahmaur was his capital, appears from local tradition and from the fact that three of his inscribed images have been found there. His dominions must have comprised Chatrāṛī, but probably did not extend further down the river.

It was Sāhilla who is said to have conquered the lower valley and made Chambā his capital. His name is remembered up to the present day and has become the centre of many a popular legend. No document of this chief has come to light, but in copper-plates I and II we have grants of his son Yagākara (or Yugākara) and of his grandson Vidagdhadeva.[1] From their titles we may conclude that they were independent rulers. The grants are dated from Chambā and therefore confirm popular tradition. The name of Sāhilla found on Plate I, as that of the donor's father, recurs in Plates III and IV, but here he has become the glorified ancestor of the donors and a considerable portion of the inscription is devoted to his praise. It is interesting that this eulogy on both plates is almost identical and has become, as it were, a formula. Some generations must have passed before Sāhilla's fame could become thus magnified, and it is therefore likely that Plates II and III are separated by a space of at least half a century.

That Plates III, IV, and V belong to the same period, follows from the names of the donors and their parents mentioned therein. It is clear that Somavarman and Āsaṭa succeeded each other and were both sons of Sālavāhana. The latter's name occurs not only in the three grants proper, but, as noted above, is found in almost effaced lettering in the margin of Somavarman's plate.

This grant apparently was first intended to be issued by Sālavāhana, who confirmed it with his signature—curiously enough before the deed was engraved on the plate. The cause which prevented him from executing his design may be surmised from the Rājataraṅgiṇī where we read that Sāla, the ruler of Campā, was uprooted by Anantavarman of Kaśmīr.[2] This Sāla has been rightly identified by Prof. Kielhorn with the Sālavāhana of the copper-plates,[3] and we have thus gained a valuable clue to the chronology of our inscriptions. Ananta reigned from 1028 until 1063, but, as he succeeded as a child, we may assume that Sāla's dethronement did not take place before 1038. The accession of Somavarman therefore lies between the years 1038 and 1063, and Plate III which is dated in the 7th year of his reign, between 1045 and 1070.[4] It would seem that the mention of a solar eclipse in connection with this grant might enable us to fix its date more precisely. But if my calculations be correct, solar eclipses took place in the month Bhādrapada of the years 1047, 1056 and 1066, so that an uncertainty still remains. Kalhaṇa's account gives the impression

[1] I take for granted that the Yagākara of Plate I is the same individual as the Yugākara of II.

[2] *Rājat.* (ed. Stein), VII, 218.

[3] Sāla is an abbreviation (*Bhimavat*) of Sālavāhana. Cunningham has confused the name of Sāhilla with Sālavāhana. He first identified the former with the Sāla of the *Rājat.* (*A. S. R.*, XIV, 115), and also with the Sālavāhana of the copper-plates (*A. S. R.*, XXI, 135), and again in his *Ancient Geography* (p. 141) he makes Sāla the father of the founder of Chambā, *i.e.* Sāhilla. His reference to Ferishta must be due to an oversight.

[4] There can be little doubt that the dates mentioned in the Chambā plates refer to regal years and not to the *Lokakāla* or *Śāstrasaṁvat* which in the later grants is used side by side with the Vikrama era. This is evident not only from the wording (*cf.* IV, 27), but especially from the fact that Yagākara's plate is dated in the year 10, whereas that of his son Vidagdha was issued in the year 4.

that the deposition of Sāla occurred towards the end of Anantavarman's reign, so that we are perhaps justified in restricting the alternative dates to 1056 and 1066. Āsaṭa must have succeeded his brother before 1087-88, the year in which he visited Kalaśa of Kaśmīr in the capacity of Rājā of Chambā.[1] Plates IV and V, therefore, belong to the second half of the eleventh century, the earliest possible date of the former being 1056, and the latest possible date of the portion added to it in Āsaṭa's eleventh year being 1099. The two earlier plates issued by Sāhilla's immediate successors we are inclined to place in the second half of the tenth century, and the reign of Sāhilla himself about the middle of that century. This would, therefore, be the approximate date of the foundation of Chambā town and of the consolidation of the State. The Turuṣkas with whom Sāhilla is said to have been at war, may have been the Muhammadans who about this time made their first inroads in the North-West.

It will be of interest to compare the data derived from our inscriptions with those contained in the *vaṁśāvalī* of the Chambā rājās. The first fifty-six names agree closely with those of the *Sūryavaṁśa* as found in the Purāṇas, and may be eliminated as mythological. After these we have the following[2] :—

Maru(t).	10. Ajyavarman.	Sāhilavarman.
Jayastambha.	Meruvarman.	20. Yugākaravarman.
Jalastambha.	Suvarṇavarman.	Dagdha or Dogdha.
Mahāstambha.	Lakṣmīvarman.	Vidagdha.
Ādivarman.	Mūṣaṇavarman.	Vicitravarman.
Devavarman.	Haṁsavarman.	Vairyavarman.
Mandāra.	Sāravarman.	Āsaṭa.
Kantāra.	Sena (or Sainya) varman.	Jāsaṭa.
Pragalbha.	Sajjanavarman.	

It will be seen that not only the name of Meruvarman occurs on the list, but also those of two of his ancestors, if we may take Ādivarman to be a corruption of Ādityavarman. Balavarman's name is omitted and the four names which separate Meruvarman from his father Devavarman must be either out of place or interpolated. Between Meruvarman and Sāhilla we have seven names ; this number would well agree with the space of time which, for reasons stated above, we believe to separate those two rulers. How far the intervening names are historical cannot be decided in the absence of any records. Yugākara is rightly put down as Sāhilla's son and successor, but the name Dagdha, which follows Yugākara, will probably have to be eliminated, unless we assume that he was an elder son of that ruler.[3] That Vidagdha was Yugākara's son is evident from Plate II. The names Vicitravarman and Vairyavarman have not been preserved elsewhere. On the contrary the genealogical roll omits both Sālavāhana and Somavarman who appear on the copper-plates as rulers of Chambā. Āsaṭa and Jāsaṭa are historical names, as they are both mentioned in the Rājataraṅgiṇī, and the former moreover figures on copper-plates IV and V. Our conclusion is that the *vaṁśāvalī* clearly

[1] *Rājat.* VII, 589.

[2] *Cf.* Cunningham, *A. S. R.*, XIV.

[3] In a period when Sanskṛt was well known, it does not seem likely that such an inauspicious name as Dagdha would have been selected for an heir to the throne. The other form under which it appears in the *Vaṁśāvalī* is hardly more plausible. The interpolation of a name Dagdha to match, as it were, Vidagdha seems quite natural.

possesses an historical base, but is by no means fully to be relied upon. The information which it contains has to be checked by the aid of documents which are less liable to alterations. Considering the number of epigraphs existing in the State, it is not unreasonable to hope that a further search for inscriptions in Chambā and the surrounding districts will, in the future, enable us to fix the chronology of its rulers and to give the outline of their history.

At the end of this paper I wish to express my sincere thanks to His Highness the Rājā of Chambā and to Miyān Bhūri Singh, C.I.E., Prime Minister of the State, for their kind hospitality and valuable assistance during my stay in Chambā territory. Only by their co-operation has it been possible to collect in a brief space of time so much material of great antiquarian value. For much interesting information regarding local traditions and history I am indebted to Dr. J. Hutchison, who in the course of more than thirty years spent in missionary work has acquired an intimate knowledge of Chambā and the neighbouring hill-tracts. In correcting the inscriptions and in restoring incomplete verses I thankfully acknowledge the assistance of my learned friend Paṇḍit Mukunda Rāma Śāstrī of the Raṇbīr Institute (Kaśmīr) and of my Assistant Paṇḍit Hīrānanda, M.A., of Lāhor.

J. PH. VOGEL.

ARMENIAN INSCRIPTIONS IN BALŪCHISTĀN.

IN July 1901 the Curator of the Central Museum, Lāhor, informed me that two inscribed stones had been received from Dīwān Gaṇpat Rāi, C.I.E., Extra Assistant Commissioner, Sibi. They originated from Kach, a station on the Sindh-Pishin railway in the Shahrig taḥṣīl, district Thalchotiali, Balūchistān. One of the stones showed only some scratchings probably intended for *triśūlas*. The other contained an inscription in a type different from any Indian script known to me. On the advice of Dr. M. A. Stein, I forwarded impressions of the latter to M. Ed. Drouin, a specialist in Semitic epigraphy and Secretary to the Société asiatique at Paris, with the request that I might be favoured with his opinion on the subject. In his reply that distinguished scholar stated that he could not discover any resemblance with Semitic alphabets but that possibly specimens of similar inscriptions would throw light on the matter. Inquiries being made by Dīwān Gaṇpat Rāi, three more inscribed stones were discovered in a spot called Ush Narāī at a distance of two miles from Kach, where the previous inscriptions had been found. One of these stones had only some scribbling of Persian letters; the other two bore inscriptions similar to the one first discovered. Impressions of the latter were sent to M. Drouin who was kind enough to forward to me the following information :—

"The inscriptions," M. Drouin wrote, "are in Armenian letters and have been "engraved on the stones by people who belonged to an Armenian colony established "in Balūchistān in the beginning of the seventeenth century. Two of these inscrip-"tions are dated 1050 and 1067 of the Armenian era (1606, 1618 A.D.). We know "from the historians that Tahmāsp (1524—'76) and Shāh 'Abbās I. (1587—1629) "ravaged Georgia and Armenia; Tahmāsp in 1547 and 'Abbās in 1600, 1603, and "1618. A large number of Armenians were transported into several parts of the "Persian Empire: Iṣfahān, Afghānistān, Mekrān, etc. The inhabitants of Djulfa, a "town of Aderbodsan, built, near Iṣfahān, a town which they called New Djulfa (Arme-"nian *Nor Djougha*).

"I have communicated my decipherment to Mr. Barmadsian, an Armenian "scholar living in Paris, who has agreed that the writing was an old Armenian writing

ARMENIAN INSCRIPTIONS FROM KACH AND USH NARAI (BALŪCHĪSTĀN).

Fig. 1.

Fig. 2.

Fig. 3.

"rudely engraved on the stone. Consequently there remains some doubt with regard "to the missing or obliterated letters. I must remark that the Armenian era is generally "accepted at 551-552 A.D., but some authors like Ed. Dulaurie (*Chronologie "arménienne*, Paris, 1859) reckon 11th July 552 to 10th July 553."

The stone first discovered (Lāhor Museum I, 144) is irregularly shaped; the inscribed flat surface measures 4" by 2½". The letters are from ¼" to 1¼" high. It contains an incomplete inscription in three lines, which M. Drouin reads:—

—*ē ordi* = son of
Khan p = khan p.—

Of the two other inscriptions, one (Lāhor Museum I, 155) is inscribed on a stone measuring 7½" by 6½" by 4½", and consists of three lines of which the first and the second, containing five letters each, measure 2½", and the third one, containing the date, 1¼". The average size of the letters is ½". It was read by M. Drouin:—

A u tch a k
B r A k a
th (or *t*) *1000 50*

The meaning being:

Autchak (a proper name?)
Br (abbreviation=son ?) Aka
Anno 1050 (A.D. 1601).
(*t* is an abbreviation for *tvin*=year).

The third inscription (Lāhor Museum I, 157) is cut on a thin slab of 10" by 7½" by ½" and contains a monogram 3¾" long by 2½" high, and a date written in two short lines to the proper left of the former, the characters being from ½" to 1⅜" high. The interpretation supplied by M. Drouin is as follows:—

Monogram= *Gh e u n t*=Leon (a proper name)
Date *th* (or *t*) *v n*, i.e., *tvin* = year.
1000, 60, 7, i.e., 1067 (=1618 A.D.).

The inscriptions hitherto discovered contain only a name and a date, but are of interest in connection with the historical facts referred to above. The explanation of their origin offered by M. Drouin possesses much probability, but cannot at present be considered certain. Mr. R. Hughes Buller, I.C.S., Superintendent, *Imperial Gazetteer*, in Balūchistān, has been good enough to provide me with the following particulars regarding the locality where the inscriptions have been found. U<u>sh</u> Narāī (*i.e.*, the Camel Pass[1]) is a barren pass on the main road from Qandahār to Sindh and the Pañjāb. In old days this road was much frequented. It ran from Sanghar in the Pañjāb to Dūki, thence through Nagau to <u>Kh</u>wās and Āmadūn and so over the U<u>sh</u> Narāī to Peshin. This is the route which was followed by Prince Dārā <u>Sh</u>ikoh, when he went to invade Qandahār, and also by Messrs. Steele and Crowther who travelled from Ajmīr to Iṣfahān about 1614 A.D. There cannot, in Mr. Hughes Buller's opinion, have been any permanent colony there.

From ancient times Armenian merchants carried on an active trade with India through Persia, which flourished especially under the reign of the Mu<u>gh</u>al emperors

[1] In Pu<u>sh</u>tū =*u<u>sh</u>* (Pu<u>kh</u>tū=*u<u>kh</u>*), from Zend *ushtra* (-camel). *Cf.* Darmesteter *Chants afghans, XXXVI.*

Akbar and Jahāngīr. In Agra and other places in India there existed extensive Armenian colonies to which numerous sepulchral inscriptions still bear evidence.[1] On the other hand, it should be noticed that no Armenian colonies can be traced now in the Kalāt agency. We should therefore have to assume that the reputed settlers of the seventeenth century, on their conversion to Islām, have become completely merged in the indigenous Brohi and Balūch tribes. It is of interest that at Kābul an Armenian colony, established in the reign of Tahmāsp and Shāh 'Abbās, has survived up to the time of Amīr Sher 'Alī Khān. They had preserved Christianity and lived in the Bālā Ḥiṣār near the Shāh Shahīd Gate, but are said to have been banished by the late Amīr Abdu-r-rahmān.[2]

In view of the above facts may we not suppose that Armenian traders left their names carved on these stones as a record of their having crossed the Camel Pass on the high road from Persia to India? Further epigraphical discoveries may perhaps help us to decide which of the two theories is correct.

J. PH. VOGEL.

---

[1] *Cf.* M. J. Seth, *History of the Armenians in India* (London, 1897), pp. 25, 37, 78. An extensive Armenian cemetery exists at Sūrat. Detached tombs are found at Behār (Cunningham, *A. S. R.* Vol. I. 37) and in the Haidarābād State (Cousens, *Lists of remains in H. H. the Nizām's Territory*, pp. 63-64).

[2] For information regarding this point I am indebted to Khān Bahādur Qāzi Jalālu-d-din Khān, C.I.E., Political Adviser to H. H. the Khān of Kalāt.

ARCHÆOLOGICAL REPORTS PUBLISHED UNDER OFFICIAL AUTHORITY.

Title of work.	Name and official designation of author.	Publishing Press, and date of publication.
INDIA.*		
1. Illustrations of ancient buildings in Kashmir.	H. H. Cole, Lieutenant, R.E., Superintendent, Archæological Survey, North-Western Provinces.	W. H. Allen & Co., 13, Waterloo Place, London, S.W., 1869.
2. Four reports made during the years, 1862-63-64-65, Volume I. (C. S)	A. Cunningham, Director General, Archæological Survey of India.	Government Central Press, Simla, 1871.
3. Four reports made during the years 1862-63-64-65, Volume II. (C. S.)	Ditto . .	Ditto.
4. Report for the year 1871-72, Volume III. (C. S.)	Ditto . .	Superintendent, Government Printing, Calcutta, 1873.
5. Illustrations of buildings near Muttra and Agra, showing the mixed Hindu-Mahomedan style of Upper India.	H. H. Cole, Lieutenant, R.E., Late Superintendent, Archæological Survey, North-Western Provinces.	W. H. Allen & Co., 13, Waterloo Place, London, S.W., 1873.
6. Report for the year 1871-72. Delhi and Agra, Volume IV. (C. S.)	J. D. Beglar and A. C. L. Carlleyle, Assistants, Archæological Survey of India.	Superintendent, Government Printing, Calcutta, 1874.
7. Report of the first season's operations in the Belgâm and Kaladgi districts. (N. I. S.)	J. Burgess, Archæological Surveyor and Reporter to Government.	W. H. Allen & Co, 13, Waterloo Place, London, S.W., 1874.
8. The Antiquities of Orissa, Volume I.	Rájendralála Mitra . .	Wyman & Co., Calcutta, 1875.

* NOTE.—The continued series of reports by A. Cunningham (Director General of the Archæological Survey of India), which extend over the years 1862-1884 inclusive, are marked (C. S.) in this list.

The reports of the New Imperial Series, which began in 1874 and are still in progress, are marked (N. I. S.).

Title of work.	Name and official designation of author.	Publishing Press, and date of publication.
INDIA—*contd.*		
9. Report for the year 1872-73, Volume V. (C. S.)	A. Cunningham, Director General, Archæological Survey of India.	Superintendent, Government Printing, Calcutta, 1875.
10. Report on the antiquities of Kâṭhiâwâḍ and Kachh. (N. I. S.)	J. Burgess, Archæological Surveyor and Reporter to Government, Western India.	W. H. Allen & Co., 13, Waterloo Place, London, S. W., 1876.
11. Corpus Inscriptionum Indicarum. Volume I, Inscriptions of Asoka.	A. Cunningham, Director General, Archæological Survey of India.	Superintendent, Government Printing, Calcutta, 1877.
12. Report on the antiquities in the Bidar and Aurangabad districts. (N. I. S.)	J. Burgess, Archæological Surveyor and Reporter to Government, Western India.	W. H. Allen & Co., 13, Waterloo Place, London, S.W., 1878.
13. Report of a tour in Eastern Rajputana in 1871-72 and 1872-73, Volume VI. (C. S.)	A. C. L. Carlleyle, Assistant, Archæological Survey.	Superintendent, Government Printing, Calcutta, 1878.
14. Report of a tour in Bundelkhand and Malwa, 1871-72; and in the Central Provinces, 1873-74, Volume VII. (C. S.)	J. D. Beglar, Assistant, Archæological Survey.	Ditto.
15. Report of a tour through the Bengal Provinces, of Patna, Gaya, Mongir, and Bhagalpur; The Santal Parganas, Manbhum, Singhbhum, and Birbhum; Bankura, Raniganj, Bardwan, and Hughli in 1872-73, Volume VIII. (C. S.)	Ditto . .	Ditto.
16. Pali, Sanskrit, and old Canarese Inscriptions from the Bombay Presidency and parts of the Madras Presidency and Maisur, arranged and explained.	J. F. Fleet, Bombay Civil Service, and J. Burgess, Archæological Surveyor, Western India.	G. E. Eyre and W. Spottiswoode, London, 1878.
17. The Stûpa of Bharhut. A Buddhist monument ornamented with numerous sculptures, illustrative of Buddhist legend and history in the third century B. C.	A. Cunningham, Director General, Archæological Survey of India.	W. H. Allen & Co., 13, Waterloo Place, London, S.W., 1879.
18. Report of tours in Central Doab and Gorakhpur in 1874-75 and 1875-76, Volume XII. (C. S.)	A. C. L. Carlleyle, 1st Assistant, Archæological Survey.	Superintendent, Government Printing, Calcutta, 1879.
19. Report of a tour in the Central Provinces in 1873-74 and 1874-75, Volume IX. (C. S.)	A. Cunningham, Director General, Archæological Survey of India.	Ditto.

Title of work.	Name and official designation of author.	Publishing Press, and date of publication.
INDIA—*contd.*		
20. Report of tours in Bundelkhand and Malwa in 1874-75 and 1876-77, Volume X. (C. S.)	A. Cunningham, Director General. Archæological Survey of India.	Superintendent, Government Printing, Calcutta, 1880.
21. Report of tours in the Gangetic Provinces from Badaon to Bihar in 1875-76 and 1877-78, Volume XI. (C. S.)	Ditto . .	Ditto, 1880.
22. Report on the Amarávati tope and excavations on its site in 1877.	R. Sewell, Madras Civil Service.	G. E. Eyre and W. Spottiswoode, 1880.
23. The Antiquities of Orissa, Volume II.	Rájendralála Mitra . .	W. Newman & Co., Calcutta, 1880.
24. The Cave Temples of India .	J. Fergusson and J. Burgess . .	W. H. Allen & Co., 13, Waterloo Place, London, S.W., 1880.
25. First Report of the Curator of Ancient Monuments in India for the year 1881-82.	H. H. Cole, Curator of Ancient Monuments in India.	Government Central Branch Press, Simla, 1882.
26. Report of tours in the South-Eastern Provinces in 1874-75 and 1875-76, Volume XIII. (C. S.)	J. D. Beglar, Assistant, Archæological Survey.	Superintendent, Government Printing, Calcutta, 1882.
27. Report of a tour in the Punjab in 1878-79, Volume XIV. (C S.)	A. Cunningham, Director General, Archæological Survey of India.	Ditto.
28. Report of a tour in Bihar and Bengal in 1879-80 from Patna to Sunargaon. Volume XV. (C. S)	Ditto . .	Ditto.
29. Lists of Antiquarian Remains in the Presidency of Madras. (N. I. S.)	R. Sewell, Madras Civil Service.	Government Press, Madras, 1882.
30. Preliminary reports by Curator, Ancient Monuments in India.	H. H. Cole, Curator of Ancient Monuments in India.	Government Central Branch Press, Simla, 1881 to 1883.
(*a*) Madras Presidency—		
The Seven Pagodas . .	Ditto . .	Ditto.
Velur	Ditto . .	Ditto.
Trichinopoly . . .	Ditto . .	Ditto.
Srirangam	Ditto .	Ditto.

Title of work.	Name and official designation of author.	Publishing Press, and date of publication.
INDIA—*contd*		
(*a*) Madras Presidency (*contd.*)—		
Madura	H. H. Cole, Curator of Ancient Monuments in India.	Government Central Branch Press, Simla, 1881 to 1883.
Tanjore	Ditto . .	Ditto.
Kombakonam . . .	Ditto . .	Ditto.
Chillambaram . . .	Ditto . .	Ditto.
Conjeveram	Ditto . .	Ditto.
Bijanagar	Ditto . .	Ditto.
(*b*) Bombay Presidency—		
Ahmedabad	Ditto . .	Ditto.
Poona	Ditto . .	Ditto.
Karli	Ditto . .	Ditto.
Ambarnath	Ditto . .	Ditto.
Elephanta	Ditto . .	Ditto.
(*c*) Bijapur . . .	Ditto . .	Ditto.
(*d*) Rajputana—		
Mount Abu	Ditto . .	Ditto.
Ajmir	Ditto . .	Ditto.
Jaipur	Ditto . .	Ditto.
Ulwar	Ditto . .	Ditto.
(*e*) H. H. the Nizam's Territory—		
Kalburgah	Ditto . .	Ditto.
(*f*) Punjab—		
(Memorandum on Ancient Monuments in Eusafzai, with a description of the explorations undertaken from the 4th February to the 16th April 1883, and suggestions for the disposal of the sculptures.)	Ditto . .	Ditto.

Title of work.	Name and official designation of author.	Publishing Press, and date of publication.
INDIA – *contd.*		
31. Second Report of the Curator of Ancient Monuments in India for the year 1882-83.	H. H Cole, Curator of Ancient Monuments in India.	Superintendent, Government Printing, Calcutta, 1883.
32. Report on the Buddhist Cave Temples and their Inscriptions. (N. I. S.)	J. Burgess, Archæological Surveyor and Reporter to Government for Western and Southern India.	Ballantyne, Hanson & Co., Edinburgh and London, 1883.
33. Report of tours in North and South Bihar in 1880-81, Volume XVI. (C. S.)	A. Cunningham, Director General, Archæological Survey of India, and H. B W. Garrick, Assistant, Archæological Survey.	Superintendent, Government Printing, Calcutta, 1883.
34. Preservation of National Monuments—Fortress Gwalior.	J. B. Keith, Superintending Monumental Preservation.	Ditto
35. Catalogue and Hand-Book of the Archæological Collections in the Indian Museum, Part I—Asoka and Indo-Scythian Galleries.	J. Anderson, Superintendent, Indian Museum.	Ditto.
36 Ditto ditto, Part II—Gupta and Inscription Galleries.	Ditto . .	Ditto.
37. Report of a tour in Gorakhpur district in 1875-76 and 1876-77, Volume XVIII. (C. S)	A. C. L. Carlleyle, 1st Assistant, Archæological Survey.	Ditto.
38. Report on the Elura cave temples and the other Brahmanical and Jaina caves in Western India. (N. I. S.)	J. Burgess, Archæological Surveyor and Reporter to Government for Western and Southern India.	Ballantyne, Hanson & Co., Edinburgh and London, 1883.
39. Report of a tour in the Central Provinces and Lower Gangetic Doab in 1881-82, Volume XVII. (C. S.)	A. Cunningham, Director General, Archæological Survey of India.	Superintendent, Government Printing, Calcutta, 1884.
40. Lists of Inscriptions and Sketch of the Dynasties of Southern India. (N. I. S.)	R. Sewell, Madras Civil Service.	Government Press, Madras, 1884.
41. Preservation of National Monuments, India.	H. H. Cole, Curator of Ancient Monuments in India.	Plates prepared in Paris, 1884-85.
(*a*) Agra and Gwalior . .	Ditto . .	Ditto.
(*b*) Golden temple at Amritsar, Punjab.	Ditto . .	Ditto.
(*c*) Delhi	Ditto . .	Ditto.
(*d*) Græco-Buddhist sculptures from Yusufzai.	Ditto . .	Ditto.

Title of work.	Name and official designation of author.	Publishing Press, and date of publication.
INDIA—*contd.*		
(*e*) Great temple to Siva and his consort at Madura.	H. H. Cole, Curator of Ancient Monuments in India.	Plates prepared in Paris, 1884-85.
(*f*) Meywar	Ditto . .	Ditto.
(*g*) Buildings of the Punjab .	Ditto . .	Ditto.
(*h*) Great Buddhist Tope at Sanchi.	Ditto . .	Ditto.
(*i*) Tomb of Jahangir at Shahdara near Lahore.	Ditto . .	Ditto.
(*j*) The temples at Trichinopoly	Ditto .	Ditto.
42. Third Report of the Curator of Ancient Monuments in India for the year 1883-84.	Ditto . .	Superintendent, Government Printing, Calcutta, 1885.
43. Report of a tour through Bihar, Central India, Peshawar, and Yusufzai, during 1881-82, Vol. XIX. (C S.)	H. B. W. Garrick, Assistant, Archæological Survey.	Ditto.
44. Report of a tour in Eastern Rajputana in 1882-83, Vol. XX. (C. S.)	A. Cunningham, Director General, Archæological Survey of India.	Ditto.
45. Reports of a tour in Bundelkhand and Rewa in 1883-84 and of a tour in Rewa, Bundelkhand, Malwa, and Gwalior in 1884-85, Vol. XXI. (C. S.)	Ditto . .	Ditto.
46. Report of tours in Gorakhpur, Saran, and Ghazipur in 1877-78-79 and 80, Vol. XXII. (C. S.)	A. C. L. Carlleyle, 1st Assistant, Archæological Survey.	Ditto.
47. Report of a tour in the Punjab and Râjpûtâna in 1883-84, Vol. XXIII. (C. S.)	H. B. W. Garrick, Assistant, Archæological Survey.	Ditto, 1887.
48. General Index to the Reports of the Archæological Survey of India, Vols. I—XXIII. (C. S.)	V. A. Smith, Indian Civil Service.	Ditto.
49. The Buddhist stûpas of Amaravati and Jaggayyapeta in the Krishna District, Madras Presidency, with translations of the Asoka Inscriptions at Jaugada and Dhauli. (N. I. S.)	J. Burgess, Director General, Archæological Survey of India, and G. Bühler, Ph. D., LL.D., C.I.E., etc.	Ballantyne, Hanson & Co., Edinburgh and London, 1887.

Title of work.	Name and official designation of author.	Publishing Press. and date of publication.
INDIA—*contd.*		
50. The Sharqi Architecture of Jaunpur. (N. I. S.)	A. Führer, Archæological Survey, North-Western Provinces and Oudh, and E. W. Smith, Architectural Assistant.	Superintendent, Government Printing, Calcutta, 1889.
51. Jeypore Portfolio of Architectural Details; Parts I—X.	Colonel S. S. Jacob, C.I.E. .	Griggs and Sons, London, 1890-98.
52. South Indian Inscriptions (Vol. I). (N. I. S.)	E. Hultzsch, Government Epigraphist.	Government Press, Madras, 1890.
53. Ditto ditto (Vol. II). (N. I. S.)	Ditto . .	Ditto, 1891.
54. The Monumental Antiquities and Inscriptions in the North-Western Provinces and Oudh. (N. I. S.)	A. Führer, Archæological Survey, North-Western Provinces and Oudh.	Government Press, North-Western Provinces and Oudh, 1891.
55. Epigraphia Indica of the Archæological Survey of India, Vol. I. (N. I. S.)	J. Burgess, late Director General, Archæological Survey of India.	Superintendent, Government Printing, Calcutta, 1892.
56. Mahabodhi or the Great Buddhist Temple under the Bodhi tree, at Buddha Gaya.	A. Cunningham, late Director General, Archæological Survey of India.	W. H. Allen & Co., 13, Waterloo Place, London, S. W., 1892.
57. Epigraphia Indica of the Archæological Survey of India (Vol. II). (N. I. S.)	J. Burgess, late Director General, Archæological Survey of India.	Superintendent, Government Printing, Calcutta, 1894.
58. Notes on the Antiquities, Ethnography, and History of Las Bela and Mekran.	T. H. Holdich, Superintendent, Survey of India.	Ditto.
59. South Indian Buddhist Antiquities. (N. I. S.)	A. Rea, Superintendent, Archæological Survey, Madras.	Government Press, Madras, 1894.
60. List of Architectural and Archæological Remains in Coorg. (N. I. S.)	Ditto .	Ditto.
61. Bower Manuscript. (N. I. S.) .	A. Hœrnle, Principal, Calcutta Madrassah.	Superintendent, Government Printing, Calcutta, 1893-97.
62. The Moghul Architecture of Fathpur-Sikri. Parts I-IV. (N. I. S.)	E. Smith, Archæological Survey, North-Western Provinces and Oudh.	Government Press, North-Western Provinces and Oudh, 1894-98.
63. On the Muhammadan Architecture in Gujarat. (N. I S.)	J. Burgess, late Director General, Archæological Survey of India.	Eyre and Spottiswoode, London, 1896.

Title of work.	Name and official designation of author.	Publishing Press, and date of publication.
INDIA—*concld.*		
64. Châlukyan Architecture, including examples from the Ballâri District, Madras Presidency. (N. I. S.)	A. Rea, Superintendent. Archæological Survey, Madras.	Government Press, Madras, 1896.
65. Lists of Antiquarian Remains in the Central Provinces and Berâr. (N. I. S.)	H. Cousens, Superintendent, Archæological Survey, Bombay.	Superintendent, Government Printing, Calcutta, 1897.
66. Monumental Remains of the Dutch East India Company in the Presidency of Madras. (N. I. S.)	A. Rea, Superintendent, Archæological Survey, Madras.	Government Press, Madras, 1897.
67. Revised lists of Antiquarian Remains in the Bombay Presidency. (N. I. S.)	H. Cousens, Superintendent. Archæological Survey, Bombay.	Government Central Press, Bombay, 1897.
68. South Indian Inscriptions (Volume III, Part I). (N. I. S.)	E. Hultzsch, Government Epigraphist.	Government Press, Madras, 1899.
69. A list of photographic negatives of Indian antiquities in the collection of the Indian Museum with which is incorporated the list of similar negatives in the possession of the India Office.	Dr. T. Bloch, 1st Assistant Superintendent, Indian Museum.	Superintendent, Government Printing, Calcutta, 1900.
70. Lists of Antiquarian Remains in His Highness the Nizam's territories. (N. I. S.)	H. Cousens, Superintendent, Archæological Survey, Bombay.	Ditto.
71. The Muhammadan Architecture of Ahmedabad, Part I. (N. I. S.)	J. Burgess, late Director General, Archæological Survey of India.	Eyre and Spottiswoode. London, 1900.
72. Report on results of explorations in the Nepal Tarai, Part I. (N. I. S.)	P. C. Mukherji, lately employed on Archæological explorations under the Government of the North-Western Provinces and Oudh.	Superintendent, Government Printing, Calcutta, 1901.
73. The Jaina Stûpa and some other Antiquities of Mathurâ. (N. I. S.)	V. A. Smith, Indian Civil Service.	Government Press, United Provinces, 1901.
74. Moghul Colour Decoration of Agra, Part I. (N. I. S.)	E. Smith, Archæological Surveyor, North-Western Provinces and Oudh.	Ditto.
75. The Architectural Antiquities of Northern Gujarat.	J. Burgess, late Director-General, Archæological Survey of India, and H. Cousens, Superintendent, Archæological Survey, Western India.	Eyre and Spottiswoode, London, 1903.

Title of work.	Name and official designation of author.	Publishing Press, and date of publication.
MADRAS—		
76. Notes on the Amarāvati Stūpa .	J. Burgess, Government Archæological Surveyor for Western and Southern India.	Government Press, Madras, 1882.
77. Notes and Inscriptions from Temples in the Madura District, Vol. IV.	Ditto . .	Ditto, 1885-86.
78. Tamil and Sanskrit Inscriptions with some notes on village antiquities, collected chiefly in the south of the Madras Presidency.	Ditto . .	Ditto, 1886.
79. List of ancient monuments for conservation in the Madras Presidency in 1884.	Ditto . .	Ditto, 1886-87.
80. List of ancient monuments selected for conservation in the Madras Presidency in 1891.	A. Rea, Archæological Surveyor, Madras.	Ditto, 1891.
81. Epigraphia Indica and Record of the Archæological Survey of India, Vol. III, 1894-95.	E. Hultzsch, Ph.D., Government Epigraphist.	Superintendent, Government Printing, Calcutta, 1895.
82. Ditto, Vol. IV, 1896-97	Ditto . .	Ditto, 1897.
83. Ditto, „ V, 1898-99	Ditto . .	Ditto, 1899.
84. Ditto, „ VI, 1900-01	Ditto . .	Ditto, 1901.
85. List of tombs and monuments of Europeans, etc., in the Madras District.	Government of Madras .	Government Press, Madras, 1898.
86. List of tombs and monuments erected in Madras.	Ditto . .	Ditto.
87. List of statues, monuments, and busts erected in Madras in honour of distinguished servants of the State.	Ditto . .	Ditto.
BOMBAY—		
88. Rock-cut Temples of Western India.	J. Fergusson, F.R.S., M.R.A.S.	R. Clay & Son, London, 1864.

Title of work.	Name and official designation of author.	Publishing Press, and date of publication.
BOMBAY—*contd.*		
89. Architecture at Ahmedabad, the Capital of Gujarat.	Colonel Biggs, R.A., Theodore C. Hope, Bombay Civil Service, and James Fergusson, F.R.S., M.R.A.S., Fellow, Royal Inst. British Architects.	John Murray, Albemarle Street, London, 1866.
90 Architecture at Beejapoor, an ancient Mahometan Capital in the Bombay Presidency.	P. D. Hart, B.E., A. Cumming, C.E., Colonel Biggs, late of the Royal Artillery, Major Loch, Bombay Army, Captain Meadows Taylor, M.R.I.A., F.R.G.S.I., and James Fergusson, F.R.S., M.R.A S.	R. Clay & Son, London, 1866.
91. Architecture in Dharwar and Mysore.	Dr. Pigou, Bombay Medical Service, A. C. B. Neill, Esq., Colonel Biggs, late of the Royal Artillery, Colonel Meadows Taylor, M.R.I.A., F.R.G.S.I., James Fergusson, F.R.S., M.R.A.S., Fellow, Royal Inst. British Architects.	R. Clay & Son, London.
92. Report on the illustration of the Archaic Architecture of India, etc.	Dr. Forbes Watson and Mr. Fergusson, General Cunningham and Colonel Meadows Taylor.	Indian Museum, 1869.
93. Photographs from Somanath, Girnar, Junagadh, and other places in Kathiawar.	James Burgess, M.R.A.S., F.R.G.S.	Sykes and Dwyer, Bombay, 1870.
94. Notes to accompany a series of photographs designed to illustrate the Ancient Architecture of Western India.	Captain Lyon, late of Her Majesty's 68th Regiment of Light Infantry.	Carey Brothers, Old College Street, 3 Geneva, 1871.
95. Rock-Temples of Elephanta or Ghárápuri.	James Burgess, F.R.G.S., M.R.A.S., and D. H. Sykes.	D. H. Sykes & Co., Bombay, 1871.
96. Memorandum on the Buddhist Caves at Junnar.	James Burgess, Archæological Surveyor and Reporter to Government, and J. F. Fleet, Bo.C.S.	Government Central Press, Bombay, 1874.
97. Memorandum on the antiquities at Dabhoi, Ahmedabad, Than, Junagaḍh, Girnar, and Dhank.	James Burgess, Archæological Surveyor, and Reporter to Government.	Ditto, 1875.
98. Memorandum on the remains at Gumli, Gop, and in Kachh, etc.	Ditto	Ditto.

Title of work.	Name and official designation of author.	Publishing Press, and date of publication.
BOMBAY—*contd.*		
99. Provincial lists of Architectural and other Archæological remains in Western India, including the Bombay Presidency, Sindh, Berar, Central Provinces, and Hyderabad.	James Burgess, Archæological Surveyor and Reporter to Government.	Government Central Press, Bombay, 1875.
100. Translations of inscriptions from Belgaum and Kaladgi Districts in the report of the first season's operations of the Archæological Survey of Western India and of inscriptions from Kathiawar and Kachh.	J. F. Fleet, Bo. C.S., and Hari Vaman Limaya, B.A.	Ditto, 1876.
101. Buddhist Caves of Ajanta, old Hills. Notes and illustrations of the—.	......	Ditto.
102. Notes on the antiquities of the Talukas of Parner, Sangamner, Ankole, and Kopergaum forming the charge ot the 2nd Assistant Collector, Ahmadnagar, with revised lists of remains in the Ahmadnagar, Nasik, Puna, Thana, and Kaládgi Zillahs.	W. F. Sinclair, Bo. C.S., and J. Burgess, Archæological Surveyor and Reporter to Government.	Ditto, 1877.
103. Architectural and Archæological remains in Khandesh in 1877.	W. H. Propert, Collector of Khandesh.	Ditto.
104. Reports regarding the Archæological remains in the Karachi, Haidarabad, and Shikarpur Collectorates in Sindh, with plans of tombs.	......	Ditto, 1879.
105. Report on the Architectural and Archæological remains in the Province of Kachh, with 5 papers by the late Sir Alex. Burnes. (Selections trom the records of the Bombay Government, No. CLII, new series.)	Dalpatram Pranjivan Khakhar.	Ditto.
106. Notes on the Buddha Rock Temples of Ajanta, their paintings and sculptures, and on the paintings of the Bagh Caves, modern Buddha Mythology, etc.	J. Burgess, Archæological Surveyor, Western India.	Ditto.
107. Inscriptions from the Cave Temples of Western India with descriptive notes, etc.	J. Burgess, Archæological Surveyor, and Bhagwanlal Indraji Pandit.	Ditto, 1881.

Title of work.	Name and official designation of author.	Publishing Press, and date of publication.
BOMBAY—*contd.*		
108. Lists of the antiquarian remains in the Bombay Presidency, with an Appendix of inscriptions from Gujarat.	J. Burgess, Archæological Surveyor and Reporter to Government.	Government Central Press, Bombay, 1885.
109. Scheme for the protection and conservation of ancient buildings in and around the City of Ahmedabad.	A. W. Crawley-Boevy, C S. .	Education Society's Press, Bombay, 1886.
110. List of Photographs of ancient buildings and antiquities, Bombay.	......	Superintendent, Government Printing, Calcutta, 1887.
111. The Antiquities of the town of Dabhoi in Gujarat.	James Burgess, LL.D., C.I.E., Director General of the Archæological Survey of India, and H. Cousens, M.R A.S., Archæological Surveyor, Western India.	George Waterston & Sons, Edinburgh, 1888.
112. List of Photographic Negatives of ancient buildings and antiquities of the Bombay Presidency.	H. Cousens, M.R.A S., Archæological Surveyor, Western India.	Government Central Press, Bombay, 1888.
113. Bijapur Guide . . .	Ditto . .	Orphanage Press, Poona, 1889.
114. Notes on the buildings and other antiquarian remains at Bijapur with translations of the inscriptions.	H. Cousens, Archæological Surveyor, Western India, and E. Rehatsek.	Government Central Press, Bombay, 1890.
115. An account of the Caves at Nadsur and Karsambla.	H. Cousens, Archæological Surveyor, Western India.	Ditto, 1891.
116. Progress Report of the Archæological Survey of Western India for the months of December 1889 to April 1890.	Ditto . .	Ditto, 1890.
117. Ditto for the months of May 1890 to April 1891.	Ditto . .	Ditto, 1891.
118. Ditto for the months of May 1891 to April 1892.	Ditto . .	Ditto, 1892.
119. Ditto for the months of May 1892 to April 1893.	Ditto . .	Ditto, 1893.
120. Ditto for the months of May 1893 to April 1894.	Ditto . .	Ditto, 1894.

Title of work.	Name and official designation of author.	Publishing Press, and date of publication.
BOMBAY—*concld.*		
121. Progress Report of the Archæological Survey of Western India for the months of May 1894 to August 1895.	H. Cousens, Archæological Surveyor, Western India.	Government Central Press, Bombay, 1895.
122. Ditto for the months of September 1895 to April 1895.	Ditto . .	Ditto, 1896.
123. Ditto for the year ending 30th June 1897.	Ditto . .	Ditto, 1897.
124. Ditto for the year ending 30th June 1898.	Ditto . .	Ditto, 1898.
125. Ditto for the year ending 30th June 1899.	Ditto . .	Ditto, 1899.
126. Ditto for the year ending 30th June 1900.	Ditto . .	Ditto, 1900.
127. Ditto for the year ending 30th June 1901.	Ditto . .	Ditto, 1901.
128. Ditto for the year ending 30th June 1902.	Ditto . .	Ditto, 1902.
129 Ditto for the year ending 30th June 1903.	Ditto . .	Ditto, 1903.
130. Paintings in the Buddhist Cave-Temples of Ajanta, Khandesh, India. Volume I (Pictorial subjects).	John Griffiths, late Principal of the Sir Jamshedji Jijibhai School of Art, Bombay, Fellow of the University of Bombay, Member of the Bombay Branch of the Royal Asiatic Society.	W. Griggs, London, 1896.
131. Ditto ditto Volume II (Decorative details).	Ditto . .	Ditto, 1897.
BENGAL—		
132. Ruins of the Nalanda Monasteries at Burgaon, Sub-division Bihar, District Patna.	A. M. Broadley, B.C.S. .	Bengal Secretariat Press, 1872.
133. Report on the Archæology of the District of Midnapore.	H. L. Harrison, B.C.S. .	Ditto, 1873.
134. Buddha Gaya, the Hermitage of Śákya Muni.	Rájendralála Mitra, LL.D., C.I.E.	Ditto, 1878.
135. List of objects of antiquarian interest in Bengal.	......	Ditto, 1879.
136. Revised list of ancient monuments in Bengal, 1886.	......	Ditto, 1887.
137. Some Historical and Ethnical aspects of the Burdwan District.	W. B. Oldham, C.I.E., Indian Civil Service.	Ditto, 1891.

Title of work.	Name and official designation of author.	Publishing Press, and date of publication.
BENGAL—*contd.*		
138. Discovery of the exact site of Aśoka's classic Capital of Pāṭaliputra, the *Palibothra* of the Greeks, and description of the superficial remains.	L. A. Waddell, M.B. . .	Bengal Secretariat Press, 1892.
139. A Brief History of the Bodh Gaya Math.	Rai Ram Anugrah Narayan Singh, Bahadur.	Ditto, 1893.
140. Sikkim Gazetteer . . .	......	Ditto, 1894.
141. Some Historical and Ethnical aspects of the Burdwan District with an explanatory Index (Reprint).	W. B. Oldham, C.I.E., Indian Civil Service.	Ditto.
142. List of Statues, Monuments, and Busts in Calcutta of Historical interest.	......	Ditto.
143. List of Inscriptions on tombs or monuments possessing historical or archæological interest.	C. R. Wilson, M.A., of the Bengal Educational Service.	Superintendent, Government Printing, Calcutta, 1896.
144. List of Ancient Monuments in Bengal—Revised and corrected up to 31st August 1895.	......	Bengal Secretariat Press, 1896.
145. List of ancient monuments :—		
Dacca Division . . .	......	Ditto.
Rajshahi Division . . .	......	Ditto.
Orissa Division . . .	......	Ditto.
Chota Nagpur Division . .	......	Ditto.
Bhagalpur Division . .	......	Ditto.
Chittagong Division . .	......	Ditto.
Burdwan Division . . .	......	Ditto.
Patna Division . . .	......	Ditto.
Presidency Division . .	......	Ditto.
146. Annual Report of the Archæological Survey, Bengal Circle, for the year 1900-01.	T. Bloch, Archæological Surveyor, Bengal Circle.	Ditto, 1901.
147. Ditto for the year ended April 1902.	Ditto . .	Ditto, 1902.
148. Ditto for the year ended April 1903.	Ditto . .	Ditto, 1903.

Title of work.	Name and official designation of author.	Publishing Press, and date of publication.
UNITED PROVINCES—		
149. Description of the antiquities at Kalinjar.	F. Maisey . . .	Baptist Mission Press, 1848.
150. List of Photographic Negatives of the monumental antiquities in the North-Western Provinces and Oudh.	A. Führer, Ph.D., Archæological Surveyor, and E.W. Smith, Architectural Surveyor, North-Western Provinces and Oudh.	Superintendent, Government Printing, Calcutta, 1889.
151. Progress reports of the Epigraphical and Architectural Branches of the North-Western Provinces and Oudh, Archæological Survey Circle, from October 1889 till 30th June 1891.	Ditto . .	Government Press, North-Western Provinces and Oudh, 1891.
152. Progress report of the Archæological Survey Circle, North-Western Provinces and Oudh, for the year 1891-92.	A. Führer, Ph.D., Archæological Surveyor.	Thomason College Press, Roorkee, 1892.
153. Ditto, for the year ending June 1893.	Ditto . .	Ditto, 1893.
154. Ditto, for the year ending June 1894.	Ditto . .	Ditto, 1894.
155. Ditto, for the year ending June 1895.	Ditto . .	Ditto, 1895.
156. Ditto, for the year ending June 1896.	Ditto . .	Ditto, 1896.
157. Ditto, for the year ending June 1897.	Ditto . .	Ditto, 1897.
158. Ditto, for the year ending June 1898.	Ditto . .	Ditto, 1898.
159. Ditto, for the year ending June 1899.	V. A. Smith, I.C.S.; and E. W. Smith, Archæological Surveyor.	Government Press, North-Western Provinces and Oudh, 1899.
160. Ditto, for the year ending 31st March 1900.	E. W. Smith, Archæological Surveyor.	Ditto, 1900.
161. Ditto, for the year ending 31st March 1901.	......	Ditto, 1901.
162. Ditto, for the year ending 31st March 1902.	......	Ditto, 1902.
163. Ditto, for the year ending 31st March 1903.	......	Ditto, 1903.

Title of work.	Name and official designation of author.	Publishing Press, and date of publication.
UNITED PROVINCES—*contd.*		
164. List of Christian tombs, and monuments of archæological and historical interest and their inscriptions, in the North-Western Provinces and Oudh.	A. Führer, Archæological Surveyor, North-Western Provinces and Oudh.	Government Press, North-Western Provinces and Oudh, 1896.
165. The remains near Kasia in the Gorakhpur District.	V. A. Smith, I.C.S. . .	Ditto.
166. Portfolio of Indian Architectural drawings, Part I.	E. W. Smith, Archæological Surveyor, North-Western Provinces and Oudh.	Griggs & Sons, London, 1897.
167. Report on the antiquities in the district of Lalitpur, North-Western Provinces.	Poorno Chander Mukherji .	Thomason College Press, Roorkee, 1899.
168. Plates illustrating the report on the antiquities in the district of Lalitpur, North-Western Provinces.	Ditto . .	Ditto.
PUNJAB—		
169. Report of the Punjab Circle of the Archæological Survey, 1888-89.	C. J. Rodgers, Archæological Surveyor.	W. Ball & Co., Lahore, 1891.
170. Revised list of objects of Archæological interest in the Punjab.	Ditto . .	Baptist Mission Press, Calcutta.
171. Progress Report of the Archæological Survey, Punjab Circle, for the period from 1st January to 30th June 1901.	Dr. J. Ph. Vogel, Archæological Surveyor, Punjab.	Lahore Caxton Printing Works, 1901.
172. Ditto, for the year ended 31st March 1902.	Ditto . .	Ditto, 1902.
173. Ditto. for the year ended 31st March 1903.	Ditto . .	Ditto, 1903.
N.-W. F. PROVINCE—		
174. Reports of Buddhist explorations in the Peshawar District by the 10th Company of Sappers and Miners.	Lieutenant C. Maxwell, R.E.	Public Works Department, Punjab, 1882.
175. Detailed report of an Archæological tour with the Buner Field Force	Dr. M. A. Stein, Ph.D., Principal, Oriental College, Lahore.	Punjab Government Press, 1898.

Title of work.	Name and official designation of author.	Publishing Press, and date of publication.
BURMA—		
176. List of objects of antiquarian interest in British Burma.	Dr. E. Forchhammer, Government Archæologist, Burma.	Government Press, Burma, 1880.
177. Notes on the early History and Geography of British Burma—		
I. The Shwe Dagon Pagoda	Ditto . .	Ditto, 1883.
II. The first Buddhist Mission to Suvannabhumi.	Ditto . .	Ditto, 1884.
178. List of objects of Antiquarian and Archæological interest in British Burma.	Ditto . .	Ditto.
179. The Po U Daung inscription, erected by King Sinbyuyin in 1774 A.D.	Taw Sein Ko, Government Translator, Burma.	Ditto, 1891.
180. List of objects of Antiquarian interest in Arakan.	Dr. E. Forchhammer, Government Archæologist, Burma.	Ditto.
181. List of objects of Antiquarian interest in Burma.	Ditto . .	Ditto, 1892.
182. Inscription of Pagan, Pinya, and Ava (deciphered from the ink impressions found among the papers of the late Dr. Forchhammer).	Taw Sein Ko, Government Translator, Burma.	Ditto.
183. Report on the antiquities of Arakan.	Dr. E. Forchhammer, Government Archæologist, Burma.	Ditto.
184. Report on the Kyaukku Temple at Pagan.	Ditto . .	Ditto.
185. The Kalyani Inscriptions . .	Taw Sein Ko, Government Translator, Burma.	Ditto.
186. Memorandum of a tour in parts of the Amherst, Shwegyin, and Pegu Districts.	Ditto . .	Ditto.
187. Note on a tour in Burma in March and April 1902.	F. O. Oertel, Assistant Engineer on special duty, Public Works Department, North-Western Provinces and Oudh.	Ditto, 1893.

Title of work.	Name and official designation of author.	Publishing Press, and date of publication.
BURMA—*contd.*		
188. Notes on an Archæological tour through Ramannadesa. (The Talaing country of Burma.)	Taw Sein Ko, Government Translator, Burma.	Reprinted from the *Indian Antiquary* by the Educational Society's Steam Press, Bombay, 1893.
189. A preliminary study of the Po U Daung Inscription of Sinbyuyin, 1774 A.D.	Ditto . .	Ditto.
190. A preliminary study of the Kalyani Inscriptions.	Ditto . .	Ditto.
191. Notes on antiquities in Ramannadesa. (The Talaing country of Burma.)	Lieutenant-Colonel R. C. Temple, late President, Rangoon Municipality, Burma.	Ditto, 1894.
192. Some remarks on the Kalyani Inscriptions.	Taw Sein Ko, Government Translator, Burma.	Ditto.
193. Inscriptions copied from the stones collected by King Bodawpaya and placed near the Arakan Pagoda, Mandalay.	Maung Tun Nyein, Officiating Government Translator, Burma.	Government Press, Burma, 1897.
194. Inscriptions of Pagan, Pinya and Ava. Translation with notes.	Ditto . .	Ditto, 1899.
195. Inscriptions collected in Upper Burma.	Taw Sein Ko, Government Archæologist, Burma.	Ditto, 1900-1903.
196. Index, Inscriptionum B. Birmanicarum, Volume I.	Ditto . .	Ditto, 1900.
197. List of objects of antiquarian and archæological interest in Upper Burma.	Ditto . .	Ditto, 1901.
198. List of Pagodas at Pagan under the custody of Government.	Ditto . .	Ditto.
199. Report on Archæological work in Burma for the year 1901-02.	Ditto . .	Ditto, 1902.
200. Ditto, for the year 1902-03 .	Ditto . .	Ditto, 1903.
MYSORE AND COORG—		
201. Mysore Inscriptions . . .	L. Rice, Director of Public Instruction.	Mysore Government Press, 1879.

Title of work.	Name and official designation of author.	Publishing Press, and date of publication.
MYSORE AND COORG—*contd.*		
202. Coorg Inscriptions . . .	L. Rice, Secretary to Government.	Mysore Government Press, 1886.
203. Inscriptions at Sravana Belgola, a chief seat of the Jains (Mysore).	L. Rice, Director of Archæological Researches and Secretary to Government, Mysore.	Ditto, 1889.
204. Epigraphia Carnatica—Inscriptions in the Mysore District, Part I.	Ditto . .	Ditto, 1894.
205. Ditto, Part II	Ditto . .	Ditto, 1898.
206. Ditto, Inscriptions in the Kadur District.	L. Rice, Director of Archæological Researches.	Ditto, 1901.
207. Ditto, Inscriptions in the Hassan District in 2 sections.	Ditto . .	Basel Mission Press, Mangalore, 1902.
208. Ditto, Inscriptions in the Simoga District, Part I.	Ditto . .	Ditto.
209. Ditto, Inscriptions in the Chitaldrug District.	Ditto . .	Ditto, 1903.
ASSAM—		
210. Report on the progress of historical research in Assam.	E. A. Gait, Esq., I.C.S., Honorary Director of Ethnography in Assam.	Assam Secretariat Printing Office, Shillong 1897.
211. List of Archæological remains in the Province of Assam.	....	Ditto, 1902.

G. I. C. P. O.—No. 2049 D. G. Archy.—15-11-1904.—450.